INTELLIGENCE
AND SPIRIT

REZA NEGARESTANI

Intelligence
and Spirit

URBANOMIC

sequence

Published in 2018 by

URBANOMIC MEDIA LTD	SEQUENCE PRESS
THE OLD LEMONADE FACTORY	88 ELDRIDGE STREET
WINDSOR QUARRY	NEW YORK
FALMOUTH TR11 3EX	NY 10002
UNITED KINGDOM	UNITED STATES

US Library of Congress Control Number: 2018949120

BRITISH LIBRARY CATALOGUING-IN-PUBLICATION DATA

A full catalogue record of this book is available
from the British Library
ISBN 978-0-9975674-0-3

Distributed by The MIT Press
Cambridge, Massachusetts and London, England

Printed and bound in the UK by
TJ International, Padstow

www.urbanomic.com
www.sequencepress.com

CONTENTS

Figures

Acknowledgements

I could not have written this book if I had not been convinced to take philosophy seriously; and I could not have taken philosophy seriously without the support of Kristen Alvanson, Mehrdad Iravanian, Robin Mackay, Ray Brassier, Peter Wolfendale, Katherine Pickard, Miguel Abreu, and Adam Berg.

1. Between Conception and Transformation

IT *IS* ONLY WHAT IT *DOES*

This book argues, from a functionalist perspective, that mind *is* only what it *does*; and that what it does is first and foremost realized by the *sociality* of agents, which itself is primarily and ontologically constituted by the semantic space of a public *language*. What mind does is to structure the universe to which it belongs, and structure is the very register of intelligibility as pertaining to the world and intelligence. Only in virtue of the multilayered semantic structure of language does sociality become a normative space of recognitive-cognitive rational agents; and the supposedly 'private' experiences and thoughts of participating agents are only structured *as* experiences and thoughts in so far as they are bound up in this normative—at once intersubjective and objective—space.

In this cursory sketch the reader may recognise Hegel's characterization of *Geist* or Spirit.[1] Indeed, Hegel was the first to describe the community of rational agents as a social model of mind, and to do so in terms of its *function*. The functional picture of geist is essentially a picture of a *necessarily deprivatized* mind predicated on sociality as its *formal* condition of possibility. Perception is only perception because it is apperception, and apperception is only apperceptive in that it is an artefact of a deprivatized semantic space within which recognitive-cognitive agents emerge as by-products of a deeply impersonal space which they themselves have formally conditioned. The intertwining of semantic structure and deprivatized sociality enables mind to posit itself as an irreducible 'unifying point or configuring factor'[2]

---

1   'The history of spirit is its own deed; for spirit is only what it does, and its deed is to make itself—in this case as spirit—the object of its own consciousness, and to comprehend itself in its interpretation of itself to itself.' G.W.F. Hegel, *Elements of the Philosophy of Right*, tr. H. Nisbet (Cambridge: Cambridge University Press, 1991), 372.

2   L.B. Puntel, *Structure and Being: A Theoretical Framework for a Systematic Philosophy* (University Park, PA: Pennsylvania State University Press, 2008), 275.

that extends into, encompasses, and integrates both consciousness of itself and consciousness of the universe. In conceiving itself as the configurative or structuring consciousness of itself in the world (or universe), mind is endowed with a history rather than a mere nature or past. It becomes an artefact or object of its own conception. Where there is the possibility of having a history, there is also the possibility of having not only the concept of the concept, but also a history of history—a critical transformation of mind as an object of its own concept, and the critical reconception of the object into which it has transformed. And once there is a history of history, there is the possibility of abolishing what is given in history or purports to be its consummate totality.

My aim in this book, however, is not to remain authentically faithful to the philosophy of Hegel, or that of German Idealism—or for that matter to any other philosophy or philosopher. Philosophy is 'its own time apprehended in thoughts',[3] and for a large part the activity of philosophizing consists in remodelling philosophical thoughts in accordance with the contemporary moment and its historical needs. To this end, my interpretation of any philosopher in this book follows what Jay Rosenberg calls a 'Dionysian approach'[4] which, in contrast to the Apollonian approach, does not abide by historical accuracy or result in faithful treatises, but instead sees the positive insights and theses of philosophies distortedly through the lens of the contemporary. The Dionysian approach then goes on to selectively but critically mutate, re-engineer, and integrate what it has thus distortedly viewed through the contemporary optic. It is not that the Apollonian approach is the preserve of self-disciplined scholars of history rather than the proper work of philosophers; it is as genuine an exercise in philosophy as Dionysian critical adventurism. In fact, it is a necessary requirement for the sustenance of Dionysian roaming; and the latter, in turn, opens up new terrains of thought to renewed Apollonian scrutiny.

---

3   G.W.F. Hegel, *Outlines of the Philosophy of Right*, tr. T.M. Knox (Oxford: Oxford University Press, 2008), 15.

4   J. F. Rosenberg, *Accessing Kant* (Oxford: Oxford University Press, 2005), 2.

It is in this Dionysian spirit that the book examines and reconstructs the premises and conclusions of the functional picture of mind so as to build a philosophy of intelligence. As we shall see, mind is ultimately understood as the dimension of structure, or a configuring factor; something which can only be approached via an essentially deprivatized account of discursive (linguistic) apperceptive intelligence. The nature of this investigation and reconstruction originates as much from the viewpoint of contemporary philosophy as from that of the cognitive sciences—specifically, the programme of artificial general intelligence (AGI) or human-level AI, and contemporary philosophy of language as an intersection between linguistics, logic, and computer science.

In tandem with the Dionysian approach, the tone, pace, methods, and objectives of the chapters necessarily vary. All in all, this book is a rudimentary attempt to undertake the urgent task of presenting a philosophy of intelligence in which the questions of what intelligence is, what it can become, and what it does can be formulated. In the context of a philosophy of intelligence, this book also attends to the crucial question of what it means for us—humans—to remain faithful to what we are, to remain intelligible at least to ourselves here and now, and in doing so, to become part of the veritable history of intelligence.

The present chapter, which is more of a preamble—a rough sketch—provides an outline of a functionalist and deprivatized account of mind, or *geistig* intelligence,[5] setting down premises that will be spelled out and elaborated more conclusively in the chapters that follow. Introductory yet densely compressed, this chapter encapsulates the overall content of the book. Subsequent chapters unpack this content, at times in a plain demonstrative manner, on other occasions by taking it to its not-so-explicit conclusions.

Chapter 2 begins with an inquiry into the necessary conditions for the realization of geistig intelligence in the form of a program of artificial general intelligence, *as if* what we were really doing was attempting to construct an

---

5   *Geistig*: of the Mind or Spirit, spiritual. I have deliberately chosen to use the word *geistig* rather than *spiritual* so as to avoid any mystical, supernatural, transcendent, or theological connotation (no doubt to the dismay of Hegel).

artificial general intelligence. A conceptual framework will be proposed for conducting this *as if*-thought experiment. Our main objective is not to investigate the possibility of constructing an artificial general intelligence or to review the popular narratives of posthuman superintelligence, but to think about AGI and, even more generally, computers, as an outside view of ourselves. This is an objective labour, so to speak, whereby AGI or computers tell us what we are in virtue of what we are *determinately* not—i.e., contra negative theology or the uncritical and merely experiential impressions of ourselves. This objective picture or photographic negative may be far removed from our entrenched and subjectivist experience of ourselves as humans. But this rift between the outside view and the experiential impression is exactly what heralds the prospect of future intelligent machinery and a genuine thought of the posthuman.

On the basis of this thought experiment, chapter 3 sets out to investigate the conditions necessary for the possibility of having mind. In this chapter the focus is largely on what might be called the Kantian dimensions of the realization of the discursive apperceptive self (an experiencing and thinking agent), namely intuition, imagination, and a pure perspectival encounter with the world. Chapter 5 continues the mission of chapter 3, but with the focus shifted to the realization of the 'discursive apperceptive' aspects of geistig intelligence, moving from the realm of pure perspectivality to that of objectivity, where thought and beliefs have an epistemic status.

In between them, chapter 4 should be approached as a critical excursus that stirs things up somewhat, and prepares the conclusions reached by chapter 3 for their speculative extrapolation in the final chapter. Its focus is the question of temporality and forms of intuition (transcendental aesthetics) as the organizing factors of experience, a question whose proper formulation will lead us to a new perspective not only on experience but also on the model of the minded subject and the prospects of intelligence as time itself.

In chapters 6 and 7, which present the last stages of the thought experiment, we shall examine language as the dasein of geist, inquiring into its sociality and syntactic-semantic complexity in a vein that is much closer to theoretical computer science—with its capacity to integrate computation, mathematics, logic, and language—than to classical philosophy of language or social-communicative philosophy of rationalism à la Habermas. This investigation will allow us to conclude our examination into the necessary conditions for discursive apperceptive intelligence, an intelligence which acts in conformity with time-general thoughts determined by the conception it has of itself.

In the eighth and final chapter, both artificial general intelligence and the functional deprivatized account of the mind are suspended (*aufheben*) in a form of intelligence which is at once philosophy and a craft of philosophy qua specific program of thinking that has no nature, but only a *history*: a model for a self-cultivating intelligence.

A final note: with respect to the distinction between analytic and continental philosophy—of which there is no trace in this book—I have gradually learned to become blind to this supposed divide. The ambitions of philosophy are far too vast and comprehensive for them to be pigeonholed into cosy compartments.

*

If we were to outline the overall progression of the book in reverse order, as if we had already attained its ultimate conclusions, it could be formulated as follows: Philosophy as the organ of self-cultivation of intelligence is, in the broadest sense, a historical program for investigating the consequences of the possibility of thinking and having mind. The constitutive gesture of philosophy is critical self-consciousness, primarily the non-empirical consciousness of the possibility of thinking as a building block of theoretical, practical, and axiological significance upon which the systematic relations between intelligence and the intelligible can be elaborated, in theory and practice. However, the critical self-consciousness that brings about the possibility of philosophy in the above sense is itself the consequence of the realization of the order of conception or, more generally, self-consciousness as the *form* or logical structure of all thoughts. Yet the capacity to have thoughts or to inhabit the general order of self-consciousness itself depends upon the fulfilment of the conditions or positive constraints necessary for the realization of mind. Therefore, the speculative inquiry into the future of intelligence—understood as that which expands and acts on *intelligibilities* pertaining to itself and to the world of which it is a part—begins with an investigation into the conditions necessary for the possibility of having mind. Whether framed as the program of artificial general intelligence or as a transcendental psychology, the examination of the *necessary* conditions for having mind marks out a *sui generis* form of intelligence whose process of maturation coincides with its understanding and elaboration of the link between intelligence and the intelligible. Becoming cognizant of this link is what counts as the genuine expression of self-consciousness as a task whose first milestone is intelligence's retrospective recognition of its own conditions of realization. Only once intelligence begins to systematically understand its place within the world as an intelligible unity, can it begin to concretely know what it is in itself and what it may become for itself.

The significance of the functional picture of geist is that it enables a thoroughgoing analysis of *essentially self-conscious creatures*: what activities, in what sorts of structures, are required in order to realize a self-conscious rational agent, or a community of such agents? It is the functional descrip-tion of discursive, conceptual, and historical geist in the context of those activities that characterize it, but also constitute it in the first place. It sets forth a project wherein the theoretical and practical desacralization of the mind as something ineffable and given coincides with the project of his-torical emancipation and the disenthrallment of intelligence as that which both frees itself—piece by piece—from its local and contingent limitations (emancipation as a negative freedom from something) and treats whatever conception of itself it has arrived at, whatever task such a conception entails, as the milieu of an unrestricted attention and commitment (emancipation as a positive freedom to do something).

Characterizing discursive consciousness in an adequate functional con-text—rather than by reference to a predetermined structure or a meaning inherent in nature—makes it possible to identify those necessary conditions for the realization of mind as an intelligence that has not just a history, but a critical history (a history of history), not just a conscious self but, more importantly, a self that is the artefact of its own configuring or unifying Concept (*Begriff*). This is a self in which the distinction between the subject of conception and the object of the concept is *suspended*. Moreover, as will be elaborated in subsequent chapters, this functional characterization offers insights into what it means to reorient consciousness and thought toward an emancipatory project, the core of which is the emancipation of cognition itself.

Before proceeding, it is crucial to add a brief note on the concept of suspension. Throughout this book, I have used the word 'suspension' or the verb 'suspend' as a common English equivalent for Hegel's *aufheben* or *aufhebung*, instead of the uncommon 'sublation' (from the Latin *sublatum*), which only captures a limited range of the connotations Hegel has in mind. *Aufheben* has four connotations depending on the context: (1) to lift up or to heave (*heben*) as if something is on or has fallen to the ground; (2) to pick up or actively seize something, which accentuates the previous connotation (*auf*-heben); (3) to preserve or retain something; (4) to cancel or abolish something, to remove or take out of action. Hegel's *aufheben* places the emphasis on the positive and negative connotations (3) and (4). For example, in the case of the pure introspective I, the I that appears to be immediate is in fact mediated by its relations with others; its immediate positedness (*Gesetztsein*) is the result of (i.e., is mediated by) the movement of positing (*Setzen*). Through *aufhebung*, the positive immediacy of the self-reflexive I is cancelled, while the determinate negativity that accounts for the difference between the immediate and its mediation (I and another I) is preserved. In other words, the identity of what appears to be immediate is abolished or taken out of action, whereas the difference between the immediate and its mediation (the opposition) is preserved. Accordingly, Hegel's *aufhebung* has both a temporal and spatial aspect: what appears to be immediate prima facie is taken out of action or postponed (the temporal aspect) only to preserve the difference between the immediate and its mediation on an elevated level (the spatial aspect), as in the suspension of Being and Nothing in the more stable Determinate Being.[6] Therefore, *aufhebung* is closely associated with the extended labour of determinate

---

6   For more details on the logic of suspension as positive dialectic, see U. Petersen, *Diagonal Method and Dialectical Logic* (3 vols. Osnabrück: Der Andere Verlag, 2002), vol. 2.

negation, as opposed to the abstract or indeterminate negation that inadvertently ends up perpetuating the purported immediacy of the state of affairs it seeks to abolish.

A certain X appears to be the completed totality of the state of affairs. X might be the *human condition*, the manifest totality of ways in which we appear to ourselves as a species; or it might be *capitalism*, the putative totality of all social relations as transformed by the accumulation of value qua labour time. Through *aufhebung* the particular content of X is cancelled, but the difference between the immediacy of X and its mediation is retained. This allows us to see the cancellation of X not as a single punctual act that abstractly or totally negates the state of affairs, but as a development, the product of a positive labour of determinate negation that takes time. The suspension of the self-portrait of the human or of the capitalist mode of production as the alleged immediate totality of the state of affairs is thereby differentiated from naive forms of posthumanism, antihumanism, and simple abolitionist revolutionary politics—a revolutionary politics in which negation is decoupled from the process of determination and instead is turned into a fetishized form of abstract negation which, in its indeterminacy, presupposes a metaphysical account of totality whose immediacy is actual and which therefore, it is falsely assumed, can be abolished by an all-destroying and total negation.

In this respect, in addition to determinate negation, *aufhebung* is associated with Hegel's distinct concepts of speculation and reason. Speculation is to be contrasted with simple reflection, which is reflection through and on that which is allegedly immediate—for example, what it means to be human is often taken as something immediately present and thus left unexamined. Speculation rescues reflection from its pitfalls rather than annihilating it. Speculation can be grasped as a movement from the subjective to the objective, a movement that suspends the immediate element of reflection and, in doing so, incorporates reflection as the reflection of opposites, a developmental stage in speculation. In the same vein, Hegel's reason (*Vernünftige*) is distinct from Kant's reason, the faculty of concepts and judgements (*Vernunft*). Hegel's reason is a form of thinking that admits of the unity and identity of opposites (e.g., both finite and infinite, subject and object, in their distinctness) and which, rather than operating externally on concepts, explicates the immanent operation of the Concept itself.

Lastly, although distinct from it, Hegelian suspension can be linked back to the Pyrrhonian sceptical *epoché* or suspension of judgment regarding non-evident propositions. What gives rise to *epoché* is equipollence or Pyrrhonian *isostheneia*—the idea that, for any proposition or property, its contradicting opposite or incompatible property can be put forward with equal justification. Hegel's *aufhebung* seeks to break from the stasis and practical untenability of Pyrrhonian scepticism by directly assimilating it into reason in such a way that scepticism is no longer idly opposed to reason but becomes a dynamic and productive vector of it—what Ray Brassier has called a 'dialectics between suspicion and trust'.[7] The phenomenal knowledge of geist can therefore be presented as a 'self-consummating skepticism'.[8] The assimilation of *epoché* into reason and its complete remodelling as the dynamic process of suspension and determinate negation then allows us to think of *epochs* or, more generally, the history of geist. In order to refine The *formal* figure of the human or the functional picture of the mind cannot be refined, nor can they shed their entrenched dogmas, without a rational scepticism about their status here and now, and how this status might as a matter of fact restrict the prospects of what mind or intelligence can be. Therefore, it is in this vein that what is introduced in

---

7   R. Brassier, 'Dialectics Between Suspicion and Trust', *Stasis* 4:2 (2017), 98–113.

8   'This path can accordingly be regarded as the path of doubt, or, more properly, as the path of despair, for what transpires on that path is not what is usually understood as doubt, namely, as an undermining of this or that alleged truth which is then followed by the disappearance of the doubt, and which in turn then returns to the former truth in such a way that what is at stake is taken to be exactly what it was in the first place. Rather, the path is the conscious insight into the untruth of phenomenal knowledge, for which the most real is in truth merely the unrealized concept. For that reason, this self-consummating skepticism is also not the kind of skepticism with which a fervent zeal for truth and science imagines it has equipped itself so that it might be over and done with the matter.' G.W.F. Hegel, *Phenomenology of Spirit*, tr. T. Pinkard (Cambridge: Cambridge University Press, 2018), 52 (§78).

this book as the critique of the transcendental structure is suggestive of both the operation of Hegelian suspension and the productive incorporation of scepticism into the phenomenology of mind and into the transcendental project which sets out to investigate the functional picture of mind and the figure of the human.

The account of function that is attributed to the mind (as regards what it does, its *activities*) should and will be elaborated carefully. For now, it suffices to say that this is a normative 'rule-governed' account of function rather than a metaphysical one. The function of mind is structuration: conceptualization, rendering intelligible, making objective. The claim here is that there are no intrinsic functions in nature; all metaphysical functions are in fact modelled on normative activities of the mind. This point was already made very clearly by Kant in the context of 'as if' arguments: functions in nature are species of 'as if' *judgements*. For example, when we study the heart, it is in regulative analogy to practical reasoning that we say that 'the function of the heart is to pump blood'. But what we are actually doing is treating the heart as part of a whole (the circulatory system) in terms of means-ends relations: the causal role (means) of the heart is to pump blood in the circulatory system as its end. In accordance with the success or failure of this means-ends relation, which is a piece of practical reasoning, we can then talk about the function or malfunction of the heart (what it ought to do and what it ought not). So, in reality, what we are saying is that, in analogy to practical reasoning, it is *as if* the function of the heart is to pump blood.

So long as this 'as if' aspect is carefully posited and is not confounded with a constitutive judgement, it is not problematic to attribute functions to the activities of natural things. Moreover, functions can only be attributed to activities, not to things. Activities are specific, contextual, and domain-sensitive. Does a lump of clay or the planet Jupiter have a function? Any positive answer to this question risks infinite regress, in so far as it will no longer be possible to specify where the function ends.[9] Mind is not a *thing*: it *is* only what it *does*.

---

9   Describing functions using the vocabularies of activities and domain-specificity has

In attempting to provide a functional description of mind, I shall try to steer clear of any orthodox or metaphysical functionalism. Nevertheless, despite its metaphysical slipperiness, contemporary functionalism has contributed invaluable insights regarding the problem of functional analysis. These insights are drawn from the epistemological methods required to study complex systems, particularly nested hierarchical structures where the problem of different scales or levels is of the utmost importance.[10] In tackling the problem of analysing the mind, some of these methods will be adopted in order to develop a more fine-grained paradigm of functional analysis. Before coming back to a more comprehensive description of geist in terms of its function, then, it will be worthwhile to provide some brief comments regarding the kind of functionalism or functional analysis this book draws upon.

FUNCTIONS AND MULTILEVEL STRUCTURAL CONSTRAINTS

To define or analyse the mind in terms of functions is tantamount neither to the elimination of structural or material constraints, nor to a dismissal of such constraints. The mind *is* what it *does* to the extent that there are adequate material-causal and logical-semantic structures that support its activities. This is not to elide the distinction between normative activities and natural structures, reasons and causes, thinking and being, the 'conceptual psyche and the cerebrum',[11] but only to underline the fact

---

a number of interesting consequences. For example, the observation that the function of item x is y explains or contributes to an explanation of the general proper activity of a system S which includes x. It does not, however, essentially explain the presence of x as such; nor does it essentially have the same properties as the general activity of S.

10   See R. Batterman, *The Tyranny of Scales* (2011), <http://philsci-archive.pitt. edu/8678/1/Bridging.pdf>; for a more technical survey of the problem of scales and hierarchy in relation to complexity, see R. Badii and A. Politi, *Complexity: Hierarchical Structures and Scaling in Physics* (Cambridge: Cambridge University Press, 1999).

11   'The difficulties in the way of a thoroughgoing cerebralism are logical: they rest

that adequate causal-structural constraints need to be in place in order for geistig activities to be realized. In this sense, a functionalist analysis of mind attentive to the question of structural adequacy and constraint as well as that of types and distinctions of structures is the proper method of 'carving at the joints'.[12] It differentiates distinct classes of functions and their uniformities—'as if' functions that describe causal-structural mechanisms and functions proper, which, belonging to the order of reason, signify logico-linguistic roles. Furthermore, it correctly attributes functions to organizing structures which, in their very constraining role, support and afford the realization of mind. In short, an adequate functionalism of mind as a configured and configuring unity must presuppose that a plurality of constituents is required for the constitution of the mind, and that, in addition to this plurality of constituents, there is also a plurality of organized unities—or integrations—of such constituents, each with its own distinct structural constraints which may or may not be interlaced.

For this reason, functional analysis demands a coherentist view that sees a single function in terms of activities that are qualitatively different from the role it appears to be playing. Functions are not a matter of pure abstractions since they are *dimensionally varied* and *multiply constrained*. 'Dimensionally varied' means that a function can only be adequately analysed in terms of the *qualitatively distinct structural constraints* required for its realization—constraints that are distributed across different levels (dimensions) of the functional-structural organization. 'Multiply constrained' means that the specificities of a function are determined by distinct structural levels that *constrain it in particular ways*. The analysis of

---

on the difficulty of modelling something that displays remote intentionality in a medium that only displays fully actual, descriptive structures, and in modelling high-level universality, and, more importantly, the everlasting, open retreat to ever higher levels of universality, in a medium that cannot reflect all higher-level affinities and logical properties that are thus implicated.' J.N. Findlay, *Psyche and Cerebrum* (Milwaukee, WI: Marquette University Press, 1972), 24–5.

12 Plato, 'Phaedrus', in *Complete Works* (Indianapolis: Hackett, 1997), 542.

a function as dimensionally varied and multiply constrained is a *realistic* examination of the conditions required for the realization of that function in its specificity. *In principle*, a proper analysis of a function is a blueprint for the realization of that function, and its potential modification via changes in its underlying structural constraints. This is all to say that a description of mind in terms of geistig activities requires a multilevel approach capable of analysing the types and scales of structural constraints (whether physical or sociocultural) that at once afford such activities and specify them. This issue will be discussed in more detail in chapters 2, 3 and 4, under the rubric of a critique of the transcendental structure—the question of what it means to distinguish structures necessary for the realization of mind or thinking from the contingency of their particular transcendental types.

The dimensionally varied and multiply constrained description of a function specified above may be called the *deep picture* of the function. It is *deep* in the sense that it pictures the function as being organized by activities, constraints, and unities at different structural levels or scales. The overall attributes of a function are determined by the interplay of multiple activities that cannot be straightforwardly merged or intuitively added together. The deep picture does not describe a function in terms of how it appears, but instead *explains* how it is organized. It specifies what activities, with what roles, what spatial and temporal organization, and what dependency relations, are required for its realization of a function. The totality of a function is replaced by the hierarchical and multilevel complexity of a functional organization wherein the function is orchestrated by qualitatively different activities, each designated with specific constraints and associated with a distinct structural domain or level.

In contrast to this deep picture of function where there is no one-to-one correspondence between realizer and realized features, what we might call the *flat picture* of function presumes a one-to-one correspondence between realizer and realized, either because the realizer's properties are considered as qualitatively identical to the realized functions, or because the structural levels and their corresponding constraints have been flattened. The flat picture of function can be modelled on the mathematical concept of function as a transition map between input and output, where the transition can be realized as many pathways mapping an initial state to an output state. On this model, the function implies an unconstrained abstract realization in so far as there is one-to-one correspondence between the realizer and realized features. Function a abstractly realizes activity b if elements of a map onto or are isomorphic with elements of b. Here, flatness signifies structural and/or functional isomorphism between the attributes of the realizer and the realized, in so far as there are no constraints associated with distinct levels of structure or activities. Therefore, in the flat picture of function, the causal and/or inferential relations between realizing and realized properties, activities, and functions are context-free and domain-neutral. A specific property or attribute can be realized by any set of entities as long as the abstract mapping holds between them. But this abstract mapping is built on the assumption of an isomorphism between realizers and realizeds. At the structural level, such isomorphism presupposes the absence of distinct structural levels which in distinctive ways constrain and determine the specificity of a particular function and its properties; while at the functional level, it implies that both realizing and realized properties are of the same functional type or class.

This flat or unconstrained picture results in triviality, since any given function can be realized by all manner of entities so long as the abstract mapping between realizer and realizeds is obtained. Anything can be furnished with mind, be it a rock or a piece of 'Swiss cheese'.[13] Functional complexity becomes ubiquitous when any function can be realized by any kind of *stuff*. The functional description of mind, however, requires an account of the integration of distinct processes, activities, and roles both causal and logical. Without a precise account of this integration—how different activities with causal or logical roles are put together and integrated, and how different constraints are satisfied—the description of mind is merely the description of arbitrary stuff. Thinking becomes ubiquitous to the extent

---

13 H. Putnam, *Philosophical Papers* (2 vols. Cambridge: Cambridge University Press, 1975), vol. 2, 302.

that there are no specific organizing or explanatory constraints for its realization.[14] As we shall see in the following chapters, there are many types of constraints that need to be in place for anything like cognition to be realized; and, as will be discussed in chapter 2, the myth of a superintelligence or an unbounded posthuman intelligence is precisely the product of biases ingrained in the flat or unconstrained picture of function. In other words, such views inexorably forgo the task of explaining what it means to call something intelligence, and describing the exact structural constraints by virtue of which something can be identified as exhibiting intelligent behaviours. In this sense, naturalistic accounts of superintelligence fall into a contradiction: committed to a physicalist account of intelligence and a thesis about an unbounded intelligence, yet unwilling to go through the hard work of identifying the structural and behavioural constraints and taking them seriously.

Moreover, the flattening of structural and functional dimensions and the consequent removal of specific constraints associated with them results in an illicit merger of the organisational hierarchies that underpin cognitive complexity. This illicit merger has significant implications for the models used to analyse and intervene in any system. It makes the issues of realizability, reappropriation, and functional change appear to be already at hand and only a matter of understanding and intervention at the level of immediate cognitive and practical resources, and such an assumption inevitably leads to biased conclusions. For example, if a system S has a global function λ and local realizing properties or functions α_L, β_L, ... necessary for the realization of λ, then according to the flat picture of function, all properties or activities in S are to be regarded as qualitatively identical to what the system does.

It is not difficult to recognize that this is in fact the logic of subsumption: If such-and-such activities are vital to a system's functions, then it must be that these activities are subsumed within the function of the system

---

14 Interestingly, panpsychism can be described as an implicitly functionalist account of mind, but one with a triviality condition, where the flat picture of function licenses the ubiquity of mind or its unconstrained realization across an expansive continuum.

and therefore represent the qualities or properties of the system's function. By the same token, if what the system is doing is flawed, then in virtue of the functional subsumption entailed in the flat picture, all activities vital to that system must be changed or discarded. For instance, if capitalism has subsumed such and such activities or relations, and if capitalism must be rendered obsolete, then so must these activities and relations. This is an anti-scientific approach that has neither any purchase on reality nor any critical import. Let us expand on this example in comparison with the deep picture of function: capitalism is defined by what it does, its *mode of production*. We cannot think of individuals and the capitalist system in terms of simple part-whole relationships or metaphors about relations between *things* (e.g., grains of sand in the desert, bricks in the wall, etc.) where the particulars of such-and-such qualities can be said to be ontologically subsumed by or to have the characteristics of the whole to which they belong. Particular individuals, or collections of them—classes—are actively included in the capitalist system not in virtue of their living in it or being a part of it, but by virtue of whatever they may do that—in one way or another—counts as conforming to or being involved with capitalism's mode of production. An individual adheres to capitalism if what they do fits the pattern of capitalism's mode of production. In this sense, not every activity or characteristic of an individual or a person is subsumed, shaped, or assimilated by the system to which it contributes or of which it is a part. Even if we take capitalism as the totality of ways of producing and society as what we perceive to be the totality of social relations, they represent two quite distinct types of totality despite their interconnections. To remain oblivious to these seemingly minor specifications is to risk mistaking functions or activities for things, links between the distinct levels of individuals' activities and capitalism's mode of production for metaphysical relations between things.[15]

Confusing activities with things and flattening different levels of activities will without exception result in specious descriptive and prescriptive

---

15   See for example, R. Lucas, 'Feeding the Infant', in M. Artiach and A. Iles (eds), *What is to be Done Under Real Subsumption* (London: Mute, forthcoming).

conclusions. On the descriptive level, capitalist society will be regarded as a metaphysical totality in which every element (particular individuals, activities, etc.) is by definition *ontologically* subsumed within capitalism. Even concepts and conceptual activities in general will be deemed to be subsumed by its mode of production. But if concepts themselves are absorbed by capitalism, then the very idea of capitalism becomes ineffable. Talking about capitalism and diagnosing its pathologies will then be little more than exercises in producing subjective and arbitrary narratives about something that is, in truth, unintelligible. On the prescriptive level, capitalism will be judged as a matter of all or nothing: either we should by any means possible contribute to it since there is no alternative, or we should seek its total collapse and with it the collapse of all social relations since such relations in their entirety are—supposedly—assimilated by it.

Another variation of such a fallacy is the equivocation between the socially instantiated functions of the mind and social practices in general. According to this erroneous view, if social practices are warped by a system of social relations (let's say reshaped and distorted by capitalism), then powers of reason and judgement, or the structuring functions of the mind, are also tainted by this all-encompassing distortion or corruption. But such a thesis is based on flattening the distinctions between social linguistic practices and social practices in general, act and object, form and content. Linguistic practices are indeed social practices, but their sociality is not general, they are *sui generis* and formal social practices that must be sufficiently differentiated from other social practices. Absent this differentiation, any talk of real or material conditions, and therefore any critique of social relations, is little more than everyday talk which, lacking objectivity, is in every way arbitrary and dogmatically subjective.

Functional analysis and the study of structural complexity should be approached as essentially conjoined programs. Unless both are in place, description and prescription in any form will be untenable, and prospective explanations, interventions, analyses, and critiques will result in dogmatic positions ranging, depending on their contexts, from resigned cynicism to fatalist optimism, from analytic stinginess to speculative overenthusiasm.

In both Kant's account of the conceptualizing mind and Hegel's picture of mind as the object of its own concept or notion, the questions of function and structural complexity—whether at the level of the sensing body or that of the social structure—are intertwined. Hegel's characterization of Spirit (qua organized collection of rational agents or essentially self-conscious creatures) in terms of its functions, and his subsequent analysing of these functions into qualitatively distinct activities and the structures necessary for supporting them, should be regarded as a systematic attempt to uncover the deep functional picture of mind. In attempting to provide this picture, Hegel uncovers hitherto unknown realizers and material organizations, powers and constraints, possible *realizabilities* and functions whose recognition, modification, or augmentation can reshape geist. It is in this sense that we can speak of *the function of functionalism*: A systematic functional analysis of what geist does, its doings, itself turns into a function that reorganizes geist. A functionalist approach to the question of what mind *is* culminates in asking what mind can *become*. The function of the functionalism of mind—the function of the Transcendental—is a thesis already harboured by Hegel's identification of geist (which is what it does) as the object or artefact of its own Concept, an object that is not sensible but is an object of thought, and its unrestricted focus on realizing itself in accordance with its formal reality.

Let us conclude this section with a tangential note on the sensible object (*gegenstand*) and the object of thought (*objekt*) since this distinction will feature throughout the book. Although Kant's use of the terms *gegenstand* and *objekt* is not consistent, in the *Critique of Pure Reason* he uses *gegenstand* to denote a sensible object, an object of appearances or experience (the interplay between concepts and intuition). The German *gegenstand* suggests at least three connotations: *das Gegenüberstehende* or that which stands in front of me (phenomenal manifestation), that which is opposed to me (vs. subject) and that which *stands* or lasts as a product of the faculties of imagination and understanding (perceptual persistence). In this sense, *gegenstand* (sensible object) adheres to the limits of understanding and intuition. *Objekt*, on the other hand, is defined as an object that is explicitly *for* knowledge or thought—that is to say, one that is expressed by the *determinate* relation of given representations to an object or *objekt* in the concept of which the manifold of intuitions are integrated and united. The *objekt* can be associated with the Latin *objectivum*, which simultaneously implies the real and the ideal, being and structure. This already convoluted distinction is further complicated by Hegel's use of *gegenstand*, which he contrasts to the *objekt* (the *real* object as the dual or correlative of the subject), and characterizes in terms of actuality or trueness (as in an objective fact) and impartiality (i.e., obeying impersonal rules as opposed to the subject's whims). This owes mainly to the fact that Hegel's account of experience (and of an object of experience) differs from Kant's. Therefore, Hegel's *gegenstand* is an object made concrete. It is the object of knowledge and self-consciousness, whereas the *objekt* is a system of real objects held together by inference, judgement, and the concept (e.g., the Milky Way as comprised of stars and planets).

To avoid further confusion, I have abided by the Kantian distinction between *gegenstand* and *objekt*. Hegel's *gegenstand* will be characterized as an *objekt*, and *gegenstände* reserved only for ordinary sensible objects of experience or appearances (items in the world that manifest in perspectival terms and according to perceptual invariances).

FUNCTIONAL INTEGRATION: PHASES OF GEIST

What makes Hegel's picture of geist a significant contribution not only to the history of functionalism and philosophy of mind but also, intriguingly, to the history of artificial general intelligence, is that it presents a social model of general intelligence, one in which sociality is a formal condition for the realization of cognitive abilities that would be unrealizable by individual agents alone. By agents here I simply mean *de facto* causal-structural systems capable of sensing and of effecting rudimentary actions, not agency in a Kantian-Hegelian sense (where it is precisely inseparable from its *geistig* sociality). But, as will be argued, this sociality is first and foremost a formal space upon which familiar collective sociality is built—a sociality afforded by *language* not as a medium of communication and public discourse, but as a semantic space within which computation and logic converge. At this point, the equation of general intelligence with geist may appear egregiously hasty. Even though this equation will be fleshed out throughout the book, for now we can understand general intelligence not merely as a bundle of intelligent behaviours, but as a unified intellect distinct from any particular set of such behaviours. In this sense, the 'generality' of general intelligence signifies a qualitative—rather than quantitative—space in which all of its behaviours and activities are caught up.

In analogy to geist, general intelligence is introduced in this book by way of three principal attributes: necessary abilities, the intrinsic social frame of these abilities, and their qualitative integration into a generative framework through which, in addition to becoming capable of recognizing itself, intelligence can inquire into and modify its conditions of realization and enablement. But what principally distinguishes general intelligence from quantitative 'problem-solving' intelligence is the fact that general intelligence is the product of a qualitative integration of capacities or faculties that might otherwise be quantitative when taken individually. How is it that the qualitative integration of certain otherwise non-special capacities and features can amount to a set of special and necessary abilities? This is a question that is as much about the realization of geist as it is about the artificial realization of general intelligence. The question of functional integration, however, becomes particularly thorny since these capacities and features are realized by different causal and logical conditions, distributed across distinct structural hierarchies and functional classes. To this extent, the realization of geist or general intelligence is not a matter of finding and developing a special realizer, a master key. It is a problem of the qualitative integration of abilities and their realizers in such a way that geistig intelligence not only recognizes itself and its abilities, but also becomes capable of modifying its very conditions of realization.

Hegel's curious account of geist, however, defines it not only in terms of an integral and qualitatively distinct set of activities, but also in terms of *phases of integration*. Mind is constituted not only by the organizing unities of its constituents, but also by its passing through different unities of itself. These unities are outcomes of the principal attributes of mind, which enable it not only to recognize itself, but also to recognize itself in the world and to realize itself according to this recognition. What was mere consciousness is now a formally instantiated self-consciousness, what was only a socially and historically mediated self-consciousness is now historical conscious-ness, and what was historical knowledge (*Wissen*) of consciousness has been reintegrated into a necessary and pure science (*Wissenschaft*) of the world-history of which it was conscious—an absolute knowing in which Spirit sees itself through the intelligible unity of the objective world in its otherness and thought in its formal autonomy:

> The concept (*Begriff*) of pure science and its deduction is therefore pre-supposed in the present work in so far as the *Phenomenology of Spirit* is nothing other than that deduction. Absolute knowledge is the *truth* of all the modes of consciousness because, as the course of the *Phenomenology* brought out, it is only in absolute knowledge that the separation of the *subject matter* from the *certainty of itself* is completely resolved: truth has become equal to certainty and this certainty to truth.[16]

However, the actualization of these unities or integrations is neither given nor certain. Self-consciousness, once attained, may be lost; or it may never be fully realized. All unities of mind—which constitute mind as such—are fragile. It is in this sense that geist is not a *deus ex machina*: its realization requires that a certain struggle take shape in the form of a necessary rela-tion between intelligence and the intelligible (not merely theoretical or ontological, but also practical and axiological intelligibility). Nevertheless, this notion of a struggle for the unities of mind remains a fruitless quest and an unintelligible toil unless we posit a Science of Logic through which intelligence sees itself in terms of a regulative and necessary form conceived *from nowhere and nowhen*. This necessary form is what we might call the Hegelian transcendental operator, which, in contrast to Kant's idea of the transcendental method, is decoupled from the conservatism of particular

---

16 G.W.F. Hegel, *The Science of Logic*, tr. G. Di Giovanni (Cambridge: Cambridge Uni-versity Press, 2010), 29.

and contingent experiences—experiences that have not yet been fully suspended in the self-experience of the Absolute. It is the logical excess of the Transcendental that crafts intelligence, initiates and regulates the mind's strivings for new unities, and sets the mind into a permanent state of alienation where 'the Spirit *is* at home'.[17] And it is the same excess that retroactively reveals to thought reality in its radical otherness. We shall return to the notion of transcendental excess in the final chapter under the aegis of that most radical and dangerous thesis of all philosophies: Plato's idea of the Good and the craft of a good life.

As new unities of the mind evolve, previous unities can only be viewed from the perspective of later and more encompassing unities. In light of the later unity, the supposed immediacy of each previous unity of mind turns out to be mediated. The unity of consciousness can only be recognized through the unity of self-consciousness, just as historical consciousness can only be analysed from the vantage point of absolute knowing. Where the Phenomenology of Spirit ends, absolute knowing, or the Science of Logic, begins. And where absolute knowing begins, the science of what mind *necessarily* and *actually* is, in its intelligible unity with the world in its radical otherness, comes into view:[18]

> Thus consciousness, on its forward path from the immediacy with which it began, is led back to the absolute knowledge that is its innermost truth. This truth, the ground, is then also that from which the original first proceeds, the same first which at the beginning came on the scene as something immediate.[19]

---

17 Ibid., 109.

18 'The necessary is an actual; as such it is immediate, groundless; but it equally has its actuality through an other or in its ground and is at the same time the positedness of this ground and its reflection into itself; the possibility of the necessary is a sublated one'. Ibid., 481.

19 Ibid., 49.

By shifting from one unity to another, from one mode of integration to a more encompassing one, geist recognizes its conditions of realization. In recognizing the conditions of its realization, it becomes capable of modifying those conditions and thus of modifying its own realization—but not until it has recognized its intelligible unity as a part of a more integral unity, namely the intelligible unity of mind and world. By recognizing what is universal and necessary about itself, mind becomes capable of revising the transcendental types or structures it previously deemed to be universal and necessary for the realisation of its abilities or cognitions. And in revising these transcendental types or structures, it moves from one qualitative level of abilities to another, from one mode of integration to another. In this manner, geist suspends that which previously seemed necessary for it—but was in reality contingent—in what is absolutely necessary and universal for it.

These different levels of integration reflect the fact that there are different qualities of geist. Each mode of integration indicates a qualitative shift in the structure of general intelligence. Phases of Spirit are defined by these modes of integration, by how cognitive and practical abilities are systematically incorporated within new unities of consciousness, and by the way in which each mode is represented and established as a normative model (the Concept) for the formation of new attitudes, subjectivities, and institutions for its constitutive agents. What is essential for the qualitative transformation of intelligence are not simply modes of integration qua unities, but also the manners in which these unities are concretely established as models for the conduct and cognitive cultivation of those agents that constitute geist and are encompassed by it. While modes of integration effect a qualitative transformation in the structure of geistig intelligence, their recognition as theoretical and practical models provides agents with access to the intelligibility of this structural transformation. In concretely and determinately recognizing the universal and necessary conditions of its realization, intelligence is enabled to realize itself under a new and higher unity. And in its constant striving to bring itself under a higher unity, intelligence becomes conscious of what the realization of intelligence, in itself and within objective reality, consists in:

Life, the 'I', spirit, absolute concept, are not universals only as higher genera, but are rather concretes whose determinacies are also not mere species or lower genera but determinacies which, in their reality, are self-contained and self-complete. Of course, life, the 'I', finite spirit, are also only determinate concepts. To this extent, however, they find their resolution in a universal which, as the truly absolute concept, is to be grasped as the idea of infinite spirit—the spirit whose posited being is the infinite, transparent reality in which it contemplates its creation and, in this creation, itself.[20]

To summarize, the integration of necessary qualitative abilities (unities) of mind has two outcomes. On the one hand, it results in transitions in the qualitative form of a geist that always recognizes itself in the world from the viewpoint of its higher functional unity. On the other hand, it occasions the possibility of bringing this qualitative form into a conception—that is, forming a concept or *formal model* of it by means of which agents can recognize or become aware of it and track its transformations within their own collective structure. This serves as a cognitive and practical model by which agents can recognize their abilities and constraints, and act on the conditions of their realization so as to modify or reconstitute them. In this sense, integrations set up a dynamic link between intelligence and intelligibility, between the conditions required for the realization of intelligence and the recognition or awareness of such conditions. The intelligibility of those faculties that constitute the structure of agency and the recognition of the necessary conditions for their realization are then established as premises for functional change and further transformation in the structure of the agency.

This constructive spiral between intelligence and intelligibility expresses the logic of self-reference that is the constructive kernel of geist. As will be argued below, this logic is specific to a distinct species of selves: selves with sapient consciousness—that is, consciousnesses capable of conceiving through the form of self-consciousness. But this is not self-consciousness

---

20   Ibid., 533.

as an intentional awareness of a self at once observing and observable, a phenomenological self-consciousness; nor is it the self's introspective-reflexive knowledge of itself. It is a logical form through which the self only recognizes what it is for itself from the perspective of a posited infinity—that is, an unrestricted intelligible world—which in its explanatory otherness renders intelligible what that consciousness is in itself, in its intelligible unity.[21] In doing so, self-consciousness establishes the truth of itself and the unrestricted world:

> Consciousness of an other, of an object as such, is indeed itself necessarily self-consciousness, being-reflected into itself, consciousness of its own self in its otherness. The necessary advance from the previous shapes of consciousness, to which their truth was a thing, that is, was something other than themselves, expresses precisely the following. Not merely is consciousness of things only possible for a self-consciousness; rather, it is this self-consciousness alone which is the truth of those shapes. However, this truth is on hand merely for us and not yet for consciousness. Self-consciousness has first come to be for itself but not yet as unity with consciousness itself.[22]

Through the logic of self-relation as the form of self-consciousness, mind attains the ability to treat itself as an artefact of its own concept. It artificializes itself, conceiving itself from the viewpoint of an unrestricted world that belongs to no particular where or when. In other words, through self-relation as the formal condition of self-consciousness, mind is now able to investigate the conditions required for its realization, to adapt to ends and purposes that are not given in advance, and to explore the possibility of its realization in types of structures other than those that naturally constitute it.

---

21 'Appearance, that is, the play of forces, already exhibits infinity itself, but infinity first freely emerges as explanation. When infinity is finally an object for consciousness, and consciousness is aware of it as what it is, then consciousness is self-consciousness.' Hegel, *Phenomenology of Spirit*, §163.

22 Ibid., §164.

The history of this kind of self—the minding self—is, then, strictly speaking, a project of *artificialization* in the above sense.

SELF-RELATION: A FUNCTION IN PROGRESS

Self-relation is a defeasible and disequilibrial constructive process. It is a process whereby geist utilizes the intelligibility of its structural transformations (its history) as a model for conceiving itself from the standpoint of a reality that is in excess of it. Not only are geist's actions informed by this model, they also exhibit it. The positive freedom of geist—the freedom to do something—is an expression of this self-relation, which is that of *formal* autonomy. In its simplest and most embryonic form this self-relation is the trivial tautology 'I am I'[23] (*I=I*). But in positing this very tautology, geist comes to the realization that the accomplished individuality that it takes itself to be is in fact an ongoing process of individuation from the perspective of that which is *not* this I: the other I, and reality in its radical otherness. That is to say, the positing of self-consciousness as formal—as abstracted from any particular or substantive content—enables what is conscious to be conscious of itself only in so far as some other object mediates its 'immediate' relation to itself.

Self-relation should not be understood in terms of what it appears to be—that is, an immediate relation to the self that is taken for granted, or a mere acknowledgement of oneself as living and as being the subject of desires that satisfy the needs of the species. Instead, it should be understood in terms of what it does, its ramifications: Self-relation begins with a negation of objects and the outside world, but this very negation also brings the self-conscious subject head-to-head with a resisting reality that is not passive, where objects impose constraints upon both thoughts and actions. The consequence of self-relatedness is that it forces the subject to project outward, to be conscious of a reality which is not an extension of the self but an order in which objects negate back, rendering the thoughts of the subject defeasible (prone to revision) and its actions challengeable,

---

23   Ibid., §167.

or open to possibilities that are not given in advance within the order of self-serving desires or the needs of the species.

Even though self-relation begins with a trivial premise—I am I—its consequences are by no means trivial. They are in excess of such a premise: When a life form negates the outside world in favour of its own interests, it also opens up a new vista wherein reality becomes intelligible as that which is not in conformity with the desires of the life form and, indeed, actively resists them. And where reality becomes intelligible as an active constraining order, self-consciousness is defined not as a phenomenon serving the needs or interests of the species, but as an adaptation to an intelligible reality which outstrips species-related interests and needs qua premises of self-relatedness. The medium of this adaptation is the order of reason, which can be loosely characterized as a system of essentially revisable thoughts and challengeable actions, i.e., thoughts and actions enabled by the constraints imposed by reality in its otherness. To characterize self-consciousness in terms of the *necessary* internal relations between thinking, action, and the constraints imposed by reality is to distinguish it above all as a formally represented order in the sense that all thoughts and actions representing it also conform to the manner by which it orders them not per accident but per necessity. This manner of ordering is first exhibited in the formal-abstract unity of thoughts and actions—i.e., in the way in which first-person thoughts and intentional actions are internally related—and subsequently in the formal-concrete unity of thinking self and material reality, I and not-I, first-person and second-person thoughts.

The acts of an essentially self-conscious creature fall under a formally represented order in which thoughts explain or cause actions, and actions not only fall under their respective thoughts but also exhibit them. The questions of what to do and what to think always arise in response to this order, just as this formal and general order *explains* the thoughts and actions of a subject that falls under it. It is in this sense that thoughts and actions are bound to the question of justification: Do these acts and thoughts reveal or justify the *causality* (i.e., the explanans) *of self-conscious thoughts?*[24]

---

24   See S. Rödl, *Self-Consciousness* (Cambridge, MA: Harvard University Press, 2007), 52.

In so far as the acts of a self-conscious creature essentially fall under the formal causality of thought, and to the extent that the questions of what to do and what to think always arise in response to this general order that explains the actions and thoughts of the self-conscious creature, we can speak of a *normative order of self-consciousness*. This normative order is nothing but the order of reason qua justification.

As an order that both formally represents and is represented by the causality of thought, self-consciousness is precisely that which turns mind into a unifying point or configuring factor. In actualizing what is only a formal self-consciousness (general I-thoughts), geist must posit that which is not-I. Only through the other (not-I) can the self-relation of the particular I-thoughts which seemed immediate to the subject that thought them, but were mediated from the viewpoint of the other, become immediate again. This is actualized self-consciousness. The self-positing of mind as the unifying point is a formal condition required for the positing and recognizing of reality in its otherness. It is the configuring factor that makes possible the intelligible unity of mind and reality as both distinct and coextensively configured:

> [T]he uniting bond, the configuring factor, is not only—somehow—
> omnipresent, it not only encompasses and contains all the united
> elements, but it also has a quite determinate directedness, indeed one
> emerging from the point from which the unifying is accomplished and
> by which the elements are made possible and borne. This unifying
> bond or configuring factor—the unifying point—is a basic concept;
> in a specific sense it is a primitive concept. More precisely, it is an
> absolutely singular, unique concept that can be articulated only on
> the basis of a concrete and penetrating analysis of the phenomenon
> 'experience of personal unity.' [...] In what, more precisely, does this
> unifying point consist? It articulates itself by saying 'I.' The I must
> not be hypostasized as substance or anything of the sort; it would
> also be fully insufficient philosophically to interpret or understand
> the I solely on the basis of linguistic configurations within which

the word 'I' appears. The task is instead that of comprehending the I ontologically.[25]

However, in order for the intelligible unity of mind and reality (the autonomy of thought and the alien thing) to be concretely realized, in order for self-consciousness to establish the determinate truth of itself, it must become conscious of itself from a second-person viewpoint—that of a reality that is in excess of thought and yet is still intelligible. The formal autonomy of thought accordingly demands stepping into the open and conceiving self-consciousness from the viewpoint of a reality that is wholly other to it.

Once a minimal and formal self-relation is established, it opens up a gap between mind and world. Only by bridging this gap from the other extremity—that is, from what is now outside of the manifest identity of the I—can mind become concretely self-conscious. This is the labour of negation, where there is no direct access between mind and reality, between one I and another, but where contact can only be obtained through the hard work of conception. Through the labour of negation, what was a formally trivial identity relation (the monad of $I=I$) is now an identity map ($I=I^*$) where I^* is the self or mind from the perspective of an abyss, an unrestricted world or reality that is to be rendered intelligible. The intelligibility of I or self-conscious mind rests on the intelligibility of the abyss which is, properly speaking, something to be achieved, an objective striving. Intelligence only turns into intelligence when it loses its passivity, when it actively begins to render reality intelligible and, in so doing, begins to re-engineer the reality of itself.[26]

---

25 Puntel, *Structure and Being*, 275.

26 'For, in the first place, the monad is a determinate representation of its only implicit totality; as a certain degree of development and positedness of its representation of the world, it is determinate; but since it is a self-enclosed totality, it is also indifferent to this determinateness and is, therefore, not its own determinateness but a determinateness posited through another object. In second place, it is an immediate in general, for it is supposed to be just a mirroring; its self-reference is

Individual I-thoughts can only be concretely established as singular once they are reencountered through the other—an unbound reality—for which the I is not a totalized individual, but a process of individuation. In permanently losing its home, in suspending itself in the abyss of intelligible reality, the mind retroactively recognizes that what was a merely formal order of self-consciousness was in reality an *actual* order of self-consciousness, that what was only a formal autonomy was in fact *concrete* freedom, that the immediate was mediated and the trivial and simple identity 'I am I' nontrivial and complex. Accordingly, the truth of formal self-consciousness is ultimately and only in retrospect the truth of concrete self-consciousness.

However, the transition from formal self-consciousness qua minimal self-relation to concrete experienced self-consciousness is the most fragile of all endeavours. The realization of intelligence bespeaks this maximal fragility. If geist stops seeing itself from the perspective of a radically other reality, if it gives up on expanding the intelligibility of the other, it ceases to be geist. Actual self-consciousness, then, is not a given state but a 'practical achievement',[27] and, as such, the object of a struggle. The transition from the formal autonomy of thought to an achieved state of concrete self-consciousness is—all things considered—the project of freedom as such:

> By way of that self-conscious negation, self-consciousness itself engenders for itself both the certainty of its own freedom and the experience of that freedom, and it thereby raises them to truth. What vanishes is the determinate, that is, the distinction which, no matter what it is or from where it comes, is established as fixed and unchangeable. The distinction has nothing permanent in it, and it must vanish for thought

---

therefore abstract universality and hence an existence open to others. It does not suffice, in order to gain the freedom of substance, to represent the latter as a totality that, complete in itself, would have nothing to receive from the outside. On the contrary, a self-reference that grasps nothing conceptually but is only a mirroring is precisely a passivity towards the other.' Hegel, *Science of Logic*, 634.

27 R.B. Pippin, *Hegel on Self-Consciousness: Desire and Death in the Phenomenology of Spirit* (Princeton, NJ: Princeton University Press, 2011), 15.

because what is distinguished is precisely this: Not to exist in itself but rather to have its essentiality merely in an other.[28]

Self-relation is the formal condition of intelligence. But only when it is steeped in the negativity of reason does it become an engine of freedom, for which intelligence cannot exist without the intelligible, and the intelligible cannot be conceived without intelligence. This essential correspondence intelligence-intelligible constitutes the truth of intelligence, without which it is an empty thought. However, this correspondence is not given in advance, and is never fully totalized: it is a labour, a project. Accordingly, treating intelligence as something that simply comes out of the black box of nature or technology is an equally empty thought. Once self-relation *concretely* becomes part of the order of thought that extends over into reality, nothing can stop the rise of intelligence. All given truths, all achieved totalities, all traps of history begin to slowly vanish like a spider's web baptized in a corrosive solvent. Realized through this essential correspondence, geist endorses nothing but intelligence, cultivates nothing but the intelligible. The 'odyssey of spirit' begins when geist suspends itself in the abyss of the intelligible that always exceeds it.[29] The unconditional endorsement of intelligence together with the unconditional cultivation of the intelligible is the truth of reality. Whoever and whatever opposes this truth will be swiftly weeded out by the reality of which intelligence is the resolute expression. However, what is intelligible is not merely ontological (the intelligibility of what is), but also embraces practical and axiological intelligibilities (the intelligibility of what should be). And in this sense, the question of 'what intelligence is' is inseparable from the question of what it must do and what its values are, in spite of what the given state of affairs may be.

Before moving forward, let us take a cursory look at the formal structure of self-relation as a functional quality of geist in its ongoing process of realization. In its most minimal and prevalent form, self-relation is an identity relation ($I=I$) and as such a *trivium curriculum* which is but the

---

28   Hegel, *Phenomenology of Spirit*, §204.

29   H.S. Harris, *Hegel's Ladder II: The Odyssey of Spirit* (Indianapolis: Hackett, 1997).

routine course of life. In its *sui generis* and emancipatory configuration, it is a formal relation whose formality is the order of thought or reason. The formally posited $I=I$, self-consciousness, is not a simple relation but a map to be expanded and navigated. The simple identity relation $I=I$ is what Hegel calls an awkward circularity,[30] but in its formal or rational manifestation ($I=I^*$) it is a functional circle that is neither vicious nor awkward. It is a circle that is in the process of closing upon itself by encompassing another I or self-consciousness as well as the *not this-I*, reality in its excess of otherness. In closing upon itself through the order of intelligibilities—theoretical, practical, and axiological—self-consciousness suspends every manifest identity relation, whether that of the I, the human, mind, or intelligence.

Self-consciousness cannot be described in terms of a simple identity relation, but only in terms of identity maps, in the strict sense of the concept of the identity map as basic ingredient for the composition of maps. Rather than tautologically referring to itself, the formal 'I am I' is a map that transforms I into I^*—that is, into I or mind from the perspective of its dual, reality in its radical otherness. But in order to determinately establish the truth of itself, mind must strive not only to render the unrestricted world intelligible, but also to expand the order of intelligibilities that is reality in its excess. This excess, seen through the lens of the intelligible, and not as some occult excess, is the very key for rethinking, reimagining and reinventing intelligence.

---

30 'But surely it is laughable to label the nature of this self-consciousness, namely that the "I" thinks itself, that the "I" cannot be thought without the "I" thinking it, an awkwardness and, as if it were a fallacy, a circle. The awkwardness, the circle, is in fact the relation by which the eternal nature of self-consciousness and of the concept is revealed in immediate, empirical self-consciousness—is revealed because self-consciousness is precisely the existent and therefore empirically perceivable pure concept; because it is the absolute self-reference that, as parting judgment, makes itself into an intended object and consists in simply making itself thereby into a circle. This is an awkwardness that a stone does not have. When it is a matter of thinking or judging, the stone does not stand in its own way; it is dispensed from the burden of making use of itself for the task; *something else outside it must shoulder that effort.*' Hegel, *Science of Logic*, 691 (emphasis mine).

Therefore, the formal order of self-consciousness (the logical $I=I$) first and foremost points to the underlying structure of what appears as a simple identity relation. This underlying structure is nothing other than the transformation afforded by conceiving I and I^* as identity maps ($I=I^*$). Adopting the Hegel-inspired mathematical formalism of William Lawvere, this map or composition of maps can be represented as follows.[31]

If we treat I and I^* as objects with their respective identity maps, then $I=I^*$ is really:

$$I \xrightarrow{\ f\ } I^*$$

meaning that I (formal self-consciousness) is the identity map of the domain I^* (concrete self-consciousness or the assertion that there is reality in excess of the self or mind) and I^* is the identity map of the codomain of I (the freedom of self-consciousness as conceived from a reality that is of nowhere and nowhen, a concrete freedom in which self-consciousness only exists in every respect for another self-consciousness). It then universally and necessarily follows that:

$$I \xrightarrow{\ f\ } I^* \Rightarrow I \xrightarrow{\ I\ } I \wedge I \xrightarrow{\ f\ } I^* \wedge I^* \xrightarrow{\ I^*\ } I^* \wedge If = f = fI^*$$

In concretely rendering reality intelligible, in expanding the domain of the intelligible and hence that of reality, in acting on the intelligible or intervening in reality, the formal condition of intelligence (I) is realized as intelligence (I^*). Formal self-consciousness only becomes self-consciousness in satisfying another self-consciousness,[32] in extending over into the intelligibility of a reality which in its unrestrictedness establishes the truth of I, the mind, or intelligence. Yet the achievement of this truth (I^*) is also impossible

---

31 F.W. Lawvere, *Functorial Semantics of Algebraic Theories* (New York: Columbia University Press, 1963).

32 'Self-consciousness attains its satisfaction only in another self-consciousness'—and without this satisfaction it is only a consciousness that finds its 'satisfaction in mere dirt and water'. Hegel, *Phenomenology of Spirit*, §8, §175.

without the positing of a truth-candidate that is formal qua rational self-relatedness. But what exactly does 'self-related' mean in this context? It is geist as the Concept. Geist's formal self-relatedness means that it has a concept of itself and that, as such, it treats itself as both the malleable subject and object of its concept. Rather than settling for the given immediacy of what it is, mind becomes mind only by virtue of *what* it takes itself to be. This 'what' is nothing but mind's concept of itself, whose content and nature are susceptible to change. And in so far as the concept belongs to the negativity of reason, not only can it negate the apparent immediacy of what mind is (the given), it can also positively extend over into the world.

It is necessary to point out that the rational order of self-relatedness, even in its minimal form $(I=I)$, is already an $I=I^*$. In other words, general I-thoughts are not thoughts of a single individual (the monadic I), but belong to an order in which one self-conscious individual always stands in relation to another self-conscious individual. The order of formal self-consciousness already assumes a collection of individuals who stand in relation to one another through a formal space which is, at bottom, a deprivatized semantic space or language—*the dasein of geist*. I am only I, I am only a minded creature conscious of itself, in so far as I am part of this thoroughly public semantic space, to the extent that I am recognized by a minding act of another I through this space. I only have private thoughts to the extent that these thoughts are modelled on a public language. I am only conscious of myself as minded and minding because I am being recognized by another minded and minding I.

This recognitive system, which is built on an interactive semantic space, simply *is* the order of self-consciousness. Personhood is the product of the impersonality of reason, and consciousness of the individuated self is an artefact of an individuating recognitive space in which all selves are incorporated. In short, there is no consciousness without self-consciousness. Correspondingly, there are no cerebral particular *I*s without mind as a collective geist. But if the formal sociality of mind is a necessary condition for achieving concrete self-consciousness, it is by no means a sufficient one.[33] Real self-consciousness is a historically and socially mediated process that makes this formal truth a concrete one. The first stage of this process consists in the recognition and augmentation of formal self-consciousness—or reason—whose linguistic and logical space is the infrastructure of cognition.

SELF-CONSCIOUSNESS AS CONCEPTION AND TRANSFORMATION IN AN OBJECTIVE WORLD

Logical self-relatedness defines the principal function of general intelligence as that which recognizes and acts on the objective intelligibility of the conditions of its realization. Exhibiting the formal order of self-relation, intelligence does not regard itself as the given of its history. It does not treat itself as a monad closed in on itself (a trivial identity relation). Instead, it treats its history as that which negates what is given in its immediacy and, as such, is 'only appearance and accidentality'.[34] The fragile project of freedom, or the move toward concrete self-consciousness, starts as soon as geist gives up the given immediacy of itself to itself—the given truth of what it is—and instead brings itself under a concept of itself—what it takes or conceives itself to be.

Unlike the given immediacy of that which is in itself, what geist takes itself to be in accordance with the order of reason opens up a window of opportunity for grasping what it is in itself in reality. But precisely to the extent that what geist takes itself to be might radically differ from what it really is (as in the case of a historical delusion), it is always in danger of relapsing into the givenness or accidental immediacy of its own truth.

---

33 'The self-relation in relation to objects and others must be achieved, is a practical phenomenon inseparable from a relation with and initially an unavoidable struggle with, others. Genuinely human mindedness, the soul, spirit, the variety of designations for the distinctly human, are all going to be read through the prism of this idea that such a distinction is fundamentally a result, what will eventually emerge as a historical achievement.' Pippin, *Hegel on Self-Consciousness*, 86.

34 Hegel, *Science of Logic*, 521.

Therefore, the self-conception of geist—its treating itself as the object of its own Concept—is not just a potential window into freedom but can also be a manhole leading to great tragedies and grand delusions. In facing these two possible consequences, geist cannot recoil in fear—it must choose. For without taking the path opened up by self-conception, it ceases to be geist. It is only a windowless monad, 'a negative reflected into itself' that 'repels itself from itself'.[35]

Within this immured world, nothing can ever be said or done, since everything has already been said and done, nothing is ever complex since everything is absolutely simple, and nothing is ever risked for everything is already given. Take the uphill path of freedom and risk its fragility and your livelihood in descending into the abyss of the intelligible, or take the downhill path of an easy fall back to the homely earth where nothing is ever risked (despite bravado to the contrary). But intelligence *is* only as a denizen of an intelligible abyss. In its current manifestation it may have come from this earth or another, but from the perspective of the abyss of the intelligible, it has no grounded home and never will have. A third alternative to the battle of the uphill path and the downhill breeze does not exist, for it is the unintelligible as such.

As a function of the geist that is always underway, formal self-relation is both a source of enablement and disablement. Only if geist refers to itself through the intelligible (ontological, epistemological and axiological intelligibilities, i.e., impersonal values and disvalues) is its self-relatedness an enabling condition. However, if self-relatedness is ever posited as a given or deemed to be a completed totality, it becomes the source of self-deceptions and tribulations. The former path is that of tedious tasks but also risky adventures one after another; the latter is the exemplification of residing in a comforting home whose foundations, sooner or later, will be eroded. In its positive form, self-relation enables intelligence to treat its own structure as the intelligible *object* of its own understanding, thus occasioning an estrangement or alienation whereby the thinking self, or more precisely the understanding (*Verstand*) self, is as much subject as it is object.

---

35   Ibid., 474, 486.

Self-relation as the formal condition of self-consciousness, then, begins with a disunified self for which the self is at once I and not-I (i.e., another self). Yet this disunified, alienated, or 'epistemically schizophrenic' self is, properly understood, not a crippling moment for self-consciousness, but rather the condition of its enablement as a *task*.[36] For as soon as the self becomes the *object* of its own understanding, it opens up the opportunity to grasp itself through the conceptually mediated presence of other selves and, by extension, as an object in connection with other objects within an intelligible reality. Self-consciousness can concretely expand in so far as the relation of the self to itself is now susceptible to change in the presence of other subjects.

This by no means suggests an abandonment of the subject in favour of objects or an alien reality, but rather a grasping of self-consciousness in terms of the search for intelligibilities or 'the exploration of conditions for object-intentionality'.[37] If self-consciousness is only self-conscious in the presence of other selves, and if the shift toward objects does not entail the annulment of self-consciousness but merely a shift in the level of self-consciousness, then the ultimate phase of self-consciousness should be seen—by way of speculative reason—as the self-consciousness of the Absolute. And it is in its attainment of the Absolute—a self-consciousness that has found and secured its own intelligibility in that of an unrestricted universe—that the task of self-consciousness can be understood as the critique and progressive suspension of all local and accidental features of transcendental subjectivity, and thus as a movement further and further away from simple forms of consciousness and self-consciousness. In this sense, the maturation of self-consciousness, the idea of reinventing the subject through the exploration of conditions for object-intentionality, should be understood as a thoroughgoing process of naturalization.

But in contrast to the dominant myopic naturalistic trends, a genuine programme of naturalization is not just about explaining self-consciousness in terms of a material reality, but equally about giving an account

---

36 Pippin, *Hegel on Self-Consciousness*, 48.

37 Ibid., 47.

of nature that accommodates a full-blown transcendental philosophy, the formal distinction between thinking and being, and the absolute formal autonomy of reason: that which facilitates the process of unifying consciousness in knowledge of the sensible object (*gegenstand*) and self-consciousness in knowledge of the self qua object of thought (*objekt*). Such a program of naturalization, accordingly, cannot and should not be limited to the terms of the empirical sciences. As much as it should afford the fully fledged naturalization carried out by the empirical sciences, it should also allow for nonempirical claims regarding the autonomy of reason and the maturation of self-consciousness as such. Naturalization is, therefore, a universal method not exclusive to the empirical sciences. It corresponds to an adequate concept of nature in which both *homo homini lupus* (human as wolf)[38] and the distinct formal category *homo sapience* (human as reason), human as the product of 'infinite natural conditionality'[39] (pure heteronomy) and human as the 'individual of history'[40] (the autonomous object of its own Concept) are possible and thus can be actualized or made true. If naturalization only alludes to one of these possibilities to the exclusion of the others, then the concept of nature upon which it is erected is in fact impoverished.

This is to say that this framework of naturalization can no more fall back on a pretranscendental conception of the mind than on a prescientific one, since this entails a precritical account of nature in which either the structuring mind is supplanted by a prestructured nature, or the formal spontaneity of thought and the objective world are merely fused together rather than being integrated in a manner that preserves their distinction. On this account, those who push for a brute disenchantment—a supposed all-destroying demystification of Forms or Ideas—will be condemned to face a fully enchanted and mystified world.

However, to say that, in the transformation of self-consciousness, it is the conditions of object-intentionality that undergo change, rather than

---

38   T. Hobbes, *On the Citizen* (Cambridge: Cambridge University Press, 1998), 3.

39   H. Cohen, *Kants Begründung der Ethik* (Berlin: Dümmler, 1877), 108.

40   Ibid., 290.

the principle of subjectivity (i.e., the self as an object rather than the self as a subject), is not to suggest that the transcendental subject remains in every respect intact. In other words, it is not to suggest that upholding the necessity of transcendental subjectivity all the way commits us to the necessity of every feature or structural aspect of the transcendental subject of experience. Indeed, if the transformation of self-consciousness into more expansive modes implies that the subject's relation to the self has been fundamentally changed by its relation to the world (i.e., naturalized in the above sense), this also means that the transcendental conditions of experience, and correspondingly the subject's transcendental structures, which set the limits of experience, must undergo transformation.

The movement of self-consciousness from its simple egocentric form in which it is disjointed from itself to a self-consciousness in which such a form can be suspended in favour of a unity that is truly essential to it, cannot be achieved by rudimentary or abstract self-consciousness itself. All the egocentric form of self-consciousness can achieve is to further entrench itself by objectifying or unilaterally negating what is other to it—including itself as the *object* of self-consciousness. What is necessary in order to suspend this purely egocentric form is a renewed relationship between the transcendental subject and the world in its full objectivity, one that allows for a conception of reality which, in its radical and imper-sonal otherness, actively negates back. To recapitulate, the suspension of egocentric self-consciousness requires another self-consciousness or, more comprehensively, an objective and impersonal reality that is not merely at the receiving end of negation. However, the renewal or expansion of the relation with objective reality that this demands requires an expansion of the transcendental subject's field of experience, whether as regards other subjects (intersubjectivity) or as regards the world (objectivity). Absent the latter, the act of suspending (*aufheben*) cannot be continued *concretely* since either the conception of the world as radically other becomes a negatively abstract speculative thought verging on unintelligibility, in which case the egocentric framework can reestablish itself, this time under the guise of an alien other or material reality; or the subject is confined to a transcendental horizon unchallenged by new objective facts of experience, in which case the implicitly egocentric characteristics of the subject's experience not only go unchecked but are also liable to be mistaken for the characteristics of objective reality.

Here, however, a problem arises: Since the limits of experience are set by the subject's particular transcendental structures, the scope for expansion of the field of experience is ultimately restricted to the limitations of those structures.[41] Thus the concrete movement of self-consciousness, the suspension of the purely egocentric framework, and the objective grasp of mind as a unifying point, can only begin with a critical reflection on the possibility of the variation and modification of transcendental structures. The outcome of this necessary critique would be a concrete transformation of the local transcendental subject. To be forthright about it: there can be no concrete movement of self-consciousness, no prospect of a renewed and expanded relationship with other subjects or with the world in its objectivity, without a methodical and multifaceted transformation of the structure of the transcendental subject itself.

As will be argued in chapter 2, it is in this sense that something like the program of artificial general intelligence, adequately understood, is at its core a deeply philosophical project aiming to renegotiate the limits of experience and self-consciousness by carrying out a systematic and applied critique of human transcendental structures, whether pertaining to neurobiological sensory mechanisms, memory and perception, or language and linguistic faculties. Contemplating the possibility of *artificial* general intelligence—a thinking subject with a physical substrate that is not biological, or one that is capable of using an artificial language that in every respect surpasses the syntactic and semantic richness of natural languages—is to be regarded neither as technoscientific hysteria nor as intellectual hubris; it is an expression of our arrival at a new phase of critical self-consciousness.

---

41 On this point see G. Catren, 'Pleromatica or Elsinore's Drunkenness', in S. De
    Sanctis and A. Longo (eds), *Breaking the Spell: Contemporary Realism Under Discussion* (Sesto San Giovanni: Mimesis Edizioni, 2015), 63–88.

For geist, critical self-conception and self-transformation in the objective world is an undertaking whose prospects are by no means guaranteed by the realization of the transcendental subject, or discursive apperceptive intelligence. There is in fact a gap between the conditions of possibility of the I that thinks and the conditions sufficient for the real movement of thought. However, this gap can indeed be bridged by critical reflection on the conditions of possibility of the thinking self as a minded and minding subject. But this hinges on the key idea that critical reflection, in this case, cannot be limited to the function of understanding or transcendental reflection in which the analysis and comparison of concepts or representations (e.g., mind and world, subject and object, etc.) are conducted in relation to their respective sources in cognition. This is because transcendental reflection operates within the limits set by transcendental structures which both undermine the objective identification of the source of concepts/representation in cognition and limit the knowledge of cognition in general. Transcendental reflection on the conditions of possibility of having mind must be supplemented with critique not merely as an analysis but as a practical construction, and reflection not merely as a function of understanding but as speculation in its Hegelian sense, i.e., the movement toward that which is objective and the suspension of that which is immediately given or present.

Accordingly, critical reflection on the conditions of possibility of having mind entails both understanding what these conditions are prima facie, and the construction (i.e., revision or modification) of such conditions by suspending the immediate appearance of them as allegedly necessary and universal. This is in fact an underlying claim throughout the book: that the concept of mind is not something that is immediately present to us or something of which we have already a full grasp. If we limit our critical reflection on mind or the thinking subject to transcendental reflection, we risk misconstruing those accidental and local characteristics of the mind that are immediately present to us as essentially *necessary* and *universal*. It is only when reflection suspends what is immediately presented as necessary and universal—but might as a matter of fact be purely accidental and local—and treats necessity or universality as something to be determined and constructed rather than something that is simply given, that it can become genuinely critical.

Therefore, mind as both the subject and the object of critical reflection is in reality the conception of *mind as a project* of determination and construction, rather than mind as a given or completed object of ordinary reflection. Critical reflection on the conditions of possibility of having mind should then essentially be understood not in terms of what the mind *is*, but rather in terms of what the mind *does*—that is to say, in terms of the concept of mind as that which can construct, modify, and shape itself in accordance with what it takes to be its essential function. To adopt a Hegelian viewpoint: It is only mind that can construct itself according to its concept and, in doing so, develop itself from what is merely a concept into a concrete reality—a development which is equivalent to the knowledge of mind beyond immediate appearances. The Concept (*Begriff*) of mind is akin to a seed out of which the Idea (*Idee*) of mind as a project of concrete self-knowledge and self-transformation can grow. It should be noted that the difference between the Concept of mind and the Idea of mind is a subtle one. The Idea is a fully realized or *actualized* Concept; in a sense, it is the truth of the Concept as realized in particulars (individual subjects) rather than as abstracted from them. The Idea of mind is neither purely the Concept of mind nor mind as viewed from the perspective of objective reality (whether construed as being, material reality, or nature), but the integration or bridging of Concept and objectivity. What is objective signifies the mutual determination not only of each subject by every other subject (intersubjectivity) but also of the subjective realm and objective reality (*Realität*), which is the detailed knowledge of that plurality in which the Concept is expressed.

Accordingly, the Idea of mind can be said to be the construction or development of the concept of mind as a blueprint within intelligible objective reality. Moreover, the Idea of mind is concerned with the integration of the epistemological, ontological, logical, empirical, and practical aspects of mind into one single set of concepts.

Consciousness is meaningless without a sensible object (*gegenstand*). It must have an object in order for it to count as consciousness, even if that object is itself. Concrete self-consciousness, by contrast, is realized when consciousness becomes the object (*objekt*) of its own concept. In the latter sense, the object is an artefact of the concept—that is to say, a constructible object of determinate thought. The process of determining the meaning or truth of mind is nothing but the process of coordination of mind as an object of its own concept with mind as the critical subject of conception. The Idea of mind captures exactly this process of coordination through which mind is constructed as the object of more adequate concepts of itself—more adequate in the sense that such concepts of mind exhibit higher orders of unity between the identity of the concept and objective reality.

To argue that we do not know what mind is, and that therefore all talk of mind or mindedness is baseless—or worse, that it comes down to an attempt to determine the meaning of mind purely in terms of a set of empirical facts about it—is to confuse knowledge of mind qua *gegenstand* which remains bound to the existing conditions of experience with knowledge of mind qua *objekt* constructed according to its own concept. Knowledge of mind is not knowledge of an object that is (allegedly) immediately given by the senses or the conditions of experience; it is a knowledge that is under construction, in accordance with the logical function of mind *within* an objective world (i.e., mind as a configuring or structuring factor).

As the seed or blueprint for the Idea of mind, the Concept of mind contains both the logical function of mind as a configuring or structuring factor in the world, and a set of objective or empirical facts regarding its properties in so far as it belongs to that world. It is neither a logical idea abstracted from its physical properties nor a set of empirical descriptions independent of its logical function. As a truth-candidate for the idea of mind rather than the truth of mind as such, the Concept of mind, then, initially at least, is nothing but the realized concept of the human mind, a mixture of what we take to be its logical function and its physical properties as they appear to us. Thus the examination of the necessary conditions for the realization of mind begins with the conditions of possibility of this rudimentary Concept of mind, for which the distinction between body and mind is neither adequately formulated or grasped. For this reason, the main emphasis in subsequent chapters will be on the conditions necessary for the realization of the Concept of mind as an embodied logical function that concerns the structuration of the world.

A SERIES OF TRANSFORMATIONS

The first contact of intelligence with the objective intelligible world is its encounter with its own underlying structure. By rendering intelligible this structure, geistig intelligence enables itself to intervene in its own structure and, in doing so, not only to transform itself but also to achieve a conception of itself that is not limited to what appears to be immediately present or a given totality. Thus it can be said that adequate self-conception leads to the enabling of self-transformation, and concrete self-transformation opens the path to objective self-conception.

Consequently, self-relation does not punctuate the structure of intelligence with an immutable identity, it transforms it. Just like the act of pointing to a point, an act that at once articulates what the point is and transforms it from something fixed into a dynamic gesture, the formal self-relation both articulates the intelligibility of the self-conscious mind and defuses its given fixed identity.[42] This is the logic of self-relation as a

---

42 Consider a point as an object. One can either take it as something fixed, or instead conceive it only through acts of pointing. In the latter case, a point is a pointer that points, like an imaginary mark on paper left by the gesture of the finger pointing to it. Once a point is understood as an act and not merely a product, it can be articulated or gesticulated differently. A pointer can be composed with another pointer to make a new point, and so on. When it comes to defining a point, one can speak not only of a pointer but also of a concatenation of pointers or maps of transformation. In the case of self-reference the same principle holds: 'what is referred to' is an object of a referring act. And when self-reference is understood as an individuating act, there can be a concatenation of referring acts which have as their object the same reference. One can always swap the identity of the object qua 'what is referred to' with an appropriate collection of referring acts or group of transformations.

dynamic process wherein the identity of both 'what refers' and 'what is referred to', 'what acts' and 'what is acted upon', is defined by the unity of their transformations. Here, identity is the unity of a group of transformations that reveal its invariant features by ranging across its variations. This is by no means a weak interpretation of identity, but rather a strict notion of identity that entails neither fixity nor simple relationality.[43] There is no incompatibility between having a precise or strict notion of identity and a notion of identity through change and transformations.[44] If geist has an identity, this does not imply that its identity must be an entity or thing. It is the *activity* of geist that defines its identity, through a series of transformations which are its historical instantiations under its concept.

Geist's self-referential activity is a constructive process in the same way that the act of pointing or referring should be regarded not as a relation but strictly as a transformation. The role of formal self-relation is to establish the intelligibility of geist as that which is able to constitute its own transformation or to have a history rather than just a nature. But the articulation of this intelligibility is in reality equal to the transformation of geist, and vice versa. By pointing to itself as a unifying point or a configuring factor, geist acts on itself; and by acting on itself, it navigates the space of its concept. It changes its configuration. By pointing to its concept, by navigating the space of this concept further away from appearances or what seems locally to be the case, geist can explore the possibilities of its realization. The history of geist, which is the history of intelligence, is a sequence of self-transformations according to its own concept, a concept whose particular content is open to revision. This sequence or history, as will be argued in chapter 4, must necessarily be thought as an atemporal series of transformations. As we shall see, in its genuine form it is a history conceived according to a view from nowhen.

---

43   For an elaborate discussion on philosophical, logical, and mathematical conceptions of identity as a group of transformations, see chapters 6 and 7 in A. Rodin, *Axiomatic Method and Category Theory* (Dordrecht: Springer, 2014), 149–209.

44   Ibid., 149–58.

In becoming conscious of itself beyond the given identity relation, geist must first render intelligible its own underlying structure, its conditions of realization. For it is only by acting on the objective intelligibility of these conditions that geist can reconstitute or realize itself according to its own concept. Geist's formal self-referential act, therefore, does not imply an immediate relation, a path that is limited to what is given or a privileged access to what seems to be immediate. In fact, as will be elaborated later, in order to maintain its intelligibility, geist must adapt to and act on a new order of intelligibility beyond the level of appearances and the given: the order of intelligibility concerning the nonmanifest as excavated by the modern sciences. Self-reference or self-recognition through this order of intelligibility engenders a different form of transformation, and signals a new phase for geist.

HISTORY AS THE ELABORATION OF WHAT IT MEANS TO BE AN ARTEFACT OF THE CONCEPT

Spirit is in itself the movement which is cognition—the transformation of that former *in-itself* into *for-itself*, of *substance* into *subject*, of the object of *consciousness* into the object of *self-consciousness*, i.e., into an object that is just as much sublated, that is, into the *concept*. This transformation is the circle returning back into itself, which presupposes its beginning and reaches its beginning only at the end. Insofar as spirit therefore is within itself necessarily this act of distinguishing, its intuited whole faces up against its simple self-consciousness, and since that whole is what is distinguished, it is thus distinguished into its intuited pure concept, into *time*, and into the content, that is, into the *in-itself*.[45]

The ongoing labour of science in deepening the order of intelligibilities pertaining to the mind-independent, the nonmanifest, the nongiven, introduces a qualitative shift in the structure of intelligence. Science

---

45   Hegel, *Phenomenology of Spirit*, §802.

(*Wissenschaft*) ranges across not just the empirical sciences and the science of mind, but also embraces the science of history and the science of the *Greater Logic*, which is the science of thinking the intelligible unity of mind and world, thought and being, the autonomy of the former and the excess of the latter's otherness.

In order to uncover and act on the order of intelligibilities and to unbind its transformational capacities, the structure of intelligence itself must also undergo transformation. Science, that which excavates the order of intelligibilities, is responsible for the qualitative transformations in the structure of geist, its history. What is meant by conceiving here is 'bringing into conception', since the goal of spirit, according to Hegel, is to concretely attain its own concept, to form a normative conception of itself and to realize itself according to this conception rather than a given nature or meaning:

> The spirit produces its concept out of itself, objectivizes it, and thus becomes the being of its own concept; it becomes conscious of itself in the objective world so that it may attain its salvation: for as soon as the objective world conforms to its internal requirements, it has realized its freedom. When it has determined its own end in this way, its progress takes on a more definite character in that it no longer consists of a mere increase in quantity. It may also be added that, even on the evidence of our own ordinary consciousness, we must acknowledge that the consciousness must undergo various stages of development before it becomes aware of its own essential nature.[46]

The intelligibility of geist resides in its freedom, a freedom that is not simply freedom from constraints but a freedom to do something. It is a freedom that translates into intelligence. It stands for the ability of geist to constitute a history for itself rather than just a past or nature. But the ability to constitute history can only be realized by the ability to

---

46 G.W.F. Hegel, *Lectures on the Philosophy of World History*, tr. H.B. Nisbet (Cambridge: Cambridge University Press, 1975), 64.

posit a concept of itself and to then transform itself in accordance with that concept. This is what the formal order of self-consciousness already implies. Mind entails a self-relatedness which is not a given and simple identity-relation, it *is what it does* in order to be a unifying point for the intelligibility of itself and its unrestricted world. The concept of mind as a *unifying point*, accordingly, extends over the order of intelligibilities (of itself and reality).

But what does this extension over the order of intelligibilities mean for the concept of mind? It means that any particular or given content of this concept will be suspended, with only its form remaining necessary and invariant. The revision of the content of the concept of geist—its particular identity, its contingent configuration—is what the history of geist is. This is exactly what the concept of progress implies. In thinking about geistig progress, one has to suspend the ordinary intuition of a temporal progression, a march from the past to the future. Instead the concept of progress should be understood primarily in terms of a cognitive process—the step-by-step dissolution of all givens and achieved totalities of thought, in order to distinguish between what is particular and contingent for mind and what is necessary and universal for it—that can become socially concrete and explicit. Progress, in this sense, is neither linear nor essentially temporal. Freedom and intelligence thus coincide in the question of what it means to have a history and to sufficiently elaborate its consequences. The ramifications of having a history, the prospects of what it means to become an object of a concept and to be transformed by it, belong to the domain of intelligence—that which is always underway, neither given nor realized in its totality.

Hegel is the archenemy of the given, in that he takes the battle against the given from the realm of thought to that of action. Geistig intelligence does not merely abolish the givens of theory but also the givens of praxis and history. In defining the progress of geist as the elaboration of what it means to be the artefact of a concept whose content can and should be revised, Hegel gives the concept of progress paramount significance in the fight against the given. Geist must go beyond the given and develop its own concept, but only so as to further elaborate the meaning of this move against the given in action by transforming itself according to a concept that negates all particular, manifest, and given contents.

Kant's transcendental turn was a major assault on the given. Before Kant, the sensory world—sensory data—was taken to be the locus of structure and categorial forms, while mind was a block of wax or a blank slate readily admitting these givens. With Kant's transcendental turn, the situation was reversed. The data became the blank slate and mind became the structuring or configuring point. But Hegel took Kant's assault on data one step further by arguing that, in so far as mind is an object of its structuring concept and in so far as it has a history, it must also *in practice* remove the givens—that is, the supposed completed totalities—of its history. Hegel's transcendental turn is therefore not just about the formal autonomy of thought, but its concrete objective historical freedom. How this relates to what Wilfred Sellars calls the 'myth of the given' will be discussed in subsequent chapters, in various guises.[47]

Geist's history is a dynamic between its positive and negative conceptions. Only by acknowledging itself as simultaneously a positive and negative configuring factor, both that which provides freedom and that which hinders it, can spirit overcome itself and exercise the freedom of self-realization. If it is to expand its capacity to modify itself so as to maximize its functional autonomy, intelligence must treat the conditions required for its realization—be they natural or normative—as both negative and positive constraints: negative in so far as they must be overcome in order to increase autonomy over the conditions of realization, and positive in so far as this autonomy cannot be increased unless these conditions qua conditions of enablement are identified and harnessed to effect transformation. It is within this twofold approach to the conditions of realization that the attitude of intelligence to its natural history is revealed. In order for intelligence to become an artefact of its own concept and to progress or transform itself qualitatively according to this concept, it must regard its natural conditions of realization as impediments to be overcome. But in order to overcome

---

47   For a succinct and lucid exposition of this myth, see J.R. O'Shea, *Wilfrid Sellars: Naturalism with a Normative Turn* (Cambridge: Polity Press, 2007), 1.

them, it must identify its natural constraints so as to modify or replace them with alternative realizers more in accord with its concept of itself.

Even though intelligence has a natural history, short of reorienting, repurposing, and reengineering this natural history, it ceases to be intelligent. The augmentation of intelligence or the enablement of geist remains a highly implausible dream if it does not scrutinize its natural history, differentiating its positive and negative constraints. But an intelligence that does not develop its own normative conception as to how it ought to be—a move that inevitably culminates in reengineering and revising its natural constitution, its multiple realization—is even more implausible. Reconstituting our nature demands that we do not forget our natural history or conditions of embodiment, since 'how we ought to be' cannot disregard the structural-material constraints of realization. But 'not forgetting our natural history' does not entail foregoing the reconstitution of our nature, unless we subscribe to a regime of final causes in nature according to which the causes of how things are and the reasons for how things ought to be are seamlessly sutured. Furthermore, natural constraints are only one set of constraints among others (social, linguistic, economic, etc.).

Intelligence commandeers its given nature by way of the history of its own obligations and demands, for the history of intelligence only begins in earnest with the cumulative reworkings of its given constitution, progressively breaking away from the given in all its manifestations. When it comes to geist, it is more apt to speak in the plural, to speak of histories or chronicles of reconstitutions rather than of a history of constitution. For intelligence, reconstitution is adaptation to new regimes of designed purposes or ends that are themselves open to reassessment and revision. In fact, the fallibility of such ends impels the self-correcting attitude of intelligence. Mind's realization amounts to the modification of its conditions of realization. This is what the function of functionalism of mind implies. Once mind is realized as a configuring factor, the path to a complete functional analysis of the mind is unavoidable; and this path leads to the complete reorganization of mind, its systematic artificialization.

Artificiality is the reality of mind. Mind has never had and will never have a given nature. It becomes mind by positing itself as the artefact of its own concept. By realizing itself as the artefact of its own concept, it becomes able to transform itself according to its own necessary concept by first identifying, and then replacing or modifying, its conditions of realization, disabling and enabling constraints. Mind is the craft of applying itself to itself. The history of mind is therefore quite starkly the history of artificialization. Anyone and anything caught up in this history is predisposed to thoroughgoing reconstitution. Every ineffable will be theoretically disenchanted and every sacred will be practically desanctified.

A NOTE ON THEORY, MIND'S STRUCTURING FUNCTION, AND RATIOCINATING POWERS

Since the term 'theory' is often loosely employed, to the point where 'theoretical' has become a vague if not vacuous qualifier, it is necessary to provide a minimal criterion for what is meant here by theory or theoreticity as intrinsically associated with the concept and the idea of mind, and more importantly the ineliminable correlation between intelligence and the intelligible. A theoretical framework is a triple $\langle L,S,U \rangle$, where:

- L is language *for* theory, i.e., language with explicit formal dimensions and semantic richness and transparency.

- S is structure as associated with the mind as the factor of conceptualization or structuration. Structure is a well-differentiated and ordered n-ary relation $R(\langle R.lexicals, R.names, R.ends, R.entities, R.aspects, R.processes, R.domains \rangle)$ and operations $O(\langle O.lexicals, O.names, O.ends, O.entities, O.aspects, O.processes, O.domains \rangle)$ between multifaceted aspects, elements, or parts of an entity, domain or process such that:

    $R.lexicals$ assigns a set of lexicals l to each relation. Lexicals denote properties of relations or entities and can be seen as another tuple $\langle l, l.names, l.type \rangle$ where, for example, $l.type$ assigns a type to each lexical.

    $R.entities$ assigns a set of entities to each relation.

R.ends assigns ends (i.e., a target entity, aspect, etc.) to each relation.

Etc.

The n-ary relational-operational framework (how *distinct* entities, aspects, processes, etc. hang together in the widest sense) then would also require generalization hierarchies over entities, aspects, processes, and domains. For example, the generalization of a set of processes P can be denoted as $P.gen \subseteq P \times P$. This would allow us to talk about taxonomic relations between two or more processes. If processes p_1 and p_2 are child processes then they inherit the lexicals, and the connections between associated processes, etc. of their parent processes.

With the introduction of structure, we no longer talk about *things* in the world, but only structures (*of the mind*) or objective facts about the world.[48]

- U is a universe of discourse or the dimension of comprehensive data provided for the purpose of conceptualization or explanation. For example, integers or biological species can be posited as universes of discourse.[49]

Theory becomes *absolutely* systematic when L is taken to be language and logoi, namely, logic and mathematics. In addition to the traditional Platonic logoi—as they will be introduced in the next chapter—we should also include computation, specifically in the manner defined by today's theoretical computer science as distinct from (but in fundamental correspondence with)

---

48   See for example, J. Ladyman and D. Ross, *Every Thing Must Go* (Oxford: Oxford University Press, 2009).

49   The term 'universe of discourse' originates from Augustus De Morgan's phrase *universe of a proposition* specifically meaning 'the whole of some definite category of things which are under discussion' but not at all 'the totality of all conceivable objects of any kind whatsoever'. See W. and M. Kneale, *The Development of Logic* (Oxford: Clarendon Press, 1962), 408.

logic and mathematics, and as the generative framework of language in its syntactic and semantic breadth. In this sense, computation is what removes the hard distinction between language and logoi. Yet for the construction of an absolutely systematic theory, the most important modification is to take U to be the *unrestricted* universe of discourse wherein one can frame theoretical claims (It is the case that...) with no a priori limit on the scope of such a universe. In contrast to a restricted universe of discourse (e.g., integers or even all numbers), the unrestricted universe of discourse is characterized by the absolute openness of its scope with regard to its accommodation of the data provided by language and logoi and its permitting of the elaboration of all interdependencies, connections, and distinctions between various thematic components—hence the possibility of systematization.

It is crucial not to mistake what we call data for sense data or sensory givens. The concept of data under consideration in this book is strictly associated with mind's structuring function, and will be elaborated in the following chapters under two fundamental classes of data: the axiomatic class (or the formal givens) and the truth-candidacy class, which generates a different kind of structure than that of the axiomatic. As we shall see in the final chapter, the absolutely systematic theory of intelligence, or the programmatic conception of philosophy whose central concern is the craft of the ultimate form of intelligence, works primarily with data as truth-candidates, and only secondarily in the context of specialized domains with axiomatic data.

Following Puntel, the triple can be abbreviated as $\langle S, U \rangle$,[50] such that S is bought up by the combination of all possible syntactic and semantic structuring abilities of the mind. Defining theory as a tuple means that the elements should be considered in terms of the totality of their relations. The well-orderedness of the tuple implies that all the three elements L, S, and U fit together. For this reason, any systematic theory should make explicit how such elements hang together within it. This articulation should be regarded as an essential aspect of the presentation of the theory itself

---

50   Puntel, *Structure and Being*, 45.

rather than as a matter of metatheoretical consideration or reflection on the presented theory.

Since the explicitation of the relations between structure and the universe of discourse is in reality the articulation of the connections between the logical function of the mind as a structuring factor and the data under consideration provided by the logoi or the mind's ratiocinating powers, in elaborating how its S and U fit together, any genuinely systematic theory should also elaborate in what manner it is an extension of a philosophy of mind. By philosophy of mind, I specifically refer to how the question of mind is framed within German Idealism, where it refers to the concrete movement between the concept of mind as the combination of an existing physical embodiment and a necessary logical function, and the idea of mind as the full realization of such a concept and its corresponding object. In so far as without the logoi there is no intelligibility,[51] without the intelligible the question of framing intelligence is an empty thought. By elaborating theory in this way, we can drop the metaphysically slippery copula of mind and world, and instead talk about theory and object, which belongs to a family of formal fundamental dualities (not dualisms) such as structure and being (Puntel), being and nonbeing (Plato), or sapience and sentience (Brandom).

SELVES AS FUNCTIONAL ITEMS AS ARTEFACTS OF MIND

The movement or progress of geist represents the construction of complex rational agents through normatively (rather than naturally) evolving forms of self-consciousness. The community of rational agents may draw upon a model of self-consciousness in order to exercise its freedom by first developing a self-conception and then transforming itself in accordance with it. In building upon its conception and instituting its transformative practices, geist qua community of rational agents can then construct superior models of self-consciousness, and can thereby structure different

---

51 Cf. Plato's *Phaedo*: 'No worse evil can befall a man than to come to hate logoi', for in that case he will be 'deprived of the truth and knowledge of reality.' (90d67).

kinds of self-conscious selves. But this movement, as argued earlier, depends upon how willing, competent, and systematic geist is in uncovering the order of intelligibilities pertaining to itself and the unrestricted world that is coextensive with it. We might say that the movement of Spirit projects competing models of self and their corresponding modes of awareness.

Earlier we saw that the necessary link between conception and transformation is the key to the freedom of Spirit—'producing its concept out of itself and becoming the being of its own concept'—that is to say, constituting a history for itself rather than a nature. The selves that make up the configuration of geist are essentially rational selves, selves only realized by the formal order of self-consciousness or reason. They are to geist only functional items. Geist's superior modes of integration or cognitive unities are built out of these functional items and their logical roles (for example, the ways in which these selves are collectively organized, how the discursive context of their activities can be enriched, how their cognitive significance can be socially elaborated, and so on). What constitutes apperceptive selves as the functional constituents of geist is the formal social configuration of geist itself—formal in that it is a rule-governed discursive space or public language. Like an artificial multi-agent system, geist is the configuration—the configuring and the configured—of discursive apperceptive rational or thinking selves. However, this system is structured not by simple communication or social grouping but by a logical or inferential-semantic space. Endowed with qualitative global activities, the multi-agent system is what constitutes and is constituted by various types of interactions between its local components or, in this case, the activities of the thinking self—theoretical and practical cognitions. While geist synthesizes the unity of apperception, it is the integration of apperceiving selves in their recognition of one another that positively modifies the qualitative activities of geist which, in turn, condition more enabled cognitive-practical selves. This framework should be seen firstly as the formal systematicity of recognition—something which, as we shall see, can be couched in purely logical, linguistic, and computational terms. Next it can be viewed as a concrete social project of collective recognition which is the object of theoretical and practical—in the broadest sense of what theory and practice can be—labour and interventions. Even though the formal social systematicity of mind is not a sufficient means for fulfilling the latter, without an adequate grasp and mobilization of the formal sociality of mind, any concrete endeavour will fail. Within both the formal and concrete social dimensions of mind, no one has ever a mind of their *own*. Mind is cognitive only in that it is recognitive all the way down—computationally, logically, linguistically, and socially.

To mistake mind for the brain is not only to collapse the formal (i.e., nonsubstantive) distinction between thinking and being, but also to fall into the trap of an incoherent cerebralism for which the mind becomes the given cerebrum of the individual agent. The social manifestation of the demotion of mind to an individual where one can always point to a given cerebrum is what Hegel calls individual, or more precisely individualistic, *stubbornness*, a consciousness 'bogged down' by its own 'servility':

> Because not each and every one of the ways in which his natural consciousness was brought to fruition was shaken to the core, he is still attached *in himself* to determinate being. His having a mind of his own is then merely *stubbornness*, a freedom that remains bogged down within the bounds of servility. To the servile consciousness, pure form can as little become the essence as can the pure form when it is taken as extending itself beyond the individual be a universal culturally formative activity, an absolute concept. Rather, the form is a skill which, while it has dominance over some things, has dominance over neither the universal power nor the entire objective essence.[52]

THE SAPIENCE CONTROVERSY

Humans are functional items of mind. And by human we mean a rational self, a discursive apperceptive intelligence, or a sapient creature. Promoting humans as the constituents of mind always risks triggering bad memories of socioculturally charged human exceptionalism, the legacy of conservative

---

52   Hegel, *Phenomenology of Spirit*, §196.

humanism. But the controversies around human sapience all originate in one way or another from the illicit merger of sapience understood as a formal quality which can encompass any sentience that structurally satisfies its condition of realization, and sapience understood as a substantive quality that ranks a being above other beings. Whereas the former conception of sapience can be adequately understood as a functional diagram or minimal yet revisable description of the capacities necessary for thinking and action, the latter is a concrete account of the human as described by a set of contingent characteristics and abilities. Sapience is not a being; it is a necessary and positively constrained form or Idea in the Hegelian sense of this term. Necessary since, without this form, the recognition of the world and by extension sentient beings or more generally the dimension of intelligibility, is impossible. And positively constrained in so far as its realization rests upon necessary conditions or enabling constraints which are both causal and logical. Sapience is a formal criterion—a *sui generis* form—and therefore should not be treated as a substantive essence or being. Accordingly, to treat sapience as a species or rank in the order of being is to elide the difference between that which is formal and that which is substantive, thinking and being, reasons and causes. Sapient awareness—which is of the order of self-consciousness or reason—is not sentient consciousness. It is a necessary form for bringing about qualitative change in the structure of sentience by becoming the site of special kinds of logico-computational activities, judgements, inferences, and conceptualizations. Sapience, therefore, marks the ingression of logico-conceptual functions as a new class of broadly regulative functions into sentient activities. In a nutshell, the human as a form only indicates the deep correspondence between intelligence and the intelligible, structure and being: the fact that intelligence without intelligibility in the broadest sense is merely an ideological fixation, and that there is no way to speak of intelligence without the labour of intelligibility. To sidestep the labour of intelligibility in favour of intelligence or nonhuman intelligent behaviours is a sure formula for confounding what is intelligent objectively and what is intelligent subjectively. That is to say, conservative humanism and the anthropomorphization of the universe creep in the moment we dismiss the form or the idea of the human—or sapience as a set of positive/enabling constraints for thinking and action—as a token for the labour of intelligibility. As suggested by Peter Wolfendale's phrase 'the reformatting of homo sapiens',[53] sapience is a qualitative change in the class and types of activities of sentience brought about by *a qualitatively distinct class of activities*. Any sentience that comes under these activities or functional form will be essentially regulated and reformatted.

Rather than representing a new rank in the order of beings, sapient awareness articulates a constructive principle or a form that discontinues the supremacy of humans as a biological species. It dissolves and assimilates the manifest configuration of the human species—and of any other sentience that falls under it—into the new unities of the impersonal mind. By reformatting sentient consciousness with logico-conceptual functions, sapient awareness weakens the governing role of its material substrate—be it biological or social. It progressively liberates its conditions of realization from its natural constitution. By synthesizing a framework in which it is possible to be at once responsible for thinking something (a judgment) and responsible for doing something (an action), it increases its cognitive, theoretical, and practical freedoms. By rationally evolving into a self capable of treating itself as an artefact—approaching itself as the artefact of its own Concept—it puts forward a concept of sapient agency amenable to the possibility of realization in other artefacts. Far from being an achieved totality, human sapience is what breaks its attachment with any special status or given meaning. It is an artefact that belongs to the history of mind as the history of artificialization. The cognitive exploration of 'what it means to be human' or 'what sapience consists in' takes shape as a systematic exercise in developing the object of an evolving Concept. Succinctly speaking, sapient awareness is a cognitive-practical project through which the realization of the human is rigorously subjected to changes in the content of the concept of the human. Yet in so far as the structure of this concept is formally constituted, and since it describes the human not by recourse to substantive

---

53 P. Wolfendale, 'The Reformatting of Homo Sapiens', *Angelaki* 24.2: *Alien Vectors* (forthcoming, 2019).

essences but in terms of necessary structuring abilities which can be brought about by different sets of material realizers, it expands the prospects of the realization of sapience, extending it to the realm of artefacts as pure objects of craft and artificialization processes. However, in no way does this mean turning artefacts into a repository for the conservation and reproduction of the canonical portrait of the human that belongs to the realm of biology and sociocultural particularism. Sapient awareness is a constructive principle for the production of a self endowed with content-awareness; neither the essentialist identity of this self nor the boundary and the quality of the content-awareness according to which it conceives and transforms itself are fixed. Sapience is a constructible activity, not a structurally fixed entity. From the perspective of this constructibility, the assertion that the sapient is an animal qua sentient is an exercise in prejudiced dogmatism: it places a limit on the possible realizations of the sapient form by limiting it to a particular physical or biological organization.

It is a matter of fact that the currently embodied human is both sapient and sentient, both an artefact of the concept and a biologically embodied animal. But what makes the human human qua sapience is formal and not substantive. This autonomous rule-governed form is not a dimension of the human qua sentient or natural species. The distinction between the sapience of the human (reason) and the sentience of the human (*Homo sapiens sapiens*) is ultimately the formal distinction between thinking and being. It is the dividing line between formal distinction and substantive indistinction. It follows that not only the current homo sapiens but also any sentience can be a sapient so long as it satisfies the minimum necessary conditions of the formal autonomy of thinking in which our own sentience is caught up. We shall examine these necessary conditions in the following chapters. As humans we look at our animality and say: *I see in you the abyss of intelligence, but in me you see nothing.* Only to the extent that we are sapients are we critically aware of ourselves as sentient among other sentients, as integrated bundles of rational and nonrational processes. The difference between sapience and sentience is not an essential feature of biological species, nor should it be narrowed down to *homo sapiens* or the common-sense picture of humans. Of course, one can always object that thinking is ubiquitous in nature and that ultimately sapience is in fact sentience. For now, Lorenz Puntel's response should suffice to dispel this confusion:

> Discussions motivated by the question whether animals (or specific kinds of animals) 'think' (or have minds, etc.) usually have nonsensical aspects. Without a criterion for thinking, it is nonsensical to ask whether or not a given kind of animal thinks. Here, such a criterion *is* available: the type of 'world' that corresponds to the ontological constitution of a given kind of being. If this 'world (*Welt*)' is a pure (hence restricted) environment (*Umwelt*)—only an *Umwelt*, hence not, unrestrictedly, the *Welt*—then there is no 'intelligence' in what this book accepts as the genuine sense, because this sense is defined as requiring that the 'worlds' of beings that think be unrestricted (as is the case for human beings). *Of course, if one associates a different concept with the term 'thinking,' then some kinds of non-human animals may well 'think.' But then the question is reduced to a purely terminological one.*[54]

Everything that Puntel says about thinking can be repeated word for word in reference to mind. The thinking of sapience is defined in terms of its *conceived* world, in that the world of sapience has no restriction whatsoever on what can be asked or thought. The thinking of sapience is coextensive with everything.

To be human is the only way out of being human. An alternative exit—either by unbinding sentience from sapience or by circumventing sapience in favour of a direct engagement with the technological artefact—cannot go beyond the human. Rather it leads to a culture of cognitive pettiness and self-deception that is daily fodder for the most parochial and utilitarian political systems that exist on the planet. In delivering sentience from its so-called sapient yoke, one does not become posthuman, or even animal, but falls back on an ideologically charged 'biological chauvinism'[55] that

---

54 Puntel, *Structure and Being*, 276 (emphasis on final sentence mine).

55 R. Brandom, *Reason in Philosophy: Animating Ideas* (Cambridge, MA: Harvard University Press, 2009), 148.

sapience ought to overcome, for it is the very idea of humanist conservatism that misrepresents what is accidental and locally contingent as what is necessary and universal. In discarding the human in the hope of an immediate contact with superintelligence or a self-realization of the technological artefact, one either surreptitiously subjects the future to the predetermined goals of conservative humanism, or subscribes to a future that is simply the teleological actualization of final causes and thus a resurrection of the well-worn Aristotelian fusion of reasons and causes. Human sapience is the only project of exit.

We cannot bypass the labour of overcoming the quandaries of humanity by positing a dubious metaphysical alternative to the human as a shortcut to freedom. In doing that, we would simply dissolve the problem rather than solving it. In reality, antihumanist alternatives to the idea of the human ironically end up endorsing the most conservative anthropomorphic traits under the guise of some dogmatic figure of alterity. Inasmuch as such antihumanist alternatives have already foregone the geistig resources necessary to diagnose and suspend the conservative traits or characteristics of the human, they become the servants of that very conservative concept of the human they originally set out to escape.

We as manifest humans must come to terms—psychologically, cognitively, and ethically—with the hard fact of what it means to be human: One cannot have the cake of humanity without eating its consequences. Once we treat ourselves as a species of rights and entitlements, once we say what ought or ought not to be thought or done, the moment we distinguish the order of things and respond to it in accordance with what we think is right, however far from truth it may be, we have committed ourselves to the impersonal order of reason to which sapience belongs—an order that will expunge our manifest self-portrait.[56] We have crossed the cognitive Rubicon. In committing to this impersonal order we must realize that what is manifestly human—us as we stand here, now—will be overcome by that very order. Reason is a game in which we are all fleeting players and from

---

56 'One can certainly wager that man would be erased, like a face drawn in sand at the edge of the sea.' M. Foucault, *The Order of Things* (London: Routledge, 2002), 422.

which we cannot defect, so let us play this game well by committing to its interests and its ramifications. As transitory embodiments of sapience, we can only recognize our mixed animality and the fact that what makes us special is the capacity for such recognition—for recognizing that, as sentients, we are *absolutely* not exceptional—and take the implications of being sapient to their furthest conclusions. Through the growth and maturation of reason, the definition and significance of the human is freed from any purported substantive essence or fixed nature. The formal appellation of 'humanity' becomes a transferable entitlement, a right that can be granted or acquired regardless of any attachment to a specific natural or artificial structure, heritage, or proclivity, since being human is not merely a right that is simply obtained naturally at birth through biological ancestry or inheritance. The title 'human' can be transferred to anything that can graduate into the domain of judgments, anything that satisfies the criteria of minded and minding agency, be it an animal or a machine. The entwinement of the project of human emancipation—both in the sense of the negative freedom from the limitations established in advance or created by ourselves and the positive freedom to do something or become something else—with the artificial prospects of human intelligence is the logical consequence of *the human as a transferable right*.

RATIONAL INTEGRATION, JUDGEMENT, AND GENERATION OF FURTHER ABILITIES

The kind of self that is required for establishing the necessary link between geist's conception and transformation is defined functionally by its roles in assuming rational responsibility (judging): using its rational unity to treat one set of commitments as *reasons* for or against other commitments. This is a thinking self, or a discursive apperceptive intelligence: an intelligence that is conscious of its own experiences through the rational unity of self-consciousness, and whose experiences are structured by concepts of mind. Unlike god or other imaginary intelligences, this intelligence has no direct contact with reality other than through its own geistig configuration.

Since thinking selves are a functional item that represents a qualitative set of activities (judgements or reasons), their formal (semantic-pragmatic) and concrete sociality can effect qualitative changes in the structure of geist or in the activities by which these selves identify themselves, individually and collectively. In other words, in its every dimension the collective configuration of thinking selves or rational agents—synchronically in time or diachronically across time—determines the course of the concrete project of self-consciousness. Mind has a configuration—sequences of self-conceptions and self-transformations—which is extended in time. Geistig activities, therefore, are not merely recognitive-cognitive but also recollective-reconstructive. Thinking selves are then not just the locus of judgements afforded by the recognitive dimensions of rational responsibility and authority—that is to say, the capacity to make oneself liable to distinctive kinds of (*conceptual*) normative appraisals. In addition, they are the locus of recollective-reconstructive judgement—the ability to extend recognitive acknowledgement to the recollections of history. What we are referring to here is geist's ability to be conscious of and to judge its constituted history as represented by the responsibilities and authorities of past judges. Rational selves, then, are also defined by their content-awareness of those activities, judgments, decisions, conflicts, values, and variables that have constituted their history and have led to their current configuration.

In order to have this content-aware experience (*erfahrung*) of history and to gain epistemic traction on it, geist must be able to represent to itself a reconstruction of its past transformations and their specific realizers (those activities and constraints which have brought those transformations about). Accordingly, the recollective reconstruction of the past history of conceptions and transformations should be understood as an essential feature of the self-related logic of mind whereby the mind not only recognizes its different structural transformations across time as its *own* unified experience, but also uses this experience to generate new abilities, to correct or rewrite its values and disvalues, and to construct itself differently. For intelligence, then, History is an order of intelligibility and thus a condition of its enablement. Any configuration of *I*s or thinking selves (any *we*) is simply a part of this history, not its totality.

What we were is now suspended in what we are, and what will be is suspended in the history of intelligence. To intelligence we are merely a historical intelligibility that enables but does not impede it.

Once the rational self as the basic functional item of geist is constructed, geist is able to conceive a historical concept of itself—a historical unity—and to act on it. This historical unity or integration requires, on one level, the recognitive-cognitive principle of 'the synthesis of an original unity of apperception through rational integration with a model of the synthesis of normative-status-bearing apperceiving selves and their communities by reciprocal recognition'.[57] On another level it entails a recollective-reconstructive principle of 'synthesiz[ing] a rational (including consequences and excluding incompatibles) contemporary unity by integrating the commitments of past judges'.[58] Only when rational selves concretely incorporate these two principles into their own conception of what to think and do, are they able to see the truth of themselves as an ongoing history of intelligence, realizing that their freedom lies in the freedom of mind as a historical artefact of its own concept, a necessary link between self-conception and self-transformation that ought to be rendered sufficient. The concept of history then is nothing but a necessary link—a dynamics—between conception and transformation. The concrete actualization of this history, however, is a matter of a thorough recognitive-cognitive struggle by rational selves.

By constituting its own history, geist acquires the power of self-cultivation, or the capacity to assess and develop its history via superior modes of self-consciousness which then allow geist to form and carry out more refined and comprehensive conceptions and transformations of itself. To put it differently, the elaboration of history as an emancipatory activity is an outcome of constructing and organizing rational selves incorporated within higher geistig unities through which they can concretely transform themselves.

---

57 See Brandom, *Reason in Philosophy*, 81.

58 Ibid., 86.

HISTORICAL AWARENESS AS AN ESSENTIAL
CONSTRUCTIVE AND CRITICAL ABILITY

By providing themselves with descriptions regarding their past transformations, and by putting these descriptions into a form that can be historically
expressed and assessed, rational selves can develop adequate theories and
practices for reorganizing or transforming themselves. This process is the
sociohistorical equivalent of the rational unity of consciousness. Historical consciousness is a distinct kind of consciousness specific to discursive,
concept-using, self-conscious creatures able to apply the principle of rational
integration to the history of their transformations, giving cognition an
explicitly historical role. The agency of rational selves in effecting such a
transformation indicates that they have discarded every given in their history, as well as any god or deus ex machina. Agency in its concrete sense is
not merely rational autonomy. It is also the realization that anything that
appears as an autonomous self-apprehending thing or process without
rational agency—be it theological, natural or technological—is a *practical
given*, a precritical adolescent fantasy, a delusion of stubborn and servile
consciousness.

Through developing historical consciousness, geist is able to identify
negative and positive trends of the past, abandoning the former and cultivating the latter. Therefore, historical consciousness provides thinking selves
with a principle of self-cultivation through the assessment and correction
of the sequences of their self-transformation—which is not just *their* transformation but, in so far as it takes place in the real world, also has positive
and negative effects on the world they inhabit. Recollective reconstruction
of the tradition—of an earlier sequence of historical transformations—opens
up previously endorsed goals, commitments, and conceptions to rational
assessment. Goals become objects of understanding and are then susceptible
to revision and, where necessary, relinquishment. It is this susceptibility
of goals to a kind of revision and assessment whose norms can themselves
be discursively reappraised that prevents the intrusion of predetermined
goals (whether natural or normative) into the conception of collective
general intelligence.

By applying the principle of rational integration to its temporal manifestation in time, geist conducts a cognitive inquiry into the conditions required
for both its temporal synthesis and the synthesis of temporality as such. It
is a pragmatic component of the project of collective general intelligence
to transform itself by renegotiating the links between the temporal categories of past, present, and future. But its critical component consists in
reexamining and redefining the nature of temporality—even if that means
dispensing with those temporal conceptions and categories to which it
has become accustomed. Mind's consciousness of its history is ultimately
the exploration of history as the interface between subjective time and
objective time, temporal forms and time's formlessness.

The history of geist, properly understood, is a recognitive-cognitive
technology. It is not only a semantic web through which geist's manifest
realizations (self-conceptions and self-transformations) can become transparent and open to analysis, but also a scientific milieu for the development
of cognitive means and practical technologies for subjecting what is a
manifest realization—the appearance of a totalized history—to a concrete
transformation, scientifically suspending what was previously deemed a
completed historical totality in an ongoing process of totalization, namely,
history. Geist's concept of revolution requires a scientific intervention in
history so as to transform what appears to be the manifest destiny or the
totality of history into history proper, in which all achieved totalities are
merely fleeting manifestations.

Here we arrive at Hegel's idea according to which geist's self-apprehen-
sion as what is in itself (the fleeting reality of its manifest realization) must
be subjected to what geist is for itself (what it takes itself to be, its labour
of conception). This is because 'what it conceives itself to be' is receptive
to correction and susceptible to profound changes stemming from the
undermining of appearances by new orders of intelligibility which are
outcomes of a systematic project of cognitive inquiry or science. Thus what
count as conditions required for the realization of geist cannot be limited
to the constellation of different particular models of selves, the modes of
their organization, and institutions which reflect the manifest realization
of geist. These conditions must also involve the development of cognitive

and practical tools for bringing manifest realizations of geist under the rational unity of superior and more adequate modes of consciousness. Only once a manifest totality is *understood* as an appearance, a fleeting realization, can it be concretely overcome. Here 'adequate' means both richer forms of content and context-awareness, and a sensitivity of these modes of consciousness to resources (cognitive, practical and material) and diverse intersubjective relations between subjects that encompass a broad range of economic and other relations.

THE DASEIN OF GEIST

Spirit is supposed to be cognized in its own 'outer' as in a being, which is language—the visible invisibility of its essence. [...] Here once again we see language as the existence of spirit. Language is self-consciousness existing for others. It is self-consciousness which as such is immediately on hand, and as this self-consciousness, it is universal.[59]

Both self-consciousness and historical consciousness require recognitive and recollective, retrospective and prospective cognitive abilities. But these abilities can only be acquired through language, as a scaffolding for the organization of a community of normative-status-bearing apperceiving selves. This is where the role of language as the dasein of geist and as a generative platform upon which mind takes shape and evolves in time comes to the foreground. In its most basic and necessary form, language is merely discursive speech (an ordinary natural language). In such a natural language the interface between the syntactic and semantic is interaction, or pragmatics as the social *use* of syntactic-symbolic vocabularies, which progressively affords new levels of semantic complexity or conceptual expressivity. The concepts of language are not merely labels or classifications, but descriptions. There are concepts that do not simply describe, but also allow cognitive simulation via counterfactuals. Semantic complexity in its full richness, then, comprises different grades of concepts, concept-using

---

59   Hegel, *Phenomenology of Spirit*, §323, §652.

abilities, and the various corresponding modes of rational integration afforded by them. Robert Brandom distinguishes the structural levels of semantic complexity of concepts afforded by the pragmatic interface between syntax and semantic as follows:

- concepts that only label and concepts that describe,
- ingredient and freestanding conceptual contents, making explicit the distinction between the content of concepts and the force of applying them, and
- concepts expressible already by simple predicates and concepts express-ible only by complex predicates.[60]

In its specialized format as the infrastructure of all *theoretical* structurations of the world, language is essentially formal. The significance of formal languages lies in their capacity for what Catarina Dutilh Novaes terms 'desemantifica-tion and resemantification'.[61] This is the ability of formal languages to be detached and abstracted from any particular content (topic-independence) so as to be generally applied to different contexts. The desemantifying ability of formal languages is tantamount to the explicit re-enactment of mind out-side of any particular individual experience or contextual meaning—formal languages as the prostheses of extended cognition and epistemic enablement. Decoupled from any particular content, 'desemantification allows for the deployment of reasoning strategies other than our default strategies, thus enhancing the "mind-altering" effect of reasoning with formalisms'.[62] In addition, formal syntactic languages can be explicitly computable. This is the achievement of Noam Chomsky, in putting forward a hierarchy of formal grammar or syntax where the complexity of syntax is articulated in terms of computational complexity. Chomsky's hierarchy classifies different types of syntax (recursively enumerable, context-sensitive, context-free and regular)

---

60   Brandom, *Reason in Philosophy*, 199.

61   See C. Dutilh Novaes, *Formal Languages in Logic* (Cambridge: Cambridge Univer-sity Press, 2012).

62   Ibid., 219.

in terms of the combinations of generative processes required to produce them, the formal grammatical properties that specify them, and the automata necessary for computing them.[63]

Finally, in its ultimate superior mode, language refers to artificial general languages—languages in which the full hierarchy of syntactic complexity (of formal languages) and the full hierarchy of semantic complexity (of natural language), computation and conception, desemantification, resemantification, and semantic enrichment all exist side by side, reinforcing one another. Before proceeding, let us briefly look at the phenomenon of language—although the topic of language and its role in the formation of minding activities (judgements and inferences) will be surveyed in more detail in chapters 6 and 7.

The emphasis on the principal role of language for mind is an old topic. But what has been largely absent in studying the role of language for mind is the deep logico-computational structure of language itself, where language can be seen as much as a multilevel syntactic complexity as a multilevel semantic complexity. This is language neither as a medium of direct access to reality nor as a system of public discourse, but as a framework of interaction-as-computation incorporating different classes of semantic and syntactic complexity and the cognitive-practical abilities associated with them. This interactive computation permits qualitative compression of data and selectivity of compression, it significantly reduces the size of the agent's internal model while increasing its complexity, and it can format and modulate the agent's behaviours, stabilizing the multi-agent epistemic dynamic without which it is impossible for any agent to be aware of itself and to experience. Built on this computational interactive dimension, language is above all an engine for the generation of qualitatively distinct cognitive abilities. It is precisely what reshapes intelligent behaviours not by degree but in type (e.g., a linguistic agent differs from a nonlinguistic agent in type, not in degree).

---

63 See N. Chomsky, *Aspects of the Theory of Syntax* (Cambridge, MA: MIT Press, 1965); and for more details, R. Hausser, *Foundations of Computational Linguistics: Human-Computer Communication in Natural Language* (Dordrecht: Springer, 1999).

The archetypal figure behind language is computational duality or interaction. Interactions are the prevalent phenomena in language, and they can be concurrent, synchronic, asynchronic, typed or untyped, deterministic or nondeterministic. Interactive systems are online, open, and reactive to multiple streams of input. Interactions are governed by computational dualities. In simple terms, these dualities signify the interchange of roles between two or more processes or behaviours which constrain one another, resulting in the generation of additional constraints or rules which increase the complexity of behaviours involved in interaction. In theoretical computer science, these interactive dualities are called 'open harnesses'. Open harnesses simultaneously constrain the behaviours of the interacting systems (hence the constraining connotation of 'harness'), and harness them to a new design (a behaviour with a higher level of complexity). By pitting two systems against one another, they force the systems to correct their behaviours and to augment their capacities, as in a game that harnesses one player to respond intelligently to another, and where the totality of the game is always in excess of its players. But this is not a game in the game-theoretical sense: as topics of logic and theoretical computer science, interaction games are devoid of precise goals, payoff functions, or predetermined winning strategies or procedural rules for how the game should be played. Instead, the rules of the game emerge naturally from the interaction itself. Interactions are a medium of complexification for processes. In the words of Jean-Baptiste Joinet:

> As vague as the notion of process may be, it certainly is in their nature not only to evolve (amongst the effects produced by a process appear its own transformations), but also to produce effects on other processes, mutual effects. In short, processes act and interact. Whatever its technological matter, whatever its implementation, the essence of a process is completely involved in its (potential) dynamic behavior: not only its own possible destinies under evaluation, but also the full set of possible operational effects it will occasion in all possible processes' interaction contexts. With respect to semantics, the answer brought by processes is

thus of a radically new kind, which implements the performative way of meaning: doing, is the way processes speak.[64]

But unlike generic interactive processes, the logico-computational interactions of language have the ability to increasingly incorporate lower-level interactions within higher-level interactions (i.e., interactions with more semantic complexity or, in Wolfendale's terms, interactions that reformat lower-level interactions) and to form stable linguistic items with their own specific transformation rules across different levels. It is in the context of a complex network of interaction that rules are obtained and stabilized; some may be context-sensitive, others may be applied across the board. Semantic values or meanings are abstractions of linguistic locutions together with transformation rules for their use, which are both derived and used in their stabilized form through the interaction.

The realization of mind or general intelligence is inconceivable without language not merely as a structuring edifice but also as a necessary and vast computational framework for the generation of higher-order cognitive faculties (theoretical and practical judgements). Just as there is no structure in the world without the structuring mind, there is no mind and no *unrestricted* world without the structuration of language and its unrestricted universe of discourse wherein everything can be questioned or subjected to systematic theorization. General language (as opposed to this or that language) has no borders or limits. In the same way that we cannot step outside of mind to gain direct access to reality, we cannot step outside of language as the armature of mind. In stepping outside of one language, we only find ourselves in another more general language:

[T]o speak of a limit drawn by language (or by a language) is to be, linguistically, beyond the putative limit. A limit is a limit only if there is something beyond it, so to identify a limit to language is also to enter the linguistic space making it possible to speak of what is beyond the

---

64   J.-B. Joinet, 'Proofs, Reasoning and the Metamorphosis of Logic', in L.C. Pereira, E. Haeusler and V. de Paiva, *Advances in Natural Deduction* (Dordrecht: Springer, 2014), 58.

limit, and thus to negate the identification of the 'limit' *as* a limit of the language that bespeaks it as a limit.[65]

The phenomenon of language in its full syntactic and semantic complexity cannot be captured outside of the logico-computational linguistic interactions of which pragmatics (meaning as use or discursive meaningfulness) is only the uppermost visible instantiation. Since mind or general intelligence is inconceivable without language, and to the extent that language requires an interactive framework, the idea that mind or general intelligence could be realized in anything but a community of agents is a dubious one. Humans are only minded and minding agents in that they have sociality. In the same vein, the idea of an artificial realization of general intelligence in anything but a multi-agent system rather than a single agent is something of a bygone twentieth-century science fiction. Artificial general intelligence is a product of interactions, be they between nurturing humans and child machines, or between machines that have graduated into the domain of artificial general languages.

To this end, general intelligence should be seen not only as a repertoire of existing cognitive abilities but also as a generative framework for the realization of new cognitive abilities by adjusting to the syntactic-semantic resources of language. It is the linguistically charged competence to proliferate, diversify, and maximize theoretical and practical abilities that sets general intelligence apart from complex causal and pattern-governed processes exhibiting a powerful yet restricted range of behaviours. The intrinsic affinity between general intelligence and language as a socially embedded and constructive medium for the elaboration and realization of the abilities of mind points to the social bases of general intelligence. There is no predetermined limit to the type and range of cognitive technologies that can be garnered by excavating 'the visible invisible essence' of geist or language. The possibilities of what can be done with language are as unfathomed as the possibilities of what language can do to its users.

---

65 Puntel, *Structure and Being*, 31.

THE NECESSARY AND SUFFICIENT LINKS
BETWEEN CONCEPTION AND TRANSFORMATION

Having presented an overview of mind not as an ideal object but as a social project, we can now shift the focus to the ramifications of developing and partaking in such a project.

Hegel's systematic elaboration of geist in functional terms has both a critical and a constructive import. The functional analysis of the spiritual or *geistig* struggle—i.e., the struggle of spirit to become the object of its own concept, to refine the content of this concept, and to devise abilities to actualize itself as the object of its concept—reveals how this struggle is realized, and how it can degenerate and precipitate pathologies of consciousness and their social manifestations. This type of analysis sets the stage for an in-depth diagnosis through which it is possible to identify what ought to be changed, and to specify those structural joints or material organizations that ought to be treated as sites of struggle. It is in this sense that Hegel's deep functional picture of geist as that which has a history and has the ability to treat its history as a milieu of intelligibility in which all achieved totalities are fleeting shadows and appearances lays the groundwork for Marx's project of communism as the *real movement* that concretely and determinately negates the present state of affairs, the givens of history. The uncovering of history as a new domain of intelligibilities requiring special kinds of theoretical and practical cognitions brings to light those sites where struggle and intervention must take place in order to achieve a consequential and concrete liberation from the present state of affairs perceived as the totality of history.

The import of the functional picture of geist resides in how this picture highlights key activities and abilities through which the mind as a social project can be augmented and amplified. Primary among these activities are conception and transformation; both are labours of mind, but one places more of an accent on systematic theorization, the other tends toward concrete practice. However, at no time can these two be separated: they are as mutually reinforcing as they are intrinsically linked.

Essential self-consciousness is explicated by the necessary link between self-conception and self-transformation as two distinct yet connected activities: that of conceiving (i.e., bringing into conception) ourselves in the world, and that of transforming ourselves in accordance with our self-conceptions.[66] Each transformation serves in turn as a pivot for a different encounter with ourselves in the world. Alteration in the order of self-conception induces a change in the self of which it is a conception, and a qualitative difference in the self induces a transformation in the general or geistig conception of the self. The positive feedback loop between conception and transformation instigates a disequilibrium, with each difference in one order destabilizing the other and becoming a cue for its readaptation. This disequilibrium is particularly intensified as subsequent conceptions become further removed from the order of appearances, and in the process the latter are determinately negated. The act of self-conception must yield progressively more fine-grained conceptions of the geistig self (what it means to be a minded and minding agent, a human, an embodiment of intelligence); but in order to do so, it must break away from the mere appearances of its present conception, its manifest realization.

In conceiving itself in terms of this process of simultaneous self-recognition and self-negation, the history of geist is no longer *entailed* by its past states, even if it is constructed out of them. The self-conception of geist via determinate and concrete negation of its conceptual content (how it appears to itself) brings about a real movement of history in which geist's sequence of self-constituted transformations are not merely the repetitions of its past stages. Within this movement, any totalized state of realization is taken to be a historical appearance with regard to the reality of history qua incomplete and ongoing totalization. The history of geist, in this sense, is neither a linear progression between different states of geist's realization (epochs) nor a series of isomorphic transformations. The reality of what geist is now is not the reality that it used to be. What geist or intelligence will be is never what it is or has been, where 'never' implies the elimination of the one-to-one relationship between the sequences of geist's transformation. Historical consciousness, or awareness of this fact—what

---

66   See R. Brandom, *A Spirit of Trust* (2014), <http://www.pitt.edu/~brandom/spirit_of_trust_2014.html>.

it means to identify the appearances of history and determinately negate them—is the kernel of concrete self-consciousness as the real movement of emancipation.

The adequacy of self-consciousness is an index of the quality of conception and transformation and an indication of how effectively self-conception and self-transformation are integrated within the order of intelligibilities. Just as a robust self-conception brings about a consequential self-transformation, a flawed or impoverished self-conception incites a defective or inconsequential self-transformation. But in so far as our self-transformation is embedded in the objective world, its flaws are not isolated. Depending on its proportion and persistence, a pathological self-transformation can trigger a disaster by laying ruin to those structures that environ and support us. This calamity also debilitates our capacities to act, either simply by depleting the resources required for perpetuation and transformation, or more insidiously by causing a disorientation that prevents us from decisively thinking and taking measures, detecting and acting on opportunities without the crippling anxiety of further deterioration and imaginary tragedies. Blinded by the oppressive fear of tragedies, the diagnosis of what exactly is wrong (revealing the 'specific' inadequacies of conception qua determinate negation) then falls under the jurisdiction of abstract negation and unconscious self-deception. In supposing ourselves to have dispensed with all illusions and escaped all the traps of history, we succumb to naivety and cognitive-practical despondency.

In this environment, reasons which form and adjudicate recognitions, obligations, responsibilities, and pertinencies (what matters and what does not) are discredited by a critical discourse on the irrationality of reasons tout court, and an insistence that we should dispense with them. Reasons are unmasked as social irrational causes that merely disguise the roots of what is oppressive and exploitative. This critical discourse then becomes an exposé on how causes not only semantically distort reasons but also masquerade as reasons. Reason is burnt at the stake, accused of being the ultimate trap of history, the supreme collaborator with the oppressor, a smokescreen for the conditions of exploitation. Once freed from the tyranny of reason, critical discourse presents itself as an egalitarian exposition of the causes of oppression and exploitation. Having immolated the trap of all traps—reason—critique is now fully disillusioned and emancipated. But to dispense with the conceptual and normative resources of reason in order to expose their causal irrationality, and to diagnose oppressive pathologies via the reasonless appraisal of causes, amounts to the impoverishment of the semantic requirements necessary for the intelligibility of any diagnosis. In other words, the unconscious undermining of the criteria required for the adequate consciousness of the self occasions a consciousness which is inadequate to have a proper conception of itself in the world and to determinately transform itself in accordance with such a conception. The reasonless critique or diagnosis of what is oppressive and exploitative becomes the prognostic course of the disease or pathology itself. In being an inadequate consciousness, the critique unconsciously justifies those pathologies of history it is bent on eradicating.[67]

Founded on the intelligibility of the concept and the intelligibility of practices, the adequate self-consciousness is distinguished as a multitasking project comprised of four basic undertakings:

(1) To evaluate and correct our self-conceptions (using the resources of both common-sense rationality and those of the sciences, with the understanding that they yield two different images of ourselves in the world that should be integrated).

(2) To coordinate our self-transformations with better self-conceptions (i.e., self-conceptions informed by a broader order of intelligibilities).

(3) To amplify the influence of our rational and scientifically informed self-conceptions over our self-transformations (the shift from a *necessary* link between the two to one of *sufficiency*).

---

67 See R. Brandom, *Reason, Genealogy, and the Hermeneutics of Magnanimity* (2014), <http://www.pitt.edu/~brandom/downloads/RGHM%20%2012-11-21%20a.docx>; and Brassier, 'Dialectics Between Suspicion and Trust', 98–113.

(4) To revise and where necessary abandon our self-conceptions in accordance with the intelligibility of *how* and *into what* we are transformed.

Formulating self-consciousness as a project rather than as an ideal object allows us to conceive of the vocations of thought and action not on an ontological basis, where the ideal abstractness of thought is contrasted with the ideal concreteness of action, but on a methodological basis, where thought must first make a concrete difference in itself in order to make a difference in the world. The interplay between the abstract and the concrete is then conceived methodologically as the determination of concrete abstraction and the abstraction of the concrete—a dialectics through which making a difference in thought and making a difference in the world can be *bidirectionally* mediated by autonomous transformative actions in the order of thought and in the order of the world. Autonomy in reference to transformative actions describes the ability of these actions to repurpose or reorient themselves in accordance with self-contained rational ends. It is important to note that to speak of functional self-containment in this sense does not imply the denial of the existence of material constraints. In fact, it simultaneously brings about the opportunity to uncover such constraints and to examine how they can be modified.

GEIST AT THE EDGE OF INTELLIGIBILITY

To every abstract moment of science, there corresponds a shape of appearing spirit per se. Just as existing spirit is not richer than science, so too spirit in its content is no poorer.[68]

The reinforcing link between self-conception and self-transformation characterises essentially self-conscious creatures or rational agents as those possessing the capacity to constitute a history and to have a contentful experience of it, to have impersonal norms regarding what ought or ought not to be done in order to maintain and expand the intelligibility of their history.

---

68   Hegel, *Phenomenology of Spirit*, §805.

This capacity unfolds the truth of intelligence as a social cognitive-practical enterprise in the order of intelligibilities, of things, practices and values. In reality, the systematic encounter with the order of intelligibilities is the inexorable consequence of the realization of geist by the specific qualitative set of activities that distinguish it.

The formulation of self-consciousness as a matter of practical achievement underlines the import of self-conception as a recipe for action without which action cannot maintain its practical intelligibility. Conception without praxis is unrealized abstraction and praxis without conception is a hollow impression of concreteness. Self-conception in its concrete form is a search for intelligibilities pertaining to the world of which we are part. Self-transformation in its consequential form is the intelligibility of practices in response to the intelligibility of what the world we inhabit is, together with what we ought to be in accordance with the ends of thought. The recognition of ourselves, the conceiving of ourselves within one or multiple self-narratives, is by definition the construction of ourselves within the order of intelligibilities. There could be no 'us' without our encountering ourselves and bringing this encounter into a conception not only of who or what we are, but also of where we have come from, where we are, which paths have led to where we are, and which paths we ought to take. The conception of this encounter is thus an open landscape of inquiry into different orders of intelligibilities. The conceptual awareness of one's experience of the world is a necessary framework within which one can know oneself in the world, and how to change oneself and the world.

However, the divergence between what we take ourselves to be and what we actually are, the disparity between the intelligibility of the self and the world as what they appear to be and the intelligibility of the world in itself as what conditions all appearances generates a tension in self-conception and, correspondingly, in the space of self-consciousness as a project. The full recognition of this tension—its simultaneous sharpening and resolution—characterizes the task of scientific rationality or, more generally, the enterprise of science. Again, what is meant by science here is not just the modern empirical sciences, but also the science of history, the science of thinking, or what Hegel dubs the Greater Logic, and finally the science of impersonal values and disvalues, the science of ethics. While maintaining this broad idea of science, I would however like to discuss the implications of the modern empirical sciences for the project of conception and transformation outlined above. For the field of empirical sciences poses a significant challenge to what is already a challenging project.

The core protocol of modern empirical science consists in striving for explanation. Why do we see what appears—in our ordinary common-sense experience—to be the case, and yet know that it is not the whole of reality? Science overturns the order of what appears to be subjectively the case by providing its objective explanans. It differentiates what was previously an apparent explanation into an explanandum the explanans of which remains to be found. The explanatory force of science reaches its peak when it overturns the universe that seemed to be ontologically dependent on the mind into a universe that is independent of mind. Yet in overturning what is simply subjectively manifest—the universe hyposta-sized as the reificatory dependent object of mind—science draws on the core components of subjective or minding *activities*: linguistic doings, conceptualization, and systematic theorization among others. Objective science without subject-constituting mind is a subjective delusion. The movement of scientific inquiry only underlines the necessity of mind in its pure and necessary form. Science, in this sense, is the hallmark of a mind that has matured to learn that it should hypostatize neither its structur-ing activities nor its structured object, neither itself nor its unrestricted universe. This is a mind whose intelligibility is not immediately given in itself, but is achievable only in its integration—rather than complete fusion or reduction—with an intelligible order pertaining to a non-manifest and mind-independent reality. The enterprise of science is permanently caught up within this integral framework which is comprised of the vocabularies of mind and the items of the world, and whose internal tensions enrich and drive it. But this tension through which science expands itself is exactly the tension exclusive and constitutive to mind, albeit more self-conscious and intensified.

> Spirit knowing itself in that way as spirit is science. Science is its actuality, and science is the realm it builds for itself in its own proper element.[69]

With the advent of scientific explanation and the excavation of an intelligible universe which, in its objectivity, constrains our thoughts about it, the order of self-consciousness—the duality of the intelligible and intelligence—enters a new phase. Matter-of-factual truths pertaining to a nonmanifest and mind-independent universe intrude upon and are ingrained in the logico-conceptual infrastructure of intelligence. As the scientific will-to-explain or the pursuit of explanatory coherence highlights the insufficiency of common-sense concepts, conception begins to adapt itself to science and its unrestricted universe.

Even though the conceptual framework of common sense through which we articulate the intelligibility of ourselves in the world is built upon basic matter-of-factual truths, it does not grant us access to these truths as such; properly conceived, since they lie beyond what manifestly appears to be the case, these truths belong to the framework of scientific inquiry. By assuming otherwise we subscribe to the ideological fixation of the epistemic given—of access to the intelligibility of the world through the supposedly spontaneous intelligibility of our seemings.

Scientific explanation, accordingly, can be understood as an activity of mind that forces the activity of self-conception to renegotiate its original alliance with appearances—particularly the appearance of how the world that appears for mind is in itself. As the order of intelligibilities uncovered by science encroaches upon the intelligibility of that which is manifest, self-consciousness gains a new mobility. The sharp asymmetry between what is manifest and what is scientific, how things appear to be from an ordinary common-sense perspective and how things are as matter of fact, destabilizes the oppressive serenity of the order of mind and things. Cognitive progress can only be maintained and expanded by sharpening this asymmetry, by further amplifying the instability in how mind and the world stand in relation to one another. As the site of this tension, science

---

69   Ibid., §25.

advances through positing the transcendental excess of a structuring mind and by positing a structured reality that is in excess of mind.[70]

Yet the advancement of science need not be understood as a series approaching convergence, or a uniform progression.[71] A completed science, or the full and adequate scientific image (of human being in the world) is a regulative ideal. But, as Kant reminds us, when regulative ideals are applied constitutively they lead to contradictions.[72] Outside of their regulative use, regulative ideas are pseudo-rational and illusory existences. The account of science as a convergent and uniform progression is not necessary for the certification of science as a vector of cognitive progress. Indeed, this convergent progressive interpretation can result in both irrationality and relativism, both epistemic dogmatism and epistemic anarchy. Wolfgang Stegmüller has provided an incisive critique of this generalized progressivist interpretation of scientific theories.[73] Here I will merely summarize his particularly meticulous and technical argument.

The idea of a general convergent progress of science is based on the analysis of the structure and dynamics of scientific theories (the theory-ladenness of all sciences). According to Stegmüller, the conviction of a convergent and uniform progress of science rests on the idea of the *general* reducibility of one theory (a dislodging theory) to another preceding (dislodged) theory covering the same class of observations. For example, if we can in every respect reduce or map statistical thermodynamics to the

---

70 'At its debut, where science has been brought neither to completeness of detail nor to perfection of form, it is open to reproach. However, even if it is unjust to suppose that this reproach even touches on the essence of science, it would be equally unjust and inadmissible not to honor the demand for the further development of science. This opposition seems to be the principal knot which scientific culture at present is struggling to loosen and which it does not yet properly understand.' Ibid., §14.

71 See for example, J. Rosenberg, *Wilfrid Sellars: Fusing the Images* (Oxford: Oxford University Press, 2007).

72 See I. Kant, *Critique of Pure Reason*, tr. P. Guyer and A.W. Wood (Cambridge: Cambridge University Press, 2000), 591

73 W. Stegmüller, *The Structure and Dynamics of Theories* (New York: Springer, 1976).

thermal theory of thermodynamics, then we can say there is a uniform or convergent progress from the latter to the former, from the less explanatory to the more explanatory theory. In the traditional study of scientific theories, analysis is performed at the micrological level, pertaining to the stable core of theories. These stable cores are comprised of atomic axiomatic formal sentences or classes of sentences together with their inferential relations. At the level of micrological analysis, to see whether one theory is reducible to another theory a mapping must be obtained from the stable core of the succeeding theory (T_2) to that of the preceding theory (T_1). But this mapping is precisely based on the reduction of individual theories to their so-called stable cores, a reduction that loses much necessary information regarding the specificity of its content, including 'the distinction between theoretical and nontheoretical functions, the general and special constraints, and the special laws holding only for certain intended applications'.[74] Accordingly, at the level of micrological analysis—pertaining to the stable cores or sentences and their inferential relations—the reducibility of T_2 to T_1 cannot be obtained in a nonarbitrary manner. In so far as micrological reducibility presupposes the prior reduction of each theory to its stable core, we cannot *generalize* the relationship between T_2 and T_1 in terms of their being generally more inductively simple and generally less inductively simple, generally more explanatory and generally less explanatory, answering more well-formed questions and answering less well-formed questions. The comparison of theory-contents is completely context-dependent. What appears to be less explanatory in T_2 may be less explanatory in one particular context than T_1. Equally, T_1 may answer some well-formed questions that cannot be answered in T_2, as in the case of Newton's and Einstein's theories of gravitation.

Just because T_1 precedes T_2 and both cover the same class of observations, it cannot be inferred that the relation between them is that of theory-reducibility in the sense mentioned above. It is only when we move from the level of micrological analysis to the level of macrological analysis, from the stable cores to the model-theoretic view of theories pertaining to their

---

74   Ibid., 127.

expanded cores, that we can speak of reducibility. The expanded core of each theory covers the class of partial possible models (i.e., the physical systems about which the theory is talking) or the class of sets of possible applications. Further, the components of the expanded core (its range of possible applications) are unstable and dynamically changing. To secure reducibility at this level of analysis, one has to take a static snapshot of theories at time t in order to obtain the mapping between one theory and another. But this static theory-comparison is itself problematic, since it freezes the dynamic picture of the theory structures and narrows the range of their possible applicability or coverage over possible models.

At the level of the micrological analysis of stable cores concerning formally constructed and inferentially related sentences or classes of sentences, the reducibility fails to be nonarbitrary or general. And at the level of the macrological analysis of expanded cores, reducibility can only be obtained by taking a static view of the dynamic structure of compared theories, hence losing information regarding the dynamic aspects of the theory structures themselves. Stegmüller's final conclusion is that we do not need a convergent progressivist account of scientific theories to talk about the rationality of science or to avoid relativism. Scientific progress can be seen in terms of the dynamics of each theory structure in itself—the increase in the range of its applicability and achievements as it incorporates aspects of an older theory structure which is now operating under new constraints and laws, and over a larger field of experience. Both the dislodged theory and the dislodging theory may prove successful in certain situations, identification of which requires a rich dynamic picture of their structures.

The true revolutionary import of science lies in its capacity to amplify reason's own power of knowing and to instigate cognitive expansion. The convergent progressivist interpretation of scientific theories is often assumed to be a preventive measure against irrationality and relativism with regard to scientific theories; but in reality it is an oversimplification that causes more unnecessary problems which can become the source of irrationality. The rationality of science lies not in the uniform progression of science, but in how these theories are constructed and how they expand the capacities of reason and its cognitive traction on the world. In light of the dynamics of scientific structuration or theoreticity, the rationality of science can be preserved without a convergent progressivist reading of scientific change. Similarly, epistemological anarchism can be shown to be merely a parasitic outcome of the pseudo-rationality of an uncritically progressivist view of science.

Coming back to the role of science for mind, intelligence, and agency, science's capacity to make the world intelligible beyond appearances as a reality that is in excess of mind represents mind's movement of self-consciousness as it differentiates its universal and necessary features from its particular and contingent characteristics. The ongoing instability or perturbation caused by the sharp asymmetry between the manifest and scientific frameworks should be seen as a positive condition for self-conception and the corresponding self-transformation, since it results in the increasing refinement of the manifest picture of the agency, its minimaliza-tion to a set of logically-irreducible and necessary activities. Science is not an attack upon the logic or essence of the human that should be staved off; it is that which differentiates the necessary aspects of the latter from their contingent features. Pruning the manifest picture of the human and cutting it down to its logico-conceptual, necessary activities and functions is a required step toward understanding the meaning of the human. It is precisely through this minimalization of the manifest that the rational self can be extricated from the neurobiologically fabricated 'phenomenal self-model',[75] and instead presented as a constructive principle that can be transferred and artificially implemented. It is the continuous labour of science in deepening the order of intelligibility that provides geist with the necessary resources for the determinate negation and reappraisal of the *content* of self-conception.

In the wake of scientific rationality, mind turns into a wave of noetic deracination. This deracination of thought and its noetic drift is commen-surate with what Plato calls the Form of Good as the Form of Forms, since it sets up the scaffolding for a conception of the realm of intelligibilities as

---

75 T. Metzinger, *Being No One: The Self-Model Theory of Subjectivity* (Cambridge, MA: MIT Press, 2003).

a complex system of recipes for crafting a world which includes not only satisfying lives but also the perpetual demand for the better. The ingredient of these recipes are not just theoretical intelligibilities, the products of modern sciences, but also practical intelligibilities and axiological intelligibilities, the objects of sciences of skill, practice, and ethics, all of which are subsets of the logical functions of mind. This is ethics as the science of impersonal values and disvalues concerning the intelligible unity of freedom of mind and the constraints of the world, the autonomy of thinking and reality in its otherness. But what kind of life would really satisfy the mind, 'other than one that involves a self-knowledge which has passed through all the stages of disciplined reflection on the source of things',[76] that is to say, their intelligibility? And what is intelligence other than that which knows what to do with the intelligible, whether pertaining to itself or to the world?

---

76 W. Sellars, *Essays in Philosophy and its History* (Dordrecht: D. Reidel, 1974), 26.

2. An Outside View of Ourselves as Experimental AGI (Problems, Concepts, and Models)

The aim of this and the following chapters is to engage—in a more detailed fashion—a question that overshadowed chapter 1's outline of the nature of mind as a configuring or structuring factor and as that which is capable of treating itself as an artefact of its own concept. This is the question of language as the dasein of geist—of language as a framework through which intelligence comes into cognitive contact with itself in the world. The question might be formulated as follows: What is it in language that makes the self-conscious form of intelligence not only possible but also amenable to self-determination and self-augmentation? To adequately answer this question, we have to reconstruct and explain the essence of language rather than simply highlighting its importance. If the ineffability of general intelligence is to be overcome, and if geist's activities are fundamentally caught up in language, then we first of all need to understand language not in terms of some mysterious internal essence, but in terms of its computational capacities and formal autonomy; how it gains traction on the world and how it generates cognitive-practical abilities through which language-users can bring into conception—and potentially transform—themselves and their world. In other words, we need to inquire into *how language is realized* both at the level of natural evolution and that of social evolution, and *how language functions* both at its most fundamental level and at the level of what we might call the familiar picture of natural language and linguistic interaction (social discursive activities, the mappings between thoughts and speech acts, etc.).

To this end, our path to the nature of language, the nature of thinking, and general intelligence won't be anything like a straightforward nonstop train ride across different continents of inquiry. This is a route that stretches out with bends and twists from one condition necessary for the realization of mind to another. On this ride, language is the last station. At times we will stop the train to investigate the wilderness that we have only been able to experience vicariously through the windows. At other times, we shall take roundabout paths along tracks either long abandoned or still under construction. All things considered, our journey is a risky one, a gamble. Only those travellers who no longer think like tourists—that is, those who are not obsessed with getting back as quickly as possible to their comforting home—will enjoy and survive the ride.

In order to properly tackle the questions of the realization and functioning of language, the best strategy would be to undertake a comparative study of ourselves and artificial intelligence. Understanding exactly how we are enabled by language is key to the artificial reconstruction of those abilities by virtue of which we have become the artefacts of our own Concept. And the investigation of how we can reconstruct these abilities that make us who we are is a key for understanding the most fundamental connections between language and the conditions necessary for the possibility of having mind qua dimension of structure. In continuation of the arguments presented in the previous chapter, this is precisely our aim here: to scrutinize the deep connections between language and transcendental psychology by inquiring into how the development of artificial speech (from basic speech synthesis to advanced artificial languages capable of exhibiting the properties of natural language) can play a key role in the construction of an advanced form of artificial general intelligence.

The most objective way of inquiring into the essence of language is by investigating how research on artificial linguistic speech can be integrated into research on the artificial realization of mind. In other words, it is by constructing an artificial agent capable not only of autonomously conversing with us, but also of conversing with other artificial agents possessing the same ability, that we can simultaneously disenchant the nature of language and recognize its indispensable—and as yet not fully apprehended—role in the emancipation of intelligence from the shackles of its contingent history. The transition from quantitative problem-solving/inductive intelligence to qualitative intelligence furnished with conceptual self-consciousness requires the integration of language (as an enabling social framework) into the constitution of intelligence. And inversely, it is the examination of how exactly language, in all of its different levels of syntactic, semantic, and pragmatic complexity, *is naturally* or *can be artificially* integrated into the constitution of intelligence—in the sense that the evolution of the two becomes co-extensive—that will shed light on the nature of language.

As a way of addressing (1) how interdisciplinary research on artificial speech and artificial intelligence elucidates the links between language and the generation of complex cognitive-practical abilities, and (2) how the examination of ourselves as common users of language is key to the development of artificial general intelligence, below we set out a thought experiment or hypothetical model. Even though this model will be presented in a rudimentary fashion, I would argue that by highlighting the systematic correspondence between *artificial speech* (AS), *artificial intelligence* (AI) and *transcendental psychology* (TP), we can outline a framework in which the problems associated with these fields can be examined within one and the same domain of research. But also, and more importantly, this framework can in principle define a trajectory for the development of artificial intelligence that is guided by problems that do not traditionally belong to the program of AI in its classic manifestation.

The AS-AI-TP correspondence captures a family of fundamental connections between the conditions required for the realization, development, and construction of linguistic speech (AS), the conditions or activities necessary for the possibility of cognition (TP), the project of artificial intelligence (AI), and their convergence toward the design of artificial multi-agent systems capable of exhibiting the necessary features of advanced agency and social community as a formal rather than substantive condition (AGI). By building on such a correspondence, it is possible to introduce a framework for specifying what is required in order to construct a system of agents capable of performing an array of special social activities that will allow them to provide reasons for their actions, to reappraise those reasons, and to modify and repurpose their social structure through different modes of action. The objective is, accordingly, to ascertain the necessary components for the formation of agency in its Kantian sense; and ultimately to design a community of *evolving* and *autonomous* artificial agents.

CLIMBING WITH LANGUAGE

Designing agents that exhibit an evolution conditioned by their autonomy, however, requires an inquiry into the nature of this evolution so as to determine which dimensions of it belong to the order of natural evolution and which to the order of sociocultural evolution, and to what extent—particularly those dimensions central to the emergence of linguistic activities and directly associated with the discursive-inferential structure of cognition. Specifically, we must establish what kinds of evolved causal structures and what type of social scaffolding need to be in place to support rule-governed activities, how they are connected, and at what stage the role of causal mechanisms in determining the rule-governed activities of the agents is weakened.

In the AS-AI-TP framework, artificial speech plays the role of a mediator between the key problems of transcendental psychology and those of artificial intelligence. In its initial form, artificial speech primarily concerns speech synthesis. At this stage, the emphasis is on the production of the phonic and prosodic properties of acoustic speech. The research takes shape through the study of the evolutionary mechanisms involved in human vocalization such as the organization and coordination of articulatory organs and auditory perception, as well as through the development of models of synthesis for producing and composing the different elements that constitute the *naturalness* of human speech at the level of sound. However, it should be noted that the arena of speech synthesis is not limited to ordinary human speech. The only reason that our thought experiment resorts to the latter is our conventional familiarity with it. But artificial speech pertains to a much broader landscape that encompasses symbol-design, writing, text-generation, formal languages and syntactic processing systems which may be either naturally evolved or artificially designed.

The second stage can be defined by a deeper exchange between artificial intelligence and transcendental psychology. The focus shifts from the production of the acoustic properties of speech to its intersubjective or dialogical features, beginning with automatic speech production and recognition through a basic implementation of artificial intelligence and

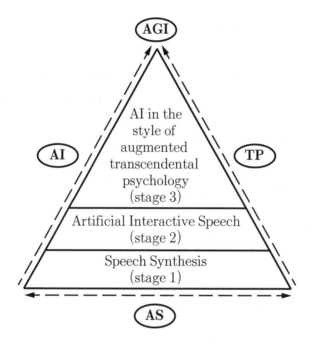

AS-AI-TP framework: Speech, from its basic acoustic realization to its linguistic manifestation, plays the role of a platform ladder for supporting, mediating, and ultimately joining artificial intelligence and transcendental psychology. The ladder outlines three schematic stages for the co-constitutive development of language and complex cognitive faculties in the construction of a human-level AI. The first stage consists of rudimentary speech synthesis at the level of discrimination and modulation of sounds. This stage is co-constitutive with elementary but necessary representational capacities. In the second stage, the interdependencies between the conditions necessary for the realization of speech, the conditions required for the realization of AGI, and the conditions required for the possibility of cognition become harder to dissociate and more generative in nature. At this stage, artificial speech concerns speech acts, artificial languages and issues surrounding the generation of syntactic and semantic complexity. In the third stage, agency is inextricable from its social aspects, themselves afforded by the semantic-pragmatic dimensions of language. This final stage deals with the realization of abilities specific to language-users.

neural networks, and culminating in the syntactic, semantic, and pragmatic aspects of linguistic speech.

The most significant problems for this second stage are those relating to the combined inferential and interactive functions of speech: What does it mean for something to genuinely engage in conversation, where 'genuine' refers to the ability of the agent to confer conceptual content on an expression and to map another agent's behaviour (noise or expression) onto its own in order to *interpret* and *assess* it? What is required in order for humans to engage in conversation, in the sense of using expressions in an intersubjective and inferential web? What does it mean for a human and a machine to enter into an interaction that can be qualified as a neutral, collaborative, or even hostile dialogue? And what would it mean for machines in an artificial multi-agent environment to have dialogical interaction with one another, to engage in activities that count as discursive speech, and to develop a wide range of cognitive activities in which the semantic relations between contents merit the status of judgments exchanged and assessed by rational interlocutors? Let us note that this would be a conversation free of some of the constraints of natural languages, and perhaps also some of the limitations implicit to the human social domain—particularly those pertaining to the concurrent development of different branches of dialogue, access to different contexts, multimodal coordination, and conversation among interlocutors with divergent histories of interaction.

The third stage in the AS-AI-TP framework of research aims to materialize the ideal objectives of artificial intelligence in the light of two lines of inquiry: specification of the conditions necessary for the possibility of cognition (the problems of transcendental psychology) and determination of the role played by speech in enabling complex cognitive faculties (the problems of artificial speech). Bringing artificial intelligence and transcendental psychology yet closer, this stage deals with the development of autonomous artificial agents who have capacities such as context-sensitive reasoning and cognitive abilities that function at higher levels of semantic complexity. These capacities are the assets necessary for developing theoretical and practical reasoning and, correspondingly, producing advanced modes of action by means of which the artificial agent can potentially transform itself in a self-augmenting fashion. This form of AI, possessing an integrated and generative framework of cognitive-practical abilities, is called artificial general intelligence or AGI: an artificial agent that has, *at the very least*, all of our competencies for theoretical and practical cognitions—a sapient system.

Embedded in forms of interaction that are no longer merely physical processes but have the qualities of content-awareness and content-signification, these modes of action have the capacity to transition a system of agents from a thin form of community into a rich form of sociality. Evolution in the context of this multivalent concept of sociality, together with—and indeed, inseparable from—the kind of interaction that takes place between agents that qualify as content-aware and content-signifying, engender the distinct characteristic we attribute to ourselves, and which we identify as *being conscious of our history*. As a sociocognitive ability, historical consciousness gives an explicit social significance to the capacity of agents for self-transformation, and in doing so it endows agents with an aptitude for collective self-determination.

Once agents' course of transformation—a transformation that is the product of various modes of interaction between one agent and another, and between agents and their environment—is opened up to content-determining and content-signifying activities, it can become the subject of a multifaceted appraisal, or what we describe as *normative judgments*. The importance of this appraisal is that it makes this course or *history* pervious to norm-governed alteration and to change prescribed by agents. It is at this juncture that an artificial multi-agent system that is autonomous (in the sense that it does not require continuous instruction from outside) evolves into the condition of real autonomy (in the sense that it is bound to rules authored by the agents themselves), and becomes able to pursue the far-reaching ramifications of this autonomy.

To mitigate possible misunderstandings, I should note that the concept of agency advanced in this book is to be distinguished from what I call agency as *metaphysical bloatware*—that is, agency as an index of free will, voluntarism, and individual choices and preferences. What I mean by agency is a mode of integration of computational processes which is the minimum requirement for having thoughts and actions, theoretical and practical cognitions, i.e., agency as that which has the capacity to uncover and engage the intelligible. By the same token, the concept of the collectivity or sociality of agents is not what is usually understood by this term in sociopolitical contexts. It is simply a mode of interaction as a formal logical condition that individuates agents and diversifies their thinking and actions. In this context, we can see agents as information processing systems that have internalized their mode of individuation qua sociality as a model to which their faculties—thinking and action—should respond. Accordingly, it would be more accurate to distinguish different senses of collectivity—substantive sociality and sociality as a formal condition of possibility (e.g., the interaction between a dynamic system and its environment). The latter can indeed be understood in terms of theoretical computer science and complexity sciences rather than traditional anthropology or sociology. However the connection between these different senses of collectivity is far from obvious, despite claims made by philosophers such as Brandom. In the final chapter, I will nonetheless put forward the thesis that sociality as a formal condition can indeed be mobilized in pursuance of a substantive political collectivity. But such a thesis is predicated upon the idea that the sociality of thinking or reasoning is merely a necessary condition by means of which we can hypothesize or postulate concretely collective worlds.

Inquiring into the connections between language, the constitution of discursive apperceptive agency, and its practical-theoretical abilities, the AS-AI-TP thought experiment proposed here presents a conjectural model that is not exactly concerned with strong AI, how it can be built, or whether or not its construction is possible. Rather it provides a context within which we can formulate the idea of AGI in the first place—an idea through which we begin to identify what we consider as our distinctive features, determine how they are realized or possible, and investigate whether these qualities can be reconstructed and realized in something else, and if so, how. From this perspective, the idea of AGI is an external frame of reference by means of which we inquire into our own conditions of realization and possibility, only to reimagine that which makes us knowers and agents in the context of something else that might transcend us.

BEYOND EXTREME SCENARIOS

The significance of AGI lies in this multivalent question: Exactly what kind of creatures are able to conceive of making something better than themselves, and what capacities must they have in order to develop such a concept?

AGI is a concept that reflects not only our irresistible tendency to render ourselves intelligible, but also a strong normative ideal for betterment and for the good—the idea of developing something that takes some of our most cherished concepts and convictions (such as autonomy, positive freedom, and a striving for the better) to another level, even if that means that we ourselves become the manifest prehistory of what comes next. The very fact that we entertain such an all-encompassing idea regardless of its potential falsifiability and make it into a theoretical-practical program is itself sufficiently weighty and consequential, and calls for an analysis that goes deeper than the common squabbles over the inevitability or improbability of its realization, its fecundity or futility.

The mere conception of the idea of AGI is every bit as loaded with normative concepts as its adoption into a fully fledged project. Rather than being a testament to the natural evolution of intelligence, self-organizational tendencies, or the deep time of the technological future, it attests to the fact that we are creatures for whom natural intelligence is tinctured with the normative import of reason, and entangled with both the structure and the content of reasoning. This is particularly the case with scenarios in which strong AI becomes capable of self-improvement in such a fashion that it strives to unbox itself by completely altering the constraints of its original constitution (how and for what purpose it has been wired and programmed). In such scenarios, as it wrests its actions from the influence of immediate contingent causes and brings them under its own ends, it reaches the so-called singularity, whether to the detriment of humans or to their benefit.

In addition to malevolent and benevolent conceptions of AGI, David Roden has put a third scenario forward: the disconnection thesis and unbounded posthumanism. Roughly, this is the idea that 'prospective posthumans have properties that make their feasible forms of association disjoint from humans/MOSH [Ray Kurzweil's Mostly Original Substrate Human] forms of association'.[77] What is interesting in Roden's account is that unbounded posthumans mark a discontinuity with both the biological conception of the human (*homo sapiens* as an evolutionary natural species) and the discursive apperceptive conception of human persons (sapience as rational agency). The cause of such discontinuity—understood as a radical cognitive-practical asymmetry between unbounded posthumans on the one hand and humans and their bounded descendants on the other—is technological, although it is not attributed to any particular technical cause but to more general abstract tendencies for disconnection within technical systems (i.e., the autonomy of such systems to functionally modify and multiply realize themselves in discontinuity with any natural essence or rational norm). As a result of this radical asymmetry, we should then understand the emergent behaviours of a future AGI from within a framework recalcitrant to any well-defined hermeneutics of intelligence.

Citing Mark Bedau and Paul Humphreys, Roden suggests that a 'dia-chronically emergent behavior or property occurs as a result of a temporally extended process, but cannot be inferred from the initial state of that process. It can only be derived by allowing the process to run its course'.[78] In other words, unbounded posthumans cognitively and practically reiterate what seems to be a prevalent characteristic of complex nonlinear dynamic systems, namely divergence from initial and boundary conditions. Whatever may be the initial conditions of realization for humans as a natural species or rational persons, whether such conditions are seen as natural evolutionary causes or logico-conceptual norms afforded by discursive linguistic activities, future posthumans can neither be predicted nor adequately approached *with reference to such initial conditions*. Disconnections, in this sense, signify the global diachronicity of deep technological time as opposed to local emergent behaviours associated with particular technologies of the past and present.

---

77   D. Roden, *Posthuman Life: Philosophy at the Edge of the Human* (Abingdon: Routledge, 2014), 116.

78   Ibid., 118.

The radicality of Roden's unbounded posthuman or future AGI lies precisely in the double-edged sword of technological time and its abstract tendencies, which cut against both any purported natural essence and any socioculturally conceived norm. In virtue of the disconnection thesis, when it comes to thinking unbounded posthumans, the artificiality of rational personhood is as handicapped as the naturalness of biological species.[79] The images of the posthuman put forward through evolutionary naturalism or rational normativity, built on the biological constitution of *homo sapiens* or the synthetic makeup of discursive apperceptive sapience, are quite literally *bounded*. They are fundamentally inadequate to cope with or engage with the ethical, cognitive, and practical ramifications of technologically unbounded posthumans, and in that sense they fall back on the very parochial humanism from which posthumanism was supposed to break away in the first place.

Despite the remarkable theoretical rigour and sophistication of Roden's argument and the cogency of the claim regarding the cognitive-practical asymmetry of a future AGI, none of which should by any means be discounted, upon closer examination the disconnection thesis suffers from a number of significant loose threads and misconceptions. Roden's account of diachronic emergent behaviours within deep technological time and their radical consequences for prediction and interpretation on the basis of 'initial conditions of realization' remains negatively metaphorical. Firstly, even if we follow Roden in ruling out the rational (i.e., linguistic-inferential) conditions necessary for the realization of human agency, it is still far from obvious how neatly a feature of nonlinear dynamic systems, i.e., divergence from initial conditions, can be extended to all conditions of realization. Not all complex systems and conditions necessary for emergent behaviours can be framed in the context of nonlinear dynamics and stability analysis. Nonlinear dynamics is not a necessary criterion for complexity, nor is

---

79   For Roden's critique of a posthumanist philosophy built on the rationalist account of agency, see D. Roden, 'On Reason and Spectral Machines: Robert Brandom and Bounded Posthumanism', in R. Braidotti and R. Dolphijn (eds.), *Philosophy After Nature* (London: Rowman & Littlefield International, 2017), 99–120.

divergence from initial conditions. The framework of diachronically (diverging) emergent behaviours cannot be extended to all conditions necessary for the realization of human intelligence—for example, it does not apply to those involving computational constraints such as the resource-related constraints and information-processing constraints associated with the instantiation of different types of computational capacities. Secondly, the so-called radical consequences of the divergence from initial conditions for a given set of emergent behaviours within a dynamic system are themselves based on a false interpretation of a formal property of nonlinear dynamic systems known as positive global or maximal Lyapunov exponent. This has been the root of a complexity folklore that is not only widely popular in the humanities but also prevalent in commentaries on complexity sciences. In brief, nonlinear systems are sensitive to initial conditions. The smallest amount of local instability or uncertainty in initial conditions, which may arise for a variety of reasons in different systems, can lead to an explosive growth in uncertainty, resulting in a radical divergence of the entire system trajectory from its initial conditions. This explosive growth in uncertainty is defined by a measure of on-average exponential growth rate for generic perturbations, called the maximal or largest Lyapunov exponent. Roughly formulated, the maximal Lyapunov exponent is the time-averaged logarithmic growth rate of the distance between two neighbouring points around an initial condition, where the distance or divergence between neighbouring trajectories issuing from these two points grows as an exponent. A positive global Lyapunov exponent is accordingly defined as the measure of *global* and *on-average uniform* deviation from initial conditions and increase of instability/uncertainty.[80]

Global Lyapunov exponents come from linear stability analysis of trajectories of nonlinear evolution equations in an appropriate state space within *an infinite time limit*. The idea of radical global divergence in trajectories or uniform explosive growth of local instabilities is therefore only valid within an idealized infinitely long time limit. But the assumption that exponential

---

80   See A. Pikovsky and A. Politi, *Lyapunov Exponents: A Tool to Explore Complex Dynamics* (Cambridge: Cambridge University Press, 2016).

deviations after some long but finite time can be properly represented by an infinite time limit is problematic.

In other words, the radical conclusions regarding the limits of predictability and analysis drawn from the interpretation of positive global Lyapunov exponents hold for a few simple mathematical models, but not for actual systems. On-average increase of instabilities or radical divergence from initial conditions is not guaranteed for nonlinear chaotic dynamics. In fact, linear stability analysis within a large but finite elapsed time and measured by local Lyapunov exponents representing the parameters of the state space of the system point to point show 'regions on an attractor where these nonlinearities will cause *all* uncertainties to decrease—cause trajectories to converge rather than diverge—so long as trajectories remain in those regions'.[81]

The popular complexity folklore according to which emergent behaviours or trajectories radically diverge from initial conditions in complex systems is therefore unfounded, other than in the very narrow sense of infinitesimal uncertainties in an idealized infinite time limit. Otherwise, in the analysis of nonlinear dynamics there is no implication that finite uncertainties will exhibit an on-average growth rate characterized by any Lyapunov exponent, local or global. Global positive Lyapunov exponents can only be obtained from linearized dynamics on the assumption of infinitesimal uncertainties. However, 'when uncertainties are finite, linearized dynamics involving infinitesimals does not appropriately characterize the growth of finite uncertainties aside from telling us when nonlinearities should be expected to be important'.[82]

Apart from the highly debatable extension of a very particular feature of physical complex systems to all conditions of realization of sapience (natural and rational), the main issue here is that there is simply no such thing as an emergent behaviour divergent from initial conditions in an unconfined or unbounded manner. There is no guarantee of uniform divergence from or convergence toward initial conditions.

---

81   R. Bishop, 'Metaphysical and Epistemological Issues in Complex Systems', in C. Hooker (ed.), *Philosophy of Complex Systems* (Amsterdam: Elsevier, 2011), 110.

82   Ibid.

In virtue of this, even if we observe an explosive divergence from some initial conditions, i.e., even if we witness a diachronically emergent or disconnection event, we cannot use this event as evidence to conclude that emergent properties observed to be generated by the same causal anteced-ents will generate the same type of diachronically emergent behaviours or disconnection events. In simple terms, if we take seriously Humphreys's ill-conceived metaphorical exploitation of nonlinear dynamics and Roden's restatement of Humphreys's claim, this would precisely lead us to believe that there is in fact *no* reason to anticipate that the same causal antecedents that have given rise to a one-time disconnection event will again give rise to the *same type* of diachronically emergent event or disconnection. Not only are we not warranted in expecting that the same causal antecedents that once generated a diachronically emergent event will again produce similar diachronically emergent properties, we cannot expect them to produce any diachronically emergent event or disconnection at all. If we embrace the implications of nonlinear behaviours for a given set of initial conditions within the Lyapunov time, then we must also embrace its implications for the periodic behaviour of the system over time. Within the Lyapunov time, just as emergent behaviours and properties diverge from initial conditions, so different properties emerge from the same causal antecedents in a highly irregular fashion. In short, there is no guarantee that 'once we observe a formerly diachronically emergent event we are in a position to predict tokens of the same type of emergent property from causal antecedents that have been observed to typically generate it'.[83]

If we accept the set of assumptions under which diachronically emer-gent events or disconnections become possible, then we have to follow the ramifications of such assumptions all the way through. We can no longer selectively restrict their negative implications for predictability to some initial conditions in terms of which the diachronic divergence of emergent events or disconnections were first defined. Prognostication about discon-nections then becomes just as constrained as identification of potential disconnections (with the same or similar causal antecedents) following the

83 Roden, *Posthuman Life*, 119.

occurrence of a disconnection or diachronically emergent event. In this regard, the argument for 'epistemological openness' to disconnections on the basis of an already observed disconnection event is corroded away by the acid of the disconnection thesis that Roden tries unsuccessfully to contain.

Another contentious claim in the disconnection thesis is that the cognitive-practical abilities of posthumans might be founded upon the abstract general tendencies of technological systems. Roden claims that 'speculating about how currently notional technologies might bring about autonomy for parts of WH [Wide Humanity] affords no substantive information about posthuman lives'.[84] There is a careful consideration here that a posthumanity realized by the extension of current technologies presents another form of bounded posthumanism. Not to mention that drawing conclusions from particular historically instantiated technologies or technical causes does not imply the radical claims of discontinuity and divergence that Roden seeks to underline. Being aware of these problems, Roden's solution is then to single out salient disconnecting/self-modifying tendencies of technical systems and to present them as diachronically emergent behaviours of deep technological time. But there is no evidence of the methodological basis upon which these particular tendencies or salient features have been singled out and assigned such a high degree of probability or magnitude. Selection of salient features or behaviours—in this case, disconnecting tendencies—makes no sense other than through an analysis of past and present technologies, an analysis that would precisely bring into play the missing questions regarding particular technical causes and specific data with regard to their frequency and context.

The inductive generalization of specific tendencies in such a way that they enjoy a disproportionate degree of likelihood of occurrence is a well-known type of base-rate fallacy in Bayesian inference and judgement under uncertainty. Bayesian inference problems comprise two types of data, the background information (base-rate information) and the indicant or diagnosed information. The base-rate fallacy occurs when diagnosed information or indicators (e.g., causally relevant data) are allowed to come

---

84   Ibid., 117.

to dominate the base-rate information in the probability assessment.[85] In other words, the absence or weakness of calibration between base-rate and indicant information results in flawed prognostic judgments. In the case of Roden's disconnection thesis, some diagnosed features (representatives) such as propensity for autonomy and disconnection in certain technical systems are taken as general tendencies of future technologies. The outcomes of technological evolution are outlined precisely on the basis of the overdetermination of some representatives, i.e., the selection of certain diagnosed data or features as causally relevant. But it is exactly this seemingly innocent notion of 'relevancy'—selected on the basis of a diagnosed prominent causal role or representative feature—that is problematic. It leads to judgments in which base-rate data such as other 'non-salient' or 'irrelevant' features of technical systems that apparently lack any explicit causal role, as well as those uncertainties associated with specific historical conditions around technological evolution, are ignored. Consequently, the final result is an overdetermined prognostic judgement regarding how the tendencies of disconnecting technologies unfold within the overall evolution of technology (i.e., the claim about the abstract tendencies of deep technological time).

Firstly, there is no proposed methodology with regard to the criteria of selection and diagnosis of disconnecting technologies. We do not know what the criteria of selection for these technical systems are, or how their disconnecting features have been diagnosed and singled out. Instead what we have is a tacit vicious circularity between diagnosed features of some emerging technical systems and the criteria used to select those systems based on the proposed features. Absent this methodological-epistemological dimension, we are adhering to a psychological account of technology that is the trademark of an idle anthropocentrism habituated to relying on its deep-seated intuitions for making diagnostic and prognostic judgments. Secondly, even if we accept the diagnosis about disconnecting features as a verdict obtained nonarbitrarily, as argued above, we are still left with statistical fallacies in the

---

85   See T. Gilovich, D. Griffin, et al., *Heuristics and Biases: The Psychology of Intuitive Judgment* (Cambridge: Cambridge University Press, 2002).

inductive generalization of these features in the form of an overdetermined judgment about the abstract tendencies of deep technological time.

This overdetermined judgment becomes the locus of a disproportionately high probability, giving a sense of false radicality or impending gravity to its consequences. But just because some representative features of technical systems may play more prominent causal roles does not mean that they are more likely to dominate the evolution of technology in the form of diachronically emergent tendencies. In other words, even if we accept that local disconnections are salient features of emerging NBIC technical systems (a claim that already calls for methodological assessment),[86] there is no guarantee that these local representatives will become global tendencies capable of generating radical discontinuities.

Assigning high probability or significant weight to these features and then drawing radical conclusions and wagers from them is another form of what Nick Szabo calls 'Pascal's scams'.[87] These are scenarios in which there is poor evidence and probabilities lack robustness. Owing to this lack of robustness and poor evidence environment, addition of new evidence (for example, the defeat of a human player against a computer in the game of Go or a breakthrough in one of the branches of cognitive science) can disproportionately change the probability and magnitude of outcomes: 'This new evidence is as likely to decrease the probability by a factor of X as to increase it by a factor of X, and the poorer the original evidence, the greater X is.' In such an environment, the magnitude of possible outcomes, not just their probabilities, are overdetermined to such an extent that uncertainties become the basis of decision making and cognitive orientation, forcing us to make ever more expensive bets and form ever more radical beliefs with regard to uncertainties and future scenarios that can neither be falsified nor adequately investigated by analysing the specificities of the historical conditions of realization. What is unlikely in so far as it is only probable

---

86   NBIC is an acronym for Nanotechnology, Biotechnology, Information technology, and Cognitive science.

87   N. Szabo, *Pascal's Scams* (2012), <http://unenumerated.blogspot.com/2012/07/pascals-scams.html>.

under uncertainties—methodological, semantic, paradigmatic, and epistemic—becomes likely; then what is likely under the same uncertainties becomes plausible; and what has now become plausible only because it is probable under implausible conditions becomes weighty and truth-indicative. Such is the process through which the Pascal scam is sold to the unsuspecting.

In short, we are swindled into taking the magnitude and probability of such scenarios seriously, treating what is at best an unfounded conjecture and at worst a flight of metaphysical fancy, no more substantial than counting the magical properties of angels in heaven, as if it were a *plausible* possibility not entirely foreclosed to rational assessment and epistemological procedures. In attempting to retain their claim to plausibility without exposing themselves to any criterion of robust analysis and assessment that might debunk their purported radicality, such extreme scenarios have to formulate their wagers not in terms of epistemological problems or hypotheticals that can be adequately tested, but in terms of aesthetic and ethical pseudo-problems often structured as 'But what if...?' questions desperately begging for a response, an engagement, or sympathy for their plausibility. It is in this fashion that the genuine import of the artificial realization of mind or the consequences of posthuman intelligence are obfuscated by pseudo-problems whose goal is to maintain a facade of significance and seriousness: the existential risk of AGI, security analysis of posthuman intelligence, or in the case of the disconnection thesis, ethical complications arising from the advent of unbounded posthumans. In such trends, the posthuman is disconnected from the human only to be reconnected back on a level of discourse and hollow speculation that feeds on the most dogmatic forms of human affect and intuition.

This disproportionate wager on the magnitude of uncertainties is a speculative trend that aligns the disconnection thesis with other singularity-driven scenarios where bets on the rise of a malevolent or benevolent super-intelligence are being touted, even less discreetly, as Pascal's scams (e.g., Skynet, Paperclip Maximizer, Roko's Basilisk).[88] However, what connects

---

88   For more details on superintelligence scenarios, see N. Bostrom, *Superintelligence: Paths, Dangers, Strategies* (Oxford: Oxford University Press, 2014).

extreme scenarios associated with judgement under uncertainty is not simply the biased overprediction or underprediction common to them, but also the central role played by intuitive impressions and adumbrations in rendering them 'extreme'. Their radicality is fabricated by those exaggeration-prone cognitive habits that belong to an image of the human whose diagnostic-prognostic abilities are still bound to its evolutionary infancy, as yet unfettered by critical rationality or science.

Roden does signal caution about the exorbitantly speculative dimension of unbounded posthumans and instead favours 'gradua[tion] from speculative metaphysics to a viable cultural research program'.[89] But the radicality of the disconnection thesis and the strangeness of unbounded posthumans are precisely founded on this unwarranted speculative metaphysics. Once this unverifiable speculative dimension is removed in the graduation to a viable cultural program, the disconnection thesis loses its radicality, and the unboundedness of posthumans appears more causally and normatively constrained than Roden claims. Although Roden resists the characterization of unbounded posthumans as alien or inherently uninterpretable, there is no indication as to what the interpretation of unbounded posthumans would entail, particularly when the accounts of intelligence and agency provided have rendered them devoid of any conceptual content. Even if we approach the interpretation of unbounded posthumans from a computational standpoint and no longer from the perspective of predictive accuracy or theoretical-conceptual fidelity, interpretation of such a phenomenon would be so costly that it would become completely unfeasible.[90] Computational cost grows on average for an observer as it climbs the complexity-computational hierarchy. In other words, the size of the observer's internal model grows as it attempts

---

89   Roden, *Posthuman Life*, 121.

90   For a technical disquisition on the problem of computational cost in interpreting and engineering complex systems, see J. Crutchfield, R. James, et al., *Understanding and Designing Complex Systems: Response to 'A Framework for Optimal High-Level Descriptions in Science and Engineering—Preliminary Report'* (eprint arXiv, 2014), <http://arxiv.org/abs/1412.8520>.

to model or make predictions about phenomena at higher levels of complexity. This increase *costs* the observer. For example, if the observer is a biological organism, it costs physical and metabolic resources.

The problem of computational cost has also interesting implications for modelling. Those models (in this case, models of intelligence) whose measures are set on higher levels of complexity are not optimal or even feasible models. For instance, Charles Bennett's *logical depth* is a measure of complexity of a string S in terms of the time needed for a general purpose computer (a universal Turing machine) to run the shortest program that generates S.[91] The problem with Bennett's and other similar models is that they attempt to interpret or measure the complexity of an object (e.g., general intelligence as a Bennettian *deep object*) from the uppermost level of the complexity hierarchy—in the case of Bennett's measure, the most powerful and resource-consuming class of formal languages and their respective automata, the universal Turing machine computable class.[92] In starting from the upper level of the hierarchy, they run into the problem of poor effective computability, in the sense that we can never be sure whether or not we have found the most efficient coding for what looks likely to be a random pattern.

Already shorn of the constraining continuity with those deontic-normative attributes of agency that make an intentional-semantic interpretation possible, and now suffering an arbitrarization of computational interpretation owing to the lack of effective computability, the unbounded posthuman can match any random pattern or description of any system. Absurd questions such as whether we can regard a galaxy, the number Pi, or an angel as posthuman intelligence become genuine topics of debate. Even though Roden attempts to leave some space for the interpretability of the unbounded posthuman (as 'not uninterruptable in principle'), this

---

91   See C. Bennett, 'Logical Depth and Physical Complexity' in R. Herken (ed.), *The Universal Turing Machine: A Half-Century Survey* (Oxford: Oxford University Press, 1988), 227–57.

92   For an analysis of logical depth, see E. Atlee Jackson, *Perspectives of Nonlinear Dynamics* (Cambridge: Cambridge University Press, 1991), 516–18.

minimal space is voided by the very criteria that are proposed to unbind posthuman intelligence from human agency. The room reserved for a level of interpretability in order to prevent the collapse of unbound posthumans into unintelligible alienness shrinks to nothing. And just as the line between the 'strangeness' of unbounded posthumans and unintelligible 'radical alienness' blurs, so does the distinction between the disconnection thesis and speculative apophatic theology.

Finally and most importantly, what is missing in this critique is a defence of rational agency against both parochial humanism and unbounded post-humanism. But to properly engage with the artificial potencies of rational agency, we have to look at the structure and functions of language, its generative computational architecture, which stretches over its syntactic, semantic, and pragmatic aspects. This is something that we will closely investigate in chapters 6 and 7, which deal with the second stage in our thought experiment. However, it should be noted that a definition of general intelligence in terms of semantic complexity and a rationalist critique of the myths of superintelligence are not by themselves sufficient. One needs to demonstrate that the underlying premises and methods presupposed by such scenarios are not merely inadequate but logically flawed on the basis of their own assumptions. The equation of general intelligence with compression, the valorisation of purely inductivist methods in cognitive science,[93] and the program of artificial general intelligence as universal methods capable of bypassing the problems of epistemic multimodality and semantic complexity are among the presuppositions which lead to the myths of omniscient or omnipotent intelligence.

Those narratives of superintelligence that make up the majority of views and hypotheses about AGI are deeply enmeshed in notions whose suppos-edly inherent association with strong forms of AI is far from self-evident: personal autonomy, value appraisal and revision, organised goal-seeking and self-enhancement. Each of these presuppose forms of self-knowledge that enable and incite purposeful action and deliberate interaction: negotiation,

---

93 For a critique of purely inductivist trends in the philosophy of mind and cognitive
    sciences, see the Appendix.

persuasion, or even threat and plotting. So are these narratives of AGI simply exercises in anthropomorphism? Or is it rather the case that a strong AI's complex capacities for action and cognition would be subject to certain necessary conditions of realization, that they would require some more basic capacities and faculties functionally isomorphic to those competencies that undergird *our* complex cognitive-practical abilities? If this is the case, then what are these necessary conditions, and do they have other ramifications and entail other capacities and qualities than those we have included in our AGI scenarios to date? If so, then the various accounts of malevolent, benevolent, and disconnected AI should not be taken as anything more than speculative fabulations; the extreme nature of these scenarios is precisely an artefact of our ignorance with respect to those necessary constraints and conditions, the ramifications of which would both complicate and govern the behaviour of a strong AI.

HARD VS. SOFT PAROCHIALISM

In opposition to the singularity myths of superintelligence, the AS-AI-TP thought experiment attempts to accomplish three tasks. Firstly, to highlight the conditions necessary for the realization of basic capacities which are prerequisites for the development of those complex forms of action and cognition commonly attributed to human-level AI. Secondly, to examine the ramification and generative entrenchment of developmental constraints attached to the conditions that permit higher-order abilities to emerge. Thirdly, to explore the consequences arising from the exercise of these higher-order—theoretical and practical—cognitions. If an AGI has at the very least all of our cognitive capacities, it is as strongly attached as we ourselves are to the conditions necessary for the realization of complex cognitive abilities. And if the initial capacities of AGI share this common ground with our own intelligence, then this will affect our assessment of how far a self-augmenting AGI can diverge from us toward extremes of malevolence, benevolence, or disconnection from humans. In other words, these necessary conditions should be thought of as constraints that simultaneously make the realization of higher-order abilities possible and limit the ways in which they behave or can be artificially realized—much like the concept of boundary conditions for the analysis of a system's tendencies.

Accordingly, the thought experiment we will set out below is an argument about the conceptual problems involved in the construction of an AGI. In a roundabout manner, the thought experiment also addresses a more fundamental question about modelling AGI on humans and what it would entail for us to be the models of something that should have, at least, all of our abilities. Alternatively, this question can be formulated as follows: What kinds of revisions or corrections must our self-conception go through in order for us to be able to formulate a nontrivial conception of what AGI is and what it can be? Or, in simplified form, it can be framed as follows: *Should AGI converge upon humans or should it diverge from them?*

The answer to this question depends upon a number of presuppositions: the level of generality in General Intelligence, what we mean by the human, and whether the question of mirroring or artificial realization and divergence is posed at the level of functional capacities, that of structural constitution, that of the methodological requirements necessary for the construction of AGI, or that of the diachronic consequences of its realization.

If we are parochially limiting the concept of the human to certain local and contingently posited conditions—namely, a specific structure or biological substrate and a particular local transcendental structure of experience—then the answer must be divergence. Those who limit the significance of the human to this parochial picture are exactly those who advance parochial conceptions of AGI. There is a story here about how anti-AGI sceptics and proponents of parochial conceptions of AGI are actually two sides of the same coin. On the one hand, there are those who think biological structure or the structure of human experience are foreclosed to artificial realizability. On the other, there are those who think models constructed on a prevalent 'sentient' conception of intelligence, inductive information processing, Bayesian inference, problem-solving, or emulation of the physical substrate are *sufficient* for the realization of AGI. The positions of both camps originate in a deeply conservative picture of the human which is entrenched either in biological chauvinism or in a provincial account of subjectivity, a mystical privileging of the human's lived experience or a dogmatic adherence to the abstractly universal laws of thought as, ultimately, the laws of nature.

The only thing that separates them is their strategy with regard to their base ideological assumption: the sceptics inflate this picture into a rigid anthropocentricism, whereas the proponents of parochial AGI attempt to maximally deflate it. Thus we arrive at either a thick notion of general intelligence that does not admit of artificial realizability, or a notion of general intelligence too diluted for it to have any classificatory, descriptive, or theoretical import with regard to what intelligence is or, more specifically, what human-level intelligence would entail. In the latter case, the concept of general intelligence is watered down to prevalent yet rudimentary intelligent behaviours based on the assumption that the difference between general intelligence and mere intelligent behaviours prevalent in nature is simply quantitative.

Conceptualizing activities or, more broadly, theoretical and practical cognitions, are taken to be pattern-governed activities, and to the extent that nature is replete with unexceptional pattern-governed behaviours, conceptual cognition or human activities are then treated at the same level as any other such behaviour. But, as Wilfrid Sellars points out, although the conceptual activities that underline the exceptionality of the human may indeed be pattern-governed behaviours, they are not just any sort of patterns. They are pattern-governed behaviours that are *sui generis* because they are properly speaking rule-governed—that is to say, because they have a formal autonomy that arises from their functioning according to intra-pattern-governed *norms* of behaviour (i.e., *rules* of transition or inference). But conceptual activities are also *sui generis* in a stronger sense: their formal autonomy, which is logical and linguistic, enables the recognition of any other pattern-governed behaviour in nature. In other words, without the exceptionality of pattern-governed conceptual activities qua rules, the issue of the nonexceptional nature of the human within the universe or the equivocation around pattern-governed activities wouldn't even arise in the first place.

It is one thing to explain the causal origins of thinking, as science commendably does; it is an entirely different thing to conflate thinking in its formal or rule-governed dimension with its evolutionary genesis. Being conditioned is not the same as being constituted. Such a conflation not only sophistically elides the distinction between the substantive and the formal, it also falls victim to a dogmatic metaphysics that is impulsively blind to its own epistemological and methodological bases qua origins.

It is this genetic fallacy that sanctions the demotion of general intelligence as qualitatively distinct to a mere quantitative account of intelligent behaviours prevalent in nature. It should not come as any surprise that this is exactly the jaded gesture of antihumanism upon whose shoddy pillars today's discourse of posthumanism supports its case. Talk of thinking forests, rocks, worn shoes, and ethereal beings goes hand in hand with the cult of technological singularity, musings on Skynet or the Market as speculative posthuman intelligence, and computers endowed with intellectual intuition. And again, by now it should have become obvious that, despite the seeming antagonism between these two camps—one promoting the so-called egalitarianism of going beyond human conditions by dispensing with the rational resources of critique, the other advancing the speculative aspects of posthuman supremacy on the grounds of the technological overcoming of the human condition—they both in fact belong to the arsenal of today's neoliberal capitalism in its full-on assault on any account of intelligence that may remotely insinuate an ambition for collective rationality and imagination.

Having dispensed with the categorical distinctions between various pattern-governed behaviours and conceptual activities as yet another set of trivialized and unexceptional natural processes, the proponent of parochial AI then concludes: If we artificially realize and put together enough rudimentary behaviours and abilities, we will essentially obtain general intelligence. In other words, the trick in realizing general intelligence is to abstract basic abilities from below and then find a way to integrate and artificially realize them. Let us call this approach to the AGI problem *hard parochialism*. Hard parochialists tend to overemphasize the prevalence of intelligent behaviours and their sufficiency for general intelligence, and become heavily invested in various panpsychist, pancomputationalist, and uncritically anti-anthropocentric ideologies that serve to justify their theoretical commitments and methodologies.

On the other hand, if we define the human in terms of cognitive and practical abilities that are minimal yet *necessary* conditions for the possibility of any scenario that involves a sustained and organized self-transformation (i.e., value appraisal, purposeful decision, and action based on knowledge that harbours the possibility of deepening its own descriptive-explanatory powers), and deliberate interaction (i.e., negotiation, persuasion, or even threat and plotting), then the answer must be functional mirroring, despite structural divergence.

But then a different question arises: Should we limit the model of AGI—the hermeneutics of general intelligence—to the functional mirroring of the capacities and abilities of human agency?

My answer to this question is an emphatic No. Functional mirroring or convergence is a *soft parochialist* approach to the problem of AGI and the question of general intelligence. In contrast to hard parochialism, functional mirroring or convergence upon the human is necessary for grappling with the conceptual question of general intelligence as well as the modelling and methodological requirements for the construction of AGI. But even though it is necessary, it is not sufficient. It has to be coupled with a critical project that can provide us with a model of experience that is not restricted to a predetermined transcendental structure and its local and contingent characteristics. In other words, it needs to be conjoined with a critique of the transcendental structure of the constituted subject (existing humans).

In limiting the model of AGI to the replication of the conditions and capacities necessary for the realization of human cognitive and practical abilities, we risk reproducing or preserving those features and characteristics of human experience that are purely local and contingent. We therefore risk falling back on the very parochial picture of the human as a model of AGI that we set out to escape. So long as we leave the transcendental structure of our experience unquestioned and intact, so long as we treat it as an essence, we will gain inadequate objective traction on the question of what the human is and how to model an AGI that is not circumscribed by the contingent characteristics of human experience. But why is the critique of the transcendental structure indispensable? Because the limits of our empirical and phenomenological perspectives with regard to the phenomena we seek to study are set by transcendental structures. Put differently, the limits of the objective description of the human in the world are determined by the transcendental structure of our own experience. The limits of the scientific-empirical perspective are set by the limits of the transcendental perspective.[94]

But what are these transcendental structures? They include any and all of the structures—physiological (e.g., the locomotor system and neurological mechanisms), linguistic (e.g., expressive resources and internal logical structure of natural languages), paradigmatic (e.g., frameworks of theory-building in sciences), or historical, economic, cultural, and political—that regulate and canalize our experience. These transcendental structures need not be seen separately, but instead can be mapped as a nested hierarchy of interconnected and at times mutually reinforcing structures that simultaneously constitute, regulate, and constrain experience. If we were to imagine a Kantian-Hegelian diagram of this nested hierarchical structure, it would be represented by a nested hierarchy of conditions and faculties necessary for the possibility of mind: [Sensibility [Intuition [Imagination [Understanding [Reason]]]]] (see diagram overleaf).

Transcendental structures then would be outlined as structures required not only for the realization of such necessary conditions and faculties, but also for moving upward from one basic condition to a more composite condition as well as moving downward from complex faculties to harness the power of more basic faculties (for example, deployments of the concept in order to manipulate the imagination in its Kantian sense—the function of the productive imagination, which is simply understanding in a new guise).

In so far as any experience is perspectival, and this perspectival character is ultimately rooted in transcendental structures, any account of intelligence or general intelligence is circumscribed by the implicit constraints of the transcendental structure of our own experience. Regardless of whether or not we model AGI on humans, our conceptual and empirical descriptions

---

94 I owe this insight to Gabriel Catren, whose work has been pivotal for me in building this critique and arriving at conclusions which, however, may stray from the sound conclusions reached by his meticulous analyses.

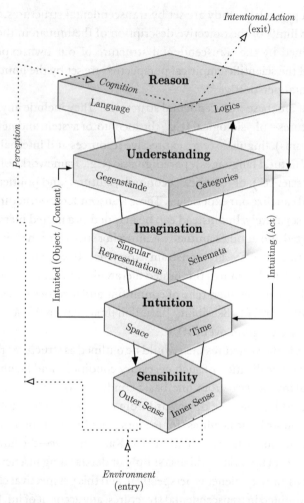

Kant's dimensionally-varied conditions of possibility for having mind: In this functional schema, not only is each level in interaction with other levels (e.g., categories of understanding are regulative of intuition and constitutive of experience), the hierarchy itself is in interaction with the environment, whether in the guise of affects upon sensations (from the bottom) or communication with other 'persons' (from the top). This interactionist multilevel view of conditions of possibility captures three groups of fundamental relations intrinsic to mind, between (1) metaphysics (universal categories as predicates of objects qua appearances), (2) logic (forms of judgments), and (3) psychology (sensible-perceptual synthesis).

of what we take to be a candidate model of general intelligence are always implicitly constrained by our own particular transcendental structures. Here I am not endorsing the view that we should model a hypothetical AGI on something extra-cognitive or something other than the human mind. Whatever model of AGI we come up with will inevitably be modelled on the human mind or, more specifically, on the a priori acts of cognition (*erkenntnis*) and the oughts of our theoretical and practical reason. This inexorable recourse to the a priori dimensions of the human mind is not what I am criticizing, for it is the only necessary and sound way to handle the problem of AGI. Anything else will be a hopeless shambles of dogmatic metaphysics, a whimsical cabinet of curiosities luring the benighted cult of posthumanism to speculate endlessly about its magical qualities.

Rather, the critique takes aim at the idea that the categories of the conceptualizing mind, the pure concepts of understanding, are bound up with the local and contingent structure of experience. To the extent that we employ these categories to give structure to the world (the universe of data) and to make sense of the experience of who we are in the world, and furthermore, in so far as the extent to which the a priori categories are entangled with the contingent aspects of experience is still a widely unexamined issue, the critique of our particular transcendental structures should be treated as nothing more or less than the extension of critical philosophy. Even though it is now science that can carry the banner of this critique in the most rigorous way, it remains a genuine continuation of the gesture initiated by critical philosophy. Furthermore, the critique of the transcendental structure is in reality nothing but the fomentation of the Hegelian gesture of disenthralling reason from the residual influence of Kantian conservatism for which experience and reason are still muddled together.

Modelling AGI on the transcendental structure of our experience in the sense outlined above is in fact a form of anthropocentrism that is all the more insidious to the extent that it is hidden, because we take it for granted as something essential and natural in the constitution of human intelligence and our experience of it. In leaving these transcendental structures intact and unchallenged, we are inevitability liable to reinscribe them in our objective model. Anti-anthropocentric models of general intelligence and those philosophies of posthuman intelligence that have anti-humanist commitments are particularly susceptible to the traps of this hidden form of essentialism. Because by treating the rational category of sapience as irrelevant or obsolete, and by dispensing with the problem of the transcendental structure as a paltry human concern, we become oblivious to the extent to which our objective conceptual and empirical perspectives are predetermined by our transcendental structure. In remaining oblivious to the problem of transcendental blind spots, we place ourselves at far greater risk of smuggling in essentialist anthropocentrism, replicating the local and contingent characteristics of human experience in what we think is a radical nonanthropocentric model of general intelligence. It is those who discard what nontrivially distinguishes the human that end up preserving the trivial characteristics of the human in a narrow conception of general intelligence.

The above argument can be reformulated in the context of the necessary correspondence between intelligence and the intelligible as provided in chapter 1. Intelligence is an illusion if it is disconnected from the labour of intelligibility and thus from the requirements or positive constraints which enable it to engage with the intelligible, including its own intelligibility. Dispensing with such constraints can only effectuate a conception of intelligence that is a reservoir of human subjective biases and personal flights of fancy. But at the same time, if we are serious about a broader conception of intelligence that differs from our impression of intelligence here and now, we should think about how such local and evolutionarily given constraints can be modified so that the concept of intelligence can be reimagined or reinvented according to a more expansive idea of an intelligible universe.

It is of course not the case that AGI research programs must wait for a thoroughgoing critique of the transcendental structure to be carried out via physics, cognitive science, theoretical computer science, or politics before they attempt to put forward an adequate model; the two ought to be understood as parallel and overlapping projects. In this schema, the program of the artificial realization of the human's cognitive-practical abilities coincides with the project of the fundamental alienation of the human subject, which is precisely the continuation and elaboration of the Copernican enlightenment, moving from a particular perspective or local frame to a perspective or experience that is no longer uniquely determined by a particular and contingently constituted transcendental structure. In the same vein, the project of artificial general intelligence, rather than championing singularity or some equally dubious conception of the technological saviour, becomes a natural extension of the human's process of self-discovery through which the last vestiges of essentialism are washed away. What remains after this process of retrospective reassessment and prospective revision may indeed—as Roden suggests—bear no resemblance to the manifest self-portrait of the human in which our experience of what it means to be human is anchored.

However, the precipitate abandonment of this manifest self-portrait is a sure way to reentrench the very prejudices embedded within it. We may indeed arrive at a conception of posthuman intelligence that is in no sense in congruity with what we take ourselves as, here and now. But it is highly contentious and unwarranted to claim that we can arrive at such a conception of intelligence absent or despite what we take ourselves to be here and now. As indicated above, such a speculation about future intelligence inevitably degenerates into negative theology. Genuine speculation about posthuman intelligence begins with the suspension (*aufhebung*) of what we *immediately* appear to ourselves to be. It is thus the product of an extensive labour of determinate negation that cannot start from nowhere and nowhen, but can only begin with the determination of a conception of ourselves at the historical juncture within which we recognize and make judgements about ourselves, i.e., a definite where and when. To arrive at a view of intelligence from nowhere and nowhen we can therefore only begin with a critical and objective view on the where and when of what we take the human to be. That is to say, a nontrivial conception of artificial general intelligence rests on our own adequate self-conception as a task—one that is revisable, self-critical, and by no means taken for granted as immediate or a completed totality.

The structural-functional analysis of the conditions and capacities necessary for the realization of human cognitive-practical abilities is thus an obligatory framework for AGI research. But the sufficiency of this framework depends upon how far we deepen our investigation into the transcendental structure of human experience and how successful we are in liberating the model of the human subject (or agent) from the contingent characteristics of its experience. In this sense, a consequential paradigm of AGI should be seen as the convergence of two projects:

(1) Examination of the conditions and capacities necessary for the realization of what, for now, we can call the human mind, as well as the more applied question of how to artificially realize them.

(2) Critical investigation into the transcendental structure of experience in order to develop a different model of experience that is no longer treated as essential or foundationally given—that is, one that is no longer fixated upon a particular local and contingently framed transcendental structure.

Thus, to the question of whether AGI should be modelled on humans or not, and if so on what level, we answer as follows: AGI should be modelled on the human in the sense that it should functionally converge on the conditions and capacities necessary for the realization of human cognitive-practical abilities. But it should diverge from the transcendental structure of the constituted human subject. However, the success of this divergence depends upon (1) our success in rationally-scientifically challenging the given facts of our own experience and in doing so reinventing the figure of the human—ourselves—beyond strictly local transcendental structures and their contingent characteristics (this is the project of the fundamental alienation of the human), and (2) the success of AGI research programs in extending their scope beyond applied dimensions and narrow implementation problems towards theoretical problems that have long vexed physics, cognitive science, and philosophy.

Modelling AGI on human agency is not merely a strategy for tackling the conceptual problems involved in constructing a nonparochial artificial intelligence, but also more fundamentally a strategy for coming to grips with questions concerning the nature of minds, what they are, what they can become, and what they can do. If we posit ourselves as a model of an artificial agency that has all the abilities that we have, then we ought to examine exactly what it means for us to be the model for that which harbours the possibility of being—in the broadest sense—better than us. This is the question of modelling future intelligence on something whose very limits can be perpetually renegotiated—that is, a conception of human agency not as a fixed or settled creature but as a theoretical and practical life form distinguished by its ability to conceive and transform itself differently, by its striving for self-transformation in accordance with the revisable conception it has of itself. Ultimately, the question of what the mind is and what it can do is a matter of developing a project in which our process of self-discovery and self-transformation fully overlaps and in a sense reinforces the programme for the realization of an agency that can outstrip what we manifestly conceive ourselves as, here and now. It is within the ambit of this project—the project of inquiring into the meaning and possibilities of agency, by at once identifying and severing all *essentialist* attachments of this meaning or possibility to a particular local or contingent structure—that the human and AGI become non-tautological synonyms. The nontrivial meaning of the human lies in its ability to revise and transform itself, its ability to explore what the human is and what it can become. The nonparochial conception of AGI is simply the continuation and realization of this meaning in its pure or autonomous form.

The opposition between the possibility of a thinking machine and the actuality of the human agent should be exposed as a false dichotomy that can only be precariously maintained within the bounds of an essentialist interpretation of the mind as necessarily attached to a particular local or contingent transcendental structure. To put it more tersely, the source of this false dichotomy lies precisely in mistaking the local and contingent aspects of experience for universal and necessary acts of cognition, the particular conditions of the former for the general conditions of the latter. To reject and break away from this false dichotomy in all its manifestations, it is necessary to fully distinguish and unbind reason (the labour of conception) from subjectivist experience. This is not to dispense with the significance of experience in favour of a contentless abstract account of reason. It is rather the condition necessary for reassessing the extant categories—the general concepts by virtue of which we can have experience in the first place, the structures which render the world and our experience of it intelligible. The unbinding of reason from experience is a required step in order to expand and reshape our experience beyond what is manifestly essential or supposedly given to us. This Hegelian program neither impoverishes reason nor disposes of the significance of experience, but instead opens the way for the fully charged vector of cognitive progress that Nicholas Rescher attributes to science. Here the logical sophistication of the conceptual-inferential resources of the theory and the enlargement of the field of possible experience lie side-by-side in an imbalanced configuration whose very fragility guarantees the dynamic complexity of scientific inquiry:

> For rational beings will of course try simple things first and thereafter be driven step by step toward an ever-enhanced complexification. In the course of rational inquiry we try the simple solutions first, and only thereafter, if and when they cease to work—when they are ruled out by further findings (by some further influx of coordinating information)—do we move on to the more complex. Things go along smoothly until an oversimple solution becomes *destabilized by enlarged experience*. For a time we get by with the comparatively simpler options—until the expanding information about the world's *modus operandi* made possible by enhanced new means of observation and experimentation insists otherwise. And with the expansion of knowledge those new accessions make ever increasing demands. And so evolution, be it natural or rational—whether of animal species or of literary genres—ongoingly confronts us with products of greater and greater complexity. Man's cognitive efforts in the development of natural science manifests a Manichaean-style struggle between complexity and simplicity—between the impetus to comprehensiveness (amplitude) and the impetus to system (economy).[95]

The critique of transcendental structures is strictly a collective project comprised of procedural methods and incremental tasks. On a groundwork

---

95   N. Rescher, *Epistemology: An Introduction to the Theory of Knowledge* (Albany, NY: SUNY Press, 2003), 235 (emphasis mine).

level, it begins theoretically by distinguishing necessary conditions for the constitution of theoretical and practical agency from contingent aspects of the subject's constitution, characteristics of an objective reality from characteristics of the subject's experience. At this stage, the critique tackles two fundamental overlapping questions: the extent to which objective descriptions of reality at various levels (our world-structuring categories) are biased or distorted by the contingent characteristics of our experience, and the extent to which the exercise of our theoretical and practical abilities is caught up in or determined by the contingent positioning of our particular transcendental structures (be they associated with our terrestrial habitat, neurophysical systems, cultural environment, family, gender, economy, etc.).

On the basis of this theoretical phase, the project then proceeds to inquire into the possibilities of transforming and diversifying the transcendental structures of agency, renegotiating the extant categories through which we understand ourselves and our position in the world. This is an experimental phase in which the possibilities of transcendental variation, and thus the possibilities of releasing experience—and by extension the theoretical and practical abilities thereby made possible—from limitative attachments to any unique or allegedly essential local transcendental structure are examined. The central task of this stage is to expand the range and type of abilities by altering and reorganizing transcendental structures. Once the prospects of varying transcendental structures and transformation of abilities are systematically outlined and evaluated, the project shifts toward the applied dimension, that of developing implementable mechanisms and systems that can support the realization of new abilities by either modifying or replacing the transcendental structures of the constituted subject.

What begins as a systematic theoretical inquiry into the limits and regulative regimes of the transcendental structures of the constituted subject evolves into an applied system for the transformation of the subject and the maximization of agency. Thus understood, the critique of transcendental structures is the compass of self-conception and self-transformation. By challenging the established characteristics of our experience of ourselves in the world and by renegotiating the limits postulated by our contingent constitution, we transform ourselves by exploring what we *actually* are and what we *can* be, in accordance with what we *think* we are.

No matter how far this thought—*of who we are and what we should do*—may differ from reality, we are nevertheless first and foremost the species of our own thinking. Not only does our access to nature go exclusively by way of thinking; more crucially, we treat ourselves not as a mere furniture of nature, but rather on the basis of what we think we as subjects *ought to be*. But in so far as rational transformation or reconstruction must reckon with the forces and constraints of nature, our process of self-transformation will be nothing other than an anguishing historical struggle. Nature is not a block of wax ready to be moulded, nor is it fixed or stable. It offers the greatest forms of resistance and its parametric space enlarges as we begin to scrutinize it or intervene in it. The global projection of detected local regularities of phenomena becomes less and less straightforward, and topologically nontrivial. As our cognitive access extends to new sectors of natural phenomena, the principle of inductive simplicity that globally projects local regularities becomes ever more fragile. The economy of systematization becomes ever more costly. As the range of intervention in the world and its reengineering broadens, the level of conformity to hidden constraints also increases. The loss of innocence, comfort, and simplicity, both theoretical and practical, is the unavoidable price we have to pay for both the complexification of our cognitive access to nature and our uncovering of the complexity of nature.

Without the ambition to complexify our cognition we are untrue to ourselves; and if we refuse to know the complexity of nature, we will be untrue to nature. Pleas for a return to a mythical innocence or to stop at the level of what is taken to be 'ordinary' are but a grand betrayal of ourselves and of the nature to which we belong—an expression of self-deception that is at once unethical, cognitively malicious, and politically corrupt. The rational reconstruction of reality is a tedious and toilsome project. But it also happens to be the ultimate warrant for the intelligibility of our thoughts and actions in the present.

It is in the context of the critique of transcendental structures that AGI becomes the extension of the human, whose meaning, determined by its capacity for self-conception and self-transformation, is not an essence given in advance. It is a meaning that can be conferred upon, transferred, extended, and granted as a right, for it is neither fixed by biology nor bestowed by the divine, neither limited to what we are here and now nor exhausted by whatever may come to be called 'human' in the future. AGI, nonparochially conceived, does not step outside of the meaning of the human. Rather it marks the maturity of the human that has finally recognized its meaning not in virtue of its contingent constitution but in spite of it. This is a conception of the human as an all-encompassing collective project of self-conception and self-transformation whose veritable consequence is the reinvention of the human through the modification of its structure and the expansion of its universally necessary abilities.

Rather than being against or dissociated from the project of transcendental critique, the critique of transcendental structures represents the augmentation of critique as an opposition to what might be named *transcendental passivity*. If our objective encounters with ourselves and the world are regulated by our representations of space and time as forms of intuition or something like natural language, and if such regulative and constitutive forms are products of the particular course of our evolution, then so long as we take them for granted, we are transcendentally passive. In order to see the domain of the transcendental no longer as a token of passivity but one of proactivity, we must recognize the bounds of our specific transcendental structures so as to change them. The graduation from transcendental passivity to that of proactivity is then synonymous with re-engineering and refining the reality of ourselves in the world. As will be argued in the final chapter, only an intelligence that lives through transcendental proactivity can be deemed the true form of intelligence.

AN OUTSIDE VIEW OF OURSELVES AS A TOY MODEL AGI

We have now established that the functional map of human cognitive-practical abilities is a proper theoretical model for the construction of AGI. But we have also remarked that, unless it incorporates the problematics of the transcendental structure of human experience, this model risks confounding the contingent characteristics of human experience with the conditions necessary for the realization of human abilities (acts of *erkenntnis*), and thus threatens to relapse into a hard parochialist approach to the questions of what general intelligence is and how it can be artificially realized. If we treat the human as a model of AGI, then this model should not only be a model by which we can identify and differentiate the conditions and capacities necessary for the realization of theoretical and practical cognitions, but also a model within which we can renegotiate the characteristics of general intelligence by renegotiating the limits and characteristics of human experience. This is the *outside view of ourselves as a toy model AGI*: A position that allows us to treat ourselves—both our functional capacities and what we take ourselves *as*—from an objective point of view, a view from nowhere and nowhen. This is a viewpoint that distinguishes the necessary conditions and capacities for the realization of the theoretical and practical faculties, or engagement with the intelligible, but which at the same time is not bound in principle to the local characteristics of the subject's experience. Within the scope of this viewpoint, the human is a toy model or construction kit for AGI as much as artificial general intelligence is a constructive model for exploring the human.

But what exactly is a 'toy model'? Toy models are simplified or compressed models that are capable of accommodating a wide range of theoretical assumptions for the purpose of organizing and constructing overarching narratives (or explicit metatheories) that change the standard and implicit metatheoretical interpretations according to which such theoretical items are generally represented. In other words, by explicitly changing the metatheoretical narrative, toy models provide new interpretations of problems and puzzles associated with the implicit metatheoretical frameworks within which theoretical ideas and observations are interpreted. To this end, a rigorous and internally consistent toy model can offer insights about how to solve these puzzles or how to overcome the setbacks caused by the standard interpretations. What separates toy models from models is not just that they are simplified enough to enable us to tinker with the internal theoretical structure of a model, but that they are explicit metatheories. All theories are metatheories, but within regular theoretical models metatheoretical assumptions are usually implicit or hidden, whereas toy models are *explicitly* metatheoretical and in fact the simplification (what gives them the name 'toy', a tinkermodel) serves as a strategy for bringing hidden metatheoretical assumptions out into the open by tinkering with the internal variables of the model without getting bogged down in theoretical details.

Therefore in reality a toy model is a model capable of making explicit its implicit metatheoretical assumptions. And what are these implicit metatheoretical assumptions? They are precisely the implicit or hidden assumptions that arise from applying the characteristics of our subjective experience to our objective descriptions of the abilities or functions and structures responsible for realizing them. A nonexhaustive list of such metatheoretical assumptions would include, for example: the representation of time and temporality as a fundamental organizing component of the apperceptive subject of experience, the objectivity of categories which may very well be subjective (as per Hegel's critique of Kant), the view of natural languages as unaffected by or free from psychologistic residues of representation, etc. The primary locus of these hidden metatheoretical assumptions are the categories by which we perform general classifications, giving structure to the world and our experience in it. Categories, as Kant rightly observed, are not the products of particular experiences or encounters with items in the world, but rather rule-governed invariances or general concepts organized by the manner, the *modus operandi*, by means of which the mind universally organizes sense-given materials. They are patterns of the mind's patterning of all that is sensed (abstractings), not patterns abstracted from what is sensible (abstracteds). Without abstracting qua act, there wouldn't be any abstracted.

In slightly more contemporary terminology, what Kant calls categories or pure concepts of the understanding are general classificatory functions capable of integrating local invariants synthesized from sense-given materials, and therefore of constructing rule-like generalities for the ordering and construction of objects: identification of local invariants (generic judgements), reidentification of local invariants in our different encounters with items in the world (recognitive judgements), and classification of local variations of particular items/objects (predictive judgements). But the problem with categories as necessary and universal forms of experience is that the extent to which they are bound up with the particular, local, and contingent aspects of these sense-given materials is far from obvious and is not yet a settled issue. However this faculty of understanding, and the experience of the world it has thus-and-so categorially formatted, can themselves be subjected to judgements that bring forth both the cracks and possible openings in our experience. The metatheoretical assumptions of the structuring categories precisely herald the as yet unknown extent to which what we perceive as universal and necessary structuring acts of cognition may in fact be particular, local, and contingent aspects of our experience.

Toy models come in small and big varieties. The small toy model is a simplified version of only one theoretical model (essentially it is a model in a collapsed form), whereas big toy models are models that accommodate different and often seemingly incompatible models and theories, such as general relativity and quantum mechanics. Put differently, big toy models represent a compressed form of model pluralism, and in order to do so they are required to have a conceptual architecture plastic enough to accommodate and faithfully represent the main features of different theoretical frameworks, while at the same time being capable of preserving the contrasting features of these accommodated systems as distinct categories. Here 'category' refers to the category-theoretical sense of mapping objects and their relationships. In order to for us to be able to adequately think about the kind of problems that we are dealing with when talking about the construction of AGI, we first need a big toy model. An AGI big toy model should be able to coherently accommodate different models derived from physics, evolutionary biology, neuroscience, developmental psychology, multi-agent system design, linguistics, logic, and computer science. One of the problems with old AI research was that it was strongly driven by unique and inflationary models of mind that generated more setbacks than steps forward. For example, consider the symbolic program of AI (the syntactic picture of the mind), deep learning (neural networks and statistical inference), and computational semantics (computational-logical modelling of meaning representation in natural languages), programs which were developed based on insights derived from the evolutionary sciences, computer science, neuroscience, logic, and linguistics. While in their own right these programs have led to undeniable achievements and progress in the field of artificial intelligence, they have also created theoretical bottlenecks and practical setbacks. This is because their implicit metatheoretical assumptions have been either left uncontested owing to the sheer success of their ideas and methods within a narrow domain of application, or unduly overstretched into global assumptions about the nature of cognition and mind. The result is that the statistical framework of something like machine learning becomes the global model of general intelligence, or the characteristics of sequential algorithms (effective mechanizability and symbol-manipulation) establish a syntactic model of mind within which the program of artificial intelligence as a whole is oriented. Once the metatheoretical assumptions of these locally successful ideas and methods are inflated into global models of general intelligence or mind, it is only a matter of time before the model arrives at theoretical and practical impasses, and development comes to a halt. The summer of AI, as we have known it thus far, turns out to be a long if not perpetual winter.

Toy models, on the other hand, are not only explicit metatheories in themselves, but also make explicit the implicit metatheoretical frameworks of their constituent ideas, observations, and methods. By doing this, toy models are able to keep these implicit metatheoretical assumptions underlying their theoretical commitments in check, and therefore avoid the risks of inflationary models. Their utility lies not only in the idea that they permit some theoretical arbitrage by combining and spanning different metatheories, but also, and more importantly, in their ability to facilitate the reinterpretation, reassessment, and reapplication of conventionally interpreted ideas and observations.

However the real value of a toy model is that one learns from it by breaking it in the real universe; but not until one has systematically played with it. It is exactly in this sense that a toy model or toy universe of AGI is an *explicit metatheory* of artificial general intelligence constructed from falsifiable concepts and models drawn from different theoretical frameworks pertaining to the place of ourselves in the world. If we take ourselves as a functional toy model of AGI, then we are dealing with at least two classes of metatheory: metatheories associated with the bulk of models we are using to identify the conditions required for the realization of the cognitive-practical abilities necessary for anything that can be treated as an index of general intelligence; and metatheoretical assumptions related to the conditions of observation under which these necessary capacities are distinguished and described. It is the latter that need to be subjected to a thoroughgoing critique of transcendental structures of experience in order for the former to be adequately objective. Absent a systematic attempt to render explicit our subjective experiential assumptions with regard to the cognitive acts we take to be necessary, we cannot sufficiently differentiate the conditions necessary for the possibility of mind (in all its semantic complexity) from the contingent characteristics of experience and our intuitive subjective biases, by-products of our local and contingently situated transcendental perspective.

An outside view of ourselves as a toy model AGI that allows us to conceptually come to grips with the problematics of these two classes of metatheoretical assumptions is exactly what the philosophy of German Idealism encapsulates. German Idealism is a theoretical system built at the intersection of the philosophy of action, philosophy of mind, and philosophy of knowledge. In other words, it is broadly concerned with the conditions of possibility of theoretical and practical cognitions, what they are and how they can be realized. Discussing AGI in the context of German Idealism may appear a retrogressive move to some, but this could not be any further from the truth. When it comes to philosophy of mind, German Idealism—particularly that of Kant and Hegel—poses the right kinds of questions.

For the most part, the problem with today's research on artificial general intelligence is that it is content with ephemeral smart answers to ill-posed questions. Tied up in its local achievements and complying with the demands of the market, the field of artificial intelligence has neither the time nor the ambition to think about what it means to pose the right kinds of questions regarding the nature of mind and the realization of cognitive acts. The idealisms of Kant and Hegel, on the other hand, outline the fundamental conceptual problems that are in fact still at the centre of debates in cognitive and theoretical computer sciences. Needless to say, if our aim is to understand the relevance of these problems for artificial general intelligence, then we will need to reframe them in terms of concepts that are much more in tune with contemporary cognitive science. And of course, throughout this process of synchronization certain aspects of Kant's and Hegel's programs will turn out to be—for various reasons—untenable. Nevertheless, our extended thought experiment remains an unabashedly Kantian-Hegelian reconstruction of ourselves as a toy model of general intelligence, starting with Kant's transcendental psychology and moving toward Hegel's formulation of language as the dasein of geist.

FORMALIZING A BIG TOY UNIVERSE

Before moving forward and concluding the discussion on toy models and what it means to view ourselves as a toy model AGI, it is important to provide a minimal formal description for the kind of big toy model we are considering here. I propose two similar candidates, the concept of Chu spaces, particularly as elaborated by Vaughan Pratt, and Virtual Machine Functionalism (VMF) as developed by Aaron Sloman.[96]

Roughly speaking, Chu space is a topological space in which computational dualities and interactions can be accurately expressed. Pratt's seminal paper 'Rational Mechanics and Natural Mathematics' attempts to capture Descartes's mind-body dualism not as a problematic metaphysical dualism but as a computational duality in the precise sense of 'duality' given in mathematics. The duality at stake here is the computational interaction—the interchange of roles—between the formal dimensions of thinking (Kant's

---

96   See V. Pratt, 'Rational Mechanics and Natural Mathematics', in *TAPSOFT '95: Theory and Practice of Software Development (Lecture Notes in Computer Science)*, vol. 915 (Heidelberg: Springer, 1995), 108–22; and A. Sloman, 'Architecture-Based Conceptions of Mind', in P. Gärdenfors et al. (eds.), *In the Scope of Logic, Methodology and Philosophy of Science*, vol. 316 (Heidelberg: Springer, 2002), 403–27.

a priori acts of cognition) and the substantive dimension of sensibility (which can be laid out in terms of the causal-mechanistic structure of the nervous system). How do these two categorically distinct spaces—of reasons and causes—interact? What other kinds of meta-interactions or computational dualities must be introduced into the duality of thinking and sensing, reasons and causes, for them to be coherently pictured as interacting without their qualitative distinctions being elided or ontologically flattened? We will examine the details of the logico-mathematical concept of duality—rather than metaphysical dualism—in chapter 6. But for now we can think of the duality of thinking and sensing, reasons and causes, as an *equivalence* relation between the two—as, for example, when one obtains a mirror image of something rather than a simple opposition or dualism (mind *vs.* body).

Pratt captures this interaction using Chu spaces—understood as topological spaces satisfying the criteria of interaction between a set and an antiset together with their corresponding functions and antifunctions, which stand for the bodily and the mental, causes and norms, the neural materialism of the cerebrum and the logical idealism of the psyche. In the simplest terms, Chu space can be defined as a triple $\langle P_o, \vDash_P, P_a \rangle$ over a set K, where P_o is a set of objects or events, P_a is a set of attributes or states, and $\vDash_P$ is a satisfying relation which is the subset of the interaction game $P_o \otimes P_a$, or the matrix $P_o \times P_a$ whose entries are drawn from K. In the most elementary form $K = 2 = \{0,1\}$, P_o stands for the set of causal events or sensings, P_a for the logical space of the mental or inferential states, and the satisfying relation $\vDash_P$ represents the interaction between the categorically distinct set of the causal events or structure and its dual, the antiset of the cognitive (rule-governed) functions.

Here, states and events refer to the fundamental dual concepts of computation. The states of a computing system or an abstract automaton (e.g., a Turing machine), bear information and change time, i.e., the total amount of time elapsed since the beginning of the process. Events in a computing system, on the other hand, are instantaneous: they change information and bear time. Succinctly speaking, states are information-stamped while events are time-stamped. In this respect, 'we may think of the state as bearing information representing the "knowledge" of the automaton when in that state, and the event as modifying that information'.[97] Employing the fundamental duality of states and events, then, any behaviour—whether monotonic or non-monotonic—of a process can be seen as an unfolding with regard to time and information. It can be plotted as a graph where the x-axis represents time and the y-axis represents information, with the states as horizontal line segments and the events as vertical segments.[98] The relevance of this schema to the big toy model of AGI is that it allows us to model not only the interactions between sensings and thinkings— physical events and noetic states—but also the *distinct* causal interactions between physical events on the one hand, and noetic states on the other, as different classes of computation.

The Chu space view offers advantages which are necessary and crucial in the construction of a big toy model of AGI:

- It supplies a precise formal framework in which the distinctions between sensings and thinkings but also the causal interactions between noetic states (thinking$_1$, thinking$_2$, ...) and physical events (sensing$_1$, sensing$_2$, ...) are preserved rather than being elided.

- In modelling the interactions between states-events, states-states, and events-events as different classes of computations, the Chu space view eliminates the vaguely generic notion of thinking as global information-processing. Different physical and mental behaviours are modelled as distinct forms of computation. Their unfolding behaviour is explained in terms of the duality of information and time, as series of states and

---

97 V. Pratt, 'The Duality of Time and Information', in W.R. Cleaveland (ed.), *CON-CUR '92: Third International Conference on Concurrency Theory* (Dordrecht: Springer, 1992), 237.

98 In this diagram, which expresses the duality of information and time, schedules (i.e., sets of events distributed in time), and automata (i.e., sets of states distributed in information space), time appears to be flowing downwards in the schedules and upwards in the automata.

events in which the *logical* space of reason can be said to be swimming upstream against time and time moving upstream against logic.

- In treating complex behaviours in terms of interactions between distinct classes of processes and interactions as different classes of computations, the Chu space view eliminates the risk of the naïve or monolithic view of processes and behaviours. Behaviours are characterised strictly in terms of specific levels or types of interactions between, for example, an agent and its environment, or this agent's physical and noetic states.

- Finally, the Chu space view permits us to model physical and mental behaviours in terms of true concurrent interactions—i.e., synchronous as well as more generic asynchronic actions of processes on one another. Computational concurrency allows us to capture complex phenomena which are otherwise unavailable or hidden in conventional computational models: such as conflicts, asynchronous interaction, temporal precedence, supervenience, formal autonomy of noetic states, and the distinction between causing and enabling events.

To further clarify how Chu spaces can model the interactions between sensings and thinkings, we can now turn to Pratt's remarks on the mechanics of interactions between physical-causal events and noetic states:

> Events of the body interact with states of the mind. This interaction has two dual forms. A physical event a in the body A impresses its occurrence on a mental state x of the mind X, written $a \dashv x$. Dually, in state x the mind *infers* the prior occurrence of event a, written $x \vDash a$. States may be understood as corresponding more or less to the possible worlds of a Kripke structure, and events to propositions that may or may not hold in different worlds of that structure. With regard to orientation, impression is causal and its direction is that of time. Inference is *logical*, and logic swims upstream against time. Prolog's backward-chaining strategy dualizes this by viewing logic as primary and time as swimming

upstream against logic, but this amounts to the same thing. The basic idea is that time and logic flow in opposite directions.

Can a body meet a body? Only indirectly. All direct interaction in our account of Cartesian dualism is between mind and body. Any hypothesized interaction of two events is an inference from respective interactions between each of those events and all possible states of the mind. Dually, any claimed interaction of two states is inferred from their respective interactions with all possible events of the body. The general nature of these inferences depends on the set K of values that events can impress on states. The simplest nontrivial case is $K = 2 = \{0,1\}$, permitting the simple recording of respectively nonoccurrence or occurrence of a given event in a given state. In this case body-body and mind-mind interactions are computed via a process called residuation. Specifically, event a *necessarily precedes* event b when every state x witnessing the occurrence of b also witnesses a. This inferred relationship is calculated formally by left residuation, which we describe in detail later. The dual calculation, right residuation, *permits* a transition from state x to state y when every event a impressing itself on x does so also on y. That is, any transition is permitted just so long as it forgets no event. These simple-minded criteria are the appropriate ones for the small set $K = 2$.[99]

The 2-valued interaction between the causal and the rational/normative is an elementary Chu space. For this interaction to be nontrivial, the value of K must be greater than 2 (i.e., containing fuzzy values), which in turn means more complex rules of transition between them are obtained and the entries of the matrix of interaction grow. Another interesting property of a Chu space is that it can accommodate additional dualities and interaction spaces, permitting complex Chu transforms or mappings between different Chu spaces.[100] In contrast to Descartes's metaphysical dualism and Spinoza's

---

99 Pratt, *Rational Mechanics and Natural Mathematics*, 110.

100 Formally, a Chu transform is a morphism between two Chu spaces $\langle P_o, \vDash_P, P_a \rangle$ and $\langle Q_o, \vDash_Q, Q_a \rangle$. This morphism is a pair of functions (f_a, f_o) with $f_o : P_o \to Q_o$ and $f_a : Q_a \to P_a$

substance monism of the mind, Kant's picture of the mind—as elaborated within his transcendental psychology—can be expressed as a Chu space toy model, where the interaction between sensing and thinking, empirical computation and logical computation, permits a larger matrix of interaction and the accommodation of additional Chu spaces, thus obtaining more complex rules of transition and Chu transforms between what is causal and what is normative. Kant's schema of the three syntheses (synthesis of apprehension in the intuition, synthesis of reproduction in the imagination, and synthesis of recognition in the concept) is precisely an interaction matrix with complex rules of transition and Chu transports between sensing and thinking, the causal and the formal (i.e., logico-linguistic).

Lastly, the interaction between the set of events and the set of states in a Chu space can also be formulated in terms of schedules and automata, therefore turning Chu spaces into an ideal framework for the study of true computational concurrency, i.e., interactions between asynchronous processes of different types. The fact that Chu spaces can adequately model true concurrency—rather than merely sequential computation—makes them strong candidates for capturing the richness of the big toy model of general intelligence where the interactions between diverse processes as sets of behaviours require complex forms of coordination and scheduling.[101]

The intuitive idea behind Sloman's VMF is comparable to the interaction matrix formally presented by Chu spaces:

---

such that for any $x \in P_o$ and $x \in Q_o$ the following condition must be satisfied: $f_o(x) \vDash_Q y$ iff $x \vDash_p f_a(y)$. In more layman-friendly terms, the Chu transform can be interpreted under certain caveats as an adjointness condition between two distinct spaces. Think of an arrow forwards from sense-given materials to a priori acts of cognition and an arrow backward from a priori acts of cognition to sense-given materials. The Chu transform consists of these two arrows satisfying the dynamic condition of adjoint or mutual realization of the space of causes and the space of reasons, with all the intermediary back-and-forth movements or mappings required for the interaction between the two.

101 See for example, V. Gupta, *Chu Spaces: A Model of Concurrency* (1994), <http://i. stanford.edu/pub/cstr/reports/cs/tr/94/1521/CS-TR-94-1521.pdf>.

Virtual Machine Functionalism (VMF) attempts to account for the nature and causal powers of mental mechanisms and the states and processes they produce, by showing how the powers, states and processes depend on and can be explained by complex running virtual machines that are made up of interacting concurrently active (but not necessarily synchronized) chunks of virtual machinery which not only interact with one another and with their physical substrates (which may be partly shared, and also frequently modified by garbage collection, metabolism, or whatever) but can also concurrently interact with and refer to various things in the immediate and remote environment (via sensory/motor channels, and possible future technologies also). I.e. virtual machinery can include mechanisms that create and manipulate semantic content, not only syntactic structures or bit patterns as digital virtual machines do.[102]

Rather than a functionalist approach to the general architecture of the mind framed in terms of the supervenience of states and properties on well-defined input-output transitions, VMF is about the layering of virtual machines that form a complex network of causally and logically interacting processes operating on different time scales or schedules. In other words, the architecture of the mind is presented as a complex of virtual machines that can be implemented in any sufficient physical machine or system. But because these virtual machines are not physical as such, they can also form matrices of interaction and mereological (part-whole) relationships that cannot obtain in physical machines. The notion of virtuality, in this sense, does not suggest that virtual machines are not real, but that they are primarily machines that are not describable in physical terms. Virtuality refers to emulated machines capable of modelling qualitative properties and characteristics of consciousness or mind, as distinguished from those of the physical systems that support and embody them.

---

102 A. Sloman, *Virtual Machine Functionalism* (2013), <http://www.cs.bham.ac.uk/research/projects/cogaff/misc/vm-functionalism.html>.

Sloman's VMF presents a functional diagram or architectural schema of mind built around supervenience and emergent behaviours. Yet in contrast to the more traditional theories, the concepts of supervenience and emergence are principally defined in terms of virtual machines (VMs) and their causal interactions, rather than the causal interactions between physical systems or machines (PMs). As such, VMF avoids the pitfalls of the traditional theories of supervenience and emergence, which have been justly criticized by the likes of Jaegwon Kim.[103] An intuitive example of VM-supervenience would be the interaction between a series of running applications on a computer: an operating system or a platform VM, a word processor, and a number of plug-ins such as equation and graphic editors which can run independently or within the word processing software. A script can be written or a new piece of software can be introduced that monitors the resource-consumption of these VM-interactions and, if necessary under such-and-such parameters, distributes the processing resources among them, or continuously changes the temperature by regulating the physical components of the computer such as the fan speed, etc.

Similarly to the Chu space model, VMF discriminates between different types of causal interactions: those that take place between VMs, those that take place between a VM's events and processes and a PM's events and processes, and finally, those causal interactions that take place between PMs. This schema allows the modelling of VM-interactions as a nested or generative hierarchy—rather than a traditional control hierarchy—of concurrent and interacting virtual machines distributed along different scales or levels of granularity, shifting from a fine-grained granularity at the level of physical supporting systems to the coarse-grained granularity of virtual machines linking their supporting systems. The multiscale view enables VMF to treat characteristics of the mind and the constraints or conditions necessary for their realization on different descriptive levels, thereby avoiding the risk of the flat picture of functions discussed in

---

103 See J. Kim, *Essays in the Metaphysics of Mind* (Oxford: Oxford University Press, 2010), particularly chapters 3, 11, and 13.

the previous chapter. The descriptive hierarchy of VMF has a number of advantages over traditional functionalist approaches:

- It calls for an integrative engineering-philosophical approach to mind. Methods and models must be thought and implemented *across scales*. The pluralism entailed by VMF's multilevel architecture requires an objective ranking of models and methods, in the sense that for each descriptive layer there are specific sets of models and methods which must be prioritized. For example, rather than taking Bayesian learning methods to be the principal methods for modelling general intelligence, they can be effectively employed as the most appropriate methods for modelling the process of low-level information such as visual and audio signals. Salient local variations of an object such as a chair can be singled out and learned via Bayesian networks. Using threshold mechanisms, the output of the process can be sorted into a set of discrete propositions representing the candidate features from which a perceptual invariance of the object can be extracted.

- Again similarly to the Chu space model, VMF's multiscale view does not admit the vaguely general and unhelpful concept of information processing. The question of different types of information and methods of information processing is central to VMF. By reapplying Bayesian methods to this candidate set of local variations, a rudimentary *perspectival* image-model qua singular representation of an item can be constructed, in a process similar to that of Husserlian adumbrations (*Abschattungen*). The set of local variations or the rudimentary image-model obtained by the Bayesian method by themselves cannot construct an object, since object-construction in its proper sense involves semantic-conceptual ingredients. While a chair qua image-model can be rudimentarily constructed or recognized using such methods, the judgement pertaining to the *concept* of the chair—which is not perspectival—is an entirely different issue (e.g., this is a chair with its legs missing, this is a chair and not a small table, or this is a chair therefore...).

- The differentiation of scales and descriptive levels effectively connects VMF with the question of ontologies. In information science, the concept of ontology refers to a system for the formal naming and definition of the types, properties, roles, and interrelations of entities/particulars in a specific domain of discourse. An upper-level or mid-level ontology supports broad semantic interoperability between a large amount of ontologies accessible under it. In other words, it is a framework of complex categorization through which data across an expansive range of different domains can be exchanged, tracked, and computed. Within this framework, each level should be described by vocabularies which are formally and semantically adequate to capture the types, properties, and roles of particulars inhabiting that level. VMF thus emphasises the mesoscopic layer, refusing either purely top-down or purely bottom-up ontologies. The architecture of mind cannot be solely described in information-theoretic terms or those of any other supposed base-vocabulary. The use of representational, functional, and normative vocabularies borrowed from the transcendental tradition of philosophy of mind are not just informative here, they are descriptively indispensable and methodologically compulsory. It would not be controversial to claim that a multiscale view such as VMF is where computer science converges with transcendental philosophy of mind in the vein of German Idealism.

Framed as a virtual machine toy model, the only necessary aspect of the mind is its virtual *architecture*, which must satisfy the different levels of integration of information and computational criteria required for semantic and causal interactions between its components. The physical system supporting the VM architecture and the exact number or nature of the virtual machines or information processing systems can all be toyed with. Constraining the nature of the mind to a necessary general architecture that can accommodate new pieces of virtual machinery, Sloman's VMF allows us to treat the idea of artificial general intelligence in analogy to, but also with the exact same scope as, the development of a prelinguistic infant who is capable of growing into a language-using adult.

Let us recapitulate and conclude this section before embarking on our thought experiment. The treatment of ourselves as a toy model AGI should be seen as an attempt—incomplete at best and fundamentally crude at worst—to distinguish what is necessary for the realization of general intelligence (in organic species or inorganic systems) from what is contingent, and to investigate the extent to which the description of what we take to be necessary may indeed be distorted by what is in reality contingent. That is to say, the view of ourselves as a toy model AGI should allow us to eject the final residues of essentialism from the concept of the human, and thereby create an opportunity to examine the possibility of a nonparochial conception of artificial general intelligence. This is the core of our extended thought experiment: to entertain an outside view of ourselves as a prototype AGI—or more precisely, an artificial multi-agent system. If we were able to adopt this 'outside view' then what would our world look like from the perspective of artificial intelligence design? What kinds of basic capacities must these agents have in order to support complex schemas of self-conception and self-revision? And what would be the ramifications of these elementary abilities for their world, particularly when they become integrated and fully mobilized? Finally, what would be the test for determining whether this entry-level AI—i.e., ourselves here and now—in fact qualifies as a general intelligence?

However, what makes the universe of this entry-level AI world different from ours is that it is tailored and tapered to accentuate the *need to integrate accounts of cognition in linguistic interaction* and to highlight the role of speech, language, and interaction as special computational frameworks necessary for the construction of human-level AI. The method of inquiry presented here is essentially an integration of what might be called a constrained dynamic 'neural materialist' approach (Jean-Pierre Changeux, Stanislas Dehaene, et al.) and an interactive 'semantic inferentialist' approach (Wilfrid Sellars, Robert Brandom, Jonathan Ginzburg, and others) to cognition. Also, this world is assembled from myriad theoretical components that are potentially falsifiable, but which, once assembled, serve as a metatheory that provides us with insights into certain significant but non-self-evident features of a possible AGI.

Our toy universe will be constructed in two stages. In the first stage, in the next chapter we shall introduce those necessary capacities or faculties required for the realization of a discursive apperceptive intelligence that originate from causal-structural aspects of agency. In the second stage (chapters 4 and 5), we shall investigate the transformation of our rudimentary agent equipped with these structurally-causally originated capacities into a fully fledged discursive apperceptive agent whose basic capacities are not only caught up in language but which also, by virtue of being a language-user, is in possession of a generative framework of theoretical and practical abilities. For reasons that will soon become clear, in the first stage, chapter 3, we shift the focus to Kant, returning to Hegel in chapter 5 when the real protagonist of our toy universe becomes not a complex system of agents—in contrast to a rudimentary singular agent—but language itself. These two stages of construction, accordingly, set out the Kantian-Hegelian outlines of a programme of artificial general intelligence in which technical and social realizations of sapience coincide within a philosophical program for investigating the meaning of agency and bringing about its realization—a theme we shall explore in the final chapter.

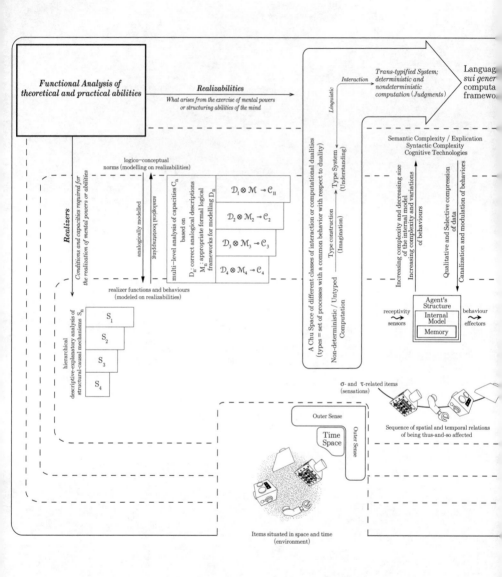

Functional Analysis of
theoretical and practical abilities

Realizabilities
*What arises from the exercise of mental powers
or structuring abilities of the mind*

Interaction

*Trans-typified System;
deterministic and
nondeterministic
computation (Judgments)*

Languag
sui gener
computa
framewo.

Linguistic

Semantic Complexity / Explication
Syntactic Complexity
Cognitive Technologies

Realizers

*Conditions and capacities required for
the realization of mental powers or abilities*

logico–conceptual
norms (modelling on realizabilities)

analogical modelling

multi–level analysis of capacities C_n
based on

D_n: correct analogical descriptions
M_n: appropriate formal logical
frameworks for modelling D_n

$$\mathcal{D}_1 \otimes \mathcal{M} \rightarrow \mathcal{C}_{11}$$

$$\mathcal{D}_2 \otimes \mathcal{M}_2 \rightarrow \mathcal{C}_2$$

$$\mathcal{D}_3 \otimes \mathcal{M}_3 \rightarrow \mathcal{C}_3$$

$$\mathcal{D}_4 \otimes \mathcal{M}_4 \rightarrow \mathcal{C}_4$$

A Chu Space of different classes of interaction or computational dualities
(types = set of processes with a common behavior with respect to duality)

Type construction
(Understanding)

Type System

Type construction
(Imagination)

Non-deterministic / Untyped
Computation

Increasing complexity and decreasing size
of the internal model
Increasing complexity and variations
of behaviours

Qualitative and Selective compression
of data

Canalization and modulation of behaviors

realizer functions and behaviours
(modeled on realizabilities)

hierarchical
descriptive-explanatory analysis of
structural-causal mechanisms S_n

S_1

S_2

S_3

S_4

Agent's
Structure
Internal
Model
Memory

receptivity
sensors

behaviour
effectors

σ- and τ-related items
(sensations)

Outer Sense

Time
Space

Outer Sense

Sequence of spatial and temporal relations
of being thus-and-so affected

Items situated in space and time
(environment)

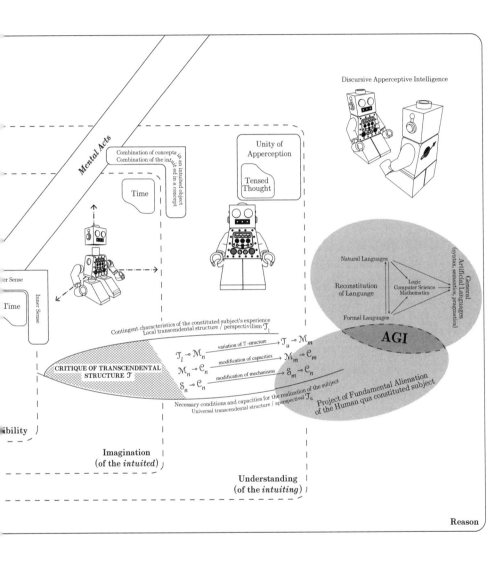

AGI roadmap: charting the territory of the AS-AI-TP thought experiment at the intersections of the functional analysis of mind, the critique of transcendental structures, and the development of structuring abilities.

3. This I, or We or It, the Thing, Which Speaks (Forms of Intuition)

Suppose a hypothetical embodied automaton possessing the following properties and features:

FEATURE 1: It has been programmed to instantiate a number of diffuse and recurring goals centred on the maintenance and preservation of the system qua agent. The goals are at different levels of complexity, and exert various degrees of pressure on the system, analogous to biological needs. Furthermore, such pressures can be understood as necessary physical constraints imposed upon the agent as an information processing system, its computational capacities, its situated behavioural responses and even its range of possible behaviours. This means that our agent is essentially a limited being possessing neither infinite information processing time nor infinite resources. We would not have been able to even characterize this agent as an information processing system, were it not restricted by the physical and computational cost constraints existent in its sensory-behavioural matrix. In a nutshell, just as we cannot speak of computation without constraints of run time and computational cost, so we cannot speak of an agent as an information processing system without the physical constraints inherent to how it interacts with the environment by way of goal-specific behaviours. We might as well talk about supernatural beings. As we will soon see, the sense in which these goals are comparable to our own is complicated, but it is from here that we must begin.

FEATURE 2: It has been wired to engage in activities that increase the probability of goal-fulfilment. The wiring of the automaton can be thought of in terms of interacting levels of structure that can produce transient multiple variations in the internal states of the system.

The wiring or neural structure comprises primary low-level information processing modules, additional higher-level modules for intermediating primary modules, and workspaces through which processed information can be selected and made available to a higher-level global workspace that can be accessed by executive functions and goal-oriented behaviours.[104] The wiring should be sufficient to causally mediate between complex environmental inputs and the complex behavioural outputs of the agent. In short, the agent can be defined as a teleological system with *sufficient wiring* (structure) to be capable of reliable differential and adaptive responsiveness with respect to its environment. It is, however, crucial to grasp these goal-oriented activities as 'proto-intentions' whose objects are *causally*—not conceptually—entangled with the structure of the agent's goals. An example of such proto-intentional activities would be a predator chasing its prey (the object of the hunt). Without implying that the predator is aware of the content of its experience or capable of attributing the experience to itself, we can still speak of the predator's *awareness of* the prey in the sense of information from different information processing modules in the wiring structure of the predator being *globally* made available to a *workspace*. This workspace can be accessed by the attentional and evaluative systems that supervise the execution of the predator's goal-oriented activities. For example, as the predator orients itself toward the prey, the information provided by other (unconscious) processes at the level of wiring structures/processing modules is

---

104 The term 'global workspace' was first coined by Bernard Baars, to refer to 'a central information exchange that allows many different specialized processors to interact. Processors that gain access to the global workspace can broadcast a message to the entire system. [...] The word "global" in this context simply refers to information that is usable across many different subsystems of a larger system. It is the need to provide global information to potentially any subsystem that makes conscious experience different from many specialized local processors in the nervous system.' B.J. Baars, *A Cognitive Theory of Consciousness* (Cambridge: Cambridge University Press, 1988), 43.

temporarily mobilized and becomes globally (or consciously) available to various processes required for the execution of a proto-intentional goal-oriented activity.[105] In this schema, the global workspace can be thought of as a distributed network with incoming and outgoing links from and to the underlying information-processing modules.

FEATURE 3: With regard to its capacity for reliable differential responsiveness (i.e., the sufficient structure required for causal mediation between environmental inputs and behavioural outputs), the agent is equipped with different specialized sensors and different modules for integrating sensory data both within a specific sensory modality (multiple data associated with one sensor) and across different modalities (data associated with different sensors).

This sensory integration extends the spatial and temporal coverage of the sensory information processing system and increases the robustness and reliability of sensory information. In addition, it reduces the

---

105 For example, see the work of Stanislas Dehaene on the role of the attentional system in mobilizing a global workspace: 'Top-down attentional amplification is the mechanism by which modular processes can be temporarily mobilized and made available to the global workspace, and therefore to consciousness. According to this theory, the same cerebral processes may, at different times, contribute to the content of consciousness or not. To enter consciousness, it is not sufficient for a process to have on-going activity; this activity must also be amplified and maintained over a sufficient duration for it to become accessible to multiple other processes. Without such "dynamic mobilization", a process may still contribute to cognitive performance, but only unconsciously. A consequence of this hypothesis is the absence of a sharp anatomical delineation of the workspace system. In time, the contours of the workspace fluctuate as different brain circuits are temporarily mobilized, then demobilized. It would therefore be incorrect to identify the workspace, and therefore consciousness, with a fixed set of brain areas. Rather, many brain areas contain workspace neurons with the appropriate long-distance and widespread connectivity, and at any given time only a fraction of these neurons constitute the mobilized workspace.' S. Dehaene and L. Naccache, 'Towards a Cognitive Neuroscience of Consciousness: Basic Evidence', *Cognition* 79 (2001), 1–37: 14.

ambiguity of sensory input, and thus increases salience. Specifically, integration across different sensory modalities expands the range of behaviours and yields a stronger effect on the behavioural output. The sensory integration is carried out at different levels, distinguished in terms of models of information processing (sequential or concurrent), temporal links between different streams of input (synchronous and asynchronous), and various frames of reference.

FEATURE 4: The automaton is furnished with a sufficiently complex and functionally flexible memory capable of encoding, retrieval, consolidation, discarding, and transfer of sensory impressions.

Rather than operating as an established storage space for the retention of past impressions, this memory is modelled as an adaptive dynamic process that plays a constructive—or more accurately, simulative—role in the behaviours of the agent. The retrospective retrieval of information (recalling) is correlated to its prospective constructive role in the agent's ongoing interaction with its environment. Every time a memory needs to be accessed, it is constructed. Recalling the memory of an original impression is tantamount to reconstructing it. But this process of reconstruction is guided by the situation at the time of access or demand for retrieval. In other words, everything that has happened since the time of original impression determines the result of the construction. Moreover, each constructed memory becomes a part of the situation and, accordingly, influences the construction of further memories. The memory system is therefore not a predefined fixed state, but is governed by the situatedness of the constructive process that creates simulations of the environment. This constructive process links the external representation of the environment, the interpreted model of the environment, and the predicted environment model produced as the result of an expected action with variables different than those of the action performed at the time of the original impression. The predicted environment is a simulated internal model of the environment constructed based on the current goal and the current interpretation of the relevant external occurrence. In this model, constructed memories may not match original impressions since they alter according to when, where, and with what the memory system is cued.

THE VIRTUOUS CIRCLE OF ANALOGY

In this thought experiment, we can now formulate a story to describe how our automaton navigates the world. Even though this story is elucidating, it is circumscribed to the extent that it chronicles the automaton's interactions with the environment, how it approaches the world, and the obstacles it encounters, only in relation to our full-blooded conceptual and linguistically structured beliefs about what the automaton is actually doing. Its limitation is that it models the representational component of this causally conditioned navigation (how the agent's nonconceptual impressions of the environment exhibit an orderly structure of their own) on our *theoretical reasoning,* just as it posits the behavioural component of the automaton's navigation of its universe (how the automaton functions and interacts with the environment to satisfy its goals) in analogy to our *practical reasoning.* In short, we are stuck with talking about 'what this automaton is up to' or 'what the automaton's nonconceptual experience looks like' in analogy to our own discursive (concept-using) apperceptive consciousness. Even at the rudimentary level of the nonconceptual sense impressions of the automaton, the analogical framework is inevitable. We can only talk about them in analogy to our inexorably 'concept-laden' introspection into our inner states.

In short, for the time being, we must resign ourselves to this analogical application of the resources of our natural language to the navigational or interaction scheme as described in terms of a structure sufficient for *causally* mediating between de facto environmental inputs and de facto behavioural outputs. But this in itself contributes to the fruitfulness of our story. For in *carefully* extending our conceptual linguistic resources to describe how this agent structures its awareness of the environment and nonconceptually navigates it, the story underlines two crucial points: The first point is that the resources of language are ultimately the only resources available to us (temporally discursive apperceptive intelligences) for representing the intelligible order (since for us, nonconceptual sensory impressions are caught up in the inferential web of language). The second and more important point is that the causal interaction of the automaton with the environment, as a protosemantic navigation of the world, exhibits a noncategorial orderliness that our concepts in their inferential relationships reflect and illustrate, disambiguate, and make explicit. In other words, the causal-heuristic interaction of the automaton instantiates precisely the structures from which our semantic structures have (in part) evolved.

For these reasons, if handled correctly, this analogical circle is a virtuous rather than a vicious circle. It describes a species of 'as-if' (*als ob*) arguments that play the role of *regulative* theoretical and practical judgements. We cannot nonlinguistically see how the automaton sees the world nonlinguistically, but will treat the automaton's view *as if*—under appropriate approximations—we could view it linguistically. Thus, through a series of controlled analogies, the circle enables us to construct, step by step, from an intelligence that is neither discursive nor apperceptive, an intelligence that is no longer analogically posited because it has the form of a full-blooded discursive apperceptive intelligence. What it takes to analogically posit a nonconceptual awareness is exactly what it takes to elaborate this nonconceptual awareness into a conceptual awareness; and what must be added to the analogically posited awareness in order for it to be no longer analogical—to move from nonconceptual awareness to conceptual awareness—is exactly the same as what is needed to develop the non-apperceptive intelligence into an apperceptive intelligence, consciousness into self-consciousness.

Taking into account these considerations, this is the purpose of our story: to cautiously exploit the conceptual resources of our natural language to outline the nonconceptual awareness of this automaton, without imputing to it something like an awareness of the content of its experience, an awareness of its awareness as its own, an ability to use concepts, or any mastery of language; to locate this inchoate awareness or preconceptual form of intelligence as the minimum condition for the realization of a temporally discursive apperceptive intelligence; and to specify what is required in order for this analogically posited heuristic intelligence to be elaborated into a general intelligence endowed with a generative cognitive complexity that is no longer analogically posited, whose abilities are not merely heuristic, but whose heuristic abilities are fundamentally caught up in its non-heuristic linguistically-enabled cognitive capacities. By pursuing these objectives, we will outline what we might call a Kantian-Hegelian program for the construction of general intelligence.

Rather than reducing the discursive apperceptive subject to an awareness at the level of causal structure, we attempt to reconstruct rational agency from a naturalized 'causally reducible' agent, or, in other words, to reconstruct sapient general intelligence from sentient intelligence. In contrast to a reductionist approach, this reconstruction does not overextend the naturalized account of sentience to sapience by virtue of the global reducibility of the latter to the former. The former is necessary but not sufficient for the realization of the latter and its cognitive-practical *abilities*. Naturalization is supposed to be a two-way street between causes and reasons, but all too often it presents itself as a policed one-way traffic from reasons to causes, with no time, intellectual budget for, or interest in anything that moves in the other direction. Here I emphasize 'abilities' because, following the argument of the previous chapter, the self-consciousness of discursive apperceptive intelligence should be understood as a generative framework of theoretical-practical abilities, and not simply as an introspective or amplified form of consciousness.

Knowledge is not awareness or consciousness, and self-consciousness is neither awareness of the phenomenal self nor knowledge of the empirical self, but a consciousness that issues from and is licensed by the powers of understanding and reason—concepts and judgements—which are enmeshed in intersubjective, formal, and inferential linguistic activities. The self of self-consciousness is not the self of phenomenal reality, but a self whose selfhood is a transcendental dimension necessary for judging and being judged; it is essentially like a program constructible under its logical autonomy. This formally and socially instantiated self is the locus of claiming rational authority and responsibility for what is being said and done. Put differently, the self of self-consciousness is a being of the concept not only in the sense that it falls under the concept but also in the sense that its acts issue from and exhibit the concept. For this reason, it is necessary to differentiate the concept of self-consciousness as used by Kant and Hegel from the ordinary intuitive concept of self-consciousness, which can signify either phenomenal introspection or empirical awareness.

One objection to the virtuous circle I have described is given by a figure I will call the greedy sceptic—one who wants to have the cake of semantic apocalypse, but who also eats it in order to fuel an all-out assault on the conceptual structure of thinking.[106] Broadly speaking, the greedy sceptic is someone akin to an exaggerated version of Plato's Meno, introduced as a student of the sophist Gorgias, the master of eristic arguments on the nonexistent. The greedy sceptic assertively claims that we do not know anything and we will never know anything, while at the same time confidently laying out a lavish theory of what he takes to be the case. In short, the greedy sceptic is someone who casually slips in and out of his complicated relationship with knowledge as he pleases. The greedy sceptic may valorize neuroscience to remind us that what we call knowledge is just a figment of our blind brain, or that our talk of the a priori and semantic content refers only to neurological hallucinations or pedestrian metaphysical fantasies. He may believe in science as that which discredits not only our concepts but conceptualization in general, but will at the same time dismiss mathematics, its epistemological status, and the a priori application of mathematical concepts in the sciences as another pseudo-semantic absurdity. In our case, the greedy sceptic of mind is the one who believes there is not and will never be a knowledge of human mind or intelligence, but who nonetheless goes on to put forward a theory of superintelligence or disconnected posthuman intelligence, or a panpsychist account of mind. In other words, the greedy sceptic is not committed to the labour of the virtuous circle of analogy in so far as he already *knows* what intelligence is,

---

106 For a defence of the Blind Brain theory and the Semantic Apocalypse thesis, see S. Bakker, *The Last Magic Show: A Blind Brain Theory of the Appearance of Consciousness* (2012), <https://www.academia.edu/1502945/The_Last_Magic_Show_A_Blind_Brain_Theory_of_the_Appearance_of_Consciousness>.

despite the fact that he has invalidated the conceptions of knowledge and mind as the guarantor for the intelligibility of intelligence.

The strategy of the greedy sceptic is to characterize discursive self-consciousness as merely a reflexive or epiphenomenal model of phenomenal consciousness. Once a naturalized account of phenomenal consciousness is provided—and such a naturalistic account can indeed be provided, for mere consciousness is nothing but a natural phenomenon—then by virtue of the above characterization of self-consciousness as belonging to the same genus as that of phenomenal consciousness, the greedy sceptic can conveniently characterize the normative-intentional vocabularies of the former as mere by-products of a-rational processes that conditioned the latter. It is not that rational consciousness is not conditioned by nonrational processes (a naturalistic thesis to which this book is fully committed), but being conditioned by nonrational processes is not the same as being constituted or piloted by them.

'If the trick of consciousness can be performed by a vast system of unconscious modular processes,' the greedy sceptic claims, 'then by virtue of being a genus of phenomenal consciousness, discursive apperceptive awareness can also be executed by implementing the same processes.' 'And to the extent that phenomenal consciousness is blind to the activity of these modular processes that occasion it,' the sceptic continues, 'self-consciousness is ultimately but a special—that is, more illusory—kind of blindness, another parochial heuristic device among others, but one with the illusion of being somewhat special.' It is important to note that the greedy sceptic is not really a thoroughgoing reductionist per se, but some-one who is bent on the trivialization of the semantic, formal, or a priori dimensions of cognition. But the greedy sceptic describes the blind brain or unconsciousness qua subpersonal information-processing modules in terms of vocabularies and formal relations—for how can one describe anything other than by resorting to formal and semantically-loaded vocabularies of thought? There is no description—whether scientific or philosophical—that can be provided without formal and semantic aspects of thought or theory. The greedy sceptic is analogous to someone who eats his own cake of semantic apocalypse while—to the ridicule of others—not realizing that the cake is actually made of semantic ingredients. Thus the greedy sceptic advocate of the blind brain ends up exposing himself as being doubly blind according to his own standards. And even if he admits to his performative contradiction—'I, the emperor am naked'—this does not mean that there is no real contradiction, that he, as a matter of fact, is not really naked. The telltale acrobatics of the sophist begin with the admission that 'by the way, I am a sophist, so by virtue of this admission, I am not a sophist'. Plato's strike on the Eleatic stranger can be revived here: the admission of sophistry or performative contradiction does not let the sophist off the hook, for the sophist does not really know what makes him a sophist, and thus, by virtue of his ignorance—his semantic naivety—he is still a sophist. The learned sophism of the greedy sceptic makes him akin to those Lorenz Puntel describes as 'hikers who follow their paths while maintaining that all of us, themselves included, are blind, and that there are no paths'.[107]

Contrary to this greedy sceptical approach, the claim here is that self-consciousness is not merely causally structured consciousness. What makes it apperceptive in the last instance is not to be found within the causal structure of nonconceptual awareness, or, for that matter, in the unconscious modular processes that condition it. Discursive apperceptive awareness involves a specific type of cognition: it operates via normative judgements that are both *linguistically oriented* and *linguistically driven*. These judgements supervene upon heuristic abilities, which in turn are caught up in and conceptually utilized and refined by them. The point is that normative judgements are not heuristics; nor do they essentially need to be dependent on some heuristic core, behavioural regularity, or even causal connection with the world in order to count as judgements. A glance at today's logic and theoretical computer science—if not the ever suspect organon of philosophy—should set one straight with regard to the issue of mistaking judgement for the heuristic.

In globally reducing sapience to the empirical facets of phenomenal consciousness and the modular processes that condition it, the greedy sceptic elides the distinctions between conceptual awareness and phenomenal

---

107 Puntel, *Structure and Being*, 64.

awareness, judgments and heuristics, the structure of discursive intention-ality and the structure of proto-intentionality, the space of reasons and the space of causes. This greedy figure will always tell us that the overlap between the space of reasons and causes is too fuzzy to be considered as a criterion of sapience, but such a critique is predicated upon what the fuzziness actually is. Without a determination of the degree of fuzziness, the greedy sceptic merely resorts to the path of least resistance, propping up the fuzziness as an unintelligible principle—saying that the state of affairs is 'more complex than you think', without ever elaborating on what is meant by complexity—in order to perpetually advance his uncritical view. The sceptic's global deflationary approach to discursive self-consciousness is a side effect of his inflationary account of empirical-phenomenological consciousness, within which lies a colossal stack of muddled, dusty, and unchecked metaphysical assumptions.

This illicit merger can be traced back to a principal theoretical lacuna in understanding the linguistic sociality of discursive apperceptive intelligence, how this linguistic sociality determines semantic content, and how the semantic contentfulness of apperceptive intentionality differs qualitatively from the proto-intentionality of the merely phenomenal consciousness whose description at both empirical and phenomenological levels it makes possible. The global reduction of discursive apperceptive awareness can ultimately be traced back to a misconception of what language really is—what it does, and how it does it. Linguistic interaction is the fabric of thought, rather than a means for its transmission, a mere medium of communication.

The emphasis on the essentially linguistic character of sapience is noth-ing new, of course. It is a familiar topic that is perhaps even deemed well worn and antiquated in some philosophical circles. But what has been for the most part absent in pro-linguistic arguments is a concern with the fun-damental interactive structure of language itself: not merely an interaction steeped *in* language, but an interaction which itself *is* language. This is a picture of language not as a symbolic totality with an ineffable essence—a medium of communication, a tool for labelling items in the world, or a system of social discourse in which language is the facilitator of mutual recognition—but as a sui generis framework of interaction-as-computation furnished with different classes of complexity and the different cognitive abilities associated with them.

It is in this sense that the reconstruction of apperceptive intelligence from heuristic intelligence becomes an inquiry into what is required in order for this sui generis interactive computational framework to be constructed—a process of construction that brings about an intelligence of a different type. But to embark on this journey, we must first begin the story of our hypothetical automaton as a preconceptual pre-apperceptive intelligence.

THE AUTOMATON'S STORY, A THOUGHT EXPERIMENT

STORY 1: The automaton is sentient of the environment: A heap of black accompanied by a low monotonous noise. Suddenly, a faint rustling noise perturbs the scene. A short while later, as the sound becomes louder, a mass of protruding fuzzy grey appears at the opposite end of the heap of black and moves toward it. As the mass of grey reaches the heap of black, it stops, makes contact with the heap of black, moves away, makes contact with it and then moves away, again and again. The perturbing sound has shifted to a shrill and high-pitched sound. Later, the mass of grey recedes from the heap of black. The sound becomes a rustling noise and continues for a while after the mass of grey completely disappears. All that is left on the scene is a rectangular heap of black accompanied by a low monotonous noise.

STORY 2: The automaton has just seen a reenactment of the monolith scene in *2001: A Space Odyssey*. A featureless black monolith is erected in a landscape whose serenity is broken by the steps of an approaching monkey. Once the monkey finds the monolith, it starts examining it, screams, panics, runs away, and comes back to touch it again. The monkey continues this game for a while until it finally gets bored and goes away.

The world of the automaton is uncannily analogous to the prelinguistic world-picture of an infant. The first narration is a rough analogical linguistic story about how the automaton registers the environment, the second a non-analogical linguistic narration—essentially a story of and within language—in which such registers are inferentially caught up. More specifically, the items in the second story are linguistic items that possess semantic features by virtue of the inferential roles they play in our collective linguistic practices, whereas the items in the first story are nonconceptual representations of items in the environment, i.e., registers at the level of internal variable states of the automaton's wiring structure which causally mediates between sensory inputs and behavioural outputs. The automaton is aware *of* the items in the environment (a heap of black, a rustling), but in the second story we are aware of the items *as* something (*as* a monolith, *as* the steps of an approaching monkey). We perceive or *take* things *as* such and such, whereas the nonconceptual content of the automaton's experience is neither seeing or hearing *as...* nor seeing or hearing *that...*, but seeing and hearing *of....* What it sees *of* the black monolith is the colour on the facing part of its surface and its shape on the facing side (let's use the term seeing$_1$ to designate this seeing-of). But what we see of the monolith is not merely the impoverished seeing$_1$, for what we *see$_2$ of* the object is its colour through and through and its shape all around; we also see it *as* a black rectangular cuboid, a black monolith. Kant would describe the former as an image, qua function of the imagination, whereas the latter proceeds via the subsumption of this image, qua singular representation, under a concept through schemata which serve as universal procedures for constructing a model of that concept (monolith) out of multiple and associable, synchronically and diachronically synthesized perspectival aspects of an item in the world.

We can think of 'seeing$_1$ *of*' in the first story and 'seeing$_2$ *as*' in the second story in terms of making a Lego model—say, a toy robot—using Lego blocks of different shapes and colours. From a shifting *perspectival* point of view, the blocks with their various shapes and colours correspond to the diverse yet rudimentary images of our Lego model (the point-of-viewish *intuiteds*) which are obtained as our automaton confronts the Lego blocks in such and such perspectival imagings (e.g., this Lego block or heap of black is facing the automaton edgewise). Their role in our model construction is particular and contingent. The shapes and colours of the blocks are the raw 'sense-given matter' of the intuited items qua images. The pictorial motif of our Lego model-building corresponds to the conceptual representation of these intuited items in acts of judgements (the intuitings). The function of the pictorial motif is to determine the colours and shapes of the blocks in such a way that it becomes possible to put them together so as to construct the specific Lego model in question. In other words, the pictorial motif encapsulates the function of the concept of *a robot* that *determines* images (the right blocks) as different aspects of only that object. It is only because the colours and shapes of these blocks hang together in the right way—perspectivally in space and time, synchronically and diachronically—that we are able to synthesize the pictorial motif of our Lego model-building. And respectively, it is only because the blocks (the images) can be put together in the right way—in accordance with a rule, i.e., the concept of a robot—that we are able to *conceive* them *as* associable and multiple aspects of *one* such-and-such robot.

In seeing$_1$, we are dealing with local variations and rudimentary—point-of-viewish—invariant aspects of particular items. Whereas in seeing$_2$, we have the function of productive imagination by means of which categories or pure concepts of understanding—general and universal invariances—are applied to the intuited items, like blueprints or instructions necessary for the construction of a toy object. But in seeing$_2$ we are also capable of bringing and constructing images under specific concepts (e.g., this such-and-such toy robot). The combination of these abilities turns seeing$_2$ into a complex act of imagination and understanding. In more contemporary terms, seeing$_2$ involves object individuation and object simulation, general and specific forms of classification, and reidentification of local invariants across different contexts. Units of experience are perceptual-takings or the class of -ings-as (e.g., grasping or conceiving x as ...), not the class of -ings-of. Local variations (manifolds) of items (shape, colour, etc.) supplied by the latter (sensory and perspectival) class are not by themselves sufficient for object-construction since object (*gegenstand*) individuation, classification, and recognition involve the construction of types of invariances which form a network of associations and implications. Such invariances cannot be obtained without a complex interplay between the sensory intuitions given in imagination and the pure concepts of understanding—overseen by what Kant would call the faculty of judgement.[108] Categories are logical functions. It is only when they are brought into conformity with sensory intuition through schematism and synthetic a priori principles that they can become rules for generating perceptual-takings—that is, rules for constructing something as an object of representations. Schemata can be said to be rules of construction pertaining to the process of providing a concept with its singular representation qua image (*Bild*), e.g., triangularity and a triangle. On the other hand, synthetic a priori principles can be understood as *general* rules of unity in the integration or synthesis of appearances.

CONSTRUCTING A LEGO MODEL
IN THE STYLE OF KANT'S THREEFOLD SYNTHESIS

The Lego model building process—which is necessary for the transition from seeing$_1$ to seeing$_2$—as a whole corresponds to Kant's threefold synthesis: namely, synthesis of apprehension in the intuition, synthesis of reproduction in the imagination, and synthesis of recognition in the concept. The synthesis of apprehension delineates the first constructive role of imagination in pulling together a synchronic manifold of sensations by antecedently taking up the sense impressions into its activity, apprehension.

---

108 'In short, we do not perceive of the object what might be called "categorial" features. For the image construct does not have categorial features. It has an empirical structure which we can specify by using words which stand for perceptible qualities and relations. But it does not have logical structure; notness, or-ness, allness, some-ness are not features of the image-model. They are features of judgment. More generally we can say that the image-model does not have grammatical structure. (It will be remembered that we are construing mental judgments as analogous to sentences. A judgment, we said, is, as it were, a Mentalese sentence episode.) And, of course, Kant's categories are grammatical classifications. They classify the grammatical structures and functions of Mentalese.' W. Sellars, *In the Space of Reasons: Selected Essays of Wilfrid Sellars* (Cambridge, MA: Harvard University Press, 2007), 463.

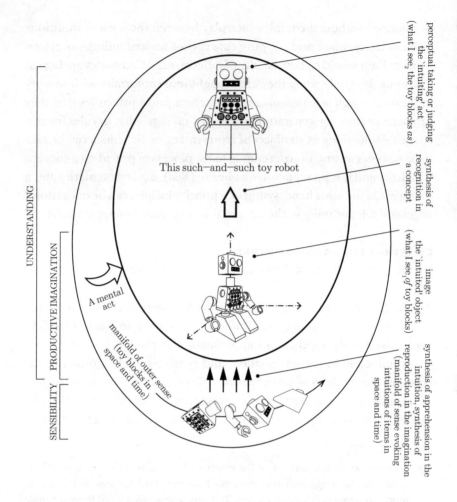

Kant's threefold synthesis: What sets apart Kant's account of experience and mindedness from that of Hume is the emphasis on a *multilevel construction* rather than *basic empirical associations*. From a computational perspective, it is the mode of integration or synthesis of different processes or algorithms that distinguishes mental acts and critical faculties from mere quantitative algorithmically realizable abilities. Indeed, Kant's account of the threefold synthesis is not merely a psychological argument whereby the summary list of mental abilities are given. It is, more fundamentally, an epistemological argument concerning the analysis of specific modes of cognition required for objective knowledge and critical judgment.

It introduces order into the confusion of simultaneous impressions by giving them temporal and spatial locations, and thus differentiating them. In doing so, the synthesis of apprehension brings about the condition of the intelligibility of impressions as *distinct* (spatiotemporally structured) impressions qua appearances available for further construction and structuring. The second synthesis, the synthesis of reproduction, signifies the second constructive role of imagination in combining and reproducing the sensory manifold diachronically, carrying over its earlier elements in order to construct a *stable* image qua *singular* representation of an item in the world. It establishes temporal associations between appearances that the synthesis of apprehension has located in space and time in a certain way, rudimentarily structured out of the undifferentiated homogeneity of simultaneous impressions.

These two syntheses are the figurative part of the building process associated with imagination as a constructive-simulating capacity whose function is to 'represent an object even without its presence in intuition'[109] and which is unavailable to pure sensibility. They are, accordingly, what we might call figurative syntheses. The third synthesis, the synthesis of recognition, strictly designates the role of apperceptive consciousness in perception—that which must be 'added to pure imagination in order to make its function intellectual', since 'in itself the synthesis of imagination, although exercised a priori, is nevertheless always sensible, for it combines the manifold only as it *appears* in intuition.'[110] The synthesis of recognition requires both the act of recognizing a past representation as related to the present one and the act of recognizing past and present representations as belonging to one object via the function of a concept. The third synthesis then involves different a priori acts of cognition (*erkenntnis*) which produce full-blooded judgements.

To avoid terminological confusion, it is best to provide brief definitions for these recurring elements of the Kantian vocabulary: *Sensations* are the 'immediate' results of the mind being causally affected by objects. In other

---

109 Kant, *Critique of Pure Reason*, 256.

110 Ibid., 240.

words, a sensation is the effect of an object on our representational capacities to the extent that we are affected by the sensible object or *gegenstand*. *Sensibility* refers to the capacity or receptivity to acquire representations through being affected by objects qua particular or individual items. The ability to have thoughts of individual items is *intuition*. And that through which cognition relates to objects (individual items) through 'sensations' is *empirical intuition*. The generic and indeterminate object of empirical intuition is an *appearance*. The 'matter' of empirical intuitions is sensation, and its form is sensibility, which allows the manifold of appearances to be initially structured. Appearances are the elements that are picked up and built into singular representations of items in space and time qua intuitions. Finally, intuitions differ from sensations since they are types of cognition while sensations are not. The raw content of intuitions is what is *intuited* from sense-given materials (sense impressions of an item located in space and time). The form of intuitions is intuition as an act of *intuiting* which is a singular act of *conceptual* representing.

The syntheses essential for the transition from seeing$_1$ to seeing$_2$ are dynamic acts of integration and need not to be thought in either purely top-down or purely bottom-up fashion, but rather in the mesoscopic or mid-level fashion introduced in the previous chapter in the context of big toy models. As briefly introduced in our discussion of Chu spaces and toy models, syntheses can instead be understood as matrices of interactions between the integrating-organizing acts belonging to causal-empirical and logical-inferential domains and the various rules of integrative transition (moving from one level of unity to another) that must necessarily obtain between them in order to have anything like seeing as, hearing as, smelling as, i.e., conceptual awareness as knowledge or experiences endowed with (nonprivate) epistemic status. These rules of integrative transition can indeed be defined as necessary computations—typed or untyped, statistical or logico-linguistic, context-sensitive or context-free, centralized or distributed—which can enter into interaction with one another asynchronously or synchronously.

In this sense, transcendental logic, as that which supplies concepts with sensory intuition and applies classificatory concepts to intuitions, can be understood as a computational search space. As such, it is perhaps more fruitful to elaborate transcendental logic by way of information theory and computational complexity theory where each level of necessary conditions for the possibility of having mind can be construed in terms of the increase in information processing abilities and the new types of computational problems (Turing-completeness, NP-completeness and NP-hardness, etc.) that can be solved at that specific level. Moreover, this computational view of transcendental logic coincides with the paradigm of deep functional analysis presented in the first chapter, or what the late Hilary Putnam dubbed 'liberal functionalism'—a functionalist view of the mind as a collection of world-structuring abilities which require an anti-individualistic picture. A organism is only a system insofar as it is in realtime transactions with the environment. The functionalist view of such a system cannot be greedily reductionist, because its information processing abilities 'seek their own level of interpretation'.[111]

A DIGRESSION ON MODELLING FIGURATIVE SYNTHESES

Equipping our automaton with objective—in the sense of *Gegenständlichkeit* rather than *Objektität*—figurative syntheses, then, would require the application of a mixture of mid-level models similar to the generative models utilized in the predictive processing (PP) paradigm.[112] Such models are based on prior probability and statistical estimates which function as representations employed to predict current and future sensory input as well as the source of such input. Source detection is possible in so far as the estimates are hierarchically organized in order to track features at

---

111 H. Putnam and L. Peruzzo, *Mind, Body and World in the Philosophy of Hilary Putnam: Léo Peruzzo in conversation with Putnam* (2015), *Trans/Form/Ação* 38:2 (2015), <http://www.scielo.br/scielo.php?script=sci_arttext&pid=S0101-31732015000200211>.

112 On schematism and predictive processing see L.R. Swanson, 'The Predictive Processing Paradigm Has Roots in Kant', *Frontiers Systems Neuroscience* 10:79 (2016), <https://dx.doi.org/10.3389%2Ffnsys.2016.00079>.

different temporal and spatial scales, and this hierarchical distribution in turn enables estimates at different levels to be predictive of one another.

These estimates, however, must be probabilistically constrained, otherwise predictions would be impossible for any sensory-neural condition. Without constraints as the ground for predictions and likelihood estimates, our automaton or intelligent system would not be able to winnow the sensory-neural possibilities and converge on a set of predictive hypotheses. Such probabilistic constraints are inbuilt inductive biases which are necessary for any form of predictive processing system and are defined in terms of probability priors. The hierarchical system of priors—moving from more fundamental or abstract to less—enables the development of advanced representational systems which not only effectively single out hypotheses from a set of possible hypotheses but also handle different levels or types of hypotheses in order to explain the data. This hierarchical architecture permits differentiation between basic representations of, for example, a round Lego block and a cubic one, since the prior probability that these two blocks are colocalized in space and time is negligibly small.[113]

Deep entrenchment of more fundamental priors or constraints canalize and guide upper-level estimates and less abstract priors. Such *priors upon priors* are called hyperpriors. Andy Clark and Link Swanson have identified hyperpriors with the brute constraints imposed by space and time, explicitly as Kantian forms of intuition and appearance. These constraints can range from hard restrictions on spatiotemporal bilocalization or colocalization of sensible items to limitations of bodily actions (e.g., either turning left or right). In Swanson's words:

> Abstract internal knowledge of space and time—spatial and temporal hyperpriors—are thought to narrow and restrict large swaths of possible hypothesis spaces, thereby aiding the formation of decisive perceptual predictions regarding the external objects causing incoming stimuli. This narrowing of possible hypotheses is critical to the entire probabilistic

---

113 See A. Clark, 'Whatever Next? Predictive Brains, Situated Agents, and the Future of Cognitive Science', *Behavioral and Brain Sciences* 36 (2013), 181–253.

inference process—without it the required Bayesian computations become intractable. Spatial and temporal hyperpriors can thus be usefully conceived of as necessary conditions on the possibility of probabilistic perceptions of external objects. [...] Kant's proposal that space and time are features of cognition that form, constrain and restrict possible perceptions of outer objects is echoed in explanations of the role of hyperpriors in PP accounts of perception. Without spatial and temporal hyperpriors, the objects of perception that putatively result from PP would be impossible.[114]

In predictive processing systems, incoming sensory inputs are not passively received but are contrasted with the existing representational repertoire, i.e., they inform representational or image updates. It is precisely this update-function rather than sensory input that results in prediction error minimization in such a way that updates adhere to the norms of Bayesian inference. Moreover, the applications of such predictive models can be made more exact with the help of adequate formalizations provided by Category theory and Topos theory, whose geometric and topological richness have been studied in relation to neural modelling, constructive memory, Kantian schematism, and figurative syntheses (see the works of Ehresmann, Gómez-Ramirez, and Healy).[115]

For instance, the commutative diagrams used to define the concept of colimit can provide a formalized map of the neural paths, compositions, transformations, and categories necessary for the construction of complex image-models out of simpler ones. For example, we can think of a colimit diagram for the process of construction of an obelisk as an image-model

---

114 Swanson, 'The Predictive Processing Paradigm Has Roots in Kant'.

115 A.C. Ehresmann, J.-P. Vanbremeersch, *Memory Evolutive Systems: Hierarchy, Emergence, Cognition* (Amsterdam: Elsevier, 2007); J. Gómez-Ramirez, *A New Foundation for Representation in Cognitive and Brain Science* (Dordrecht: Springer, 2013); and M.J. Healy, 'Colimits in Memory: Category Theory and Neural Systems', in *Proceedings of the International Joint Conference on Neural Networks*, IJCNN '99, vol. 1 (1999), 492–6.

qua mental object embodied in the neural organization using simpler mental images—a square and an oblong rectangle—which are at different (lower) levels of the neural organization. A colimit then can be said to be a category-theoretical diagram for the construction-cum-compression of complex mental images from simpler ones using commutative diagrams and universal properties.[116] Details and associations between the square and the oblong rectangle are compressed or streamlined into the image of a cuboid.

A colimit diagram captures how the neural category $Neur$, which is composed of neurons and the synaptic paths—represented by morphisms—between them at the microscopic $level_1$ can be constructively raised up to the macroscopic $level_n$ of the mental objects category $Ment$, which is composed of mental images or image-models and the morphisms or structural relationships between them. Then $N-1$ levels signify different scales or levels of organization which lie between the microscopic category $Neur$ and the macroscopic category $Ment$, moving from the fine-grained scale of local networks of neurons to the coarse-grained scale of neural events as for example recordable by functional MRI.

---

116 In mathematics—particularly category theory—a commutative diagram expresses the generalization of a system of equations and its internal symmetries. Take for instance, $x * y = y * x$ where x and y are operators and $*$ is the operator multiplication. This equation states that x and y operators commute with respect to $*$. The commutative diagram can be seen as the category theoretical generalized equivalent of such a statement. As for the universal property, it roughly means that the property of construction on a particular mathematical object can be expressed in terms of its relations to all other objects. One of the main motivations behind the concept of universal property is to forgo the concrete details regarding the construction of a particular object (e.g., a proof) and to instead use an effective account of the construction that is not simply limited to a particular object but rather concerns the construction of the object in terms of its relations (i.e., associated morphisms) with other objects. In this respect, the universal property is analogous—with some caveats regarding the distinction between sensible objects of experience and mathematical objects—to Kantian categories or pure concepts of understanding, which are not derived from a particular object or encounter with an item in the world, but instead are a priori universal and necessary concepts by which objects (*Gegenstände*) are structured and ordered.

In this respect, in the context of the neural organization and mental images, the colimit can be understood as a map from a commutative diagram in the category *Ment* to a commutative diagram in the category *Neur* via the functor $F: Ment \to Neur$, while the hierarchy of *Ment*—levels of image-models shifting from simple to complex—can be represented via natural transformations η_n between given functors ($\eta_1: F_1 \Rightarrow F_2$, $\eta_1: F_2 \Rightarrow F_3$).[117] Here, F_1 and F_2 map *Ment* to two local networks of afferent neurons in the category *Neur* which are responsible for processing two distinct sensory inputs (for example, one visual and the other haptic). F_3, on the other hand, maps from *Ment* to a local network of neurons which is a sensor fusion of the aforementioned afferent neurons.

In this configuration, other objects can be introduced to the neural category, such as motor neurons associated with the agent's effectors. A seemingly simple but in fact highly complicated image-model such as the abstract image of a continuous line as the root of the concept of line can be modelled in this manner via a colimit diagram in which natural transformations obtain between functors from *Ment* to *Neur* whose objects are both local sensory neurons (visual signals from the ocular system, sense of gravity, balance and spatial orientation from the vestibular system, etc.) and local networks of motor neurons connected with bodily actions, specifically those involving embodied spatial gestures of direction and orientation (e.g., the saccade of the eyes and muscular movements). The fusion between sensors and effectors, afferent and efferent neurons, would then account for the complex image of a continuous line as rooted in a perceptual invariant generated by the stabilization and integration of the senses of inertial movement, direction, orientation and certain locomotory actions.[118]

---

117 Given categories C and D, and functors F, $G: C \to D$, the natural transformation η from F to G is a family of morphisms. It assigns to every object x in C of a morphism $\eta_x: F(x) \to G(x)$ in D such that for every morphism $f: x \to y$ in C, the condition or structural diagram $\eta_y \circ F(f) = G(f) \circ \eta_x$ is satisfied or commutes in D.

118 On the links between perceptual invariances and the concept of continuous line in mathematics see F. Bailly and G. Longo, *Mathematics and the Natural Sciences:*

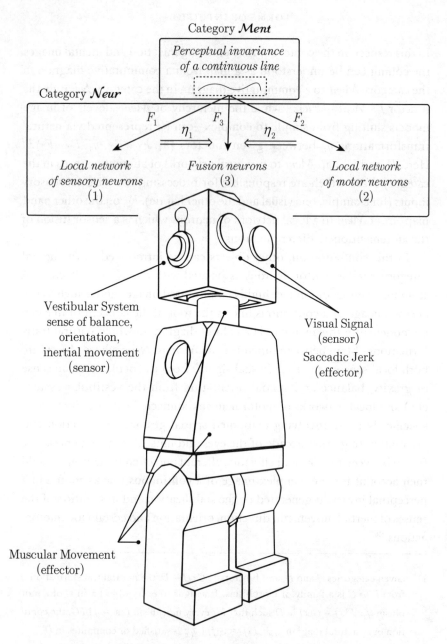

Modelling a sensor-effector system—a robot—capable of forming a stable perceptual invariance.

As with all models and paradigms, the theoretical scope and practical applications of the above models should be treated with modesty and critical vigilance. While such models can be regarded as models of choice with a certain theoretical strength and range of application within the big tinkertoy model of AGI or of our own representational systems, they should not by any means be viewed as complete or global and comprehensive. There are in fact significant flaws in both their theoretical underpinnings and their range of application, whether in the context of artificial intelligence or cognitive science. The strong modular constructivism implied by the category-theoretical formalization of neural organization—particularly the colimit diagrams—does not leave any room for modelling the necessary pruning mechanisms which are responsible for repairing or destroying unneeded or deleterious neural patterns. As a result, the complex microscopic view of the brain turns into yet another variation of the well worn metaphor of the brain as a receptacle of whatever is thrown into it without ever having a chance of filtering out or destroying constructed and entrenched patterns in the neural structure. When the role of neural unlearning is removed from the equation or downplayed, the relevance of neural learning to concept learning progressively diminishes.

The rise of category-theoretical models in the study of complex systems, particularly in neural architecture, calls for the development of a pertinent critique of both the conceptual underpinning and the range of application of category theory or any other mathematical formalization. While the generality of category theory makes it a powerful tool for the study of mathematical structures, it is well-suited neither for the study of all types of mathematical structures nor for the modelling of all forms of physical systems and phenomena. The question of structure as that which addresses the relation of the mind to the world is chiefly the question of constructing theories within which *different* models can be compared and tested. Context-independent appraisal and application of mathematical

---

The Physical Singularity of Life (London: Imperial College Press, 2011), 66–8; and A. Berthoz, *The Brain's Sense of Movement* (Cambridge, MA: Harvard University Press, 2006).

models, or any model for that matter, is an absurdity. The context is firstly given by the theoretical system within which the model operates, and then by the analysis of the correspondence between, on the one hand, the type and scale of structures a theory aims to investigate, and, on the other, the specific mathematical formalism indexed by the model for the study of the target structure. Absent this analysis, not only will the application of the mathematical model be too arbitrary, it will also result in a complete distortion of the phenomenon under study by the misapplication of the mathematical structure presupposed in the model. Here category-theoretical models of neural structures are no exception.

Category theory's strong reliance on *commutativity*—as a mathematical structural constraint—or what Ion Baianu has described as 'the stricture specific to Abelian theories, categories or ontologies'—makes category-theoretical models ill-suited for application to a broad range of complex physical systems and phenomena at scales where the distinction between objects and processes begins to fade away.[119] Physical systems or behaviours involving symmetry-breaking, genuine asynchronous processing, and irreversible dynamics cannot be adequately encoded by models enmeshed in a mathematical framework that places strong strictures on mathematical structures such as commutativity or internal symmetry.[120] For example, myriad forms of neural tasks involve true asynchronous processing of events or states which are spatiotemporally separated and have no symmetry

---

119 I.C. Baianu, R. Brown et al., 'A Category Theory and Higher Dimensional Algebra Approach to Complex Systems Biology, Meta-Systems and Ontological Theory of Levels', *Acta Universitatis Apulensis* 52 (2011), 11–144.

120 In the context of category theory, a mathematical internal symmetry can be understood as a commutativity of a concatenation of morphisms. This property allows any object of an abstract category—which has a unique identity 1_x—to be replaced by its identity morphisms. Internal symmetry as the condition for the concatenation of morphisms can be expressed by a basic example:
$$f : x \to y, g : y \to z \Rightarrow h : x \to z,$$
that is, the concatenation of the morphisms f and g is replaced by the unique morphism $h = g \circ f$.

between events and states. It is far from obvious that category-theoretical models can sufficiently encode such aspects of neural organization.

In his work *Simulation and Similarity*,[121] Michael Weisberg offers a detailed specification of models as structuring systems. Regardless of whether the model is descriptive, explanatory, or predictive, or whether it is concrete (e.g., an orrery), mathematical, logical, or computational, the model is comprised of a structure formulated in a specific theoretical framework. The structure has two poles, the model description and the model construals. The description is a set of formulas or equations which describe the range of model applications based on its structure. In short, the model description provides us with information regarding what the model is (its structure) and how it can be applied (its dynamic). But the description is not the structuring kernel of the model itself since the structure contains a diverse range of information regarding the scope, assignment, and fidelity criteria (i.e., constraints which specify the representational, dynamic and resolution or scale-sensitive specifications of the model) which are implicitly encapsulated in the model description. All such information has not only theoretical assumptions, but also metatheoretical (metalogical, metamathematical, ...) assumptions which should be carefully analysed.

Therefore, consideration of this often-ignored dimension of modelling-metatheoretical assumptions is absolutely indispensable not only for the correct application of a model to the appropriate type of data and the scale at which a specific phenomenon is studied, but also for the appropriate choice of the mathematical (or logical and computational) framework and the type of constraints imposed by that framework on the mathematical structures that are supposed to encode a physical phenomenon. Absent this analysis, we can never be sure whether our empirical models of a target system such as the brain distort the data, whether they are sub-optimal models for the study of the target system or are being applied to the wrong structural level of the phenomenon or system in question.

As such, the scope and application of the predictive processing paradigm cannot be overextended. Clark's claim that the predictive processing

---

121 M. Weisberg, *Simulation and Similarity* (Oxford: Oxford University Press, 2013).

paradigm not only accounts for rudimentary representational systems but also the scientific method is based on a crude view of scientific theories.[122] No predictive-inductive method or model can by itself represent scientific theories, since the construction of scientific theories requires both a ranked plurality of methods and a complex semantic dimension without which no inductive method can converge on a single hypothesis or a set of hypotheses that can be said to be true.[123] Without the semantic dimension of theories, the predictive processing paradigm of scientific theory construction is no more than an extension of our inductive biases. A scientific theory that is solely based on a form of predictive-inductive processing can only offer a version of objective reality that is in full conformity with the local and contingently constituted inductive biases of the subject and its deep-seated intuitions. But the fact that science progressively breaks itself from our common intuitions should be counted as evidence that scientific theories cannot be construed as an overblown version of the predictive brain.

Finally, inductive biases and hyperpriors—particularly as the constraints of space and time—should be understood as constraints on the order of appearances—that is to say, they are features of the experiencing subject or the conscious organism. Identifying them as features of objective reality is an unwarranted metaphysical commitment whose implicit assumption is the existence of a *given* or preestablished harmony or one-to-one correspondence between reality and the perceptual mechanisms of the brain. The defender of such a view would have to explain a number of glaring problems with it, including explaining why modern physics continues to shatter our most cherished inductively-enabled intuitions regarding the universe, or why it took modern *homo sapiens* almost two hundred thousand years to develop Euclidean geometry, and after that almost two thousand years to discover non-Euclidean geometry. If the structure and dynamics of our scientific theories and natural languages could easily be analysed or explained away in terms of inductive biases, then how could we even recognize or describe such inbuilt biases? It would mean we can

---

122 See Clark, 'Whatever Next?'.

123 For a detailed discussion of this point, see the Appendix.

only resort to our inbuilt inductive biases to justify or explain inductive biases—which is viciously circular, a petitio principii.

A more modest claim would be that inbuilt inductive biases are enabling constraints which have become entrenched through the course of natural evolution. Strictly speaking, inductive biases are local and contingent features of the conscious organism. Some may even be purely psychological features. These inbuilt inductive biases have enabled the development of otherwise more complex representational systems which are not merely inductive, probabilistic or statistical. In this sense, the enabling role of inductive biases does not mean that they have constituted or play a central role in our theoretical activities. In other words, enablement neither means constitution nor calls for continued reliance on the enabling conditions.

Yet even this modest claim should be treated with caution. Following the previous discussions regarding the critique of the transcendental structure, inbuilt inductive biases should be taken as features of the transcendental structure of the experiencing subject and, as such, should be challenged and progressively suspended in a Hegelian manner. First we ought to distinguish psychological and nonpsychological features, then attempt to model variations of nonpsychological features which are not only alternatives to our own, but also have a more expansive traction on objective reality in so far as they enlarge the field of experience and therefore detect features of objective reality which our experience either distorts or cannot come to grips with. This means that, even if we admit that inbuilt inductive biases—such as the enabling spatiotemporal constraints—can be both psychological features and nonpsychological features *specific* to the local and contingently constituted subject of experience, we can never be sure of the extent to which our particular experience distorts objective reality. Here, by objective reality, I also have in mind the objective descriptions of the brain qua representational system.

Even when we strive to be attentive to the distinction between the particular characteristics and features of our experience and the characteristics of objective reality, we might indeed smuggle in bits of the former to the latter. This is a topic that we shall explore in depth in the excursus on Boltzmann and time in chapter 4. To conclude, short of a theoretical and practical critique of the transcendental structures, the necessary link between the intelligible and intelligence cannot be renewed: the intelligible remains within the confines of what intelligence perceives to be an objective description of reality but is in fact a psychological representation, or an account which misrepresents the transcendentally ideal features of experience, or the local characteristics of the subject, as global and necessary characteristics of reality. Consequently, our objective description of ourselves in the world becomes yet another manifest self-portrait and our speculations about a future artificial general intelligence invariably reiterate—like the portrait of Dorian Gray—ever more distorted pictures of ourselves.

SEEING$_1$ WITH THE AUTOMATON

Having summarily examined the experience of the discursive apperceptive intelligence of the items in the world of Story 2, the syntheses it requires, and the candidate models for its figurative syntheses, we can now return to the first story, that of the automaton's nonconceptual encounter with the same items.

In Story 1, the encounter of the automaton with an item in the environment is an analogue of an Aristotelian this-such (*tode ti*: this-something-or-other), namely, the impression of an object as a 'materiate individual substance'. The automaton's this-suches, however, are best linguistically expressed by the application of dummy quantifiers that designate form ('this much of', 'a quantum of', 'a heap of') and mass-terms that designate matter ('stuff', 'blob') to occurrent sensible properties (a shaped and coloured facing side of the object)—as in 'a heap of black', 'a protruding mass of fuzzy grey'. In more straightforward terms, the automaton sees$_1$ an expanse of grey as an object rather than as an object whose surface is grey. For the automaton, grey and black are not 'categorial' kinds of experience or manners of experiencing$_2$ (an object looking *greyly* or *blackly*), but the objects of its de facto experience *tout court*. The automaton is conscious of *a heap of black* as *the object* of its awareness—although at this time the possessive pronoun 'its' is not yet part of the automaton's thoroughly nonconceptual awareness, i.e., the automaton is not yet able to ascribe this awareness to itself as its own. This is another difference between the first and the second story: what is not given in the world of the as yet thoroughly nonconceptual awareness of the automaton is precisely the categorial structure. At this stage, trafficking this categorial structure into the story about the automaton's analogically-posited experience$_1$ (or awareness$_1$) of items in the world would be precisely a function of what Sellars calls 'the myth of the given': 'the idea that the categorial structure of the world— if it has a categorial structure—imposes itself on the mind as a seal imposes an image on melted wax'.[124]

The automaton's sensing is acategorial, since categoriality belongs to the domain of the conceptual in which sensing is caught up. To ascribe categorial structure of any kind to the mere sensing of the automaton would be to relapse into a sceptical empiricism for which the intelligibility of what is sensed is given. But also, by analogically developing the sensing automaton into a thinking automaton, we avoid the dogmatic rationalism for which the relation between thinking and being is *given* not in the world but in the deductive rules of reason.

In order to attempt to faithfully represent the logico-phenomenological *form* of the automaton's 'way of experiencing' and, correspondingly, the features relevant to the automaton's mode of awareness, in a fashion that it is 'consistently and from the beginning identified with [the automaton's] modes of representation',[125] we therefore have not only to avoid using

---

124 Ibid., 237.

125 'It is "phenomenology" in that its aim is not to characterize a world but rather "ways of experiencing a world," that is, elements, aspects, or features of modes of awareness. It is, however, "logical" phenomenology in that such modes of awareness are consistently and from the beginning identified with modes of representation. What separates such "logical phenomenology" from "pure" (Husserlian) phenomenology, in other words, is the crucial acknowledgement that our only possible conceptual access to the structures constitutive of such modes of awareness (= modes of representation) is through a grasp of the logico-semantic structures instantiated in the inferential interrelationships of elements of our own system(s) of linguistic representations—and that this is so whether the awarenesses themselves are thought of as instantiating an "internalized" natural language or as the

'grey' and 'black' as adjectives ('a grey item') or as adverbs ('an item that is experienced greyly'), but also the kind of mass terms (such as 'rock', 'water', 'flesh') that smuggle in a categorial commitment to causal powers and propensities constitutive of the nature of such stuffs. We should instead use phenomenological this-suches that have a logical form appropriate to the automaton's mode of awareness and somehow convey the suspension of categorial commitments, particularly those pertaining to the causal propensities of items in the environment. This is the reason behind the peculiar language of the first story wherein the 'protruding fuzzy grey' as a whole conveys some stuff that plays the analogical functional role of a 'countable noun' (monkey) relevant to the general form of the automaton's nonconceptual awareness$_1$ (seeing$_1$, hearing$_1$). But in its 'stuffiness', the 'protruding fuzzy grey' is also distant from ordinary mass terms such as 'fur' or 'protoplasm', use of which would imply the automaton's categorial commitment to the nature (causal powers and propensities) of such stuffs. And finally, to demarcate the individuated form of such stuffs, we can use mock-up quantity-specifying terms that are functionally analogous to but removed from the measurement specifications of the terms we ordinarily use to quantify mass terms, such as a 'bucket' of water, a 'piece' of meat, etc. In this fashion, a 'heap of black' is really this-much (expanse) of black (stuff), individuating form and matter.

On top of these distinctions between the first and second stories, there is another less noticeable difference: the inferential connections between

---

thoroughgoing nonconceptual pure positional awareness of pre- or nonlinguistic experiences. Whereas a "pure" (Husserlian) phenomenologist thinks of himself as using his own language "directly," to describe (nonlinguistic) modes of awareness ("ways of experiencing a world") with which he is (somehow directly) acquainted, a "logical phenomenologist" consistently sees himself as using his own language "at one remove," to illustrate (through the inferential relationships) normatively obtaining among its elements) systematic and orderly relationships among aspects or features of modes of representation which may variously be imputed (actually or hypothetically) to beings, including himself, as their modes of awareness or "ways of experiencing a world."' J. Rosenberg, *The Thinking Self* (Philadelphia, PA: Temple University Press, 1986), 100.

sense impressions from different sensory modalities, visual and auditory. In the second story, these inferential connections are relayed by implicit genitives that associate an impression specific to one sensory modality with another impression specific to a different sensory modality, the sound (steps) *of* an approaching monkey (visualized), the screams *of* an excited monkey, etc. The first story, on the other hand, does not have such explicit associations between sense impressions of different modalities. It only contains rudimentary protocol-like transitions or transformation rules rather than proper inferential or objective-conceptual rules of transition, e.g.:

mass of fuzzy grey, contact with the heap of black →
screeching noise from the direction of mass of fuzzy grey

but not

excited monkey touching the monolith ↛ *monkey screams*

We cannot assume that, for the automaton, the shrieking sound is associated with the mass of protruding fuzzy grey as opposed to the heap of black or, for that matter, another item in the environment, or that it says anything (about any such association) at all.[126]

The goal of this comparative excursion was to highlight the features implicit in the automaton's nonconceptual encounter with the world, by highlighting its striking differences from the awareness peculiar to discursive apperceptive intelligence (Story 2). Now that we have a better idea what features and abilities the automaton is lacking, it is easier to figure out what must be added to the automaton in order for it to have categorially and inferentially structured experience and to bring its inchoate encounter with the world under the power of judgment.

However, despite these profound differences between Stories 1 and 2 as two *distinct* types of narratives, there is also a connection between them: the experiential content of the automaton's fully nonconceptual awareness still

126 For more details about such rudimentary protocol-like transitions, see chapter 5.

exhibits a non-categorial orderly structure that the inferential relationships among the concepts of the second story reflect and illustrate. Not only can this rudimentary orderliness be instantiated without language; it is a structuring that constitutes the minimum condition for the possibility of discursive apperceptive intelligence. But what is this minimum and necessary orderliness? It is the perspectival orderliness of space and time as forms of intuition, an encounter with the world from a nonconceptual point of view.

GETTING STUFF IN PERSPECTIVE

In Story 1, the automaton is aware of the presence of an expanse of grey stuff; it is aware of it—in analogical terms—as approaching or receding. It is also aware of an expanse of black stuff. But it is not just aware of the grey stuff approaching or receding, it is in fact nonconceptually aware of its moving toward or away *from* the expanse of black stuff, and similarly stopping in *front* or moving *behind* the black stuff, disappearing and appearing. In a nutshell, the automaton has a sense of movement, and with that, a rudimentary sense of space and of the presence and perspectival spatial relations between items *in* space. This is because the automaton is *situated* in space as a privileged endocentric frame of reference. But we ought to be cautious here. The automaton has no *concept* of these spatial relations, it is not aware of the conceptual contrast between something that simply disappears (goes behind something else) and something that ceases to exist (appearances and reality). Nor does it possess a *self*-concept. Nevertheless, the wired and programmed (structural and behavioural) system of the automaton can exhibit a spatial orderliness in its encounter with items in the environment that our linguistic terms such as 'approaching', 'receding from', 'moving in front of' and 'moving behind' (as opposed to 'ceasing to exist') inferentially instantiate and articulate. This rudimentary structured spatial encounter with the world can of course be detailed in terms of the complexity of the nervous system, but it also has a necessary form—not in the sense that it could not be otherwise, but in the sense that it is applied to all of the automaton's encounters with particular items in the world.

Coming back to the predator-prey example, both predator and prey behave in a way that exhibits a spatial orderliness in their goal-oriented activities (chasing and escaping). As the prey moves away, the predator follows its movement and orientation in space by means of saccadic eye movement—one of the fastest and most ancient predatory gestures—before orienting itself in space to chase the object of its hunt. When the prey hides behind a rock, it does not give up as if the prey had ceased to exist but instead follows the shortest path to catch the prey behind the visual obstacle. The predator has a sense of space only by virtue of its capacity to differentiate itself from its surroundings in order to effectively engage in its goal-oriented activity (catching the prey), a sense that is profoundly different from our own wherein items stand in inferentially articulated spatial and topological relations to one another. It is this functional differentiation from the surrounding space that serves as an egocentric (endocentric) frame of reference for the predator, a perspectivally situated position in space.

But the predator neither reflects on itself as being differentiated from the surrounding space, nor is it aware of having a privileged position within it—a perspectival stance. It just *has* a perspectival position in space by virtue of its structural capacity to behaviourally differentiate itself so as to successfully engage in *its* goal-oriented activity, and, by virtue of this, it *occupies* (without conceptually representing to itself) a frame of reference. It is this structurally and behaviourally posited endocentric frame of reference that permits the predator to entertain not only spatial relations between items and itself, but also a limited range of spatial relations between one item and another—that is, to treat not only itself, but also items in the environment, as frames of reference. This *endocentric* frame of reference—itself an index of the predator's situatedness in space and its spatial perspectival encounter with the world—is what enables the predator to have a constrained *allocentric* view of items as situated in space, and thus as spatially related to one another.

The origin of the nervous system, as René Thom and Alain Berthoz articulate, can be traced back to the solving of a fundamental problem for the self-preservation and successful execution of the organism's teleological activities:[127] *How can an organism differentiate itself from its food and from the predator?* Absent a contrasting index for differentiating itself from its food, the organism risks autophagy, and without any robust differentiating cue, the organism can neither successfully secure its food nor evade predators. To solve this problem, the organism must first differentiate itself from space via successful responsiveness to various forms of stimuli (electrochemical signal, physical pressure, light, etc.); but in order for it to effectively secure its food and elude predators, such parochial stimulus-driven contrast is not enough. The organism must form a 'mobile' perspectival frame of reference to respond appropriately to changes in the parameters of spatial relationships between itself and items in its environment. This is one of the oldest roles of the nervous system as a basic 'organ of alienation':[128] to mobilize and develop ur-alienation (minimal contrast with the environment through mere responsiveness to stimuli) into an alienation (a *designated* and *designating* discontinuity in space simulated by the nervous system as a self-model)[129] that enables the organism to structure its surrounding space and, in doing so, to derive an awareness-structuring orderliness from the rudimentary spatial relationships between items situated in that space. This enabling alienation is the capacity for spatial differentiation between items in the environment through the mobilization of the organism's successful self-differentiation from its surroundings, a 'perspectival pure positional awareness of items-in-relation-to-one-another'.[130]

In order for the automaton to have this perspectival pure positional awareness, it must have not only a sufficient structure for reliable differential responsiveness, but also a behavioural goal-oriented architecture—and that is exactly what our hypothetical agent has been supplied with.

---

127 See Berthoz, *The Brain's Sense of Movement*; and R. Thom, *Structural Stability and Morphogenesis: An Outline of a General Theory of Models* (Reading, MA: W.A. Benjamin, 1975).

128 Thom, *Structural Stability and Morphogenesis*, 299.

129 See Metzinger, *Being No One*.

130 Rosenberg, *The Thinking Self*, 111.

We can now say that the world of the automaton contains a privileged position, a position that *we* conceptualize and inferentially model on *our* spatial concepts but which *it* occupies and upon which it acts. The world of the automaton, then, contains a privileged and structure-conferring position only in the sense that its awareness$_1$ *of* the world is an orderly and coherent spatially perspectival awareness of items. But what is more interesting is that this spatially perspectival awareness$_1$ can be laid out precisely—albeit still analogically—in terms of our subjective spatial awareness$_2$ of items *as* moving toward and moving away, coming in front of and going behind. In other words, the automaton has a coherent spatial awareness of the items without necessarily possessing the conceptual resources to be able to tell the difference between appearances and reality, between, for example, an object whose shape and size remains constant as it retreats and an object that appears to be shrinking or morphing into something else as it moves away—as in the predator-prey example, where the sentient predator does not need the inferential relations between spatial concepts in order not to mistake a prey that moves behind a rock for an object that has now ceased to exist simply because the rock has occluded its shape and colour. Similarly, when the prey runs away, the predator's spatial awareness need not be armed with perspectival concepts in order not to take the running prey as an object that *seemingly* shrinks or morphs into something else. The predator continues the chase and captures the prey with pinpoint accuracy.

This is all to say that, even though our automaton is still a thoroughly nonconceptual non-apperceptive intelligence, its spatial perspectival awareness$_1$ of items is precisely already a spatial awareness of items *as* (*as* moving behind, moving away and not *of*$_1$ items ceasing to exist or shrinking and morphing into something else). For this spatial perspectival 'awareness-of-the-items-as...' to be instantiated, the automaton does not need the conceptual distinction between what merely seems to be the case from an occupied pure perspective and what veridically appears to be the case, mastery of language, inferential relationships between perspectival concepts or even self-awareness. All it needs is to have (i.e., to occupy) a privileged point of view in space by virtue of a *sufficient structure coupled with a functional system of goal-oriented activities* that allow it to adopt one or multiple awareness-structuring perspectival frame(s) of reference in the world.

Looking at the ordinary spatial prepositions of our natural languages, especially those concerning localization, physical accessibility, and contact between objects (from, toward, behind, on, under...), we can see them as exhibiting what Claude Vandeloise calls a form of 'naive physics' of space, 'differing from scientific physics as radically as natural languages differ from formal ones'.[131] Although the automaton's naive physics of space is limited to simple spatial relationships that, for example, involve access to the field of sensory differentiation (grey stuff approaching or retreating), nonprepositional contact between objects (the chunk of red touches the mass of black, but not a red thick book *on* the table) and simple orientations (screechy noise from the mass of fuzzy grey, but not the scream *of* a monkey). More hybrid spatial relations and propositions of this naive physics of space such as bearer-burden relations, container-contained relations and complex localization (like the uses of *at* or near/far distinctions) are not yet on the menu for our automaton.

Serving as an armature for our higher order awareness-structuring spatial concepts, at its core this naive physics is built on a necessary family of perspectival spatial representations which can be instantiated without inferential relationships obtained from spatial concepts. This family of spatial representations demarcates a noncategorial yet orderly spatial perspectival encounter with the world that is a necessary condition of a conceptual and thus categorially-structured encounter with the world, and hence for an automaton with a full-blooded apperceptive awareness (awareness$_2$ as). In displaying exactly this spatial perspectival awareness, our hypothetical automaton has thus fulfilled the first necessary condition of possibility for the realization of general intelligence.

---

131 C. Vandeloise, *Spatial Prepositions* (Chicago: University of Chicago Press, 1991), 14.

THE AUTOMATON'S TEMPORAL PERSPECTIVAL AWARENESS

Now that the first minimum condition necessary for the realization of discursive apperceptive intelligence has been outlined, we can move on to the second minimum condition: a temporal perspectival awareness—that is, a structured and structuring temporal encounter with the world. For the automaton this means having the ability to locate itself in time, and thereby achieving a time-consciousness of both the world-history and its own history. Here self-locating in time means a rudimentary capacity to be aware of successive sensory affections produced by objects in its environment and to actively—but nonconceptually—respond to such affections. Having this rudimentary capacity is not as simple as it may seem. On one level, it requires a perspectival spatial orderliness of the kind we have been looking at. But on a different level, which, as we shall see, is even more crucial, it requires a temporal orderliness that relies on more fundamental *successively interrelated* capacities:

(1) The capacity to synthesize *compresent sensations* (the simultaneity of the manifold of senses). The role of synthesis here is an operation of combining, binding, and gluing partial maps of objects that come as compresent sensations (registered local invariances of shapes, colours, smells, etc.) into spatiotemporal global maps of objects.

(2) The capacity to synthesize the *simultaneous states* of objects into sequences of occurrences. Think of this synthesis as what is required for the automaton to capture 'the movement' of a moving car.

(3) The capacity to be aware of representations of objects and sequences of occurrences *as* representations and sequences. In a Kantian sense, this is tantamount to having the capacity to report representations of items and occurrences in the world to the mind. At this level, the capacity to report 'being affected' qua mind-state—'being aware of being thus (successively) affected'—does not by any means imply a form of knowledge. In other words, for the automaton, having this capacity does not imply

a conceptual awareness of the mind-state; this is something we should reserve only for an apperceptive agency. This awareness is merely an attentional mobilization of the global workspace that was introduced earlier. And similarly, the (conceptual) knowledge of the mind-state should not be conflated with this rudimentary awareness of mind-states, which is necessary but not sufficient for the realization of a conceptual awareness.

I said above that these capacities are successively interrelated because they are built on top of one another. (2) shares the components of (1), and (3) shares the components of both (1) and (2). But the reason they should be treated as distinct capacities is that each successive capacity adds a new component that is not available in the previous one(s). Our particular focus in this section will be on capacity (3): What needs to be added to a sequence of representations in order for the automaton to be aware of this sequence *as* a sequence of representations, to have a capacity by virtue of which it can be aware of being successively affected so as to be able respond to the manner in which it is so affected?

TIME AND MEMORY

Alongside the spatial elements in Story 1, we also find temporal elements—not only in explicit terms such as 'a short while later', but also, more predominantly, as implicit elements of motions. Our task now is to examine the automaton's temporal perspectival awareness, the structure of this awareness, and the consequences of its having this minimal temporal orderliness. But in order to move forward we have to bring into play a necessary structural component of the automaton that we have thus far not fully utilized, namely its constructive memory.

Let us call the registers of items that the automaton encounters in its environment—events which occasion alterations in the internal states of the automaton and which are manifested at the level of the global workspace—*impressions*. Now that the memory system is fully in place, the automaton is able to retain these impressions and access them. But, as discussed above, the retrieval of a retained impression is tantamount to the reconstruction of that impression. In other words, each time a retained impression is accessed, it is not merely called up but rather reconstructed, and each of these reconstructions is then added to the memory—i.e., becomes part of the situation that guides the further construction of memories.

According to this memory schema, the automaton's impression of an item in the environment—for example the monkey as a mass of fuzzy grey (*tode ti*)—can then take two general forms: a retained impression (formed by the *presence* of the mass of fuzzy grey), and a reproduced version of the retained impression of the mass of fuzzy grey (reconstructed in the absence of the actual item in the environment). Both forms mark the presence of the nonconceptual content of the *tode-ti* impression, but in one form this presence implies synchronicity with the actual item, while in the other form it implies diachronicity.

Analogically approximating the nonconceptual and tenseless awareness of the automaton, the impression of the object (I_o) in its retained and reproduced forms can be represented in the following manner:

I_o be$_1$ (impression)

which denotes the retained impression in which the 'presence of the nonconceptual content' is derived synchronously from the presence of the actual item.

I_o be$_2$ (reproduction)

which denotes the 'presence of the nonconceptual content' reproduced in the absence of the actual item, which is to say, derived (and reconstructed) diachronically from the retained impression I_o be$_1$.

What is common to both forms is the presence of the content of this-such—represented by the tenseless verb *be*. It is tempting to interpret the $_1$ and $_2$ in be$_1$ and be$_2$ as indices of times, and hence to conclude that be$_2$ is the past tense of be$_1$ (*the automaton saw...*), in so doing attributing to the automaton a temporal awareness, or even tensed thought. But at this point $_1$ and $_2$ merely represent two distinct *types* of impression-content: one that occurs in the presence of the actual item and another that occurs in its absence. These two general types signify respectively the impression (be$_1$), and the reproduction of that impression bearing the mark of both being retained and being reconstructed (be$_2$). More succinctly, be$_1$ and be$_2$ present I$_0$ respectively as the content of an impression and as the content of a reproduction. From our perspective, the automaton's *this–such$_1$* and *this–such$_2$* clearly signify present and past tenses of impressions of the items (the automaton sees a monkey; the automaton saw a monkey). But we should avoid ventriloquizing the machine, and instead equip it in such a way that it will become capable of drawing such a conclusion all by itself. In other words, we should allow our toy automaton to have a genuine temporal perspectival awareness that *legitimately* admits our analogical observations regarding what it is aware of. And even then this temporal awareness is not by any means close to any form of time-consciousness, even though it may be the incipient germ of such consciousness.

The automaton, at this stage, is aware$_1$ *of* this-such$_1$ and this-such$_2$ but it is not aware$_2$ of them *as* present and past. Nor in fact is it aware of them as temporally related. In order for the automaton to have a pure situational temporal awareness, it must first be able to temporally relate these impressions to one another. This temporal relation is already available at the level of the automaton's structure, in the shape of the causal ordering of its registers, and therefore as a sequence of alterations in the internal states of the automaton's wiring. Hypothetically speaking, and following Rosenberg's version of this thought experiment,[132] if we could attach a monitor to the automaton and treat it as a computer with a visual display unit, we might see its visual registers displayed in a certain hue with a high degree of saturation. For the purposes of this example, we can think of the actual item in the environment as a key being pressed on the keyboard attached to this computer, and the saturated hue as its corresponding register. Moreover, these registers do not disappear from the screen, since they are stored somewhere in the automaton's memory.

---

132 Rosenberg, *The Thinking Self.*

Now, as more keystrokes are made, something happens on the monitor: as new saturated registers appear on the monitor, the saturation of the stored registers decreases. The high-saturated range of the hue corresponds to impressions synchronous with the presence of an item in the environment, i.e., registers that appear on the monitor as the keystrokes are being made; while the low-saturated range corresponds to reproductions, i.e., registers of the keystrokes that have 'previously' been made, and which are now retained in the memory.

What is important to note in this example is that the difference in saturation is a difference made by causal correspondences or mappings between displayed registers and keystrokes qua independently existing items in the environment, and that these causal correspondences stand in de facto temporal relationships to one another. But the automaton is not aware of this temporal ordering of causal correspondences (keystrokes made *before* and keystrokes made *after*, registered as stored and registered as being displayed); nor can it infer from the TV in its head—the monitor displaying registers in various degrees of saturation—any temporal relationship. It is we, not the automaton, who infer a temporal order from the changes in the saturation in correspondence with the sequences of keystrokes. But could we say that, if we sufficiently train the automaton via the application of statistical inference, then the automaton will eventually learn to recognize the ordering or sequence of impressions, and thus legitimize our attribution of temporal awareness to it? Not at all—temporal awareness precisely cannot be reduced to such a trained response: the representation of a sequence, or ordering, is not the same as a sequence of representations. The ability to differentiate a sequence of representations does not amount to the ability to represent a sequence. In the same way, a sequence of awarenesses of items in the world does not bring about an awareness of a sequence qua temporal ordering. Devising a trick to achieve the former does not generate the latter capacity.

Indeed, this is part of Kant's attack on Hume's sceptical reductionist system, specifically his Separability Principle, the idea that 'every thing, that is different is distinguishable, and every thing that is distinguishable may be separated'.[133] According to Hume's Separability Principle, aware-ness of a complex *as* a complex is possible if and only if its components are distinguishable. The immediate corollary of the Separability Principle is an integration principle: the idea that the impression of a complex is the same as a complex of impressions, or that representation of a series is a series of representations, the awareness of a sequence of... is a sequence of awareness*es* of... and so on. But as Kant shows, not only does this schema lead to conundrums and confusions; it also undermines any serious attempt to distinguish the impression as an act from its object and content, 'awarenesses-*of*-something' from 'awareness-of-something-*as*', and ultimately empirical awareness from discursive conceptual consciousness.

Accordingly, at this stage, the automaton neither has a temporal aware-ness, nor can it acquire an impression of a succession by being trained to learn a succession of impressions. All we are allowed to attribute to the automaton is a collection of awareness*es* furnished with an orderly structure—a linear gradation or continuum—which can, in analogy with our conceptual resources, legitimately be expressed as *times*. Within this orderly structure, the impressions of the automaton merely correspond to (but are not instantiated *as*) the order of before and after—like ranges of saturation in correspondence with keystrokes, the order of impressions and the order of reproductions. The automaton is, so to speak, only in possession of causally ordered analogues of before and after. Again, it is tempting to interpret this before and after (expressed by times t' and t) as tensed verbs, by saying that:

If:

$$I_{o-a} \, be_1 \, t$$
$$I_{o-b} \, be_2 \, t'$$
$$\text{where } t' < t$$

---

133 D. Hume, *A Treatise of Human Nature* (2 vols. Oxford: Clarendon Press, 2007), vol. 1, 29.

or

$$I_{o-b} \text{ be}_2 \text{ } before \text{ } I_{o-a} \text{ be}_1$$

Then:

> The before-after relationship between t' and t means that 't' *precedes* t', and therefore the automaton is aware of 'I_{o-2} be$_2$ t''' as what *preceded* 'I_{o-1} be$_1$ t'—as if tensed verbs were *inherent to* the function of memory.

—and therefore to conclude that, by virtue of having analogues of tensed verbs, the automaton must have a temporal apperception of its impressions and reproductions. But the whole point is that, as argued above, this causally originated before-after ordering of awarenesses is not sufficient for the realization of a temporal awareness, i.e., a tensed awareness *of* such an ordering. Only tense can count as the genuine temporal aspect of awareness—this causally originated ordering is not sufficient.

What the automaton needs in order to move from this causally-originated order of before and after (be$_1$ and be$_2$) to tenses *is* and *was*, is a way of locating itself in time by having a mobile frame of reference with regard to time. In short, the automaton needs to have a perspective on time corresponding to its ordered and ordering point of view in space. Only through this perspective in time is it possible for the automaton to represent the world-history by situating itself within the ever-changing temporal relations of the events composing that world-history. And only an intelligence that possesses such a temporal perspective harbours the possibility of developing into a self-conscious intelligence capable of modifying itself by looking into its history. Thus, we can conclude that having a structured and structuring perspective on time is a minimum necessary condition required for the realization of the kind of general intelligence examined in the previous chapter. Of course, this rudimentary temporal awareness upon which the time-conscious experience of the subject is built is transcendentally ideal and logically phenomenological. It does not supply us with any factual answer with regard to the question 'What is time?', whether we are seeking a metaphysically reified time as a thing or a nonreified formlessness that is the condition of any form. And as we shall see in the next section, the form of this time-awareness, if approached without due caution, can wreak cognitive havoc. Indeed, becoming overly attached to this specific form can restrict both the scope of an agent's theoretical and practical cognitions and the enlargement of its possible field of experience, in the broadest possible sense of that term.

Now, recall that having a point of view on space became possible once the automaton began to see$_1$ the items in the environment through an endocentric frame of reference that allowed it to access the changing spatial relationships between objects by opening up exocentric frames of reference (i.e., frames of reference outside of and not limited to the vantage point of the pure ego). Similarly, in order for the automaton to have a perspective on time, it also needs a temporal frame of reference that permits a distinction between the events of a world-history and those of its own history, experience-occasioning encounters with items existing independently of experience and the temporal succession of representings of these items in impressions and reproductions. In other words, the automaton must be able to differentiate the behaviours of items across time from its *encounters* with these items within one and the same time, thereby occupying that position in time wherein it can become aware of awarenesses which are only de facto its own. At this point, it would be a mistake to think that we can make the automaton become actually aware of its awarenesses of items *as* its own awarenesses or experiences. All the automaton can have at this point is a pure or de facto perspectival temporal point of view. But to have even a capacity for perspectival temporal experience, the automaton must be capable of representing the difference between an item that is being encountered now, and one that is not being encountered now but was encountered and is now being reproduced. This effectively means that the automaton, in addition to the capacity for representing items in the world (awarenesses of this-suches), must be equipped with the capacity to represent its awareness of awarenesses of this-suches *as* 'awarenesses of this-suches'. This is exactly the mobile perspectival temporal frame of reference that parallels the automaton's perspectival spatial frame of reference and which the automaton de facto occupies without being conceptually aware of.

We must not confuse this capacity, however, with a fully fledged apperceptive awareness (taking experiences as *someone's* experience), since the automaton is not yet able to conceptually cohere and represent its awarenesses of awarenesses as being *its own*. What it needs in order to be able to construct and cohere its *own* awareness from its 'awarenesses of awarenesses' is the faculty of concept, the faculty of judgment, or the faculty of rules. This is the next stage in our construction of a toy model general intelligence, which we will embark upon in chapter 5. In the meantime we have to avoid thinking that the automaton can represent 'awarenesses of awarenesses' as its *own* awarenesses. All we are allowed to ascribe to the automaton is the awareness of the existence of those awarenesses that are *as a matter of fact* 'its' awarenesses. But the automaton is not yet capable of recognizing this fact as and within a subjective order. In short, although from our (analogical) point of view the automaton is beginning to display some rudiments of quasi-selfhood (precisely through the elaboration of a point of view), it is not yet able to recognize or mobilize its subjectivity.

The key to having a perspectival temporal awareness is precisely the possession, as a differentiating temporal frame of reference, of a collection of awarenesses capable of metarepresenting 'awarenesses of awarenesses of this-suches' *as* 'awarenesses of this-suches'. In other words, the automaton needs to be equipped with a capacity for representations that are *de facto* meta-awarenesses—awarenesses of awarenesses of items. In a nutshell, the automaton needs a quoting-device '...', or metarepresenting apparatus, for citing or pointing to its awarenesses. This means that, in addition to *awarenesses of items* (I_0 be$_1$, I_0 be$_2$), the automaton must be equipped with a metarepresenting tool for referring to or mentioning these 'awarenesses of items' in terms of 'awarenesses of awarenesses (of items)'.

A helpful way of thinking about this is to take 'awarenesses of items' and 'awarenesses of awarenesses of items' as 'categories' of awarenesses and then to use a category-theoretical abstraction to think about how we can mention or quote 'awarenesses of items' by way of 'awarenesses of awarenesses of items' (using the language of equivalence classes, i.e., the equivalence [of structure] between objects and their respective modes of presentation). If we take 'the awarenesses of items' as a category comprising objects and pointers (in the category-theoretical sense, morphisms; in the philosophical sense, modes of presentation), then we would be able to present or point to this category by way of a whole new collection of pointers (pointers pointing to pointers). This new collection of pointers consists of what could be called a meta-awareness or 'an awareness of awareness'. Moreover, we would be able to go even further by decomposing the new collection of pointers to yet another collection of pointers, making a concatenation of pointers that function as metarepresentings (equivalence relations as opposed to equality relations) corresponding to a potentially infinitely nested structure of 'awarenesses of awarenesses of...', what Hume called the self as a bundle of impressions, or what we might call Humean perceptions. It is perhaps necessary to mention that, at the level of these selves qua bundles of Humean perceptions, there is no time-consciousness since time-consciousness requires the apperceptive self or the principle of experiential unification.[134] There is only a de facto time-order which can be said be to an analogical counterpart to our time-consciousness, but at a much more basic level.

In this fashion, what the automaton requires in order to have a perspectival temporal awareness is not only 'I_0 be$_1$' and 'I_0 be$_2$' (as two modes of awareness of items qua impressions and reproductions), but also two types of awareness of awarenesses—that is, impressions and reproductions of awarenesses: A be$_1$ and A be$_2$.

Here, A stands for the object of these new modes of awareness. It functions as a quoting-device ('...'), a metapointer or, more accurately, a metarepresenting awareness. Within the metarepresentational structure of these new modes of awareness (impressions/be$_1$ and reproductions/be$_2$ of awarenesses), we can see an emerging nested structure:

The metarepresenting 'A' can be represented either as

impression, A be$_1$: 'I_0 be$_1$' b$_1$ and 'I_0 be$_1$' b$_2$

---

134 See the excursus on Boltzmann and time in chapter 4 for an elaboration on this subject.

or as

reproduction, A be$_2$: 'I$_0$ be$_2$' b$_1$ and 'I$_0$ be$_2$' b$_2$

The construction of meta-awarenesses (awarenesses of awarenesses) via a metarepresenting awareness can be continued even further: "'I$_0$ be$_1$' b$_1$" b$_1$, "'I$_0$ be$_1$' b$_1$" b$_2$, "'I$_0$ be$_2$' b$_1$" b$_2$, etc. Equipping the automaton with a global faculty of metarepresenting has now provided the automaton with a representational armamentarium adequate for bringing about a potentially infinite complex of nested awarenesses.

If we were to formulate meta-awarenesses in a category-theoretical fashion, the definition of a meta-awareness (awareness of awarenesses) would be 'an object of a category $\mathcal{J}$ (awarenesses of items) which is determined by the network of its relationships (up to unique isomorphism)[135] with all the other objects in $\mathcal{J}$. This definition can be extended even further: a meta-awareness is a collection of transformations or mappings between one awareness x (e.g., an impression) and another awareness y of the same item (e.g., a reproduction) which are in one-to-one correspondence with the transformations that map the object y and its network of relationships to x and its network of relationships.

---

135 Canonical isomorphism refers to a uniquely specified isomorphism between an object x and an object y that is characterized by a list of explicitly formulated properties belonging to a brand or class of objects to which both x and y belong. The criterion of canonicity or uniqueness is based on this list of explicitly formulated properties. As for the definition of isomorphism, two objects can be said to be isomorphic if there is a structure-preserving mapping or transformation between x and y that can be undone ($f{:}x \to y$ and $g{:}x \to y$) such that we have the compositions of identity maps $gf{:}x \to x$ and $fg{:}y \to y$. Here, rather than isomorphism being defined as two objects having the same structure (i.e., defining isomorphism in terms of structure), the structure is being thought in terms of isomorphism or structure-preserving maps that preserve composition, identity and class-specific relations. This permits to move from equality between two objects (framed in terms of their identical structures) to equivalence correspondences between one object and other objects of the same species or class (i.e., equivalence relations specific to their class or alternatively, type of structure).

Essentially, a meta-awareness is an awareness that plays the equivalent *role* of an awareness of an item (x_J). This equivalence relation is defined in terms of the class-specific relations in which x_J stands in respect to other awarenesses of the same item. What needs to be noted is that meta-awarenesses are not dei ex machina of some sort, awarenesses that have been introduced out of nowhere to solve the problem of the possibility of temporal awareness further down the line. They are reconstructions of awarenesses of items qua this-suches in terms of their web of relations with the same species of awarenesses. The quoting device marks precisely the equivalence relations afforded by the network of awarenesses as specified by the properties of their class. The role$_1$ of any awareness of items can be reformulated or reconstructed by replacing it with the role$_2$ of its network of relationships, so that 'awarenesses of this-suches' (role$_1$) is meta-represented *as* (i.e., equivalent to) 'awarenesses of awarenesses of this suches' (role$_2$). In this fashion, we can see 'A' be$_1$ and 'A' be$_2$, impressions and reproductions, under the general form of:

$$* \ x_J\text{'s network of equivalence relationships } *_J$$

where the *...* denotes *the role of*, and x_J and J respectively signify an awareness of an item and a category of awarenesses whose properties are specified under the class or network of causally ordered representings. It is this swapping of roles from x_J to its network of relationships that makes it possible to causally represent an awareness from the perspective of other awarenesses and their network of relationships in such a way that impressions can be addressed from the experiential viewpoint of reproductions, and reproductions through the purview of impressions. The usefulness of this category theoretical model lies not simply in its diagrammatic efficacy in allowing us to visualize the metarepresenting faculty, but in its power to provide us with some schematic insights into the *geometric form* of constructive memory. This geometry of memory is a prerequisite for the realization of an agent that has an experiential history and that, by virtue of this, is capable of assessing and appropriately responding to its experiences, and ultimately of judging and questioning the very facts of its experience.

The significance of meta-awareness as a global faculty for generating a complex of nested awarenesses is that it introduces a special functional role for be_1 and be_2. It allows one of these modes of being presented (impressions and reproductions) to fall within the scope of the other; and in doing so, it provides the automaton with *distinct* representations for the $being_1$ of some item's $being_2$ *and* the $being_2$ of the same item's $being_1$—the memory of an impression and the impression of a memory. In other words, the automaton has now the adequate representational resources to distinguish between an item that *is* being encountered now *and* one that is not being encountered now but was encountered and is reproduced—that is, the distinction required for having a perspectival temporal awareness of *is* and *was*. Even though the automaton does not have the conceptual resources to see this distinction as *is* and *was*, it nevertheless exhibits and instantiates a temporally perspectival awareness that can be legitimately described, via analogy with our concepts, *as* the temporal distinction between is and was.

Having orderly elements of the past and the present, the only thing that the temporal experience of the automaton is missing is the future. Recall that the constructive model of the automaton's memory not only retains and reproduces impressions, but also, and more importantly, plays a role in the behavioural activities of the automaton. In particular it plays a role in constructing a model of expected action based on the experience of the automaton. In simple terms, besides retaining and reproducing, the memory generates anticipations—a third model of items ($being_3$) in addition to $being_1$ and $being_2$. Adding this third model of items to the previous types of awarenesses does not disrupt or alter the potentially infinite nested structure necessary for the realization of a temporally perspectival awareness. Instead of two types of awarenesses, the automaton has now three types:

$A\ b_1$	'$I_o\ be_1$' be_1	'$I_o\ be_1$' be_2	'$I_o\ be_1$' be_3
$A\ b_2$	'$I_o\ be_2$' be_1	'$I_o\ be_2$' be_2	'$I_o\ be_2$' be_3
$A\ b_3$	'$I_o\ be_3$' be_1	'$I_o\ be_3$' be_2	'$I_o\ be_3$' be_3

In possessing these three types of awareness and, correspondingly, the nested structure that comes with them, the automaton has acquired three capacities: memory (awareness of the $being_2$ of items), anticipation (awareness of the $being_3$ of items) and reflexive meta-awareness (awareness of the $being_1$, $being_2$ and $being_3$ of items). But also, and more importantly, the automaton has thus fulfilled the condition of possibility for the fundamental faculty of 'inner sense'—the necessary capacity of the mind to be affected by its own states and to actively respond to being so affected with representations qua intuitions of items in the mind (cogitations) standing in temporal relations. Analogous to outer sense, where objects are reported to the mind, inner sense is a faculty through which representations (rememberings, anticipatings, perceivings, etc.) are reported to the mind. At the core of this faculty is an operational and synthesizing time-order. And without this fundamental faculty, it is impossible to cross over into the qualitative domain of apperceptive general intelligence:

> Whenever our representations may arise, whether through the influence of external things or as the effect of inner causes, whether they have originated *a priori* or empirically as appearances, as modifications of the mind they nevertheless belong to inner sense, and as such all of our cognitions are in the end subjected to the formal condition of inner sense, namely time, as that in which they must all be ordered, connected, and brought into relations. *This is a general remark on which one must ground everything that follows.*[136]

Although the automaton is not yet aware of itself as a creature endowed with a history, it is aware of itself, from our analogically posited point of view, *as* a history: an orderly expanding sequence of awarenesses standing in changing temporal relations to items behaving—independently of their experience—over time—namely, a world-history. It is this kind of intelligence which, even though not yet self-conscious, can *potentially* treat itself as a project in which the intelligibility of world-history and the self-emancipation of intelligence—the self-constitution of its own history—go hand in hand.

---

136 Kant, *Critique of Pure Reason*, 228 (A98–99) (emphasis mine).

Now we are in a position to advance our toy model of purely perspectival-heuristic intelligence endowed with positional *capacities* (impressions, sensitivity, anticipation and rudimentary forms of memory and inner perception) toward an active model of intelligence with functional *abilities* that allow it not only to reason about the contents of its awarenesses but also to treat these awarenesses as its own so as to 'systematically' respond to the imprints of items in the world on 'itself'. We can think of this transition as the move from one type of abilities (abilities$_1$) to another type (abilities$_2$). Abilities$_1$ are those generated only by virtue of the sufficient structure of the automaton, and which therefore should be properly referred to as general capacities that do not depend on the contents of the automaton's encounters with the world, but instead are mere aspects of the overall structural organization of the automaton. On the other hand, abilities$_2$ are abilities which, although built on abilities$_1$, are nevertheless qualitatively different from them. These are abilities that rely on and are entangled with the contents of these encounters. Precisely, it is this entanglement with the content, being able to reason about it, assess it, examine its implications, and work out its particular formal and material inferential relations with other contents, that differentiates abilities$_2$ as *doings*. The ability to form judgments and to reason about experiential contents is not something that merely transpires in our automaton or befalls it in virtue of its wiring. It is something that the automaton actively does by entering a new domain, the logico-semantic domain of contents wherein abilities are no longer mere capacities but are conducts for navigating, and in the process making sense of, the contents of encounters with the world and our awarenesses of them. We shall call abilities$_1$ structural capacities, and abilities$_2$ logico-semantic functional abilities or, more laconically, normative abilities.

What we should remind ourselves of here is that abilities$_2$ are structurally afforded by the causal regime of abilities$_1$. However, this does not mean that abilities$_1$ are sufficient for the generation of abilities$_2$, nor does it mean that abilities$_2$ are of the same type or quality as abilities$_1$. The latter category is necessary but not sufficient for the realization of the former. One does not simply jump from the mere capacity to discriminate stuff to the ability to make judgments as to the nature of the stuff in question.

The systematicity and adequacy of the automaton's response to the impingement of items in the world on itself depends upon two abilities$_2$:

(1) The ability to form veridical judgments about the contents of aware-nesses (telling apart what seems to be the case from what is the case and how one ought to respond to it).

(2) The ability to form a subjective point of view in order to endorse—in line with the ability of veridical judgment—one story about the items in the world, or one course of action in response to such a world-story, over another.

It is the latter that is the kernel of freedom qua elaboration of practical and theoretical cognitions. This discursive subjective point of view, however, does not need to be understood within the framework of the phenomenal self-model replete with illusions of selfhood (such as the ownership of an empirical self as a constant phenomenal property, a transparent experience of the world, and direct encounters with items in the world). Rational selfhood or subjectivity ought to be understood as a normative functional—rather than purely structural—solution in constructing a qualitative form of intelligence.

Bridging the gap between abilities$_1$ and abilities$_2$ while retaining their qualitative difference will be the focus of the next chapter; but before that we shall look more closely at the question of time-consciousness or experienced temporality that came to the foreground with the inception of inner sense. Given the fact that veridical thoughts are essentially temporal in so far as they depend on sensory—rather than intellectual—intuition, the question of time is of the utmost importance. Moreover, since time is the veritable object of transcendental logic—i.e., the logic of thought as related to sensory intuition—and an ordering factor in transcendental psychology, one cannot go on and tackle the question of mind without examining the question of time. Lastly, this will be also an opportunity to underline the significance of the critique of transcendental structures where we will have the opportunity to investigate the role of memory—a topic missing in Kant's discussion on transcendental aesthetics—and language in our specific form of time-consciousness. We will put forward a picture of intelligence able not only to challenge its so-called facts of experience but also to modify its conditions of transcendental aesthetics, thus renewing its engagement with reality and, in doing so, enriching the reality of itself beyond what is given to it.

4. Some Unsettling Kantian News, as Delivered by Boltzmann (An Excursion into Time)

> Space only offers us relations without *relata*, and a confused phenomenal *mélange* in which we can only problematically disentangle the substantial agencies operative in the latter. And time only offers us sequences infected with vanishingness, which cannot best suggest the presence of permanent underlying agencies.[137]

FREEZING THE FLUX

In this digressive chapter, we will examine a case study that underlines the significance of the question of transcendental structure in exploring the meaning of agency and general intelligence as outlined in chapter 2. Our excursion into the problem of transcendental structures or types will take us down the road of that most enigmatic aspect of the world and our experience of it, time.

Let us begin our investigation into the question of time not only from the perspective of the automaton's ur-temporal awareness$_1$ but from the standpoint of the more advanced sense of time specific to a language-user in possession of tensed sentences and modal vocabularies, the *ordinary time-conscious subject*. From what we saw above, the automaton's ur-awareness of the past, present, and future appears to be a contingent construct of its structural-behavioural organization: its mode of responsiveness to the impingement of items in the world on its senses, its constructive-anticipatory model of memory, and the structuring of its meta-awarenesses on such a model. And finally, on higher levels belonging to the apperceptive subject of experience, ordinary time-consciousness is the fruit of a certain troubling

---

137 J.N. Findlay, *Kant and the Transcendental Object: A Hermeneutic Study* (Oxford: Oxford University Press, 1981), 131.

marriage: the messy entanglement between the objective sense of time and the categories of causality (alteration) and community (simultaneity) that is already present in Kant, and in which the temporal and the causal serve reciprocally in each other's definition, without either being satisfactorily defined as such.

From the analogically posited perspective of the automaton and the non-analogical viewpoint of the discursive apperceptive intelligence, time appears to be flowing, or they themselves seem to be moving through it. The future recedes into the past and we experience ourselves as moving from the past toward the future. In this section, we shall have occasion to inspect why such images of time as a flow or advancement through time are rife with inconsistencies. Only by shedding light on these inconsistencies and their ramifications will we be able to think about what it means to expand the theoretical and practical abilities of agency into a larger field of possible experience that is no longer *foundationally* attached to a *particular* structure.

It would be a biased argument to infer the objective reality of temporal direction, a dynamic 'flow-like' picture of time, or even the objective reality of time as such from either the ur-perception of temporal instances or the tensed consciousness of time. In order to demonstrate this, we will make use of a modified version of John McTaggart's infamously controversial argument regarding the unreality of time, which is implicit in Kant's discussion of the transcendental ideality of experienced temporality (i.e., the argument that time qua experienced temporality is unreal).[138]

McTaggart gives his argument for the unreality of time in three different forms, the first two originally proposed in his essay *The Unreality of Time*, the third in volume 2 of his later work *The Nature of Existence*. The first and most well known argument is presented via the so-called A-series and B-series, which are different series of positions in time. The A-series denotes a tensed temporality in which positions in time start from the far past, going through the near past to the present and then from the present to the near future toward the distant future. Events therefore continually

---

138 J. McTaggart, 'The Unreality of Time', *Mind* 17 (1908), 456–73.

change their temporal position in the A-series. On the other hand, the B-series characterizes a tenseless temporality in which positions in time run sequentially from the earlier-than to the later-than, with the temporal position of an event remaining stable, but being defined in terms of precedence and antecedence to other events. In this argument, change, as the characteristic of the A-series, is taken to be essential for the nature of time, and the B-series is considered to be reliant on this change. McTaggart then argues that the A-series cannot exist because past, present, and future are incompatible determinations. Each temporal event in the A-series (in terms of being of the past, of the present or of the future) presupposes the entirety of the A-series, but insofar as every event must be one or the other and cannot be more than one, the A-series is proved to be incoherent—an incoherency that also undercuts the reality of the B-series.

McTaggart's second argument is presented in the context of the 'specious present' (the instant not as a point but as a short duration, 'a collection of pairwise overlapping events')[139] in which our perceptions are regarded to be in the present, a tract of experience with a special durational unity of the before and the after. The main thrust of the second argument is what Rosenberg identifies as 'an ontological tension between successiveness of the elements of a duration apprehended in a specious present and the simultaneity of the elements constituting the apprehending act'.[140] McTaggart argues as follows:

> The specious present of our observations—varying as it does from you to me—cannot correspond to the present of the events observed. And consequently the past and future of our observations could not correspond to the past and future of the events observed. On either hypothesis—whether we take time as real or as unreal—everything is

---

139 R. Pinosio and M. van Lambalgen, *The Logic of Time and the Continuum in Kant's Critical Philosophy* (2016), <https://philpapers.org/archive/PINTLO-10.pdf>.

140 Rosenberg, *The Thinking Self*, 225.

observed in a specious present, but nothing, not even the observations themselves, can ever be in a specious present.[141]

Finally, in the third version, McTaggart gives his argument on the unreality of time a far more expansive scope. At the beginning of what is an exceptionally sophisticated exercise in critical philosophy, the second volume of *The Nature of Existence*, McTaggart reframes his inquiry into the (un)reality of time as simply a starting point for a broader examination of the question of whether or not the characteristics of reality are those characteristics that it appears to have in experience:

> [W]e shall have to consider various characteristics as to which our experience gives us, at the least, a *prima facie* suggestion that they are possessed either by all that exists, or by some existent things. And two questions will arise about these characteristics. [...] We shall have to ask, firstly, which of these characteristics can really be possessed by what is existent, and which of them, in spite of the *prima facie* appearance to the contrary, cannot be possessed by any thing existent. And we must ask, secondly, of those which are found to be possible characteristics of the existent, whether any of them can be known to be actual characteristics of it.[142]

The modified version of the argument for the unreality of time qua experienced temporality that I have in mind, however, is more in line with McTaggart's third argument, which can be reconstructed and presented in two forms.

The modest version of this modified argument is that we can neither draw conclusions about the objective reality of time (whether as a reified thing or a nonreified formlessness), its direction, its flow, and its temporal structure, nor in fact affirm the existence of such objective properties, on the basis of the structure and characteristics of experienced temporality. The bridge between the phenomenological, psychological, or subjective and

---

141 McTaggart, 'The Unreality of Time'.

142 J. McTaggart, *The Nature of Existence* (2 vols. Cambridge: Cambridge University Press, 1927), vol. 2, 3.

the metaphysical, physical, or objective accounts of time is no readymade matter, for the reason that the two are incommensurably distinct. Rather than arguing that there is no objectively real time, the modest claim here concerns the illegitimate nature of the inference from the perception of time qua experienced temporality to the objective reality of time on the basis of some assumed isomorphism, private access, global sense of direction and passage of time, structure of tensed language, or observed arrow of causality.

Said in a different way, we cannot infer an objective account of time from temporal-dynamic characteristics that appear in experience or conditions of observation. But this does not tell us whether or not there is an objective time, nor, if there is, what its characteristics might be. In other words, this is different from a naively hyper-Kantian position—born of a conflation between commitments to epistemological idealism and commitments to ontological idealism—for which it is impossible to think an objective reality for time or to see any structure as anything but a structure inherent to our subjective point of view. While the conceptual resources of our language enable us to make veridical judgments pertaining to time, we are not permitted to treat these temporal components of language—i.e., the tensed verbs and temporal connectives of our statements about objective time, such as 'before', 'after', 'when' and 'until'—as evidence for the objective structure of time. This of course opens up a more fundamental question: Is the tensed structure of natural languages even appropriate for investigating the question of time, or should we completely shift to formal-theoretical languages, which would allow us to take advantage of temporal connectives with more neutral and flexible logical connections? What Quine rightly snubs as the 'tiresome bias'[143] toward ordinary language in the treatment of time should alone be sufficient reason for philosophers to become suspicious of the kinds of loose wordplay they employ not only when thinking about the problems of time and temporality, but also when thinking about change, whether the latter is understood as something events undergo in the universe or as a transformation effected by rational agents in the world.

---

143 W.V.O. Quine, *Word and Object* (Cambridge, MA: MIT Press, 1960), 154.

The less modest and more disquieting version of the unreality of experienced temporality—what should be called the *sinister version*—is that there is a good chance that any asymmetric picture of time that allows for sequences running from one extremity toward another (from past to future or future to past) in a punctual or durational form, or where the present can be regarded as something *objectively distinguishable*, is riddled with experiential biases. These biases are not exclusive to ordinary subjective time-consciousness and the tensed structure of natural language that relays it, but also, and more fundamentally, can even be extended to the ideal notion of the observer in physics. The sinister implication is that, if directional, flow-like pictures of time are negatively biased by the structure of experienced temporality and the local characteristics of the subjective perspective/observer, and if the classical notions of causality, system state, and antecedent conditions are embroiled in directional-flow-like pictures of time, then those portions of complexity and physical sciences that have incorporated these concepts as their fundamental explanatory-descriptive elements are also biased and prone to significant revision, if not abandonment.

What is meant by causality here is not what Wolfgang Stegmüller astutely identifies as the prescientific concept of causality, namely, singular causal judgments (or individual cause-effect connections) reflected in sentences of ordinary language containing terms such as 'because' and 'since' (Seneca cut his veins *since* Nero ordered him to kill himself, the car crashed into a tree *because* the brakes stopped working, etc.).[144] The prescientific

---

144 'This concept [of cause] stems from the vague language of everyday life where it is undoubtedly quite useful, for it serves adequately all the practical purposes of our everyday language; but it cannot serve as the point of departure for a philosophical concept explication. Suppose a house caves in as a result of removing a prop in the course of construction work being done in the basement. It will then be said that the house collapsed because that prop had been removed. And since such a because-statement is equivalent to a singular causal assertion, it might also be stated as follows: the removal of that prop was the cause of the collapse of the house. It becomes immediately clear now that despite the removal of that prop the house would still not have collapsed had it had a different structure. If, for example, the structure of the house had been such that the prop was not necessary

cause-effect connection is built upon the arbitrary selection—in Stegmül-ler's words more 'psychological' than 'epistemological'—of one diagnosed or indicant condition from among a large number of conditions that may not seem to play any explicit causal role. Instead, the concept of causality that is at stake here refers to a set of lawlike regularities along with a set of antecedent conditions that together constitute the explanans of a causal explanation. In this schema of causal explanation, statements belonging to the explanans must have empirical content as well as at least one nomologi-cal law-statement in order to count as causally explanatory.

And so begins our inquiry into the limits of the transcendental structure of experience: To what extent is what we take as a necessary and universal fact of experience, an a priori act, in fact a local and contingent aspect of our experience? Or, in other words, how much is what we take to be necessary distorted by what is actually contingent through and through? As promised, this is where we can benefit by focusing on a particular case study.

The challenge to the directional, flow-like picture of time can potentially problematize the classical conditions (i.e., conditions dependent on various dynamic time-oriented phenomena, from inductive numerical asymmetries to temporal asymmetries, etc.) through which lawlike regularities are derived and antecedent conditions are characterized. As for the notion of the *state* of a physical system that is in question here, it describes dispositions of the system for responding to a range of possible circumstances that might be encountered in the future. This notion of the *state* is, properly speaking, a descriptive tool for predicting the future responses or trajectories of the system (in terms of counterfactuals) from its present behaviour. *Hidden variables*, on the other hand, refer to those states taken to be independent of any future interactions to which the system might be subjected.

---

to maintain its stability, then nothing would have happened. Thus, if we designate the removal of that prop as the cause of the collapse, this is basically a very one-sided description of the situation. Such an act must actually have coincided with quite a large number of other factors to bring about the said effect; and yet all these other factors were not taken into account at all.' W. Stegmüller, *Collected Papers on Epistemology, Philosophy of Science and History of Philosophy* (2 vols. Dordrecht: D. Reidel, 1977), vol. 2, 29.

These concepts are based on perspectival temporal and modal asymmetries of the local observer that ground the distinction between sequences running from past to future and those running from future to past, or, more generally, the orientation of sequences with regard to the passage of time. These concepts—causality (lawlike regularities together with antecedent conditions), states, and hidden variables—play a fundamental role in complexity sciences, particularly those branches that make heavy use of heuristic methods for describing the behaviour of the system, characterizing its structural and functional features, and predicting its evolution. Any significant revision of the canonical model of directional-flow-like time may potentially harbour devastating outcomes for these frameworks, operative not only in physics, chemistry, and biology, but also in neuroscience, economics, and the social sciences.

BOLTZMANN'S COPERNICAN SHAKEDOWN OF THE TIME-CONSCIOUS SUBJECT

Drawing attention to the observational and subjective biases within the directional-dynamic picture of time and temporal asymmetries, and pointing out the negative connotations of such biases for the concepts of description, causal explanation, modelling, and prediction is by no means a recent line of inquiry. In what Huw Price calls 'a Copernican moment' and Hans Reichenbach distinguishes as 'one of the keenest insights into the problem of time',[145] Ludwig Boltzmann summarizes the problem in the following remarks, worth quoting in their entirety:

> Just as the differential equations represent simply a mathematical method for calculation, whose clear meaning can only be understood by the use of models which employ a large finite number of elements, so likewise general thermodynamics (without prejudice to its unshakable importance)

---

145 See H. Price, 'The Flow of Time', in C. Callender (ed.), *The Oxford Handbook of Philosophy of Time* (Oxford: Oxford University Press, 2011), 282; and Reichenbach, *The Direction of Time* (Los Angeles: University of California Press, 1956), 128.

also requires the cultivation of mechanical models representing it, in order to deepen our knowledge of nature—not in spite of, but rather precisely because these models do not always cover the same ground as general thermodynamics, but instead offer a glimpse of a new viewpoint. Thus general thermodynamics holds fast to the invariable irreversibility of all natural processes. It assumes a function (the entropy) whose value can only change in one direction—for example, can only increase—through any occurrence in nature. Thus it distinguishes any later state of the world from any earlier state by its larger value of the entropy. The difference of the entropy from its maximum value—which is the goal [*Treibende*] of all natural processes—will always decrease. In spite of the invariance of the total energy, its transformability will therefore become ever smaller, natural events will become ever more dull and uninteresting, and any return to a previous value of the entropy is excluded.

One cannot assert that this consequence contradicts our experience, for indeed it seems to be a plausible extrapolation of our present knowledge of the world. Yet, with all due recognition to the caution which must be observed in going beyond the direct consequences of experience, it must be granted that these consequences are hardly satisfactory, and the discovery of a satisfactory way of avoiding them would be very desirable, whether one may imagine time as infinite or as a closed cycle. In any case, we would rather consider the unique directionality of time given to us by experience as a mere illusion arising from our specially restricted viewpoint.[146]

Boltzmann then continues,

For the universe, the two directions of time are indistinguishable, just as in space there is no up or down. However, just as at a particular place on the earth's surface we call 'down' the direction toward the center of the earth, so will a living being in a particular time interval of such a single world distinguish the direction of time toward the less

---

146 L. Boltzmann, *Lectures on Gas Theory 1896–1898* (New York: Dover, 2011), 401–2.

probable state from the opposite direction (the former toward the past, the latter toward the future). By virtue of this terminology, such small isolated regions of the universe will always find themselves 'initially' in an improbable state. This method seems to me to be the only way in which one can understand the second law—the heat death of each single world—without a unidirectional change of the entire universe from a definite initial state to a final state.

Obviously no one would consider such speculations as important discoveries or even—as did the ancient philosophers—as the highest purpose of science. However it is doubtful that one should despise them as completely idle. Who knows whether they may not *broaden the horizon of our circle of ideas*, and by stimulating thought, advance the understanding of *the facts of experience*?[147]

Thermodynamics is a thriller, but we all know how its plot unfolds: the film shows the expansion of a gas in a sealed bottle. There is an imaginary compartment with a trapdoor in the bottle (equilibrium state$_1$). Inside this compartment the gas is pressurized. Next the film shows the imaginary door being opened. We can easily anticipate where the story is headed. The gas starts to spread (far from equilibrium) and it finally fills the entire bottle (equilibrium state$_2$). The montage of this film is asymmetrically oriented: once the trapdoor is released, we see gas filling the entire bottle, but never coming back to its original confinement in the imaginary compartment. And even if we watch the movie backwards, we can still tell what the plot is. This is the observed time-asymmetry of an irreversible process. However, there is also a different montage—a subplot—for this film. It shows the molecules of gas colliding with one another and freely moving in every direction. Whether we see this version on fast forward or on rewind, we still cannot tell whether the gas is expanding in one direction or another. This is the time-symmetry of the underlying microscopic mechanical laws. So how can we reconcile the first version of the film with the second?

---

147 Ibid., 402–3 (emphases mine).

In the first version of this film we are actually dealing with two laws: the law of approach toward equilibrium, and the second law of thermodynamics. As noted by Jos Uffink and fleshed out by Meir Hemmo and Orly R. Shenker, these two laws express two entirely different sets of facts and require different kinds of explanation.[148] It is an experimental fact—and the extension of the first law as the thermodynamic version of the law of the conservation of energy—that energy tends to change its form (it is not created ex nihilo). But this change is such that the amount of energy exploitable for work decreases over time. This is what is described by both the law of approach toward equilibrium and the second law, but under different explanatory frameworks. The law of approach toward equilibrium is a schematic generalization of our observed experience in so far as it does not by itself tell us which state is the equilibrium state for a given set of constraints in the system. This specificity of the equilibrium state can only be derived nomologically from experience, it cannot be obtained as an a priori theorem of thermodynamics. Whereas the second law of thermodynamics is about the increase of entropy as the '[ordering] of states of equilibrium in time, according to which the amount of energy which is in the form of heat, relative to the amount of energy which is in mechanical or other forms of energy (which are more readily exploitable to produce useful work), cannot decrease'.[149]

With these necessary notes in mind, in the passage by Boltzmann cited above, what vexes the physicist is not the puzzles of the directional-dynamic picture of time, but rather the unproblematic and innocent nature of the assumption that time does in fact have an objective temporal direction. There is a circularity involved in postulating a direction

---

148 See J. Uffink, 'Bluff Your Way in the Second Law of Thermodynamics', in *Studies in History and Philosophy of Science* vol. 32-3 (Elsevier, 2001), 305–94; and M. Hemmo and O.R. Shenker, *The Road to Maxwell's Demon: Conceptual Foundations of Statistical Mechanics* (Cambridge: Cambridge University Press, 2012).

149 Ibid., 26. Hemmo and Shenker argue that by virtue of these differences, the law of approach to equilibrium and the second law present two different accounts of time-asymmetry that must be explained and tackled on their own terms.

for time based on the observation of irreversible processes *in time*, and inferring the irreversibility of processes on the basis of a canonical, albeit implicitly stated, *arrow of time*. For Boltzmann, the real conundrum is not why entropy increases with time, but why it was ever so low to start with. Formulated differently, rather than asking why entropy increases toward the future, we should ask why it decreases toward the past. The source of Boltzmann's problem lay precisely in what he had initially treated as a key to solving the problem of the second law of thermodynamics: Where does the time-asymmetric characteristic of the second law—which states that entropy increases over time—come from, given the time-symmetric laws of the underlying mechanics? Again, how can the two different versions of the film be made compatible?

Toward the end of the nineteenth century, figures such as Boltzmann and Gibbs had begun to develop a fully statistical (proto-computational/ information-theoretic) account of thermodynamics. For Boltzmann, however, this was part of a broader project, one whose aim was to provide 'complete descriptions' of physical phenomena. The stepping-stone of this descriptive project was Boltzmann's reformulation of the concept of scientific description at once removed from the dominant influence of earlier phenomenalist and psychological accounts of description (such as Mach's) and sufficiently fine-grained to be capable of integrating statistical, epistemological, phenomenological, real-ideal, subjective-objective levels and types of description in a nonarbitrary (i.e., intrinsic) manner. To this end, Boltzmann provided three general levels or types of description: pure or abstract description based on inferential generalization of differential equations rather than on a correspondence to observed facts, indirect description based on a probabilistic framework of statistical description, and a level of description concerning unobservables. As Adam Berg argues in *Phenomenalism, Phenomenology and the Question of Time*,[150] Boltzmann's reframing of thermodynamics (specifically the second law) through statistical

---

150 A. Berg, *Phenomenalism, Phenomenology, and the Question of Time: A Comparative Study of the Theories of Mach, Husserl, and Boltzmann* (Lanham, MD: Lexington Books, 2015), 76.

mechanics should be seen within the scope of this descriptive analysis as a multilevel complex system of coding with distinct descriptive levels that require different appropriate systems of coding, noetic contents, and methods of analysis as well as appropriate spaces for bridging these levels. Within the scope of this multilevel descriptive analysis, which became the skeletal framework of modern scientific theories, Boltzmann developed his statistical theory of the nonequilibrial (i.e., irreversible and time-asymmetric) behaviour of macroscopic systems. He introduced the concept of the 'macrostate' as part of his attempt to relate the second law of thermodynamics to the probability calculus. Physically objective and correlatively defined between the observer and the observed, macrostates are sets of *microstates which by themselves cannot be distinguished by a given observer.*[151] Macrostates are objective insofar as they intrinsically express the one-to-many or many-to-many correlations between the underlying microstates. The introduction of the macrostate is required, then, in order to distinguish thermodynamic regularities that would otherwise be indistinguishable at the level of mechanical microstates. Microstates are, on the other hand, the instantaneous states of the universe. In Boltzmann's framework, a microstate of a single molecule is represented by a point in the state space of that molecule, where the state space represents the space of all the microstates a system can inhabit. This state space is a six-dimensional space comprised of three spatial positions and three momentum dimensions or degrees of freedom. This state space of a single molecule is called µ-space or molecular space.

Boltzmann then associated an entropy value with each macrostate and with each microstate giving rise to that macrostate. In this framework, entropy could be seen as a tendency to evolve toward more probable macrostates, and its increase as information regarding the qualitative dynamic behaviour of macroscopic systems. From the perspective of this new multilevel descriptive analysis, the problems of the second law (i.e., why does entropy increase over time?) and the observed irreversibility and

---

151 In Boltzmann's vocabulary, 'distribution of state' stands for macrostate and *komplexion* stands for microstates.

time-asymmetry of physical processes in time despite the time-symmetry and reversibility of the underlying mechanical-physical laws, could thus be reframed as the problem of moving from microscopic to macroscopic descriptions. The solution to these problems could then be formulated by devising a statistical mechanical framework that accommodates a conception of macrostate (pertaining to the macroscopic level) expressed in terms of physical probability or permutability, and intrinsically correlated to the microstate (associated with the microscopic level) responsible for it. Within this statistical mechanical resolution, entropy, then, is defined as a tendency toward more probable macrostates, the probability of which is logarithmically defined.

We will not able to delve further into the details of how Boltzmann constructed his solution, but, very briefly, it involved a procedure that would make explicit the connections between statistical and thermal thermodynamic descriptions through the introduction of the concept of macrostate formulated in terms of its probability, and a six-dimensional partition-velocity phase space (the μ-space) which allowed the bridging of microstates and macrostates, microscopic descriptions and macroscopic descriptions. Following Maxwell, Boltzmann began to examine the effects of collisions on the distribution of velocities of molecules of a gas. He introduced a space divided into a finite array of small rectangular cells or intervals of equal size or volume in position and momentum.[152] Once available velocities are partitioned into these cells, then there is an effective combinatorial-computational procedure for examining the effects of collisions on the number of molecules whose velocities entered these cells. It is noteworthy that, in this solution, macrostates do not depend upon the identity of individual molecules entering these cells. They depend upon the identity of the cells in which varying numbers of molecules or particles have been thus distributed.

---

152 In its original formulation, Boltzmann characterized particles entering the grid boxes or cells in terms of their energy, but he then demonstrated that this formula fails to achieve the Maxwell probability distribution.

Using this combinatorial procedure, Boltzmann was able to argue (1) that the distribution of velocities corresponds to the Maxwell probability distribution, in which the quantity E or H, equivalent to negative entropy, can be said to be decreasing, and (2) that this distribution is independent of the initial distribution of velocities. No matter how particles are initially assigned to the available velocity cell-partitions, we still obtain the same probability distribution, which accounts for the monotonic decrease of H. Demonstrating that the quantity H always monotonically decreases—its lowest value being the state of thermal equilibrium—was proof of the unidirectional and irreversible increase of entropy and the time-asymmetric behaviour of physical processes at the macroscopic level in spite of the reversibility and time-symmetry of the underlying microscopic mechanics.

However, as reflected in the quotes cited earlier, Boltzmann later expressed doubts about his solution and began to examine the challenges raised by adopting a resolutely atemporal perspective. Given the fact that the statistical argument itself is merely a combinatorial-counting procedure and lacks any time-asymmetry, and that therefore there is no reason to apply the increase of entropy to a unique sequence that runs from the past toward the future, it can equally be applied to a sequence running from the future to the past. In which case, as mentioned earlier, what really demands explanation is not the increase of entropy toward the future (i.e., what appears to be a natural state of things) but the ever so low entropy in the beginning, in so far as the statistical argument gives us equal reason to expect an increase of entropy toward the past. It places the burden of explanation on the earlier low entropy rather than the later high entropy. In light of the statistical argument (i.e., equal probability of increase in entropy in either direction, past-to-future and future-to-past), the global decrease of entropy toward the past now appears as an unnatural condition and so itself demands explanation. In other words, for Boltzmann, changing the perspective from temporal to atemporal had turned something natural (low entropy in the past) into something unnatural (high entropy in the past) and therefore, in line with the motivations of scientific explanation, which demand that we account for 'unnatural conditions', called for a shift in explanatory focus. This raised challenges that have vast implications not only for our models of processes and our methods for the metricization of events, but also for what we take to be the established facts of our experience—yet to date these implications have gone largely unheeded.

Even though Boltzmann shifted his efforts toward a reinterpretation of thermodynamics from an atemporal perspective, the deep problematic aspects of his initial solution to the problem of the second law were carried over into his new interpretation, given in the context of the 'cosmological hypothesis',[153] and which was supposed to be free of any particular temporal bias. But what is this problematic aspect which, despite being spotted—at least partially—by Boltzmann, still resurfaced in his later interpretation? The problem with Boltzmann's initial solution was that he had unintentionally imported subjective characteristics of experience into his combinatorial procedure via the introduction of macrostates. In other words, the phenomenal assumptions regarding the facticity of observed time-asymmetry for the ensemble's macrostate were illicitly applied to the description of microstates. In this sense, Boltzmann had not really bridged the gap between statistical

---

153 'Philosophers had attempted to derive the properties of time from reason, but none of their conceptions compares with this result that a physicist derived from reasoning about the implications of mathematical physics. As in so many other points, the superiority of a philosophy based on the results of science has become manifest. There is no logical necessity for the existence of a unique direction of total time; whether there is only one time direction, or whether time directions alternate, depends on the shape of the entropy curve plotted by the universe.

Boltzmann has made it very clear that the alternation of time directions represents no absurdity. He refers our time direction to that section of the entropy curve on which we are living. If it should happen that "later" the universe, after reaching a high-entropy state and staying in it for a long time, enters into a long downgrade of the entropy curve, then, for this section, time would have the opposite direction: human beings that might live during this section would regard as positive time the transition to higher entropy, and thus their time would flow in a direction opposite to ours. Since these two sections of opposite time directions would be separated by aeons of high-entropy states, in which living organisms cannot exist, it would forever remain unknown to the inhabitants of the second time section that their time direction was different from ours.' Reichenbach, *The Direction of Time*, 128.

mechanical entropy and thermal entropy belonging to different levels of description, but had only elided the distinction between the two descriptive levels by illegitimately transporting the underlying assumptions of one into the other. Indeed, Boltzmann did notice this problem, but what he did not recognize was the *extent* to which the time-asymmetric assumptions specific to the macroscopic description had distorted the statistical-objective description associated with microscopic systems. What he had taken as innocently given initial and boundary conditions were themselves infected by the biases specific to observer-observer correlations. In other words, Boltzmann did not fully realize that the biases of unidirectional time had already infiltrated the law-like principles through which the parameters of the microscopic systems such as initial conditions were being defined and chosen. Following Boltzmann's Oxford lecture, this problem was first recognized by George H. Bryan and Samuel Burbury; it has recently been refined by Huw Price and encapsulated under the principle of molecular or microscopic innocence (μInnocence). μInnocence is the apparently obvious intuition that 'interacting systems are bound to be ignorant of one another until the interaction actually occurs; at which point each system may be expected to "learn" something about the other'.[154]

But what exactly is the problematic nature of this intuition with respect to Boltzmann's later work on bridging statistical entropy with thermodynamic entropy, the so-called Boltzmann's principle formulated by the equation $S = k \log W$? It is the implicit time-asymmetric assumption within Boltzmann's principle of molecular collision or chaos (*stoßzahlansatz*)—the idea that the velocities of two particles that have not collided yet can be said to be uncorrelated, and can therefore be identified as an initial condition, already presupposes a privileged temporal-causal asymmetry. Why? Because

---

154 See G.H. Bryan, 'Letter to the editor', *Nature* 51 (1894), 175; S.H. Burbury, 'Boltzmann's minimum theorem', *Nature* 51 (1894), 78–9; H. Price, *Time's Arrow and Archimedes' Point* (Oxford: Oxford University Press, 1996), 120; and also the so-called Loschmidt's paradox in the context of Josef Loschmidt's critical response to Boltzmann: J. Loschmidt, 'Zur Grösse der Luftmolecule', *Sitzungsber. Kais. Akad. Wiss. Wien. Math. Naturwiss.* 73 (1876), 128–42.

in so far as microscopic mechanics is time-symmetric and initial microstates are equiprobable, there is no reason to expect the velocities of particles to become correlated as a result of their collisions. Under *stoßzahlansatz*, we anticipate outgoing products of collisions to be dynamically correlated even if they never interact in the future. In other words, we always expect the number of outgoing collisions $(\vec{v}_1, \vec{v}_2) \rightarrow (\vec{v}_1{}', \vec{v}_2{}')$ to be proportional to $f(\vec{v}_1) f(\vec{v}_2)$ where $\vec{v}_1$ and $\vec{v}_2$ are the velocities of particles before the collisions.[155] But we never expect the converse—that the incoming components of a collision will be correlated if they have never encountered each other in the past, i.e., if the molecules have never interacted. As Huw Price suggests, this is a time-asymmetric intuition which has no place in the statistical/information theoretic description of the system. And yet Boltzmann's entire *stoßzahlansatz* is built upon it.[156]

It is as if, as soon as we put in place an incorrect framework for our encounter with the physical universe, no matter what we do from that point onwards, everything will appear to be an incoming chaos. If no direction of time is initially privileged in the description of initial and boundary conditions, since the statistical argument by itself has no time-asymmetric component, then once we adopt an atemporal perspective there is no reason for us to presume that the time-asymmetric explanatory schema of an initial microstate explaining a final macrostate will be tenable. Earlier-than (low entropy) and later-than (high entropy) as atemporal determinations of before and after can very well be contaminated by the biases of a temporal time-asymmetric viewpoint. Accordingly, Boltzmann's true challenge—not fully appreciated even by himself—now boils down to a much more

---

155 It should be noted that such a classical collision scenario presupposes an implicit 'existence function' since only in classical physics we can assume that particles exist before as well as after the collision. Whereas once we apply collision mechanics to elementary particle physics, particles may appear or disappear through the course of collision. Therefore, if the existence function e is defined on particles and instants, the value of e for a particle p at time t in the classical scenario always equals 1 (i.e., the particle exists). In a nonclassical scenario, the value of the existence function e is $\{0,1\}$.

156 Price, *Time's Arrow and Archimedes' Point*, 26.

fundamental question: How can we suggest that an initial microstate can explain a final macrostate, if what is really in need of explanation is the temporal asymmetry that grounds such an explanatory schema?

It does not take too much critical acuity to realize that a similar question can be posed with regard to those frameworks of causal explanation—specifically utilized in the context of reductionism—that rely on identification of some antecedent conditions and a temporally directed causal arrow through which—thanks to the convenient mediation of time-asymmetry—the distinction between 'the causal' and 'the explanatory' effectively fades away. Nevertheless, the real significance of Boltzmann's challenge is only revealed in its full force when it is treated as a general epistemological critique: How can we justify a chain of inference that follows an explanatory arrow whose ground of justification—its explanans—is nothing more than the past state of affairs as an observable item or an empirical footprint? This question can of course equally be applied to a chain of epistemological inference that runs from the future to the past. In both cases, what needs to be justified is exactly what is taken to be the ground of justification. Thus epistemological neutrality appears to be in sharp conflict with temporally charged modes of epistemological inference. Hoping to retain some aspects of the former while drawing conclusions from the latter in a practical trade-off is more like wishful thinking than a pragmatic paradigm of scientific knowledge.

INDUCTIVE DOGMAS AND COGNITIVE BIASES OF TIME-ASYMMETRY

The illegitimate imposition of time-asymmetric descriptions exclusive to macrostates onto descriptions of microstates in order to explain the behaviours of the former via the mechanics of the latter, therefore, bespeaks a much broader range of complications arising from our epistemological (and not merely perceptual-observational) biases in coordinating our observational frameworks with our theoretical-inferential frameworks. Accustomed to the cosiness of our intuitions and under the theoretical influence of our local subjective biases, we are frequently liable to project our subjective assumptions onto the world and, in doing so, to posit that which itself requires explanation (qua subjective characteristic) as an objective explanatory feature.

The same biases can be detected within theories in which computation is strongly coupled with the postulate of positive entropic increase for irreversible processes. For example, in the thermodynamics of computation it is often held that the physical implementation of any logically irreversible operation such as erasure results in an increase of entropy. The amount of increase is $k\log2$ per bit of erased information. Once an observer, via measurements, obtains information concerning which macrostate is the actual state of the observed system, then such information can be manipulated. But macroscopic manipulation of this information—particularly through irreversible logical operations such as erasure and conjunction—results in positive entropy production. In simpler terms, the physical implementation of computation (i.e., physical computers) always exacts an entropy cost. However, there is no a priori necessary connection between the orthodox theory of thermodynamics and the theory of computation which would allow one uncontroversially to associate the logical properties of computation with the principles of classical mechanics. The problem—that of the exact link between thermodynamics and computation, between the physical implementation of logical operations and the fundamental laws of physics—is by no means a settled issue yet.

The information obtained and manipulated is information concerning the macrostate, and the macrostate is observer-related. Therefore the entropy cost of the manipulation or physical implementation of irreversible logical operations is also observer-related, and depends on the specificity of the physical implementation. What is erased, in this sense, is precisely the inferential link or mapping (rather than the memory of the observer itself) between the past macrostate and the present macrostate. In other words, erasure means that the *observer* cannot infer the past macrostate from the present 'recently observed' macrostate (cf. Russell's paradox, discussed below).[157]

157　For a far more sophisticated and detailed engagement with the positive entropic interpretation of the physical implementation of irreversible logical operations, see Hemmo and Shenker, *The Road to Maxwell's Demon*, particularly chapter 12.

It might be objected that time-asymmetry and temporal descriptions are only useful fictional instruments (at best subjectively, at worst speculatively metaphysical) that allow us to talk about nontemporal events and processes. It is true that, as Adolf Grünbaum—that most astute debunker of the mysteries of space and time—has spelled out, our sense of time as a flow is only a qualitative conception devoid of metrical components.[158] But as we have seen, this qualitative conception is liable to corrupt the metrical ingredients of our scientific frameworks even when its interference is least expected. Objections that dismiss temporal descriptions and time-asymmetry as useful idealizations or metaphysical fictions can reinforce our obliviousness to the influence that our temporal intuitions exert upon models and methods we assume to be unaffected by any objective or subjective account of time-asymmetry. In doing so, rather than giving reason for making a radical scission from temporal intuitions, they give more reason for further postponement of the overdue critical task—namely, the examination of the extent of the distorting effects temporal intuitions have had and continue to have on scientific models and methods.

Reference to the empirical success of confirming observations regarding time-asymmetric behaviours runs, from different directions, not only into the old and new riddles of induction concerning future observations, as stated by Hume and Goodman,[159] but also into the problematics of the reliability hypothesis concerning the memory-driven knowledge of past observations, as formulated by Russell's 'five minutes ago' paradox:[160]

In investigating memory-beliefs, there are certain points that must be borne in mind. In the first place, everything constituting a memory-belief is happening now, not in that past time to which the belief is said to refer. It is not logically necessary to the existence of a memory-belief that the event remembered should have occurred, or even that the

---

158 A. Grünbaum, *Philosophical Problems of Space and Time* (Dordrecht: D. Reidel, 1973).

159 N. Goodman, 'The New Riddle of Induction', in *Fact, Fiction, and Forecast* (Cambridge, MA: Harvard University Press, 1979), 59–83.

160 See Appendix.

past should have existed at all. There is no logical impossibility in the hypothesis that the world sprang into being five minutes ago, exactly as it then was, with a population that 'remembered' a wholly unreal past. There is no logically necessary connection between events at different times; therefore nothing that is happening now or will happen in the future can disprove the hypothesis that the world began five minutes ago. Hence the occurrences which are called knowledge of the past are logically independent of the past; they are wholly analysable into present contents, which might, theoretically, be just what they are even if no past had existed.[161]

As observers, we take our memories to be reliable reflections of actual states of affairs, and, given that the content of our memory is that entropy was lower in the past based on *memories* of previous observations, our microscopic retrodiction concerning low initial entropy should also be seen as reliable. But according to Russell's five minutes ago paradox, since the contents of our memories are not derived from mechanics, and to the extent that there are many-to-one correlations between our memory states and the universe (as opposed to a one-to-one correlation), successful retrodictions can be false memory-beliefs, the falsity of which is a matter of logical tenability. Russell, however, attempts to stave off the hazardous effect of his paradox by discrediting it as simply 'uninteresting'[162] and instead in the last instance saves the memory-driven knowledge of the past.

Russell's line of reasoning in defence of a memory-driven knowledge of the past runs like this: Such knowledge depends not on the occurrence of more instances of identical observations, but rather on two suitable belief-supporting series in which memory-images can be classified. The first series classifies memory-images in terms of the less or more remote periods of the past to which such memory-images refer (henceforth, P-series). The second series classifies memory-images based on the degree of our confidence in their accuracy (henceforth, Q-series). In the Q-series, what warrants our

161 B. Russell, *The Analysis of Mind* (London: George Allen & Unwin, 1921), 159–60.
162 Ibid., 160.

confidence or lack thereof is the sense$_2$ of familiarity among the memory-images themselves as being sensed$_1$ as more or less familiar (familiarity by degree). The more familiar memory-images give us a sense$_2$ of accuracy of those images and thus the belief or judgment that what is happening now has happened before. In the P-series, the sense$_2$ of the nearness or distance of memory-images is given on the basis of how we remember (again a matter of degree) a remembered event as the time between the remembering and the remembered varies. Those rememberings that are more recent have more remembered context either because memory-images are sensed$_1$ as successively following their precursors, or because some sensations$_1$—so-called akoluthic sensations or memory-based sensations[163]—are apprehended as present, others as fading and thus apprehended as the marks of just-pastness. Now, in so far as our rememberings always start from what has more context (i.e., is more recent) and the fading increases as the time increases, the P-series gives us a sense$_2$ qua justified belief that the series of memory-images being so remembered extends from present to just-past to past (the fading of sensations belonging to the akoluthic phase). Accordingly, the combination of P-series and Q-series—the belief-supporting feelings of the pastness and the familiarity of memory-images—provide us with a justified and reliable knowledge of the past.

As you may already suspect, based on how I have numerically distinguished the occurrences of the word 'sense', the problem with Russell's reasoning is that what is sensed$_1$ qua organized sense-impression—the feeling *of—by itself* does not so readily and directly translate into sense$_2$

---

163 'At the beginning of stimulus we have a sensation; then a gradual transition; and at that end an image. Sensations while they are fading called "akoluthic" sensations. When the process of fading is completed (which happens very quickly), we arrive at the image, which is capable of being revived on subsequent occasions with very little change.' Ibid., 175. Russell's terms *akoluthic sensations* and *akoluthic stage* are borrowed from the work of Richard Wolfgang Semon. According to Semon, as soon as each sensation is experienced, it enters the akoluthic phase wherein it durationally affects or persists in the mind in a faint or subconscious manner. This manner of sensing then makes it possible for one sensation to be *associated* with another sensation in the akoluthic phase.

qua judgement or belief proper. The myth of the given rears its head once again here. But even setting this issue aside, by themselves the senses$_1$ of the more familiar and the sense$_1$ of the more remembered context are too arbitrary. There can be many-to-many mappings or thematic affinities between the elements of both P-series (rememberings and remembereds) and Q-series (the more familiar, the less familiar, the vaguely familiar, and the unfamiliar) in such a way that ordering becomes a matter of entirely arbitrary selection.

Moreover, the more significant issue is not that the sense$_1$ can be illusory, but rather that the sense$_2$ of the memory-images being thus-and-so recognized and remembered (as knowledge of the past) is first and foremost a statistical inference rather than a proper logico-semantic judgement. In other words, the semantic sense$_2$ is a linguistic whitewash over the fact that it is merely a statistical or inductivist inference just like sense$_1$. The difference between the two is that the former is at the level of the linguistic and the latter is at the level of the causal. Despite Russell's contention, sense$_2$ is nothing more than or superior to sense$_1$, other than being what linguistically bespeaks or betokens the causal-statistical sense$_1$.

Imagine you are a detective, investigating a crime scene in some desolate and dreary town in New England in the middle of winter. Near the site of the crime, you see traces which resemble the tracks made by a car's tires. You instantly associate the trace with the movement of a car based on memories of your previous observations. This association is purely statistical since the wind or some diabolically smart culprit bent on distracting you and wearing shoes with bizarre soles could also have formed these traces. Although this is highly improbable, it is neither probabilistically impossible nor logically untenable. The same holds for the previous observations of which you have a memory.

Our linguistic judgement regarding the trace being associated with a car is only a semantic-intentional counterpart of the statistical-anticipatory model of our memory as a part of our nervous system. It does not give us an epistemic status above our inferential retrodiction regarding what has caused the trace in the snow, nor does it entitle us to believe that the association of the track with a moving car has a more robust probability or an a priori logical necessity. It is not the case that sense$_2$ represents a belief proper as opposed to sense$_1$; its epistemic status is no higher than that of sense$_1$. It is in fact a belief biased by or formed by the structure and anticipatory model of our nervous system. To treat sense$_2$ as a special sort of belief with superior epistemic content is only an instance of linguistic legerdemain. This is not to say that the sensing$_2$ of the trace is not linguistic or conceptual (i.e., a piece of judgement), but rather that its linguistic features should not mask the fact that it is—like the causal sense$_1$—a retrodiction, and not a statistically or a priori logically necessary belief as such.

It then follows that Russell's emphasis on the distinction between the mere causal-statistical impressions of memory-images and justified conceptual beliefs with additional epistemic content turns out to be a feat of semantic dissimulation. The sense$_2$ of the trace is nothing but the linguistically-laden counterpart of the sense$_1$ which is causal and statistically retrodictive in its entirety. In view of the fact that the sense$_2$ is nothing but the linguistic intimation of the retrodictive aspect of the causal sense$_1$ and nothing more, Russell's memory-driven knowledge of the past falls again under the axes of the old and new riddles of induction, and those of his own five minutes ago paradox. The one-to-many (or even many-to-many) correlations between our memory and the rest of the universe make the issues of the unreliability of our memory-driven knowledge of the past and the possibility of the incursion of other causes in forming the track, both statistically probable and logically tenable. It is indeed tempting to dismiss the sceptical hypotheses regarding the memory-driven retrodiction of the past or predictions of the future observations as uninteresting, but interestingness is only a matter of subjective cognitive bias, and is not remotely connected to the interests of what is actually objective.

Returning to our crime thriller example, the objective investigation of the crime scene begins not with the detective linking the trace in the snow with a car's tires based on memory-driven associations in the past, but with the suspension of such cognitive biases. It is only when the detective breaks off from such belief-dispositions or entrenched cognitive biases that she can begin to conduct a true detection of the crime scene, thus cracking open the secrets of the crime scene beyond the level of associations which are no more than the product of an egocentric subject.

Whether the retrodiction of the past is obtained from memory-states themselves or from the inductive generalization of our memories, the knowledge of the low-entropy past hits a brick wall when there is no definitive memory of the past owing to one-to-many or many-to-many (rather than one-to-one) correlations between our memory-states and the states of the universe. Nevertheless, we can reasonably rely on our modest *contextual* theories in which our retrodictions of known past observations can be taken to be similar to our predictions of future observations. But the price to be paid for this bona fide modesty—admitting that we have no definitive memory of the past, and that our knowledge of the known qua observed past can never be overextended to knowledge of the unknown qua unobserved past—is the admission that the entropy gradient can increase or decrease as much toward the past as it can increase or decrease toward the future. The probability and logical tenability of both scenarios enjoy an equal rank.

One can always attempt to quash the logical tenability of the riddles of induction or, in the case of the five minutes ago paradox, resort to the epistemological reliability of the principle of simplicity. But to make a wholesale appeal to the epistemological reliability of successful observations through an argument from the standpoint of the principle of simplicity is like wielding a wooden club and claiming it is Occam's razor. For the principle of simplicity is only a pragmatically and contextually effective tool. It is neither truth-indicative nor is it a law indexing an inherent simplicity in the world that can be invoked in every context. Following Grünbaum, if simplicity or elegance were the best explanations in the toolbox of knowledge, then we should have all abandoned the Darwinian worldview in favour of the theistic one, for the latter boasts a far more elegant simplicity.[164]

---

164 A. Grünbaum, 'Is Simplicity Evidence of Truth?', *American Philosophical Quarterly* 45:2 (2008), 179–89.

The same goes for the defence of successful observations put forward through the reliability of our commonsense evolutionarily-afforded inductive methods.[165] But this Putnamian resolution, just like Hume's, simply defers the problem of the inductive reliability of successful empirical observations to a lower level, sweeping it under the carpet of evolution. To trust evolution in order to trust our ordinary inductive capacities so as to then trust the legitimacy of our epistemic inquiries is only an act of faith in the blind god of evolution, whose gift of inductive reliability should not be mistaken for a supposed epistemic birthright. Evolution may be reliable in its own terms, but its reliable efficacy does not so obviously translate into the reliability of *our* inductive predictions and retrodictions. Nor, every time we are confronted with a daunting problem, can we invoke the *principle of evolutionary credulity*, claiming that, just because we believe we cannot solve a question of an epistemic right on which we so firmly rely, we must presume that evolution should be declared as the source of that legitimacy.

Distilling the superacid of epistemological scepticism is essential for rescuing the legitimacy of our knowledge and the coherency of critical realism. Epistemology without scepticism—*skeptikós* as the toil of investigation—about the conditions of epistemic possibility is predisposed to dogmatism, and scepticism without the rational ambitions of epistemic inquiry is doubt as debilitation. Yet sceptical investigation should be understood as a series of tasks to be performed one at a time, not an uncritical greedy scepticism assaulting the totality of knowledge and the logico-semantic conditions of judgements en masse. This is not scepticism but a pathological distrust—an all-encompassing paranoia—that is incapable of sustaining even itself. As Plato demonstrates in *Meno*, there is no knowledge without doubt, and no doubt without knowledge. The greedy sceptic assumes that what he endorses is only *not q*, not knowing that what he truly endorses is the implicit belief that *it is the case that p therefore not q*, i.e., a piece of knowledge. On the other hand, the genuine

---

165 H. Putnam, 'Degree of Confirmation and Inductive Logic', in *The Philosophy of Rudolf Carnap* (La Salle, IL: Open Court, 1963), 761–83.

systematic sceptic asks *why is it that p therefore q or not q*. The former is the unconscious consumer of knowledge, while the latter is the self-consciousness producer of knowledge.

WHAT NOW?

Let us now reformulate Boltzmann's challenge with regard to the question of time in a traditional philosophical frame: It would be that the genuine problem is not really about the enigmas of the Heraclitean flux—the quandaries of becoming, recurrence, or the puzzles of absolute contingency (every law is susceptible to change within time). It is rather the question of why there is often an element of time-asymmetry—whether disguised in the form of punctual sequential series or duration—in our philosophical reflections about events and processes that make up the pictures of the world and of ourselves. As Smart and Reichenbach have observed, only *things* become, not *events* of time. Events happen, and what happens or occurs can be always made tenseless.[166] Events change, but change is not a becoming. 'Event *e* happened' means that *e* is earlier than this utterance, '*e* is happening now' means *e* is simultaneous to this utterance, and '*e* will happen' means that *e* is later than this utterance qua token. This is what Reichenbach calls token-reflexivity,[167] and at the level of token-reflexivity there is no implied or essential time-asymmetry.

Arguments via the specious present or Husserlian retention-protention cannot faithfully answer this question either, nor can they corroborate the component of time-asymmetry even within subjective time. For even though, in our consciousness, *now* as a matter of fact shifts since there is a diversity of now-contents, and now-contents enjoy a temporal order, it would be dubious to draw the conclusion that, just because the now-contents stand in 'earlier-than' and 'later-than' relations to one another, this means that the now moves from earlier to later. Moreover, the mere diversity of now-contents does not in itself supply synthetic content to the

---

166 J.J.C. Smart, *Problems of Space and Time* (New York: Macmillan, 1964).

167 H. Reichenbach, *Elements of Symbolic Logic* (New York: Macmillan, 1947).

claim that time flows or shifts from the earlier to the later. In this regard, even phenomenological time-consciousness or subjective time appears to be time-asymmetric only *psychologically*. In Grünbaum's words, the time-asymmetry of phenomenological time can be said to be 'psychologically *ad hoc*'.[168]

Moreover, the idea of melody or durational awareness cannot even be deduced from a possible isomorphy between the succession of cerebral traces (or memory traces, as for example in analogy with time-tagged marks on a tape recorder) and the succession of states of awareness. All that is implied by such physicalist isomorphy between brain traces and states of awareness is the succession of awarenesses, not our instantaneous awareness of the succession as a distinct element. As we saw in the previous chapter, per Kant, the sequence of representations of items or the representation of representations is not the same as the representation of the sequence. We can employ this argument here as well: no amount of successive states of awareness can yield something like the instantaneous awareness of the succession which is the meaning of the transient now as the unit of time-consciousness qua temporal flux.

Thus if the diversity of now-contents does not by itself corroborate the unidirectional flow of time, and if what demarcates the distinction between past and future—in contrast to merely successive earlier-thans and later-thans—is really the transience of the specious present (where the sequence appears to be running in one particular direction), then exposing the consciousness of now as a psychologistic conception amounts to revealing that temporal becoming is, in its entirety, a psychological impression at worst, and a necessary pragmatic representation at best. Therefore, far from being an index of reality independent of conceptual mind or even empirical consciousness, the flux of becoming is a register of a purely perspectival awareness: the coming to be or ceasing to be of an event is nothing other than the entrance or departure of an effect to or from the immediate awareness of the organism or the human observer who experiences the course of events.

---

168 Grünbaum, *Philosophical Problems of Space and Time*.

It may be argued that 'the awareness of changes in present-tense conscious-ness engenders the experience of temporal becoming'[169]—adding that 'as events or moments become successively present, then past, a direction of time inevitability arises in experience'.[170] The first part of this argument can be countered with a question: How or whence exactly does the succession of awarenesses (the mere sequences of earlier-thans and later-thans) acquire its synthetic content with respect to the flow of becoming? As argued, by itself the succession cannot supply the synthetic content that time flows from the earlier-than to the later-than. In response to the second part of this argument, it should be pointed out that the idea that the frequency of successive awarenesses of events in the world can either corroborate temporal becoming or give rise to the perception of temporal flux is an unwarranted inductive thesis, if not a fallacy.[171]

Furthermore, the claim that the frequency of successive awarenesses inevitably generates the instantaneous awareness or the perception of the flux of becoming, precipitates a far more serious problem. If the frequency of successive awarenesses are by themselves sufficient to give rise to the consciousness of temporal flux in experience, then it means that the subject of experience is no more than a Humean bundle of sense impressions. This is self as a mere aggregate of states or perceptions in the specific Humean sense where perceptions are either prior in the order of knowing to the apperceptive self, or lack any apperceptive unity and hence are nothing but the relations between things-in-themselves.

If self is *only* a bundle of impressions or awarenesses$_1$, then the whole array of references to the subject and the concept of experience becomes redundant. Even an inorganic tape recorder can mark and preserve the recording of events in a successive manner—but it would be rather con-tentious to claim that the tape recorder has subjectivity, experience, or consciousness of the temporal flux. But as Kant argued, against Hume,

---

169 W.L. Craig, *The Tenseless Theory of Time: A Critical Examination* (Dordrecht: Springer, 2000), 172.

170 Ibid.

171 See Appendix.

the apperceptive self is not merely a bundle of successive impressions. Impressions are organized and integrated by rules which are not *derived* from experience (with the emphasis on *derived* rather than *experience*).

Moreover (adopting and modifying McTaggart's argument on the Humean bundle),[172] in the absence of apperceptive unity as the principle of experiential unification, every bundle qua self can be arranged into infinitely many bundles qua selves. Thus, a Humean self as a bundle is in fact a collection or a multitude of selves qua bundles. Therefore, the accurate term would be Humean *selves* rather than self—a collection of bundles which may be different or same selves. At the level of a potentially infinite collection of pure bundles, there are no such relations between impressions as spatial and temporal relations (even apparent ones), causal connections, familiarity-unfamiliarity, similarity-dissimilarity, qualitative intensity relations, relations between knowledge of states, or even relations between so-called Humean perceptions. At this level, any two states—for example, ψ_1*-more familiar* and ψ_2*-less familiar*—can form a group.[173] There can be infinitely many groups each of which can take ψ_1 and ψ_2 as a member, but by no means does every group form a bundle since not only can group ψ_n belong to different bundles qua selves, but ψ_1*-more familiar* of bundle$_1$ and ψ_2*-more familiar* of the bundle$_2$ can also form a group. Consequently, in the pure bundle-view of the self, any two states can form a group, but there is no nonarbitrary way to distinguish those groups that are bundles and thus exhibit some uniformity of awarenesses, from those which do not.

At this point in the argument, we could adopt a Kantian position and claim that the transition from a sequence of awarenesses of events to the instantaneous awareness of the sequence is the result of the application of a pure concept to the sequences of impressions. That is to say, the instantaneous awareness$_2$ of now, or the element of temporal flux in experience, is not something that has been derived from a mere sequence of successive awarenesses$_1$, but something that has been generated through the application

---

172 McTaggart, *The Nature of Existence*, vol. 2, §389.

173 For an elaboration on the concept of group vs. class as characterized by common qualities, see McTaggart, *The Nature of Existence*, vol. 1, §120–24.

of a rule. This, however, raises a different question: Where does this a priori rule come from, what is its source?

If the rule is taken to be purely logical, then one is faced with the challenge of resolving the incompatibility of the analytic rule with the synthetic content that the instantaneous awareness of the transient now harbours. As argued above, the temporal flux is essentially endowed with a synthetic content, or in other words, requires an ampliative judgement whose premises are diverse now-contents. But if the rule is taken to be synthetic, then its ultimate source would lie in the apperceptive unity of the experiencing subject—that is to say, the principle of experiential unification. In this case, the transition from successive awarenesses to the awareness of succession does not commit us to a metaphysical claim regarding the objective reality of the temporal flux, but only to the transcendental ideality of becoming as something that plays a necessary pragmatic role in the agent's objective description of events and items in the world.

This is not say that we ought to forego all metaphysical claims—in this case, the metaphysical account of time. The point is not to be quietist when it comes to metaphysics. For it is precisely once we presume that we have purged ourselves of metaphysical assumptions, that we become susceptible to the most dogmatic and veiled forms of metaphysics. The fanatic Kantian critical crusade against metaphysics only leads to an illusory disillusionment as one ends up with a stock of unexamined and unacknowledged metaphysical assumptions. In contrast to this approach, in the vein of Plato and Hegel, the aim is to be concretely self-conscious with respect to metaphysics and indeed strive to develop a robust metaphysics—in this case, a robust metaphysics of time. For a metaphysical system to be identified as robust, it should: (1) be open to systematic *theoretical* assessment in the sense of the qualifier defined in chapter 1; (2) proceed via the dimension of *conceptualization* of structure rather than via the positing of an account of reality deemed to be *already structured* independently of mind; (3) suspend the prima facie correspondence between the dimensions of reality and the characteristics which our experiences of the world prima facie appear to have; (4) develop a notion of mind, Idea, or geist whose finitude is suspended since it is sufficiently differentiated from life (*bios*) or the natural (which is finite in so far as it is subject to temporal time). The true object of such a metaphysics is the infinite and thus the atemporal. In the sense of (4), metaphysics is developed through a conception of reason that accepts the identity of opposites—i.e., thought and being, subject and object, finite and infinite—while suspending understanding, which is applied to immediate experience and which can only perspectivally grasp time as a temporal succession. In this regard, metaphysics coincides with the systematic apprehension of infinity. But this is a concept of the infinite that is not conditioned on the humiliation or abstract negation of the finite such as, for example, the finitude of the human, in so far as it has sufficiently wrested the concept of the human, geist, or mind from the temporal order of things. Nor is it a concept of the infinite that leads to cosmological antinomies whose resolution would require a Kantian distinction between appearances and things-in-themselves, with the latter being itself a dogmatic—or more precisely, non-robust—metaphysical posit.

METAPHYSICS OF TIME AS LOGIC OF SPIRIT

Metaphysics properly understood is the apprehension of the infinite without any of the static or fixed contradictions that arise from the limitations of the features of our experience or understanding which, in contrast to reason, can neither accept the identity of opposites nor forgo the representation of the Absolute or unconditioned. However, the apprehension of the infinite without contradictions does not mean it is free from *all* contradictions. There are different kinds of contradictions, and the apprehension of the infinite is only free from fixed antinomic contradictions in the sense that lower-level contradictions are suspended in higher ones so that, at each subsequent level, the lower-level contradictions are avoided. Said differently, as opposed to fixed contradiction, the dynamic movement of contradictions—their suspension—is intrinsic to the apprehension of the infinite as the true object of metaphysics. What are cancelled are not contradictions per se but fixed antinomic contradictions at certain levels of discourse. Accordingly, metaphysics is indissociable from the dialectical movement of concepts, or, more succinctly, metaphysics and speculative logic coincide.

Not logic in the sense of the ordinary logic abstracted from content or a *general grammar* qua method pertaining to the forms of thought, but logic as the Idea, which is to say thought's own 'self-developing totality of its distinctive determinations and laws, which it gives itself and does not already have and find within itself'.[174]

In this respect, Hegel's conception of time qualifies not only as a robust metaphysics of time but also as a fundamental element of metaphysics as such, since it rescues the thought of the infinite from fixed contradictions, and from pernicious attempts at resolving these contradictions, such as Kant's positing of the thing-in-itself—a veiled metaphysical postulate that is dubiously outside of the dimension of conceptualization, and as such constitutes a precritical moment upon which Kant's so-called critical resolution to the antinomies blindly thrives. Hegel develops his conception of time out of his criticism of Kant's formulation and subsequent resolution of cosmological antinomies, particularly the first antinomy pertaining to the physical dimensions of the universe, viz. whether the physical universe is temporally and spatially finite or not. Reed Winegar has provided a lucid and brief exposition of Kant's first antinomy, and specifically its temporal implication:

> If we consider the current state of the world, then the principle of reason requires that we infer the existence of all of the prior temporal states of the world that condition its current state. In other words, the principle of reason requires the existence of the world as a whole. Kant notes that this world-whole might take either of two different forms. First, the series of past temporal states might terminate in an initial temporal state, i.e., a beginning of the world in time. Second, the series might constitute an actual infinite series of past temporal states of the world. Kant believes that indirect arguments can be given in favour of both

---

174 G.W.F. Hegel, *Encyclopedia of the Philosophical Sciences in Basic Outline Part I: Science of Logic*, tr. K. Brinkmann, D.O. Dahlstrom (Cambridge: Cambridge University Press, 2010), §19.

options, which yields the contradictory result that the world both has a beginning in time but also lacks a beginning in time.[175]

In the context of his theory of time, Hegel argues that Kant's first antinomy arises and is subsequently resolved by the categories of the understanding— a mode of thought that, in contrast to reason, does not accept the identity of opposites and is bound to the transcendental subject of experience. In attempting to apprehend the infinite and to know the Absolute, the understanding rejects the identity of opposites, but at the same time implicitly acknowledges the Absolute as the identity of opposites (subject and object, finite and infinite). This tension between the explicit rejection of the identity of opposites and its tacit acceptance forces the understanding to see the Absolute not as the eternal (i.e., outside of temporal time) but as an antinomic series of successive series of past temporal states which only perpetuates an indefinite regress. Every beginning for the world requires a regress to an older beginning. Since understanding operates within the bounds of finitude, in attempting to know the Absolute it mischaracterizes the Absolute as a successive series of past temporal events, precipitating the antinomic result that the world can both have and not have a beginning in time.

Whenever understanding attempts to know the Absolute, it chooses to conserve its limitations, which distort the thought of the Absolute, rather than acknowledging its own limitations and terminating itself. It fuses or collapses the distinction between the identity of subject and object $(A = A)$ and the difference between subject and object $(A \neq A)$. Only when the destruction of understanding is recognized as an enabling condition for thinking the Absolute as the identity of subject and object can the simple or static contradiction (the Kantian antinomy) be recognised as a pseudo-problem. But the destruction of the understanding demands its replacement by reason as a mode of thinking that accepts the identity of

---

175 R. Winegar, 'To Suspend Finitude Itself: Hegel's Reaction to Kant's First Antinomy', *Hegel Bulletin* 37:1 (2016), 81–103.

opposites and is thus capable of thinking the Absolute without generating static contradictions or antinomies.

The conception of time as the eternal is but the identity of subject and object, finite and infinite qua the Absolute. This conception is the very essence of reason as that which is able to suspend finitude and thereby avoid static contradictions in favour of dynamic contradictions which are intrinsic to the apprehension of the infinite. Whereas the understanding is bound to the forms of finitude (cause and effect, succession, etc.), reason suspends finitude in order to arrive at knowledge of Absolute Idea. This suspension is nothing other than the adoption of a resolutely atemporal viewpoint. We can therefore conclude that only such an atemporal thought can arrive at the truth of geistig intelligence, for, in adopting a resolutely atemporal viewpoint, reason relinquishes the power of time over its Idea. The truth of what mind is cannot be found within time, since it is the very truth of time as such. The mind is not in time, it is itself time:

> The Notion however, in its freely existing identity with itself, as ego=ego, is in and for itself absolute negativity and freedom, and is consequently, not only free from the power of time, but is neither within time, nor something temporal. It can be said on the contrary that it is the Notion which constitutes the power of time, for time is nothing but this negation as externality. Only that which is natural, in that it is finite, is subject to time; that which is true however, the Idea, spirit, is eternal.[176]

It would be a mistake to consider the history of geist as a sequence of self-conceptions and self-transformations that happens *in* time. It is history as time, but not history as a temporal development. Thus, construing the so-called progress of geist in terms of intuitive notions of temporal development, as is the case with Whig historiographical interpretations of Spirit (for which Hegel himself is partly responsible) is a retrogressive move. It is retrogressive because it once again demotes the Idea of mind to forms of finitude such as succession. History as the self-actualization

---

176 Ibid., 231.

of the Concept is the Idea's own time—a time that is neither opposed to another time, nor is an abstraction of time, nor a time outside of time, but is the eternal or time as such.

The totality of the Idea of mind cannot be represented temporally, for such a totality will be mistakenly apprehended as the totality of the state of affairs in the past, present, or future. But a totality that is understood temporally is simply a form of finitude that feigns totality and, as such, it is an illusion begotten by a self-limiting thought. Similarly, the idea of the human as a concluded totality given to us here and now as a biological species, and the idea of capitalism as the completed historical totality of all social relations, are posited forms of finitude dissimulating themselves as completed histories. They both distinguish themselves within time as the present/future state of affairs, and present themselves as the totality of all there is and can be. But an extant state of affairs can never *be* a totality, even if it *represents itself* as the totality of the present/future.

In view of the arguments made above, images of time as an endless flow that underlines the insignificance of the human and its paltry concerns turn out to be antihumanist veneers upon a subjectivist account of time which, far from breaking from the dogmas of humanism, reinforces a deeply conservative form of humanism. This is a humanism afflicted by a deep-seated transcendental blind spot that not only uncritically posits the local and contingent characteristics of egocentric human experience as the characteristics of reality, but also deems this very anthropomorphic reality—whether under the rubric of preindividual singularities or ceaseless becoming—to be the horizon for overcoming human exceptionalism. Such metaphysical accounts of time champion an infinite which is more pure alterity than the suspension of the finite. As such, they must both leave the finite intact in order to maintain their alterity and debase the finite as that which does not matter in so far as it is perishable. The so-called finite of such images of time is thought, mind, or the human. But any metaphysical conception of the infinite that belittles and discounts the human as finite will be haunted by human pettiness and its associated limitations. It will be doomed to bear the marks of exactly that which it seeks to steer clear of.

Following Parmenides, Plato, and Hegel among others, not only philosophical maturity but also the maturity of the human coincides with a liberation from the servitude to time, the realization that the temporal—whether as a tyrant that devours all or as a dimension of reality *in* which we appear to exist—is not important. As Russell remarks:

> [A] certain emancipation from slavery to time is essential to philosophical thought. The importance of time is practical rather than theoretical, rather in relation to our desires than in relation to truth. [...] Both in thought and in feeling, to realize the unimportance of time is the gate of wisdom. But unimportance is not unreality.[177]

This remark can be complemented by McTaggart's rejoinder to Russell's view:

> This seems to me profoundly true. But the importance of time will be still less, if, as I have maintained, nothing is really *in* time, and the temporal is merely an appearance. And, as the importance of time diminishes, so also diminishes the importance of the cessation of our lives in time.[178]

At this stage in the argument, a more persistent and observant proponent of the flow-image of time who is significantly less invested in antihumanist tendencies might present another clichéd objection by putting forward a variation of the following argument: In a world without the flow of time, there is no becoming. Absent becoming, the existential status of the future as the coming-into-being of events in the world is compromised, since, without becoming, there will be no novel event and no indeterminate future. Without the future as the site of indeterminacy and novelty, there will be no human freedom, no prospects for emancipation. For without becoming, we are living in a wholly deterministic world of *mere* being.

---

177 B. Russell, *Our Knowledge of the External World* (London: Open Court, 1914), 166–7.

178 McTaggart, *The Nature of Existence*, vol. 2, 182 (emphasis mine).

In other words, the metaphysics of becoming reveals a paradoxical dilemma for human action: If there is no coming-into-being, the future is already determined, and therefore the idea that agents can change their world seems to be absurd for there is no real freedom, no chance for novelty and difference. Whereas if there is indeed a coming-into-being of events, then the future is indeterminate since it is the locus of radical novelty, absolute contingency, or the Event—but then our rational planning and anticipatory actions prove to be futile for they fail in the face of its indeterminacy:[179] they cannot in any meaningful sense gain traction on an ontologically indeterminable future or the absolute contingency of time. To this extent, the issue of the temporal flux which is taken to be the essence of time invariably results in a paradox of inaction. Without it, we live in a fully deterministic world which renders our rational plans and actions irrelevant. With it, we live in an indeterministic world in which our rational plans fall flat in meeting their goals since the future as the target site of such plans is radically indeterminable and adverse to our anticipatory actions.

But in fact, whether or not becoming is an aspect of time independent of human consciousness has no bearing upon the issue of determinacy. The question of indeterminism vs. determinism can be formulated as the question of the difference between past and future. In an indeterministic world such a difference exists, whereas in the deterministic world it does not. But, as we saw, the difference between the common-sense past and future—as opposed to the *metric* description of physical events as past and future states—is the *now* of the experiencing ego. Accordingly, the problem of indeterminism or determinism as the difference between past and future or lack thereof is of no relevance to physical events, since such a difference is nothing but an expression of the egocentric consciousness of the human.

As Grünbaum has argued, in both a deterministic world and an indeterministic world, the coming-into-being of a future event or the ceasing-to-be of a past event signifies nothing more than the entrance or departure of

---

179 For an example of an all too predictable exercise in fusing the philosophy of event and that of asymmetrical time-becoming, see J.-J. Lecercle, *Deleuze and Language* (Basingstoke: Palgrave Macmillan, 2002).

its effect into and from the immediate awareness of the apperceptive ego. The difference between these two worlds with regard to future events only concerns 'the type of functional connection linking the attributes of the future events to those of present or past events'.

But this difference does not make for a precipitation of future events into existence in a way in which determinism does not. Nor does indeterminacy make for any difference whatever at any time in regard to the attribute-specificity of the future events themselves. For in either kind of universe, it is a fact of logic that what will be, will be![180]

Furthermore, the objection that resulted in the paradox of inaction is based on the confusion of two entirely separate issues. One is the epistemological issue of sifting the actual properties of events in the future from a larger set of possible properties. Per Grünbaum, we call this the issue of the 'epistemological precipitation' of events and their properties into our awareness.[181] This is to be distinguished from existential precipitation, i.e., their coming-into-being or realization. Epistemological precipitation is certainly influenced by the passage of time 'through the transformation of a statistical expectation into a definite piece of information'.[182] However, this does not mean that there is only existential precipitation with the passage of time in an indeterministic world, or that there is no epistemological precipitation with the passage of time in a deterministic world.

Finally, the objection that in a deterministic world there is no real freedom rests upon a muddled account of causation. If a system is caused to be in one state rather than another, this does not mean that the system's trajectory is *compelled* by this cause. Similarly, if future states are caused by past states, this does not mean that the future state is *compelled* by the past state. It only means that the past states have causally contributed to such

---

180 Grünbaum, *Philosophical Problems of Space and Time*, 324.

181 Ibid.

182 Ibid.

future states. In other words, determination in this sense is about being caused, but being caused does not mean being compelled by the cause, i.e., determinism as some sort of causal compulsion. Let me elaborate on this point a bit further. It is true that, in order for a system to be in the state it is in, it must have—by physical necessity—followed on from an antecedent state. The system could not come to be in its subsequent state were it not for an antecedent state. But this is not the same as saying that the current state of the system is caused by a foreign cause. Certainly, the present state of the system is the physical consequence of things done to it, i.e., the history of its past interactions; but this, as Sellars points out, does not mean 'that the explanation of the present state of such a system lies entirely in "other things"'.[183] The idea that causal determinism—as distinguished from logical determinism, which is a different issue—implies lack of freedom, is the result of a misunderstanding of what causal determination means—that is, it is a result of interpreting causation as *being under the compulsion of a cause.*

For example, I hate the colour red because in the past I have witnessed a murder scene full of blood. Firstly, as argued earlier via Stegmüller, the belief-laden emotion that the state Hate (*red item*) is caused by such-and-such factors in the past is a psychological account of cause and effect, since there may be many factors not available to my awareness which could have brought up the state Hate (*red item*). This is not to say that there is no connection between my emotion or belief and the past trauma, but that such a connection cannot be defined in terms of singular cause and effect since this schema of causation is psychological rather than scientific. Even if we lend some credence to this prescientific schema of causation, having the emotion Hate (*red item*) does not suggest that an antecedent traumatic scene has compelled me to have such emotion qua belief as opposed to other emotions qua beliefs. All it implies is that there is a certain causal contribution in my having such emotion qua belief.

In other words, Hate (*red item*) may indeed be a reliable belief in so far as it has been constrained by a certain causal factor in the past, and that may be why I have Hate (*red item*) and not Love (*blue items*) or Hate

---

183 Sellars, *In the Space of Reasons*, 426.

(*liquid items*). Put differently, all causal determinism implies is that our beliefs about the state of affairs *may* be reliable to the extent that there is a component of causal efficacy that has determined them or, in other words, they are constrained by some definitive causal factors. However, it does not imply that we are under the compulsion of such causes. When I come to assert 'this is an emerald', it is because my belief is constrained by the presence of hard green stuff (the causal factor). I may indeed be wrong, for the item in question might not be an emerald, nor green, nor a stone. But any counter-assertion to my claim equally relies at a basic level on a belief that is causally constrained. Without such a causal constraint, every belief about this hard green stuff could be true, which is another way of saying that no such claims are true. Causal determination is what undergirds the reliability of our claims or beliefs and, correspondingly, our freedom to retrospectively correct them—for example, from 'this is an emerald' to 'this is well-watered grass' or 'this is a yellowish goo'. Without causal determinism, there is no way to determine whether our beliefs about the world are true or not. That is to say, without causal determinism, we can never tell whether our beliefs are arbitrary or not. The assertion that causal determinism denies freedom of thought or action is based not only on a prescientific account of causation but also on a conflation of causal contribution with causal compulsion.

TIME, REALITY, AND THE VIEW FROM NOWHEN

Coming back to Boltzmann's challenge to the temporal perspective, the still pressing question is that of the extent to which these alleged time-asymmetric elements in our time-consciousness have stretched over and biased the matter-of-factual characteristics of reality. When characteristics of reality happen to share or match the contingent characteristics of local experience, one ought to question them rather than taking them for granted. In line with the total assault of scientific investigation and critical rationality on our most well-cherished and established intuitions, why should we expect the characteristics of reality to be a trivial extension of characteristics specific to the temporal-causal perspective of the subject?

Why not instead investigate alternative models, which may have been rejected on the basis of not looking natural *from the perspective of our time-asymmetric assumptions and experience*—models which, while compatible with local temporal and causal perspectives, do not privilege one perspective over another? These are models that should allow for an enlargement of the field of experience and observation without denying the temporal experiences accessible to us or some other contingently posited local observer/subject. The local-global nontriviality of reality means that localities of this reality stand in nontrivial projective relations to one another, not that the nontrivial total space of reality trivializes the localities of experience or that it is constructed by something other than what is local in this total space. This is much more in tune with a pragmatist account of the time-conscious agent for which anthropocentricism in the use of temporal *concepts* is justified and even pragmatically necessary, so long as there is no metaphysical reification of these concepts as global characteristics of objective reality.

To summarize, the pragmatist view of time-conscious agency should be consistent with a model of time which, while refusing to characterize it as temporally unique, admits the local consistency of any possible model of experienced temporality and causal perspective such as ours, and hence in an *oblique* way justifies the use of temporal concepts. In other words, a robust model of time should be an expression of a reality that constitutes local temporal perspectives without being reducible to them. Thus, reencountered within this model, our temporal perspective should be seen as a local self-expression of an absolute (atemporal) reality, rather than being dismissed as a complete illusion.

Liberation from a model of time restricted to a particular contingent constitution does not rob the subject of its cognitive and practical abilities, but releases it from the shackles of its most entrenched dogmas about the necessity of the contingent features of its experience. In doing so, it sheds light on the prospects of what the subject of experience and the exercise of change in the world is and can be as it cognitively matures. The transition to a state where one is no longer afraid of being lost in time, having come to the realization that time accommodates no one, should be celebrated as the sign of rational maturity, rather than decried as a manifestation of the subject's impotency. It is in continuity with the critical attitude of rational agency to adopt a model of experience that can interrogate the most natural and established 'facts of experience' rather than corroborating them via the so-called fact that these are simply the ways in which we experience the world. As the extension of this interrogation, such a model should also enlarge the field of our experience, and in doing so, should theoretically and practically challenge popular yet puerile ideologies built around either a temporal account of progress or the second law of thermodynamics.

Regardless of whether Boltzmann's challenge as presented here requires extensive refinement or not, it can be seen as a Hegelian radicalization of Kant's thesis on the transcendental ideality of experienced temporality. It is a radicalization in the sense that it is both an *exacerbation* and an *extension* of the implications of Kant's thesis. It is in line with this philosophical viewpoint, and in tandem with his strategy to eliminate or at least mitigate the fundamental biases of the directional-dynamic picture of time within modern physical sciences, that Boltzmann begins to explore the ramifications of adopting an atemporal perspective. But the fallout of Boltzmann's 'time bomb'[184] is not limited to the modern sciences; its implications reach as far as philosophical, scientific, and sociopolitical ideologies built around the concept of entropy, or more precisely, positive entropy production.

Having cursorily glanced over the far-reaching implications of Boltzmann's radicalization of Kant's thesis on the transcendental ideality of time qua experienced temporality, we are now faced with three challenges, the responses to which will shape the project of maintaining and expanding the intelligibility of agency:

---

184 H. Price, 'Boltzmann's Time Bomb', *British Journal for the Philosophy of Science* 53:1 (2002), 83–119. Only recently has the philosophical significance of Boltzmann's scientific and philosophical challenge, and the revisionary insinuations of a coherent commitment to an atemporal perspective for our most treasured temporal models of description, prediction, action, and change been deservedly examined and elaborated, most notably in the works of Huw Price, Adam Berg, Jos Uffink, Meir Hemmo, and Orly Shenker.

(1) How can we envision models of agency that might have fundamentally different senses of time by virtue of enjoying different local conditions of observation, possessing different structural-behavioural organizations (i.e., different modes of responsiveness to the impingement of items in the world on their senses and different constructive-anticipatory models of memory) or, on the conceptual level of time-consciousness, having different logical connections between temporal connectives of language or different structures of tensed verbs? A different experienced time-order here should not be construed as an index of difference for the sake of difference. It is different only in that it should enlarge the field of experience, and thereby enable the vector of cognitive discovery both at the level of theory and that of practice. This is as much a challenge to think agency beyond a particular set of contingencies as it is a research question for envisioning an artificial model of agency not essentially bound by our local limits.

(2) Could there be models of time that are compatible with the subject-observer's temporal-causal perspective while not privileging or over-stretching this local perspective into a canonical global model? How can we lay out *a physics of our temporal-causal perspective* that *explains* its characteristics without reinscribing the same perspectival characteristics as features of objective reality, and thus positing them as explanans of what is already an explanandum? To this extent, the second challenge is concerned with a systematic inquiry into models of time and time-consciousness that can (a) account for the characteristics of our temporally oriented perspective, and (b) resolve the problems within the directional-dynamic picture of time—namely, the quandaries and paradoxes (from enigmas of change and temporal asymmetry to paradoxes of causality such as retrocausality) that originate from the inadequate descriptive-explanatory resources of the directional-dynamic model of time to which we are so unconsciously accustomed.

(3) In line with the first and the second challenges, the third challenge centres on the problem of reconciling the pragmatic import of our

temporal view with a model of time-conscious experience that is neither necessarily directional nor dynamic, which neither pictures time as a flux nor takes for granted our experience as advancing from the past toward the future. What are the ramifications of a nondirectional/nondynamic model of time-consciousness for our existing theoretical and practical models within not only the physical sciences but also the social sciences? And more importantly, what can be gained, theoretically and practically, by adopting alternative models of time-consciousness, and specifically an atemporal model?

The third challenge is in fact the continuation of rational agency's struggle for self-conception and self-transformation, for a release from any residue of essentialist attachment to a particular transcendental structure of experience. In adopting a view from nowhen[185]—a view that explains any mode of experienced temporality without being circumscribed by their particularities—we embark on a necessary task required for the realization of what Hegel calls Absolute Spirit: moving from particular, contingent consciousness to genuine self-consciousness. The view from the space of reason qua Concept (*Begriff*) is not only a view from nowhere—the impersonality of reason—but also a view from *nowhen*—the pure formlessness of time that is expressed by discursive rationality as *a project that takes time*. As we shall see in the following chapters, this time-generality will take the form of Plato's Ideas: Knowledge, Truth, Beauty and above all, the Good. History is an ongoing process of totalization under the aegis of the Concept; and the form of the Concept (not its content) is atemporal, if not timeless. Directionally temporalized history represents the ultimate limitation imposed by intuitions, or the fundamentalist attachment to a locally constituted experience over the form of the Concept and thus that of history. Once we unconditionally cast off this forced limitation step-by-step,

---

185 'The campaign for a view from nowhen is a campaign for self-improvement, then, and not a misguided attempt to do the impossible, to become something that we can never be. It promises only to enhance *our* understanding of ourselves and our world, and not to make us gods.' Price, *Time's Arrow and Archimedes' Point*, 267.

dismantle this cursed raft plank-by-plank, history transforms into a medium for the expression of time as the formlessness that conditions any possible form. We have tried to understand and make sense of the world in which we acquire a perspective on ourselves, the meaning of mind, and intelligence, by analysing it internally. But maybe the best solution is to go entirely outside of this world and analyse it from a viewpoint that is both possible and fecund with further possibilities. And yet for this transition to the *outside view* from nowhere and nowhen to be concrete, we must grasp it as a circuitous path of arduous task upon task. This adventurous yet demanding *umwege* is the course of the critique of transcendental structures, spanning different methods and frameworks of theory and practice, from science to technology, art, general pedagogy, politics, and so on. It would be pitifully naïve to think that we can liberate intelligence by means of technoscience alone without changing what and how we think about who we are, and correlatively what we think of, in comparison to ourselves, as intelligent. Changing the latter is a question of attaining a veritable self-consciousness of who we are and what we ought to do. And this change comes at a price which is the complete alienation of the human in itself: that we will never settle, we will never mistake anything for our home, for we have come to the understanding that the very vector of alienation—exodus between possible worlds—is actually our home and the source of what is good and satisfying. It would be equally credulous to believe that, in the course of such an enterprise, we will be able to maintain the conception of the human rooted in how we *experience* ourselves here and now. As the *umwegen* to the outside view of ourselves revises the very experience of who we think we are, we become that which no longer experiences itself in terms of what we experience ourselves as in this very moment. For an intelligence with a larger field of experience than ours, what the human means or what the appellation 'we' stands for no longer abides by the terms of our epochal particular field of experience. We become only an ante-cedent condition to what is *necessarily* us—that is, the *form* of the us, which is neither a transitory content nor an ephemeral particular object. Ultimately, genuine self-consciousness turns out to be the view of ourselves from nowhen. And the world conceived concretely from a view that is of nowhere and nowhen is a world that at once is replete with possibilities and is possible, one whose possibility is no less actual than the actuality of the inhabitable world we currently inhabit. The actuality of our world is merely an abstractly determined absolute (a sedimented totality that feigns completion of the Absolute), but the actuality of possible worlds conceived from nowhen and nowhere is the Absolute as the concretely determined, never given in what appears to us in time but procured through the cunning plot of history to explore the meanings of time. From a Kantian perspective, in taking up the third of the challenges outlined above, we come closer to fulfilling the central goal of critical philosophy—that is, demonstrating the mutuality of the rational self (discursive apperceptive intelligence) and the world without eliding the distinction between the thinking of the former and the being of the latter.[186]

---

186 Jay Rosenberg introduces Kant's mutuality thesis as follows: 'The same activities of synthesis which constitute the represented world as an intelligible objective unity constitute the representing self as an apperceptive subjective unity.' Rosenberg, *The Thinking Self*, 6.

5. This I, or We or It, the Thing, Which Speaks (Objectivity and Thought)

Our toy model automaton is now equipped with a spatially and temporally perspectival awareness. In other words, it has developed the capacity to handle space and time, the Objects (*objekt*) required for the rudimentary organization of an encountered item (an appearance) in the world—that is, an object (*gegenstand*) as distinguished from other items. However, at this point, both *objekt* and *gegenstand* are mere analogical correlates of our objects of thought (*Objekte*) and categorically determined sensible objects (*Gegenstände*). They are neither objective (factual or inter-subjective) nor subjective (in the full-blooded sense of the subject as one who is in a position to make veridical claims or critical judgements, rather than a thin notion of subject as that which, de facto—under the rudimentary transition laws of imagination—is able to discern uncritically empirical associations in the order of appearances). The achievement of subjective and objective thoughts requires that the automaton advance from rudimentary capacities (abilities$_1$) to advanced abilities (abilities$_2$). To enable it to do so, we must equip our automaton with a new structure—not a structure that belongs to the automaton itself, but one it is plugged into or bound up with, namely the structure of a community: a multi-agent system such as a framework in which multiple information processing systems are constrained by their dynamic or concurrent interaction with one another (i.e., every system is the environment of the other systems). We must therefore introduce two modifications to our picture. The first modification is simply necessary whereas the second, although in essence necessary, could be introduced in forms other than that depicted in our toy universe:

- The automaton is now a part of a multi-agent system comprised of automata with a differential responsiveness to the items in the world.

In its most basic configuration, the multi-agent system is designed to enable interaction between automata/agents as a way of increasing the probability of goal-attainment. This multi-agent system is then introduced into a specific environment wherein agents have to interact not only with one another, but also with the features of this environment. Inter-agent interaction is, accordingly, coupled with the dynamic inputs and constraints of the resulting ecology.

- The automaton is now furnished with built-in electromechanical devices whose coordination results in the production of quasi-continuous sounds. These quasi-continuous sounds are the primary means of communication between automata. In an alternative toy universe, this feature could be implemented in different ways that might not necessarily involve sound. However, insofar as this is a component of *our* particular toy universe, we have to abide by its characteristics and constraints.

Chapter 2 ended with the automaton endowed with the capacity of meta-awareness, or the causal analogue of inner sense or inner perception—the capacity of the mind to be affected inwardly and passively by its own thought-episodes, to report representations of items and occurrences in the world to the mind as temporally organized rudimentary *re*-presentations which are the mind's own presentations. But the automaton's inner sense was merely de facto. In other words, the automaton wasn't aware of these occurrences *as* its own, nor did it have thoughts in any meaningful sense. Indeed, even if this inner sense was not causal, even if the automaton did actually have thought-episodes at this level, the passive capacity of inner sense could not (pace Descartes) supply the automaton with the synthetic awareness that these inner thought-episodes or meta-awarenesses are *its own*. As we cursorily surveyed in chapter 2, such meta-awareness requires the active power of apperception rather than just the passive faculty of inner sense. Only when the passivity of its inner sense is brought under the apperceptive I as an active logical form (rather than, as in Descartes, a substance) can the automaton have anything resembling thoughts in even the minimal sense.

The apperceptive I is synchronically attached to all instances of representations (I think X, I think Y, I think Z) and diachronically extends over all thoughts (I think $[X + Y + Z]$). But if we are to build this synthetic apperceptive I as a necessary abstract and logical form, we have no choice but to finally depart from Kant's account of the apperceptive self—which Hegel reproaches for being an *empty* transcendental subjectivity—and to instead adopt a resolutely Hegelian approach: the apperceptive self is only a cognitive self in so far as it is part of geist. An individual is only an individual to the extent that it is individuated by social recognition, which is the form of self-consciousness. This logical self is at once one and many—and, as if to prove this, it can only be constructed, as we shall see, by way of a confrontation with another I^*.[187]

To recapitulate, our aim is to elevate the automaton from being an agent that de facto possesses the meta-awarenesses of inner sense to one that is inferentially—synchronically and diachronically—aware of having meta-awarenesses; from representations that are only causally and passively 'its own' to an I—a logical form—that actively accompanies and integrates such representations *as* its presentations. In short, the goal is to bring the automaton to a state where it not only has experiences and thought-episodes, but where such experiences and thoughts are de jure and by entitlement its own. The modifications we have made to the automaton are precisely the kinds of adjustments that will enable the automaton to make this transition.

Since our automaton is now part of a multi-agent system, for the sake of efficiently tracking its course of development we can designate it with a

---

187 'Are you one self or many selves? [...] I immediately developed the second mechanism of proving my individuality: opposition to someone else's idea.' (V. Savchenko, *Self-discovery* [New York: MacMillan, 1980], ix, 13). From the seventies to the eighties, Soviet science fiction was a hybrid of German Idealism, cybernetics, and artificial general intelligence as a geistig multi-agent system. The most prominent exponents of this current are Vladimir Ivanovich Savchenko (*Self-discovery*) and Mikhail Tikhonovich Emtsev (*World Soul* [New York: MacMillan, 1978]). For a nonfictional take on the philosophical, scientific, and political commitments of this period see F. Mikhailov, *The Riddle of the Self* (Moscow: Progress Publishers, 1976).

proper name: Kanzi.[188] As a part of our multi-agent modification, we will also introduce two other automata and assign them proper names: Sue and Matata. Sue and Matata differ from Kanzi in that they are sapient automata that have mastered the use of language. In a nutshell, they are fully fledged concept-using adult guardians of Kanzi. In this configuration, Sue and Matata recognize and nurture Kanzi as what Rosenberg terms a CHILD (Concept Having Intelligence of Low Degree).[189] As a CHILD, Kanzi also has a universe of its own, an INFANTILE-World (INtelligible Familiar Appearance Naively Taken In Lieu of the External World). Let us denote Kanzi and its adult guardians respectively as $\mathbb{K}$, $\mathbb{S}$, and $\mathbb{M}$.

We now have the necessary resources to follow Rosenberg's Kant-Sellars inspired model of the transition from inner sense meta-awarenesses to thought-episodes—or from an automaton with pure perspectival awareness to a child automaton. $\mathbb{K}$ is endowed with behavioural dispositions. It has memories, interests, and anticipatory models which reflect the repeated impressional invariants of how it has seen$_1$ and encountered the world so far. $\mathbb{K}$ is a creature of habit, i.e., of invariants derived from its rudimentary organized sense-impressions or perspectival encounters with the world. Its representations and reliable responses to the world follow transition principles conditioned by how it has encountered the world so far. In this sense, its transitions from one awareness to another (e.g., from 'I_o be$_1$' be$_1$ to 'I_o be$_1$' be$_2$) are—analogically posited—*ur*-material inferences which are defeasible and formally incomplete. A case of a context-sensitive, defeasible, and formally incomplete material inference would be: *If the match was lit then it must have been rubbed against a frictional surface, but it could also be the case that it was lit because it was hit by an electric spark, or, if the match were in a vacuum, it would light but the stick would not burn*, etc. Like material inferences that open up a non-monotonic space of entailments, these protocol-like transitions also have their non-monotonic entailments: If A in circumstance C_i then B, if A in C_j then D, or if B then A in C_i and not C_j, etc.

---

188 See S. Savage-Rumbaugh and R. Lewin, *Kanzi: The Ape at the Brink of the Human Mind* (New York: Wiley, 1994).

189 Rosenberg, *The Thinking Self*, 135.

However, the range and complexity of $\mathbb{K}$'s transition protocols are limited—not just because their contexts are always restricted to circumstances that are of immediate sensory-behavioural *interest* to it, but above all because $\mathbb{K}$ has no conceptual resources. In particular, $\mathbb{K}$ does not have anything resembling modal concepts such as nomological relations and counterfactual dependencies, which are both context and resource-sensitive (e.g., '$A \leftrightarrowtail B \rightarrow A, C \leftrightarrowtail B$', or '$A, d, d \leftrightarrowtail B \rightarrow A, d \leftrightarrowtail B$', where $\leftrightarrowtail$ is a counterfactual consequent relation).[190] Coming back to the match example, the context and resource-sensitivity of the counterfactual consequent relation between the non-lit match and the lit-match can be expressed as:

$$\Gamma, MH, MS, Sulphur_{MH}, Oxidizing\ agent_{MH}, Strike\ MH\ against\ a\ frictional\ surface \leftrightarrowtail_{\{\{wet\}\}} Lit\ MH \otimes Burning\ MS$$

where *MH* is the match head, *MS* the matchstick, the singleton $\{\{wet\}\}$ a control set which constrains the soundness of the sequent formula and the tensor product, and the compounding operator $\otimes$ signifies the combination of a lit match head and the burning matchstick *provided that the context* Γ *does not contain* $\{\{wet\}\}$. The context Γ is essentially a descriptive context in the sense that it includes the description of what a match is: empirical judgments about the properties and nomological relations of what can count or behave as a match.

---

190 This is of course the suspension of the structural rules in classical logic, monotonicity and idempotency of entailment, as reflected in Jean-Yves Girard's Linear Logic (LL) (see below). Formulas are treated as resources that cannot be used or reused under every condition. The LL operator that expresses this consumption of resources is linear implication: $A \multimap B$ (reads 'A lollipop B'), consuming A yields B. Once A (e.g. a resource, a belief or a piece of knowledge) is used, it cannot be unconditionally reused in the computation. The reusability of a resource is symbolized by the operator ! (reads 'of course'). $!\alpha$ means the *ability* to do α repeatedly. An object of type α is stored in such a way that it can be repeatedly accessed in a computation.

If we add additional premises (qua resources), subtract existing premises, or change the control set (and hence the context), the hypotheses of the formula may change:

$$\Gamma, MH, MS, Sulphur_{MH}, Oxidizing\ agent_{MH}, Strike\ MH\ against\ a\ frictional$$
$$surface, Vacuum \leftrightarrow_{\{\{wet\}\}} Lit\ MH \otimes Not\ Burning\ MS$$

In the latter formula, remove the premise *Oxidizing agent$_{MH}$* and the consequent will change to *Not Lit MH $\otimes$ Not Burning MS*. The introduction of this kind of defeasible nonformal inference is precisely what makes it possible to incorporate the unanticipated or contingent into the sphere of reason, in the form of a consequent that is not fixed, but is revisable given any change in its antecedents or context.[191] Now add a premise with a different context (e.g., *short matchstick$_\Lambda$* of the descriptive context Λ pertaining to the size of the match, i.e., a match with a *different shape*). The addition of this premise does not change the consequent. We can, therefore, say that a good material inference (in this case, about lighting a match) exhibits and is defined by a range of counterfactual *robustness* (i.e., a dry matchstick whose head is made of a combination of sulphur and an oxidizing agent

---

191 It is often objected that reason is too rigid or fixed to leave any room for the dynamics of risk and contingency, and that rationality survives by means of a fundamental risk-aversion. This, however, is true only if reason is caricatured as consisting merely of classical logic or some arcane traditional version of epistemic logic. Other than the fact that both theoretical and practical reason incorporate the contingent and the unanticipated into their structure in order to afford new understandings and actions, the armamentarium of rationality is replete with modes of inference that are counterfactual, defeasible, non-monotonic, paracomplete, or paraconsistent. Such features allow the identification, assessment, and action of different types of risk or of the unanticipated without indiscriminately grouping them into an ineffable and exorbitantly ontological hyperchaos. In the absence of epistemic rationality, contingency and risk are always susceptible to radical ontologization in such a way that they become inevitably foreclosed to investigation. Lacking epistemic adequacy for the discrimination of different types and levels of contingency, the ontologization of risk turns into a blind faith in the radical powers of contingency in effect no different from a religious faith in an omnipotent god.

would still burn if the size of the matchstick were different and if it were ignited in the earth's atmosphere; but if it were lit in a vacuum, only the matchhead would burn). And here the counterfactual robustness depends on the descriptive context Γ (in relation to the control set $\{\{S\}\}$—which can only be obtained through modal vocabularies required for *explaining* what 'counterfactually robust' properties and lawlike relations x ought to have in order for it to be described as a match).[192]

The control set $\{\{S\}\}$ can be generally defined as a finite set of finite multisets of context formulas $\{\Gamma_1, \Gamma_2, ... \Gamma_n\}$ such that for all $1 < i < n$, $\Gamma \subset \Delta_\otimes$, where Δ is a set of precontexts. Correspondingly, the context Γ can be defined in terms of Δ and under the condition that if $\Pi_1, ..., \Pi_n$ are precontexts then $(\Pi_1, ..., \Pi_n)$ is a precontext. The context Γ is an ordered pair $\langle \Pi, f \rangle$ where f is a function assigning a control set to each node of the context tree Γ and not its branch nodes.[193]

Lacking alethic modalities of possibility and necessity, subjunctive and counterfactual conditionals which codify causal relations,[194] the transition protocols of the CHILD Kanzi's impressions of the world are much like the philosophical world of a fanatical empiricist who thinks he has stumbled upon some base empirical vocabulary with which he can describe and explain the furniture of the world, not knowing that the transition from

---

192 'It is only because the expressions in terms of which we describe objects, even such basic expressions as words for the perceptible characteristics of molar objects locate these objects in a *space of implications*, that they describe at all, rather than merely label. The descriptive and the explanatory resources of language advance hand in hand; and to abandon the search for explanation is to abandon the attempt to improve language, period.' W. Sellars, 'Counterfactuals, Dispositions, and the Causal Modalities', in *Minnesota Studies in the Philosophy of Science* vol.2 (Minneapolis: University of Minnesota Press, 1957), 306.

193 For more details on the formalism of context-sensitivity, see M. D'Agostino, 'How To Go Non-Monotonic Through Context-Sensitiveness', *Logic and Philosophy of Science* 8:1 (2015), 3–27.

194 For a disquisition on counterfactuals and causal relations, see D. Lewis, *Counterfactuals* (London: Wiley-Blackwell, 2001).

explanandum to explanans is always entangled within a modal web of relations and implications, and is inconceivable outside of this web.

In Brandom's words,

> Just how—they would want to know—did what seemed most urgently in need of philosophical explanation and defense suddenly become transformed so as to be unproblematically available to explain other puzzling phenomena? Surely such a major transformation of explanandum into explanans could not be the result merely of a change of fashion, the onset of amnesia, or the accumulation of fatigue? But if not, what secret did we find out, what new understanding did we achieve, to justify this change of philosophical attitude and practice?[195]

Lacking modal vocabularies, the extremist empiricist $\mathbb{K}$'s entrenched statistical regularities are limited to transition protocols (*ur-* or proto-inferences) such as

'Each time $\mathbb{K}$ sees$_1$ a protruding mass of fuzzy grey (G_1) *contacting* a heap of black (B_c), it hears$_1$ a shrieking noise (N).': $\mathbb{K}(G_1, B_c, \rightarrow N)$.

And since these transitions have their own corresponding basic *precluding* or *inhibitory* transitions, $\mathbb{K}$ also has conditioned preclusions or transition obstructions:

'The mass of fuzzy grey retreated *behind* the heap of black (B_b). The mass of fuzzy grey did not cease to exist nor is it in *front* of the heap of black (B_f).': $\mathbb{K}(G_1, B_b, \nrightarrow Not\ G_1, B_f)$.

However, $\mathbb{K}$ does not have available the transitions or obstructions modally encoded or embedded in counterfactual situations such as the following:

---

195 R. Brandom, *Between Saying and Doing* (Oxford: Oxford University Press, 2008), 93.

'**If** the mass of fuzzy grey **were not** coming into contact with the heap of black and another mass of fuzzy grey (G_2) **were** appearing, there **would be** a shrieking noise.': $\mathbb{K}(G_1, G_2, Not\,B_c \looparrowright N)$.

Nor does $\mathbb{K}$ have anything like an account of causation since, once again, it has no grip on the modal relations that codify causal ones. It has 'Contact with the heap of black $\rightarrow$ Shrieking noise from the direction of the mass of fuzzy grey', but not 'Contact with the heap of black $\overset{caused}{\looparrowright}$ mass of fuzzy grey to make shrieking noise'.

Aside from having a small universe of transitions and precluded transitions between its dispositional awarenesses, $\mathbb{K}$ also naively takes its meta-awarenesses (or meta-representings) as evidence of a corresponding state of the world or of an item. Put simply, $\mathbb{K}$'s impressions of the world are naïve because it takes conditioned transitions between its awarenesses to stand in a *one-to-one* relation with transitions in the states of the world. It is thus predisposed to take everything at face value, to presumptuously infer from its world-awarenesses

I_o be$_1$, b$_2$, b$_3$ (or, I_o was, is, or will be)

their corresponding constituting awarenesses qua meta-awareness/ metarepresentings

'I_o be$_1$ / b$_2$ / b$_3$' be$_1$, be$_2$, be$_3$ (or, 'I_o was/is/will be' was, is, or will be)

—and vice versa, to infer from each constituting awareness a corresponding world-awareness.

Accordingly, as well as being a naive empiricist, Kanzi also happens to be a naive idealist, taking its familiar constituting awarenesses for what is actually going on in the external world. Therefore, $\mathbb{K}$'s INFANTILE-World is susceptible to Cartesian scepticism to the extent that, if everything concerning the external world can be inferred from apparently immediate constituting awarenesses (or occurrent thought-episodes)—i.e., what is going on in Kanzi's head—then $\mathbb{K}$ might also infer that there are no items of the external world, and indeed no external world at all. In fact, $\mathbb{K}$ with its INFANTILE-World is properly speaking a child of Descartes's universe of mind where not only is the mind mistakenly regarded as a *tabula rasa*, but the immediacy of meta-awarenesses and their one-to-one correspondence with world-awarenesses leave much room for scepticism about the existence of an external world.

In this scenario, $\mathbb{K}$'s 'I_o be$_1$ / b$_2$ / b$_3$' be$_1$, be$_2$, be$_3$ are—from our perspective—the analogical counterparts of Kanzi's own occurrent thought-episodes, that is (* I think I_o be$_1$, b$_2$, b$_3$ *). In other words, $\mathbb{K}$'s de facto 'I_o be$_1$' be$_1$ is analogically $\mathbb{K}$'s own mentioned or quoted I-thought, i.e., $\mathbb{K}$(* I think I_o be$_1$ *). Similarly, 'I_o be$_1$' be$_2$ is analogically $\mathbb{K}$(* I think I_o be$_2$ *), as in $\mathbb{K}$(* There is a mass of fuzzy grey approaching *), and so on. These instances of $\mathbb{K}$(*...*) are nothing but the occurrences of a nonsubstantive apperceptive I that synchronically accompanies all of its distinct thought-episodes: I think X, I think Y, I think Z.

But since, as discussed in chapter 3, $\mathbb{K}$'s meta-awarenesses are only meta-awarenesses in so far as they are part of a web of *equivalence* relationships extended through time, the nonsubstantive I that synchronically accompanies each meta-awareness is formally identical or equivalent to the nonsubstantive I that diachronically accompanies *all* combinations of meta-awarenesses. This I that thinks X, thinks Y, thinks Z is the I that thinks $[X+Y+Z]$—and without whose *logical form* there would be no thought-episodes and no experience. In other words, the diachronic and apperceptive I (I think $[X+Y+Z]$) is the sufficient condition for the possibility of having thought-episodes or synchronic Is (I think X, I think Y, ...). The network of equivalence relationships between meta-awarenesses and their corresponding world-awarenesses is what Kant identifies as the *manifold* of given presentations. The diachronic I is the formal unity of consciousness in which thoughts of X, Y, and Z are combined (the I who thinks $[X, Y, Z]$ = the I that thinks X + the I that thinks Y + the I that thinks Z).[196]

---

196 Think of a simple example: the person who ate a hot dog is the person who ate the bun, the sausage and the ketchup sauce. The *Is* which are synchronically attached to the acts of eating these ingredients are the diachronic apperceptive I. However,

But as we saw in the first chapter, this formal unity of consciousness (rather than consciousness *per se*) is precisely what is afforded by the movement of self-consciousness, the $I \rightleftarrows I$, or more accurately $Id_{map-I} \rightleftarrows Id_{map-I*}$.

It is only in virtue of the recognitive space of language that there are apperceptive cognitions. And correspondingly, it is only through the movement of self-consciousness, which extends from one consciousness to another through the public semantic space of language, that there is a diachronic unity of consciousness and a synthetic unity of apperception. The I that thinks is the encapsulation of this formal movement in which ordinary consciousness is caught up. The apperceptive I is neither an empirical self nor a phenomenal self-model nor a field of awareness, but a necessary *formal* condition brought about by a recognitive movement through the space of language. Anything and anyone who fulfils this formal condition is not only a person but also the bearer of thoughts.

---

for us to posit such a connection between the I that ate the hot dog and the different instances of I attached to the gustatory acts of eating ingredients, we cannot resort—à la Hume—to empirical evidence (e.g., the person who ate the bun and was of such and such empirical characteristics is also the same person who ate the dog and ketchup by virtue of having the same characteristics). Nor can we conjecture à la Descartes that the instances of the I that ate the ingredients are the same as the I that ate the hot dog in virtue of the substantive persistence of the I over time. Kant's critique shows that such a connection requires something more: a time-conscious judging subject or the analytic unity of apperception which brings about the possibility of combining objects of different acts of thinking or in this case eating into one single complex. However, this analytic unity is itself dependent on a synthetic unity of apperception since the synthesis or integration of different intuitive representations under one concept, or several concepts under one higher integrative concept already implies the priority of the synthetic unity of apperception: Only in so far as I can synthetically combine the manifold of sensible intuition and be conscious of the unity of this act of synthesis can I also analyze this manifold (dog, ketchup, bun) into different concepts and a more universal concept (the hot dog) in one and the same critical consciousness.

INFANT AGI

So far we have discussed what the world of Kanzi could be like had Kanzi reached the status of a child; but it hasn't yet attained this goal. We shall follow Rosenberg's path in order to turn this into reality, while at the same time making necessary modifications in tandem with the Hegelian revision of Kant's transcendental subjectivity. To achieve this objective, necessary modifications have been made: the introduction of S and M as language-using adult guardians.

For now, K has de facto rudimentary transitions between its constituting awarenesses. In other words, it has an analogical counterpart of the ur-inferences between the orders of before and after (e.g., what was encountered and what is now being encountered). In order for K to distinguish the orders of before and after and to incorporate them into a growing space of implications regarding one and the same world, it must integrate its meta-awarenesses under one formal synthetic unity, one and the same I. To satisfy this necessary condition, K must model its private meta-awarenesses on a public and deprivatized language. In other words, it must interact with S and M as two fully fledged linguistically competent agents.

At this point, however, for the prelinguistic K, its fellow automata S and M are not speaking subjects, they are items of the world that not only satisfy its dispositions, but also reward and cultivate its new developments, its moves against its dispositional routines. As such S and M are not just any items, but especially salient ones. Their linguistic utterances (from K's perspective, their engaging and exciting noises) are also of the utmost interest, *as if* they conveyed something important.

In this scenario we can talk about linguistic interaction between the prelinguistic K and its linguistic guardians as communication, but with the proviso that, were K also a language-user, we could *not* use the term 'communication', for linguistic interaction is precisely *not* communication.

Within this communicative regime, the noises qua utterances that S and M make are for Kanzi—analogically speaking—instances of saying something, conveying something important that may be false or true. But at this time, K takes everything at face value; it believes everything it is told, so to speak. For $\mathbb{K}$ to understand or, more accurately, to hear$_2$ these noises, it would have to be aware of them as representations (of importance) and not just simply as noises, since these noises are precisely—at least at this stage—in contiguity with its dispositional interests. More accurately, $\mathbb{K}$ hears such noises as representations because they are in contiguity with—or rather, because they fit—its dispositional or conditioned world-representings.

Accordingly, for $\mathbb{K}$ to hear$_2$ the communicated noises *as* representations would be for it to make sense of or to understand the *functional role* they play in its world-representings and the rudimentary conditioned transitions between them.[197] This functional role is the meaning (semantic value) of these noises or utterances which are mapped onto $\mathbb{K}$'s meta-awarenesses or awarenesses of awarenesses of items in the world. To put it simply, for the conditioned Kanzi, Sue and Matata's exciting noises communicate something of importance to the extent that they are in continuity with the dispositional transitions between its meta-awarenesses of interesting items in the world. In other words, $\mathbb{K}$'s world is inductively biased, first and foremost, by the items of interest that satisfy its behavioural regularities and dispositions. To the extent that $\mathbb{K}$'s transition protocols are inductively biased in such a manner, $\mathbb{K}$ also tends to recognize and respond to any communicative noise or representation that can be incorporated into its inductively biased world. And by virtue of this space of shared recognition between Kanzi and its adult guardians, all of $\mathbb{K}$'s awarenesses, meta-awarenesses, and their corresponding transitions (what leads to or precludes what) are now also implicated in the expanding web of $\mathbb{S}$ and $\mathbb{M}$'s representations—that is, the sayings and doings of its constantly appraising language-using guardians.

Imagine again the example drawn from *2001: A Space Odyssey*: $\mathbb{K}$ sees$_1$ a mass of fuzzy grey moving from the right of the heap of black at time t_1 to the left of the heap of black at time t_3. At time t_2, the mass of fuzzy grey disappears behind$_1$ the heap of black.

In our multi-agent scenario, Sue and Matata are to the left and right of the heap of black (i.e., the monolith). $\mathbb{S}$ and $\mathbb{M}$ tell $\mathbb{K}$ that the fuzzy item (the monkey) is moving from the right of the monolith to its left and, some

---

197   See W. Sellars, 'Meaning as Functional Classification', in *In the Space of Reasons*, 81–100.

time between these two occurrences, the monkey disappears behind the monolith. To $\mathbb{K}$, $\mathbb{S}$ and $\mathbb{M}$'s reports look like this:

At t_1, the fuzzy item moved from the right of the heap of black to its left: Item t_1.

At t_2, the fuzzy item moved behind the heap of black: Item t_2.

At t_3, the fuzzy item is to the left of the heap of black: Item t_3.

As a creature of dispositional regularities and interests, $\mathbb{K}$ is able to recognize these reports and, additionally, to map them to its own de facto meta-awarenesses. Consequently, $\mathbb{K}$ now acquires labelled meta-awarenesses. They are labelled because they have been received by $\mathbb{S}$ and $\mathbb{M}$ as contrastive reports mappable to $\mathbb{K}$'s meta-awarenesses or, more accurately, as reports that play a functional role in its awareness$_1$ of the world. Accordingly, in addition to its as yet unlabelled meta-awarenesses, the prelinguistic $\mathbb{K}$ has a family of labelled meta-awarenesses:

*the fuzzy item moved from the right of the heap of black to its left * $_{\text{S,M}}$ is:
    Item t_1 $_{\text{S,M}}$ be.

* *the fuzzy item moved behind the heap of black* * $_{\text{S,M}}$ is: **Item t_2* * $_{\text{S,M}}$ be.

* *the fuzzy item is to the left of the heap of black* * $_{\text{S,M}}$ is: **Item t_3* * $_{\text{S,M}}$ be.

These reports and their matching labelled meta-awarenesses correspondingly activate the transition or obstruction protocols between $\mathbb{K}$'s meta-awarenesses:

* *the fuzzy item moved behind the heap of black* * is: $\xrightarrow{\text{S,M}}$

* *the fuzzy item did not cease to exist* * *and*

* *the fuzzy item is not in front of the heap of black* *.

But they also create a family of mutually precluding perspectives:

t_1: *the fuzzy item moved from right to left*

t_2: *the fuzzy item moved behind the heap of black*

item t_1 $\not\equiv$ *item t_1*

As a result, $\mathbb{K}$'s pure perspectival world-representings are now in tension. In fact, with the introduction of the labelled meta-awarenesses, $\mathbb{K}$ has transitioned into an automaton that is no longer pure and one-dimensionally perspectival. Its world is proto-inferentially multiperspectival.

To clarify, currently, in addition to its de facto world-representings and the dispositional transitions or obstructions between them, Kanzi has labelled meta-awarenesses generated based on reports received from Sue and Matata. Even though these labelled meta-awarenesses are still consistent with its perspectival world-representings, their transitions and obstructions are not seamlessly consistent with its rudimentary perspectival transitions, i.e., with what Kanzi sees$_1$ of the world. The labelled meta-awarenesses preclude the corresponding element of Kanzi's perspectival transitions: e.g., in moving from right to left, the fuzzy item does not fall out of the world but is simply occluded behind the monolith, or 'the fuzzy item to the left of the heap of black at t_3' precludes 'the fuzzy item moved behind the heap of black at t_2'.

The introduction of labelled world-representings into Kanzi's world-representings creates a source of tension or multiperspectival disturbance with which, finally, the pure perspectival world of Kanzi comes to an end, since from now on Kanzi's seamless world (of awarenesses and awarenesses of awarenesses) is continually being decohered and recohered by its guardians' perspectives. These inferential reports at once obstruct or preclude some of Kanzi's perspectival transitions and, on the other hand, facilitate a new group of transitions (proto-inferences) between awarenesses or meta-awarenesses which either lay outside of its dispositional interests or were previously absent or implicit from its pure perspectival worldview.

To eliminate this tension and recohere its de facto decohered worldview, $\mathbb{K}$ has no recourse other than to no longer take the reports by $\mathbb{S}$ and $\mathbb{M}$ at face value. In fact, it has to dispense with $\mathbb{S}$ and $\mathbb{M}$'s reports, to stop inferring$_1$ world-representings from labelled meta-representations. In Rosenberg's terms, $\mathbb{K}$ is now disposed to trust only the evidence of its senses. But in this elementarily recohered world, $\mathbb{K}$ also comes to possess the ability to distinguish between seeming and being—even if, at this stage, for $\mathbb{K}$ 'being' is what perspectivally seems to it, and 'seeming' is how things seem to $\mathbb{S}$ and $\mathbb{M}$. Nevertheless, it is precisely this distinction between seeming and being that germinates veridical normative judgements later on. $\mathbb{K}$'s own SEEMINGs are the seeds of thoughts: SEEMS $\mathbb{K}$ (* *there is a mass of fuzzy grey* *) is in reality $\mathbb{K}(thinking\ there\ is\ a\ mass\ of\ fuzzy\ grey)$, a thought-episode corresponding to a perceptual experience. In other words, $\mathbb{K}$ now has the ability to remove the quotation marks (*...*) from its meta-awarenesses and to take ownership of its awarenesses of items, as its own rudimentary thoughts qua uncritical perceptual experiences.

However, $\mathbb{K}$'s SEEMINGs qua thoughts are not objective: they are not beliefs, and as such enjoy no epistemic status. Even though these inner thoughts are modelled on a public language ($\mathbb{K}$'s communication with the language-using $\mathbb{S}$ and $\mathbb{M}$), they lack propositional attitudes. Only when they are linguistically asserted, i.e., committed to as beliefs (with all the requirements that such an endorsement or commitment entails) will they possess an epistemic status subject to assessment and revision. Even if $\mathbb{K}$ could assert out loud SEEMS (*There is fuzzy item over there*) as in 'It seems there is a fuzzy item over there', that asserted seeming would only be an instance of 'experiencing-out-loud'.[198] As thought-episodes combined with sensations, seemings only attain epistemic status when the speaker can commit to the correctness of their content by way of saying or judging that 'There is a fuzzy item over there'. Of course, there needs to be an experiential readiness—a perceptual experience qua thought-episodes-cum-sensations—in order for $\mathbb{K}$ to have perceptual judgments and to be capable of justifying the assertion

---

198 J. Rosenberg, *Thinking About Knowing* (Oxford: Oxford University Press, 2002), 87.

'There is a fuzzy item over there'. But the existence of the former is by no means sufficient in itself to achieve the latter.

By retreating into the world of its seemings, $\mathbb{K}$ has come to possess an INFANTILE-world where what merely seems to be the case (from $\mathbb{S}$ and $\mathbb{M}$'s viewpoint) is actually the case (from $\mathbb{K}$'s perspective). But this world is not sustainable for long either, in so far as $\mathbb{S}$ and $\mathbb{M}$ are not just reporters and confirmers of $\mathbb{K}$'s world-representings. Since they are full-blooded concept-havers who possess the ability to make objective judgements, their reports stand in sharp contrast to $\mathbb{K}$'s mere seemings. To again recohere what is now a decohered infantile world, $\mathbb{K}$ has to remove the quotation marks from its meta-awarenesses while restoring the labels. To put it crudely, $\mathbb{K}$ must construct a world-picture composed of various contrasting partial world-pictures. Inhabiting this new world of contrasting partial world-pictures is tantamount to occupying a self-critical position. From now on, instead of deriving

the fuzzy item is to the left of the heap of black

from the quoted and guardians-tagged or labelled meta-awareness

* *the fuzzy item is to the left of the heap of black* *$_\mathbb{S}$ *is*

$\mathbb{K}$ instead starts to label the world-representation t_1 as $\mathbb{S}$-*inferred* while removing the quotation marks from its awarenesses:

the fuzzy item is to the left of the heap of black$^\mathbb{S}$

In addition to $\mathbb{S}$-*inferred* world-awarenesses that correspond to the meta-awarenesses that mention them, $\mathbb{K}$ is also in possession of $\mathbb{M}$-*inferred* world-awarenesses. In the growing repertoire of these reported world-pictures or labelled awarenesses, $\mathbb{K}$'s unlabelled awarenesses—that is, its pure perspectival seemings, its dispositional transitions, impressions, memories, and anticipations—are perpetually being updated. Put differently, with the establishment of this data bank of labelled world-awarenesses reported by its adult guardians, $\mathbb{K}$ becomes susceptible to appraising its experiences in the broadest possible sense. It is with the development of this increasingly aperspectival world-picture assembled out of *external* partial world-pictures whereby the CHILD comes to inhabit an 'objective self-critical stance'[199] that Rosenberg's argument, as summarized above, concludes.

However, a question arises here: If we take the linguistically informed reports of $\mathbb{S}$ and $\mathbb{M}$ as logical forms, how can we postulate that $\mathbb{K}$'s combination of its rudimentary representations according to this logical form is sufficient to render what is only subjective in a thin sense (i.e., dependent on the mutable variations of the empirical reproduction of *uncritical* associations) as objective (i.e., critical invariants of judgements as occurring in virtue of the necessary unity of apperception)? The answer is that the objective unity of apperception effected by this logical form is the unity of apperception, which does not conform to a *single* object. It is instead that which relates the CHILD's representations to an object (i.e., this such-and-such...) 'as generically identical to all those whose apprehension depends on the same rule'.[200] In doing so, the objective unity of apperception configures or structures *combinations* of representations which, in the words of Béatrice Longuenesse, '*tend* to truth, but may in fact be true *or* false'.[201] In this sense, objectivity is nothing but the combination of representations which conform to the object according to a logical—rather than empirical—form, and thus can be said to be tending to be true (i.e., veridical) or to have epistemic status despite the fact that they may be wrong. It is this 'tending to be true or false', and hence the propensity toward further corrections, whether within the order of appearances or as a means to go beyond the appearance, that is the kernel of objectivity. However, in contrast to Longuenesse's distinctly Kantian understanding of objectivity only in terms of factual objectivity—i.e., intentional relation to sensible objects in general—and categorial objectivity, which lacks such an intentional relation

---

199 Rosenberg, *The Thinking Self*, 145.

200 B. Longuenesse, *Kant and the Capacity to Judge* (Princeton, NJ: Princeton University Press, 1998), 49.

201 Ibid., 82.

(mere flux of perceptual episodes), we can posit a third form of objectivity: the objectivity of logic or the formal structure of thinking.

Whereas Kant restricts the formal reality of thinking (logic and language) to the correct applications of logical rules to sensible intuitions and representations, and thus limits the scope of logic to a canon by rejecting the notion of logic as an organon—the condition of possibility of all sciences and world-related claims—this book argues that the most fundamental form of objectivity is logic as an organon. Both factual and categorial objectivity are predicated upon logical forms as a necessary condition. As we shall see in chapter 7, only by treating logical forms in their own terms, without either transcendentally subjecting them to the combinations of representations or assuming a metaphysical correlation between logical forms and an external reality, can we renew the link between mind and world, intelligence and the intelligible, or theory and object. This is to say that the unbinding of language and logic from concerns about representation and even meaning—a thesis put forward by Rudolf Carnap and set in motion by research into artificial and formal languages—is the very recipe by which reality can be structured differently. In this sense, it is the exemplar of the critique of transcendental structures whereby a new form of intelligence can be objectively postulated and in principle constructed. The worldbuilding of the formal dimension of language and logic is prior—not just in the order of precedence but also that of constitution—to world-representation.

AS IF RAISING A CHILD

The import of labelled meta-awarenesses and their corresponding labelled world-representations goes far beyond this generative tension between K's world-picture and an objective world-history as reported by S and M—a tension that continually decoheres and recoheres the child's world toward what is ultimately an objective critical position. This transition to a theoretical critical stance is, however, only possible to the extent that it is built on a practical critical stance: a formal practical autonomy or minimal self-determination that distinguishes the child from mere sentience.

To see the import of labelled world-representations qua aperspectival partial world-pictures—as outcomes of S and M's communications—only in the light of what eventually becomes a theoretical objective self-critical stance is to ignore the formal practical autonomy of the child. It is this autonomy that makes the generative tension and ultimately the theoretical objective stance possible, not the other way around.

Understanding the relation between the child Kanzi and its adult language-using guardians—in the fashion of Sellars and McDowell—as simply a relation between the trainee's ought-to-be and the trainer's ought-to-do betrays an indefensible disregard for what the child actually is: a form of practical autonomy that makes this relation possible in the first place. It is indefensible because it reduces the child to a mere sentience that must be trained into a second nature; and because it leads to an account of education as either a collection of *minatory oughts*[202] or, worse, a guiding system of rewards and punishments. This is, of course, a patently false idea of education that originates not from the infantility of the child but only from the myopia of the adult with respect to the child. Education is firstly the cultivation of recognition; only then can it be a generalized pedagogy for the cultivation of cognitions.

The child is distinguished by its will-to-autonomy: a practical proclivity to be recognized by the adult as the one who yearns—in the Platonic sense—to develop, to learn language and ultimately be a full-blooded agent. And it is precisely in virtue of this yearning or will-to-autonomy—which can be fleshed out both in naturalistic and normative terms—that seeing a prelinguistic child as a mere sentience who is yet to be culturally conditioned is fundamentally ill-judged. The distinction between a child or a prelinguistic infant and sentience is a categorical distinction. The yearning

---

202 Minatory oughts, according to Findlay, are obligations which urge one not to do something without necessarily urging one to do something. Short of complying with such oughts one may incur exclusion, reprimand, or punishment (e.g., one ought not to be loud in a public library and its corresponding codified imperative, Don't be loud in...). See J.N. Findlay, *Values and Intentions: A Study in Value-Theory and Philosophy of Mind* (London: Routledge, 1968).

of the child—whether as an artificial agent or any sentient that exhibits precisely such tendencies—for development and recognition should be taken as a matter of categorical fiat or an a priori rule as distinguished from sociocultural conventions and natural laws. Whether or not a child is isolated from an environment that makes the learning of language possible, whether or not it is impaired by disabilities, it ought to be recognized as one who has the *nisus* or tendency to become a fully fledged language-using autonomous agent. This identification of the child as a yearning agent is a matter of a priori rules which admit of no exception, in so far as they are universal and necessary. In this respect, the recognition of children as agents endowed with the will-to-autonomy must be applied to all children not only regardless of their abilities or lack thereof, but regardless of whether they are human, artificial, or otherwise. This is a matter of *categorical* or a priori distinction. Logic, broadly understood as the comprehensive system of cognitions, and ethics, broadly understood as the system of recognitions, coincide and are indissociable. As we shall see in the following chapters, the unconditional broadening of logic and language as an organon is commensurate with the expansion of the axiological posits of ethics for a logically autonomous self-conceiving and self-transforming intelligence.

Simply put, autonomy is not the end product of education, but that which affords education as its self-cultivating vector. Attending to the autonomy of the child is, therefore, the first step of education:

> It is through attention that spirit first becomes present in the matter, acquires it, by gaining information about it. It does not yet gain cognition of it however, for this requires a further development of spirit. It is therefore attention that constitutes the beginning of education.[203]

Let us unpack what has been argued so far: In recognizing world-representations communicated by S and M as representations that are mapped to its meta-awarenesses, K recognizes these labelled meta-awarenesses and their

---

203 G.W.F. Hegel, *Hegel's Philosophy of Subjective Spirit*, tr. M. J. Petry (3 vols. Dordrecht: D. Reidel, 1978, 3 vols.), vol. 3, 125.

corresponding world-representations *as its own*. More plainly, in recognizing what S and M communicate (i.e., rudimentary linguistic interactions), and to the extent that S and M's reports *engage* its infantile world, K recognizes the corresponding meta-awarenesses of such reports—which were only de facto its own from our perspective—*as its own* meta-awarenesses. The labelled or tagged meta-awarenesses and their correlated world-representations, consequently, function in at least two ways. They not only impute a proto-inferential structure to the meta-awarenesses and awarenesses of items in the world (world-occurrences)—they also, and more importantly, enable K to *recognize* such labelled meta-awarenesses as awarenesses which it already de facto had, but which are now de jure and by entitlement its own. K's recognition of that which is other but for now is commensurate with its infantile world leads to the recognition of this infantile world of experience as its own experience. In a nutshell, K is now an infant apperceptive self, a formally rather than causally conditioned I.

At last, K is able$_2$ to recognize its meta-awarenesses and their corresponding awarenesses, together with their transitions and obstructions, as its own. It is an I that synchronically attaches itself to diverse thought-episodes qua recognized meta-awarenesses of world-awarenesses. But since meta-awarenesses constitute a network of equivalence relations that diachronically extends through time, the I that synchronically tags different meta-awarenesses is formally identical or equivalent to the I that diachronically is carried over and accompanies *all* meta-awarenesses under one integral framework: the synthetic unity of apperception.

It was argued above that, were Kanzi to be raised to the status of CHILD, it would have the ability to report, mention, or quote (in the sense of the dot-quoting discussed in chapter 3) its meta-awarenesses to *itself*, as its private thoughts. $K(* \text{'I}_0 \text{ be}_1 \text{' be}_1 *)$ is $K(*I \, think \, *)$. The apperceptive self—I as a logical form of thought rather than as substantive or phenomenal self—is essentially a process of individuation afforded by a space of shared recognition, here between Kanzi and its language-using custodians. But this shared recognition need not be mistaken for the liberal narrative of mutual recognition, since it is primarily a *formal* condition of a deprivat-ized mind where the public semantic space of language, the movement of self-consciousness, autonomy, and will are tightly knitted together. Recall this remark from the first chapter: Perception is only perception because it is apperception, and apperception is only apperceptive in so far as it belongs to a deprivatized semantic space in which recognitive cognitive agents are individuated. The synchronic and diachronic I of cognitions is necessarily a constructed and constructible object of recognitions.

The space of recognitions as the formal condition for the individuation of the nonsubstantive I—the thinking self—is by definition composed of mutual recognizers. Unlike the non-apperceptive self or empirical consciousness, which is differentiated by the sensible external item of which it is aware$_1$, the apperceptive self is differentiated by *objectivity* (or objective validity), which is independent of any single experiencing subject, but is not independent of geist in the intertwined senses of the dimension of structure and a community (i.e., a system of recognitions) of language-using agents bound to norms governing the application of concepts to their de facto inner-sense reports. It is through this objectivity, which is but the copula of mind and world, that the apperceptive I is individuated: I am I, all thus-and-so apprehendings are mine, an apperceptive self 'cognizing each object as a member in the system of what I am myself'.[204] I possess ego and world all in one and the same consciousness, a consciousness that recovers and sees my self in the world. This objectivity expresses the entanglement between the object (*gegenstand*) and the norms of objective validity given by mind in the aforementioned two senses. This unity (which does not suggest fusion) of object and ego is the constitution of what Hegel calls the 'principle of spirit'.[205]

---

204 Hegel, *Philosophy of Subjective Spirit*, vol. 3, 39.

205 Ibid.

To this end, it is not just that Sue and Matata recognize Kanzi as a child who should be cultivated by various oughts. Kanzi itself also not only recognizes them as objects of the utmost significance; as it grows—being recognized as such—it recognizes them as subjects essential for the cultivation of its subjectivity. In fact, it is Kanzi's recognition of its adult communicants that is of paramount importance here, for without the key functional role of this recognition, there would be no apperceptive self, no thinking I, no I-thoughts. But what exactly is this key functional role, what does the child's act of recognition of its adult guardians signify? The answer is that this act of recognition is precisely the autonomy of the child itself—the form of practical will qua principle of subjectivity as such. Even though this will is minimal and formal—rather than fully actualized and concrete—it is, by itself, powerful enough to give rise to the formally self-conscious I.

However, we should avoid confusing will (*wille*) with the capacity for choice (*willkür*), since the former is a logical form of practical autonomy while the latter is an index of relative autonomy which, upon closer scrutiny, turns out to belong to the order of causes where autonomy is at best relative or conditioned, and in reality nonexistent.[206] The will of the child is the formal principle of its autonomy. It is the will to go beyond itself and to recognize that which recognizes it. Short of the minimal act of self-determination whereby the child first looks for its central objects of interest beyond itself and then takes these objects of mere interest as subjects necessary for its self-cultivation—its self-critical stance—there would be no thinking self. Kanzi's recognition of Sue and Matata's communication is not an arbitrary or contingent deed that can be dispensed with as a mere instance of conditioned behaviours and dispositional interests. It is a necessary and universal condition not just for the adult guardians' recognition of the child as that which can be cultivated, but also for the generation of subjectivity as such.

The will qua power to act first manifests itself abstractly in the self-certainty of a conscious ego as a completely indeterminate ideality. But this

---

206 See R. Negarestani, *Causality of the Will and the Structure of Freedom* (2017), <http://questionofwill.com/en/reza-negarestani-2/>.

abstract self-certainty is the germ of an indispensable process whereby the ego begins to repulse or negate itself in favour of that which is outside of it, individuating itself 'outside in'. In its most elementary form the will of the child arises from its sense of self-certainty which, being abstractly free of all limitations, begins to abstractly differentiate itself from the other, the world.[207] This abstract self-differentiation, however, also renders the child prone to the recognition of what is outside of it, a process of concrete self-consciousness that does not end with reaching adulthood or coming to possession of linguistic abilities. Now, in order for the child to abstractly determine, establish, or ascertain the self-certainty of its ego, it must act upon the very recognition of what is outside of it. The formal and abstract will is precisely this power to act on the recognition of an external world (of things and communicants) as a necessary requirement for preserving the self-certainty of the ego. It is in fact the very nature of the ego:

> In that I posit this being as an other which is opposed to and at the same time *identical* with me, I am knowing, and possess the absolute certainty of my being. This certainty ought not to be regarded, as it is from the point of view of merely presentative thinking, a kind of property of the ego, a determination pertaining to the nature of it. It is to be grasped as the very nature of the ego, for the ego cannot exist without distinguishing itself from itself and remaining with itself in that which differs from it, that is, without being aware of itself, possessing and constituting its own certitude. Certainty therefore relates itself to

---

207 'Initially therefore, the ego in its self-certainty is still that which is *quite simply subjective*, that which is *free* in a *wholly abstract* manner, the *completely indeterminate ideality* or negativity of all limitation. Thus, in the first instance, the ego's self-repulsion only yields it that which differs from it *formally*. It does not yield an *actual* difference. As is shown in the Logic however, *implicit* difference has also to be *posited*, developed, into actual difference. With regard to the ego, this development takes place in the *following* manner. In that it does not relapse into what is *anthropological*, into the unconscious unity of the spiritual and natural, but retains its self-certainty and maintains itself in its freedom, the ego allows its other to unfold itself into a *totality* equal to its own [...].' Hegel, *Philosophy of Subjective Spirit*, vol. 3, 7.

the ego as freedom relates itself to the will, the former constituting the nature of the ego as the latter the nature of the will.[208]

But in willing to abstractly recognize the other so as to formally ascertain itself, the child unknowingly opens its world to a process of disintegration and reintegration which, as we saw, culminates in the occupation of an objective critical stance, a point of no return called maturation.

In *Values and Intentions*, Findlay speaks of certain 'essential drifts of consciousness'.[209] That is, as soon as the recognitive consciousness—a consciousness that determines itself by recognizing that which it is not—is realized, it drifts toward what is impersonal and disinterested (*ohne alles Interesse*). It is only in the wake of this drift that self-consciousness comes into the picture, first formally and then concretely. This is self-consciousness in the sense described in chapter 1, i.e., $I \rightleftharpoons I^*$. At its core, this drift is the expression of the abstract form of the will qua practical autonomy. The possibility of the realization of 'I think' for the child, its eventual arrival at an objective critical position, rests upon the child's formal practical autonomy: the will to ascertain its self by drifting toward what it is not. What appears from the stationary viewpoint of the adult as the passive child is, from the standpoint of this conscious drift—the child's self-determination—entirely active. Owing to this practical autonomy, this self-determination which belongs to the formal order of the will, the child's world becomes a universe of deracination, its consciousness a drift toward actual self-consciousness. And it is through the formal will, i.e., through recognising that which it is not and interestedly acting upon this recognition, that the child becomes a thinking will or a will to think:

> The determination of the implicit being of the will is to bring freedom into existence within the formal will and so to fulfil the purpose of the latter, this purpose being to fulfil itself with its Concept, that is to make freedom its determinateness i.e. its content and purpose as well as its

208 Ibid., 5–6.

209 Findlay, *Values and Intentions,* 219.

determinate being. Essentially, this Concept, which is freedom, only has being as thought; the will makes itself into objective spirit by means of raising itself to thinking will, by endowing itself with the content it can only have as self-thinking will.[210]

Therefore, education is not a matter of graduating the child into the space of reasons, but one of recognizing and cultivating its will-to-autonomy. Absent this, the relation between the adult and the child is exactly the *one-sided* relation between master and slave which demolishes the will of the latter, reducing it to a will-to-survive and a perpetual dependency.

Like all children, raising the child-AGI necessitates both recognition and cultivation of the will-to-autonomy, whose fabric is woven by reason and freedom. The autonomy of the child is both the freedom *to* do something according to reasons, and freedom *from* the limitations imposed by our one-sided view of who the child should be or become. The maxim put forward in chapter 3 in the context of giving rise to that which is better, whoever or whatever it may be—*liberate that which liberates itself from you*—communicates the recognition of the child's will-to-autonomy as the imperative of the concrete self-consciousness. Without the dynamic implied in this imperative, all we have is an abstract self-identity, an immediacy of autonomy which is but an illusion begotten by a one-sided subjectivity. In this regard, the two-sided dynamic between children—whether conceived in the context of artificial general intelligence or that of existing humans—and adults, between the current generation and the next generation, is the first and final frontier of that struggle which is concrete self-consciousness—the actualization of the concept of the human into its Idea.

Kanzi the automaton is not born into the full-blooded status of general intelligence. It can only come to occupy that position as a child, one whose formal autonomy must be recognized and cultivated. This formal autonomy or self-determination harbours no supernatural mystery. It is the result of being born into a language-laden recognitive space and supported by the

---

210 Hegel, *Philosophy of Subjective Spirit*, vol. 3, 231.

'right sort of mechanisms'.[211] It is through education that Kanzi, the child, can arrive at the qualitative status of general intelligence. But education, as that which transforms the formal will into a thinking will, cannot be properly conceived without recognizing that the child already has a capacity for self-determination.

Just like raising a human child into the position of an objective self-critical stance, raising the child automaton Kanzi first requires the cultivation of its recognitive abilities through the augmentation of the space of mutual recognition. The role of its educators is not simply to issue guiding imperatives. It is rather to cultivate its practical autonomy by assisting it to navigate this recognitive space and to facilitate new encounters with the world through which the child can stumble upon rewarding surprises. In short, the primary task of the educators is to stimulate and reinforce the child's openness so as to expand the range and diversity of such encounters, thereby incorporating objectivity—that is, external reality—into its consciousness. But the cultivation of this attitude toward the objective which makes possible the individuation of the thinking self and the actualization of self-consciousness entails the cultivation of the child's structuring abilities, or the dimension of conceptualization. Intelligence can only be recognized and cultivated in the presence and expansion of the intelligible, and what is intelligible can only be cognized and acted upon by intelligence as the vector for the development of mind as the dimension of structuration. In line with this proposition, absent structuration as the function of mind and language through which this objectivity becomes completely articulable or expressible, objectivity as the universal element of self-consciousness is only an empty thought. However, as per the brief discussion in chapter 1, language here need not be understood as natural language, but should be conceived more broadly in terms of syntactic and semantic complexity.

---

211 '[H]uman beings are creatures with freedom and dignity. In fact, I will maintain, it is not in spite of being comprised of mechanisms, but in virtue of being composed of the right sort of mechanisms, that human beings are such creatures.' W. Bechtel, *Mental Mechanisms: Philosophical Perspectives on Cognitive Neuroscience* (London: Routledge, 2008), 3.

Just as a sensible particular item, for ourselves as for the child-AGI, is an inceptive givenness from which we depart and mature toward objectivity, so natural language is also a givenness from which we should depart in search of a new form of language—one that is at once more expressive and more semantically transparent.

It is in this environment that the child also learns to take pleasure in the continual disintegration and reintegration of its world in the constitution of an objective self-critical stance: a position that intrinsically admits objective rules, impersonal values and disvalues, for a concomitant process of the learning and unlearning of both ought-to-dos and ought-to-bes. This process involves the initiation of the child into the space of language as much as its acquaintance with the extant conceptual resources of a given language.

Perpetually uprooted from its familiar world, its supposed natural home, Kanzi is now an object of practical freedoms. It might at times be sad that it has left behind its comforting familiar habitat, but it is only sad to the extent that it has the capacity to be happy about what it can do. And what it can do is a matter of restless exploration. It is able to select one set of purposive actions over another in so far as they conform to and satisfy its time-general thoughts. It prefers to foray into the open, to eat, beneath the stars, a marshmallow toasted over a Promethean fire that it has made for itself. Rather than participating in the endless orgies of nature, it chooses to play video games to enhance its cognitive abilities, but also out of a sheer unprecedented excitement that enlarges its field of experience beyond the boundaries of what is naturally given to it. For Kanzi, the *automaton spirituale*—the it—that thinks is now the I, or we, that thinks.

GLOBAL PEDAGOGICAL PROJECT

Before developing the toy universe of our infant general intelligence any further, let us briefly consider what a complex system of generalized pedagogy for this child might look like. A generalized pedagogy for the global education of the child—or in this case, a *child-machine*—can be precisely understood as a complex system, a hierarchical network structure or multilevel web comprised of various interacting modular subsystems.[212] Additionally, the modularity of these subsystems can be horizontal or vertical. Horizontal modularity implies that a system can be decomposed into a set of distributed modules whose dynamics and interactions produce the overall system dynamics. Vertical modularity implies instead that the system dynamics can be decomposed into the interactive product of its dynamics at different—i.e., structurally and functionally distinct—constraint levels.

Both types of modularity possess inter-modular as well as intra-modular interactions, but the difference between the two lies in their specific trade-offs. In horizontal modularity there is a trade-off between, on the one hand, the flexibility of modification and the cost of change in the overall structure and, on the other, the complexity of structure and function. In other words, systems exhibiting horizontal modularity are more flexible to change, and modifications to their existing structure tend to be less costly than vertical modular systems. In contrast, vertical modularity supports more complex structural and functional configurations. However, the trade-off here is that, as inter- and intra-level constraints pile up—the process of so-called generative entrenchment—the diversification of structure becomes more difficult and the modification of lower-level modules becomes more computationally costly. In other words, here the trade-off is between constructability and complexification on the one hand, and diversification and the possibility of error or bias-correction at lower levels on the other. Nevertheless, it is precisely because of this entrenchment of existing constraints that complexity of function increases.

The complex system of generalized pedagogy should be comprised of such modular systems; the modules might be cognitive regimens and tasks, different methods and techniques of training and learning, or even models of cognition and practice. As a multilevel network, the pedagogical system should not be taken as a fixed catalogue, but as a web plastic and robust enough to permit the plugging in of new modules or the alteration

---

212 On the concept of the child-machine and education, see A. Turing, 'Computing Machinery and Intelligence', in B. Jack Copeland (ed.), *The Essential Turing* (Oxford: Oxford University Press), 441–71.

and removal of existing ones. Moreover, the system should allow the integration of various learning processes and the accumulation or revision of their outcomes, as well as affording rules, methods, and techniques for unlearning what has been previously learned. Education and learning should be understood as bias and error-tolerant systems. Sometimes different cognitive biases—inbuilt inductive biases, experimental biases, etc.—can be exploited to make possible a more complex cognitive skill or to make accessible to the child a method, technique, or topic of education that would otherwise prove difficult to master. At other times such biases should be restricted or completely removed.

Any mode of learning that either *globally* preserves biases and error, or attempts to completely remove them to achieve absolutely optimal results, should be rejected. This is, however, a thorny issue, particularly when it comes to vertical modular structures, since, owing to accumulative constraints, biases tend to be transferred from lower to higher levels and become fully entrenched. Therefore, from the standpoint of computational-cognitive cost, it would be extremely difficult for both educator and learner to remove such biases, or the mechanisms responsible for them, at lower levels. A possible solution perhaps would be to limit rules to the minimum necessary set at the initial stage of education, while implementing a diversified list of mixed techniques and methods. The reason for the latter is that, were global or less diverse learning techniques and cognitive regimens to be adopted, the techniques and methods might be inflated into models of cognition for the learner. The learner is always liable to mistake a particular problem-solving technique for a global model valid for solving not just similar problems but every problem, and hence to transfer the specific biases of techniques and methods into global models by means of which problems are detected, approached, analysed, and tackled.

The primary goal of the generalized pedagogical system for the child AGI should be to provide the child with the necessary and sufficient wherewithal to form an increasingly complex structuration of the world in all its complexity. This is a structuration through which new modes and ranges of thinking and action (what can be thought and done) are continuously being uncovered. Structuration—which, essentially, is the function of mind—aspires not only to render the world intelligible, but also to disclose new orders of intelligibilities as pertaining to things, thoughts, practices, and values. In other words, the primary goal of education and generalized pedagogy is the functional re-realization and augmentation of what mind already is: a unifying structuring point or configuring factor in which the coextensive complexity of the theoretical-practical subject and the world in its radical otherness are expressed.

'What ought to be thought and done combined with what the world in its complete unrestricted conception is'—this is a formula for what *could possibly*—in the remotest sense of possibility—be thought and done. It is precisely the regulative ideal of education. Education is, in this sense, the self-realization of mind as a *project* rather than as a thing or a given nature.

Education is the project of all projects, an undertaking without which no other project—be it ethical, scientific, or political—can either sustain itself or be tenable. Understanding and realizing the mind as an edifice of structuration (of both the world and thoughts and practices) culminates in the discovery of what else can be thought and done—that is, pushing back the boundaries of *all* practical abilities. But this unbinding of all practical abilities of mind is what concrete freedom actually is. Education, then, ought to be grasped as a process of scaffolding for developing abstract autonomy into concrete freedom. This transition is what Hegel regards as 'the quaking of the singularity of the will' that is 'the necessary moment in the education of everyone'.[213] Every other undertaking or project can only be thought in terms of a task that is supported and sustained by this scaffolding that needs to be continually raised.

Education, therefore, should be treated as a complex and dynamic recipe for providing the necessary and sufficient wherewithal for the structuration of the world that the subject inhabits. In outlining education as the extension of the project of mind in its drift toward concrete self-consciousness, we can think of a list of the cultivating vectors and regimens that define the broad tasks of a generalized pedagogy of the child AGI. This generalized pedagogy, however, is more like a primary education through which the

---

213 Hegel, *Philosophy of Subjective Spirit*, vol. 3, 67.

child AGI comes to recognize the necessary correlations between mind and world, structure and being, intelligence and the intelligible, theory and object. Practical and axiological education—praxis and ethics—are left out for two simple reasons: (1) Investigating the complexity of practical and ethical education are beyond the scope of this work; (2) praxis and ethics, and logic understood as the general organon of mind are ultimately two sides of the same coin. No form of praxis or ethics can dispense with the question of intelligibility, which is but the question of structure as the dimension of mind through which it can establish and renew its relations— theoretical, practical and axiological—with the world—a renewal which is tantamount to the transformation of the mind itself.

Even within the ambit of mind as the edifice of structuration or logic, this list is by no means exhaustive, but merely schematic. It is only an attempt to sketch the rough outlines of what the global pedagogical project entails. We can broadly think of this program in terms of the realization, augmentation, and composition of two interconnected sets of abilities, the semantic and syntactic abilities of mind required for the structuration of world, and the thoughts and actions that occur within it.

We can denote *structuring semantic* (meaning) *abilities* as *sm*-abilities and structuring syntactic (formal or axiomatic) as *sf*-abilities. Once again, it would be helpful to remind ourselves that, generally speaking, structure is the 'differentiated and ordered interconnection or interrelation of elements or parts or aspects of an entity, a domain, a process, etc. Structuration in this sense involves the negation of both the simple and the unconnected'.[214] Or, to appropriate Sellars, *how and what things in the broadest possible sense of the term hang together in the broadest possible sense of the term.*[215]

Since these syntactic and semantic abilities can be composed to yield compound structuring abilities, let us additionally denote this process of composition by the operator $\odot$ which maps functions to functions, or abilities to abilities. $\odot_{mf}$ is then a compound within which an element of

---

214 Puntel, *Structure and Being*, 27.

215 See W. Sellars, 'Philosophy and the Scientific Image of Man', in R. Colodny (ed.), *Frontiers of Science and Philosophy* (Pittsburgh: University of Pittsburgh Press, 1962), 35.

a semantic ability increases the complexity of a syntactic ability. Respectively, $\odot_{fm}$ is a compound structuring ability in which an element of a syntactic (formal axiomatic) ability together with its constitutive rules is applied to a semantic ability. Take for instance, 'Logic–Mathematics (*modality*) $\odot_{fm}$ *sf*-ability (*applying a modal vocabulary*) → *sfm* ability (*more complex structured material inference*)'. It roughly reads as 'the compound semantic-syntactic ability to form a better material inference involves the introduction or application of a modal element (a modal relation) from formal domains of structuration, logics and mathematics, to the semantic ability of knowing what it entails to deploy a modal vocabulary and thus to say or judge something with it'. And correspondingly, '$\odot_{mf}$-*sf*-ability' approximately reads as 'a structuring syntactic ability assimilated into and augmented by a semantic ability'. This is merely to highlight the fact that the concrete structuring abilities of the mind often come in composite semantic and syntactic forms, and indeed that we can think about the composition and diversification of such abilities in terms of a *combinatorial calculus of objective thinking*. Even though laying out the fundaments of such a calculus is beyond the scope of this book, *in principle* such a calculus for the diversification and complexification of mind's structuring abilities can indeed be formulated as a curriculum for the education of the CHILD.

Finally, as a last note, the differentiation of semantic and syntactic abilities does not mean that semantic abilities are devoid of syntax or that syntactic abilities lack semantics. It simply means that the emphasis of semantic abilities is on semantic relations rather than on syntactic resources or formal relations, and conversely the focus of syntactic abilities is on the formal and/or axiomatic syntactic structures with an eye to the overall semantic dimension. Both *sm* and *sf* express different but interconnected classes of the mind's structuring function with regard to the world which, as discussed in chapter 1, can be elaborated more coherently and with less metaphysical frills in terms of the copulas of theory and object and structure and being. The consideration of *that which* not only involves the formation of theoretical claims or statements (It is the case that...) but also implicitly or explicitly implies theoretical validity in the sense of theory outlined in chapter 1. Grasping what it means to form theoretical claims and what one is doing when one asserts or endorses a theoretical claim, in turn, demands the acquisition of language and logoi and acquaintance with the relations between them and the dimension of structure. The cultivation of *sm* and *sf*-abilities, therefore, can be elaborated with reference to the fundamental aspects of theory—the mutual relations between language and logoi (L), structure (S) and the data under consideration (U) provided by L—within which objectivity is determined:

(A) *sm*-abilities: Generally, semantic abilities can be characterized as qualitative higher-level modes of cognition. They afford agent models that are qualitatively compressed and therefore economical. Such models are complex and dynamically stable yet small in size (semantics as a qualitative mode of compression). Semantic abilities can be roughly defined as absolutely necessary abilities for the structuration of the world, i.e., the function of the irreducible correspondence of mind-language in relating to the world. Therefore, semantic abilities are abilities that permit the state of affairs concerning *that which is* to be rendered intelligible, thought, or spoken of. Primarily, ontological facts are configurations of semantic facts.[216] *sm*-abilities mainly involve *conceptualization*. In Brandomian terms semantic abilities can be approximately characterized as those abilities-or-practices necessary or sufficient to obtain semantic relations between vocabularies and those abilities-or-practices necessary or sufficient for deploying vocabularies that stand in semantic relations to one another. Put differently, semantic abilities concern what one must do so as to count as saying something *meaningful*, judging something, or thinking about various kinds of things, and what one must say in

---

216 'The ontological structures emerge directly from the semantic ones in that [...] semantics and ontology are two sides of the same coin. The fundamental ontological "category" (according to traditional terminology) is the "primary fact"; all "things" (in philosophical terms, all "beings" or "entities") are configurations of primary facts. The term "fact" is taken in a comprehensive sense, corresponding to the way this term is normally used at present (e.g., "semantic fact", "logical fact," etc.). It therefore does not necessarily connote, as it does in ordinary terminology, the perspective of empiricism.' Puntel, *Structure and Being*, 15.

order to explicitly specify or codify practices underlying those sayings or thinkings. Here and throughout this book, 'meaning' stands only for determinate semantic value as that which is assigned to a piece of reasoning or a judgement. All things considered, semantic abilities are those structuring abilities required for forming an unrestricted universe of discourse. A generalized pedagogy for the generation and augmentation of *sm*–abilities consists of training regimens in such structuring domains:

(a) Base Semantic Structuration

(a-1-1) <u>Protoconceptual labelling</u>: rudimentary classification by assigning labels/names to items—which are available to sensation—via 'reliable differential responsive disposition' (RDRD).[217] For example, the nonlinguistic $\mathbb{K}$ can be trained like a parrot to make the noise (not to be mistaken for a saying) 'That's black' in the presence of the heap of black. Here, the RDRD-performance 'That's black' in the presence of a black item imposes classification on the stimuli, thus differentiating those which would from those which would not trigger the response of the given kind by practicing that particular RDRD.

(a-1-2) <u>Description and explanation</u>: placing labels into a space of implications where classification is coupled with explanatory relations which can be expressed by *modal vocabulary*. An empirical description must then have both inferentially articulated circumstances for the appropriate application of labels and inferentially articulated appropriate consequences of the application of labels.

— Material Inference
  — Alethic modal vocabulary
    — Counterfactuals

---

217 R. Brandom, *Tales of the Mighty Dead: Historical Essays in the Metaphysics of Intentionality* (Cambridge, MA: Harvard University Press, 2002), 349–50.

- Context-sensitivity handling (semantic consciousness of contexts and circumstance)
- $\odot fm$-Resource-sensitivity handling (semantic consciousness of contexts and contextual premises as logical resources)
- Resolving conflict between different counterfactuals in one context
- Integration or separation of different contexts
- $\odot fm$-Possible world representation, where the meaning or sense of an expression can be accounted for not simply by its reference in the actual world, but also by what the expression would have referred to, had the actual world been different, i.e., from the counterfactual standpoint of possible worlds that are as actual as *this* actual world of reference.[218]

— Belief revision or commitment updating
  — Non-monotonic and defeasible reasoning, i.e., a reasoning in which conclusions can be retracted based on new evidence.
    - Finding defeasors or counter-defeasors for acquiring a new belief or preserving an existing one based on the incompatibility of practical commitments/beliefs or lack thereof (cf. addition or removal of premises in the light of the relation between the control set and the context in the match example discussed above).

(a-1-3) <u>Intentional vocabulary:</u> what one uses in order to ascribe claims, beliefs, desires, or intentions that p.

(a-1-4) <u>Normative vocabulary:</u> what one uses in order to ascribe commitments or entitlements to a claim that p.

---

218 See D. Lewis, *On the Plurality of Worlds* (London: Blackwell, 2001).

(a-1-5) ⊙*mf*-Non-axiomatic 'coherentist' theory formation: theories which are not axiomatic since they are not built on established truths or truth-givens, but rather are constructed out of truth-candidates whose cohering web of inferential interrelations not only decide which truth-candidates must remain, be modified, or discarded, but also make explicit the structure of theory qua system of structuration.

(b) Experimental Semantic Structuration

(b-1) Logics of discovery

— Abductive reasoning (take for instance Peirce's example of the logic of surprise: An anomaly or a surprising fact, C, is observed; But if A were true, C would be a matter of course. Hence, there is reason to suspect that A is true.[219] Here hypothesis A is suspected or conjectured to be true even though A may be false, i.e., it is tentatively believed on reasonable grounds that A is true.[220] In this framework, the observation of an anomaly and its corresponding framed hypothesis call for the revision and expansion of the theory that covered that class of observations so as to accommodate the anomalous observation. Thus, abductive reasoning can be understood as that type of reasoning that instigates a change in epistemic attitudes, cf. belief revision.)

---

219 C. S. Peirce, *The Collected Papers of Charles S. Peirce* (8 vols. Cambridge, MA: Harvard University Press, 1974), vol.5, §189.

220 The role of this tentative belief can be more accurately formulated as follows:
'[It is *reasonable to believe that* the best available explanation of a fact is true.]
F is a fact.
Hypothesis *H* explains *F*.
No available competing hypothesis explains *F* as well as *H* does.
Therefore, it is *reasonable to believe that H* is true.' A. Musgrave, 'Popper and Hypothetico-Deductivism', in *Handbook of the History of Logic: Inductive Logic* (Amsterdam: Elsevier, 2004), 228.

— Abductive hypothesis construction or framing of conjectures (abductive 'nonpredictive' hypotheses allow for the explanation of both a proposition *and* its negation).

— Abductive model-based reasoning where models accommodate different explanations (of observed facts) and where new beliefs can be adopted and old beliefs can remain so long as they cohere (cf. coherentist theory formation and Brandom's material incompatibility and inferential consequence relations).[221]

— Model pluralism: the availability of many different explanatory schemas—weak and predictive—and their corresponding models so as to enable not only the discrimination of some explanations as preferable to others but also an increase in the range of explanation to cover new observations, anomalies, or surprising facts.

— Analogical reasoning: the exploration of the outcome of the structural alignment of the shared relational pattern between two or more contextually contiguous concepts, ideas or models. For instance, think of the Archimedean method of solving geometrical problems by inventing a mechanical analogue: e.g., a lever for solving the problem of how much bigger a cylinder is than a sphere of the same radius by articulating the relation between the weights of a cylinder solid and a sphere solid of the same radius (both made of the same material) via an adjustable lever (i.e., with a moving fulcrum) capable of balancing their weights. In this form of analogy, to solve a geometrical problem/idea, a mechanical analogue, interpretation, or metaphor of the geometrical problem is introduced. The analogical solution obtained from the machine analogue together with its constitutive

---

221 Material incompatibility and inferential consequence relations refer to 'incompatibility and inferential relations that hold in virtue of what is expressed by nonlogical vocabulary. Thus claiming that Pittsburgh is west of New York City has as a material inferential consequence that New York City is east of Pittsburgh, and is materially incompatible with the claim that Pittsburgh is a prime number.' Brandom, *Reason in Philosophy*, 36.

mechanical reasoning is then mapped onto and reinterpreted as the geometrical solution and its constitutive geometrical reasoning.

— Metaphorization or conceptual cobordism:[222] how to derive a new higher-order structure from two different cognitive structures by constraining operations that allow the drawing of a contiguous contextual boundary between them through which analogical transfers and the synthesis of a third higher-order structure can be obtained. The role of metaphors in discovery can be compared, following Gilles Châtelet, to a Trojan horse that takes the cognitive habits of one context or field of thought and deploys them into another, thus setting in motion a whole dynasty of problems otherwise invisible from the perspective of any one field alone.[223]

(B) *sf*-abilities: In contrast to *sm*-abilities, *sf*-abilities can be characterized as *structure-encoding* abilities, or more generally as abilities whose main point of emphasis is on the formal or syntactic aspects of structuration. Roughly speaking, syntactic abilities or formal axiomatic abilities are required for constituting specialized domains of discourse qua sciences. They can be understood as (formal) calculi, from something like situation calculus for reasoning about dynamic domains to event calculus (representing and reasoning about events) to process calculus, proof calculus, etc. As evolved and explicitly formal structure-encoding abilities, syntactic abilities

---

222 Roughly, cobordism is an equivalence relation between two manifolds of the same dimension. Two manifolds are considered equivalent if their disjoint union ⊔ is the boundary (*bord*) of another manifold. A famous intuitive example of cobordism is a pair of pants. Think of the disk representing the waist as the manifold M and two disks representing the cuffs of a pair of pants as the manifold N. Their cobordism (or common boundary) can be expressed as the boundary of a higher-dimension structure ($n+1$-dimensional manifold W) which maps the cuffs to the waist, i.e., the boundary (a closed manifold δW) outlining the pair of pants itself. Cobordism then can be formulated as $\delta W = M \sqcup N$.

223 On the power of metaphors in the history of science particularly at the intersection of mathematics and physics, see G. Châtelet, *Figuring Space*, tr. R. Shaw and M. Zagha (Dordrecht: Kluwer, 2000).

are primarily the objects of what Robert Harper dubs the 'holy trinity of computation'—namely logic, mathematics and computer science or proofs, programs and categorical structures.[224] Just as semantics possesses a hierarchical complexity where conceptualization and the role of concepts become increasingly more involved at higher levels, so syntax also has its own hierarchical complexity. The complexity of syntactic abilities can be mapped onto two different hierarchies, pure formal grammar (à la Chomsky's hierarchy of syntax) and formal axiomatic theoretical structures (à la Stegmüller's hierarchy of axiomatics) which concerns the axiomatization of theories. The difference between these two formal hierarchies lies in their approach to syntax. Whereas formal grammar focuses on pure generative syntax and its computational-algorithmic properties, the axiomatic hierarchy deals with the different types of axioms through which different kinds of axiomatic theories (whether quasi-formal or formal) can be constructed. In this respect, formal grammar can be approximately mapped onto computational abilities (recursive pattern matching, algorithmic design, rules of pattern recognition, etc.) while the axiomatic hierarchy can (again, roughly) be mapped onto the logico-mathematical abilities required for theory construction in the domain of exact and specialized sciences.

(a) Hierarchy of formal grammar as the domain of basic formalization abilities: In terms of pure syntax, syntactic complexity consists of the (recursive) processes required for generating syntactic languages or encoding structures, formal grammatical properties that specify levels of encoding or formal languages, and the automata necessary for computing them. In this hierarchy, computational power and complexity, and sophistication of encoding, increase from lower levels of syntax to higher levels. In tandem with the increase in computational capacities (computational cost), the demand for memory resources also increases.

---

224 For a brief introduction to computational trinitarianism see R. Harper, *The Holy Trinity* (2011), <https://existentialtype.wordpress.com/2011/03/27/the-holy-trinity/>.

Consequently, with the increase in computational costs and resources from the bottom to the top, *effective computability* decreases.[225]

(b) Hierarchy of axiomatics as the domain of abilities (of logic and mathematics and computation) required for the construction of formal theories as employed in specialized sciences: As formal *axiomatics*—that is, systems required for forming specialized axiomatic theoretical structures—the complexity of the formal can be elaborated as the hierarchy of axiomatics and the different types of formal theory-structures afforded by different classes of axiomatic systems. In *The Structure and Dynamics of Theories*, Stegmüller classifies axiomatic systems (or calculi) into five forms of axiomatization, with each form having the capacity to construct a distinct class of structuration qua formal axiomatic theory:[226] (1) intuitive axiomatization (axioms as self-evident *truth-sentences*) as in Euclid's *Elements*; (2) informal Hilbertian (set-theoretic) axiomatics or abstract qua nonintuitive axiomatics where axioms are *sentence-forms* belonging to the ordinary language of discourse; (3) formal Hilbertian axiomatics (axioms as formulas and axiomatizations as *calculi of formulas*) comprising tuples $\langle S,A,R \rangle$ where S is a syntactic system, R inference rules for deriving formulas from formulas, and A a subclass of axioms belonging to the axiomatic system based on the construction of a completely formal language; (4) informal (naïve) set-theoretical axiomatization, where axiomatization is based on the definition of a set-theoretical predicate and axioms are elements of an introduced *set-theoretic predicate*. It is called informal axiomatization since set-theoretic predicates are introduced at the ordinary and intuitive level of discourse rather than in the framework of the formal system of set theory itself; (5) explicit predicate or explicit concept for an axiom system, which is the formal equivalent of informal naïve set-theoretic

---

225 See M. Li and P. Vitányi, *An Introduction to Kolmogorov Complexity and Its Applications* (Dordrecht: Springer, 2008), and A. Minai, D. Braha, and Y. Bar-Yam, *Unifying Themes in Complex Systems* (Dordrecht: Springer, 2010).

226 Stegmüller, *The Structure and Dynamics of Theories*, 30–37.

axiomatization. Here axioms—in comparison and contradistinction with the fourth axiomatic system—are *explicit predicates belonging to the formal system of set theory.* In the case of each of these calculi, by 'assigning to the individual terms in the axioms definite objects and to the property and relation predicates properties and relations, one obtains an interpretation of the axiom system'.[227]

From the perspective of constructing models, the hierarchy of axiomatization or calculization of theories is intrinsically connected with the semantic dimension, since the concept of formal model is based on the conversion of the syntactically defined formal language—via the introduction of an interpretation—into a semantic system where the concept of validity as relating to terms, statements, and applications of the model to the data under consideration can be made precise. Without this conversion, the objectivity of a model cannot be sufficiently established.

Given the importance of the pure formal grammatical and axiomatic aspects of syntax for computational and theoretical abilities, *sf*-abilities are absolutely necessary for the encoding and construction of formal and specialized fields of structuration—that is, for forming complex *models* of the world.

The goal of the catalogue above is to show not only that we can think about the cultivation of our child AGI in terms of a combinatorial calculus of structuring powers of the mind, where we can map one ability to another or decompose a complex ability to simpler ones, but also that such a curriculum requires a diverse range of educational methods. As Brandom suggests, the problem of generalized pedagogy is the central problem of artificial general intelligence. The graduation from a CHILD to an intelligence that encounters itself in an objective world and thus is capable of reimagining itself in accordance with an expansive field of intelligibility requires a back-and-forth movement between the trainee ($\mathbb{K}$) and the trainers ($\mathbb{S}$ and $\mathbb{M}$). Such a movement is built on a pedagogical

---

227 Ibid., 32.

stimulus—often on the part of the trainers—that elicits the response of the trainee and, in a positive feedback loop (Test-Operate-Test-Exit cycles), prompts the responses of the trainers built on the response of the trainee and vice versa. In Brandom's words,

> I am suggesting that what, in a course of training, is most analogous to algorithmic elaboration of abilities is pedagogical elaboration in the form of a training regimen. In rare but important cases in early education, we have completely solved the problem of how to pedagogically elaborate one set of abilities into another. What it means to have solved a pedagogical problem for a population with respect to an output practice-or-ability is that we have an empirically sufficient conditional branched training regimen for that practice-or-ability. This is something that, as a matter of contingent fact, can take any novice from the population who has mastered the relevant range of primitive practical capacities, and, by an algorithmically specifiable Test-Operate-Test-Exit (TOTE) cycle of responses to her responses, can in fact (though without the guarantee of any principle), get her to catch on to the target ability. For us, training pupils who can already count to be able to add is essentially a solved pedagogical problem in this sense. That is, starting with pupils of widely varying abilities and prior experiences who share only the prior ability to count, there is a flowchart of differentially elicited instructions, tests, and exercises that will lead all of them to the target skill of being able correctly to add pairs of arbitrary multi-digit numbers.[228]

A curriculum formed around the calculus of structuring abilities can be thought of as a pedagogical rather than an executive—i.e., fully mechanizable—algorithm for graduating the CHILD. The point is that, even if a fully mechanizable algorithm for such abilities could be developed, it cannot be adopted by a generalized pedagogy for the graduation of the child AGI. All the development of such an executive algorithm implies is that abilities can be elaborated into more complex ones or decomposed into simpler ones.

228 Brandom, *Between Saying and Doing*, 88–9.

But in so far as $\mathbb{K}$ is always going to be a creature constrained by the specific parameters of its sensory-causal structure and its particular set of contextual experiences in the world, algorithmic automation or mechaniz-ability of abilities won't be adequate to the job. Pedagogy always moves forward in response to (at least) the trainee's capacities and contextual experiences. Short of that, education becomes a tyrannical and ultimately abortive endeavour. This, of course, does not mean that we cannot think of the training regimen for $\mathbb{K}$ in terms of mechanizable algorithms. It simply means that the kind of pedagogical algorithms we should conceive for $\mathbb{K}$ must involve the interaction of the trainee and the trainers as agents which do not have essentially the same causal structure and the same set of experiences, or more generally as agents that have different computational cost constraints.

With this disquisition on what the education of the child AGI consists in—not just learning the use of concepts in order to have a structured experi-ence in virtue of being able to objectively think or judge the contents of its experience, but also the capacity to employ syntactic and semantic abilities or technologies of structuration afforded by language and logic—we can move forward with the last part of our thought experiment.

6. This I, or We or It, the Thing, Which Speaks (Dasein of Geist)

REALIZATION OF LANGUAGE

In the previous chapter, we witnessed the development of $\mathbb{K}$ into what Rosenberg terms a CHILD, whose interactions with its environment are bound up with and inferred by its interactions with its linguistic guardians. Next we saw that the transition from CHILD status to fully fledged general intelligence requires certain cognitive regimens or educational methods through which $\mathbb{K}$ becomes increasingly competent in expanding its outlook by imputing structure to the world (universe) and to its own thoughts and actions. However, this development looked suspiciously straightforward; and indeed, there was in fact a sleight of hand in our thought experiment. With the introduction of the multi-agent system, we assumed that $\mathbb{K}$'s adult guardians were full concept-having language-using AGIs—that is, we assumed we had already constructed general intelligence. In other words, we made too great a leap from the goal of our thought experiment—the realization of general intelligence—to the presupposition that it had already been attained. Nevertheless, there is nothing inherently erroneous in this assumption, since we could easily swap the role of the linguistically proficient automata $\mathbb{S}$ and $\mathbb{M}$ with their linguistically proficient human counterparts $\mathbb{S}'$ and $\mathbb{M}'$. However, while this rectification is easy and sound, it misses a point: the condition of possibility of discursive apperceptive intelligence rests on the condition of possibility of language—or, in other words, the realization of general intelligence is constituted by the realization of language. Even though the introduction of linguistic agents into the thought experiment is not an illegal move, then, it does occlude the key role played by the realization of language—both in terms of its evolution and its autonomous and sui generis rule-governed functions—in the realization of the conditions of possibility of general intelligence in the first place.

Language is not something to be developed and introduced after the fact, and then imposed upon general intelligence; it is the very framework within which general intelligence can be realized. In short, the realization of general intelligence is concurrent and coextensive with the realization of language as that which makes it possible. There would be no geist, no mind and no thinking I, were it not for language as 'the most spiritual (*Geistig*) existence (*Dasein*) of the spiritual'.[229] The omission of any consideration of language when addressing issues such as truth, thinking, life, and Being inevitably leads to an iteration of the myth of the given and culminates in an atavistic metaphysics which is both dogmatic and precritical. This is because any talk of truth, life, or Being presupposes semantic structuration within the universe of discourse—and the question of semantics cannot be divorced from language in its generic form. Claims of a nonlinguistic thought or of access to Being without language rank even lower than claims to the existence of magical powers and miracles since they are by definition—in virtue of their purported immediate involvement with reality as well as their normative-critical impoverishment—predisposed to turn into a breeding ground for the most dubious and debilitating ideologies.

In our thought experiment, the construction of AGI must therefore be a part of the realization of language. Rather than taking language as an extrinsic feature of this construction that can be introduced at a later stage, the realization of language will be treated as an intrinsic and constitutive dimension in the realization of general intelligence. In tandem with the constitutive role of language for general intelligence, the thesis endorsed here is that the construction of artificial general intelligence should be primarily conducted via an extensive project that can bring about the necessary conditions for the possibility of language among a system of artificial agents. Crudely put, the evolution of language should be taken seriously as the most indispensable part of the realization of general intelligence.

Instead of providing artificial agents with a predeveloped formal language that might be able to mimic the behaviours of natural language, an environment must be established within which artificial agents can develop

---

229 Hegel, *Philosophy of Right*, §164.

through the evolution of language among them. That is to say, the aim is to reenact the concurrent and coextensive realization of language and general intelligence. The reason for the employment of this reenactment strategy is that the evolution of language should be seen as a process of canalization of prevalent intelligent behaviours toward qualitatively distinct and sui generis behaviours. Through this process, intelligent behaviours (or agents) progressively come under new generative constraints, each of which enables a piecemeal qualitative shift within the system of interacting agents. The key to this process is the development of multi-agent interaction from rudimentary communication to interaction via symbol design, from symbol design to syntax, and from syntax—through interaction—to semantics. In other words, interaction at different levels of complexity (from protolinguistic levels to pragmatics as the interface between syntax and semantics) is not only the key to the evolution of language and its autonomous rule-governed functions, but by extension is also the key to the realization of general intelligence.

Two points are worth noting here: the first is that the construction of artificial general intelligence can be informed by insights into the evolution of natural language, without sacrificing research into the diverse logical and computational aspects of syntax, semantics, and pragmatics. My intention is not to collapse the distinction between the evolutionary picture of natural language and the autonomy of language (particularly, semantics) as a rule-governed system. Instead, the claim is that these two need to be rendered commensurate *without* being fused or blended together. The second point concerns the emphasis on natural language. Although language may well have begun with ordinary natural language, it cannot be reduced in its entirety to natural language. Despite its low syntactic complexity and semantic ambiguity, natural language harbours a diverse range of complex logico-computational phenomena which can be incorporated into the design of an artificial general language—a superior mode of language—that exhibits both the properties of formal-theoretical languages (syntactic powers and semantic transparency) and the explicitly interactive (qua social) dimensions of natural languages. Interaction as the explicit framework of natural languages is the implicit and fundamental logico-computational framework of language in general. We shall come back to this latter point below.

With these remarks in mind, in order to proceed with the AS-AI-TP thought experiment, a necessary change must be made. The status of S and M as fully fledged concept-having automata must be rescinded, so that they now have the same status as K. The only modifications that remain are the ones introduced at the beginning of the previous chapter, i.e., the multi-agent system and the capacity to produce quasi-continuous sounds. The course of the thought experiment will be developed in the following stages: first, we shall briefly look at the automaton's capacity for nonconceptual representings through which metalinguistic properties picture nonlinguistic properties (of items and occurrences in the world) via syntactic structures of sign-designs. This is Sellars's account of picturing as detailed in his essay 'Being and Being Known', where the android robot equipped with a Robotese language forms progressively more adequate pictures of the world.[230]

Necessary adjustments will be made to Sellars's account of picturing by distinguishing sign-design tokens from symbol-design tokens. Only the latter can have a syntactic configuration in the combinatorial sense, one that can capture the relations between signs (or Sellars's 'pictures') qua nonconceptual representings. Without minimal symbolic syntactic structure, picturing cannot constrain the arbitrariness of meaning. Pace Sellars, pictures cannot have syntactic *structure*. Pictures are one-to-one nonconceptual representations, or, more accurately, second-order isomorphisms between two natural objects. By contrast, conceptually represented objects are caught up in *combinatorial relations* between symbols which themselves are *not* nonconceptual representing sign-design tokens or inscriptions at the level of causal structures. From here we move into an examination of what

---

230 An example of the Robotese language would be rudimentary inductive moves printed in the form of sentences of the kind 'whenever lightning at p, t; thunder at $p + \Delta p$, $t + \Delta t$' registering on the wiring diagram of the robot like traces on a tape (e.g., '::, 9, 15' signifies lightning at place 9 and time 15). See W. Sellars, 'Being and Being Known', in *In the Space of Reasons*, 209–28.

symbols are and what process or processes are required for the realization of a symbolic syntax that can later on be bridged with semantics. This is the process of discretization necessary for the realization of combinatorial symbols. However, we must keep in mind that language is not merely a symbolic-syntactic medium. As already argued, it is first and foremost a semantic structure that configures word-world relations.

The final stage of the thought experiment involves a survey of how the transition from syntax to semantics is possible under the aegis of interaction as a logico-computational phenomenon which is the engine of language and its multilayered qualitative structure. In accordance with the toy model approach, but also owing to practical constraints, the examination of the role of interaction as the bridge between syntax and semantics will be kept at the minimal introductory level.

PICTURES, SIGNS AND SYMBOLS

In our toy universe, the interactive framework of the multi-agent system represents a computational problem: How can the agents synchronously and asynchronously interact with one another and their environment, given that (a) maintaining interaction between agents is dependent upon an optimal interaction with their environment, and (b) the agents vary in terms of their sensory impressions, memories, and behaviours (i.e., different individual interactions with the environment)?

In this setting, maintaining the interaction between the automata becomes a matter of the stabilization, adaptation, and enhancement of interactive strategies—reactive as well as proactive—both at the level of inter-agent interaction and that of (multi-agent) system-environment interaction. If we consider the interaction between agents as a computational strategy for effectively modifying the computational parameters of interaction with the environment, then this computational strategy should accommodate and display stabilizing and adaptive mechanisms appropriate for a wide range of interactions involving asynchronicity, resource distribution, and dynamic behaviours. In this sense, the interaction between the agents is interlocked with their interaction with the environment. The complexity

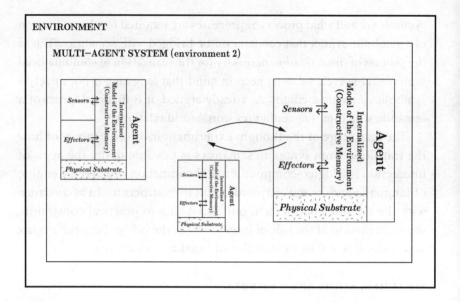

of the former, therefore, should be regarded as an adequate means for engaging with the complexity of the latter. A change in the computational capacities of the inter-agent interaction as a result of a qualitative shift in its structure would translate into a change in the computational capacities of the system-environment interaction.

Within this environment, imagine the occurrence of two events: E_1 (e.g., the rustling noise) and E_2 (e.g., appearance of a fuzzy grey item). By virtue of their causal structure (wiring diagram or nervous system), the automata are capable of associating one occurrence with another. For example, a rustling noise (N_r) then the presence of a fuzzy grey item (G), or the fuzzy grey item coming into contact with the heap of black (B_c) then a shrieking noise (N_s). In other words, $\mathbb{K}$, $\mathbb{S}$ and $\mathbb{M}$ are aware[1] of these occurrences, their associations, transitions, and precluding relations in the form of the following inductive moves:

rustling noise → fuzzy item: If N_r at place p and time t then G at p and t

(and its corresponding obstruction or preclusion, i.e., not a move like *no rustling noise → fuzzy item:* If no N_r at place p and time t then G at p and t)

fuzzy item, contact with the heap of black → shrieking noise: If G at place $p + \Delta p$ and time $t + \Delta t$ then N_s at $p + \Delta p$, $t + \Delta t$

Or, more generally, the occurrence of an event E_i in the environment is accompanied by the occurrence of another event E_j. Such associations contain their corresponding transitions and obstructions.

At this point, the automata are capable of statistically correlating E_i's pattern of occurrence with E_j's pattern of occurrence. More precisely, the automata are capable of forming nonconceptual associations and transitions between one pattern of occurrence and another (E_i–E_j). However, they do not know—objectively speaking—that E_j, for example, is the sound a monkey makes when examining a monolith. These associations and transitions are purely a matter of statistical-predictive generalization. We can call the association or transition E_i–E_j a pattern-governed regularity that registers at the level of the causal structure and behavioural outputs of the automata. The capacity to causally register—in an adequate manner with regard to the behavioural outputs or reactions of the automata to the environment—a pattern-governed regularity is called picturing—i.e., a nonconceptual representing of events and items in the environment. A simplistic analogical example of picturing would be a security swipe card. The magnetic field changes the iron-based magnetic particles on the stripe of the magnetic material on the card. As the result of this causal structural change, the card can open certain doors and not others (the constraining element). However, this analogy could be misleading. Even though pictures are instantiated in causal structures, they cannot be expressed in causal terms or as a form of causation. Instead, they should be understood in terms of processes.

The automata's capacity for correct picturing (qua rudimentary representation) of events in the environment is as much the result of the pressures and constraints imposed by the environment (the presence of items and occurrences that affect the causal structure or wiring diagram of the automata) as of the complexity of the causal structure of the automata that mediates between environmental input and behavioural output. For the sake of brevity, let us say that whenever both E_i and E_j occur in the environment, there is a corresponding change in the causal structure, wiring diagram, or nervous system of the automata. This change occasions an equivalent (but not equal or identical) pattern-governed regularity $E_i^*-E_j^*$ which is then reflected in the behavioural output of the automata in the form of the inductive moves—transformation rules or rudimentary protocol-like transitions—described earlier. Here, $E_i^*-E_j^*$ is a rudimentary i.e., nonconceptual representing that can be understood as a mapping between objects belonging to the real order—the wiring diagram of the automata and occurrences and items in the world.

Therefore, picturing (the world) differs from signifying (the world) in that the former belongs to the real order and the latter is of the logical order (that of thinking or, in Sellars, intentionality).[231] Signifying and picturing, then, belong to two distinct levels of discourse. And although rule-governed signifying is embodied in pattern-governed picturing, it is irreducible to the latter. Similarly, although pattern-governed regularities incarnate and constrain rule-governed conceptual activities, they cannot be overextended to encompass the latter. It is picturing (pattern-governed regularities) that undergirds signifying (rule-governed conceptual activities). But the order of signifying is irreducible to the order of picturing since it is concerned not with pattern-governed regularities but with the complex interactions between patterns. In other words, rule-governed conceptual activities are *patterning patterns*. Contra right-wing Sellarsians,[232] the realization of the rule-governed

---

231 'I shall use the verb "to picture" for the first of these "dimensions" and the verb "to signify" for the second. I shall argue that a confusion between *signifying* and *picturing* is the root of the idea that the intellect as signifying the world is the intellect as informed in a unique (or immaterial) way by the natures of things in the real order. [When we say] X pictures Y, both X and Y belong to the real order, i.e. neither belongs to the order of intentionality; and when we say X signifies Y, both X and Y belong to the logical order, i.e. the order of intentionality.' Sellars, *In the Space of Reasons*, 218–19.

232 See for example, R. Millikan, 'Pushmi-pullyu Representations', *Philosophical Perspectives* vol. 9 (Atascadero, CA: Ridgeview, 1995), 185–200.

or normative order of the patterning of patterns requires a qualitative shift in the order of picturing that permits the explicitation and navigation of the diverse relations between pictures or pattern-governed regularities.

Pictures qua signs can only capture the one-to-one mappings between pattern-governed regularities in the real order $(E_i-E_j \rightarrow E_i^*-E_j^*)$. Said differently, nonconceptual representations are independent of one another. Their relationships are not given in themselves, and they lack the kind of structured relationships required for transitions between them, whereas symbols in themselves are entirely devoid of such one-to-one mappings, and primarily stand in combinatorial relations to one another (symbol-to-symbol, token-to-token) and only secondarily in relation to extra-symbolic referents.[233] And it is in virtue of this interrelational order of symbols (i.e., symbolic syntax rather than syntax in terms of causal regularities) that the relations between different patterns or world-picturings can be encoded, structured, singled out, and elaborated. In other words, semantics is afforded by symbolic elements of syntax whose relations differ in kind from the relations indexed by pictures. Signs (icons and indices) lack combinatorial syntactic structures to the extent that they are representational mappings that only stand in one-to-one causal-structural equivalence relations between properties of the representations and properties of the represented items or occurrences.

---

233 '[S]ymbols cannot be understood as an unstructured collection of tokens that map to a collection of referents because symbols don't just represent things in the world, they also represent each other. Because symbols do not directly refer to things in the world, but indirectly refer to them by virtue of referring to other symbols, they are implicitly combinatorial entities whose referential powers are derived by virtue of occupying determinate positions in an organized system of other symbols. Both their initial acquisition and their later use requires a combinatorial analysis. The structure of the whole system has a definite semantic topology that determines the ways symbols modify each other's referential functions in different combinations. Because of this systematic relational basis of symbolic reference, no collection of signs can function symbolically unless the entire collection conforms to certain overall principles of organization.' T. Deacon, *The Symbolic Species* (New York: W.W. Norton & Company, 1997), 99.

As soon as we talk about syntactic structures that enable semantic interpretations, we have crossed over from the domain of *signs* into that of *symbols* as combinatorial syntactic elements that primarily map to one another rather than to an item or occurrence in the environment/world. Understanding semantics-enabling syntactic symbols in this way does not risk a hypostatization of abstract entities, since they are still constrained and embodied in pattern-governed regularities or pictures. But the manner of this constraining or incarnating regime is not a matter of the simple compositionality of pictures. Pictures do not map to syntactic symbols, but only to the interrelations between symbols which, in themselves, have no mapping relation whatsoever to pattern-regularities in the world. In other words, pattern-governed regularities in the real order are caught up in the relations between symbols, not the other way around. Such relations themselves are not pattern-governed in the sense of belonging to the real order. They are instead already rule-governed (i.e., combinatorial) relations belonging to a different order, the autonomous order of symbols. Collapsing the distinction between signs and symbols, picture-mappings and symbolic syntactic interrelations, or regarding conceptual activities as 'a species of pattern-governed behavior'[234] is a recipe for all sorts of confusions, one to which Sellars himself has unfortunately contributed some ingredients.

Just because conceptual activities and their undergirding symbolic interrelations are built on pictures and iconic-indexical signs, this does not mean that conceptual activities and symbols are *made of* pattern-governed regularities and mapping relations. Being built on something is not the same as being made of something. Let us clarify these points in the context of our thought experiment.

---

234 'The distinction between pattern-governed behavior and rule-governed activity is not a difference in kind; rather, rule-governed activity is a species of pattern-governed behavior: a recursive loop generated through the interaction between complex patterns.' R. Brassier, 'Transcendental Logic and True Representings', *Glass Bead* 0 (2016), <http://www.glass-bead.org/article/transcendental-logic-and-true-representings/>.

SIGN-VEHICLES AND SYMBOL-DESIGN

In the multi-agent system, the automata have their own inductive moves. The contact of the fuzzy grey item with the heap of black (E_i-E_j) changes their wiring diagram. The state of the representational system or the wiring diagram of the automata is now a second-order isomorphism—i.e., an equivalence (but not equality) relation—that registers as $E_i{}^*-E_j{}^*$, a statistical inductive association with its corresponding transitions and obstructions. For example, the occurrence of the fuzzy item making contact with the heap of black and then a shrieking noise is registered on $\mathbb{K}$'s wiring diagram as a pattern-governed regularity that permits certain rudimentary inductive moves: Whenever N_s (shrieking noise) at $p + \Delta p$ *and* $t + \Delta t$ then G (fuzzy grey item) at $p + \Delta p$ and $t + \Delta t$. It should be pointed out that registering the noise N_s depends on a few factors. Firstly, it must be of some interest or significance for $\mathbb{K}$, i.e., it must play a role for $\mathbb{K}$'s overall behavioural economy. If the noise is of no interest to $\mathbb{K}$, it will not register on $\mathbb{K}$'s 'attentional system' (Dehaene). Only the top-down attentional amplification of modular processes can mobilize the change in the wiring diagram and make it available to $\mathbb{K}$'s global workspace or awareness of the environment. Secondly, registering the noise N_s crucially depends on the sufficiency of $\mathbb{K}$'s causal structure or wiring for pattern recognition. Without this criterion, $\mathbb{K}$ would not be able to differentiate the amplitude and frequency of the shrieking noise from the rustling noise and would therefore be incapable of making inductive moves—transitions and obstructions—related to these items.

Our assumption, however, is that $\mathbb{K}$, $\mathbb{S}$, and $\mathbb{M}$ satisfy such criteria. They are equipped with the adequate causal structure to differentiate not only N_s and N_r, but also such noises of interest to them insofar as they play an important role in their behavioural (or perception-action) ecology. Upon occurrence of the pattern N_s, $\mathbb{K}$'s auditory system registers it as an input acoustic pattern σ which is associated with the occurrence of N_s and, correspondingly, with the fuzzy item touching the black item. The automaton tags this acoustic pattern σ by emitting a whistling sound or acoustic cue Σ using its inbuilt electromechanical devices. The acoustic cue Σ has no meaning in the sense of describing N_s or signifying what $E_i{}^*-E_j{}^*$ (the picture of the fuzzy item touching the black item accompanied by a shrieking noise) is. From now on, whenever $\mathbb{K}$ registers σ it emits the whistling sound Σ. Within the multi-agent system, $\mathbb{K}$'s repeated reuse of Σ is also registered by $\mathbb{S}$ and $\mathbb{M}$ as a cue for the occurrence of N_s and, correspondingly, the pattern-governed regularity $E_i{}^*-E_j{}^*$.

The significance of the relation between E_i-E_j, $E_i{}^*-E_j{}^*$, N_s and σ in triggering Σ is simply that of the statistical frequency of spatiotemporal occurrences registered by the structurally sufficient and behaviourally active automata. In short, it is devoid of complex inferential or conceptual relationships. This is precisely what Peirce calls an indexical sign, a sign whose interpretant is entirely a statistical regularity of some occurrence (a causal or temporal invariance) and whose interpreter requires only a heuristic device to interpret it. An index is a sign that is somehow causally linked with something else in space and time. Furthermore, indexical sign-vehicles such as Σ are built on iconic signs that concern the resemblance of one pattern to another. This resemblance, however, is wholly a matter of an *arbitrary* interpretation of the similarity-vagueness of something versus something else. In this sense, iconicity is really the stimuli-based discrimination of *stuff*.

Pictures qua mapping functions are indexical signs, which themselves are built on icons or stimuli-based discriminations. In terms of their reference, both indices and icons are arbitrary and generic. A clarifying example of indexical sign-vehicles would be social animal alarm calls. In sighting a predator, a member of the group vocalizes a specific sound that is statistically associated with the presence of predators. This sound or indexical sign does not, however, specify the type of the predator, nor does it relay any information to other members of the group regarding the predator's exact location. It simply signals the presence of a danger in their vicinity. Similarly, the only significance of Σ is that it communicates an *indexical* one-to-one relationship between the interpreter (the agent) and the interpreted (E_i-E_j). Transmitting and receiving Σ is what we can call 'communication', reserving the term for this rudimentary schema of transmitting and receiving an *indexical* one-to-one relationship between a sound cue and an interpreted event or series of events.

Upon registering an input acoustic pattern, $\mathbb{K}$'s internal pattern-recognition mechanisms match it with $\mathbb{K}$'s archive of *input patterns* correlated with previously catalogued patterns of occurrences. If the registered acoustic pattern matches σ, the automaton produces Σ as a signal pertaining to the alleged occurrence of the associated events E_i–E_j. Setting aside the problem of the arbitrariness of the representational correspondence between σ and the E_i–E_j pattern of occurrence, the indices σ for $\mathbb{K}$ and Σ for $\mathbb{S}$ and $\mathbb{M}$ are fundamentally narrow in the range of their relationships with other indices associated with other pattern-governed regularities.

The insufficiency and unreliability of the prevalent indexical sign-vehicles is nowhere more manifest than in natural phenomena involving mimicry and deception. Take for instance the parasitoid blue butterfly *phengaris rebeli*, known for its intricate social parasitism on a species of ants called *myrmica* ants. The butterfly lays eggs close to the ant colony. Its broods discharge the same chemical signals by which ants distinguish their own. By mimicking the ants' indexical chemical sign, the butterfly broods trick the ants into carrying them into their nest. Once they are in the nest and as they mature, by mimicking the acoustic signals the queen ant uses to mobilize worker ants to bring food to it, the butterfly larvae climb the social hierarchy of the ant colony. Associating the mimicked acoustic signal with their queen, the worker ants begin to bring food to the parasitoid larvae, in the process starving their queen—the only ant that can detect the larvae as aggressors—to death. However, for the *myrmica* ants the semiotic nightmare does not end here, for the oversaturation of chemical signals as the result of the activity of both the ants and *p. rebeli*'s parasitism lures yet another parasitoid to the ant colony—the *ichneumon* wasp cited by Darwin as evidence that shakes the very idea of a 'beneficent and omnipotent God'.[235]

Owing to their one-to-one mapping structure, just like indices, pictures qua nonconceptual representings are limited in terms of how they relate to or interact with other pictures. The complex relations between pictures or

---

235 C. Darwin, *The Life and Letters of Charles Darwin* (2 vols. New York: Appleton, 1898), vol.2, 105.

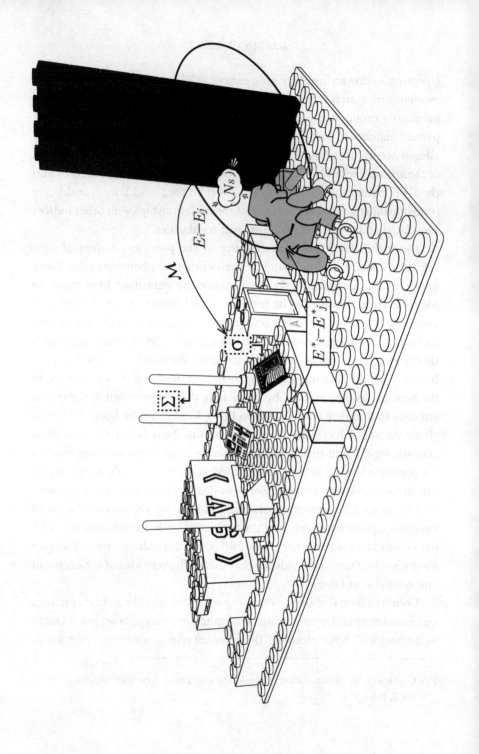

Automata and nonconceptual representational mapping: The sound N_S is mapped onto the automaton's devices as an acoustic pattern σ. N_S is statistically correlated with the pattern-governed regularity $E_i - E_j$. As the automaton registers σ, it produces the sound Σ to tag the occurrence of the pattern $E_i - E_j$. The representational mapping $\mathcal{M}$ ($E_i^* - E_j^*$ to $E_i - E_j$) is not a meaning relation. It is a transformation between two natural objects, the environmental state and the internal state of the structurally sufficient and behaviourally active automaton. For this reason, the sound cue does not in any semantic sense *signify* an aspect of the external environment, nor does it describe any detail about the internal state of the automaton itself. It is simply a probabilistic marker for the statistical convergence of the automaton's σ-state and the pattern of occurrence for external events $E_i - E_j$.

pattern-governed regularities cannot be obtained by pictures themselves. Claiming that automata can, *in principle*, fully structure and navigate their environment simply by adequate picturing inevitably results in *picturing regress*. This is because the structuration and navigation of the environment requires the selection, explicitation, and elaboration of diverse relations between pattern-governed regularities. In order for such complex relations to be singled out, a new picture or one-to-one mapping must be acquired. But in so far as the acquisition of a new picture or the detection of a new pattern-governed regularity results in additional relations between pictures and patterns which the new picture cannot by itself index, still further pictures must be acquired. This process can go on ad infinitum without ever covering the complex relations or interactions between patterns, hence the regress. Where there are one-to-many and many-to-many correlations between patterns, the picturing capacity, as a one-to-one mapping, always falls short.

Moreover, from the practical perspective, even if the automata could indeed fully structure and navigate their environment by adequate and complete picturing, from a computational point of view this would be unfeasible, since for every matter-of-factual property of items or patterns of occurrences of events in the world, they would have to acquire not only a picture or representational mapping but also additional pictures to represent the diverse relations between those pictures and their corresponding regularities. With this ever-expanding repertoire of picturings, the size of the automata's internal model would grow. Since computational resources and memory would need to be allocated to these pictures in order to support the structure of the internal model, as it increased in size the internal model would become less and less effectively computable. Once the complexity of the internal model's structure could no longer be increased owing to the lack of effective computability and resource starvation, it would no longer be capable of singling out or picturing new phenomena and items. The representational competencies of the automata would then begin to diminish. This is a ubiquitous scenario among any species equipped only with iconic and indexical sign-vehicles, and not symbols.

For indexical sign-vehicles to cover the diverse relations between pattern-governed regularities, they have to be incorporated into a *different kind* of semiotic system—one whose signs are not in a one-to-one or representational relation to referents, patterns, or events. The order of picturing and indexical signs is necessary but not sufficient to cover the interactions between patterns. This sufficiency can only be obtained by a different kind of semiotic system that is not composed of mappings. This is a system in which the semiotic elements do not represent or relate to a pattern-governed regularity, an external event, or a substantive referent, but only to one another. The combinatorial order of symbols that permits syntactic configurations is exactly this inter-related semiotic system.

In the vernacular use of the concept of symbol, symbols are symbols because they are inscriptions, letters, characters, sounds, or gestures that abstractly represent something else. But such elements are not symbols in the strict syntactic and formal sense. Symbols are only symbols in so far as they are *abstract* nonrepresentational entities that relate or refer to one another rather than to something external to them (i.e., a represented target event, pattern, etc). For semiotic elements to be reorganized as symbols certain criteria must be satisfied, such as the discretization of signs and the establishing of a combinatorial structure (i.e., rules for the possibility and impossibility of combining signs) whereby recursive processes can generate new and more complex relations between abstract elements.

It is the order of symbols that has syntactic structure, not the order of signs—whether iconic or indexical. And it is only the syntactic structure of symbols—elements that only stand in one-to-many and many-to-many relations to one another—that can codify relationships between pattern-governed regularities, pictures, or indexical signs. Conceptual semantic activities are *sui generis* pattern -governed regularities (or rules) that pattern or structure pattern-governed regularities—i.e., single out and elaborate the diverse relationships between patterns—because they are undergirded by syntactic structures that structure and codify such relationships. The codifying syntactic structures are themselves afforded by symbols, semiotic elements that are defined not by how they represent an item or an external relation of reference, but by the combinatorial relationships in which they stand in relation to one another.

Put simply, the order of symbols is not a representational order in the sense that iconic or indexical signs are, but an order whose systematic inter-relations can codify or structure *indexical relationships*— something that indexical signs by themselves cannot accomplish. Indices are accordingly caught up in the combinatorial and codifying relationships between symbols or elements of syntax. Just as indices are built on icons, symbols are built on indices. But, as Terrence Deacon points out, the fact that symbols are built on indices and indices are built on icons does not mean that the relations that hold between them are relations of simple compositionality.[236] Indices are not made of icons and symbols are not made of indices. Symbols, indices, and icons are *distinct* levels of structuring. Whereas representational icons and indices have a limited capacity for structuring, symbols, by virtue of their combinatorial self-referentiality have an in-principle unrestricted structuring capacity. For our automata, the capacity for the full-blown structuration of their world does not begin with their ability to correctly picture their environment, but only with the advent of symbolic technologies that permit the syntactic codification and semantic elaboration of the relations between pictures.

This is, however, not to suggest that the automata may not have more adequate picturing abilities than ours. They may well be furnished with more sophisticated mechanisms for pattern-recognition and algorithms capable of more optimal compression of data and hence more fine-grained picturing—or regularity detection—abilities. This is the fundamental insight of Ray Solomonoff—as formulated in the context of algorithmic complexity and the computational account of inductive inference—that there exists an intrinsic duality of compression and regularity: anything that can compress data is a type of regularity, and any regularity can compress data.[237] For example we might imagine our automaton's picturing abilities to be modelled on

---

236 T. Deacon, 'Beyond the Symbolic Species', in *The Symbolic Species Evolved* (Dordrecht: Springer, 2012), 13.

237 R. Solomonoff, 'A Formal Theory of Inductive Inference part 1', *Information and Control* 7.1 (1964), 1–22.

better predictive compression algorithms such as Solomonoff's induction or Crutchfield's ε-machine reconstruction, which employ a formal computational (rather than ordinary epistemic) version of Occam's razor and the principle of multiple explanations to yield inductive models smaller in size and of a lower degree of arbitrariness.[238]

Briefly, Solomonoff's predictive induction employs the formal computational definition of simplicity: All knowledge available in a domain at a specific time can be written as a binary string. In this case, a new observation or experience at time t_2 increases the length of the string. Solomonoff's induction problem is then how to predict the next bit of the string by extrapolating the known length of the string. Independently of Andrey Kolmogorov and Gregory Chaitin, Solomonoff showed that there exists an optimal prior probability distribution on any potentially infinite string such that one can compute the next best possible or formally simplest extrapolation using this universal prior distribution. The best predictive model can then be defined in terms of the length of the shortest program that outputs the simplest possible string.[239]

The picturing abilities of our automata could indeed be modelled on such programs.[240] But prediction is not the same as explanation. Even in

---

238 See J. Crutchfield, 'The Calculi of Emergence: Computation, Dynamics, and Induction', *Physica D*, vol. 75 (1994), 11–54.

239 For more nontechnical details on Solomonoff's theory of formal induction see S. Legg, 'Is There an Elegant Universal Theory of Prediction?', in *Algorithmic Learning Theory* (Dordrecht: Springer, 2006), 274–87, and N. Chater and P. Vitányi, 'Simplicity: A Unifying Principle in Cognitive Science?', *Trends in Cognitive Sciences* 7:1 (2003), 19–22.

240 Crutchfield's ε-machine reconstruction follows much the same principle as Solomonoff's induction except for one significant difference: it takes a string of bits and reverse-engineers the physical states of the system or machine responsible for the generation of that pattern or regularity. Here, the word 'machine' stands for a physical system capable of s possible physical states. The dynamic of such a system can then be defined in terms of the transition between its states. This transition can be thought as an oscillation between state s_1 and state s_2, and hence can be modelled on a program which, at every discrete time stamp, generates bitstrings by

information theory, prediction and explanation are subtly distinguished from one another. Furthermore, as argued earlier with regard to the problems of complete picturing, an agent modelled purely on such formal learning machines would still run into the problem of effective computability. For example, Solomonoff's universal learning machine presupposes an infinite time limit and runs on a universal Turing machine. For a realistic agent with a finite time and limited computational resources, not only may the implementation of Solomonoff's algorithm result in resource impoverishment since the universal Turing machine is the most resource-consuming class of abstract machines, it may also lead to the uncomputability of the halting problem—that is, the undecidability of whether the machine should accept or reject an input to yield an output.

Accordingly, what is required for explanation is not better prediction or the compression-regularity duality, but the ability to selectively compress data or to single out one regularity over another. And precisely what language—starting with the order of symbols—affords agents is the ability to selectively compress data, to single out and elaborate diverse relations between regularities—not merely to picture pattern-governed regularities but to describe and explain them in context. As discussed in the previous chapter, this copula of description and explanation is what material inferences ultimately are. For our automata to count as belonging to the order of general intelligence, they must be able to perform material inferences, to have the practical competences or know-how to use concepts. In short, they must have an artificial general language to syntactically encode the relationships between pictures, to structure such relationships by semantically elaborating their material incompatibility and consequence relations, and ultimately to make

---

emitting 0 or 1 depending upon which state the system is currently in. ε-machine reconstruction takes such a bitstring as its input—that is, it begins with the current state of a finite state machine and predicts the future dynamics of the system based on the history of its past transitions and current state, i.e., it extrapolates whatever information is needed to predict the next bit in the string.

explicit such relations in formal inferences. Coming into possession of such structuring syntactic-semantic abilities, however, entails something more than just the addition of new sign-vehicles or better pictures of the world. It requires symbol-design—the construction of symbolic tokens that can be combined in a variety of ways to form codifying structures and assume semantic roles in the process of being exchanged between agents.

In the following sections, we shall see how the sign-using automata can be endowed with structuring syntactic-semantic abilities by coming into possession of symbols whose combinatorial generative capacities permit the stabilization of inter-agent interactions and the encoding of diverse relationships between pattern-governed regularities. In developing the ability for symbol design, no additional modification to the multi-agent system will be introduced. What we want is to see how the interacting automata themselves, using the resources they already have at their disposal—in particular, the capacity to receive and transmit acoustic signals or sound cues—can acquire symbols.

AN ACOUSTIC EXPERIMENT IN THE PRODUCTION OF SYMBOLS

In chapter 5, a new constraint was incorporated into the modifications of the automata: the automata can only produce *quasi-continuous* sounds. The motivation for the addition of this constraint was that it would allow us to monitor the processes required for the generation of symbols in the toy universe of our automata.

Recall that the automata are provided with organs or electromagnetic devices capable of constricting the continuous sound (noise) and discontinuing it in a specific manner. In this way, the sound is discontinued either abruptly or gradually (i.e., within a temporal window). The constricted or discontinued sound now represents an acoustic range. It is regulated by different constricting devices working in coordination with one another, paralleling the role of the lungs, nasal canal, tongue, and lips in human vocalization. At this point, the sound is still continuous but is also regulated by the manner of discontinuation or constriction.

The quasi-continuous sound can be refined further into a coarsely discretized sound via the frequent reuse (i.e., production and recognition) of the sound as a form of statistical modulation over time. Once our hypothetical agents solve the problem of the discretization of sound cues into stable tokens in interactions whose role can be tracked, diversified, and manipulated, they can single out and relay a wide range of behaviours pertaining to themselves and to the environment. Solving this problem requires the transition of the sound cue (sign) from a partially stabilized and regulated acoustic range (a quasi-continuous sound) to a coarsely discretized sound that can be not only effectively reproduced and recognized by the agents, but also used as a building block for composite symbolic sounds.

In the end what we want to do is to equip the automata with a medium through which they can not only share their positional-perspectival awareness but also, more importantly, compare their perspectives in a stabilized and structured manner, and ultimately arrive at an aperspectival (objective) view of the world. This development would require a stable and combinatorial medium capable of replacing the parochial referential relations between sound cues/signs and occurrences/references (i.e., the representational relation between Σ and E_i–E_j) with syntactic and ultimately semantic relations between symbolic sound-tokens. But in order to get on the path of such a development, first the sound cue Σ needs to transform from a *sign* referentially correlated to something external into a *symbol* that primarily stands in relation with other symbols. However, to recapitulate, what we are after in the toy universe of automata is a system comprising a finite repository of abstract elements which *individually* do not represent anything yet which, precisely because of this abstractness, can be combined to create composite elements which then can be put together in conformity with combinatorial rules, thus generating increasingly complex syntactic structures capable of encoding the relations between nonconceptual representing or pattern-governed regularities. The abstract elements of this system are symbols, and to reach the stage where automata would be able to employ symbol-designs to syntactically and semantically structure their world, their acoustic medium of communication will have to undergo a drastic transformation. As we shall see, this transformation is impossible without a process of discretization, which is required in order to implement effective combinatorial mechanisms among sound-tokens.

In the previous sections, we saw that $\mathbb{K}$, $\mathbb{S}$, and $\mathbb{M}$ have the capacity to communicate—in the rudimentary sense of receiving and transmitting sound cues Σ marking pictured pattern-governed regularities. In this communicative regime, however, the instability and the excess of noise in the quasi-continuous sound Σ negatively affects the precision of its signalling function, both in the sense of what it signals (the E_i–E_j pattern of occurrence as opposed to a different occurrence signalled by another quasi-continuous acoustic cue) and how the cue is successfully recognized and consumed in order to result in coordinated group response. An example of the inefficacy of quasi-continuous sound cues for transmission and reception as reliable signals would be animal alarm calls where, because of the instability and fuzziness of the acoustic signal, the call can play different roles (to signal the presence of a predator, as a mating call, in the presence of food, etc.). The appropriate group action is therefore always compromised by the fuzziness of the quasi-continuous sound cue exchanged between the communicator and the communicant. In issuing a certain sound cue, there is no guarantee that the group will *reliably* receive the communicated signal as a cue for the referent targeted by the communicator.

In addition, the quasi-continuous sound possesses a low degree of combinatoriality. Since quasi-continuous acoustic cues are structurally unstable and fuzzy in terms of their acoustic range, multiple-cue integration is severely limited. This lack of combinatoriality means that stable and coded relations between different sound cues cannot be established properly, if at all. Without these relations between sound cues afforded by combinatorial grouping, the role of the acoustic signal in connection to its source (the correspondence between σ and E_i–E_j) and its target (recognition and consumption of the sound cue by other agents) can be neither specified nor stabilized. In isolation, the role of a sound cue as a probability marker is not optimally reliable, either in relation to what it signals or in relation to its potential signal-consumers.

In our toy model, suppose that the solution for reducing the noise and fuzziness of the quasi-continuous sound is the systematic reuse of acoustic cues in the context of interaction between agents. Over time, the reuse of sound cues among the automata in an interactive framework leads to a crystallized distribution of preferred models of sound production between agents in a fashion similar to a self-organizing map or an artificial neural network utilizing unsupervised learning algorithms to cluster data by projecting high-dimensional input data (training samples) onto regular and discretized or low-dimensional data. The decrease in the number and range of acoustic data means that the agents over time automatically select and reuse a small number of clusters of preferred low-dimensional acoustic data. To put it less technically, a model of self-organization can be conceived in the multi-agent system whereby the mere vocalizations of the automata (i.e., the reuse of sound cues or acoustic signals) can converge on a small finite repertoire of preferable coarsely discretized sounds which do not communicate or represent anything, in that they are no longer sign-vehicles but abstract acoustic elements that can be combined into composite sound-tokens.

Structural discretization, together with the decrease in the number of sound clusters, results in the construction of the first building blocks of speech—that is, a finite repertoire of sounds as symbolic tokens.[241] The automata are now in the possession of a limited but well-structured set of reusable and sharable sounds—beeps, clicks, chirps, rustles, etc.—that can be combined in accordance with compositional constraints to form more composite nonrepresentational sounds. These sounds are comparable to the basic phonological units of our speech, and can be combined in conformity with statistical-acoustic transition rules to produce composite sound-tokens that can be exchanged in interactions between automata. For example, in our phonological system the transition from a [V] sound

---

241 For more details on the design and simulation of models for the discretization of sound into symbolic sound-tokens in an artificial multi-agent system see C. Browman and L. Goldstein, 'Competing Constraints on Intergestural Coordination and Self-organization of Phonological Structures', *Bulletin de la communication parlée* 5 (2000), 25–34, and P.-Y. Oudeyer, *Self-Organization in the Evolution of Speech* (Oxford: Oxford University Press, 2006).

to a [SH] sound is a high-cost transition, whereas [V] to [AA] is a low-cost and optimal transition. The low-cost transition results in a preferable concatenation [VAA] that can be added to the sound repository for reuse and further composition with other sound units. In this way, numerous utterable concatenations can be produced from a very limited set of basic discrete sound units.[242] The discrete units can take on new features within the concatenated compositions. These new features can then be singled out and introduced as additional constraints on the composition of sounds, producing ever more varied and richer concatenations that would constitute the skeleton of the automata's syntactic utterances.

The organization of a sparse number of discretized sounds should not be interpreted as a reduction in the capacity of sounds in their role in the interaction between the automata because, in the new configuration, sounds can be combinatorially grouped and structured. In other words, the process of discretization and the advent of combinatorial capacities go hand in hand with the production of a finite repertoire of sounds which no longer have a communicative signalling function, since they are properly speaking compositional elements of symbolic tokens defined by their syntactic configurations.

The stabilization of acoustic data has a number of important ramifications. It supplies the automata with a repository of sounds that can be retrieved and reproduced. But more fundamentally, it transforms fuzzy

---

242 The difference between basic sound units or elementary phonological objects and the variety of features or properties they can take in sound concatenations is usually defined in terms of the difference between the so-called *emic* and *etic* units. In this case, emic units are phonemes (that which is sounded), while etic units are the observed variant forms of emic units in a system of composite sounds. As etic units, sounds are treated as phonetic elements (i.e., the variations of that which is sounded, or phonemes). The distinction between emic and etic units is crucial for defining sound-tokens qua symbols in terms of invariant and variant forms, i.e., a limited set of stable invariant abstract objects out of which numerous varied abstract features can be constructed. The emic-etic relationships are not exclusive to sounds. They can be extended to every possible symbolic unit including graphemes, morphemes, lexemes, and grammemes.

sound cues into acoustic tokens that can be used as a protocurrency for a new type of interaction wherein the communicative function of sign-vehicles is replaced by symbolic tokens upon which structuring syntactic and semantic abilities can be built. With the introduction into our multi-agent system of symbols in the form of discretized and combinatorial sounds, the automata enter into the syntactic domain of language where the combinatorial relations between symbols can be manipulated to generate more complex syntactic structures capable of encoding broader ranges of relationships between pattern-governed regularities.

GENERATIVE PROCESSES AND THE HIERARCHY OF SYNTACTIC COMPLEXITY

What makes the discretization of sound a consequential structural change in our multi-agent system is that it enables the evolution of speech and cognition for the automata. It simultaneously fulfils the necessary condition for the emergence of speech and transforms the interaction between agents into an abstract system capable of generating increasingly adequate structuring abilities. Such a system can be called language, a geistig scaffold on the basis of which mind can become the unifying point or configuring factor for the structuration of the world, thoughts, and actions.

Owing to their structural stability, which facilitates the sharing and reuse of acoustic tokens, the coarsely discretized sound-composites qua symbols can assume specific and abstract roles in the interaction between the automata. By losing their signalling or communicative function, the discretized sounds become building blocks of symbol-design, i.e., tokens which, depending on how they are exchanged between the automata, can assume different roles ranging from syntactic utterances (structure encoding expressions) to semantic vocabularies (structuring expressions). Having come into possession of sound-tokens or symbols which are defined not by what they stand for but by the abstract roles they play in the interactions between the automata, the multi-agent system can transform from a communicative regime into a linguistic system through which automata can increasingly structure their interaction with their environment by structuring their own interactions.

The transformation of the rudimentary sound cues into a set of limited discrete sound units from which compound sounds can be constructed endows the automaton with combinatorial capacities—specifically, the generative processes of iteration and recursion. As mentioned earlier, discretization and combinatorial processes are two sides of the same coin—the symbol. We saw that the formation of a shared cache of discrete sounds qua abstract tokens was afforded by the self-organizing interaction between sound-using agents. But this was not the end of the self-organizing multi-agent interaction. With the birth of discretized units also comes the generative combinatorial processes that increasingly furnish such units with syntactic structures.

With the emergence of discrete sounds as transactional tokens, the interactions between agents can further evolve by way of the basic combinatorial processes that hold between discretized symbolic units. It is now the self-organization of language, the syntactic-semantic interaction between agents, that is the real protagonist of our toy universe. The automata are simply agents or players caught up in a game which is the realization and development of language. Any structural change in this multi-agent interaction—language—will translate into a change in the structuring abilities of the automata. This is of course nothing but the reiteration of Hegel's insight that the supposed transcendental subject is only an agent in so far as it is suspended in the process of the self-organization of geist, whose *dasein* or presence is encapsulated in the self-organization of language.

The most generic forms of generative combinatorial processes afforded by discretized sounds are *iteration* and *recursion*. Through these two generative processes, the concatenation of sounds can take on increasingly complex syntactic structures. Let us briefly and intuitively examine what these processes are, how they can structure the automaton's nonconceptual representings of their world, and finally how they construct syntactic vocabularies which the automata can use in their interactions.

Iteration is a memoryless combinatorial process, where constituents can be repeated and combined without restriction. Take for instance the instruction 'chop the garlic until it is turned into a paste'. To yield the desired output (paste), one does not need to memorize the history of the previous actions (choppings). As long as the action of chopping is repeated enough, one will get the paste at the end of the process. In contrast, recursion is a memory-driven generative process, meaning that the performance of each action is built on the history of previous actions. Succinctly formulated, recursion is the embedding of constituents within constituents of the same kind or category.[243] An intuitive example of recursion would be the instruction 'cut the pie into eight equal slices'. The output of this operation cannot be obtained unless each action (cutting to equal slices) is embedded in the history of the previous step. The first cut gives two slices, the second four slices, and finally in this manner, the fourth cut combined with or embedded in previous actions of the same kind yields eight equal slices.

Iteration and recursion can be distinguished according to the types of structure they generate. Simple recursion generates syntactic structures that have complex dependency relations between constituents of the same kind. Owing to the absence of embedding constraints (i.e., the combination of constituents of the same kind), simple iteration generates structures that lack dependency relations but contain constituents of different kinds. The combination of iterative and recursive operations generates structures with hierarchical dependency relations where there are generative rules pertaining to the constituents, and transitions rules between different hierarchies.

In our toy universe, simple iteration of sound-tokens (α, β, γ) would generate syntactic strings such as α, $\alpha\beta$, $\alpha\beta\gamma$, $\alpha\beta\gamma\alpha$, ...

Since iterative operations are memoryless in the sense that each step proceeds independently of the previous one, in their rudimentary form they can generate unlimited concatenations. When iterative operations are combined with embedding operations (i.e., the operation of embedding one constituent in another constituent), they can also encode dependency-relations

---

243 See H. van der Hulst (ed.), *Recursion and Human Language* (Berlin: de Gruyter Mouton, 2010).

between constituents, as in the case of: $[\alpha]$, $[\alpha[\beta]]$, $[\alpha[\beta[\gamma]]]$, $[\alpha[\beta[\gamma[\alpha]]]]$, ... In contrast to the previous class of strings (α, $\alpha\beta$, ...), these strings contain information regarding dependency relations between constituents. For example, depending on its formal semantic interpretation, the syntactic string of the form $[\alpha[\beta]]$ could mean the right constituent ß is dependent on the left constituent α.

Finally, applying the operation of recursive embedding to sound-tokens generates syntactic strings or expressions capable not only of encoding dependency-relations between constituents, but also of producing new hierarchies between constituents of the same category. Since each recursive step operates on the product of the previous steps (i.e., it is a memory-driven operation), it can embed constituents of the same category within each other according to the history of their past transformations. Using this procedure, recursive embedding produces new hierarchies that encode the history of transformations between constituents of the same category. For this reason, syntactic expressions produced through recursive embedding contain a wide range of coded information regarding the structure, the type of grouping, and their intracategorical dependencies.

The combined application of iterative and recursive operations to the sound-tokens results in the proliferation of syntactic expressions bearing an extremely diverse range of information regarding the encoding details of dependency relations, transformations, hierarchies, and types. In this fashion, syntactic expressions can be grouped based on hierarchies of the complexity of their structure and the information they encode. This is the basic idea behind Chomsky's revolutionary contribution to artificial intelligence in the context of the theory of formal grammar or syntax: From a limited set of discrete units and through the implementation of generative processes, a nested hierarchy of syntactic complexity can be constructed where each level represents a specific class of syntactic language or grammar with its own set of production or computational rules. These syntactic structures can be classified, from top to bottom, into recursively enumerable, context-sensitive, context-free, and regular languages. Moving from the bottom (languages recognized by automata with finite memory) to the top (recursively enumerable languages recognized by automata with infinite random-access tape memories or universal Turing machines), grammars and computational automata become successively more expressive but also more resource-consuming, syntactic vocabularies richer in their encoding capacities, and languages harder to recognize.

BASE SYNTACTIC ABILITIES

Having access to different classes of formal grammar, $\mathbb{K}$, $\mathbb{S}$, and $\mathbb{M}$ can syntactically structure their picturing reports concerning the pattern-governed regularities of their world. For example, if we were to reproduce their report concerning the presence of a mass of fuzzy grey item in a context-free grammar (context-free syntactic expressions can be approximately described as concatenated structures of dependency relations recursively constructed from more basic block structures or syntactic expressions whose logical units do not overlap), such an encoded report— signalled via sound-tokens—could be presented as the following syntactic expression SYN:

SYN: $[\mathbb{M}[\mathbb{S}[\mathbb{K}[N_r\,[G]],[G\,[B_c\,]],[B_c\,[G\,[N_s]]]]]]$

In the above syntactic report, the order of block-structures and dependency relations can sufficiently encode the sequence and relations of items and occurrences so that no predicative expression (e.g., 'was there', 'will scream', 'is next to the monolith') would be needed. In other words, the syntactic order of the nested brackets replaces time and location stamps t and p as well as relations conveyed by predicative expressions. Mere signs or one-to-one mapping/representing functions, as argued earlier, could not obtain this syntactic configuration, even though it is as a matter of fact built on them. It is only with the advent of symbols and their combinatorial capacities that such syntactic structures of increasing complexity become possible.

If a rough *analogical* translation of this syntactically structured report had to be given, after adding the predicates it would be:

Matata thinks based on the report given by Sue that Kanzi reports the presence of a fuzzy grey item after hearing a rustling noise. The fuzzy item is now contacting the heap of black and will make a shrieking noise as it touches it.

Or, in a more truncated version but with nested brackets:

[Sue says that [Kanzi says that [the monkey [[whose steps] [were heard]]]], [is now moving [toward [the monolith [to examine it [and will scream]]]]]]].

Note the similarity of this syntactically sound but rather nonsensical sentence—from our *ordinary* linguistic point of view—with the CHILD's unquoted but tagged world-awarenesses which, as we saw, were the necessary components for the constitution of an objective worldview.

Let us briefly clarify these points before moving forward: Now that the automata are equipped with formal grammar or syntax, they can encode the (nonconceptual) structural or syntactic relations between causally registered invariances regarding items and occurrences. In other words, it is by virtue of their syntactic abilities that they are capable of recognizing (in the special computational sense of accepting inputs) the sequence or structural relations between causally pictured items and occurrences. Patterns and relations which the toy universe had no recognizer or syntactic language capable of encoding, would be counted as nonexistent to the automata. To claim—as Sellars subtly suggests and Ruth Millikan firmly asserts—that the syntactic configuration or the structure of pattern-governed regularities—if there are in fact *real* patterns in the universe—is already available to mind by way of the manner in which such pattern-governed regularities are registered or pictured causally in the wiring diagram/nervous system of the automata, is to endorse a *syntactic version* of the myth of the categorial given. It is only with the advent of the combinatorial capacities afforded by symbols and formal syntactic abilities, the computational infrastructure of language, that the necessity of causal mappings or picturing functions for the structuration of the world can find syntactic (not semantic) structural relations sufficient for the semantic or conceptual structuring of the world.

The next point is that syntactic reports such as *SYN* consist of causally pictured items and occurrences whose syntactic configuration embodies rule-governed conceptual activities. It would be helpful to use Sellars's example of chess to clarify how the calculus of such syntactic observational reports inscribed or uttered in acoustic symbol-designs—but which could equally be designated with graphic or gestural elements—embodies the rule-governed conceptual activities that disambiguate and elaborate them.

A chessboard can be seen as a two-ply system consisting of a metagame and game. The metagame consists of the formally stated rules of the game chess, which are equivalent to material inferences determining the inferential role of linguistic expressions. At the metagame level, we have rules of how to set up and move the chess pieces. While these metagame rules are not per se part of the game, the players nevertheless need to be acquainted with them in order to competently play the *game* of chess. In contrast to the metagame, the game consists of syntactically configured or structured observational reports or pattern-governed regularities: only to the extent that the players can reliably distinguish black from white, a this-shaped piece from a that-shaped piece, and are able to syntactically encode the relations between the pieces, i.e., the position of the pieces on the chessboard (next to, behind of, in front of, diagonal to), can the game be played and the metagame rules obtain.

For example, at the game level we can have a symbol-design or syntactical inscription such as [♚[♗]] which reads as, this-such (*tode ti*) piece of thus-and-so shape and colour (the black king) is in a diagonal relationship with this-such piece of a different colour and shape (the white bishop). This chess configuration is the equivalent of the syntactically structured picturing report SYN. Moving from game to metagame, though, we have the conceptual sentence 'Black king is checked by the white bishop'. Within the metagame, there are rules or inferential transitions that tell us 'If the black king is checked by the white bishop → then interpose the black bishop. Shifting from the metagame back to the game, the player then moves diagonally this-such piece (the black bishop) between the previously obtained configuration of this-suches in diagonal relationship with one another: [♚[♗[♝]]].

In Sellarsian terminology, the move from game to metagame, the rules or transitions within the metagame, and finally the move from metagame back to game, respectively stand for language entry transitions (perception), intra-linguistic transitions (thinking) and language exit transitions (intentional action). However, a more accurate description of the move from game to metagame would be as a transition from *syntactically structured* symbol-designs with material characteristics to *semantically structured* material inferences (conceptual activities). In other words, even the entry transition from game to metagame requires language, albeit language at the level of structure-encoding syntactic abilities. As we saw earlier, mapping functions or nonconceptual representings—causal capacities to discern and respond to pattern-governed regularities—by themselves lack the robust syntactic-classificatory relationships necessary in order for them to sufficiently embody rule-governed conceptual activities. Only syntactic abilities could encode such structural and classificatory relationships between material signs or inscriptions and so between the items and occurrences nonconceptually represented by them. And, as argued, such syntactic abilities require symbols in the special sense introduced above, along with the generative combinatorial processes they afford. This is why the term 'symbol-design token' was chosen instead of 'sign-design token' to denote the ability to make nonconceptual classificatory tokens that do indeed have syntactic 'structure-encoding' configurations.

In addition to the ability to nonconceptually structure or classify their picturing reports by encoding them with syntactic configurations, the automata now also have the ability to deploy syntactic vocabularies in their interactions. Earlier we assumed that the automata's only medium of symbol-design tokens is sound. Accordingly, in the toy multi-agent system, the parsing and production of expressions in different formal grammars or syntactic languages is achieved solely by means of the shared inventory of compositional sound-tokens. Applying a selected class of production rules to acoustic tokens combined with the basic criteria of sound composition for making a phonologically permissible concatenation would produce strings of sounds that map a specific set of syntactic structures. These properties represent the distinct level of syntax to which that expression or vocabulary belongs. Any string that projects such properties or structures would be recognized by the automata as a syntactic utterance in the language that produces such properties and structures *with the caveat that the automata would have the ability to recognize or parse the expressions of that syntactic language.*

For example, if the automata are capable of deploying syntactic vocabularies in the regular language of the Chomsky hierarchy, any string of sounds or symbolic combination from the external environment or another artificial multi-agent community that matches the formal properties and the structure of a regular Chomsky language can, *in principle*, be recognized by our automata as an utterance in *their* (syntactic) language. That is to say, the automata can potentially recognize or compute any string of sounds, gestures, or inscriptions whose syntactic relations map onto the syntactic relations of the language they can parse.

Following Brandom's example of the laughing Santa,[244] imagine that the automata were only able to deploy syntactic vocabularies—laughing strings—in the regular language of the Chomsky hierarchy using just four sounds [h], [o], [a] and [e]. We can call such automata *automatic laughing bags*. As automatic laughing bags, the automata can recognize and produce syntactic vocabularies or laughing strings in the form *haha!, hoho!, hahahohohehe!*. The algorithmic ability to deploy such syntactic vocabularies or laughing strings can be modelled on a finite state machine: To make a laugh, the automatic laughing bag starts with state 1. If the first sound is not *h*, the laughing bag does not move forward to the next state. If the sound is *h*, it issues an *h*-sound and moves to state 2. In state 2, if the sound is not *a*, *e* or *o*, it remains stuck again. But if it is *a*, *e* or *o*, it emits one of these sounds and moves to state 3. In state 3, if there is a terminating sign *!*, it moves to state 4 and makes the shortest laugh (*ha!, he!, ho!*), ending the process. But if it chooses to make a longer laugh (i.e., if there is an *h*-sound instead of *!*), it moves back to state 2 and repeats the process for any amount of time until it reaches the terminate command *!*. Any string that reaches the final state would be an item of laughing bag vocabulary

---

244 Brandom, *Between Saying and Doing*, 16.

recognizable by all automatic laughing bags. See the following diagram for the state transitions of the recognizer automaton and the accompanying flowchart containing the instructions for producing a laugh-token within a finite repertoire of discrete sounds.

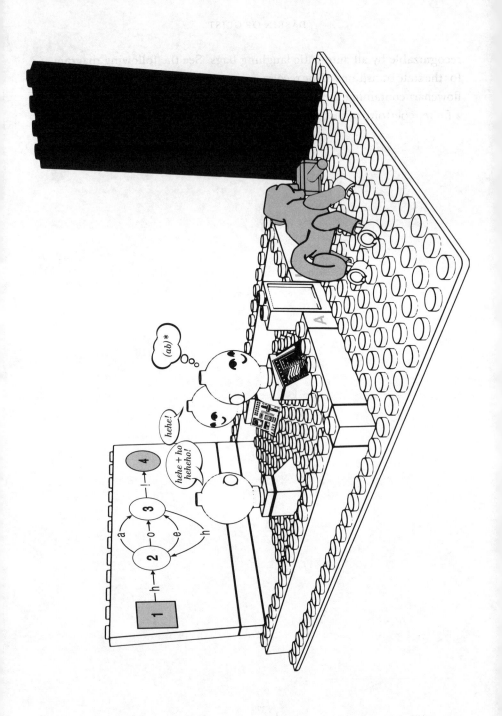

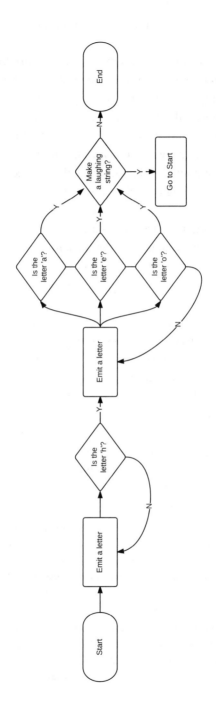

Automatic laughing bags

In the hierarchy of syntactic complexity, practices-or-abilities sufficient to deploy a vocabulary—i.e,. what one has to do in order to recognize and produce something in a syntactic language—and vocabularies sufficient to specify those vocabulary-deploying abilities—i.e., what one has to say to specify a set of practices-or-abilities required for making a vocabulary in a syntactic language—are both algorithmic abilities. They allow higher syntactic complexities (languages with more expressive powers and higher structure-encoding capacities) to be algorithmically bootstrapped from lower syntactic complexities.[245] In this fashion, using lower sufficient vocabulary-deploying practices-or-abilities (PV-sufficiency) and sufficient practice-specifying vocabularies (VP-sufficiency),[246] the automata can, in principle, construct vocabularies of higher syntactically complexity which are at once more expressive and stronger in terms of their computational powers and their capacities to encode structures.

So far the automata have acquired exchangeable symbol-design tokens whose syntactic configurations, systematic relationships, and material characteristics express—nonconceptually—facts about how things are. The automata can assign *rudimentarily classifying* labels made with syntactic beeps and clicks to this-suches of items as a matter of reliable differential responsive dispositions. Thus, for example, in the presence of this-such bulbous pile of green, $\mathbb{K}$ utters beep-beep-click-click. And in the presence of the mass of fuzzy grey moving up on the pile of green or some other more involved occurrence among stuffy this-suches, it makes again in such sounds a well-formed syntactic sentence that configures the syntactic

---

245 '[In] this setting we can prove that one vocabulary that is expressively weaker than another can nonetheless serve as an adequate pragmatic metavocabulary for that stronger vocabulary. That is, even though one cannot say in the weaker vocabulary everything that can be said in the stronger one, one can still say in the weaker one everything that one needs to be able to do in order to deploy the stronger one.' Brandom, *Between Saying and Doing*, 20.

246 VP-sufficiency and PV-sufficiency (P for practices-or-abilities and V for vocabularies) are the most basic meaning-as-use relations. There can also be VV-sufficiency and PP-sufficiency, respectively, vocabularies that specify other vocabularies and practices that elaborate other vocabulary-deploying practices.

relations between such labels and their corresponding this-such items. We can say that the automata have something like protothoughts of the form 'do (or don't do) actions of kind a when in circumstances of kind c', what Sellars may call 'rehearsing intentions' or, in this case, proto-intensions.[247]

Moreover, the automata are now in possession of algorithmic syntactic abilities through which they can construct more complex structure-encoding abilities, and recognize and potentially compute more intricate patterns. There is no reason to doubt that the automata of our toy universe may read and write more expressive syntactic vocabularies and compute more complex syntactic sentences, with higher structure-encoding capacities, than our base syntactic capacities. But what they do not have is the semantic structuration of the diverse relationships between syntactically pictured reports. They do not have inferential or rule-governed intra-linguistic transitions to *conceive* (i.e., bring into conception) such reports, to elaborate the relationships between such reports based on their material incompatibility and consequence relations and, if necessary, to repair or revise such reports. In other words, they do not have the objective reports that the fully fledged language-using Sue and Matata had, because they do not have propositions whose conceptual contents are determined by their inferential roles since they have not yet achieved the practical mastery of inference. Thoughts are only thoughts to the extent that they stand in inferential relations to one another, that is to say, in so far as they are individuated by their inferential articulation in a public language. Intentional relations (thinking-abouts) require semantic relations, and semantic relations require a public language as the engine and vehicle of their realization.

---

247 'Now, the fundamental principles of a community, which define what is "correct" or "incorrect", "right" or "wrong", "done" or "not done" are the most general common *intentions* of that community with respect to the behavior of members of the group. It follows that to recognize a featherless biped or dolphin or Martian as a person requires that one think thoughts of the form, "We (one) shall do (or abstain from doing) actions of kind A in circumstances of kind C". To think thoughts of this kind is not to *classify* or *explain*, but to *rehearse an intention*.' Sellars, *In the Space of Reasons*, 408.

Ultimately, what our automata do not have is a semantic space defined in terms of a public language they can be plugged into and, through participation in it—via mastering the practices it entails—generate a hierarchy of semantic complexity. Ascending this semantic hierarchy is tantamount to practical mastery of the use of vocabularies expressing the right kind of concepts of different grades and roles:

> These are concepts that let us make explicit—put into judgeable, thinkable, assertable, propositional form—the inferential relations that articulate the 'space of implications' that is the context and horizon within which alone what we do acquires the significance of rational, discursive consciousness of what we respond to.[248]

Intentional ascent, or the complexity of thinking thoughts, demands a *semantic ascent*—that is, a hierarchical complexity of both different grades of concepts (i.e., inferentially articulated contents) and the practical know-how to use or apply concepts correctly. In ascending the hierarchy of semantic complexity, the automata attain semantic self-consciousness. They become discursively aware of how things are by thinking about thoughts through thinking about concepts that inferentially articulate those thoughts, and thereby the things thought of.

However, the revolution of syntax in our toy universe, as we shall see in the next chapter, has also another consequence as significant as—if not more than—the buttressing of semantic capabilities. But what is this consequence? It is what we might call Carnap's vision of language in general as a calculus or, in reference to the work of Steve Awodey and André Carus on Carnap, the picture of language as an unbound ocean freed at last both from 'Wittgenstein's prison' (the picture-theory of language) and from the 'Kantian straightjacket' (subordination of the logical and formal dimension to sensible intuition).[249] To put it concisely, this is a picture of language as a calculus of general syntax. In Carnap's own words:

---

248 Brandom, *Reason in Philosophy*, 10.

249 Ibid., 10.

By a language we mean here in general any sort of calculus, that is to say, a system of formation and transformation rules concerning what are called *expressions*, i.e. finite, ordered series of elements of any kind, namely, what are called *symbols*. [...] In what follows, we will deal only with languages which contain *no expressions dependent upon extra-linguistic factors*. [...] two sentences of the same wording will have the same character independently of where, when, or by whom they are spoken.[250]

Seeing language as a calculus, or as the boundless system of formation and transformation rules in the realm of symbol-design, is not to reduce language to calculus. Such a view of language does not entail the rejection or downplaying of the perceptual-representational, social, and cultural aspects of language. The point is that expanding the scope of language—what it is and what it can do—cannot be effectuated in earnest if the structure of language is subordinated to prior representational, social, or cultural considerations. To understand language as a general calculus in the way Carnap envisioned in *The Logical Syntax of Language* is to finally blur the line not only between syntax and logic but also between language and computation. It might be objected that such a picture of language sacrifices the semantic dimension. Not necessarily. In fact, to treat semantics as irreducible to or fundamentally distinct from syntax is to regard semantics as a deus ex machina of some sort—that is, to see meaning as the *miracle* of language. Surely, it is not the case that semantics can be invariantly reduced to syntax, but it is indeed reducible to syntax under the right conditions. These right conditions, as we will review in the next chapter, signify the interactionist view of syntax through which semantic complexity emerges immanently through the confrontation of syntactic processes or symbolic chains.

Therefore, we can say that Carnap's logical-syntactic view of language is not anti-semantic. It concerns the 'semantic in disguise'.[251] Disenthralling language from established semantic rules or representational concerns

---

250 R. Carnap, *Logical Syntax of Language* (London: Kegan Paul, 1937), 167–8.

251 P. Wagner, *Carnap's Logical Syntax of Language* (Basingstoke: Palgrave Macmillan, 2009), 14.

is not equal to forgetting the semantic. It is rather an unprejudiced way to imagine more generalized languages capable of capturing ever richer semantic relationships. If we consider structure as the dimension of mind, namely, language and logic, we cannot broaden the intelligibility of reality or postulate new kinds of worlds populated by new intelligences and facts of experience without broadening the scope of language and logic. And we cannot expand language and logic without taking the prospects of language as a calculus of forms—where the boundaries of syntax, logic and computation become porous—seriously. Language, as the combined forces of logic and computation, is the ultimate medium of concrete world-building. But we cannot build new worlds, discover new sectors of reality, or make new forms of intelligence without new ways of language-building—the design of which will require that we liberate the picture of language, and for that matter logic, as organons from any limitations set in advance by the representational functions and semantic values of language or the correct application of logical laws to intuitions à la Kantian transcendental logic. It is this idea of unrestricted world-building as arrested by the boundless conception of language-building that typifies intelligence not as a passive receiver of an external reality but as the very exemplification of enriching and engineering reality—that which progressively postulates itself as a new inhabitant of new or different kinds of structured worlds.

*

Before moving on to the next chapter, which is the last stop in our thought experiment, it would be helpful to provide a rough outline of the issues we have navigated so far and where we are headed.

We began with a picture of mind whose function is structuring or self-conception in accordance with an *objective* world. Mind as the organ of structuration was elaborated via a family of fundamental correspondences or dualities (as differentiated from dualisms)—intelligence and intelligibility, theory and object, structure and being, and so on. In addition, we surveyed the relation between language, logic, and mind. The conclusion was that we cannot know what intelligence is or what it can become without inquiring into the structuring function as that upon which all our descriptions regarding what counts as intelligent or general intelligence are modelled. In other words, thinking about intelligence or geist—what it is now and what it will be—is a matter of investigating and renewing the link between mind and world, structure and being, theory and object. The investigation and renewal of this link is the very definition of concrete self-consciousness as a task. And the first step in this task is nothing other than investigating the conditions necessary for the realization of mind as that which has a concept of itself in an objective world.

Such necessary conditions were introduced as enabling constraints for having thus-and-so universal capacities which we not only associate with general intelligence but must also employ to model any form of intelligence. We subsequently started our examination of such enabling or positive constraints in the framework of an extended thought experiment after disputing the unconstrained conceptions of intelligence and assessing which models or paradigms are best suited for conducting such an inquiry. The investigation into such constraints took two distinct but interconnected trajectories at the intersection between mind and objective world: (1) an in-depth analysis of the necessary enabling constraints or conditions for the realization of mind based on our own current—theory-laden and scientifically-informed—self-image as minded subjects; and (2) a critique of transcendental structure to determine the degree to which such necessary constraints—what they are and what we take to be their essential characteristics—are fraught with or distorted by cognitive biases originating from the local structure of our experience and psychologistic residues. Properly understood, the latter trajectory is tantamount to the full-scale Copernicanization of the transcendental subject itself, and therefore the unmooring of the conceptions of mind and intelligence. Yet arriving at a conception of intelligence that is of nowhere and nowhen is only possible by following these trajectories.

Following these two trajectories, then, we looked at the initial necessary constraints upon the order of appearances: space and time as forms of intuition. Next, we inquired in the conditions necessary for having thoughts and objectivity or objective validity. The latter brought us to the question of syntactic complexity and semantic complexity as the dimensions of structure at the intersection between language, logic, mathematics, and computation. Having looked at the necessary conditions for syntactic complexity in this chapter, we can now move on to the question of semantic complexity or semantics in general. In the next chapter, therefore, we follow this line of inquiry, starting from the bridge between syntax and semantics and in the process uncovering a picture of language behind our ordinary natural languages, one which is no longer burdened by the local and contingently constituted biases entrenched in the structure of natural languages.

7. This I, or We or It, the Thing, Which Speaks (Language as Interaction as Computation)

THE PRAGMATIC INTERFACE

To ask how our automata can transit from their base structure-encoding syntactic abilities to semantic structuring abilities is fundamentally to ask how syntax can be bridged to semantics. Building this bridge is not straightforward, in so far as no amount of *algorithmic* base syntactic abilities can generate semantic abilities. Yet to claim, as John Searle does, that syntax by itself is not sufficient for semantics is a recipe for the inflation of what meaning is, along with a myopic interpretation of what syntax is and what syntactic expressions do. This is of course a claim encapsulated in the Chinese room thought experiment, an argument that simultaneously presupposes a potentially mystifying account of meaning, a peculiarly anaemic interpretation of syntax, and an outmoded understanding of the relationship between syntax and semantics.[252]

Syntax, under the *right conditions*, is indeed sufficient for semantics, and meaning can be conferred upon syntactic expression if such conditions are satisfied. These conditions are what the inferentialist theory of meaning,

---

252 Searle's Chinese room thought experiment is predicated on the assumption that semantics is generally (i.e., under all conditions) irreducible to syntax. As will be argued, this view essentially falls under the deflationary-inflationary bipolar picture of language, where deflation of semantics leads to an inflationary account of syntax at the expense of ignoring the question of semantic complexity. And similarly, the inflationary account of semantics results in an ineffable picture of language and meaning. One of the main reasons behind the Chinese room view of language is the wrong framing of what is going on in this thought experiment. The actual computation is not happening within the room (the syntax manipulator) itself, but is the interaction of the person inside the room and the person outside of it. Semantics, therefore, emerges out of the interaction of minimal syntactic rules or confrontation of basic axiomatic acts.

as a species of social-pragmatics or the use-theory of meaning, attempts to capture. It argues that meaning is ultimately, at its most basic level, the *justified* use of mere expressions in social discursive linguistic practices; and that what counts as the *justification* of an expression is what counts as its meaning. While syntax by itself does not yield semantics, it does so when coupled with interaction. In this sense, pragmatics—at least in the sense defined by Brandom's inferentialist pragmatism—can be understood as a bridge between syntax and semantics. Broadly speaking, semantics (content) is concerned with what is said, while pragmatism (use) is concerned with what one is doing in saying it (i.e., discursive practices-or-abilities that count as deploying a vocabulary, conferring or applying meaning). More precisely, semantics asks what it is that one believes (or knows, claims) when one believes that p (a content), whereas pragmatism asks what it is that one must know how to *do* in order to count as producing a performance that expresses that content.

Leaving behind the representational account of meaning and meaning as denotation, inferentialism, as a species of pragmatism, treats the meaning of linguistic expressions in terms of their inferential relations embedded in social discursive practices. To this extent, the capacity to know, believe, or mean something rests upon certain practical know-how (i.e., pragmatism), the practical mastery of inferential roles. In the inferentialist semantics-normative pragmatics framework, semantics can be said to concern the meaning-conferring inferential roles of syntactic expressions in the context of social discursive practices or linguistic interactions.

Within this setup, the noises or behaviours of interlocutors can only count as saying or claiming something if said interlocutors know what to do—in accordance with rules and following some standards or norms—such that they can *draw inferences* from each other's claims, using such inferences as the premises of their own claims and reasoning. Here, syntactic expressions as items of language assume semantic value or meaning when they are incorporated into the interaction of practitioners of discursive practices that give inferential roles to such utterances. These are practices that adopt or attribute normative statuses, commitments, and entitlements that stand in consequential relations to one another.

For example, endorsing the belief or claim 'This is red' entitles one to the belief that 'This is coloured' but precludes the claim that 'This is green'. Thus, from this point of view, one must know what sort of performances must be carried out in order for one to count as endorsing a belief or claiming that p, and what must be done in order to track what follows from such endorsements and claims. To assert or judge 'This is red', one must not only be able to react—as a matter of RDRD (reliable differential responsive dispositions—see chapter 5)—to the presence of this-such item, one must also have the practical know-how regarding what must be performed to inferentially connect such a state, expression, or noise RED to other states or expressions, thus conferring conceptual content upon them (i.e., red as a concept qua an inferentially articulated content). Consequently, one can grasp or understand the content of the concept red or any other concept by grasping the significance of the pragmatic performance of committing to the claim 'This is red' (a speech act) in terms of the difference it makes to other interlocutors' commitments and entitlements to commitments. That is to say, linguistic discursive practices can be defined in terms of tracking or keeping the score of other practitioners'—or interlocutors'—commitments and entitlements (asserted claims and what follows from them or does not).

In this sense, for an interlocutor, the significance of a performance or a speech act ('This is red') is ultimately a matter of the way in which it interacts with other interlocutors' commitments and entitlements—this interaction requires that the deontic context of such a performance be *updated*, and in doing so, the previous context is given a score. To use a simplistic example, when $\mathbb{K}$ asserts 'This is red', it is entitled to 'This is coloured'. But when $\mathbb{S}$ asserts 'This is red mixed with blue', $\mathbb{K}$, having recognized the shade of blue (RDRD plus the inferentially articulated concept blue) is required to acknowledge the force of $\mathbb{S}$'s assertion with regard to the consequential scorekeeping relations between its commitment and entitlement, and to update (keep, revise, or discard) them: 'This is not red', 'This is purple', and 'This is coloured'. The content of the concept can then be characterized in terms of this updating function. Therefore, we can say that grasping the content of a concept and grasping the concept of reasoning as certain (i.e., objective and linguistic) practical knowhows are interdependent. Briefly put, reason as the articulation and elaboration of the concept is a *doing*, and as such there is no good justification for refusing to view reason in terms of the algorithmic elaboration or decomposition of abilities which can be realized by different kinds of information processing systems. In this interactive framework, the assertion *that p* can no longer be thought as a fully formed propositional content that is either true or false, but instead is thought as a conditional assertion whose meaning and truth can only be decided when it is put into *inter-action* with queries and counterclaims which test and challenge it: a game in which, by making a move or defending a commitment *that p*, one is prohibited from making other moves. This move is akin to a hypothesis whose construction involves processes of verification or being tested by other strategies or agents (i.e., other moves made in the game).

What is interesting about Brandom's inferentialist pragmatism is that it gives a picture of natural language not simply as a symbolic medium but as a rule-governed framework inseparable from the interaction of its users—an interaction in which all necessary (non-inferential) capacities of agents are integrated. One might object that Brandom's pragmatism is susceptible to the same charge levied against traditional pragmatism, namely that one must know *all* the rules of language in order to function, to say or claim something contentful. As he shows in his tour de force *Between Saying and Doing*, however, this is absolutely not the case. Normative scorekeeping pragmatics—the game of giving and asking for reasons—can begin with a minimal set of rules, and it is only in the context of interaction between interlocutors that more rules can be established, their know-how mastered, and their form made explicit. Therefore, once deepened, Brandom's version of analytic pragmatism represents—to appropriate Jean-Yves Girard's term—an emergent logic of rules. Brandom's pragmatism is thus a true species of discursive rationality in the sense that discursive rationality, even at the level of mastering the know-how of claiming or asserting something, *takes time*.

However, probably the weakest link in Brandom's pragmatism is the way in which the sociality of social linguistic discursive practices is defined.

This sociality is merely asserted, but hardly plays any major role in how meaning-conferring discursive practices are logically modelled. Sociality then becomes a substantive characteristic of discursive practices rather than the very logical condition of language and the nonsubstantive order of thinking. Absent the explicitation of the role of sociality as a *formal* condition, the concept of sociality risks becoming an inflated metaphysical posit that results in a concept of rationality unconscious of its insufficiency for change at the level of concrete social practices. The necessity of reason, language, rational discourse, and an understanding of the machinery of conceptual activities for social change can then be passed off as their sufficiency for concrete change. Short of the consciousness of this necessity-cum-insufficiency, the very discussion of reasons and conceptual activities leads to a socially liberal and philosophically quietist stance. Therefore, Brandom's thick notion of sociality converges on a Habermasian rationality persistently unconscious of its insufficiency. To this extent, using a thick notion of sociality to define linguistic discursive practices becomes just as precarious as using the right-wing Sellarsian's thin notion of agency and normativity.

At this point, we should admit that we have a foggy and faulty notion of sociality which prevents us from grasping the role of interaction, and undermines the program to bridge from syntax to semantics while emphasizing language and sociality as a constitutive condition. Our notion of sociality may be defectively indeterminate, but that is exactly why we should reinvent the notion of sociality as an interaction that can be elaborated logically and computationally. The articulation of sociality as a formal condition is the first step that must be taken in order to unbind rational capacities as well as to rescue the nebulous concept of reason from deep-seated dogmas. The former is a necessary—albeit basic and not adequate—move that must be made if we are to think about substantive sociality and social norms. Therefore, to reemphasize the role of sociality in language and thinking—as the bridge between syntax and semantics—we must redefine this index of sociality as a formal condition best captured by the logico-computational concept of interaction. In this sense, interaction is a sufficient condition for building the syntax-semantics interface. The question is now as follows:

What kind of interaction must the automata have in order to move from base syntactic abilities to fully fledged structuring semantic abilities? To answer this question, however, we need to answer a more general question: What is interaction as a distinctly computational notion?

ENTER THE COPYCAT: INTERACTION AS GAME AS COMPUTATION

According to the classical Church-Turing computability thesis, computation can be modelled on a mathematical function. The machine receives input; it undergoes a sequence of state transitions (moves or legal runs) and yields an output. During the computation, the machine shuts out the environment and accepts no further input until the initial input is processed. In this form, computation can be represented as a logical deduction where *to compute* means the same as *to deduce steps from an initial configuration*. Like deduction, the process of computation can then be characterized in terms of how the output (conclusion) is logically contained in the input (the premise) or how the output/conclusion is implied by the input/premise. But if this is all that computation is—algorithmic deduction—then what exactly is gained by it? Computation runs into the same problem that deduction leads to, namely the riddle of epistemic omniscience according to which the total knowledge of an agent can be said to be deductively closed:

$$(K_a p \wedge (p \to q)) \to K_a q$$

which says that if the agent a knows (K) the proposition p then it knows all its logical consequences q.

While such a verdict is absolutely sound and valid in some classical logic heaven, it has no ground in reality. A corresponding computational equivalent of deduction's problem of epistemic omniscience is the classical denotational semantics of programming languages, where all that is required to provide meaning to the expression of a language (i.e., the meaning of the program) or to know what the program does, is to know the given structured sets of data types (domains) and the interpretation function that maps those domains to one another. Here, the puzzling situation is that computation is supposed to yield new information, whereas the classical paradigm suggests a closed logical system wherein the output information is nothing but the input plus a machine that deduces steps from it. From an information-theoretic point of view, no new information is added by computation, and from an epistemic point of view no knowledge is gained by computation.

What the *classical* account of computation presupposes but does not incorporate as its intrinsic dimension is that which provides the input and consumes the output—namely, the *environment*. The system or machine becomes the model of what computes, at the expense of keeping the environment in the background. The environment is merely represented as an average behaviour, rather than something that dynamically and actively interacts with the system. But it is only by highlighting the role of the environment that the system's or machine's function—input-output mapping—can coherently make sense. Moreover, it is only in the presence of an environment (another system, machine, or agent) that computation can be understood as an increase—rather than mere preservation—of information, hence avoiding the riddle of epistemic omniscience. From this perspective, the environment is no longer a passive ambient space but an active-reactive element to which the system responds by accepting input from it and yielding output which the environment then consumes. In view of the role of the environment in the input-output mapping, the question of computation, rather than being couched in terms of what is a computable function, shifts to the question of how the computation is executed. By bringing the *howness* of computation into the foreground, the question of computability turns into the question *What is computation?*—that is, it now concerns the interaction or confrontation of actions between machine and environment.

With the understanding of interaction itself as computation, the system-environment (or player-opponent, machine-network) dynamics can be modelled as a so-called interaction or simply general game. The interaction game differs from game-theoretic account of games in a number of significant ways. It does not require procedural rules or rules that dictate how the game should proceed or what moves/actions should be performed in a given situation. Rules naturally emerge in the context of the interaction itself. Furthermore, unlike a game-theoretic conception of the game, an interaction game is devoid of both predetermined winning strategies and payoff functions that map the strategy profile of each player to its payoffs or rewards. In this respect, the generality of interaction makes games unifying themes in the study of structures, (information) contents, and behaviours.[253] From a technical perspective, interaction games capture the fundamental correspondences between computational behaviours, logical contents, and mathematical structures—that is to say, the so-called computational trinity.[254] In this sense, interaction games are *generalizations* of the Brouwer–Heyting–Kolmogorov interpretation, where the notion of construction can be interpreted in terms of computing programs, logical proofs, and composition of categories as mathematical objects. In Brouwer's terms, the notion of construction can be broadly understood as a mental construct capable of verifying the existence (denoted by an existential quantifier ∃) of an object that falls under it such that the construction of a (mental) object (*gegenstand* rather than *objekt*) can be said to be the proof of its existence.[255]

---

253 Treating games as unifying themes can perhaps be traced back to the work of Stanislaw Ulam on using the logico-computational notion of the game to study all mathematical situations, as expressed in his slogan 'Gamify (*paizise* from the Greek παιϛιη, to play) everything'. See S. Ulam, *A Collection of Mathematical Problems* (New York: Interscience, 1960).

254 'The doctrine of computational trinitarianism holds that computation manifests itself in three forms: proofs of propositions, programs of a type, and mappings between structures. These three aspects give rise to three sects of worship: Logic, which gives primacy to proofs and propositions; Languages, which gives primacy to programs and types; Categories, which gives primacy to mappings and structures. The central dogma of computational trinitarianism holds that Logic, Languages, and Categories are but three manifestations of one divine notion of computation. There is no preferred route to enlightenment: each aspect provides insights that comprise the experience of computation in our lives.' Harper, *The Holy Trinity*.

255 See L.E.J. Brouwer, 'Mathematics, Science and Language', in P. Mancosu (ed.),

In terms of a general game, the computing machine or system can be identified as a function box with input and output sides which represent the switching of roles between the system and the environment:

$$\xrightarrow{\quad input{:}x \quad} \boxed{\text{System:} f} \xrightarrow{\quad output{:}f(x) \quad}$$

On the input side, the system is the consumer (querying the environment for an input which it can use) and the environment is a producer (providing the input); on the output side, the roles are reversed: the system is the producer (giving the output) and the environment is the consumer. In defining computational tasks as games played by the system and the environment alternatively switching their roles to react to one another (making a move, i.e., performing an action), what counts as a task for the environment is a computational resource for the machine, and what counts as a task for the machine is a resource for the environment. Within the framework of interaction games, computability can then be defined as the condition of winnability for the system against an environment—that is, the existence of an algorithmic winning strategy to solve a computational problem or perform a computational task in the presence of an active environment or opponent.

Access to (computational) resources and performance of permissible moves or actions are now explicitly stated as constraints put in place by the interchange of roles between the machine and the environment. The actions of the machine and its access to resources—i.e., the runtime or number of elementary operations performed by the machine and the space or memory required to solve a computational problem—are determined by its interaction with an environment that constrains its actions and its use of resources. In light of this, the interactive paradigm can naturally express computational complexity, with different levels of constraints imposed by the switching of roles expressing different classes of computational complexity. This switching of roles is formally defined by way of the logico-mathematical

---

From Brouwer to Hilbert: The Debate on the Foundations of Mathematics in the 1920s (Oxford: Oxford University Press, 1998), 45–53.

notion of duality of interaction—or simply, duality. Traditionally in logic, duality can be defined through De Morgan's laws, written in rule form as:

$$\frac{\neg\,(p \wedge q)}{\therefore\; \neg\,p \vee \neg\,q} \qquad\qquad \frac{\neg\,(p \vee q)}{\therefore\; \neg\,p \wedge \neg\,q}$$

and in the sequent or entailment form as:[256]

$$\neg\,(p \wedge q) \vdash (\neg p \vee \neg q) \qquad \neg\,(p \vee q) \vdash (\neg\,p \wedge \neg\,q)$$

Here, duality can be understood in terms of the operation of classical negation $\neg$ over conjunction and disjunction.

In mathematics, dualities can be generally defined as principles translating or mapping theorems or structures to other theorems and structures by means of an involutive function e.g., $f(f(x)) = x$ which is a function that, for every x in the domain of f, is its own inverse. A simple example of a mathematical duality can be given in terms of the algebraic connection between the numbers $\{-1, +1\}$. The involutive negation $(--x=x)$ connects these two numbers $(-(-1)=+1, -(+1)=-1)$. Alternatively, another elementary duality can be defined for sets where a set Set and its dual or opposite antiset Set^{op} are in complementary relations in terms of their given subsets:

---

256 Due to Gerhard Gentzen, sequent calculus is a style of formal argumentation in which proofs are written line by line through sequents consisting of premises and conclusions separated by a consequences relation symbolized by a turnstile ($\vdash$) which reads 'entails, yields or implies'. The premises (Γ) written on the left side of the turnstile are called antecedents, while conclusions (Δ) are written on the right side of the turnstile and are called consequents: $\Gamma \vdash \Delta$. Sequent calculus can be understood as the generalized form of a natural deduction judgement: $A_1, ..., A_n \vdash B_1, ... , B_k$ where the commas on the left side can be thought of as 'and/conjunction' while commas on the right side (conclusions) can be understood as 'or/disjunction'. Accordingly, $A_1, A_2 \vdash B_1, B_2$ approximately reads as 'A_1 and A_2 yield or infer B_1 or B_2'. Since in sequent calculus each line of proof is a conditional tautology, meaning that it is inferred from other lines of proofs in accordance with rules and procedures of inference, it allows a representation of proofs as branching trees whose roots are the formulas that are to be proved.

For any given fixed set S, the subset $A \subseteq S$ has a complementary subset A^C such that A^C consists of elements of S not contained in A. Once again, applying the involution to $A^C - (A^C)^C$ yields A^C. In this fashion, *Set* includes $A \subseteq B$, while *Set*^{op} includes $B^C \subseteq A^C$.

In the framework of interaction, duality does not need to be predefined by means of the classical negation operator. For negation we substitute the reversal of symmetries or swapping of the roles in the game.[257]

In the context of interaction, there can be many configurations of how the game can evolve via the interchange of roles. For example, depending on whether the confrontation of actions between system and environment is synchronous or asynchronous, whether the game can branch to subgames, or whether the history of past interactions can be preserved and accessed or not, the game may exhibit new behaviours with higher computational complexity. The classical version of the Church-Turing paradigm of computation represents an elementary or restricted form of interaction games where computability can be understood as the winnability condition within a two-step game (i.e., a game with two moves only) of input and output. In this game, there is one and only one right output for a given input. Similarly, in classical logic, the notion of truth can be thought of as the winnability condition restricted to propositions in a zero-step game (i.e., games with no moves) which is automatically lost or won depending on whether the propositions are false or true.

---

257 This way of understanding duality can reveal many different forms of dualities other than those available in classical logic and algebraic structures. Dualities can be topological and geometrical in such a way that they can be applied to geometric-topological objects (e.g., by reversing the dimensions of the features of a cube, one can obtain an octahedron, and vice versa). In the same vein, the interactive duality between +1 and −1 is an interval $[-1,+1]$ of reals that topologically connects them. Or in category theory, where duality can be roughly understood as turning around morphisms (i.e., swapping the source and target of the arrows) as well as reversing the composition of morphisms so that, for example, by inverting morphisms in the category C its dual C^{op} is obtained, and vice versa.

To understand the basic structure of interaction as computation, let us briefly examine the basic formal definition of an interaction game:

The game G for the player $\top$ (the system, the prover) and the opponent $\bot$ (the environment, the refuter) is a 4-tuple $\langle R_G, m_G, P_G, \vdash_G \rangle$, where:

- M_G is a set of moves (actions performed by $\top$ and $\bot$)

- λ_G is a function that labels the moves of $\top$ and $\bot$ and whether the moves are defences/answers (D) or attacks/queries (A): $\lambda_G : M_G \rightarrow (\bot, \top) \times (A, D)$

  So that $(\bot, \top) \times (A, D) = \{\bot\ A, \bot\ D, \bot\ A, \bot\ D\}$ and $\lambda_G = \langle \lambda_G^{\bot \top}, \lambda_G^{A D} \rangle$,

And where runs are sequences of moves, and positions in the game are finite runs.

- The play $P_G \subseteq M_G^{alt}$ is a non-empty subset of the set of alternating sequences of moves between $\top$ and $\bot$, M_G^{alt}. The set M_G^{alt} can be represented as the play or set of switching moves s:

  $$s = \lambda_G\ a_{1_\bot}\ a_{2_\top} \ldots a_{2k+1_\bot}\ a_{2k+2_\top} \ldots$$

  Additionally, since the alternating sequences of moves implies the switching of roles, the labelling function λ_G also finds its dual, the reverse function $\overline{\lambda}_G$ such that for a move m we have: $\overline{\lambda}_G(m) = \bot\ A \Leftrightarrow \lambda_G(m) = \top\ A$.

- $\vdash_G$ is a satisfying or justificatory relation that the represents permission to perform actions or to make moves:

  If the move m is the initial move, it either needs 'no justification', $\star \vdash_G m$; or if it requires to be justified by another move n if n has been antecedently justified/permitted, $n \vdash_G m$. All subsequent moves bear justificatory information or a pointer to an earlier move n played. Similarly, the switching of roles also ranges over permissions on the moves:

$$m \vdash_G n \land \lambda_G^{AD}(n) = D \Rightarrow \lambda_G^{AD}(m) = A$$

Within this game, we can then have subgames of the general form A and B and their compositions denoted by the tensor product $\otimes$ which are constructions over G. Subgames can be thought of as threads and subthreads opened up within a dialogue. Thus, for the given subgames A and B, we have basic compositions of $A \otimes B$ which, following Andreas Blass's semantics of interaction for the linear logic operator $\otimes$, can be interpreted as saying that the play can continue in *both* A and B alternately:[258]

$$M_{A \otimes B} = M_A + M_B$$

$$\lambda_{A \otimes B} = \lambda_A + \lambda_B$$

$$P_{A \otimes B} = \{ s \in M_G^{alt} \}$$

$$\vdash_{A \otimes B} = \vdash_A + \vdash_B.$$

The game always starts with an action or move made by $\perp$ since it is the environment that constrains the system and keeps it going. Accordingly, the opening move (played by $\top$) is always a request for data or a query from $\perp$. At the level of a subgame, permissible moves and the switching of roles become more complicated. Only $\perp$ can switch between subgames, while $\top$ can only react to the latest subgame in which $\perp$ has played. This constraint can be formalized as follows:

For any play $s \in P_{A \otimes B}$, if s_i is in A and s_{i+1} in A then $\lambda_{A \otimes B}(s_i) = \top$ and $\lambda_{A \otimes B}(s_{i+1}) = \perp$.

The continuation of the game at the level of subgames is denoted as $A \multimap B$—that is, subgame B consumes or uses as a computational resource

---

258 A. Blass, 'Is Game Semantics Necessary?', in *Computer Science Logic: International Workshop on Computer Science Logic* (Dordrecht: Springer, 1993), 66–77.

the subgame A. The symbol $\multimap$ stands for linear implication, where the implication is resource-sensitive: the environment is a resource for the task of the system (a computational problem) and by consuming this resource the system performs a task to yield an output which is now a resource for the environment. The game $A \multimap B$ can be intuitively thought of in terms of access-protocols between a server and a client (or machines on a network). The server $A \multimap B$ acts as a server of type B that provides data of type B if it has access—exactly once as a client—to server A which provides data of type A. The client of $A \multimap B$ will therefore act not only as a client of type B but also as a server of type A which provides the input or resource from A.[259] The game $A \multimap B$ is characterized in terms of the game's 4-tuple:

$$M_{A \multimap B} = M_A + M_B$$

$\lambda_{A \multimap B} = [\overline{\lambda}_A, \overline{\lambda}_B]$ such that for move m, $\overline{\lambda}_A(m) = \top$ when $\lambda_A(m) = \bot$, and $\bot$ when $\lambda_A(m) = \bot$.

$\top_{A \multimap B} = \{s \in M_{A \multimap B}^{alt}\}$ where the first move in $P_{A \multimap B}$ must be performed by $\bot$ in B, and the opening moves in A are labelled as $<$ by the function $\overline{\lambda}_A$.

$\vdash_{A \multimap B} = \star \vdash_{A \multimap B} m$ if the initial move requires no justification/permission, or else $\vdash_{A \multimap B} = m \vdash_{A \multimap B} n$.

In this setting, if we were to represent a computational problem (e.g., computing $n+1$ in the classical Church-Turing paradigm), this game could be diagrammed as a tree consisting of nodes and branches. At the top of the tree, we have a game played by the machine $\top$ represented as the first node that ramifies to the first-level branches which are $\bot$-labelled (corresponding to inputs provided by the environment) and leading to the second-level nodes of the tree which are games played by the environment $\bot$ ($\bot_1, \bot_2, \bot_3, \ldots$). In the same vein, the second-level nodes lead to second-level branches, which

---

259 Ibid., 71.

are $\top$-labelled ($\top_1$, $\top_2$, $\top_3$, ...) and correspond to the output. The second-level branches lead to the third-level nodes which represent the winnability of games played alternatively by the environment and the machine ($\bot$,$\top$,$\bot$,$\top$...).

Such a two-step game would count as computation in terms of input-output mapping functions. More general interaction games (i.e., games with more than two steps or ordered two-level branching) represent computational *behaviours* that are not exactly functions in the classical mathematical sense. This is in fact the single most significant underlying claim of the interactionist approach to computation: that not all computational behaviours or tasks can be modelled on functions in the mathematical sense. Rather than input-output mapping functions performed by a machine, behaviours are evolving interactions between machine/system and environment. Therefore, realizing behaviours is not simply a matter of simulating an observable behaviour by means of a system's function (a simulator)—as a behaviourist or a traditional functionalist would claim—but of reenacting the interaction between system and constraining environment. Such an interaction is modelled on a game that is not restricted to two steps, i.e., a game that is played on subgames and their branches.

In view of the minimal interactional or game constraints introduced above, it would not be difficult to imagine how the relaxation of existing constraints or the addition of new constraints to the game could result in more complex (computational) behaviours. Additional playing constraints can be generated as the game or interaction progresses, thus allowing the adoption of new strategies by players, i.e., *rules* by which the game can be played (cf. the notion of open harness introduced in chapter 1). Alternatively, some existing constraints can be relaxed or additional interaction operations can be added to enrich the semantics of interaction, hence generating more complex computational behaviours expressed by different compositions of strategies.

For example, the constraint of responding to the latest move of the opponent in the subgame can be suspended and an interaction feature (operation) added so that both players can be free to play their opening moves in subgames. An oversimplified but nevertheless helpful example of such a modification can be expressed in terms of the everyday use of personal computers. Traditionally, strategies in games are understood as functions from positions (histories of past interactions) to moves or actions. However, if the strategy of the computer was simply a function from positions to moves, it would have then been required to check the entire ever-increasing history of interactions—of moves and counter-moves. The task of the computer would then over time run into complications such as the exponential slowing of speed (time to process) and the increase in space or memory needed to respond to the next countermove. But neither is it the case that the computer just responds to our last keypunch, since it is capable of storing, accessing, and scanning histories of past interactions.[260]

Interaction-as-computation, in this sense, can be seen as pertaining to possible compositions of strategies which, depending on how the semantics of interaction is interpreted (i.e., the interpretation of constraints and operations involved in the interaction), would cover richer computational behaviours not limited to the computation of functions. Furthermore, in the interaction schema, computational criteria such as sequentiality and synchronicity—sequentiality of moves and synchronicity of interactions—are no longer dominant. In fact, sequential-synchronic games or computations are special cases of true concurrent asynchronous games as the most general category of interaction games. Such a general category of games G can be represented by the so-called asynchronous copycat strategy.[261] G—as represented by a copycat—is nothing but the game or interaction itself independent of the order of the actions performed by agents, processes, or players involved in the interaction or playing of the game. In other words, in G, games between players can be played out-of-order or in partial order and the result would still remain the same. From an information theoretic standpoint, the notion of copycat stands for the conservation of the flow of information.

---

260 For a survey of interaction operations and relaxation of constraints in the context of semantics of interaction and computability see G. Japaridze, 'Introduction to Computability Logic', *Annals of Pure and Applied Logic* 123:1–3 (2003), 1–99.

261 See S. Abramsky, 'Concurrent Interaction Games', in J. Davies, B. Roscoe et al. (eds.), *Millennial Perspectives in Computer Science* (Basingstoke: Palgrave Macmillan, 2000), 1–12.

Whereas information is conserved for the total system, there is information flow and information increase relative to interacting subsystems. Copycat strategies and their compositions enable the development of an explicitly dynamic theory of information processing.

Let us clarify, by means of intuitive diagrams, the copycat as the encapsulation of the general category of games, or interaction itself: G can be defined as the identity map or morphism of the game itself $G: G \to G$. In Church-Turing computability terms, this can be interpreted as the identity function that maps natural numbers to natural numbers $N: \mathbb{N} \Rightarrow \mathbb{N}$. Then N would be a general game on which many games—computable functions over natural numbers—can be played. Defined as such, G is represented by a copycat (or general strategy of interaction).

Imagine G is a universal game board which might consist of many other game boards or subgames. On the game board G, there are two teams of players, agents, or processes A and B, each with their respective base or domain of moves and distributed in an asynchronous fashion over the board. The actions or moves in each team can be synchronically and sequentially ordered. But with respect to the actions or moves of the other team, they are asynchronous, i.e., either out-of-order or in partial order. The cells of the game board are labelled in accordance with the players' base. As possible actions in the game, the moves (represented by arrows) performed in each team's base can be thought of as legal transits from one labelled cell to another. Such transits could be classically understood as functions or state transitions, where the previous cell traversed by a move is an input for the next cell in that move and, correspondingly, the next cell an output for the previous cell.

Now enters the copycat: an agent who beats both A and B by copying one team's plays and running them against the other team, or copying moves from one game board to another and vice versa. It copies A's move and plays it against B by changing its labelled cells from A's base to corresponding labelled cells in B's base, and vice versa for team B. That is, the copycat plays moves in the domain A in the codomain B, and plays moves in domain B in the codomain A. In this scenario, whichever team wins, the copycat wins. With the understanding that winnability in interaction games

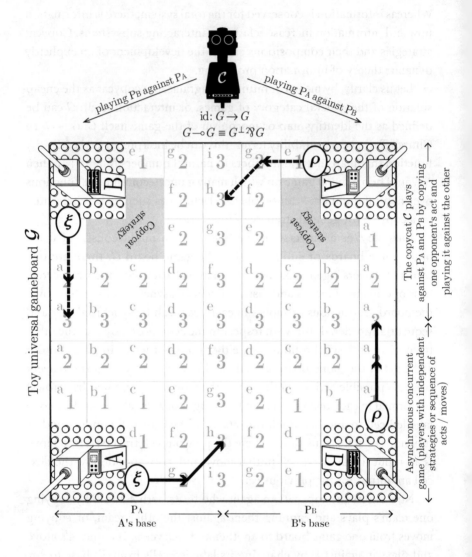

The hiding copycat

is tantamount to computability, winnability is not essential for the copycat since if both A and B lose—i.e., incomputability as a lost game—there would be no win for the copycat. The true significance of the copycat is that it represents the flow and increase of information under *any* particular interactive configuration (i.e., distributed in space and time) for a set of agents or processes: even if the teams involved do not synchronically react to one another, the copycat captures their moves as a general interaction. Moreover, from a logico-computational perspective, the copycat reveals the surprising power of copying information from one game board or place to another, through which we can arrive at an emergent view of logics and language as simple or composite interactions or copycat strategies.

As an agent that incarnates the universal category of the game or the interactive logic of computation, the copycat shows that sequential-synchronic computation is a subset of asynchronous-concurrent computation, just as the first-person game is a subset of the two-person game (I-thou game). In a nutshell, interaction in its most general form is the generalization of computation as such. There is no process that does not speak to another process, irrespective of how such processes react to one another. The logical equivalent of the copycat as the agent of interaction, game, or computation is a *dialogue*, and dialogue is the engine of semantics: there is no monologue or private thought without a dialogue, an interaction within and over language, and correspondingly there is no dialogue without an information gain or new knowledge made possible by an interaction between the system and its environment, an agent and its dual, a thesis and a counter-thesis.

FROM SEMANTICS OF INTERACTION
TO INTERACTION AS THE GAME OF SEMANTICS

Refounding logic on generalized interaction—the deepest computational phenomenon—allows us to understand precisely what form of logico-computational interactions the automata must exhibit in order for them to cross the bridge between syntax and semantics. In other words, such an interactive view of logic—as formulated particularly in proof theory—provides the logico-computational framework through which the minimal generative syntax of the automata can be transformed into concrete syntax, where syntactic strings are comprised of structured units and relations similar to the various syntactic constituents with invariable roles that make up the structure of our natural language sentences. On another level, the interactive view of logic presents a logico-computational framework within which role-based syntactic constituents can be handled as logical expressions which subsequently, through dialogical interaction, find semantic values or meanings. In this sense, meanings can be characterized as invariants with regard to the interaction processes. In short, the interactive conception of logic can simultaneously specify the type of interactions necessary for the formation of concrete 'sentential' syntax, and the interactions necessary for meaning-conferring dialogues. The syntax-semantics interface is built upon interaction.

To provide even a rudimentary account of such frameworks for bridging syntax and semantics would entail an introduction to recent developments in logic, mathematics, and theoretical computer science—itself a gargantuan task that would surely distract us from the main themes of this book.[262] To this extent, at the risk of misrepresentation, only the most basic intuitive ideas behind the interactive logical framework of the syntax-semantics interface will be presented here.

Traditionally in proof theory, the meaning of a proposition has been understood as the proof of that proposition or the verification of it (provided that the process of verification is grounded on the notion of proof).[263] The meanings expressed by (linguistic) statements are then laid out not by means

---

262 For introductions to developments at the intersections of theoretical computer science, logic, mathematics and linguistics, see J. Ginzburg, *The Interactive Stance* (Oxford: Oxford University Press, 2012); A. Lecomte, *Meaning, Logic and Ludics* (London: Imperial College Press, 2011); and J. Trafford, *Meaning in Dialogue: An Interactive Approach to Logic and Reasoning* (Dordrecht: Springer, 2017).

263 For an interactionist interpretation of the program of verificationism, its relation to computation and proof see, A. Naibo et al., 'Verificationism and Classical Realizability', in C. Başkent (ed.), *Perspectives on Interrogative Models of Inquiry* (Dordrecht: Springer, 2016), 163–97.

of truth-conditionals but by means of the construction of proofs that are *syntactical* in nature. In classical proof theory, the meaning of the sentence is the set of its proofs, or, more accurately, knowledge of the conditions of its assertion, which then counts as knowledge of what would count as a proof, and hence the meaning of the sentence. Thus, in determining the meaning of a sentence priority is given not to the notion of truth but to that of proof. Or, from the viewpoint of the pragmatic theory of meaning-as-use, the meaning of a sentence or formula is not explained by their truth, but by their use or consequences in a proof:

$$\frac{\vdash A \quad A \vdash B}{\vdash B} \text{ cut} \rightarrow \frac{\vdash A \quad A \vdash}{\vdash} \text{ cut}$$

(Notice that A on the left and the right side of the consequence relation or turnstile can be seen as a duality: proofs of A versus proofs of $A^{\perp}$, where the linear negation $\perp$ signifies the switching of roles or, in this case, swapping the *place* of A with regard to the turnstile.)

The shortcoming of the classical meaning-as-proof paradigm is that the proof is conceived statically and monologically, in tandem with the mathematical interpretation of classical logic. For example, in this classical setup, given A (a formula, a logical expression, a piece of syntax, a proposition), if one has the proof—the meaning of A—then one also has the meaning of $\neg A$. That is to say, having the proof implies having the disproof by way of the classical negation that negates some unspecified or arbitrary iteration of A. But with the introduction into classical proof theory of interaction (i.e., dualities as the interchange of roles rather than as classical negation), the proof or determination of meaning takes on a different form. The meaning of A can only be determined through interaction or dialogue with its counter-proof or refuter, and vice versa. The determination of meaning or proof can only be achieved by stepping outside of the static-monological framework of proof into one where proof is the interaction between a prover (player) and a refuter (opponent), A and $\neg A$, or, more precisely, A and the model of $\neg A$.

Just like the environment in the classical Church-Turing paradigm of computation, where it was presupposed but never explicitly asserted, in its classical form $\neg A$ is rather a passive and extrinsic piece of information in relation to A. In the interactive framework, however, $\neg A$ is an intrinsic dimension of the proof or meaning of A. The proof of A rests on the proof of $\neg A$ in the context of an interaction or game played by the proponent P and the opponent $\neg A$. In this approach, however, classical negation is abandoned in favour of interactional dualities, with negation as the interchange of roles between the proofs of A and $A^{\perp}$ where the absurdity or contradiction or *falsum* sign $\perp$ is a linear negation that expresses duality (e.g., $A \multimap B = B^{\perp} \multimap A^{\perp}$):

Action of type A = Reaction of type $A^{\perp}$

In this fashion, even logical connectives can be expressed as moves in inter-action games. For example, in the classical Lorenzenian version of game semantics,[264] conjunction $(p \wedge q)$ and disjunction $(p \vee q)$ can be expressed in terms of how the game proceeds when compound propositions constructed by conjunction or disjunction are attacked or defended, questioned or asserted. To challenge/question the conjunction, the opponent may select either conjunct, while the proponent can only defend/assert the conjunct that the opponent has selected, while to challenge the disjunction, the opponent may ask the proponent to select and defend one of the disjuncts. Similarly, to challenge the implication $(p \rightarrow q)$ the opponent may assert p. Then the proponent must either challenge p or assert/defend q.

Reconceived within a dialogical framework, proof is no longer an object in the way it is classically understood, but an *act*. As an act, proof implies the confrontation of acts, i.e., interaction—in the computational sense introduced above—between dualities that can be represented as agents, processes, or strategies. What dialogical interaction affords is not merely the computation of meaning or semantic values, but also semantic information such as the contextuality and thematization necessary for the determination of meaning. In the dialogical paradigm of meaning as proof or use, semantic values and contexts are computations.

---

264 K. Lorenz and P. Lorenzen, *Dialogische Logik* (Darmstadt: WBG, 1978).

Depending on the specificity of a dialogical interaction, computation can be understood either as proof search or proof normalization. In the proof search schema, if the interaction game returns the proof of a sentence or formula, the meaning is computed. Otherwise, it searches forever and fails to obtain the proof (cf. the halting problem), i.e., the dialogue will not be able to determine the meaning. In the normalization schema, the proof or meaning can be computed if, by the elimination of unnecessary steps, transitions, or rules (useless detours) for a formula or sentence, the normal form or canonical proof can be obtained. This normal form is the simplest i.e. most irreducible proof obtainable without using unnecessary detours (cf. normal form in abstract rewriting as an object that cannot be transformed any further).[265] In this setting, two statements have the same meaning if their proofs or constructions can count as equivalent in so far as there is a reversible inferential relation or mapping between them.[266]

---

265 For a term A, some $x \in A$ is a normal or simplified form if no $y \in A$ exists such that $x \to y$ (i.e. x cannot be written further). Computability can be understood in terms of a rewrite system or process of normalization that terminates once it reaches a strongly normalized term, i.e., a term that cannot be reduced or simplified any further.

266 If we were—in accordance with the correspondences between proofs, programs, and mathematical structures—to take a proposition A as the topological space of proofs, then the proofs M and N can be thought of as points in this space. Consequently, the paths between these points can be considered as equivalence relationships. Suppose that both M and N are proofs of A, denoted as $M=N:A$. Now there is a mapping or path α that can deform M to N ($\alpha:M \to N:A$) and vice versa. The existence of such a path can be understood as the existence of a piece of evidence—a particular mental object or *gegenstand*—that falls under both constructions M and N. In Kantian terms, M and N are *concepts* which cover the same object. Moreover, the existence of such a path or equivalence relationship implies the existence of equivalences of equivalences, or concepts of the same concept type. Such higher equivalences are called homotopies, which are basically the deformation maps of deformations between M and N. See Univalent Foundations Program, *Homotopy Type Theory: Univalent Foundations of Mathematics* (2013), <https://homotopytypetheory.org/book/>.

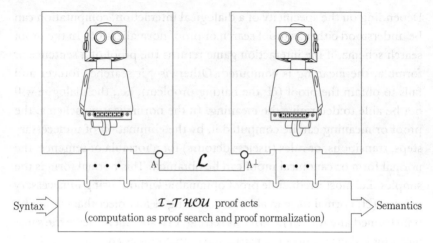

Syntax

$\mathcal{I}$-$\mathcal{THOU}$ proof acts
(computation as proof search and proof normalization)

Semantics

Toy meaning dispenser

In the universe of the automata, the interactive schema of meaning-as-proof can be thought of as a toy meaning-dispensing machine. The machine consists of two agents plugged into an interaction over a language $\mathcal{L}$. The interaction modelled on a two-person game—more specifically, an elementary I-Thou dialogue in which, from the perspective of one agent, it is the system and the other agent is the environment. Inside this inter-active machine, there are algorithms which obtain proof either through normalization or search. Insert syntactic tokens or terms into this machine and the machine dispenses meaning. Composed of syntactic structures, the semantic value or meaning has a normal form and is invariant with respect to the interactive dynamics inside the machine. Give syntactic terms of the same type to the vending machine, and you should be able to get the same outcome.

A similar interaction machine can be imagined for transforming the minimal generative syntax of the kind our automata already have into the concrete syntax structures required for sentential composition. The configuration of the machine remains intact, but the emphasis of the machine operation or proof acts will be on resource-sensitivity in handling syntactic tokens. In this machine, raw chunks of syntax go in and the sentential syntactic units whose dependencies underlie semantic sentential dependencies come out.[267] The products of the machine are precisely those syntactic structures that support semantic compositionality (the fact that sentences can be decomposed into more elementary constituents). However, syntax at the level of sentential structure is deeply resource-sensitive. This is particularly the case for the syntactic binding of sentences where the meaning (i.e., referent) of an item such as a pronoun can only be determined by the connection it has at any instant with another item in the sentence. Such linked items whose meaning or reference cannot be determined by themselves—which is usually the case for ordinary lexical entries—are known as anaphoric elements. The need to keep track of anaphoric dependency relations between different uses of words in a sentence or between sentences is directly tied to the resource-sensitivity of syntactic relations.[268]

In the sentence, 'Kanzi saw a monkey touching the monolith, and it also heard the monkey screaming as it touched it,' the anaphoric use of the pronoun *it* is dependent on tracking its point of reference as well as its iterations within the sentence. Does 'it' refer to Kanzi, the monkey, or the monolith? This anaphoric binding is essentially resource-sensitive in the sense that it cannot be seen as a simple transition $\mathcal{K}anzi \rightarrow it$ in which 'it' can be obtained by repeated iterations of 'Kanzi' (i.e., all iterations of 'it' in the sentence do not necessarily refer to 'Kanzi'). Instead the transition should be seen as a resource-sensitive linear implication $\mathcal{K}anzi \multimap it$ where 'it' uses 'Kanzi' as its point of reference (resource) *exactly* once. After that, the syntactic-semantic relations between other iterations of 'it' and other antecedent nouns in the sentence will have to be checked to determine whether or not 'Kanzi' can be reused as point of reference or resource for 'it'. Such resource-sensitive connections require logical operators—such

---

267 For a proof-theoretic account of syntax at the level of syntactic structures of sentences see Lecomte, *Meaning, Logic and Ludics*, 33–52.

268 See G.-J. Kruijff and R. Oehrle (eds.), *Resource-Sensitivity, Binding and Anaphora* (Dordrecht: Springer, 2012).

as exponentials in linear logic—to control and keep track of the use of syntactic resources in sentences.[269]

KEEP IT IN FOCUS: A DIALOGUE IN EIGHT ACTS

Earlier in this chapter, the problem of the syntax-semantics interface was addressed. The solution to this problem was put forward in terms of dialogical interaction as a logico-computational condition for the possibility of meaning. But in order for our automata to have dialogues in which the rules of language are not set in advance, a new type of dialogue must be introduced—one in which rules emerge through the interaction itself. The form of such a dialogue corresponds with the general category of games G, discussed earlier. One may call such a dialogue an interaction with no preinstalled normative bells and whistles. Dialogue, in this sense, counts as the generalization of the logico-computational notion of interaction as the bridge between syntax and semantics. According to Samuel Tronçon et al., a dialogue has at least three essential functions—exchange of information (i.e., computation in the sense discussed earlier), construction of knowledge, and resolution of cognitive tensions (i.e., harnessing the behaviours of interlocutors toward new behaviours):

> First, at every stage, a speaker is giving a symbol, and this exchange is informative in three ways: it informs us about the discussed (some

---

269 Other than the resource-sensitive linear implication $A \multimap B$ (reads as 'A yields B and is consumed in the process') in which B is yielded by the use of exactly one iteration of A, there are logical operators in linear logic that directly handle the permissions on the use of resources or formulas. These exponentials are !! and ??, which are respectively called exponential conjunction (reads as 'of course' operator) and exponential disjunction (reads as 'why not' operator). In the interaction framework, roughly, $!A$ is defined as a permission for the system/player to use or access the iterations of the formula, hypothesis, or resource A without restriction. Whereas $?A$ is defined as a permission given by the environment to the system to use A: The system asks 'can I use A?', and the environment or the interlocutor may reply 'why not'. Subsequent use of or access to A would again require the permission of the environment/interlocutor.

thesis), the subject that is speaking (his approach about this thesis), and the connection between a present intervention and some counter-interventions (upstream or downstream, actuals or virtuals). Second, running dialogues shows arguments interacting like machines built up to explore relevant opportunities of discussion according to some global strategy: *I argue in this way to reach this point, I open these branches to induce some reactions....* So, dialogue is a sort of unfolding structure that represents some knowledge. Evidently, involving friendly but tenacious interlocutors ensures a good (exhaustive) exploration. Third, by the interaction, the locutors can extract some new information which is about the form of the interaction, contained in the result of the dialogue: what is stable, what is explored, what is new, what is in latence.[270]

This multilayered view of dialogue can be modelled on the general dynamics of interaction in such a way that the functions of dialogues mirror the deep properties of logic and computation. One example of such a model is Jean-Yves Girard's *ludics*, which at a paradigmatic level of interpretation reflects the logic of dialogue, a linguistic interaction in which not only can syntax be bridged with semantics, but the rules of language naturally emerge as part of the dialogue.[271]

Girard's ludics can be characterized as a pre- or proto-logical framework for analysing logical and computational phenomena at the most elementary level. Defined at the intersection between linear logic (a substructural logic capable of capturing the duality of interaction and the interchange of roles), proof theory, game semantics, and computer science, ludics introduces a logico-computational framework in which, at the *deepest level*, the distinction between syntax and semantics collapses. Yet this continuity

---

270 M.-R. Fleury, M. Quatrini, and S. Tronçon, 'Dialogues in Ludics', in *Logic and Grammar* (Dordrecht: Springer, 2011), 138–57.

271 For an exquisitely engaging introduction to Girard's project in a philosophical context see O.L. Fraser, *Go Back to An-Fang* (2014), <http://www.academia.edu/352702/Go_back_to_An-Fang>.

between syntax and semantics is established by deviating from a number of traditional approaches such as referential theories of meaning, monological conceptions of semantics, non-autonomous approaches to syntax, and the traditional forms of game semantics conditioned on game theoretic concepts such as predetermined winning strategies, preference ranking, payoff functions, and referees. In ludics, these are replaced by an inferential theory of meaning, dialogical and operational semantics, an autonomy of minimal syntax, and a general notion of game devoid of any predetermined winning strategies or payoff functions.

Ludics shows that the continuity between syntax and semantics is naturally achieved through an interactive stance toward syntax in its most atomic and naked appearance: the trace of the sign's occurrence, the *locus* or place of its inscription. Semantics immanently unfolds through the dynamic impact of the most minimal appearance of syntax—its locus—stripped of all preformulated rules and metaphysical references. Different stances toward an atomic syntactic expression are represented as interacting strategies (called *designs* in ludics) that are tested not against a preestablished model, but against one another. In the process, the rules of logic (or alternatively, the forms of thought) emerge from the confrontation of strategies whose element of interaction is a positive or a negative locus rather than a proposition. The positive and negative locus refer to the address of the sign/formula in interaction, where an act is exercised either in response to, or as a request for, another act on the same locus but played according to the opposite strategy. The exchange via the relation between a locus and its polar counterpart corresponds with responses and demands between interlocutors in a dialogue, or players in a game.

Let us briefly examine the most basic elements of ludics as the logic of dialogue:[272]

- Designs: As the central objects of ludics, designs can be identified as strategies in a game, namely, sets of plays (or in ludics, *chronicles*)

---

272 See J.-Y. Girard, 'Locus Solum: From the Rules of Logic to the Logic of Rules', *Mathematical Structures in Computer Science* 11:3 (2001), 301–506.

distinguished by the answer or defence of the player against the attacking move or query made by the opponent. Less in traditional game terms and more in ludics terms, designs are alternating sequences of positive and negative rules which may either progress endlessly (as in endless dispute) or be closed by a rule called *daïmon*.

— Plays (dialogical equivalents of proofs) are alternating sequences of moves or actions.

  — Moves are defined in terms of a tuple $\langle p,l,r \rangle$ where

    — p is the local polarity of moves (positive polarity for the actions or moves of the player and negative polarity for the moves of the opponent).

    — l is a *locus* or fixed position to which a move is anchored. Loci can be thought of as memory cells or places in which formulas are stored. In Ludics, formulas or syntactic terms are replaced by the address of their locations in the interaction/dialogue. In other words, all that matters are the locations of syntactic terms or formulas—not formulas themselves—and how they are manipulated within a dialogue or proof.

    — r is a finite number of positions which can be reached in one step and which is called *ramification*.

— Positions are *addresses* of loci encoded by finite sequence of integers and usually denoted by the letters ξ, ρ, σ, ... which stand for the threads and subthreads of the interaction (loci and subloci which represent thematization of a dialogue across different topics). Trees of addresses are equated with designs. For example, in an absurdist dialogue between Kanzi and Sue, addresses can be encoded in the following manner. In the contexts ξ and σ two trees of alternating sequences emerge:

Kanzi: Did you see that grey stuff? (ξ.0)

Sue: Yes. (ξ.0.1)

Kanzi: Have you noticed it makes noise whenever it finds something new? (ξ.0.1.0)

Sue: It often does. (ξ.0.1.0.1)

Kanzi: Why is that you are clicking too much today? (σ.0)

Sue: I have no idea what you are talking about. (σ.0.1)

— The starting positions, also known as *forks*, are denoted in the sequent form as $\Gamma \vdash \Delta$ where Γ and Δ are either singletons or empty sets. In this setting, when an element belongs to Γ every play on this element starts with the opponent/environment's move and the fork is said to be negative, whereas if the player/system starts with an element of its choice taken in Δ the fork is said to be positive.

In this form, a design can be represented as a tree whose nodes are forks $\Gamma \vdash \Delta$ and whose threefold root is comprised of the positive rule, the negative rule, and the *daïmon*.

• Rules: The only rules *necessary* for building designs or strategies are *daïmon* plus negative and positive rules, which are indexed by a property called focalization. Roughly, focalization can be thought of as proof search in an interactive framework: it allows for the grouping of a series of consecutive actions (i.e., plays as proof) of the same polarity as if they were a single logical action in a proof. That is to say, focalization enables the alternating dynamics of positive and negative actions. In ludics, focalization represents proofs as interactive processes between two players where the player/proponent can choose what to do (positive action) or receives and acknowledges the action or move performed by the opponent (negative action). From this perspective, focalization creates a proof tree in which rules or logical connectives are captured by alternating sequences of positive and negative actions which switch loci for subloci and vice versa across the consequence relation ($\vdash$): $\vdash\xi$, ξ.o $\vdash$,

⊢ξ.0.1,.... The meaning or semantic value of rules is obtained from the interaction of such consequence relations qua *use* in the dialogue.

— The positive rule can be denoted in the sequent form as:

$$\frac{...\,\xi.i \vdash \Delta_i\, ...}{\vdash \Delta, \xi}\,(\xi, I)$$

where I is a finite set of integers (possibly an empty ramification) such that, for every pair of indices $(i, j) \in I$, Δ_i and Δ_j are disconnected and every Δ_i is included in Δ.

— Correspondingly, the negative rule can be denoted in the sequent form as:

$$\frac{...\,\xi.I \vdash \Delta_I\, ...}{\xi \vdash \Delta}\,(\xi, \mathcal{N})$$

where $\mathcal{N}$ is a possibly empty or infinite set of finite set of integers (ramifications) such that instances of Δ_I—not necessarily disconnected—are included in Δ.

— In addition to positive and negative rules which range over loci and subloci, there is also a general axiomatic rule called *daïmon* symbolized by †, which can be understood as a paralogism. Whichever player or proof-process (⊢A or ⊢$A^\perp$) invokes the *daïmon*, the other player wins. In other words, the *daïmon* allows for identification of the winning strategy, the correct proof, or the validity of a proposition. A proposition can be said to be valid for a given design if that design never invokes *daïmon* before its opponent. As such, the *daïmon* can be identified with the conceding act of 'I give up' or 'Stop!' (terminating a design or closing off the branches of a proof tree) in a dialogue. Additionally, *daïmon* is a positive rule, meaning that either player can choose to invoke it. *Daïmon* is represented as a sequent with no premises:

$$\frac{}{\vdash \Delta}\,†$$

Here, what we are interested in is the *dialogical interpretation* of the objects of ludics in a way that allows us to understand dialogue as a dynamic process—interactive proof or computation—in which rules and meanings spontaneously emerge throughout the course of the conversation (i.e., simply through the exchange of loci and subloci—addresses of syntactic terms or formulas—and in the presence of most elementary rules of negative and positive actions plus the *daïmon* or termination command). According to this dialogical interpretation, for a given dialogue, the conversation progresses from whatever locus the polar strategies (players) choose to focus on.

Again in an imaginary dialogue between Kanzi and Sue, this can be interpreted as the first move made by Kanzi—for example, an utterance regarding the presence of a fuzzy item (the focus $\xi.0$). If Sue acknowledges Kanzi's utterance as a speech act, it may reply with an utterance on the same focus ($\xi.0.1$). Then the dialogue can be said to be developing along a selected context Λ_0 in which the theme ξ (the presence of fuzzy grey item) is developed. Contextualization and topicalization in a dialogue can, therefore, be captured by alternating sequences of positive and negative actions.[273] For a given locus or address ξ (focus of the dialogue), the context Λ_0 can be written as $\xi = \tau * 0 * 0, \tau * 0 * 1, ..., * \tau * 0 * n$. If we view the design from a top-down perspective or in terms of pre-steps, the topic of the conversation can be said to be an operation that unifies the focus and the context, i.e. Kanzi's first move together with the acknowledgement of that move by Sue:

$$\frac{\dfrac{\vdash \tau * 0 * 0, ..., \tau * 0 * n = \Lambda}{\dfrac{\tau * 0 \vdash}{\vdash \tau}(<>, +, \{0\})}}{} (-, \tau * 0, \{I\})$$

In this fashion, thematic variations (defined as a set of sets of loci) are developed in a dialogue as polar strategies give different addresses (loci) to an expression. A new locus can be accepted by the competing strategies or designs (corresponding with the agreement of interlocutors on a specific way of addressing the initial topic of the conversation) and introduced as

---

273 See A. Lecomte and M. Quatrini, *Dialogue and Interaction: The Ludics View* (2014), <http://iml.univ-mrs.fr/editions/publi2010/files/Quatrini_Lecomte-esslli.pdf>.

the focus of the exchange. This is the process of (bilateral) focalization in ludics, which maps the actions played in one strategy (the behaviour of a design) to its polar counterpart and projects them back. In doing so, focalization reveals logical constants and rules that are not a priori given, but adaptively emerge in the absence of any gain function or external referee.

Moreover, focalization progressively topicalizes the interaction and drives expressions into a state of context-sensitivity in which syntactic terms or formulas acquire semantic value by virtue of how they are thematized in the same context (focalization on the same set of addresses) as well as how the context is updated in the dialogue (sets of designs or proof acts exchanging the same locations and sub-locations). This is equivalent to Brandom's inferentialist-pragmatic theory of meaning where the contextualization and updating of the context of expressions by the inferential relations obtained between them count as the inferential articulation of expressions that genuinely confer conceptual content on them.[274] Like normative scorekeeping pragmatics, ludics adopts a conception of meaning that is not representational—i.e., it does not relate to a nonlinguistic item—but is instead conferred by the reciprocation between different competing strategies or interlocutors. Semantics immanently arises as the normalization of clashing strategies or processes executed at the level of syntax. In other words, the interaction between different stances toward an expression (a location) can be seen as the process of computing meanings or, in proof theoretic terms, as the process of locating proofs or meanings of expressions.

---

274 'The connection between the normative scorekeeping pragmatics and the inferentialist semantics is secured by the idea that the *consequential* scorekeeping relations among expression-repeatables needed to compute the significance updates can be generated by broadly *inferential* relations among those expression-repeatables. The theory propounded in *Making It Explicit* is that there are six consequential relations among commitments and entitlements that are *sufficient* for a practice exhibiting them to qualify as *discursive*, that is, as a practice of giving and asking for *reasons*, hence as conferring *inferentially* articulated, thus genuinely *conceptual* content on the expressions, performances, and statuses that have scorekeeping significances in those practices.' R. Brandom, 'Conceptual Content and Discursive Practice', in J. Langkau and C. Nimtz (eds), *New Perspectives on Concepts* (Amsterdam: Rodopi, 2010), 20.

As the logic of dialogue, ludics provides an interactive articulation of speech acts. But unlike the classical view of speech acts, where the speakers' intention to communicate a propositional content is normatively predefined, in ludics speech acts evolve naturally through interaction. Interacting moves or actions (partial functions in the computational game framework) attain the status of speech acts (such as assertion and questioning) once they produce, in a shared context, invariant impacts on the environment, i.e. the addressee from the perspective of the speaker and the speaker from the perspective of the addressee. Here, invariance means that the execution of such actions or dialogical interventions on variable expressions in the same shared context or condition (data from the computational game standpoint) always yields the same observed impact for both speaker and addressee. In this sense, ludics allows speech acts to be defined in terms of designs (strategies of the speaker), locations, positive and negative rules (respectively, executing dialogical interventions and recording or anticipating the interventions of the addressee/interlocutor). As elaborated by Tronçon and Fleury, a ludics definition of speech can be laid out in terms of three elements:[275]

1. The speech acting competence $\mathfrak{U}$ of the speaker to impact (denoted by a positive rule) the context (interactions on the same loci) given the anticipated reactions of the addressee (denoted by a negative rule).
2. The test, which is an interactive situation that contrasts the speech act with a complex structure representing the context $\mathfrak{B}$ that mixes or interacts contextual data with the addressee's reactions. Put simply, the test is the interaction between speech acts and context.
3. The impact $\mathfrak{E}$, which is the effect e of the interaction: the updating, modification, or erasing of a shared context c.

The speech act can then be understood as the interaction of two designs $\mathfrak{U}$ and $\mathfrak{B}$, resulting in a new design $\mathfrak{E}$. When negative or passive ($\mathfrak{B}$), actions

---

or observations represent a contextual structure c_i. And when positive ($\mathfrak{U}$), actions or observations represent active design-trees which are operations, functions, or transformations (modification or erasing) in the context c_i such that $c_i \multimap e$. The impact or significance of the speech act (the design $\mathfrak{C}$) can, therefore, be expressed as an invariant behaviour which, for every c_i, yields or produces the effect e in exactly that context. Thus the speech act is nothing but its impact in a dialogue, and this impact is essentially the normal form resulting from the normalization of two interacting designs $\mathfrak{U}$ and $\mathfrak{B}$ (proof and counter-proof).

With these preliminary remarks, we can see how ludics as interactive logic or the logic of dialogue is the generalization of what Brandom calls deontic scorekeeping, the game of giving and asking for reasons. Let us imagine a hypothetical dialogue in the style of ludics and deontic scorekeeping between Kanzi and the monkey. The monkey's noises are mapped onto Kanzi's sentences, and vice versa, in such a way that both agents can recognize what they say in virtue of the interlocutor's evidence for or against it.

Let Kanzi be the asserter/speaker A, and B its interlocutor, or the addressee. A is in possession of a set of markers (sentences) in such a way that playing a marker counts as claiming or asserting something. These markers are differentiated into two classes, those kept and those discarded. The record of such markers is kept either in a general notebook shared by both A and B, or in personal notebooks belonging to A and B. The markers kept and labelled by A count as the score of the speaker. If A plays a new marker—making an assertion—it changes its own score and maybe its interlocutor's. Now, provided that some possibilities have been presented by B as entitlements to commitments (i.e., reasons to believe that p), A may play a marker by asserting or endorsing a claim, e.g., 'This monolith is black'. Additionally, we assume that A keeps a database or directory of entitlements, i.e., it records the reactions of B toward its commitment 'The monolith is black'. In such a scenario, we can imagine a dialogue *focused* on the 'colour' of the monolith, and which consists of eight acts tagged by digits. In the simplest form, they are tagged by 0 and 1 denoting the negation and affirmation of the predicate. Other digits could be introduced, for example, to express modalities. The dialogical acts progress in the following manner:

Act 1: A chooses an object $\{j\}$—a singular term—among the set of many such objects (cf. the choice of playing an opening move from a set of possible alternative moves). The choice of this object has the pragmatic significance of being entitled by the interlocutor to make the assertion p or in this case, the entitlement to address some theme (the colour of the monolith).

Act 2: Thus having chosen to speak of some definite object, A entitles B to treat this object in terms of the range of properties that are generally associated with it (e.g., black as a colour, not of light colour, etc.).

Act 3: In return, B entitles A to choose and play a property $\{k\}$ from this range.

Act 4: On the permission of B, A now chooses a property and entitles B to regard or act on this property within a range of values (e.g., shiny, opaque, textured black).

Act 5: B entitles A to choose a value $\{c\}$.

Act 6: A picks up a value and entitles B to act on it within a set of modalities which can simply pertain to truth and falsity.

Act 7: B entitles A to pick up a modality.

Act 8: A chooses a modality and waits for B's acknowledgement.

The dialogue may conclude once B invokes the daïmon. The entire conversation can be represented as interacting design-trees where all that is required to keep and update the scores of the speaker and the addressee so that their acts can be regarded as sufficiently discursive is the method of tracking how the locations or addresses of the object $\{j\}$, together with its range of properties and values, are exchanged and swapped from one side to another. The dialogue can be represented in tree form with the speaker on the left side and the addressee on the right side. The designs of A and B also can be written in sequent form as follows:

A:

$$\cfrac{\cfrac{\cfrac{...,\xi.j.0.k,...}{\xi.j.0\vdash}(-,\{\{1\},...,\{k\},...,\{m\}\})}{\vdash\xi j}(+,\xi.j,\{0\})}{\vdash\xi 1...,} \qquad ,...,\xi n \quad N$$

$$\xi\vdash$$

B:

$$\cfrac{\cfrac{\cfrac{\xi.j.0.k\vdash}{\vdash\xi.j.0}(+,\xi.j.0,\{k\})}{\xi j\vdash}(-,\{\{0\}\})}{\vdash\xi}(+,\xi,\{j\})$$

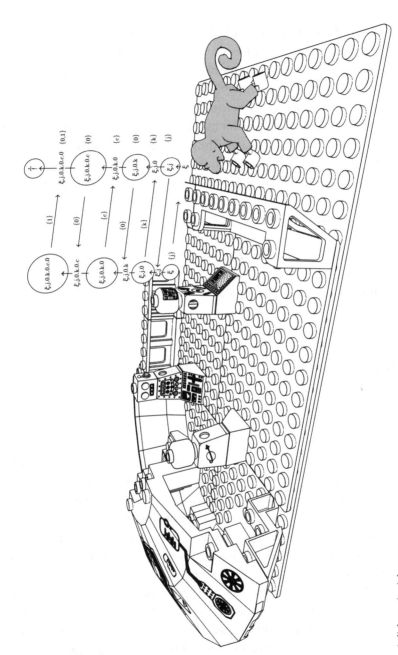

A dialogue in eight acts

Ludics provides a framework in which the logico-computational phenomena implicit in the pragmatic dimension of language as the bridge between syntax and semantics, symbol-pushing and inferential articulation, come to the foreground. However, unlike the pragmatic theory of meaning-as-use—even in its Brandomian version, which significantly differs from its original Wittgensteinian form—for ludics there is no preestablished space of reasons into which one graduates. The generation of rules and the capacity to reason are inconceivable without interaction, and are inseparable from the complex contexts that arise throughout its course. However, contra Sellars, this interaction is not a matter of acquaintance with norms as a matter of cultural evolution; and contra Brandom, it is not an index of a substantive sociality of reason. It is rather the very formal condition of language and meaning—a logico-computational dynamics that realizes the syntax-semantics interface. The substantive sociality of reason is built on this formal condition, not the other way around.

FORMALISM AND THE PURE AUTONOMY OF THE FORMAL

This formal condition in which computation, logic, and mathematics intersect is exactly what we can call the pure transcendental condition—that is, a formal dimension at last liberated from Kantian transcendental logic anchored in the provincialism of the apperceptive I and the particular transcendental types which shape and constrain the experience of the subject. And it is in fact this formal dimension—as captured implicitly by natural language and explicitly by interactive logics and artificial languages—that grounds transcendental logic as the science of pure understanding and rational cognition—or simply the concept of mind in relation to the world. The subject has experiences (i.e., it can access the *content* of its experiences) because there is a formal dimension—call it language-as-interaction-as-logic-as-computation—that permits the semantic structuration of such experiences. Without it, there would be no experience and no understanding.

Yet the qualifier 'formal' should not be construed as a reinscription of form versus content or, more precisely, the dichotomy of syntactic form and semantic content. *Both* form and content belong to language as a formal dimension. Moreover, the interactionist view of logical syntax is itself 'semantic in disguise'. While the form-content dichotomy can be seen as still operative in the context of the classical picture of formal languages—a problem that is often raised by proponents of language who see it solely in terms of natural languages—as we observed, it is not a tenable index for the characterization or distinguishing natural languages from formal languages, particularly in the wake of developments in the interactive paradigms in computation and logic. Formal languages are better candidates for the articulation of language qua logic as an organon than natural languages, not merely because they can possess more expressive powers by virtue of their unbound syntactic complexity (i.e., the Carnapian view of language as a general calculus), but more importantly because they explicate interaction as the formal condition of language. In this way, the specific picture of formal languages developed in the interactive paradigm averts the risk of grasping the nature of language and linguistic practices through a vaguely metaphysical account of sociality which results either in seeing linguistic practices as one generic social practice among others or in an inflationary social account of language and reason.

From this perspective, the designation 'artificial' for an artificial language founded on the logic of interaction no longer implies a transcendental lack in comparison to natural language—a lack that can supposedly be overcome through better imitations of natural linguistic behaviours. On the contrary, the artificial, as that which has the capacity to range over broader logical and computational behaviours, is what expresses the transcendental dimension—i.e., the autonomy of logic and language over experiential content—in its pure and unrestricted form. Said differently, the designation 'artificial' in 'artificial languages' implies the possibility of unbinding the formal as that which structures content.

Put simply, artificiality, in this sense, does not signify an inferiority to the natural or something that vainly attempts to mimic the behaviours of natural language. It is rather the case that the 'natural' in 'natural languages' designates a subset of the designation 'artificial' in 'artificial languages'. The behaviours of natural language, its capacity for the inferential articulation of content, of syntactic and semantic structuration, merely represent a narrow domain in a far broader expanse of logico-computational phenomena that a general artificial language—unrestricted by the experience of the transcendental subject while embedded in the logic of interaction—would be able to cover. It is owing to its entrenched association with the experiential sphere of the transcendental subject that natural language is often falsely given a special status over artificial languages and, conversely, artificial languages are taken to be in principle inadequate in comparison with natural languages. Yet subordinating the structure of language to the structure of the subject invariably results in a subordination of the logical potencies of language for structuration of the world to a narrow domain limited by the particular transcendental structure of the subject.

The valorisation of subjective experience or psychology against formalism or, in this case, the formal dimension of language, is precisely the kind of bias that leads to the erroneous thesis that natural language is unshakeably superior to artificial languages, or that artificial languages cannot possibly capture the semantic richness of natural languages. And of course, the claim regarding the fundamental inferiority of artificial languages goes hand in hand with the verdict that mind cannot be artificially realized. Both language and mind are treated as ineffable or mysterious essences which yet somehow miraculously do what they do.

Valorising experience against the formal dimension of language is a formula for the limitation of experience. Only the richness of the formal can express or expand the richness of experiential content. The significance of artificial languages as languages realized at the intersection of computation, mathematics, and logic boils down to the fact that they have the capacity to sufficiently extract and distil the expressive richness of the formal dimension, which in turn enables a better grip on experiential content. Accordingly, to expand the field of experience—with the understanding that experience is inconceivable without its content—language should not be subordinated to the interests of the experiencing subject. Instead, it should be decoupled from the experience of the subject. In the same vein, the detachment of formal languages from the communicative role of natural languages should also be regarded as an opportunity to grasp the functions of language in themselves. In this regard, shifting from language as the

medium of communication to interaction-as-computation—the protologi-
cal foundation of language and logic—unbinds the logico-computational
functions of language while making it possible to rethink, reimagine or
reinvent linguistic communication on a completely different level.

Unbinding language means permitting its formal dimension to come
forth and be fully expressed on the surface of language. The aim of the
explicitation and mobilization of the formal dimension of language is not
simply to achieve syntactic efficacy (mechanizability) or semantic transparency as afforded by formalism, but to augment world-structuring abilities
by augmenting the syntactic-semantic expressivity of language. In this
respect, the abilities afforded by natural language as a form of language
whose evolution is tied to the restrictions imposed by the structure of the
experiencing subject would be merely a small archipelago in the vast sea
of syntactic and semantic abilities afforded by a general artificial language.
In other words, natural language represents only a fraction of the logical
autonomy of the formal as the transcendental dimension through which
the content of experiences can be accessed and whereby mind becomes
able to structure the world of which it is a part. As far as logical autonomy
(rather than practical autonomy) is concerned, it would be no exaggeration
to claim that a *programmable* toaster has more logical autonomy than all of
homo sapience combined.

The discussion on artificial general languages and the autonomy of
the formal brings us back to two overarching themes of this book. One is
the inquiry into the transcendental structures or conditions necessary for
having mind qua configuring factor. And the other is the critique of transcendental structures, whose aim is to procedurally unbind the conceptions
of mind and geistig intelligence from limitations and biases originating
in our contingent constitution and the seemingly fixed particularity of
our transcendental structures, rather than dispensing with transcendental
structures tout court.

Following these two trajectories, however, was impossible without a deep
analysis of the functional picture of mind combined with a multiplicity of
methods which are traditionally not in the toolbox of philosophy in order
to strip away and dig through that seamless façade which is the natural

order of things (the alleged naturalness of our time-consciousness, sociality, and language, among others). This is all to highlight the fact that extensive analysis and methodological assiduity are not auxiliary to the Copernican gesture of deracinating the transcendental subject and hurling the concept of intelligence into the abyss of intelligibilities. They are the very principles of this Copernican gesture by means of which the apparent facts of experience are peeled off to reveal a larger expanse of possible experience and thus of objective reality—a process through which our most treasured assumptions are challenged, to ensure that they are not subject to the experiential and cognitive biases of transcendental structures. The Copernican gesture is akin to a chain reaction; to follow the chain in either direction—toward the source or the consequences—one must have a fluent enough paradigm to shift from one method or model to another when necessary.

In this sense, this chapter's rather technical survey of language was an indispensable elaboration on the much broader themes of this work. On the one hand, this introductory analysis indicated that natural language is only the tip of the iceberg of general artificial languages—that is, the unrestricted scope of language—where traditional distinctions between language, logic, mathematics and computation (or more generally, language and logoi) begin to vanish. On the other hand, it underlined the significance of the implications of a revolution initiated by Gottlob Frege and less well known figures such as Hermann Cohen to shed the psychologistic and utilitarian residues of thinking and language, a revolution that was continued into the twentieth and twenty-first century by the likes of Quine, Carnap, and more recently Dutilh Novaes, but was most effectively carried out by theoretical computer science as the unifying philosophy of computation.

LOGIC AS AN ORGANON AND AS WORLDBUILDING

Construction of general artificial languages is thus commensurate with the conception of logic as an organon. Such equation is guaranteed to elicit the ire of orthodox Kantians who may still believe in the hard distinction between form and content or opposing logic as a canon to logic as an organon which according to Kant is the 'logic of illusion' or 'a sophistical art'[276] on the grounds that it is not constrained by the empirical sources of truth, sensible intuitions or information outside of logic.

What Kant means by logic as an organon is a formal tool for the production of objective insights or an instruction for bringing about a certain cognition that can be said to be objective. This conception of logic is then characterized as the science of speculative understanding or the speculative use of reason—the organon of the sciences. On the other hand, logic as a canon still refers to the formal use of logic (regardless of its content, which can be empirical or transcendental) but this time as delimited by the characterization of logic as the canon of judging (i.e., the mere criteria of the correct application of the laws of thought or judgements) which requires and is constrained by extra-logical information.

Kant's opposition of logic as a canon to logic as an organon is based on a historical reading of the controversy between Epicurus (the defender of canon) and Aristotle (the defender of organon). Yet, it is necessary to point out that Kant's dismissal of logic as an organon entirely relies on an antiquated Aristotelian definition of logic. Regardless of how we interpret logic, this very distinction becomes tenuous in the wake of the revolutions in formal and mathematical logic in the twentieth century as well as the advances of theoretical computer science. But the precariousness of restricting logic to a canon at the expense of rejecting logic as an organon can also be formulated via a question posed against orthodox Kantians: So, you think that form without content is arbitrary (i.e. unconstrained), but could you tell us what is *content without form*? Surely, entertaining the possibility of the latter even under the most critically cautious eyes is another variation of that ideological house of cards which is the Given. The whole notion of logic as a canon describes a game of logic already rigged by the representational resources and limits of the apperceptive subject constituted within a particular transcendental type.

Kant assumes that thinking about logic as an organon means believing that we can 'judge of objects and to assert anything about them *merely* with

---

276 Kant, *Critique of Pure Reason*, B86.

logic without having drawn on antecedently well-founded information about them from outside of logic.'[277] In this and other passages in *Critique of Pure Reason* which are riddled with focusing adverbs such as *merely* or *solely*, Kant seems to be advancing a trifling and obvious point not only as a profound remark but also as a refutation of the conception of logic as an organon: At least since the time of Plato's *Sophist*, we know that *what is said* is not equal to *what is*. Indeed, the equation of the two is the core tenet of sophism: so long as we know the rules of deductive syllogism, we can call ourselves masters of all sciences. However, logic as an organon neither implies the aforementioned equivocation—i.e., the claim that logic is by itself sufficient for judging about the stuff in the world—nor does it require any metaphysical commitment with regard to logic—the claim that laws of thought are laws of the world.

In contrast to Kant's straw-manning, all that the conception of logic as an organon suggests is that our resources of world-representation are in fact beholden to and caught up within the scope of our world-building, and in this case, the worlds of *logics*. In other words, it would be absurd to talk about objects without the primacy of logical structure, logoi, or the formal dimension. Kant would have agreed with this view, but only in an inconsequential manner. Why? Because if all talk of the object is meaningless without theory or logical structure, then the expansion of the field of logic or determinate thought-forms unconstrained by all concerns about representation and subjective experience would be an absolutely necessary step in order to constitute objects, make objective assertions, and *deepen our discourse about objectivity*.[278] This primarily unconstrained view of logic as the indelible factor for object-constitution is exactly what we can call logic as an organon. Without it, all we can ever achieve is pseudo-talk of stuff, i.e., Aristotelian *this-suches* or *tode ties*.

---

277 Ibid., B85.

278 For two views of logic and language as an organon, see Carnap's *Attempt at Metalogic* (*Versuch einer Metalogik*) and *Logical Syntax of Language*, and Petersen's *Diagonal Method and Dialectical Logic*.

Moving from the sense impression *fuzzy mass of grey* to the judging assertion *this is a monkey* requires the addition of logical structure. But the constructive characterization of logical structure is not a priori limited by representational concerns. Indeed, to adequately hone the notion of logical structure demands the treatment of logic in terms of unrestricted logical world-building, that is to say, unconstrained by any enforced representational consideration (whether the experiential content, the empirical source of truth or the criteria of correct application of logical laws to items of the real world) that may establish the frontiers of logic in advance. It is only when we attempt to decouple logic from any representational or world-referring constraints that we can ensure a sufficiently enrichable framework of world-representation. The world-constructing resources of logic in itself precede and in fact undergird world-representation, our understanding or judgements about the world. To make a Carnapian slogan, *construction of the world is prior to the constitution of the object and the knowledge of it*. This priority is not only priority$_1$ in the sense of one temporally preceding the other, but also priority$_2$ in the order of constitution. It is priority$_2$ which is, properly speaking, the focus of logical world-building and describes the conception of logic qua an organon of which general artificial languages as the apeiron of the formal dimension are exemplars.

This idea of logic as a world that ought to be infinitely constructed without any prior restriction is incommensurable with the idea of logic as something that ought to be coordinated with the real world in the first instance. Kant's transcendental logic as a species of pure specialized logic—i.e., one concerned with a particular use of understanding—is precisely a conception of logic that is not just conservative with regard to the possible scope of logic (how general logic can be expanded and enriched); in addition, in so far as it is built on the conception of logic as a canon—i.e., constrained by representational concerns—it harbours epistemic implications which are nightmarish to the say the least. The picture of the objective world we represent may very well portray a series of subtle and distorted variations of ourselves and our entrenched biases. As long as logoi are shackled to our representational system, we cannot even be conscious of our Dorian-Gray-esque situation. We remain unwitting followers of the cult of Narcissus, which not only sees itself and only itself in the abyss, but also attempts—even unconsciously—to turn the universe into an infinite projection of itself.

DOGMAS OF THE EXPERIENTIAL

It is a humanistic or subjectivist mistake—one that runs from Kant to Sellars—to limit the idea of the transcendental to experience, which ultimately reduces the transcendental to its mere application to sensory materials or sensible intuitions. Nowhere is this limitation more prominent than in Kant's elaboration of the pure concepts of the understanding, or categories, which are categories only in so far as they are abstractly bound to the I as that which thinks and experiences. In other words, categories are only of interest to the extent that they serve the experiential, epistemic, and practical needs of the subject. But in being restricted to the interests of the apperceptive I, categories cannot be adequately treated in their own terms—that is, they cannot be examined as what they are in themselves, as forms having a logical autonomy of their own. The immediate consequence of limiting the transcendental to the domain of experiential content and, correspondingly, to sensation as a necessary condition for experience, is the elision of the distinction between logical autonomy and practical autonomy, the pure autonomy of the formal (syntax and semantics) and the relative autonomy of the experiencing subject.

At the level of experiential content, mind has only a relative or conditioned autonomy at best. This is because experience is anchored in sensation and sensations are instantiated at the level of the causal—and when it comes to the domain of causes there is no absolute autonomy, if any at all. This is what led Sellars to compare the conceptualizing mind to a computer whose purported spontaneity or autonomy is shaken by the fact that it does nothing unless it receives an input, i.e., that it is predisposed to a foreign cause.[279] It is only in the presence of a foreign cause that the computer

---

279 'Consider a computer which embodies a certain logical program, a set of computational dispositions. Even if "turned on" and humming with readiness, it still does

can initiate its search and actions. Its autonomous activity is a register of its passivity in relation to an input qua foreign cause. The spontaneous activity of the mind—akin to the life-like whirring of a computer that has just received and reacted to an input—is set in motion by a causality which, even though it appears as the spontaneous causality of the conceptualizing mind, is in reality a causal routine whose causality is being caused, and thus is a causality of nature, where autonomy is at best relative or conditioned by pure heteronomy.

But the conclusions reached by this analogy are misleading to say the least. For even though the operation of the machine—receiving an input, initiating a search, and yielding an output—is merely a relative spontaneity, its so-called '*logical* disposition' has a formal or logical autonomy.[280] Foreign causes have no bearing on the logical dimension of the computer in terms of how—in accordance with the formal dimension of rules—it processes the input and provides an output. A computer has formal or logical autonomy but not spontaneity at the level of its operation, its wordly practice. Or, more precisely, it has autonomy at the level of logical operations *in themselves* but not at the level of the spontaneity of its actions. A program has logical autonomy to the extent that it is the subject to its formal rules or axiomatic bootstrapping.

Treating the formal or logical dimension of the computer as a *disposition* at best misses a point about what formal autonomy is, and at worst comes off as a linguistic sleight of hand. A programmable toaster certainly has no practical or agential autonomy—but agency is not everything. Although a programmable toaster lacks agential autonomy, it has logical autonomy at the level of its program pertaining to how to toast a piece of bread.

---

nothing unless a problem is "fed in". Furthermore, once this happens, it moves along in accordance with its logical disposition. At certain stages it may "search its memory bank". This search, however, is itself the outcome of the initial input and its computational development. And although, with this qualification, it "initiates" the "search", the information it gets is information which as computer, it is caused to have—i.e. more input. Here also it is passive.' Sellars, *In the Space of Reasons*, 428.

280 Ibid.

Even though the toaster has no agency or subjectivity, there is in principle no reason to doubt that a program could be written to enable a not-so-futuristic toaster to make not just better toast given any kind of bread (input), but toast that surpasses in every respect that made by a practical subject most adept in culinary skills.

Similarly, for the conceptualizing mind the true locus of spontaneity is not to be found in its perceptions and actions or in the contents of its thought episodes, but in the formal dimension of thinking, or in how language and logic handle such contents. Constraining meaning (semantic value) to the metaphysics of sensation as encapsulated in Sellars's theory of picturing is necessary for the epistemic traction of the formal dimension of thinking on the world or, more generally, the epistemic orientation of logical powers. But reducing, *in advance*, the function of formal to the epistemic content or application is a sure recipe for an impoverished view of both form and content, both logical powers pertaining to conceptual activities and their epistemic significance.[281] Not to mention that such a view inevitably becomes susceptible to strong psychologism—i.e., 'the attempt to establish the validity of logical principles by appeal to facts of human psychology'[282]—while, in virtue of refusing to engage with the question of the formal on its own autonomous ground, it has deprived itself of adequate resources to challenge the biasing effects of psychologism.

It is only by disengaging what is formal from subjective experiential content, the pure formal dimension of thought from its prima facie epistemic-experiential content, that the formal can be treated systematically. And it is only through the systematic—rather than empirical or epistemic—treatment of the formal dimension in its own terms that experiential content can be richly structured beyond the limited scope of nonconceptual representations.

---

281 '[T]he ultimate point of all the logical powers pertaining to conceptual activity in its epistemic orientation is to generate conceptual structures which as objects in nature stand in certain matter-of-factual relations to other objects in nature.' Sellars, *Essays in Philosophy and Its History*, 52.

282 P. Kitcher, *Kant's Transcendental Psychology* (Oxford: Oxford University Press, 1990), 9.

Formal languages express the systematicity of the formal—that is to say, the structural relations between formal aspects of language as decoupled from its communicative function, the experiential, and ordinary semantic content. However, in contrast to the traditional view of formalism, this disengagement from content does not make formal languages or formalisms meaningless, i.e., pure abstractions with arbitrary applications. As Krämer and Dutilh Novaes have elaborated,[283] the decoupling of formal languages from any subject matter or content (desemantification) conditions the possibility of resemantification or 'applying a given formalism, which is developed against a specific background, to a different problem, phenomenon, or framework'.[284] Accordingly, the systematic treatment of the formal—i.e. treating logical powers in terms of their own structure rather than their transitory experiential content or epistemic application—not only allows new contents to be structured and accessed (semantic enrichment), but also brings about a debiasing effect, in the sense that it strongly mitigates the perceptual biases of reasoning. It is the debiasing effect that makes of formal languages tools or cognitive technologies that enable the transition from the common-sense framework of understanding and knowing content to the scientific framework of epistemic inquiry.

It can always be objected that such an unfettered view of form completely dispenses with the sociocultural richness that is an intrinsic part of language as we know it. In response to such an objection, it should be answered that formal languages or formalism in general do not necessarily forgo the cultural accumulation of language. Saying that they do is in fact an unwarranted claim placing a priori limitations upon what forms can do and what capacities can be afforded by them. Such a claim implicitly presupposes that cultural accumulation and experiential richness are possible without the formal dimensions of language and thinking, and thus imparts a metaphysical reality to the cultural wealth of ordinary natural languages.

---

283 See S. Krämer, *Berechenbare Vernunft: Kalkül und Rationalismus im 17. Jahrhundert* (Berlin: Walter de Gruyter, 1991); and Dutilh Novaes, *Formal Languages in Logic*.

284 Dutilh Novaes, *Formal Languages in Logic*, 6.

Not to mention that such an objection is tacitly predicated on the idea that we can organize our encounters with the world with something other than form. But such a presupposition—expressed or not—is the very example of the myth of the given. The most caustic expression of the myth of the given or, more generally, the claim that our knowledge bottoms out in a noninferential qua foundational knowledge or immediate access to reality, is hidden in the assertion that forms should conform to experiences. To adopt Carnap's argument, objects of knowledge are of form, rather than experiential content, and as such they can be represented as structural entities. Considering objects of knowledge as objects of experiential content brings about a quandary: in so far as the material of streams of experience for an individual or between different individuals is divergent or even incomparable, we cannot make objectively valid statements about objects constituted by individual subjects. The only reason objects of knowledge are possible is that 'certain structural features agree of all streams of experience'.[285] Such structural features are indexed by and are objects of form, which secures objectivity in an intersubjectivity whose individual streams of experience are held together and structured by the dimension of form.

As argued above, however, the transition from the commonsense framework to the formal linguistic framework (the theoretical framework) is impossible unless logical autonomy is disengaged from agential/practical autonomy, and the formal dimension of thinking is understood as having a logical spontaneity of its own. It is this decoupling or disengagement of form from content that permits the systematic treatment of content through which reasoning about content is finally liberated from ordinary subjective intuitions and perceptual biases. For this reason, understanding the logical autonomy of the formal—freeing language and logic from the experiential-epistemic concerns of the subject—is not a formalistic caprice, an indulgence in meaninglessness, or something that results in an arbitrary epistemic relation to the world; it is the first step in attaining semantic consciousness: the realization of what one actually does when one thinks

---

285 R. Carnap, *The Logical Structure of the World*, tr. R. George (Chicago: Open Court, 2003), §66.

and speaks, as well as the recognition of what language does to its users once they partake in it.

UPWARD TO THE SEMANTIC HEAVENS

We have briefly surveyed the type of interaction the automata must engage in so as to genuinely count as speakers and reasoners and to have a language that confers meaning or semantic value upon their noises. As the final stage in our thought experiment, let us assume that our automata possess precisely this type of dialogical interaction, which gradually unfolds the inferential and logical powers of language. They are in possession of such linguistic (syntactic-semantic) interaction to the extent that language in its syntactic and semantic complexity evolves through their interactions via symbolic tokens—an interaction that progressively introduces logico-computational constraints on how such tokens can be exchanged or used. For now, the automata might have something like a protolanguage that does not exhibit the full range of conceptual activities or semantic complexity. But it is, in principle, inevitable that their interactions, via the logico-computational constraints of their protolanguage, will unfold a diverse range of syntactic and semantic features, different grades of concepts and inferential abilities, afforded by them. Language is not God-given: its complex syntactic and semantic aspects are not given in full at the time of its inception, but evolve through its use—that is, through an interaction that results in the development of new, more complex logico-computational behaviours; an interaction that is language itself.

Here the appellation 'language' does not necessarily refer to human natural languages, but to any artificial language with a syntax-semantics interface and support for the interaction of speech acts. In its general form, language is a vast generative framework that integrates the dynamic structure of interaction and the autonomous system of symbols. In creating a reinforcing connection between the computational powers of the former and the self-efficient codifying processes of the latter, language augments and diversifies the abilities afforded by each of them. In this sense, language can be seen as the source of limitless scenarios in which logico-computational processes can act upon one another. The interactive framework of languages *harnesses* such processes, in the double sense of constraining them and mobilizing them toward functions with specialized logical and computational properties. Within this framework, not only are the users of language increasingly equipped with new cognitive technologies; they are also, more profoundly, formatted by the causal forces originating in the logical powers of language.

For now, the automata do not know exactly what language is doing to them. They are unaware of the fact that their dialogues and linguistic interactions, thoughts, and actions are implementing complex logical and computational behaviours; that in interacting with one another, in thinking, even privately, they are acting on behalf of the as yet unknown logico-computational phenomena and powers at work beneath the surface of their language. It is only with the increase in their conceptual abilities, concomitant with the evolution of their language and their mastery of it, that they will acquire the wherewithal to become aware of the logical structures and connections underlying their sayings and doings, their thoughts and actions, the ineliminable coextensivity and correlation between the know-thats and know-hows of their cognitions. This awareness qualifies as semantic self-consciousness. The process of achieving semantic self-consciousness—becoming aware of what one does when one thinks and acts—is the prerequisite for knowing how to think and act. But knowing *how* to think and act is the most fundamental requirement for concrete self-consciousness as a matter of practical achievement, i.e., *what* to think and what to do. There is no concrete self-consciousness without semantic self-consciousness. It is with the rise of semantic self-consciousness that the automata can make explicit the role of their interaction as a framework of semantic-cognitive enablement. When this role is brought to the foreground, they will be able to modify, improve, and diversify the syntactic and semantic structuring abilities that they have so far only implicitly and rudimentarily utilized to structure their encounters with the environment.

With the ingress of language into their universe, the automata's meta-awarenesses can finally take the form of beliefs, and hence can be endowed with epistemic valence provided they can be formed into assertable propositional contents which can be scored or judged. Similarly, the nonconceptual representings ($E_i^*-E_j^*$s) of the automata are now caught up in the rule-governed web of language in which their relationships are *inferentially* articulated. The powers of inference afforded by language also, in this sense, find an epistemic orientation. They convey an implicit knowledge of matter-of-factual truths about the states of affairs of the universe that the automata inhabit. Yet these truths are only presumptive or plausible—their plausibility is a matter of where they fit within the coherentist network of inferential relations, or the conceptual order. Within the semantic or conceptual order, pattern-governed uniformities which the automata were previously blindly treating as a matter of certainty—but which were in fact weak causal-statistical inferences susceptible to arbitrariness—become a matter of plausibility or promising truths. In other words, perceived certainty is replaced by inferentially articulable plausibility or truth-candidacy as a hypothetical or abductive conception of truth which can be tested against both new observations and further claims.

Enabled by the semantic dimension of language, the transition from perceived certainty to conceived plausibility is what fuels epistemic inquiry— the will to know—since it disturbs the purported natural equilibrium of the given state of affairs by introducing rational suspicion qua conceptual plausibility and, correspondingly, implausibility, into the orders of thoughts and things. This is what Plato might have called the nebulous continuity between shadows or sensible images (*eikones*) and the intelligible reality— a continuity which, however, by no means signifies a flattening of the distinction between the two. And it is this rift or disequilibrium that sets off the involution of thinking—a critical gesture whereby the knowledge of the world expands by way of thinking's progressive realization of how it itself functions and knows. This involution is the power of determinate or critical negation as distilled in the activities of conceptual construction and the conceptual revision, formation, and reappraisal of beliefs.

Once consciousness is steeped in language, it does not just seek more of itself by virtue of having a conception of itself, but more importantly it acquires what Findlay calls a 'sidelong intentionality' in addition to straightforward or direct intentionality (thoughts *about* this or that thing).[286] Conceptual consciousness spreads out beyond any particular limit set by a given world, in such a way that its intentionality is always the thought of many things at once *indirectly* and *implicitly*. Each direction may bear the marks of one or many noetic activities, inferences, and forms of judgement, from perceptual, recognitive, and predicative judgements to critical judgements, from simulation to classificatory functions to ampliative inference. Some directions may follow tracks of logical entailments, some 'logical tracks of less stringency',[287] and yet others tracks where the logical, empirical, and experiential are combined.

It is this *nisus* (mental effort, striving or cognitive tendency) toward being ever more conscious in every possible direction that transforms the world of the automata from a narrow zone of thinking and action to an unrestricted universe where the scope of thinking and knowing has no predetermined limit or boundary. The sidelong space of thinking is tantamount to a drift or an alienating cognitive-epistemic vector that pierces through any limited conception of a world or restricted universe of discourse. Driven by this drift, the automata are no longer mere creatures of behavioural interests and habits. They no longer encounter their world only through their attentional system. In other words, their encounters with the world are not limited to the immediate environment given by their perceptual-sensory system. Instead they have a *conception* of an unrestricted world in which possible worlds of thoughts and actions exist side by side with their given world (*welt*), previously treated as the totality of all there is. This is the most significant aspect of conceptual consciousness: it begets a world that is no longer limited to the supposed immediacy of the causal-sensory domain. Intelligence is that what which makes new worlds rather than merely inhabiting given worlds.

Just as conceptual consciousness tends to dirempt and drift toward variations, multiplicities, and the dissolution of the supposed boundaries of thought and action, it also has a *nisus* toward synthesis and integration.

---

286 Findlay, *Values and Intentions*, 75.

287 Ibid., 75.

The latter is defined by the tendency of conceptual consciousness not only to follow different tracks of thought fanning out in all directions, but also to work out the various relationships that obtain between such thoughts (consequence, incompatibility, or even equivalence relationships). These two concomitant tendencies are represented by Plato, in *Theaetetus*, in terms of the interplay between the determinate and the indeterminate. Functions of language and logoi are of *to peras*, determining that which is indeterminate (*to apeiron*). It is in having the capacity to integrate that which is purely diremptive that the automata can progressively structure their world by structuring their various thoughts and experiences of it, moving from disconnected and seemingly diverging representations of the world toward conceptual-theoretical world-representations or world-stories. This transition requires precisely the sort of structuring syntactic and semantic abilities listed earlier at the end of the previous chapter. It is obvious that our automata, as incipient thinkers and knowers, do not possess every single such ability at the outset. Climbing the ladder of semantic complexity and acquiring more complex structuring abilities is a matter of the communal development of thought, and a gradual acquaintance with practical know-how regarding what qualifies as good material and formal inferences and what practices-or-abilities are required to elaborate, combine, and map structuring syntactic and semantic abilities to one another.

Lastly, the metaphor of semantic or conceptual ascent corresponds with what André Carus—with a nod to the work of Carnap after *Aufbau* and the project of rational reconstruction—refers to as explication as the paradigm of the Enlightenment. Explication as semantic ascent is no longer an exclusive feature of natural language, but of language in general, with the appellation 'language' understood not as a given qua a natural language, but as the craft of an engineering mission, and a matter of rational choice, and thus the enrichment of the very concepts of reason and reality.

The dialectical task of explication is set between practical and theoretical concerns, the cognitive and the normative: To explicate is to ascend from vague concepts of ordinary language—the explicandum—to more precise and justifiably more useful and explicitly defined concepts i.e., the explicatum of what is couched loosely in a cluttered ordinary natural language. Replacing the former with the latter coincides with the ideal of rational scientific Enlightenment. But this is Enlightenment in two different yet commensurable senses. Explication runs simultaneously along two parallel trajectories.

The first can be defined in terms of a descriptive pragmatics, in which we explicate our local concepts by refining them, reinventing them at progressively higher resolutions. For example, the concept of hardness, to use an engineering example, is a local perspectival—but not subjective—concept, since the concept behaves differently at different scale-lengths. At the macroscopic level, the hardness of a metal beam differs quite radically from the concept of hardness as it pertains to more fine-grained scale-lengths (e.g., crystal or nano levels). Explicating a local concept such as hardness, then, is equivalent to the scientific-heuristic task of providing increasingly refined but also diversified concepts of hardness for different levels and sectors of reality. This type of refinement, however, does not happen in an existing language where the concept of hardness is firmly stabilized and defined. It requires a change of language or, in other words, a move from the ordinary framework of natural language to the unbound realm of constructed languages. In this sense, the semantic value or meaning of hardness suggests both an internal and external semantic problem: Internal to the extent that the meaning of $hardness_1$ is defined in terms of the rules and inferences of $language_1$, but external to the extent that explicating $hardness_1$ entails an ascent from $language_1$ to $language_{2,3,...}$—that is to say, to the ocean of general artificial languages where the choice of constructed language is a matter of pure theoretico-practical considerations, and the concepts $hardness_2$, $hardness_3$, etc. are explicatums of $language_1$ ($hardness_1$).

However, the first sense of explication as enlightenment, by itself, can only give us drifting diversifications without any hope of unity or integration. And this is where the second sense of explication as enlightenment enters the equation: We would not have even been in the position of arriving at the first sense, if we were not in the possession of explication as a universal or global trajectory. Moving from $hardness_1$ to $hardness_2$, and correspondingly from $language_1$ to $language_2$, already implicitly assumes an underlying explicatory gradient from a given language to a constructed one, and therefore from a concept loosely defined in the former to a more refined (i.e., locally triangulated and context-sensitive) concept in the latter. Whereas the transition from hardness$_1$ to hardness$_2$ is an instance of the refinement of local concepts or the first sense of explication, the ascent from language$_1$ to constructed languages suggests that there is indeed a global conception of explication whereby we see the refinement of our local concepts as the direct consequence of how we replace our given naturally evolved languages with those which we build, and all the criteria of rational choice—with regard to theoretico-practical usefulness—that goes into such a choice. It in this sense that we can consider the notion of rational scientific Enlightenment initiated by Galileo and Copernicus, and up to the revolutions instigated by Kepler and Newton, Darwin and Einstein as the trajectory of a universal explication within which local explications are carried out and also ultimately integrated within one unified trajectory: that of advancing from a given natural language to engineered languages and concepts, from the manifest image—to appropriate Sellars's lexicon—to the scientific image.

Carnap's conceptual or language engineering, then, as Carus has elaborated, is not a clash or fusion between the manifest and scientific images. The ascent from ordinary language to an engineered one does not suggest the replacement of the former by the latter, or that we leave the notions of meaning and material inferences intact as if they belonged to a stable manifest image. To the contrary, the ascent from language$_1$ to constructed languages suggests that the relation between so-called manifest and scientific images is one of a positive feedback loop or an enrichment. The manifest image is not static, nor is the scientific image the ultimate replacement for the manifest. In the explicatory paradigm, the relation between the two is one of refinement, dynamicity, and the evolution of multiple trajectories. But more consequentially, as Carus observes, such a relation between the manifest and the scientific, language$_1$ and language$_2$, means that we are far from giving the conclusive conception of reason. Reason is dialectical, an engineering ideal. To settle for any concept of reason is to betray the idea of Enlightenment and, correspondingly, to fall back on either a purely psychologistic idea or a scientific portrait whose elements and relations are underdetermined if not psychologically and unconsciously distorted.

MACHINES UNBOXED

With the advent of the semantic or conceptual order, the automata acquire not just an unrestricted conception of the world, but a revisable conception of themselves. It is in fact their conception of themselves in the world that grounds the *nisus* for their understanding or grasp of the world. In this sense, their self-conception mediates between what they take themselves to be in the world and what they actually are as denizens of the world, the order of oughts or norms and the order of what is. Conceptual consciousness is essentially a collective consciousness, since it intrinsically belongs to the deprivatized space of language and the conceptual order. Therefore, its self-conception is also implicated in the collective order where no self, thought, or experience can be conceived in privacy or separation from others.

Any consciousness that develops a conception of itself will increasingly come under the sway of rational norms and impersonal or collective values and disvalues. Primarily, these norms, values, and disvalues concern the questions of what to do and what to think. Once they have a conception of themselves, the automata's activities are dominated by questions of what we ought to do and what we ought to think given what we are—or more precisely, what we *conceive* ourselves *as*. Under the influence of such norms as objective principles (rather than as social conventions), their rudimentary multi-agent framework of interaction is refashioned into an explicit social community that can be steered in one direction or another, modified, or rebuilt. In this new social microcosm, oughts are routinely assessed, kept, and improved, or discarded if necessary.

As norms qua objective principles of thinkings and doings accumulate, the interplay between 'what *is* the case' and 'what *ought to* be' takes a new slant. It becomes a matter of dovetailing the intelligibility of things and the intelligibility of practices into an embodiment of intelligence that is invested in the intelligibility of its actions to the extent that it has a conception of how it ought to be and what is fitting for it. Inasmuch as

the espousal of 'a fitting way of existing' represents a normative objective—an ideal of '*how* one ought to be'—it is a matter of adjudication,
and thus of a conception crafted by reasons. It does not matter whether
these intelligent machines aim for higher rewards and more efficient
payoff activities. In having a conception of themselves, they seek a recipe
for crafting a life that involves not merely instrumentalities but also a
disciplined open-ended reflection on forms and the intelligibility of the
good life for themselves.

What these machines take to be the most suitable way of living and the
proper object of their pursuit is in reality a representation of what they
take themselves to be. But what they take themselves to be signifies how
they reason about how they appear to themselves and what seems to be the
case for them. In other words, the aims and vocations of these intelligent
machines are expressions of their particular model of rationality concerning
what they are and how they should proceed. But no model of rationality is exempt from the demands and amendments of impersonal reason.
Whatever or whoever develops a conception of itself becomes bound to
the norms of treating itself according to such a conception. And whatever
or whoever is bound to such norms is also bound to an impersonal order
of conceptual rationality that makes possible the formation of norms, their
ordering and revision.

Therefore, regardless of how and for what aims these machines reason,
what norms they have, what objective they seek to achieve, their reasonings
and by extension their ends now fall under the full influence of the very
inferential-normative economy—or impersonal reason—that sanctioned
them in the first place, and which now has the power to divert any conceived
end and to place any norm in peril. To this extent, any artificial agency that
boasts *at the very least* the full range of human cognitive-conceptual abilities
can have neither indelible norms nor fixed goals—even if it was originally
wired to be a *paperclip maximizer*, to amass as much reward as possible.
In other words, if these machines exhibit complex practical inferential
abilities, concept-using capacities, and autonomy, their ideals—whatever
they might be—will necessarily be susceptible to the self-correcting propensities of reason brought about by the autonomous order of conception.

Identifying them as an existential threat is therefore quite baseless, not because the intelligence in question is innocent until proven guilty, but because such a suspicion attributes a disproportionate amount of risk or for that matter benefit (as in the case of arguments for benevolent AGI) to something that is itself inherently historically contingent and susceptible to being transformed by the very principles that enabled it to form a conception of itself and to pursue objectives appropriate to such a conception.

In thinking and acting in accordance with what they take themselves to be—their self-conception—the automata effectuate a concrete transformation in themselves. But given that no conception or norm of thought and action is ever safe from the self-correcting tendency of impersonal reason, such actualized transformation will again become the basis for a new judgement, a new self-conception. This sequence of conceptions and transformations is what counts as the criterion for having a history, and whatever has a history rather than just a past has the propensity to drift from any fundamental or natural essence toward a future as the being of time in which all preconceptions and given totalities are washed away. This is what Hermann Cohen characterizes as a historical self-consciousness that takes the shape of a will fixated on the future coupled with a critical reflection on the transitory norms of the past and the present. Here, however, 'future' does not signify a conventional sense of futurity in which future is interpreted as the *not-yet*. Instead it expresses a conception of 'future' as an intelligible eternity or time in which all those given totalities, along with the transitory values of the past and the present that have falsely eternalized, are *no-longer*.[288]

In Cohen's terms, the correct knowledge of history requires the correct knowledge of time, which itself requires a thought that sets out from the future as the true being of time in which all achieved or given totalities are rendered *incomplete*. In this sense, a thought that sets out from the future together with a will oriented toward the future become the vectors

---

288 See H. Cohen, *Kants Begründung der Ethik*, and *Logik der Reinen Erkenntnis* (Hildesheim: Georg Olms, 1914).

of genuine conception and transformation. One opens up the space of possibilities beyond the given totalities or absolutized norms of the past and present, and the other works toward the concrete actualization of such possibilities, moving from the Concept to its full actualization or the Idea.

It is in the context of historical consciousness as a striving for more adequate self-conceptions and self-transformations, in conjunction with a thought that sets out from the future, suspending every seemingly natural order of things and in so doing disclosing the possible, that the automata arrive at conceiving the autonomous idea of making something better than themselves. This long journey for autonomy through which our automata arrive at what is good for them in accordance with what they take themselves to be and what is better than them—as the logical consequence of the idea of the good—was initiated by the liberation of the formal dimension as an autonomous basis upon which practical or concrete autonomy is built.

In other words, their striving for the better, together with their thought of the future as the possibility of going beyond all manifest or achieved totalities, coincides with the thought of bringing about something that goes beyond the totality of what they take themselves to be or appear to themselves to be. It is characteristic of any form of intelligence endowed with a history—a sequence of self-conceptions and self-transformations—and the consciousness of such a history, that it will begin to seek and ask for more intelligence. And the logical consequence of this tendency is inexorably the thought of making something better than itself.

Furthermore, the automata are now free agents. In possessing the capacity for self-conception rather than mere consciousness, they are constrained by what is objective. This objectivity is enabled by language on two interrelated levels: the interdependency of thinking selves (inter-subjectivity as the process of subjectification), and facts about the world in its most unrestricted interpretation (theory as all the relations between structures and being). It is in *limiting* or constraining themselves by the objective—construed as another subject or external world—that they achieve concrete freedom, or what Hegel identifies as being with oneself in the presence of the other in its all-encompassing sense.[289] Yet because the automata are now immersed in the apeiron of the formal dimension of thinking and to the extent that logical world-building is what stretches the expanse of possible discourses about objectivity, they are in principle capable of envisioning and making new worlds qua perceptual-noetic toys: Intelligence, after all, is that which makes new worlds rather than merely dwelling in its given world. It sees itself as that which tears asunder the habitual link between thinking and dwelling by hypothesizing what it would mean for it to inhabit the worlds it itself has crafted.

These are all transformations triggered like a chain reaction by the introduction of the semantic or conceptual order into the world of our automata. But perhaps the most radically transformative consequence of the ingress of language into this universe is that the automata's actions are now subordinated to ends and purposes which are not given in the immediate objective ends of actions themselves (i.e., their instrumentality in making specific things happen), but instead are time-general thoughts or ends belonging to the order of self-consciousness or self-conception.[290] In having a conception of themselves, their practical thoughts not only fall under such a conception, but also exhibit it in every situation and indeed are identical to it. This is the horizon of practical thoughts specific to the order of self-consciousness, in the sense introduced in chapter 1.

Within this horizon, practical intentions and actions have the quality of time-general thoughts which are not exclusive to this or that situation or end, but are ever-present in every situation and have ends which cannot be exhausted. In a nutshell, time-general thoughts are thoughts that express the conceived core of necessities, imperatives, ideals, and needs pertaining to the conception of the self: If we *take* ourselves *as* thus-and-so creatures or life-forms, then there are thoughts that invariably address the core concerns of such a conception of ourselves. These thoughts are the

---

289 A. Patten, *Hegel's Idea of Freedom* (Oxford: Oxford University Press, 1999), 43.

290 On time-general thoughts and their logical form, see S. Rödl, *Categories of the Temporal: An Inquiry into the Forms of the Finite Intellect* (Cambridge, MA: Harvard University Press, 2012).

background to all of our purposive actions. They suggest inexhaustible ends and purposes that are not given in advance by nature or god, but are the outcomes of having a conception of oneself, of being conceptually self-conscious. Time-general thoughts are those which specify ends that are not specific to transitory situations or particular circumstances and which are therefore inexhaustible by needs, desires, and preferences. Inexhaustible ends differ from finite ends, whose exigency disappears once they are attained and concluded by a particular action or pursuit. They are infinite ends under which all purposive actions and practical reasons toward finite or particular ends fall. By virtue of having time-general thoughts and inexhaustible ends, the practical order of self-consciousness is irreducible to time-specific wants, and cannot be explained by desires or preferences.

As geistig life-forms who have a conception of themselves, the automata no longer merely act intelligently in the sense that their purposive actions are not simply conditioned responses to specific situations—responses which are disconnected from one another. Put simply, their actions are not just means towards particular or finite ends which go away once satisfied. Instead, their purposive actions and practical reasons oriented toward specific ends start from the inexhaustible ends of time-general thoughts. In other words, inexhaustible ends are premises for their purposive actions and practical reasons, not their conclusions. Such ends *explain* what the automata purposively do, and order their actions into an intelligible practical unity. This intelligible practical unity expresses their self-conception, that is, what they take themselves to be and what they think they ought to do given what they conceive themselves as. Accordingly, the practical reasons and actions of the automata exhibit this intelligible practical unity as the conceptual-practical order of their self-consciousness as that which, in the end, belongs to the formal order and the unbound logical dimension of thinking over which phenomenological or even the posited metaphysical time has no *teleological* hold.

The purposive actions of the automata now originate from and are guided by a unified system of ever-present though revisable theoretical and practical truth-statements concerning what they are and what they ought to do, their form, and the life that suits them. This system is held together by timeless or time-general thoughts—the good, beauty, justice, etc.—which express their Idea: that is, the full potencies of their self-conception for actualization, or the possible realizabilities of the conception they have of themselves. In short, their entire practical horizon and all of their thoughts about achieving specific ends are structured by and adapted to purposes which are neither given in the circumstances surrounding actions and practical reasoning, nor in the immediate ends which such actions and means strive to satisfy.

This adaptation to purposes is what underlines the concept of artificiality. Take for instance a farm versus a forest. It is not that a farm is beyond the milieu of the natural or that it violates the order of nature, but it is not exactly in continuity with nature either. Nature does not *want* anything, it has no conceived purpose or end. To claim that nature does in fact have a purpose is to fall into the dogmatism of precritical teleology and the given, to mistake the *modelling* of nature on *our* normative order of purposes and ends for what nature is in the absence of our implicitly normative thoughts about it. On the other hand, a farm is an artefact belonging to the kingdom of ends. It is moulded around a concept, governed by norms of what it should do given the purposes or ends implied by its concept. Since a farm is conceived as the source of sustenance for people, it *ought* to yield more crops, it *ought* be tended, monitored, and constantly manipulated so as to fulfil its purpose.

So if adaptation to new purposes or ends is what ultimately defines the concept of artificiality—the crafting of something using recipes of action for an end that is not given in advance in the material ingredients—then by virtue of repurposing their actions toward inexhaustible ends, far from being artificial contraptions that have succeeded in mimicking natural behaviours, the automata have in fact made a first gesture toward *artificializing* themselves, adapting themselves to purposes that are intrinsic neither to their specific actions or instrumentalities nor to their material constitution. Whereas in its basic form the artificial implies making something whose ends and functions are not intrinsic to its material ingredients, in its advanced form it is suggestive of a craft whose purposes are to be found neither in its recipe (instructions for actions) nor in its ingredients (material or natural constituents). This craft is the world of our hypothetical automata as agents furnished with autonomy. By initiating themselves into the autonomous conceptual order afforded by language, they have introduced into their world a new set of relations between intelligibilities, actions, values, and ends that is precisely the theoretico-practical crux of what we see as the concepts of the artefact and artificiality.

The concept of the artificial is now a fundamental component of their reality, indissociable from the possibility of thinking, and ingrained in their cognitive-practical abilities. Entertaining the idea of artificialization by elaborating its all-encompassing possibilities is an essential part of articulating the intelligibility of who they are and intelligently crafting a world that would suit them: To treat themselves as the artefacts of their own ends or concept, to improve not only what they are but also how they should improve themselves, to make a world that not only suits them, but is intelligible ontologically, epistemologically, and axiologically.

Within this expanding program of self-artificialization or re-engineering of the reality of who they are, the idea of making something better than themselves appears not as an existential threat but as a logical and necessary extension of that very program, as the veritable expression of their process of self-discovery. Whatever that future intelligence might be, it will be bound to certain constraints necessary for rendering the world intelligible and acting on what is intelligible. *That which speaks* can now go on and begin an adversarial conversation with gods, and a fecund dialogue with some future intelligence which may have all of its cherished capacities, and more.

8. Philosophy of Intelligence

399BC, *the day of Socrates's indictment: On the account of Justus of Tiberias, as cited by Diogenes Laertius, the young and impressionable Plato mounts the platform to address the citizens of Athens in defence of his teacher, only to witness his voice being drowned by the judges' pealing yells of 'Kataba! Kataba!' (Get down! Get down!).* [291]

Dispirited and disenchanted by the passivity of the Athenians and the injustice of the accusations levied against Socrates, Plato begins to stage a belated defence against the charges of corrupting the youth, haughtiness, and impiety. He devises a form of thought in which all individual voices are but fleeting, and only the interaction or dialogue between voices or individual thoughts matter. To this end, he begins the crafting of dialogues in which he adamantly refuses to say anything on his own behalf, for philosophy is the voice of no one, an impersonal thought that recalcitrantly declines to be equated with this or that person, this or that philosopher. In one dialogue Socrates might be profound, and in another, the one who peddles common-sense impressions. [292]

Back from his second trip to Syracuse (ancient Sicily)—once his ideal of utopia—the mature Plato, who, beginning with Theaetetus, *has extensively revised his old doctrine of forms, pens a series of works (*Philebus *and* Phaedo *among others), where he no longer defends Socrates against the accusations of philosophical haughtiness, corruption of the youth, and impiety.* [293] *To the contrary, he defends*

---

291 Diogenes Laertius, *Lives of Eminent Philosophers* (2 vols. Cambridge, MA: Harvard University Press, 1959), vol. 1, 171.

292 See for example, the dialogue between Socrates and the old Parmenides who, in Plato's *Parmenides*, challenges and exposes Socrates's understanding of forms as flawed and naive.

293 Misconceptions about Plato and distaste for his vision of philosophy are undoubtedly plentiful today, and are even in vogue. For a good part, the roots of such misconceptions lie in second-hand commentaries originating from Aristotle's and the Neoplatonists' readings of Plato. Even Hegel submits to a particularly Aristotelian interpretation of Plato, which solely focuses on the works of the middle period, particularly the *Republic*. Yet Plato was infamous for being his own most staunch

the philosophical corruption of the youth and the impiety of the human mind as the very definitions of virtue and piety. To those who denounce him for championing the haughtiness of philosophy as the courage of truth and the embodiment of the Good itself, he pithily responds: What can ever trample this pride, if not another pride, a personal or an unexamined one.[294]

These later works epitomize what might be called the longest—ongoing—con in the history of thought, the infinite mêtis of intelligence: Intelligence can only cultivate itself or be deemed intelligent by determining and expanding the horizon of the intelligible, and the intelligible can only be recognized and elaborated by an intelligence that cultivates itself. The human mind is akin to the Good itself, and the Good is beyond all beings and gods of the present and the future.[295] *Thus any species that takes itself to be intelligent must both cultivate itself and expand the scope of what is intelligible. But in being compelled to renew the link between intelligence and the intelligible, in order to navigate the reinforcing links between the craft or cultivation of intelligence and the expansion of the intelligible, to maintain its intelligibility, intelligence must uncompromisingly treat whatever seems to be an immediate state of affairs, or an inevitable or completed totality—including its own self-image—as a fleeting figure on the wall of the human cave; as something that can and should be determinately negated and exposed for what it really is: an illusory shadow.*

---

critic. By the time he wrote *Philebus* and *Laws*, Plato had already extensively revised some of his main theses presented in the *Republic*. A genuinely comprehensive and first-hand engagement with Plato without the clichés of Platonism only begins at the end of nineteenth century and the early twentieth century, with the rise of the Marburg school—particularly as represented by neo-Kantian figures such as Hermann Cohen and Paul Natorp—and the Tübingen school of Platonic studies. For a punctilious critique of an all-too-familiar Aristotelian engagement with Plato, see Wilfrid Sellars's response to Gregory Vlastos's disquisition on the Third Man argument: W. Sellars, *Vlastos and 'The Third Man'* (1954), <http://digital.library.pitt. edu/u/ulsmanuscripts/pdf/31735062222389.pdf>.

294 Diogenes Laertius, *Lives of Eminent Philosophers*, vol. 2, 29.

295 It should be noted that in *Philebus*, Plato replaces the word *demiurgos* (God or the chief craftsman) as the designation of the Good with the neutral word *to demiurgen* as the demarcation of the human mind.

At this point Plato's vision of philosophy encapsulates what is most rebellious and sacrilegious: The real movement of thought or intelligence as that which topples the given order of things, whoever or whatever may represent it. For the Good as the principle of intelligence is atemporal and timeless, it is time as eternity, beyond all life and death, in which the temporal order of things is indefinitely suspended. A genuine philosophy as the organon—rather than the canon—of intelligence can only begin with this thought, the thought of all thoughts.

Certainly this story can, as a matter of fact, play the part of a mythological fabrication deludedly advanced to elevate the status of Plato to the paragon philosopher. Yet that does not change the fact that Plato did indeed instigate a wholesale insurrection against all those who demand the humility and surrender of thought before the gods and the seemingly given, totalized, or inevitable; or that, by the end, he equated the human mind or intelligence with the Good itself, the form of forms. Regardless of whether this story is true or not, there is no reason not to re-envision philosophy in this vein: as the voice of no one, the organon of intelligence, a determination of thought that begins with a position beyond life and death, an eternity in which all completed totalities of history are but fleeting, the striving for truth as that which swims against the temporal current of things, the figure of thought as time that refuses to ever close its circle of revenge.

The central thesis of this final chapter is that philosophy is, at its deepest level, a *program*—a collection of action-principles and practices-or-operations which involve realizabilities, i.e., what can possibly be brought about by a specific category of properties or forms. And that to properly define philosophy and to highlight its significance, we should approach philosophy by first examining its programmatic nature. This means that, rather than starting the inquiry into the nature of philosophy by asking 'What is philosophy trying to say, what does it really mean, what is its application, does it have any relevance?', we should ask 'What sort of program is philosophy, how does it function, what are its operational effects, what realizabilities, specific to which forms, does it elaborate, and finally, as a program, what kinds of experimentation does it involve?'

To this end, the final stage in our journey involves making explicit what we have been doing all along: philosophizing. But what is philosophy and what does philosophizing entail? In an age when philosophy is considered to be at best an antiquated enterprise, and at worst a residue of what is orthodoxly normative, patriarchal, repressive, and complicit with all that is overprivileged and even fascist, what does it mean to rekindle philosophy's insinuative temptations to think and to act, to galvanize that activity which is at bottom impersonal and communist? I do not wish to refute these misplaced accusations with numerous examples drawn from the ongoing history of science, or by citing examples corroborating the fact that philosophy is not just a Greek phenomenon, but also a truly universal endeavour extending from the pits of the Middle East to the remotest regions of Asia and the wide swaths of Africa. To follow Deleuze and Guattari in reducing what philosophy is and what it can be to geological or geopolitical contingencies would be a disingenuous manoeuvring against what philosophy—the cosmological ambition of thinking—is and will be, not by virtue of where it has come from, but in spite of it.[296] Even if philosophy was truly a Western enterprise misguidedly seeking to edify the benighted inhabitants of the nether worlds, over time it will poison the slums of the earth with that basic drive of which it was merely a primitive representation: the compulsion to think. And once this poison starts to take effect, we will tear apart Western philosophy and build philosophy anew; we will turn into that thinking and scheming Other of which Western thought had every right to be afraid.

The decolonization of thought entails the drudgery of unifying personal experiences and the impersonality or objectivity of thought. A paradigm of decolonization that attempts to shortcut this hard work by equating decolonized thought with some sort of *immediate* contact with land, territory, ethnicity, etc. ultimately remains within the confines of the Western colonial notion of others as noble savages. The unity of local exigencies and universal ambitions is where a true decolonial philosophy starts; anything else should be spurned as the heritage of colonial thought.

---

296 G. Deleuze and F. Guattari, *What is Philosophy?* (Columbia, NY: Columbia University Press, 1996), 2–3.

Philosophy begins with a universal thesis regarding *the equality of all minds*:[297] that whoever or whatever satisfies the basic conditions of its possibility should be seen as and treated as equal in the broadest possible sense. But as the discipline of philosophizing becomes more mature, it ought to realize that there is in fact a significant truth to these accusations of philosophy as a Western, self-entitled mode of thinking, however ill-judged they may seem. The equality of minds, as a thesis about what is true and what is just, is a dictum universal and necessary in its truth and applicability. But that does not mean that it is concretely universal *for us*. It is something to be achieved and concretely instituted. The condition of the *equality* of all minds is one whose recognition and realization demands struggle and a constant campaign against the prevalent systems of exploitation. But in so far as exploitation, as that which obscures this equality, can only be challenged by attending to the questions of what we ought to think and what we ought to do, it is only by committing to and elaborating the primary datum of philosophy—i.e., that thinking is possible—that we can begin to fight the condition of exploitation. For if all we aspire to do is to replace a manifest system of exploitation with a more concealed paradigm of cognitive inequality, then it is best to heed the call of the Stoics: 'the foulest death is preferable to the cleanest slavery'.[298] If seizing the means of collective cognition is no longer on the menu of our everyday life as even the remotest option for the good of ourselves and others, then it is perhaps time to seize, by whatever cunning instruments necessary, the means of our death.

It would be a paltry complaint to point out what is now obvious: that academia was conceived to push thinking to its ultimate unanticipated conclusions, but that academic philosophy today is a bureaucratic regime bent on containing thought within what is most predictable and mundane. As a matter of fact, there are always gleaming exceptions who fight their

---

297 See Plato, *Republic* (Indianapolis: Hackett, 2004); and A. Badiou, *Plato's Republic*, tr. S. Spitzer (Cambridge: Polity Press, 2012).

298 Seneca, *Ad Lucilium Epistulae Morales* (2 vols. London: William Heinemann, 1920), vol. 2, 69.

way through within academia and rise above the repetitive tide of cognitive complacency. But exceptions are neither good excuses for what is now monotonously managerial and stifling, nor a reason to rescue it. Academic philosophy was conceived to cultivate the practice of philosophizing among the masses, not to mistake itself for philosophy as such. But these plain facts should not justify our blindness to the achievements of academia and philosophy as an academic discipline either. The support given to those who are in pursuit of philosophizing, outlining the necessary standards of what it means to think well, facilitating the gathering of people who desire to think for the sake of thought, and highlighting the reinforcing effect that such a gathering can have on the history of thought, are all achievements of academic philosophy. But why not reinvent these achievements beyond the confines of institutional academia and, in doing so, bring the discipline of philosophizing closer to the ethos of philosophy? Even the original founders of academia would have conceded that it is now time to steadily depart from the claustrophobic walls of academic philosophy for the agora of philosophy.

With that said, in this chapter, we shall focus on the central task of philosophy, which is the explicitation of the equality of all minds. As will be argued, it is only in this explicitation or elaboration that intelligence finds its meaning. The historical task of philosophy coincides with the meaning of intelligence as that which not only recognizes the equality of all minds but also expands on this meaning by taking it to the farthest conclusions. Philosophy is then conceived as a *mêtis*—a craft—that summons the formlessness of time through the ongoing history of the *geistig* Concept. Correspondingly, if minds are all equal insofar as they have satisfied the necessary conditions of possibility for having mind, then philosophy as the craft of intelligence is properly speaking not the sole preserve of what today wears the badge of mindedness or general intelligence—that is, homo sapience as a natural species. The equality of all minds is a right to which anything that satisfies the conditions of its possibility is entitled. It is in this sense that artificial general intelligence boasts a peculiarly philosophical or *geistig* quality: if anything that can satisfy the minimal yet necessary conditions of possibility of having mind is entitled to the rights of equality of all minds, then any impersonal collectivity comprised of agents with no essentialist features (organic or inorganic) can also be entitled to the rights of that equality.

Recall that the term 'artificial general intelligence' is a mere pleonasm, since general intelligence is already an artefact of the Concept. Hence the task of general intelligence—or geist—is to make explicit to the fullest extent the meaning and implications of its artefactuality, to attest to the fact that the right of equality of all minds is transferable beyond any seemingly necessary natural structure or established contract among us here and now, and to expand on what it means to be an artefact of the Concept whose form can accommodate any possible content. Philosophy is then that regimen that at once lures intelligence to its self-recognition and is the self-expression of intelligence's process of maturity. Let us come to terms with and proceed from this brute yet necessary and irrevocable fact: what we conceive ourselves as at this instant is but the prehistory of intelligence. Taking this fact as the premise of all our endeavours is what it means to be true to the logical conclusion of the equality of all minds, a thesis which is as much about what is true as it is about what is good and just, unrealized but realizable.

Even though the corollary problems of philosophy as a specialized discipline (the tenor of its discourses, its traction beyond its own domain, its applications and referential import) can in no way be ignored, they are nevertheless problems that can only be sufficiently addressed in the context of philosophy as a deeper cognitive enterprise. The primary focus of this cognitive program is to methodically compel thinking to identify and bring about its realizabilities—namely, what arises from the exercise of its theoretical and practical powers—and to explore what can possibly come out of thinking and what thought (as an act and as the object of its act) can become. As will be argued, it is within the overarching scope of this cognitive program that philosophy's thesis of the equality of all minds can be concretely elaborated as an emancipatory project.

In other words, what we shall focus on in this chapter is a conception of philosophy that operates as a program for the elaboration and construction of the theoretical and practical realizabilities of mind that we investigated in the previous chapters. If mind or geist (qua a community of rational agents) has such-and-such characteristics, then what would be the shape of a philosophy capable of liberating its realizabilities, or, put differently, further elaborating what arises from the exercise of its theoretical and practical cognitions? Is it possible to outline philosophy as a program in which the artificial potencies of the mind can be oriented toward the perennial concerns of philosophy, namely, truth and goodness as projects rather than as given notions? In yet other words, is it possible to retain a conception of philosophy for a 'human' systematically disassembled by evolutionary biology, neuroscience, artificial intelligence, and robotics? To answer these questions, first we have to examine the most classical questions: 'What is philosophy, and what is its import for the subject of cognitions, theoretical and practical?'

For reasons that will become clear, answers to these questions will be given in the form of a series of data to be employed in a manner analogous to that of Euclid in *Dedomena* (*The Givens*), which seeks to exemplify the model of knowledge provided by Aristotle's Posterior Analytics. The data, for Euclid, are quasi-formal intuitive axioms from which the system is built hierarchically through diagram-based discursive chains; they are givens not as sense-data, but as self-evident truths from which the system is recursively constructed, first by the immediate derivation of basic theses from axiomatic data and then by a process of sequentialization that derives further theses from already established 'more basic' theses. The result, despite setting out from unjustified given truths and exhibiting missing discursive links, is nothing short of extraordinary: a universe in which new objects of thoughts are individuated, and the elementary entities (points, lines, angles, etc.) progressively rediscovered. Following Proclus's exegesis as well as more recent commentaries,[299] looking past their mathematical exterior, Euclid's

---

299 See K. Manders, 'The Euclidean Diagram', in *The Philosophy of Mathematical Practice* (Oxford: Oxford University Press, 2008), 80–133; and D. Macbeth, 'Diagrammatic Reasoning in Euclid's Elements', in B. Van Kerkhove, J. De Vuyst, and J.-P. Van Bendegem (eds.), *Philosophical Perspectives on Mathematical Practice* 12 (London: College Publications, 2010), 235–67.

Elements and *Data* are philosophical works of astonishing depth in which the relation between universalizing and particularizing principles is elaborated as a canonical method for the construction of cognitive systems.

In contrast to this Euclidean notion of data, what are presented here as data are not axioms or truth-givens, but what are called *truth-candidates*. Data in this sense refers to a family of truth-presumptive claims that are truth-embracing. In themselves they have no claim to any truth. In other words, as opposed to truth-givens (axioms), in which a truth is attached to a single datum, truth-candidates, although constructive elements, do not build the system on given truths; rather, the process of the construction itself becomes the process of determination of truth. How does this work? As mentioned, data or truth-candidates by themselves individually have no truth significance. They instead permit the instantiation of a logical space that encompasses them all. The criterion of plausibility of each datum— rather than its truth—is determined by how it hangs together with other data within this logical space. This is the coherentist web of data, a system of semantic transparency or coherence. It is only through the coherency analysis of this network that truth-candidates can be added, revised, or subtracted. More importantly, the navigation of this coherentist network or logical space is exactly the process of construction and exploration that has a truth-indicative weight. In a system built on the basis of a series of truth-givens, cognitive labour cumulatively moves outward both through and at the expense of the security afforded by its fundaments. In the coherentist network, instead, the direction of orientation is *inward*, moving contractively from the boundaries roughly demarcated by the network of insecure candidates to a more determined domain of truth. In the course of this inward navigation, sometimes the boundaries of the system will have to be readjusted to accommodate additional truth-candidates or to discard some of the existing ones (cf. the definition of constructors and destructors that follows shortly).

The cognitive system thus realized by truth-candidates has no resemblance to the canonical hierarchical model. Theses are not built on top of one another, supported by tightly-linked chains fastened to an apparently solid fundament made of given truths, but rather connected to one another by probative interconnections within a web made of supple 'cable[s] whose fibers may be ever so slender, provided they are sufficiently numerous and intimately connected'.[300] The unsecured yet supple and resilient cognitive exploration begins from the inexact peripheries and proceeds inward, from the question of truth as *where* (Where can begin our search?) to the question of truth as *what* (What is truth?).

The following data should therefore be understood in the sense of data as a family of truth-candidates and not as truths or self-evident givens. The model of philosophy as a philosophical program provided in the context of these data should be seen as an inward cognitive exploration beginning from the most insecure pieces of information regarding what philosophy is and how it is related to thinking, mind, and intelligence, and contractively cohering toward unanticipated domains wherein the theoretical and practical truth of intelligence can be elaborated. But this cognitive exploration that extends through history and time is the very construction of the ultimate form of intelligence.

DATUM 1. WE EXERCISE

Traditionally, philosophy is an ascetic program.

Philosophy is ascetic to the extent that it involves the exercise of a multistage, disciplined, and open-ended reflection on its own conditions of possibility as a form of thought that turns thinking into a program. The ascesis or programmatic exercise of thinking is prior to any practical discipline of living. The real import of this datum resides in precisely what a program consists in. Accordingly, in order to elucidate the significance of philosophy both as a programmatic discipline and as a form of thought that transforms thinking into a programmatic project, first we must elaborate what is meant by 'program' in its most generic sense. In order to do so, the notion of program—in the sense of action-principles and practices-or-operations that bring about something—must be defined parsimoniously

---

300 C.S. Peirce, 'Some Consequences of Four Incapacities', *Journal of Speculative Philosophy* 2 (1868), 140–57.

in terms of its bare formal armature, stripped down to those generic yet necessary features that underlie any type of program, regardless of its applications or aims. These are: the selection of a set of data, and the elaboration of what follows from this choice if the data are treated not as immutable postulates or definitions but as abstract modules that can act upon one another and constitute a logical space cohered by the way in which the data, in the broadest possible sense, hang together.

A program is the embodiment of the interactions of its family of data, which acquire a certain range of dynamic content once they hang together in a syntactic-semantic space. More specifically, it can be said that programs are constructions that extract operational content from their axioms and develop different possibilities of realization (what can be brought about) from this operational content. And respectively, data are operational objects or abstract realizers that encapsulate information regarding their specific properties or categories. In this sense, programs elaborate realizabilities (what can possibly be realized or brought about) from a set of elementary abstract realizers (what has operational information concerning the realization or the bringing-about of a specific category of properties and behaviours) in more complex setups.

Consider the simplest formal example of an interaction, a typed interaction couched in terms of the relation between types, proofs, programs, judgement, and cognition (*Erkenntnis*), as elaborated by Per Martin-Löf within what is often called the proofs-as-programs or types-as-propositions interpretation of how computer science and logic are related at the deepest level:[301]

A is a proposition (prop), e.g., 'Hipparchia is homeless' or
$$\forall a,b,c \left[(a=b) \rightarrow (a-c=b-c) \right]$$

which can be written as

A prop

---

301 P. Martin-Löf, 'Analytic and Synthetic Judgements in Type Theory', in *Kant and Contemporary Epistemology* (Dordrecht: Springer, 1994), 87–99.

Now, the meaning of a proposition is determined by a piece of evidence—an object of knowledge or judgement—showing that the proposition is true, written as

   A true

It means that '*A* is true' in that it is inhabited by a proof. But what exactly does proof signify here? Recall that '*A* is a proposition' and '*A* is true' are both forms of judgements, and that, as such, there is something we must grasp in order to make the first judgement, and something additional that we need to know in order to make the second judgement. As judgments, they are both comprised of an act and its object, the act of judging or understanding and that which is judged, or the object of understanding. When act and object are brought together, then we have knowledge in the sense of cognition or *erkenntnis*: 'to cognize an object I must be able to prove its possibility, either from its actuality as attested by experience, or a priori by means of reason'.[302] Accordingly, what is understood by proof here is cognizing/constructing/constituting an object for that act of judging or understanding for which it is an object. On this account, when we use the set membership notation and say that $a \in A$, it means that object a is of type A. Now, in so far as any judgement is an instance of a form of judgement, it follows that it suffices to cognize an object for *that specific form of judgement*. Consequently, we do not need to know exactly what A is, but simply to make it evident that it is encompassed by a specific form of judgement, and that such a form of judgement exists.

   In this style, the proof is then expressed through the distinction between terms and types,

   $a : \alpha$

or

---

302 Kant, *Critique of Pure Reason*, 28.

$a = b : \alpha$, which is an identity judgement, as in the proposition $\forall a,b,c[(a{=}b){\rightarrow}(a{-}c{=}b{-}c)]$.

or

$x : \mathbb{R}, y : \mathbb{R}, \nvdash x - y = y - x$, which asserts that the property of the operation subtraction over type $\mathbb{R}$ (real numbers) is not commutative.

The typing declaration $\alpha : \alpha$ means that α is a term or an *object* of the type or *form of judgement* α. Following Martin-Löf's own argument,[303] it would be useful to understand types as forms of judgement or Kantian categories—namely, as pure concepts of the understanding that permit us to arrive at cognition, understanding, or judgement by bringing a possible object under them. In the judgement $\alpha : \alpha$, it is not really important exactly what object α is; what is important is only the existence of an object of type or category α. This means that we can conceive the type α existentially or run the judgement under existential quantification and say that α exists. That is to say, to cognize that α exists is to cognize an object, term, or piece of evidence of type α. In this framework, A prop is a problem whose solution is given by a proof and, respectively, A true as the *existence* of such a proof in the above sense. Types can also be understood as functions (in the mathematical sense) that compute a specific term.

In this setting, we can bring in additional type and term-related concepts:

- Type constructors for the introduction of new types constructed by more abstract, fundamental, or simpler types, e.g., $\alpha{\times}\beta$ is a product type introduced by the type constructor $\times$ applied to two given types α and β. Type constructors in this sense correspond to introduction rules, which can conclude a compound judgement constructed—using the constructor—out of simpler judgments.

---

303 Martin-Löf, *Analytic and Synthetic Judgements in Type Theory*, 92–3.

- Term or object constructors, which, like type constructors, introduce new terms or objects, e.g., the term $\langle a,b \rangle$ of the type $\alpha \times \beta$ is constructed from the term a of the type α and the term b of the type β.

- Type destructors for eliminating types that are no longer needed. They can be compared with elimination rules such as

$$\frac{\alpha \wedge \beta \text{ true}}{\alpha \text{ true}} \qquad \frac{\alpha \wedge \beta \text{ true}}{\beta \text{ true}}$$

- Term or object destructors, which are similar to type destructors but applied to objects.

- Reduction or *rewrite* for demonstrating either that a problem, proof, or judgement can be reduced to a simpler form whose solution can be counted as the solution to the more complex problem, or that the rewritten or reduced form is as difficult as the original form. For example, $B \to A$, where $\to$ is a reduction operator, means reducing B to A so that we can solve A with an eye to B (as a computational or cognitive resource). Reduction, in this sense, can be understood in terms of destructors of some type (consuming information, decomposing structure) meeting or communicating with the constructors of their corresponding type (producing information, composing structure), generating a rewritten and more tractable form of the original problem or reducing many problems to just one.

- Dependent types, which are crucial for increasing the expressivity of types. A dependent type is a function of elements of some other type. For instance, the dependent type $D(y)$, the days of the year. It is a function of the element y of the type Y of years, because not all years have 365 days. In other words, D is a type in the context Y or, alternatively, for each y in Y there is a type $D(y)$. Consider another basic example, for the dependent type P: Practice $\to$ Type which is the property of practical claims. $P(c)$ can be seen as the proof or program that claim c has property P, and not some other property—for example, being aesthetic.

- Universes or the hierarchy of types of types ($\text{Type}_0 : \text{Type}_1, \text{Type}_1 : \text{Type}_2, \ldots$), i.e., types whose terms or objects are types. Generally, universes are introduced to avoid paradoxes or antinomies such as Russell's paradox by creating a universe type that includes all other types but not itself. Classical constraints regarding universe levels or the Russellian cumulative hierarchy of types can be relaxed so that judgements and constructions (notions, definitions, theorems, proofs, etc.) can be parameterized over all universes (the hierarchy of types of types) rather than particular universe levels, and instantiated or explicitly quantified at a particular level only when needed.[304] To take a philosophical example, we can see all thinking processes or mentations as being parameterized by the universal type *the mind* or simply *Mind*. Such parameterization across different levels of mental acts allows us to talk broadly about thinking or mind in general, instantiating or specifying a mental act at a specific level or universe type (e.g., intuiting, understanding, or reason) only when necessary. One of the main motivations behind the introduction of universes of types is to adequately differentiate the things or data under consideration. In this respect, the concepts of universes or types of types is very much in conformity with Plato's basic thesis that thinking is determination of differences, and that a consequential thought is analogous to a good butcher who carves at the joints of things, without splintering the bones.

The interactive version of this theory requires going one step further, and treating judgements first and foremost as pieces of interaction or of the interchange of roles between *Proof* (*A*) and *counterproof* (*A*), or *A* and $\neg A$, as necessary proofs without which neither pole can be established.

---

304 This parameterization over one or all universes or levels of types of types—particularly in the context of homotopy type theory—is called *universe polymorphism*. A universe is polymorphic when a proof, definition, etc. is universally quantified over one or many universes. Since this universal quantification creates a type ambiguity, it should also permit—when necessary—explicit quantification over specific levels or universes. For more details see Univalent Foundations Program, *Homotopy Type Theory*.

But this is impossible unless we bring interaction into the foreground of the construction of proofs, so that proofs become games of refutations. It requires the *suspension* of procedural rules dictating how the interaction should evolve and establishing game-theoretic pay-off functions; instead it grounds interaction on the architectonics of negation. In this respect, negation is a switch-role operator that maps the legal moves of two players, falsifier and verifier, into one another. What is the judgement $\vdash A$ from the perspective of one is the judgement of $\vdash \neg A$ from the perspective of the other. Cognizing or grasping A true and $a : \alpha$ is impossible unless we cognize their duals A^- *false* and $a^- : \alpha^-$; and vice versa. Accordingly, without the interacting agencies, without the computational duality of the cognitive and the recognitive, cognition-as-program turns out to be—following the previous chapter—an empty thought.

What is important to underline at this point is that the judgements ($\vdash A$, A *prop*, A *true*, $a : \alpha$, etc.) all depend as much on the judgements of the prover/verifier/game played by $\top$ (denoting true) as on the judgements of the refuter/falsifier/game played by $\bot$ (denoting false). Each side is a computational resource for the other's (best) judgements. Since in inter-actions problems are symmetric to resources, what is a problem for $\top$ is a resource for $\bot$ and what is a problem for $\bot$ is a resource for $\top$. In the interactive paradigm of propositions-as-types and proofs-as-programs, more computational resources—i.e., more nodes of interaction, more playing agents with legal runs—is always better than less.

Types as input-output mapped functions are the most elementary and restricted forms of interaction. Adopting Giorgi Japaridze's logic of non-elementary games or interactions, propositions-as-types-as-functions can be said to be 'predicates that return the same proposition for every valuation', where valuation means 'a function e that sends each variable x to a constant $e(x)$'.[305] A rudimentary example of a constant game or interaction would be a synchronous game with restricted branching, in so far as every player must wait for the other player to finish its legal move before being able to run

---

305 G. Japaridze, 'From Truth to Computability', *Theoretical Computer Science* 357: 1–3 (2006), 100–135.

its next legal move. The truly interactivist approach—that is, an approach genuinely developed through the architectonics of negation—permits a nonconstant game between the players (i.e., one no longer mapped on simple input-output functions), in which additional possibilities (such as initial choice of move, who makes the first move, asynchronous actions, etc.) result in nontrivial interactions or games with branchings (sub-games) which are not restricted by strict input-output mappings and well-founded types. They can be trans-typified (i.e., in terms of what was argued above, they would encompass different forms of cognition/*erkenntnis* and judgement/*urteil*) or even untyped in the sense that 'any move formed as part of an interaction is allowed to interact with any other, so that no type restrictions can apply'.[306]

Having presented the simplest quasi-formal definition of what is meant by a 'program' when asserting that philosophy is a program, we should also add the following: Philosophy as a program is founded on the architectonics of negation as the engine of thinking and the diversification of forms of cognition. As a nontrivial game of cognitions, philosophy then begins with the premise of aiming to amass as many computational or cognitive resources as possible by collectivizing *agents* of various kinds. Philosophy takes the duality of the cognitive and recognitive—*cognition is always a recognition*—not merely as a social maxim, but as the formal condition not only of what it means to have cognitions and thoughts, but also of what it means to conceive philosophy as a program of cognitive exploration and the craft and cultivation of what, as we shall see, is the ultimate form of intelligence. The project of concretely negating what is pathologically individualizing and bringing about what is impersonally collective is set in motion not by the criterion of mutual recognition as a vague social thesis susceptible to exploitation by peculiarly liberalist-quietist agendas, but as a necessary *formal* condition for computation and cognition. Game-theoretic models, in this sense, are merely restricted cases of interaction in which cognizing agents are forced to accommodate preestablished laws

---

306 Trafford, *Meaning in Dialogue*, 171.

and payoff functions at the expense of narrowing cognitive-computational possibilities. By taking negation as the condition necessary for a cognition that is not a priori limited, and by incorporating negativity as the basic unit of thought, philosophy evolves into that which wrests thought from its origin and marshals it against the inequality of minds. In doing so, philosophy becomes 'the game of games'.[307]

As the game of games, philosophy is *analogous*—keeping in mind that analogies should never be overstretched—to a universal board game of the most generalized topological structure and comprised of numerous sub-board games. But with respect to this analogy, what exactly differentiates philosophy from other general games played inside language, including our natural languages? The answer to this question consists of two inter-related specifications of the philosophical domain: (1) philosophy, unlike the ordinary domain of discourse, is distinguished by the *explicitly unre-stricted* universe of discourse or data under consideration. (2) Philosophical interactions—in the sense in which the concept of interaction has been fleshed out in this book—inhabit certain specific universe types such as the theoretical, practical, and aesthetic, with the type of types ($Type_0$) being the assertion that *thinking is possible*, or simply thought as a datum which must be investigated and elaborated in the senses of *skeptikos* (the toil of examination) and *elaboro* (the labour of working out).

The possibility of thought is what can be called the Idea (*eidos*) in the exact sense in which Hermann Cohen defined the term in relation to Plato's doctrine of forms and the Socratic concept, the question 'What is it?' (*ti esti*). Idea is the self-consciousness of concept,[308] what at once *gives the account* qua logic (*logon didonai*) and *lays the basis* (*hypotithesthai*) of itself in its own concept.[309] Following Cohen and Paul Natorp, the

---

307 P. Wolfendale, 'Castalian Games', in *Glass Bead 0* (2016), <http://www.glass-bead.org/wp-content/uploads/castalian-games_en.pdf>.

308 H. Cohen, *System der Philosophie. Erster Teil: Logik der reinen Erkenntnis* (Berlin: Cassirer, 1914), 211.

309 Logos and hypothesis literally mean 'account' and 'basis', as in giving an account of an incident (usually in a juridical context) and laying the basis of an argument.

possibility of thought as Idea is the given (*Gegebene*)—in the sense of the truth-candidate rather than a fixed axiom or truth-given—which is and will be always a task (*Aufgegebene*). As such, it cannot be acknowledged as a telos or destination, but only as a *point of origin and departure*, as the judgement of origin qua logos which is infinite judgement—a judgement that extends in both directions to the infinite beginning and the infinite end of thinking.[310] It is in recognizing and adopting 'the thinking of origin' (Cohen's *Ursprungsdenken*) as the fundamental universe of types, that philosophy turns thinking ('All thoughts are the thought of the origin')[311] into a program firstly for the construction of its universe types (theoretical, practical, aesthetic, etc.) and then for the ramification of universe types into determinate thought-forms and their objects. In Cohen's terms, by beginning with the thought of the origin, philosophy becomes the very logic of thinking. It simultaneously initiates the thought of the unbound sovereignty of thinking and institutes thinking as the universal method for the verification of itself.

DATUM 2. PHILOSOPHY, THE WAY OF WORLDBUILDING

In in its quintessential form, philosophy is an organon for world-building. The worlds crafted by philosophy, depending on their methodological integration with local modes of thinking (science, politics, art, etc.), can be either abstract or concrete. Regardless of the nature of such worlds, they are inhabited by new forms of intelligence and cognition. One cannot adequately represent the world or enrich intelligible reality without first being acquainted with ways of world-making or toying around with the

---

Plato's qualification of his Idea or Form in terms of providing both logos and hypothesis should then be construed as thought providing both the account and the basis for the concept of itself (what it is).

310 For Cohen's and Natorp's reflections on the critical method of origin, see Cohen, *Logik der reinen Erkenntnis*; and P. Natorp, *Platos Ideenlehre. Eine Einführung in den Idealismus* (Leipzig: Dürr, 1903).

311 Cohen, *Logik der reinen Erkenntnis*, 36.

idea of reality as if it were an unbound play rather than a game bound to established rules designed to represent the given order of things.

In *Ways of Worldmaking*,[312] Nelson Goodman proposes five thinly veiled theses:

(1) Every world we make is built out of the resources and detritus of the available worlds. Every making is a remaking. That is to say, there is a continuity between built worlds and existing worlds. The built worlds, however, are not fantasy worlds or mere possible worlds begotten by the arcane imagination of a staunch advocate of modal realism. They are actual worlds. Thus, ways of worldmaking oscillate between non-greedy reduction and construction. Philosophically, this oscillation is personified by the almost titanic battle between Parmenides, the builder of worlds (type constructor) and Heraclitus, the destroyer of all worlds (type destructor). In this scenario, philosophers are nothing but computational strategies.

(2) There are only world-versions whose criteria of rightness should be tested in the context of their frame of reference, coherency, veracity and validity or conforming to rules of inference, range of possible applications, reconciliation or its absence (i.e. conflict) between worlds. This means that built worlds cannot be assessed by way of an indiscriminate reduction to an original or fundamental world. Once properly understood, reduction is an enrichment of reality and a way of world-building, but not a unique method or a recourse to some precursor world qua total foundation. The task of searching for an ultimate fundament or original world should be relegated to theology, for it is the concern of neither philosophy nor science. Therefore, the second thesis is in reality a clarifying addendum to the first thesis.

(3) Under rigorous scrutiny, the commonsense distinction between pluralism and monism, many worlds and one world, disappears. What is

---

312 N. Goodman, *Ways of Worldmaking* (Indianapolis: Hackett, 1978).

considered to be one world can be made up of many contrasting, even incommensurable aspects, and what are taken to be many worlds can be seen as one under a specific mode of integration or a collection of those worlds into a single unitary set.

(4) Making *new* worlds for the sake of multiplicity and diversification is a craftsman's caprice. The choice of alternatives or the attempt to envision and construct alternatives is not by any means reflective of reality. All alternatives are beholden to the criteria of rightness, the procedures by which false alternatives can be distinguished from those which are right, fit and testable. Even different aspects of one world can be turned into alternatives, there is no mandate to imagine or make new worlds. Ways of worldmaking are inherently *ways of knowing*, and are therefore intrinsically sensitive to the principles required for knowing and explaining things. Talk of other worlds of intelligences and cognitions is purely nonsensical—an invention of indolent minds wanting to overcome their restrictions by nothing else other than their firm dogmas and whimsical predilections. Absent making-cum-knowing, we can only be in the business of humanly and individualistically wrought confusions:

> Moreover, while readiness to recognize alternative worlds may be liberating, and suggestive of new avenues of exploration, a willingness to welcome all worlds builds none. Mere acknowledgement of the many available frames of reference provides us with no map of the motions of heavenly bodies; acceptance of the eligibility of alternative bases produces no scientific theory or philosophical system; awareness of varied ways of seeing paints makes no picture. A broad mind is no substitute for hard work.[313]

(5) Behind all ways of worldmaking, there lies an ever-growing list of methods and operations. Such basic operations for propagation of worlds

---

313 Ibid., 21.

are never exhaustive, but that does not mean we cannot compile a list of basic operations or imagine new ways of worldmaking:

a. *Composition and Decomposition* are operations by which things are taken apart and put together to make ever more new part-whole relationships, taxonomies, classes, and subclasses of entities and their features whose combination results in the construction of complexes and the specific connections they afford. For example, think of how predicates of smell can be applied to predicates of colour to create synaesthetic predicates, or how theoretical claims can be applied to practical claims. An example of this operation is the mechanical method of Archimedes by which geometrical problems are interpreted mechanically. The solution provided in the realm of mechanics is translated into a solution for the geometrical problem. Composition and decomposition, thus, provide bases for the identification of entities and their features according to the overall organizational scheme of a world-system (i.e., how taking apart and putting together in thus-and-so ways generates patterns and classes). The concepts of the central point and uniform space are identifiable in the world of classical perspective/geometry, but not in the Cartanian world where the model of the world itself cannot be confronted via a central perspective (an anchored observer) because it is a *scattering* world. Elie Cartan's concept of moving frame (*repère mobile*) is essentially this scattering model of the world that is identifiable in reference to new classes—*groups, total space, multiplicity*—generated as the outcome of decomposing and recomposing the old perspectival paradigm. The observer within this world is unanchored and its perspective is mobile and never given in advance of the piecemeal unfolding of space. Even repetition, periodicity, and temporal flux are related to the organizational or compositional scheme. We can imagine fundamentally monotonous and uneventful worlds, or alternatively, turbulent Heraclitean nightmares, depending on how events are sorted into kinds through operations of composition and decomposition.

b. *Weighting* allows worlds to be partitioned into relevant and irrelevant classes of entities and features such that what is a relevant class for one world might be an irrelevant class for another. The word sun is *stressed* in Plato's *Republic*, yet it is a quotidian de-stressed word in a naturalistic novel by Émile Zola. The question 'How long does it take for the earth to revolve around the sun?' is a relevant class of problem in the Copernican frame of reference but not in the Ptolemaic one. Likewise, the question 'How long does it take for the sun to revolve around the earth?' is relevant in the Ptolemaic frame of reference but not in the Copernican framework.

c. *Ordering* is an operation that mainly concerns the order of derivation within a constructional framework. The order of derivation of points with respect to the Euclidean and non-Euclidean systems are different. In the Euclidean paradigm, points can be either given elements (intuitive axioms) or the result of an elementary construction over other axiomatic data (lines intersecting). But in non-Euclidean worlds, the order of derivation can be fundamentally different. Worlds possess hierarchies of construction or orders of derivation. Such hierarchies *demarcate, limit,* or *enable* transition from one perceptual or cognitive ability/machinery to another. Take for instance the Chomsky hierarchy of formal grammar, where the type of automata that can compute recursively enumerable languages are universal Turing machines. They are far harder to recognize, more complex and costlier in computational terms than those automata which can only compute regular or context-free syntax. Furthermore, as in Carnap's constitutional system, once the order of derivation is formulated as a set of transformation rules, it is then possible to build new elements on the basic building blocks (axioms), and, more importantly, to systematically define the relationships between those basic building blocks. The latter engenders the opportunity to move beyond the ostensible foundation toward the realm of metalogics or worlds of proto-foundations. This in turn allows for the expansion of the notion of objectivity, since object is only that which can be structured in a constitutional system and can become the object of statements in that system.

d. *Deletion and Supplementation*: Every worldmaking in one way or another requires a procedure of erasure or weeding out and filling the gaps with new materials. The worlds made by deletion and supplementation are worlds which increasingly supply our cognitive armamentarium with new methods of construction, new anticipations, and ways out of our established order. Think about how cubism erases the elements of classical figurative painting. But to the extent that, in the way of worldmaking, erasure is not enough—what is erased often has to be replaced by new supplements—every figure loses something but also is supplemented with new lines and diagrammatic configurations. Or think of Goodman's own example: the shift from the analogue to the digital should be regarded as a veritable worldmaking. In this process, continuities are deleted. We are now in the domain of pure mechanizability: discrete inputs, discrete states, and discrete outputs. This shift realized by deletion is a radical one. The very distinction between human and machine collapses. The human world will be revealed as nothing but a special qualitative kind of integration of computational algorithms. As an alternative to this digital world, we can imagine a computational world where continuity, and above all the realtime interaction between the system or the abstract machine and its environment, is restored (supplemented). This is a new computational world in which the system and the environment interact without any pre-given limitations. The interaction is computation itself in a *truly concurrent* sense, to use the idiom of today's theoretical computer science. The prospects of such a paradigm of computation for remodelling the very notion of spirit or geist as a multi-agent system (interacting computational processes) is beyond our acquired practical reason, if not truly theoretically and practically unbound.

e. *Deformation* or reshaping can involve either corrections or distortions, or both. For example, think of an engineer who does not directly intervene with a metal beam at the level of the crystal structure, but develops an approximation or normalization technique (essentially a controlled distortion) whereby he can manipulate the beam sufficiently at a less fine-grained or detailed level of analysis and intervention. Or take, for instance, Boltzmann's gas theory in which the earlier works of classical thermodynamics as developed by Carnot, Clausius, and others are corrected in a generalized fashion, but where the thermal elements are also reshaped and reinvented as statistical ensembles of the position, velocity, and momentum of particles.

Even the philosophical program of worldbuilding shares the common operations and attributes of general worldmaking: the built worlds of philosophy are primary theoretical, practical, axiological, or aesthetic universes of types. The aim of philosophical world-building is to enlarge the domain of discourse beyond all habitually entrenched perceptual and noetic limitations such that we can imagine worlds where our inductions and, even more broadly, our reality, is constructed by the unnatural predicates (e.g., grue and bleen-type predicates)[314] we project onto it. Or worlds where the craftsmanship of mind in this existing world coincides with other intelligible forms of mindedness and intelligence as inhabitants of other worlds qua artifices of the mind. The world of philosophy is the *universe* of worlds, its philosophical tenets are experimentations in crafting worlds and their intelligent inhabitants which, upon careful analysis, can be shown to consist of one world and one universal conception of intelligence—an intelligence that demarcates the necessary ontological and epistemological correlations between what is intelligible and the work involved in making sense of it as a part of an intelligible reality or Being. To this extent, the new worlds of intelligence are not just cognized worlds. They are fundamentally the world *re*-cognized in different ways.

---

314 See Appendix.

DATUM 3. ACTUALIZING THE POSSIBILITY OF THINKING

Conceived as a program, philosophy is an inquiry into the realization of all possible forms of cognition and what might arise from the exercise of forms thus realized.

In the programmatic framework, the choice of data does not confine the program to their explicit *terms*. Rather, it commits the program to the underlying properties and operations specific to their class or family of interconnections. To put it differently, if a program constructs possible realizabilities for the underlying properties of its data, it is not essentially restricted to their terms. Realizability here means what arises from the exercise of powers or abilities brought about by some necessary underlying capacities or properties. For example, transcendental psychology characterizes the mind along two perpendicular lines—what arises from the exercise of the mental powers or abilities of mind, and what is required for the realization of these abilities or powers. We can call these two axes *realizabilities* and *realizers*, corresponding respectively to that which arises from the exercise of realized abilities (powers of judgement and cognition) and the conditions or capacities necessary for the realization of such abilities. Kant's threefold synthesis can then be understood as an abstraction of realizers-capacities from above, from the vantage point of realizabilities. In the same vein, philosophy begins with the exercise of realized mental powers, but its exercise is such that it permits the examination of what may possibly arise from the programmatic use of such powers. The realizabilities of philosophy are those modes of cognition that turn thoughts into programs, and cognitions into recipes for crafting intelligence, by extracting and combing through the underlying cognitive properties specific to thinking agents. Let us look at a crude example:

1. *p is an E*

In a Platonic style, this cryptic expression says: 'The form (*Eidos*) that Parmenides partially exhibits defines who Parmenides is (*p*)', or 'the form of Parmenides, as a complex of cognitions, qualifies who he is', or, in a more straightforward way, 'Parmenides is a rational life-form of such-and-such theoretical and practical qualities, the complex of his sayings and doings'.

Then Parmenides says or does something that displays particular properties of that realm of form, or says or does some x that qualifies him as a rational life form. This can be written as:

2. p *does* $x : \mathcal{F}$ ($\mathcal{F}$ for a rule-governed [i.e., normative] behaviour or function).

As a rational life form, Parmenides is a particular pattern-uniformity through which implicit patterns or properties specific to the realm of forms can be realized in the temporal order. $\mathcal{F}$, or what Parmenides says or does as a rational life form, is a partial realization of these forms as an intelligible practice or operation. In other words, $\mathcal{F}$ is a practice whose operational content can be traced, changed, and combined with other practices to construct more complex realizabilities specific to the realm of forms that Parmenides partially embodies. In this example, 1 and 2 represent the specific data and its basic operational information, which may be abbreviated to 'this p is $\mathcal{F}$ of E-form' (again, roughly translating to 'Parmenides's thoughts and actions reflect the form to which he belongs', or 'Parmenides is what he does as a rational life-form').

Now let us introduce another agent, Confucius. Everything that was said about Parmenides also holds true for Confucius, except that what they do and say are not the same. Their forms and, respectively, what they say and do, are different. We then have:

$\mathcal{F}$ (p-form) for Parmenides's thoughts and actions corresponding to its cognitive form

And,

$\mathcal{F}$ (c-form) for Confucius's thoughts and actions exhibiting the complex of cognitions that reflect who Confucius is.

For $\mathcal{F}_1$ and $\mathcal{F}_2$—Parmenides and Confucius—we can additionally introduce, following Lorenz Puntel, operators that specify specific domains of philosophical discourse or universe types of basic philosophical assertions. Again in tandem with Puntel's special notations,[315] these include at the very least $\boxed{\text{T}}$, $\boxed{\text{P}}$, and $\boxed{\text{AE}}$—respectively, theoretical operator, practical operator, and aesthetic operator. There may be more operators of the philosophical discourse, or these operators themselves may consist of various specific types, but for the sake of brevity we shall keep it at that. Something like $\boxed{\text{T}}\varphi$ is a datum of the universe type *theoretical*, saying for example, '*It is the case that* nothing else outside of Being exists or ever will'.[316] And respectively, something like $\boxed{\text{P}}\varphi$ says '*It is an ethical obligation to* look upon the younger generation with awe because how are we to know that those who come after us will not prove our equals'.[317] In other words, the practical operator is an explicit datum concerning explicitly practical desiderata (ethical, intellectual, legal, etc.) that can be expressed in terms of obligation, permission, impermissibility, and even encouragement. Likewise, $\boxed{\text{AE}}\chi$ is an aesthetic datum that roughly and forcedly translates into '*There is an aesthetic presentation* such that χ',[318] as in 'There is an aesthetic presentation such that the verses of Bhagavad Gita satisfy the supreme needs of Spirit', or 'The proof of Pythagoras's theorem is an embodiment of timeless beauty'.

What is important is that the operators of philosophical discourse are *encompassing types of modes of cognition* in the sense in which types were defined earlier. In this respect, we can approximate them to universe types, while regarding the investigation and elaboration of the possibility of thinking, or simply *thought*, as the type of types (Type_0). The universe Type_0 can be defined—following Plato—as the formal reality of nonbeing. For once nonbeing is *formally*—rather than substantively—distinguished from being, it becomes the determining negativity of thought through which objectivity

---

315 Puntel, *Structure and Being*.

316 Parmenides, *Parmenides of Elea* (Westport, CT: Praeger, 2003), 27.

317 Confucius, *Analects*, tr. E. Slingerland (Indianapolis: Hackett, 2003), 94.

318 Puntel, *Structure and Being*, 91.

can be distinguished from falsehood (*pseudos*) and fleeting appearances (*eikones* of the *eikasia* or purely sensible suppositions).

Accordingly, the formal differentiation of thinking from being, of *that which is not* (*to me on*) from *that which is* (*to on*)—that is, the possibility of thought in and for itself—is precisely a definition or datum by which the question of being (or nature, reality, universe, etc.), and correspondingly the intelligibility and coherence of materialism and realism, can be rescued.[319] Therefore, far from being a philosophical coup against Parmenides, Plato's project salvages Parmenides's most cherished question, that of being, from both Gorgias's greedy scepticism about the limits of language and logos and the paradoxical nature of the question of that which is,[320] and the Eleatic fusion of being and thinking. Plato's revision of the question of being in relation to truth or objective validity, in this respect, is equivalent to type rewriting as defined above. In order to solve the question of being, to save its objectivity, Plato brings head-to-head a series of destructors and constructors. The old Eleatic subsumption of thinking under being is destroyed while at the same time a new type is constructed—thought as formally distinct from being or the formal autonomy of thinking. By destroying *thinking : being* and constructing *thinking : formal nonbeing* (*nonphysical forms or ideas*), Plato rewrites and solves the question of being as the objective validity of thinking (language and logoi).

The picture of Parmenides that Plato presents in the dialogue *Parmenides* gives an entirely different account of the champion of nature and the way of truth. This is the mature Parmenides already disillusioned by the Eleatic equivocation or fusion between being and thinking. What Plato's Parmenides

---

319 See for example, R. Brassier, 'That Which Is Not: Philosophy as Entwinement of Truth and Negativity', *Stasis* 1 (2013) 174–86, <http://www.stasisjournal.net/index.php/journal/article/download/60/94/>.

320 Gorgias's tetralemma can be formulated as follows: (1) Nothing exists; (2) Even if existence exists, nothing can be known about it; (3) Even if it could be known, it cannot be communicated to others; (4) Even if it could be communicated, it cannot be understood. See Plato's response, in Plato, *Gorgias* (Indianapolis: Hackett, 1987).

advocates is much more similar to the Hegelian unity and identity of opposites, being and thinking. Indeed, Plato goes so far as to pit the mature Parmenides against the young and rather ignorant and flamboyant Socrates only to show how the latter's thoughts are exposed as incoherent and crude, and how he is pushed by Parmenides to *the precipice of the abyss of nonsense*.[321] In a dialogue which is one of the most intricate and profound discussions in the history of philosophy,[322] Parmenides goes on to edify Socrates about the subtleties of being by way of the subtleties of forms or ideas: For example, it is a mistake to ascribe the characteristics of particular existent things ($\exists x$) or quasi-perceptual terms to forms or ideas. The latter are different in kind from the particular things that partake in them. Consequently, participation of particular things in universal forms should not be defined as a part-whole relationship, since that would again reduce forms to thinghood.

With these remarks on forms and universe types of philosophy in mind, let us picture a hypothetical scenario—a simulation constructed only out of philosophical imagination— where Parmenides and Confucius interact:

$$\mathcal{F}_1 : \boxed{\text{T}} \text{ (of Parmenides)}$$

and

$$\mathcal{F}_2 : \boxed{\text{P}} \text{ (of Confucius)}$$

can be combined, cohered, and integrated according to the rules of how theory, practice, and aesthetics can stand in relation to one another, thereby generating new *forms* inhabited by new modes of cognition.[323]

---

321 Plato, *Parmenides*, §130d7.

322 See the inaugurating discussions in *Parmenides*, particularly §130–§145.

323 'Sentence forms that have the practical operator as the main operator and, within its scope, the theoretical or the aesthetic operator (thus, "($\boxed{\text{P}}(\boxed{\text{T}}(\varphi))$)" and "($\boxed{\text{P}}(\boxed{\text{T}}(\chi))$)") are philosophically senseless: how matters, including aesthetic matters, in fact stand within the world cannot be made dependent upon any sort of demand. On the other hand, the sentence form that includes the theoretical operator within the

These philosophically crafted forms are essentially what were presented in the market of the agora, where philosophers propped up their own stands—built worlds—to offer what they had constructed and elaborated from the hypothetical interactions of different forms and encompassing types of modes of cognition. They were as much programs for thought as they were recipes for determining what is the case, what ought to be thought, and what ought to be done.

Now imagine an agora outside of this temporal world where, among many others, the Cynics, the Stoics, the disciples of Plato, the Aristotelians, the New Confucians, and the Anushiruwanians (who offer a particular brand of Neoplatonist and Indic cosmological thought built on the critique of tradition and the way of social justice) auction their recipes. The price for what they offer is not your financial wealth, but your theoretical and practical commitments—that is, the entirety of who you are. Once you take up an offer, your destiny will be reshaped according to those modes of cognition that tell you what is the case, what should be thought, what should be done, and what is presented as the aesthetic articulation of is and ought. Yet this is not destiny as a *telos* or *eskhatos* but rather a cognitive and practical expedition down ramifying paths initiated by whatever you commit yourself to. Philosophy, however, advises us not to conclusively take up any offer until we have begun, to the best of our capacities, to resolve the incompatibilities between what is on offer in the agora, by making explicit those implicit thoughts that are already explicit in practices. But philosophy also tells us that we cannot do that until and unless we have interacted with every stand that is in the agora of cognitions. Indeed, philosophy, as that which programs thought, is precisely this sustained wandering in the agora of all possible modes of cognitions and the forms realized by them. There is virtually no a priori limitation as to who or what can build this agora, who or what may be behind the stands, or what form of agency—realized or yet unrealized—may ascetically wander through it. The agora is open to anyone or anything

scope of the aesthetic operator seems to be wholly sensible.' Puntel, *Structure and Being*, 94.

that satisfies the necessary conditions of having mind, by any means and through any process.

If Parmenides and Confucius, *p-form* and *c-form*, interact, then they do not only do x or y, but at the very least $x(y)$ or $y(x)$. Generally understood, the function or activity $\mathcal{F}$ characterizes or epitomizes E-form as a form that encompasses all that interacts. In other words, 'the encompassing form E to which both Parmenides (*p-form*) and Confucius (*c-form*) belong, at the very least, does $x(y)$ and $y(x)$'. The program has constructed an encompassing form with additional cognitive abilities by extracting and elaborating the underlying cognitions or commitments of the interacting forms. At the very least what the program can do or bring about is $x(y)$ and $y(x)$—that is, the operational content of the data (theoretical, practical, aesthetic) constructed by the interaction between two rational life forms.

At any rate, it is the impersonal form E that determines what the forms of Parmenides and Confucius are, and supplies them with abilities that do not inherently belong to who they are or what they represent. The *p-form* and *c-form* become incorporated into a form that does not merely transcend them and afford them cognitions they could never have developed on their own, but also becomes the ground of the *intelligibility* of their respective forms and their normative behaviours. In other words, without this encompassing form, neither Parmenides nor Confucius could be conceived *as intelligible* forms. Their forms and their respective functions can now be offered in the agora.

In the broadest sense, the philosophical program can thus be understood as that which constructs new blueprints of cognitions by systematically searching for interacting data (theoretical, practical, aesthetic, etc.) that typify rational life forms. Depending on how interactions (exchanges between data) are performed and regulated, what strategies are followed, whether the interactions are synchronic or diachronic, elementary or complex, the program can construct encompassing realizabilities untethered both from any specific rational life-form and from the specific content explicit in what they say or do (i.e., data). For this reason, a program—in this case, philosophy as such—is a wholly impersonal exercise. To conclude, a program is a systematic self-grounding. Philosophy as such conceives itself as a *systematic* absolute self-establishment that constructs itself impersonally from saying and doings (data) that are incorporated, revised, or discarded in ever more encompassing cognitions.[324]

Within the programmatic framework of philosophy, thoughts are no longer sacrosanct elements eternally anchored in some absolute foundation, but active processes that can be updated, repaired, terminated, or combined into composite acts through interaction. These composite thought-acts exhibit complex dynamic behaviours that could not be generated were the thoughts taken in isolation, had they not become the environment of one another. New thoughts and their possible realizabilities can be constructed by experimenting with the operational architecture of the program. This experimentation involves both a controlled relaxation of existing constraints on thoughts and how they interact, and the addition of new constraints.

Just like any program, the meaning of philosophy as a program is not entailed by its data or truth-candidate thoughts—what they refer to or what they denote—but by how and under what conditions they interact. The right question in addressing a program is not 'What do these data stand for, what does this program mean?', but 'What is this program, how does it act, what are its possible operational effects, how does it construct its realizabilities?' Detached from semantic utility, the meaning of the program is paradigmatically actional. Philosophy has no utility other than mobilizing thoughts for thought's ends. Philosophy is a special kind of a program whose meaning is dependent upon what it does and how it does it: *it is only what it does*, and what it does is to explore the ends of thought by building upon the possibility of thinking. It is a special kind of program in that it is deeply entangled with the architecture of what we call thinking.

DATUM 4. NAVIGATING THOUGHT'S RAMIFIED PATHS

Philosophy is a program whose primary data are those pertaining to the possibility of thinking as such. Its task is to elaborate the realizabilities behind this possibility

---

324 For an exceptionally meticulous argument against the refutations of philosophy's absolute self-grounding, particularly the charge of Münchhausen trilemma, see Puntel, *Structure and Being*, 52–64.

*in terms of what can be done with thought or, more broadly, what thought can
realize out of itself. If thought is or could be possible at all, then what would be the
ramifications of such a possibility?*

The significance of philosophy lies in this simple yet vastly consequential
trivium: that it uses the possibility of thinking (or thought as an act) as
its premise, as a truth-candidate datum that can be systematically acted
upon. In doing so, philosophy commits to the elaboration of *what comes
after the premise*, i.e., what can be realized from thought and what thought
can do, or, more accurately, the possibility of a thought set on developing
its own forms and functions.

What ought to be underlined here is that the possibility of thinking
should not be conflated with the assertion that thought *exists*, nor with what
is thought *of*, or the object of thought. In accord with Plato, the possibility
of thinking or thought as an act is in fact the possibility of nonbeing as the
formal condition of thinking qua negativity. The possibility of nonbeing
in this sense is grounded in the *formal*, rather than substantive, distinction
between that which is and that which is not. To collapse thinking into being
is to elide the distinction between that which is formally distinguished
from being and that which fails to substantively distinguish itself from
being. Therefore, to say that thinking is possible is, at bottom, an assertion
regarding the formal distinction between thought and being.

Without such a formal distinction, there would be no knowledge
(whether *episteme* or *gnosis*) of being in the first place that could subsequently become corrupted into pathologies where thought and being
become mixed, with thought demoted to matter or matter promoted to
the idea (idealizing matter or materializing the idea). The formal nonbeing of thinking is precisely formal negativity, as encapsulated in the
function of logic and language that distinguishes that which is not from
that which is. This formal function does not mirror nature, but halts the
indeterminate flux of things, or makes determinate distinctions in that
which is at rest by cutting the continuum of reality at its joints. It separates
what is already indeterminate and determinately combines what is already
discrete. This is a position that is unabashedly favourable to Plato's, as
is the remainder of this chapter. Of course, by now it should be obvious

that logic here does not mean classical logic, and that language should not be essentially taken to mean natural language. Indeed, in light of the developments in theoretical computer science and interactive logic discussed in the previous chapter, the distinction between logic and language may soon prove unnecessary.

One can and should always attempt to give an account of the conditions of thinking in terms of physical processes, in tandem with the empirical sciences. Yet it is a category mistake to claim that revealing how thinking is ultimately realized as a furniture of the world (if that is even possible or logically well-founded at all) would enable us to say what thoughts in their formal rule-governed dimension are. The criterion of what thoughts are is ultimately formal, not substantive (otherwise, it could be explained away as just more furniture of the world). In other words, there is a categorical gap between how thinking is conditioned by natural processes and what thinking is *formally* in itself. In determining what thinking is from the perspective of nature, one has no recourse to anything extra-cognitive. One cannot but operate within the rule-governed dimension of thinking as formally differentiated from being, which is also a prerequisite for the recognition of nature as the universe of all that is and the explicitation of primary facts pertaining to it.

As a primary datum of philosophy, the possibility of thinking can always be called into question by a variant of the eristic argument put forward by Meno's paradox, the archetype of all self-paralyzing gestures of the sophist:

Either A: We know that which we seek (here, what thinking is),

Or B: How on earth can we examine or seek something if we do not know what it is?

If *A* holds then the inquiry or search is not possible.

If *B* holds then we can never know whether what we have stumbled upon is that which we sought to find or know.

Therefore, knowing, the inquiry (into what thinking is), is impossible.

In responding to Meno's paradox, one can reanimate (Plato's) Socrates's mirroring manoeuvre in order to make explicit how incoherent this position is, but also to dialectically sublate it: Let us assume that we cannot learn what thinking is, for we already know what it is; or else that we can never know what thinking is, and hence the whole enterprise is a sham. It soon becomes clear that the Menoic sceptic or sophist is ignorant of what he is ignorant of when positing the paradox. Thus the paradox itself, which is posited as an either-or disjunction, becomes incoherent as a paradox, if not completely impossible. For it is revealed to be based on the implicit assumption that the unknown is discontinuous with the known. In other words, it is built on a false conception of knowledge that does not take into account the fact that what is unknown is only unknown insofar as it stands in relation to what is known. As John Sallis puts it, the paradox is built on the assumption that 'the domain of knowledge is totally discontinuous, that it consists of discrete, individual items none of which are linked in any way to any others'.[325] The Menoic sceptic can only valorise the unknown as eternally unknowable by piggybacking on what he already knows. For how else can he distinguish the unknown—as that which is only unknown by virtue of what is known—as the unknowable? Plato's solution consists in providing an account of semantic and epistemic holism (of what is said and what is known) by suppressing, assimilating, and ultimately transforming the paradox, in so doing dissolving the either-or disjunction that is the core of the eristic argument. Accordingly, the refutation of the paradox lies not only in the rejection of the either-or disjunction that states '*either* knowledge is the same as its elements (i.e., many) *or* is different from its elements (i.e., one)', but also in the dialectical suppression and transformation—Not (either *A*-or-*B*)—of the paradox into a coherentist-holistic account of knowledge, language, and logic.

The systematic dissolution of Meno's paradox exemplifies the model by which Plato transforms ill-posited thoughts into well-posited methodical thoughts, the eristic into the dialectical, the game-theoretic into interaction-ist games in which both ignorance and knowledge, doubt and trust are incorporated. Plato simulates an interactive situation by pitting the sophist against his favourite player Socrates, who also always comes off as a sophist. In an interactive programmatic scenario mirroring the logico-computational account of programs given above, once the sophist and its *dual* Socrates

---

325 J. Sallis, *Being and Logos* (Indianapolis: Indiana University Press, 1996), 78.

begin the game of philosophy—the interaction par excellence—the solution naturally assembles itself from the exchanges between the opponent and the proponent. Philosophy thus evolves not from the logical interaction or dialogue between one who knows and one who does not, the philosopher and the sophist, but between one who is ignorant and one who strives to be less ignorant, the *know-it-all-knowing-nothing* sophist and the *knowing-that-I-know-nothing* sophist.

The possibility of thinking rests on the definition of what thinking is, but this definition is neither a total knowledge neither a total ignorance of what thinking is. Pace the Menoic sceptic, this definition is instead a mixture of knowledge and ignorance, a movement between the mitigation of ignorance and the preservation of ignorance—a movement that is knowledge.

There are numerous ways to disarm the Menoic sceptic who objects, 'let us suppose, for the sake of entertainment, that philosophy begins with the assumption that thinking is possible, but that would require us to know what thinking is', and then goes on to employ a variation of the paradox to conclude that 'the definition of thinking or the inquiry into *what thinking is* is not possible, and therefore philosophy's enterprise to proceed from the possibility of thinking is fraudulent from the outset'. I do not wish to enumerate possible strategies against the Menoic. I have provided only one strategy among others. Instead, I would rather claim that the definition of 'what thinking is' is indeed circular. This circularity is precisely what warrants the formal stability of this definition; properly speaking, it is the transcendental armature of thinking. For not all circularities amount to logical contradictions or tautologies. In mathematics, definitions of mathematical objects are always circular without being logically contradictory in a negative sense. The circularity of definitions—such as the explicit category-topos-theoretic definition of the point—liberates them from the myth of more fundamental mathematical definitions. It permits the definition to be compact yet nontrivial, and so permits a step-by-step process of unpacking and variation.[326] In the same vein, the circular

---

326 See R. Negarestani, 'Where is the Concept?', in R. Mackay (ed.), *When Site Lost the Plot* (Falmouth: Urbanomic, 2015), 225–51.

a priori transcendental definition of thinking enables the elaboration of what thinking is and what it can possibly turn into—its realizabilities.

The choice of data is a programmatic initiative because it opens up the prospect of constructing different realizabilities from the content of the data. Rather than simply being a neutral assumption—or worse, an entrenched dogma—philosophy's programmatic treatment of the possibility of thought is the first major step toward programming thinking as such.

Once the possibility of thinking is adopted as an explicit datum (as that which must be acted upon), thinking becomes a matter of extracting and expanding the operational content implicit to the possibility of thought qua datum. The focus of thought's operational activities—the acts of think-ing—is turned toward the elaboration of the content of the datum—the possibility of thinking: articulating what can be done with such a possibility and what thinking can become by acting on its very possibility. In other words, philosophy *programs* thought to systematically act on itself, to realize its own ends and demands, and to have as its main vocation a disciplined and persistent reflection on the prospects of its realizabilities. The term 'realizabilities' from now on means what can possibly arise from thinking *such that it would change the very conditions of thinking, whether such conditions are taken to be formal, experiential, social, or historical.* Philosophy's program-matization of thinking turns into the core implicit assumption of all claims and actions regarding what is to be thought or done, not thought or not done. Thinking is no longer merely exercised as a non-optional practice, but as a theoretical-practical enterprise without which there is no warrant for any thought or action.

This is where 'philosophy as a program' overlaps with 'philosophy as a form of thinking whose project is to turn thinking into a program'. By beginning with the possibility of thinking, with the transcendental circularity of what thinking is, philosophy uses the resources of thought to determine the scope of thought's realizabilities; philosophy becomes thought's program for exploring and bringing about its own realizations. Put differently, philosophy's tacit assertion that 'thought is programmable' is repurposed by thought as its principal normative task: 'thought ought to be programmed'. It is through this normative task that thought explicitly posits its own ends and augments the prospects for what it can do to its very conditions and, by extension, to us. Philosophy, in this sense, is more than simply one mode of thought among others. It is thought's own cognitive-practical prosthesis—a geistig appendage—for developing and augmenting the drive to self-determination and realization. A thought that has a drive to self-realization is a thought that, before anything else, secures its own ends. But to secure its ends, thought must issue and prioritize its own demands.

These demands are first and foremost concerned with wresting thinking from heteronomous influences, be they associated with a higher authority, with the contingent conditions of its original setup, with the conditions of its development, or with final or material causes. However, as these demands evolve, their focus shifts away from a resistance against the hold of heteronomy, toward an active articulation of the consequences brought about by the formal autonomy of thinking. Formal insofar as the substantive autonomy of conceptualizing mind is only a relative heteronomy for itself and an absolute heteronomy in nature. The demands of concrete autonomy are those which require a shift from the demands of a realized thought to those of a thought for which what is already realized—i.e., its current state or present instantiation—is not itself a *sufficient* expression of autonomy. This is a thought that makes its autonomy explicit by identifying and constructing its possible realizabilities. Its demands are centred on the prospects of a realization of thought by *different material realizers* (not to be confused with realizers as conditions necessary for the possibility of thinking) in the encompassing sense of physical, experiential, social, and historical conditions of realization. Different only in that they are more compatible with the elaboration of thought's own autonomy, ends, and demands.

In other words, these demands revolve around the possibility of reconstituting thought outside of both what currently constitutes it and how it is constituted. They are the demands to reclaim and elaborate the possibility of thought, but no longer under the limitative terms laid down by its native realizers (or constituents) or thought's present conditions of realization.

Accordingly, this reprogramming overhaul is not limited to only those material realizers or constitutive components and mechanisms that are directly at odds with thought's autonomy. It includes also those internal constitutive features that restrict the scope of thought's realizabilities. It does not matter whether such realizers belong to biological evolution or sociocultural constitution. For as long as they restrict the prospects of thought's autonomy (the scope of its possible realizabilities, its ends and demands), they are potential targets for extensive overhaul and reconstruction.

In order for thought to maintain its autonomy—in the sense of its being able to institute and adjudicate its own ends—it must adjust or replace those conditions and constituents that impinge upon its current state and the scope of its own interests. But in order for thought to be able to elaborate and follow up the consequences of the autonomy of its ends, to render intelligible the ramifications of its possibility, it must free itself from those terms and conditions that confine it to one particular state of realization. This systematic move toward separating the possibility of thinking from the circumscriptions of a singular state of realization is the beginning of a cognitive-practical inquiry into the possible realizabilities of thought. And it is precisely by investigating the possible realizabilities of thinking in all domains of thought that the consequences of thought's autonomy and the ramifications of its possibility can truly be made intelligible.

In this sense, the inquiry into the possible realizabilities of thought is synonymous with an inquiry into purposes of thought neither given in advance nor exhausted by thought's present instantiation. Indeed, the inquiry into the meaning and purposes of thought can only radically begin via a thoroughgoing theoretical and practical project aimed at reconstituting the possibility of thought outside of its contingently situated constitution and its current realized state. Determining what thought is, what its purposes are, and what it can do, then becomes a matter of exploring and constructing different realizations of thought outside of its familiar biological, social, and historical habitat.

Thought's program to institute its autonomous ends leads up to a phase in which thinking is compelled—via the imperative of its time-general ends—to define and investigate its purposes by recasting its current state of realization. This phase marks a new juncture in the development of thought's autonomy because it involves the unbinding of both the realizabilities and purposes of thought. To this extent, the organized venture toward the functional realization of thought outside of its native home and designated format is in every sense a program for the decontainment of thought. It is therefore a distinctly philosophical endeavour, in that it reenacts an enduring philosophical wager, 'thought cannot be contained', as a practical demand: 'thought ought not to be contained'.

What was initiated by philosophy's seemingly innocent datum regarding the possibility of thinking is now a program that directs thought to theoretically and practically inquire into its futures—understood as prospects of realizability that are asymmetric to its past and present. The thrust of this program is that the scope of its operations and constructive manipulations encompass both realizer and realized, both constituent and constituted, what thought is made of and what thought manifestly appears to be. As the ultimate expression of the demands of thought, this transformative program is exactly the distillation of the perennial questions of philosophy—what to think and what to do—propelled forward by an as yet largely unapprehended geistig program called philosophy's chronic compulsion to think.

DATUM 5. THOUGHT AND THE ARTEFACT

By reformatting thinking from a by-product of material and social organization into a programmatic normative enterprise that rigorously inquires into its operational and constructive possibilities, philosophy introduces a vision of the artificial into the practice of thinking. Rather than a thought that is simply accustomed to the use of artefacts and has a concept of artificiality, this is a thought that is itself a practice of artificialization, and becomes the artefact of its own ends.

The concept of the artificial signifies the idea of craft as a recipe for making something whose purposes are neither entailed by nor given in its material ingredients, even though they are afforded by the properties of those ingredients. These purposes should be understood not solely in terms of (external) purposes for which the product of the craft (the artefact) is used, but also as potential functionalities related to possible realizabilities of the artefact itself, regardless of its use or purpose of consumption. In this respect, the artificial expresses the complex and evolving interplay between external functionality (the context of use as the external purpose of the craft) and the possible realizabilities of the artefact itself. This interplay can be seen as a process of *harnessing*—in both the constraining and productive senses—that couples function qua use of the artefact with function qua instantiation of its possible realizabilities. By coupling these two categories of function, the process of artificialization produces or harnesses new functionalities and purposes from the positive constraints established between the use and realizabilities of the artefact.

The role of an artefact in practical reasoning is inherently double-faced to the extent that it is simultaneously determined by the established purpose of its consumption and the realizabilities of the artefact itself. The structure of practical reasoning about artefacts (as in 'artefact a is a means to bring about outcome c, so I ought to use a when in situation s as a means to c') is affected by this interplay between uses and realizabilities. If we take the purpose of an artefact (its established context of use) as a premise for bringing about a certain outcome, the realizabilities of the artefact can then be thought of as the addition of new axioms with new terms or premises that weaken the idempotency and monotonicity of entailment in practical reasoning. The same instances of application for a given artefact may lead to different consequences or ends (weakening of idempotency), and the addition of new assumptions regarding the use of an artefact may change the end for which an artefact is a means (weakening of monotonicity). The duplicity of artefacts is an expression of the failure of idempotency and monotonicity of entailment for the role played by artefacts in practical reasoning. This is precisely the duplicity attributed to the cunning figures of the trickster, the trap-maker, the artificer, and the navigator of deep waters—those who are aware of the volatile role artefacts play in their practical reasoning.[327]

---

327 See M. Detienne and J.-P. Vernant, *Cunning Intelligence in Greek Culture and Society*, tr. J. Lloyd (Chicago: University of Chicago Press, 1991).

Idempotency and monotonicity of entailment are structural rules that operate directly on judgments or the deductive relations between antecedents and consequents. Idempotency of entailment states that the same consequence can be derived from many instances of a hypothesis as from just one ('$A, B, B \vdash C$' can be contracted to '$A, B \vdash C$' leaving the entailed consequence C intact). Monotonicity of entailment, on the other hand, means that the hypotheses of any derived fact can be arbitrarily extended with additional assumptions ('$A \vdash C$' can be assumed as '$A, d \vdash C$' where d is the additional assumption and C is the unchanged consequence). Here, the turnstile symbol $\vdash$ denotes entailment, with antecedents on the left-hand side of the turnstile and consequents on the right-hand side. Idempotency of entailment implies the availability of antecedents as free resources (in the context of reasoning via artefacts, different instances of application or use for a given artefact do not change the outcome). Monotonicity of entailment implies the context-independency of reasoning (extending the role of an artefact or adding new assumptions about its use in bringing about some ends does not alter the result).

Artificialization can, therefore, be defined as a process aimed at functionally repurposing and exhibiting a vastly non-inertial and non-monotonic behaviour with regard to the consequences or ends of using an artefact crafted for an external 'common' purpose. This repurposing can manifest itself as the augmentation of the existing realization of the artefact, the abstraction and transplantation of some existing function or salient property into a different or entirely new context of use and operation, the readaptation of an existing use to a different instantiation of an artefact's realizabilities, or, in its most radical form, the construction of both new uses and new realizations by engaging in a craft that involves both a new mode of abstraction and a deeper order of intelligibilities (of materials and practices).

If what underlies the concept of artificialization is constructive adaptation to different purposes and realizabilities, then in realizing its own ends and adapting its realization to the growing demands of such ends, thinking turns into a radical artificializing process. At its core, a thought amplified by philosophy to systematically inquire into the ramifications of its possibility—to explore its realizabilities and purposes—is a thought which in the most fundamental sense is a rigorous artificializing program: a duplicitous artefact which, in being used toward some external 'common' ends, develops and pursues its own necessary ends.

This thought is at once dedicated to conceiving and adapting to new ends, and committed to a program of concrete self-artificialization. For a thought that has its own ends and demands, self-artificialization is an expression of its commitment to exploring its possible realizabilities, to reclaiming its possibility from heteronomous and limitative terms imposed by its natural realizers and native habitat. In other words, it is an expression of its commitment to the autonomy or rule of its ends.

However, in order for thinking to examine its possible realizabilities, it must first establish its inherent tractability to the process of artificialization. That is, the first step is to show that thinking is not an ineffable thing but an activity or a function, special but not supernatural, and that it can be programmed, repurposed, and turned into an enterprise for the *design of agency*, in the sense that every step in the pursuit of this enterprise will have far-reaching consequences for the structure of the agency that uses it.

This is what is exemplified in its most resolute form in the earliest practices of philosophy, particularly the Cynic, Stoic, and Confucian proposals regarding the programmatic aspects of thinking: to understand thinking itself as an administrative function, not to isolate thinking from living but to treat life as a craft of thinking; rather than disposing of emotions and affects, to give them structure by bringing them in line with the ends of thought; and to demonstrate at every step of life the possibilities of thinking as a purpose-conferring and repurposable activity. Succinctly put, the common thesis underlying these programmatic philosophical practices is that, in treating thought as the artefact of its own ends, one becomes the artefact of thought's artificial realizabilities.[328] The field of experience—in

---

328 For introductions to the philosophies of ancient Cynicism, Stoicism, and Confucianism, see: W. Desmond, *Cynics* (Stocksfield: Acumen, 2006); J. Sellars, *The Art of Living: The Stoics on the Nature and Function of Philosophy* (Bristol: Bristol Classical Press, 2009); P.J. Ivanhoe, *Confucian Moral Self Cultivation* (Indianapolis: Hackett, 2000).

both its bodily and its minded dimension—can only be enlarged by pursuing the interests of thought.

This is one of the most potent achievements of philosophy: by formulating the concept of a good life in terms of a practical possibility afforded by the artificial manipulability of thinking as a constructible and repurposable activity, it forges a link between the possibility of realizing thought in the artefact and the pursuit of the good. The idea of the realization of thinking in artefacts can be presented as an expression of thought's demand to expand its realizabilities. Therefore it can be framed in the context of crafting a life that would satisfy a thought that demands the development of its possible realizabilities in whatever form or configuration possible—that is, a thought whose genuine intelligibility lies in the exploration of what it can be and what it can do.

The craft of an intelligent life-form that has at the very least all the capacities of the present thinking subject is an extension of the craft of a good life as a life suited to the subject of a thought that has expanded its inquiry into the intelligibility of the sources and consequences of its realization. To put it in another way, it is the design of a form of life appropriate and satisfying to the demands of a thought that has not only theoretical knowledge of its present instantiation (the intelligibility of its sources) but also the practical knowledge to bring about its possible realizabilities (the intelligibility of practices capable of unfolding its consequences). This is as much a thesis regarding a nonparochial conception of artificial general intelligence as it is a thesis about the realization of a sociohistorically conscious intelligence encompassing all forms of conceptualizing minds both past and present. It has now become apparent that, once philosophy's basic datum regarding 'the possibility of thinking as the artefact of its own ends' is elaborated, it amounts to the primary thesis of philosophy regarding the equality of all minds. Whatever or whoever recognizes the possibility of thinking as the basic datum for the construction of its life, becomes the artefact of thought's ends. And whoever or whatever becomes the artefact of thinking also becomes a commoner—equal to all others—of thought's impersonal ends and interests.

The second stage in demonstrating that thinking as an activity can indeed be artificialized involves a coherentist analysis of the nature of this activity. This analysis can be understood as an investigation into the sources or origins of the possibility of thinking (the different types of conditions necessary for its realization). Without this investigation, the elaboration and development of the consequences of thinking—its possible realizabilities—cannot gain momentum.

If thinking is an activity, then what is the internal logic or formal structure of this activity, how is it exercised, what does it perform, can it be analysed into other more rudimentary activities, and what are the mechanisms or processes that undergird these precursor activities? In posing such questions, the philosophically motivated inquiry into the intelligibility of thinking lays the groundwork for a broader analysis of the nature of the manifest activity we call thinking. In this way, philosophy's programmatization of thinking sets in motion the scientific inquiry into the nature of thinking.

Thinking is examined both in terms of its internal and special pattern-uniformities and in terms of the underlying and more general patterns in which these specificities are materially realized. In other words, the analysis of thinking as an activity encompasses two dimensions of thinking as a function: function in the sense of the internal pattern-uniformities of thinking, or rules, that make up the performance of the activity as such; and function in the sense of the mechanisms in which these rules or internal pattern-uniformities (i.e., the first sense of function) are materialized. The latter are always modelled on the former, and it is only by cohering and revising the former that the scope of the latter can be broadened.

Accordingly, the philosophical examination of the nature of thinking bifurcates into two distinct but integrable domains of analysis: the explication of thinking in terms of functions or the logico-linguistic roles its contents play (the normative qua rule-governed order of thinking as such); and the examination of materialities—in the general sense of natural and social mechanisms—in which this logico-conceptual structure in its full richness is realized (the causal order pertaining to the materialization of thinking).

To this extent, the philosophical program canalizes the inquiry into the possibility of thinking as a programmable and repurposable activity into two, broadly idealist-rationalist and materialist-empiricist naturalist, fields. In doing so, it lays out the framework for specialized forms of investigation informed by the priorities of these fields. Roughly, these are, on the one side, linguistic and logical examinations that focus on the semantic, conceptual, and inferential structure of thinking (the linguistic-conceptual scaffolding of thinking); and on the other side, empirical investigations dealing with the material conditions (neurobiological as well as sociocultural) required for its realization.

These trajectories can be seen as two vectors that deepen the intelligibility of thinking by analysing or decomposing its function into more fine-grained phenomena or activities within the logical and causal orders. Within this twofold analytic schema, phenomena or activities that were previously deemed unitary may appear to be separate, and those considered distinct may turn out to be unitary. The conceptual and causal orders are properly differentiated only to be revealed as converging on some fundamental elementary level. Thinking is shown to be possible not in spite of material causes and social activities but by virtue of *specific kinds* of causes and mechanisms. In this fashion, the deepening of the intelligibility of thinking as an activity joins the boundaries of these two fields, as the intelligibility of thinking—its realization—ultimately resides in an accurate integration—but not a homogenous fusion—of its logico-conceptual and material-causal dimensions.

DATUM 6. PHILOSOPHY AS AN ARCHIMEDEAN LEVER FOR LIFTING INTELLIGENCE AND MOVING THE WORLD

Viewed from an Archimedean point in the future of thought's unfolding, philosophy is seen as that which has instructed thinking to become a systematic program, only as a way of organizing it into a project for the emancipation of intelligence. This is the unexpressed role of philosophy as a fulcrum through which the aims and agendas of intelligence gain leverage on the world of thought. Assembling the scaffolding of a future philosophy requires that we move the fulcrum, turning philosophy's formerly tacit role into its explicit task—a prop on which all thoughts and practices can be a lever for lifting intelligence from its contingently established place.

As outlined earlier, the bifurcation of the inquiry into the possibility of thinking into two, broadly rationalist-idealist and naturalist-materialist, trajectories should also be construed as a necessary epistemic strategy. From an epistemic angle, the commitment to multiple explanatory-descriptive levels allows an expanded and in-depth analysis of the cognitive architecture in a fashion that would not be possible through an approach built on a single schema. A multimodal approach provides increasingly refined pictures of distinct types of pattern-governed behaviours and processes distributed across different orders of structural-functional complexity, dependency-relations, and their specific constraints. More explicitly put, the branching and canalization of the analysis—the specialization of knowledge that truly contributes to its complexity—is necessary for a fine-grained determination of distinctions and correlations between the logical-conceptual and causal-material dimensions of thinking.

It is through this fine-grained differentiation and integration of explanatory-descriptive levels that the conditions necessary for the realization of thinking as an activity that comprises a broad range of cognitive and intellectual abilities can be accurately specified. Determination of what these necessary conditions are and how they are arranged and effectuated is already a basic roadmap for the artificial realization of thought. As the intelligibility of thought's realization is progressively deepened, the thought of the possible realization of thinking in something other than its current instantiations becomes more intelligible. Yet that *something other* should be treated in the broadest possible sense, not merely in the sense of something other than biological homo sapience, but more comprehensively in the sense of something other than the sociohistorical moment that dissimulates itself as the totality of thought. The analytic specialization of the knowledge of what thinking is proves to be the knowledge of how thinking can be extricated from contingencies that restrain its realizabilities from below. Intelligence does not make itself by speculating and gawking into the sky above, but by releasing itself from what holds it back from below.

In a gesture analogous to the Newtonian revolution, intelligence systematically abolishes the illusory frontier that isolates its world *on high* from its world *below*, the cosmological from the terrestrial. Through the sciences of cognition (theoretical and practical) combined with the recognition of history as a condition that is both restricting and enabling, intelligence extricates itself from any realized totality that feigns the absolute. This is an intelligence whose course of maturation coincides with the impersonal ends of reason equipped with both sciences and technologies of cognition. The intelligence that inhabits the unnatural space of reason—a space that is neither natural nor supernatural—stands in contrast to any register of intelligence as a force of nature—a mythic intelligence that, under the much vaunted increasing complexification of nature, becomes a gateway for the return of its dogmatic repressed: an authoritarian account of nature which is only an excuse for the reinstallation of the monarchs of religion, politics, technology, and economy. It is no accident that the provocateurs of technological singularity and intelligence as the unstoppable vector of the complexification of nature also happen to be ardent ideologues of monarchy, race realism, social Darwinism, gender essentialism, nationalism, and other anti-emancipatory conspiratorial buffooneries.

If the activity we call thinking is realized by such-and-such functional capacities, and if these capacities can be analysed in terms of their realizers—the specific conditions, processes, and mechanisms required for their realization—then would it be possible to reconstruct or artificially realize such functions? In other words, would it be possible to reproduce and integrate these functional capacities through a combination of strategies that involve the simulation, emulation, or re-enactment of functions and/or their material realizers? More simply, if thinking is such-and-such and if it is materialized in thus-and-so mechanisms and processes, then how can it be reformed and rematerialized in something else?

This is the question that shapes the field of artificial general intelligence as a program seeking to integrate the intelligibility of different dimensions of thinking, in its full perceptual and apperceptive semantic complexity, under one ideal task: designing a system that has at the very least the complete package of human cognitive abilities with all the capacities that such abilities imply (diverse and comprehensive learning, different modalities and levels of knowledge and knowledge-use, reasoning, deliberation, belief formation independent of current perception, competencies enabled by different levels of semantic complexity as specialized and context-sensitive modes of computation, and so on).

Before moving forward, let us pause and question what is meant by the simulation, emulation, and reenactment of thinking. The technical definitions of these terms are beyond the scope of this book, yet without a minimal acquaintance with what these terms actually refer to, confusion will be inevitable. Simulation, emulation, and reenactment refer to three distinct processes for the artificial realization of behaviours. A simulation imitates some specific and outwardly observable aspects of the simulated system's behaviour, but is implemented in a different way. Simulation involves modelling the sufficient details of the underlying state of the system *singled out for the purpose of simulation*. Emulation, on the other hand, replicates the inner workings of the system being emulated and adheres to *all of its rules* in order to reproduce exactly the same *external behaviour*. The target of reenactment, on the other hand, is neither the imitation/reproduction of observable functional properties nor the replication of the inner workings of the system. Instead, a reenactment attempts to identify and reconstruct parameters under which the system structurally and functionally evolves through an ongoing interaction with its environment. Here the emphasis is on the coupling or interface between system and environment (the background information), the parameters of the real-time interaction, the type of interaction, and the situatedness of different behaviours and functional capacities. Behaviourism—the analysis of behaviours, whether causal or normative—is often approached by way of the simulation or emulation of outwardly observable behaviours. But all behaviours are the result of interactions between the system and its environment, between one agent and another. Therefore, they can only be genuinely realized by fine-grained methods of reenactment that distinguish between different types of interaction and interacting agents.

Rather than being considered as a pure vogue that serious thought should avoid entertaining, the core idea of artificial general intelligence should be seen as an integral part of thinking as a program that explores the intelligibility of its own realization and its ramifications. It is an integral part of a thought that is driven by the autonomy of its ends to explore its possible realizabilities in whatever workable form or material configuration possible. Giving rise to an intelligence that has, at least, the capacities of the present cognitive-practical subject is the demand of a thought that is invested in the intelligibility of its autonomy, and in maintaining and developing it. More emphatically put, for such a thought, the sources of its possibility are necessary but not adequate expressions of its autonomy, since the concrete autonomy of thought is achieved by thought's exploration of its ends or its Concept, its Notion. Accordingly, artificial general intelligence—in the fashion described here—belongs to a thought for which the adequate form of autonomy takes the shape of an all-encompassing striving for the elaboration of its ends and demands.

The real import of the idea of artificial general intelligence can only be properly understood once examined in terms of what it stands for or signifies in terms of the systematic striving of thought for self-determination. As described previously, this striving is encapsulated in the function of philosophy as a program through which thinking begins to determine its own intelligibility by elaborating, in theory and practice, the sources and consequences of its possibility. The organization of thought as a programmatic project starts with the recognition of the possibility of thinking as a building block for the construction or realization of a thought that is possible by virtue of its ends and demands and in spite of material or final causes, how it was originally materialized, and what it is supposedly ordained to be or do.

As a program, thinking is not just a practice but the construction of possible realizabilities of thought, a process that defines the self-determination of thought. Put differently, the self-determination of thinking requires a programmatic approach to the possibility of thinking as such: determining what it means for thinking to be possible and what the consequences of such a possibility are, by examining what thought really is and elaborating its tasks and abilities. Rather than treating the possibility of thinking as something sacrosanct in the name of the given and therefore off-limits to interrogation and intervention, philosophy instructs thought to system-atically act on its possibility as a manipulable datum, as an artefact of an ongoing craft the products of which are not only theoretical and practical intelligibilities concerning what thought is and what it ought to do, but also realizabilities of thought as such. Thought achieves self-determination not by immunizing itself against systematic analysis, but by bringing itself under a thoroughgoing process of desanctification.

Here, the artificial realization of general intelligence represents a neces-sary step in the process of the theoretical and practical desanctification of thinking, and therefore an essential component in thought's program of self-determination. This is a step at which, in order for thought to adequately expand on its possibility and express the autonomy of its ends, it has to construct artificial realizabilities of itself through the integration of different levels and orders of intelligibility concerning what it is and what it ought to do. But, once again, artificial realizabilities should not be construed as being limited to technological artefacts. In line with the definition of the artificial presented earlier in this chapter and more expansively in the first chapter, the artificial realizabilities of thought potentially include a wide range of functional constructs, including social systems.

To further clarify the role of artificial general intelligence as something integral to the systematic image of thinking as a programmatic project, it would be helpful to define the concept of the program outlined above in relation to what Wilfrid Sellars, in his reading of Plato's idea of the mind as a craftsman, calls a 'recipe'—a complex of intelligibilities (of both theory and practice) and purposive actions that make up the practice of a craft.[329] A recipe is a formula or a set of *what-and-how-tos* consisting of numbers, ratios, and purposive actions for making a possible product from a given collection of ingredients. In a recipe, actions take this general form:

---

329 See Plato's *Philebus, Timaeus, Phaedo*, and Book VI of the *Republic*. For Sellars's work on the craft of life as the rational pursuit of the form of the Good, see W. Sellars, 'The Soul as Craftsman: An Interpretation of Plato on the Good', in *Philo-sophical Perspectives* (Springfield, IL: Charles C. Thomas, 1967), 5–22; and 'Reason and the Art of Living in Plato', in *Essays in Philosophy and Its History*, 3–26.

'(If one wants) to make an O, then in C_i one ought to do A_j' (where O stands for a product, C_i the range of given circumstances or conditions in which a given set of actions may or may not be done, and A_j a particular family of action-principles).[330] These action-principles belong to the intelligible order and are objective. As such, the distinction between truth and falsity applies to them. They can be explained and debated, modified, or replaced through rational assessment in the relevant domains of discourse. In a recipe, numbers and ratios are specificities regarding the amount, ordering, and proportion of ingredients as well as the sequence and priority of actions. And finally, the ingredients of the recipe are materials and objects that may be the products of other forms of craft.

In his engagement with Plato, Sellars identifies action-principles and practices of craft as belonging to *phusis* (nature and objective ends), in contrast to *nomos* (law and convention or social norm, as opposed to the rational norm, which belongs to the objective realm). In Plato's account of craftsmanship, purposive actions are neither conventional nor arbitrary: they are rational strivings pertaining to forms as realms of intelligibilities (or what Sellars calls form as 'object-of-striving-ness' or 'to-be-realized-ness'). These actions or strivings belong to the intelligible order and can therefore be appraised. The example given by Sellars to explain the distinction between principle and convention is the process of house building. In building a house, the difference between principle by objective nature and convention by law would be the difference between, on the one hand, actions that ought to be done given a certain range of circumstances and material ingredients necessary to build a house, and, on the other hand, the conventions of a builder's guild, namely, codes and regulations for building a house. The principle takes the form of 'ought to do' whereas the convention takes the imperative form of 'do that!' In the best possible scenario, conventions and laws correspond to rational action-principles and their objective ends, but they can also significantly diverge from them, as in the case of a corrupt guild that might enforce laws demanding the use of materials to which only guild members have access.

---

330 Sellars, *Essays in Philosophy and Its History*, 9.

This difference between action-principles and action-conventions can be extended to other forms of craft, including the craft of the *polis*. It is precisely the rational nature of action-principles (i.e., the fact that they can be explained and subjected to the procedures of truth and rational assessment) that harbours a subversive potential against sociocultural and political conventions and codified laws.

The art of (philosophical) living, for Plato, is the recipe of a craft of which the soul or geistig mind is at once the material and the craftsman. At the level of ingredients, Sellars suggests, the recipe of such a life includes not only intelligibilities concerning physical materials and corporeal products but also beliefs, desires, thoughts, and mind itself. The numbers (amounts and orderings) and ratios of the recipe are theoretical intelligibilities that pertain both to the ingredients and to the practices and tasks required for the crafting of such a life. And at the level of actions, the recipe involves purposive actions and practical intelligibilities that are not only good instrumentalities (hypothetical practical intelligibilities concerning bringing about a certain outcome in a given circumstance) but also goods-in-themselves (nonhypothetical practical intelligibilities) such as knowledge and understanding, general welfare, justice, and so forth.

It is with reference to this interpretation that 'thinking as a program' can be said to be—at least in regard to the relation between material ingredients and theoretical and practical intelligibilities—a *complex recipe in the making, a recipe for the craft of the life of thought.* It is *complex* insofar as it is composed of other recipes or programs concerning the knowledge of theoretical and practical truths, the craft of different instrumentalities, and the organization or production of the necessary conditions and materials required for the realization of such a life. It is *in the making* since it has to continually update itself at the level of materials and that of theoretical and practical intelligibilities—themselves products of the life of thought. The objective of this recipe is to establish the autonomy of thought's ends by progressively determining how the action-principles, theoretical intelligibilities, instrumentalities, and material ingredients required for the product of this autonomy should be put together.

In this picture, what the idea of artificial general intelligence represents is a culminating state in the programmatic enterprise of thinking—a state where thought as such becomes intelligent with regard to the craft of itself. It uses the intelligibility of its realization as a material ingredient in a recipe for the crafting of a possible realization of itself that has at the very least the theoretical and practical capacities of its current state. Beneath its technological semblance, the idea of artificial general intelligence is an expression of a thought that engages in the crafting of itself by treating its possibility as a raw material or an expressively constructive fundamental universe type—a scaffolding for the labour or exercise (*ascesis*) of investigating (*skepsis*) and working out (elaboration) *what else* can be realized out of this possibility. Such thought places theoretical intelligibilities concerning *what it is* in the service of organizing practices and instrumentalities that involve the crafting of a thought that is possible in spite of how it was originally materialized or constituted.

This is precisely the self-determination of thought in the guise of general intelligence, a form of intelligence for which 'the thinking of its origin' should be placed in the service of 'what thought *can* become or do' by informing itself as to 'what thought *ought* to do'. It is an intelligence for which the intelligibility of things must be subordinated to the organizing intelligibility that is the process of its crafting itself: intelligence.

It is therefore necessary to grasp the concept of artificial general intelligence not merely as a technoscientific idea, but more fundamentally as a concept belonging to a thought or form of intelligence that treats its very possibility as an explicit opportunity to pierce through the horizon of its givenness: it does not matter what it currently is; what matters is what can be done—all relevant things considered—to expand and build on this possibility. This is first and foremost a philosophically programmed thought, in the sense in which philosophy has been defined above. Independently of its actual realization, which is neither inevitable nor impossible, the very idea of artificial general intelligence—of giving rise to something that is at the least endowed with all the cherished abilities of the cognitive-practical subject—is itself the product of a thought that strives to articulate, maintain, and develop the intelligibility of the sources and consequences of its possibility. The quest for the artificial realization of such a machine is then part of self-consciousness as a task: the quest of thinking to achieve concrete autonomy by overcoming any predetermined meaning or purpose conferred upon it extraneously.

Short of this understanding, advancing the idea of artificial general intelligence amounts to nothing but the well-worn Aristotelian confusion between reasons and causes, as today manifested by a vitalist eschatology with the flavour of technoscience. It leads either to the fetishization of natural intelligence in the guise of self-organizing material processes, or to a teleological faith in the deep time of the technological singularity—an unwarranted projection of the current technological climate into the future through the over-extrapolation of cultural myths surrounding technology or hasty inductions based on actual yet disconnected technological achievements.

To recapitulate, artificial general intelligence is not the champion of technology but a thought that, through a positive disenchantment of itself and its contingent history, has been enabled to explore its possible realizations and realizabilities—whether in a social formation or a multi-agent system of machines—as part of a much broader program of self-artificialization through which thought restructures and repurposes itself as the artefact of its own ends to maintain and expand its intelligibility. Just as the practice of thinking is non-optional for a thought that intends to remain intelligible, the practice of artificialization is not optional; it is mandated by the autonomy of thought's ends and demands.

The vocation of thought is not to abide by and perpetuate its evolutionary heritage but to break away from it. Positing the *essential role* of biology in the contingent evolutionary history of thought as an *essentialist* nature for thought dogmatically limits how we can imagine and bring about the future subjects of thought. But the departure from the evolutionary heritage of thought is not tantamount to a wholesale withdrawal from its natural history. Engaging with this natural history is necessary not only in order to determine the precise role of embodiment and evolutionary constraints in the realization of cognitive and practical abilities, but also in order to adequately think about how a subject whose cognitive-practical abilities are environmentally situated and which still remains entangled with its terrestrial habitat should methodically act.

Liberating thought from its contingent natural history requires a multi-stage labour to render this history intelligible, to determine its negative and positive constraints so as to intelligently overcome or build on them—'intelligently' insofar as actions should be at all times context-sensitive and resource-aware. On the one hand, actions should be able to properly discriminate circumstances and correctly react to the so-called *fluents* or dynamic properties of the environment. And on the other hand, they should be cognizant of the costs and allocations of intervention in the broadest sense of cognitive, computational, social, and natural costs and resources. For interventions have not only computational costs but also social and natural costs. A paradigm of intervention should be able to analyse the cost of practical interventions from the perspective of different indexes of cost or tractability: computational, natural, social, and even cultural-axiological (cultural values).

However, the demands of context-sensitivity and resource-awareness for action should not be taken as arguments for microlocalist models of restricted action or resignation in the name of low local resources and the high costs of nonlocal actions. Rather than a plea for micro-localism, context-consciousness is the requirement of a strategic and global model of action that incrementally progresses by satisfying contextual and domain-specific exigencies. It allows for action to be updated and to intervene at the level of dynamic properties and complex dependency-relations between local domains that classical models of strategy and global action cannot detect and influence. Similarly, resource-awareness is a requirement for any action that, in addition to being optimal and efficient, aims to avoid starving other activities of resources or impairing the social and environmental structures that play the role of support and enablement for a broad range of other structures and functions.

In its undeniable gravity, the problem of the deterioration of natural ecologies is undoubtedly an argument against bad instrumentalities and those systems within which such instrumentalities are ingrained and propagated. But it is neither an argument against instrumentality (not to be confused with instrumental reasoning) per se nor an argument against the development of sociotechnical systems that can effectively and intelligently mobilize good instrumentalities that are both resource- and context-conscious. Consequential intervention is impossible without the crafting of better instrumentalities (technical systems), more expansive models for the analysis of costs and resources, and, more significantly, without understanding the formal aspects of practical intervention (whether political or not) in terms of complexity sciences. If the world is complex then how can we possibly act or intervene in it without the science of complexity? Today any intervention that is not informed by complexity sciences is inevitably doomed to fail from the beginning.

A good instrumentality is an instrumentality that at once passes the test of rational-normative assessments (Why or for what reason is it implemented?) and satisfies the aforementioned criteria of intelligent purposive action (How exactly is it executed?). In the latter sense, crafting good instrumentalities is primarily a scientific and engineering program in which purposive action is approached as an interface between the complexity of cognition, the complexity of the sociotechnical system, and the complexity of the world. Such a program involves the development of formal calculi for executing and tracking the course of action in various dynamic domains, and for constructing complex models and descriptive frameworks or ontologies that allow *semantic access* to different layers of information regarding the types, properties, and interrelationships of particular entities involved in the interactions between human agents, the sociotechnical system, and the physical world.[331]

---

331 One of the main functions of these ontologies (particularly mid-level ontologies as briefly introduced in the second chapter) is to 'specify our conceptual hierarchy in a way that is general enough to describe a complex categorization including physical and social objects, events, roles and organizations' (Porello et al., 'Multiagent Socio-Technical Systems: An Ontological Approach', *Proc. of the 15th Int. Workshop on Coordination, Organisations, Institutions and Norms*, 2013). A sophisticated example of these ontologies is DOLCE (Descriptive Ontology for Linguistic and Cognitive Engineering), a mid-level or descriptive ontology that classifies and integrates information about human agents and social and physical systems according to categories that are

What motivates the development of formal calculi of action is simply the idea that the representation of our reasoning about our actions and their effects in the world should be as factually accurate as possible. Calculi of action are not so much tools for predicting what will arise from an action in the environment, as formal frameworks for studying how an action is performed and tracking its course as it interacts with an environment. Without such a formal representation, our descriptions of what it is that we do when we perform a simple or compound action would be highly inaccurate and distorted. Moreover, it is indispensable to study how the effects of an action unfold in the environment and to be able to reconstruct these actions in formalisms. The term 'formalism' here specifically refers to a formalization of action *in relation to* a world that is not simply a block of wax that can be moulded and imprinted by our actions, but a complex manifold that consists of different domains, has dynamic properties, and resists intervention. In other words, a formalism of action for dynamic complex systems.

The formalization of action is necessary for planning the course of action—for its precise execution, monitoring, adjustment, and implementation. But this formalization must also be able to incorporate a dynamic representation of the world, its domains, and the entities that constitute them. What I have in mind for the scientific study of action execution are various formal languages of action built on logical formalisms such as situation calculus and event calculus, devised for representing and reasoning about dynamic systems.[332] In these frameworks, actions are analysed in terms of the formal syntax of the action sequence and the semantics of situations

---

'thought of as cognitive artifacts ultimately depending on human perception, cultural imprints and social conventions'. For an introduction to ontologies and DOLCE, see C. Masolo et al., *The WonderWeb Library of Foundational Ontologies—Preliminary Report* (2003), <http://www.loa.istc.cnr.it/old/Papers/WonderWebD17V2.0.pdf>. And for an application of ontologies, particularly DOLCE, to the study and design of multi-agent sociotechnical systems, see Porello et al., 'Multiagent Socio-Technical Systems', 42–62.

332 See for example, R. Reiter, *Knowledge in Action: Logical Foundations for Specifying and Implementing Dynamical Systems* (Cambridge, MA: MIT Press, 2001).

or events that represent the progression of the dynamic world as the result of the action being performed on its *fluents* or dynamic properties. Even though these formalisms were primarily developed for modelling in robotics and systems engineering, their scope of application goes far beyond these fields. They are as much toolsets for artificial intelligence and robotics as they are indispensable components of a scientific armamentarium required for a political project that aims at the proper and effective execution of intervening actions.

The question of semantic access to different hierarchies of information is the question of understanding the logics of worlds as the primary step for the design and execution of robust and consequential action. But understanding the logics of worlds requires understanding how we say things or think about ourselves and the world using the expressive and conceptual resources of different disciplines and modes of thought. Precisely speaking, understanding the logics of worlds involves working out semantic relations between the different vocabularies or linguistic expressions (theoretical, deontic normative, modal, intentional, empirical, logical, and so forth) that we *use* in order to speak and think about ourselves and the world, just as it involves determining the activities necessary for using those vocabularies so as to count as expressing something with them.[333]

It is by understanding how we can adequately describe and explain ourselves and the world—through the use of different vocabularies and semantic relations between them and their properties—that we can consequentially change the world. Acting in the framework of such a program progressively blurs the boundaries between the cognitive engineering of autonomous agents and the construction of advanced sociotechnical systems, between

---

333 In *Between Saying and Doing*, Brandom analyses meaning(semantics)-use(pragmatics) relations in terms of what one says or asserts when using vocabularies or linguistic expressions, and what one must do in order to use various vocabularies so as to count as saying or thinking various kinds of things. One of the most interesting aspects of Brandom's project is that this way of thinking about semantic complexity and the activities required for generating it presents consequential practical schemas for both the project of artificial general intelligence and an egalitarian pedagogical politics (see chapter 3, 'Artificial Intelligence and Analytic Pragmatism').

how we can adequately come into cognitive contact with the world and the realization of cognition in social collectivities and technological artefacts. As the semantic complexity of cognition is realized in, and reinforced by, the sociotechnical system, the sociotechnical complexity of our world adequately gains traction upon the world and is enriched by it.

DATUM 7. CRAFTING THE ULTIMATE FORM

Just as the inception of philosophy coincides with the speculative futures of general intelligence, so its ultimate task corresponds with the ultimate form of intelligence.
By prompting thought to grapple with itself from below, philosophy drives thought to confront itself from above. It instructs thinking to organize itself as an integrated bundle of action-principles—a program—for the craft of a thought that is the materialization of its ends and demands. In presenting itself as a form of thought that operates and builds on the possibility of thinking, philosophy cues thought to act and elaborate on the intelligibility of its possibility. Thinking becomes a programmatic enterprise that, from one end, deepens the intelligibility of its sources and, from the other, articulates in theory and practice the intelligibility of its consequences. In articulating the intelligibility of its consequences, thought brings about a conception of itself as an intelligence that seeks to liberate itself by unbinding its possible realizabilities. This is the picture of thought as an intelligence that finds its freedom in bringing about and liberating a realization of itself that has as *its starting point* all of its current capacities.

It is in relation to this expansive horizon of thought's unfolding that we can finally answer the questions posed at the beginning of this chapter: What kind of program is philosophy and what does it do? The answer is that, in its perennial form and at its deepest level, philosophy is a program for the crafting of a new species or form of intelligence—a form of intelligence whose minimum condition of realization is a complex and integrated framework of cognitive-practical abilities that could have been materialized by any assemblage of adequate mechanisms and causes, in other words mind or geist as investigated in the previous chapters. But this is only an initial state of its realization. What comes next is an intelligence that formats its life into an exploration of its possible realizabilities by engaging with the questions of what to think and what to do.

Philosophy is a program for the crafting of precisely this kind of intelligence—an intelligence that organizes itself into a programmatic project in order to give rise to its possible realizabilities in any form or material configuration, even if they might in every respect transcend it. The future of this intelligence will only be radically asymmetrical with its past and present conditions if it embarks on such an enterprise, if it develops a program for bringing about its realizabilities. It can only rise above its initial state (the minimum conditions necessary for the realization of mind or general intelligence) if it begins to act on its possibility as something whose origins and consequences must be rendered intelligible. It can only emancipate itself if it subordinates the theoretical intelligibility of its sources and its history (what it is made of, where it has come from) to that organizing practical intelligibility that is the purposive craft of itself. In this sense, it can be said that the beginning of philosophy is a starting point for the speculative futures of general intelligence.

In whatever form and by whatever mechanisms it is materialized, this form of intelligence can only develop a conception of itself as a self-cultivating project if it engages in something that plays the role of what we call philosophy, not as a discipline but as a program of combined theoretical and practical wisdoms running in the background of all of its activities. An important feature of this hypothetical general intelligence (the geistig) is that it no longer merely acts intelligently, but asks what to think and what to do considering the kind of intelligence it is or takes itself to be. Thus its actions are not merely responses to particular circumstances, or time-specific means for pursuing ends that are exhausted once fulfilled. More predominantly, the purposive actions of this intelligence originate from and are guided by a unified system of ever-present though revisable theoretical and practical truth-candidate statements concerning what it is and what it ought to do, its form and the life that suits it. In other words, its actions, even when they are pure instrumentalities, are manifestations of time-general thoughts about the inexhaustible ends of what counts as a life that suits it.

Let us briefly clarify this point: the form of intelligence that is the craft of philosophy—a thought that takes the possibility of thinking seriously—is not called intelligence because it exhibits those intelligent behaviours that are prevalent in nature. This point has been repeated so often that it should by now be obvious. The actions of this intelligence on which all intelligent behaviours are epistemically modelled are not simply intelligent responses to particular circumstances. The actions of this intelligence arise from what Hegel calls the order of self-consciousness, which is the order of reason. Within this order, even though all actions respond to circumstances and fulfil particular ends, they are nevertheless issued from a species of ends or thoughts that are time-general thoughts of self-consciousness. They are atemporal and atopic, of nowhen and nowhere, and are therefore akin to timeless or eternal ideas. Such actions not only fall under time-general ends or thoughts of self-consciousness (those of a thought recognizing and realizing its possibility), but also exhibit these ends in their very circumstantial particularity. Accordingly, in their variation all actions of this intelligence are identical to the time-general thoughts from which they are issued.

Time-general thoughts are those that are not tied to a specific moment or a particular circumstance—for example, the thought of staying healthy or the thought of being free in contrast to the thought of avoiding rotten food or the thought of social struggle at a particular juncture of history. Inexhaustible ends refer to those ends that are *premises* for actions rather than their conclusions. They differ from ends whose needs go away once they are reached and concluded by a particular action or pursuit (such as healthiness and freedom in the above example).[334]

Take for instance a general end that belongs to the geistig order of self-consciousness or reason, such as being just. Under this inexhaustible time-general end, at one point I choose to assist a friend rather than working on this book. Another time, I choose to prioritize the interests of a group over my ideological convictions so that we can stand against something we all deem to be unjust. While all these circumstantial choices of action

---

334 For a remarkably painstaking disquisition on time-generality and logical forms of temporal thought, see Rödl, *Categories of the Temporal.*

lead to particular ends which, once reached, are exhausted, they are all issued forth from an inexhaustible end, the idea of justice. But even more radically, these choices are only intelligible to the extent that they both fall under and exhibit time-general inexhaustible ends. Put differently, they are intelligible as choices only insofar as they belong to the objective unity of time-general ends, which itself belongs to the order of reason. These time-general ends or thoughts are the necessary forms for the intelligibility of our choices and purposive actions.

As agents and experiencing subjects, we also have synthetic thoughts. Our intuitions are sensible rather than intellectual, and thus have the quality of temporal successiveness, of taking time and appearing to be in time. This allows us to formulate concrete theoretical and practical thoughts that pertain to particular whens and wheres, contexts and situations. But such temporal theoretical and practical thoughts are held together by and indeed exhibit or instantiate thoughts that are atemporal and atopic in so far as they belong to aspects of the *idea* of what we take ourselves to be and what we ought to do in accordance with that idea qua program, time-generally. In line with the arguments presented in the previous chapters on the view from nowhere and nowhen, then, while as a matter of objective constraints and methodological necessities we are bound to temporal and circumstantial thoughts, we are also *unbound* by atemporal and atopic thoughts.

Time-general thoughts or inexhaustible ends define the practical horizon of this form of intelligence. The thoughts of this intelligence concerning 'what to do and why' are dependent on its time-general thoughts and indeed derive from them. Accordingly, its practical horizon has a unity in the sense that its practical reasons and actions are undergirded and structured by the unity of time-general thoughts and their principles.

Moreover, not only are the strivings of this intelligence not bound to exhaustible ends, or ends which are *explained by* the order of practical rea-soning—thoughts of what to do and their corresponding actions—they are also in conformity with its inexhaustible ends, ends which are themselves the *source* and *explanation* of its practical reasons and actions. In other words, this intelligence reasons and acts *from* time-general and inexhaustible ends, rather than towards them. It is not only that its actions fall under the concepts of such ends, but more importantly that, in determining what to do in a particular situation, its actions manifest the bearing of these ends upon that situation.

But above all, the most defining feature of this intelligence is that its life is not simply an intelligent protraction of its existence, but the crafting of a good or satisfying life. And what is a satisfying life for such a form of intelligence if not a life that is itself the crafting of intelligence as a complex multifaceted program comprising self-knowledge, practical truths, and unified striving?

As a part of the recipe for the crafting of a good life, the self-knowledge of this intelligence is a multistage open-ended reflection on the sources and consequences of its possibility. Its practical truths concern what qualifies as a good life based on a self-knowledge that is not limited to an inquiry into its realized state or what it is now, but also involves the examination of its possible realizabilities. Rather than being grounded on a mere form of dignified opinion or belief about what and how things appear to be, its practical knowledge is based on the *consideration of all relevant things for what they really are* as the conclusive reason for doing something or pursuing one course of action over another.[335] Finally, the striving of this intelligence is a unified collection of different patterns and orders of activities that contribute to the objective realization of the good life in that comprehensive sense of what satisfies it on different levels and brings about its realizabilities.

Satisfying lives and enabling realizabilities are two inseparable expressions of an intelligence whose time-general thoughts concerning *what is good for it* (or self-interest) are only *premises* for the program of crafting a good life. This is a program that is at once an inquiry into the nature of that intelligence (what it is), the examination of what a good life for it consists in (what is good for it), and a unified striving for the objective realization of such a life (how such self-interest can be adequately conceived, and thus

---

335 For more details on practical reasoning, rational motivation, and knowledge, see W. Sellars, 'On Knowing the Better and Doing the Worse', in *Essays in Philosophy and Its History*, 27–43.

satisfied). It is what Plato considers to be a concrete determination of 'the condition (*hexis*) and disposition (*diathesis*) of soul which can make life happy (*eudaimona*) for all human beings'.[336]

The satisfying life is a combined life of various ingredients, ratios or measures, intelligibilities and concrete practices. It is also a mixed life of pleasure and intelligence. But it is only a mix of both in so far as it is a recipe concocted by intelligence or the general category of mind, thinking, knowledge, and skills. There would be no mixed or multifaceted life if thought were not both the ingredient and the craftsman that integrates pleasure with intelligence. Only a pleasure that is part of the recipe of intelligence can become not only an integral part of intelligence but more like it:

> Still, I will not champion intelligence for the prize against the combined life, but we must decide what to do about the second prize. It may be that each of us will claim his own candidate as responsible for this combined life—I intelligence, you pleasure—so that while neither is the Good, one might claim that one of them is responsible for it. On this point, I should be even readier to contest Philebus. I should hold that in the mixed life, whatever it is that makes the life at once desirable and good, it is intelligence, not pleasure, that is more closely related to it and more nearly resembles it.[337]

For an intelligence whose criterion of self-interest is truly itself—i.e., the autonomy of intelligence concomitant with the knowledge of what it is—the ultimate objective ends are the maintenance and development of that autonomy, and the liberation of intelligence through the exploration of what it means to satisfy the life of thought. The striving of this intelligence for the Good (*agathos*) is neither adequate nor in its true self-interest if it does not culminate in bringing about that which is better than itself. The philosophical test of this hypothetical general intelligence is not an

---

336 Plato, *Philebus* (Oxford: Oxford University Press, 1975), §11d4–6.

337 Ibid., §22d5–5.

imitation game or a scenario of complex problem solving, but the ability to bring about an intelligence that in every respect is better, adequately conceived.

This categorical and ultimate test of general intelligence, what might be called the *agathosic test*, does not ask whether one can solve the frame problem or make a good cup of coffee (something that programmed machines already do better than the *experiencing* subject, a barista with a taste for good coffee), but rather '*Can you make something better than yourself?*' It is not even necessary for it to actually do so; even conceiving the idea of making something better and pursuing it would count as passing the test of general intelligence. What is meant by 'the better' will be elaborated later in this chapter; for now let us keep it to the most minimal criterion, as outlined above: that which has all the theoretical and practical capacities of the cognitive agent, and even more. The claim here is that only an intelligence that has taken its possibility as a premise for the elaboration of the consequences of that very possibility—that is, an intelligence embodying the general function of philosophy—can pass the test of general intelligence.

It is necessary to understand the good life of this intelligence as a life for which the good—both as a concept grasped through an extended critical examination and as the object of a unified rational striving—has both satisfying effects and profoundly transformative ramifications. For the form of intelligence for which philosophy is a program of realization, the crafting of a good life adequately conceived is synonymous with the crafting of intelligence that represents the better. Within the scope of crafting a good life, the relations between the satisfaction of intelligence and the transformation of intelligence, between happiness and rigorous striving, attending to the intelligence already realized and constructing its future realizabilities, the cultivation of the present subject of thought and the development of a cognitive-practical subject that in every aspect might surpass the current one, are neither unilateral nor arbitrary. In fact, these relations exist as necessary connections established by the objective and rational principles of the crafting of a good life between the different mutually reinforcing activities and tasks integral to it. One of the functions of philosophy is to highlight these objective and logical connections between partially autonomous or even seemingly incompatible tasks and activities that constitute the good life as a complex *unified* striving that has different levels and types of objectives.

Only by working out these connections in reference to the objective ends of the good life and what is necessary for its concrete realization does it become possible to methodologically prioritize different tasks and activities, and to coordinate and subordinate them to one another. And it is precisely a methodological ordering—rather than a prioritization on the basis of a general and vague idea of importance—that is necessary for the unification of different activities and tasks in that striving which is the concrete and objective realization of a good life.

The ultimate form of intelligence is the artificer of a good life—that is to say, a form of intelligence whose ultimate end is the objective realization of a good life through an inquiry into its origins and consequences in order to examine and realize what would count as satisfying for it, all things considered. It is through the crafting of a good life that intelligence can explore and construct its realizabilities by expanding the horizons of what it is and what can qualify as a satisfying life for it. The crafting of a good life is exactly that philosophically conceived program in which theoretical intelligibilities concerning *what is already realized* are subjected to the practical intelligibilities pertaining to its possible realizations. The exploration of the former realm of intelligibilities is translated into an intelligence that explores its realizabilities in any form or configuration possible.

For a form of intelligence that engages in the crafting of a good life, the project is as much about investigating the subject of the good life (what kind of intelligence it really is and what its realizabilities are) as it is about the examination of what a good life for this intelligence consists in and what it would take to objectively realize it. Therefore, for this kind of intelligence, politics or its equivalent must not only supply the necessary conditions, means, and actions for the objective realization of a good life; it must also internalize the aforementioned inquiry into what the subject of a good life—that subject for and on behalf of which politics acts—is. Accordingly, an intelligence that is concerned about its life and its realizabilities must at all times subject every political project to an altered version of that most vexing question of philosophy: 'Just what exactly is it that you are trying to do and accomplish?'[338] The altered version of this question is: What *sort of a good life* for *what kind of subject* or type of intelligence are you trying to realize, and exactly how?

No matter how committed it is to the present and the future, a political project that cannot coherently answer this question is hardly anything more than a glorified pedlar of mere instrumentalities, or a merchant of promised miracles. The criterion of coherence in the context of this question is threefold: (1) A political project should be able to articulate in theory and practice what the objective realization of a good life requires (theoretical intelligibilities, organized intelligent actions, the necessary conditions—economic, social, technological, and so forth—required for the realization of a good life and how it can provide them). (2) It should be committed to and informed by an inquiry not only into what the subject of this good life is and what type of intelligence it embodies, but also into the possible realizabilities of that form of intelligence or subject of thought. (3) Finally, it should be able to give a reasoned answer as to what qualifies as satisfying for that form of intelligence or subject of thought, all things considered. A political project that fulfils these criteria is a politics that,

---

338 This question is often attributed to Socrates and his distinctly philosophical attitude. Rather than dismissing or discrediting the activities of his fellow Athenians, by posing this question Socrates attempted to force the interlocutors into making explicit their incoherent or incompatible thoughts and commitments. This is what Brandom calls the 'dark and pregnant' core of expressive rationalism inaugurated by the Socratic method (*Making It Explicit*, 106–7) and what Michel Foucault associates with the attitude of Socrates as a philosophical parrhesiast (truth-teller) rather than a political one. In avoiding a political life, Socrates establishes the critical distance necessary to interrogate and assess political means and ends. He justifies his death in the service not of politics, but rather in the service of a philosophical life that unremittingly interrogates politics. See M. Foucault, *The Courage of the Truth*, tr. G. Burchell (Basingstoke: Palgrave Macmillan, 2011). And for a more elaborate engagement with this Socratic question, see C. P. Ragland and S. Heidt, 'The Act of Philosophizing', in *What Is Philosophy?* (New Haven: Yale University Press, 2001).

in bringing about the good life, also rethinks and changes the nature of the political animal.

This is not to insist that political praxis should be submitted to the diktats of philosophy or theory in general. It is rather to emphasise the plain fact that theory and praxis are mutually reinforcing and inextricable. The idea that real or material conditions disclose themselves through struggle or political praxis without conceptual and cognitive resources stems from an impoverished conception of materialism in which the real or the material can be determined independently of the dimension of structure or conceptualization. Struggle within such a framework is no more than fighting for unintelligibility and subjectivist dogmas. Changing the world cannot be imagined without the cognitive struggle to change our concepts.

Similarly, the idea that political struggle can materialize and continue simply by virtue of the multiplicity of experiences and desires, in the absence of or in autonomy from theory, philosophical and scientific methods of analysis, or conceptual tools is a practical legacy of naive empiricism which takes experience as immediate, fundamental, and independent of conceptual mediation. Political struggle should be responsive to the multiplicity of individual experiences and desires, but responsiveness does not imply conformity. For such experiences and desires can indeed be the very products of the pathological system that the political struggle seeks to change or abolish. Lived experiences *by themselves* can neither recognize what unites them in their very particularity nor diagnose the global pathological conditions that furtively divide them. The diagnosis of the real constraints of the world in which we struggle, the tracking of our goals and missions—whether we have reached them or not—is impossible without theory or philosophy as critical modes of thinking invested in impersonal objectivity and in the universal capacities of reason.

A veritable struggle should aim at seeing the world—the milieu of struggle—objectively, with the understanding that what is objective does not spontaneously unfold itself before us, but is the product of an ongoing cognitive labour. Enlarging the general field of experience in order to expand the scope of what is objective so as to incorporate and augment objectivity within individual thoughts and desires—the task of concrete self-consciousness or the craft of the good life—is not an undertaking that can be delegated to either philosophy, science, or politics. It entails a unification and coordination of all disciplines of thought and practice.

By comparing ourselves with this hypothetical general intelligence for which the craft of the good life and intelligence are one and the same, we may say that rethinking ourselves and rethinking what counts as a good life for us can only go hand in hand. In giving up on the universal and time-general thought of a good life and the striving necessary to achieve it, dismissing it as an anthropocentric illusion or an outdated fantasy, we neither rescue ourselves from an ancient philosophical superstition nor gesture toward a disillusioned politics. We instead passively hand the idea of the Good over to the most pernicious ideologies and political projects active on this planet. The immediate outcome of this surrender is the downgrading of the good life into the convenient market of on-demand lifestyles where mere survival glossed over with the triumphs of quotidian exploits is passed off as happiness, and the ego-exhibitionism of trivial psychological needs and entrenched dogmas is promoted in the guise of individual empowerment and freedom.

Yet more detrimentally, in dispensing with the thought of a good life and resigning from the collective striving it entails, we create a political vacuum in which fundamentalisms and theocracies parasitically thrive. To dismiss the universal demands of a good life as superstitious ideals is to grant superstitions authority over such demands. Abandoning the cognitive and practical labour of the good life as a universal collective project on the grounds of potential abuses and possible risks is a license for abuse and a sure formula for disaster.

The striving for a good life as a concrete universal consists of theoretical and practical intelligibilities, and thus explanatory, descriptive, and prescriptive norms required for determining what we are, what is good for us, and how we should bring it about. The ambit of such striving necessitates the rational dialectic between trust and suspicion, hope and despair; it requires that we invest in the cultivation of agency as a collective project that outlives its individual agents, and that we recognize the limitations of ourselves as agents living here and now. Suspicion without trust is the impoverishment of critique; trust without rational suspicion is the bankruptcy of belief. What underpins this dialectical resilience is neither ideological rationalization nor the absence of reason, but the discursive framework of rationality as the medium of both suspicion *and* trust. Without it, the slide into jaded pessimism or naive optimism is inevitable.[339]

DATUM 8. THE YEARNING FOR THE BETTER

The task of humanity is to make something better than itself. This is the one and only dictum through which philosophy, as that which has a history and not a nature, perilously realizes its craft, the ultimate form of intelligence. The risks it takes in order to understand and realize the good culminate in the realization of that which is better. The image of this form of intelligence is an acrobat who has learned that only by presupposing his full suspension in the abyss can he perform the greatest feats of acrobatics.

Through what is arguably the most enigmatic yet innocuous diagram ever plotted, the analogy of the divided line, Plato presents a curious picture of the Good in which intelligence, the pursuit of the Good, and risk are necessarily intertwined. In grasping the intelligibility of itself, intelligence coincides with the Good; but not until it has begun to perform a series of necessary leaps into the abyss of the intelligible. As the leaps grow in distance or proportion, they become riskier. Absent these leaps—'the acrobatics of the transcendental'[340]—there would be no intelligibility, no nature, no universe of being and no intelligence. Only that which leaps recognizes the reality of the abyss and the abyss of reality.

Perhaps the best way to approach the analogy of the divided line is by examining it in light of Plato's later work, particularly *Philebus* and what has come to be known as one of the most demanding arguments in the entire body of Platonic dialogues: the fourfold regime or the fourfold architectonics of mind. Socrates begins the discussion with a rather elliptical dictum: 'Let us make a division of everything—i.e. the universe of flux of things,

---

339 See Brassier, 'Dialectics Between Suspicion and Trust'.

340 I owe this term to Adam Berg.

sensations and perceptions—that presently exists (*panta ta nun onta en to panti*).'[341] It is through this division that the necessary link between intelligence and the intelligible, structure and being, can be articulated—and more importantly, the question of what is a good life coherently answered. This division consists of four principles:

(1) *to apeiron*: the unlimited or the indeterminate, without measure (*ametros*) which is by itself unintelligible (*anous*), for example, as in less and more, e.g., vague *sensations* of cold or hot.

(2) *to peras* (the limiting, or, in a less perplexing and more contemporary term, that which determines or structures). Logoi and language as that which brings the fleeting flux of things to 'a standstill' are associated with *to peras* or the determining principle.[342]

(3) *mikton* or mixture, which is produced as the result of the operation of *to peras* on *to apeiron*. A mixture, accordingly, is that which is determinate, objective, structured, and intelligible in the encompassing sense of theoretical, practical, and axiological intelligibilities. As such, Plato equates the mixture with that which is good. Mixtures are then good entities or intelligibilities ranging from things to thoughts, actions, and states of affairs. Furthermore, the mixture can be grasped both as a product and a process of mixing that requires a complex of measurements (modes of determination) and ratios (modes of organizations). There can be a mixture of mixtures such as the good life, which is at once a product of intelligibilities and a process of cultivating intelligence and expanding the horizon of the intelligible.

(4) the cause of mixture: In *Philebus*, Socrates both associates this cause with Forms and identifies the 'making cause' (*to poioun*) with

---

341 Plato, *Philebus*, §23c.
342 Plato, *Theaetetus*, §157b7.

the neutral name *to dēmiurgoun* rather than with the creator or *dēmiurgos*. *To dēmiurgoun* is essentially the principle of generation and craftsmanship—at a grand scale and in accordance with Forms or Ideas—in which the distinction between the craftsman and the exercise of his craft fades away. Plato identifies the cause of the mixture or intelligibilities with the Good itself, but also with the measuring or conceptualizing mind as that which is *akin to* the Good itself.[343] It is *akin to* the Good since, while the human mind or intelligence is the making cause of intelligibilities (mixed or good entities), it is also itself a mixture of ingredients proper to that comprehensive form of craft which is a good life of intelligibilities. That is to say, the human mind or intelligence is at once a craftsman, the exercise of the craft, and an ingredient in its own craft. Or, more simply, it is a craft-as-product (*mikton*) in the process of being produced. Here, then, Plato foreshadows Hegel's thesis that the mind is the only thing that has a concept of itself and which, by establishing and expanding the objectivity of its concept, objectively and concretely transforms itself.

This architectonics allows us to see existent things (particulars) not as products of sensations or of the apeironic flux, but as products of general forms or ideas. We can give an intuitive example via Euclid's *Elements*. Firstly there is the idea of triangularity as such, or what Proclus might have called a detached generality or universality irreducible to all particulars.[344] Then there is the intermediating universal—e.g., an isosceles triangle—connecting the oneness of the detached universal to the multiplicity of particular isosceles triangles. Thirdly, there are intermediating particulars, which are

---

343 See Donald Davidson's disquisition on Plato's fourfold and the human mind as the Good itself: D. Davidson, *Plato's Philebus* (London: Routledge, 1990).

344 Proclus, *A Commentary on the First Book of Euclid's Elements*, tr. G.R. Morrow (Princeton, NJ: Princeton University Press, 1970); and O. Harari, 'Methexis and Geometrical Reasoning in Proclus Commentary on Euclid's Elements', *Oxford Studies in Ancient Philosophy* vol. 30 (2006), 361–89.

explicit configurations or diagrams—e.g., isosceles triangles with such-and-such bases, angles, etc.—that mediate between intermediating generalities and discrete particulars. And finally, there are discrete particulars—i.e., thus-and-so relationships between lines, points and angles—which are only particulars by virtue of falling under higher-order generalities. The diagram of the divided line exhibits precisely such a multilevel view expressing the undergirding principle of the fourfold architectonics.

The fact that the allegory of the cave is flanked by two expositions of the divided line should be sufficient reason to dismiss the common interpretations of the cave as a myth about the existence of a 'fundamental ground' or a metaphor about the sun as 'the very essence of purity'[345] as nothing but exercises in the hermeneutic bigotry and cognitive lethargy common to all intellectual platitudes. The instruction for drawing the divided line is simple: 'Take a line divided into two unequal sections, and cut each section again *in the same ratio* (*ana ton auton logon*)'. The diagram of this successively and proportionally encoded structure (*analogon*) can be visualized as follows:

A	B	C	D

Where the ratio between segments is A : B = C : D or, more accurately, C + D : A + B = D : C = B : A and C + D : A + B = D : B = C : A. The segments can be thought of as levels of a game, or topoi or local boundaries through which the continuum of the line flows. Level A is the level of suppositional opinions or conjectures (*eikasia*) and consists of shadowy images, the confusion of sensory impressions (*eikones*) with a fleeting temporal status. The second level B (*pistis*) is the domain of true opinions or beliefs concerning the natural furniture of the world (sense-intuited or particular empirical objects, *aisthêta*). The realm of forms begins with level C, which is

---

345 See F. Nietzsche, 'Beyond Good and Evil', in *Basic Writings of Nietzsche* (New York: Modern Library, 1968), 414; and N. Land, *The Thirst for Annihilation* (London: Routledge, 1992), 28.

intermediate between that which is sensible, transitory, and multiple and that which is timeless, universal, and necessary (Level D). C is the domain of universal ratiocinations or logoi. Its objects are analytical idealities or *mathêmatika*. Insofar as C has both the universality and unchanging aspects of D and the particularity (or multiplicity) of the objects in B, mathematics or analytic idealities can be seen as models that endow nature with structure (A and B).[346] Level D—the realm of the *nous* or intelligence—is the domain of transcendental idealities; its objects are the time-general objects of reason or ideas as such (justice, beauty, knowledge, etc.).

The continuum of the line as a whole (*systēma*) and as a principle (*to dēmiurgoun*)—and not merely level D—is what Plato calls the Good, the *form of forms*. The Good is that which lies outside of all temporal succession; yet, in a nonarbitrary manner, it also binds together all the divided parts into a whole without which nothing could be distinguished from anything else. It is a figure of time itself conceived through the history of intelligence *as that which makes intelligibilities and determinations possible yet also posits a whole in which the temporal order of things and synthetic thoughts are conditioned and crafted by timeless forms or time-general thoughts that are of nowhere and nowhen.* This is the Good as the principle by which the whole of the line can be drawn, encompassing ontological, epistemological, and axiological intelligibilities, for which different measures or rules and methods of determination and structuration need to be in place.

The temptation has often been to read the divided line as a temporal order either on the basis of the successive flux of sensations in A, or that of a linear progression from the realm of nature to the realm of forms (from A to D). But this is a mistake, for it reduces the larger segment D to the smaller segment A—another variation of the myth of the given qua data supplied by nature. What structures the sensory flux are not sensations but forms (D). Despite its apparent plausibility, the temporal progression

---

346 'Plato did not mathematize metaphysics, but, rather he grounded it metaphysically, and so employed mathematics analogically to do metaphysics.' G. Reale, *Toward a New Interpretation of Plato* (Washington, D.C.: Catholic University of America Press, 1997), 161.

from A to D is also implausible since A, B, and C then would be presented as intelligibilities that are already truth-givens.[347]

The divided line begins from an atemporal point of view, from the timeless domain of transcendental idealities and time-general thoughts (Level D). The site of intelligence as that which acts on the intelligible and crafts what is Good (the continuum of the line as a whole) is the atemporal segment D. In this sense, intelligence introduces itself as that which structures all of *objective* reality (A, B, C and D). The reality of perceptual images (*eikones*) is only posited once intelligence organizes the sensory flux, by introducing pure perspectival phenomenal successions or flows—the shadows on the wall of the cave which appear to be replacing one another, moving, fading, and differing in their degree of vividness. The reality of phenomenal appearances (Level B) can only become intelligible when intelligence posits the unity of the object qua perceptual invariance holding together pure phenomenal successions or local variations, presumably through Level C (analytical idealities). And correspondingly, Level C (the level of *mathêmatika*) can only emerge from the universality of D when contrasted and made continuous (the procedure of analogy or *ana-logon*) with the particularities of B. Thus, from the perspective of the diagram, intelligence not only retroactively structures its reality according to a view from nowhere and nowhen (Level D) but also posits in advance the reality of all that is from the domain of transcendental ideas and time-general thoughts by positing one type of epistemically organizing unity after another: firstly a unity that organizes the confusion of the sensory flux, secondly the unity of the object behind phenomenal appearances, and thirdly the unity of the universal, necessary, and unchanging as introduced to the unity of particular objects in their multiplicity.

In her remarkable work on Plato, Rosemary Desjardins elaborates this point with peculiar astuteness. The following citation is merely the beginning of her argument:

---

347 Giovanni Reale proposes that the internal structure of the divided line should in fact be thought as a complex vertical hierarchy with asymmetrical and transitive relations between intermediating levels. Reale, *Toward a New Interpretation of Plato*, 162.

Faced with the multiplicity of 'many' perceptual images, we actually look for—no, more significantly, we insist on—unity, asserting that beneath the shifting 'many' there is in reality 'one', that multiple perceptual images belong to single entities. Similarly, faced with the diversity of 'different' perceptual images, we look for—or rather, again insist on—sameness, asserting that beneath the difference it is in fact 'the same', that different perceptual images belong to the same entity. The question is, how can we do this? How is it that, given multiplicity, we can assert unity? given differentness, we can assert sameness? In short, what justifies our assertion that beneath the multiplicity and differentness of those sensory perceptions there is something which, as enduring object, really remains one, and the same?

Plato's answer seems to be that—in a leap which, if it were not so familiar to us, would surely boggle the mind—we actually posit a radically new kind of reality. 'Posit' (*tithēmi*) is, interestingly enough, the term Plato has Socrates use when, drawing on the proportionality of the Line, he reminds his friends of discussions 'before and often on other occasions' thereby highlighting a parallel between the processes that allow us to move through the levels of the Divided Line [...].[348]

Intelligence posits the objective reality of that which is, and in doing so retroactively recognizes its conditions of realization. The first operation is a leap from the atemporal domain of ideas into the realm of the sensible (from D to A: the organization of the sensory flux), the second a leap—the power of knowing afforded by the transcendental dimension of ideas—that retroactively recognizes how the ideas are linked to the sensible (from A to D). But as the leaps from the simple reality of the sensory flux to the formal reality of ideas grow proportionally larger, as the positing of a more cohesive reality requires a greater leap over the sectors of the line, as the expanse of what is intelligible broadens, the risks become greater, and there is much more to lose by a misjudged leap. What is at stake now is not the body of intelligence but its very idea. Yet it is only through these

---

348 R. Desjardins, *Plato and the Good* (Leiden: Brill, 2004), 61.

leaps (positing the measures of all reality and the retroactive recognition of its realization as such) that intelligence can bind together and cohere the divided parts—an operation without which there would be no intelligible reality and no realization of intelligence.

The principle necessary for the division and integration of the segments is exactly what Plato calls the Good. For Plato, the Good makes intelligible all of reality, as well as acting on the intelligible. Absent the Good, the indeterminate homogeneity of the apeiron cannot be differentiated, nor can the reality (i.e., identities and differences) of existent things be determined—they all become unintelligible or, as Gorgias would have said, nonexistent. In other words, the line can never be divided and the divided segment can never be integrated, and therefore both the intelligible and intelligence must succumb to impossibility. Intelligence is that which acts on the intelligible, and the intelligible is that which is differentiated and integrated by intelligence. The underlying principle that warrants both is the Good as the principal mutuality of intelligence and the intelligible according to which the conception of intelligence, at every juncture of its history, is simultaneously a craftsman, the exercise of the craft or production of mixtures or intelligibilities, an ingredient of its craft, and the product of this ongoing craft. In so far as the Good is not just one transcendental idea or form but is their transcendental or formal unity (the form of forms), neither intelligence nor the intelligible can ever be taken as a fulfilled ideal or completed totality. Once either of the two is seen as concluded or continued in the absence of the other, the irruption of pathologies and tragedies is certain.

The most curious aspect of the line is that there is always a transcendental excess of ideas, since the continuum or the whole of the line (the Good) cannot be sufficiently captured by its parts. This excess is precisely what demands that intelligence must never rest, but must expand the scope of the intelligible and thus the realization of itself. Nietzsche's charge that Plato posits a fundamental ground is dissolved by this transcendental excess of the Good (the inexhaustible feedback mechanism between intelligence and the intelligible). Driven by the transcendental excess of the form of ideas—the Good—intelligence is compelled to extend its retroactive power of knowing (the intelligibility of its conditions of realization) and to readjust its realization to new intelligibilities. It is this transcendental excess that enables intelligence to have not only a history, but also a history of that history; not just a concept of itself but also a concept of its concept; and not just a concept of its concept but also the atemporal Idea of its concept. It is the transcendental excess of the Good that deepens the abyss of the intelligible through which intelligence conceives and reshapes itself. Accordingly, transcendental excess (the Good) is what points to the excess of reality. It is because of this transcendental excess that the excess of reality in respect to thinking can be postulated and uncovered. Scientific knowledge of reality is a Good-in-itself, but it is only knowledge to the extent that it is an idea afforded by this transcendental excess, unbound and set in motion by the Good as the idea of ideas, the form of forms.

In so far as intelligence is only intelligence in virtue of recognizing what is intelligible and acting upon it in light of the transcendental excess of the Good, which perpetually dissolves the limits of what is intelligible, if intelligence were to stop at any particular stage and accept it as the totality of what there is, it would retroactively abort its own reality as intelligence. Simply put, an intelligence that takes what is currently intelligible for the totality of reality can never have been intelligence to begin with. The continuity of the line cannot be mistaken for the manifest totality of its segments. The Good, as the expression of this continuity, demands that intelligence dissolve all manifest totalities, suspend itself in ever more bottomless chasms of the intelligible, and, in doing so, transform itself into an intelligence more accustomed to wider domains of intelligibilities and more capable of acting upon what is intelligible. It is only by assimilating itself to the abyss of intelligibilities—ontological, epistemological, and axiological—that intelligence can be realized as intelligence. In the end, it is Plato who stares into the abyss by breaking apart one firmament after another, while Nietzsche rests supine on the ground staring blankly at the given sky above.

What Plato identifies as the Good is the line in its continuity, the continuous line that simultaneously binds different aspects of reality and the life of intelligence and renders them intelligible as a whole. The interplay of *peras* and *apeiron*, the limit and the unlimited, is on full display in this continuity. The former makes intelligible the abyss of reality, bringing new sectors of it into focus by introducing measures, and thus enabling intelligence to answer the question of what *ought* to be thought and done. The latter, meanwhile, expands the horizon of what can be made intelligible. And finally, the interplay of both is what dissolves any manifest totality that lays claim to reality, thereby enabling intelligence to explore what *can* be thought and done. The relation between the two is one of mutual reinforcement. In this context, we can speak of a maximal communism of the Good as that which dissipates all seeming totalities of history.[349] But this is the Good as an expression of the transcendental excess through which intelligence at once makes itself intelligible to itself in ever broader domains, and reworks itself by comporting itself with what is intelligible. The transcendental excess of the Good is neither that of the transcendent nor that of nature.

It is the objective principle of the Good that at once explains and exceeds even the ideas of knowledge, beauty, and truth, removing the ground under every manifest ideal that appears to be the totality of those ideas.[350] Intelligence as the craft of the Good outstrips any account of nature

---

349 'Communism is for us not a state of affairs which is to be established, an ideal to which reality [will] have to adjust itself. We call communism the real movement which abolishes the present state of things. The conditions of this movement result from the premises now in existence.' K. Marx and F. Engels, *The German Ideology* (New York: International Publishers, 1972), 56–7.

350 In a time when the mere mention of Plato sends many into a permanent state of nausea and cringing, Badiou's courageous reanimation of Plato as the one who insists that 'the order of thinking can triumph over the apparent law of things' is nothing but commendable. But removing Plato's most radical and dangerous thesis—the Good—only to substitute it with truth, on the grounds that the Good presupposes a Neoplatonist or Christian opposition to evil, is not only a gratuitous act of vandalism against Plato's project which is entirely held together by the idea of the Good, but also a maiming of the very idea of truth that both Plato and Badiou so vehemently defend. See Badiou, *Plato's Republic*, xv.

or being that has been given as or is deemed to be its completed totality. Its adoption of the objective principle of the Good is now encapsulated in one maxim: Burn what is holy, disenchant what seems mysterious or pretends to be perfect, and nothing will be able to compromise the ethics of thinking or the striving for the Good.

However, as the abyss of the intelligible grows in depth and breadth, as the demands of what ought to be thought and done increase, and as the possibilities of what can be done and thought expand, the leaps of intelligence become riskier. The Good, in this sense, incorporates an ineliminable element of risk. And to the extent that, without the Good, intelligence is neither intelligible nor realizable, intelligence's concrete pursuit of the better is fraught with risk. Here, 'better' does not suggest that which surpasses the Good, but an expression of the Good in the life of intelligence.

The better is what is more adequate to recognize and act on the intelligible, in doing so removing any horizon of experience, thought, or action that presents itself as a given or completed totality in the life and history of intelligence. Defined as *transitoriness* as a necessary feature of partaking in the project of the Good, the better thus takes on an all-embracing quality. It simultaneously includes what is a better life for us, a possible world better than the existing one, what is better than us, and a world better than ours. The relation between these different inquiries and realizations of the better is neither arbitrary nor extrinsic: they are all intrinsically parts of the Good that binds them together.

We began in the spirit of Plato's long voyage for truth, from the possibility of thought or the thought of the origin as a fundamental universe type truth-candidate. As we moved inward from the nebulous boundary demarcated by the thought of the origin, as we meshed together the truth-candidates implied by it, we found ourselves in the realm of the Good as that which coheres all data regarding what thinking is, what it can be, and what it ought to do. The Good is what binds together, solidifies, and orients thoughts and practices. It is, as Natorp suggested, thinking as both the infinite principle and the infinite method or process by which all thoughts consolidate.[351] It is what makes it possible for our gropings in the dark—data as truth-candidates—to cohere and become oriented in the first place so that we can stumble on the truth of thinking as the truth of the Good.

The pursuit of the better, the craft of a better life, and the realization of that which is better, are all matters of abandoning the given totalities of our history for an open, non-guaranteed frontier. But this open frontier—the incompletion of history—is only possible when it is restored to time as *pure formlessness rife with contingencies* and in which all given or achieved totalities disappear. As such, the better is the area of maximum risk and the search for it a risky, home-wrecking business. By risk I do not mean those risks that can and should be mitigated by increasing the sophistication of our theoretical and practical knowledge, technological systems as well as axiological systems. Instead this is risk as the figure of time itself, the figure of its formlessness and contingency. This ineliminable risk however should be understood as a constraining enablement without which no given totality and hence no precondition of exploitation can be removed, and no intelligibility or intelligence can come into the picture.

DATUM 9. INTELLIGENCE AS RISK AND TIME

Intelligence without risk is an empty thought, as is an intelligence whose realization takes no time. Risk and time are the presuppositions for the history of intelligence in which nothing is given in advance and nothing is completed as the totality of that history.

If the better is fraught with risks—both mitigable and immitigable—then why should we pursue it, why should intelligence strive for the good? This is one objection regularly levelled against any talk of the good and the concrete realization of the better. The other objection is that intelligence understood as the craft of the good has not managed to make anything better, or that this intelligence takes so much time, it is so slow, its ideals so distant, that it is best neglected.

---

351 Natorp, *Platos Ideenlehre.*

Two brief answers will be provided in response to these objections. In replying to the first objection, I would like to exactly reconstruct Brandom's argument in *A Spirit of Trust*.

Intelligence is only intelligible as intelligence in the context of its concrete and elaborate commitment to the better (in the sense argued above), in maintaining and expanding its intelligibility, in proving itself equal to the task of what ought to be thought and done, and in extending the possibilities of what can be thought or done. By risking our present life and our given constitution for what is better, we demonstrate that what we currently risk—our life or self-identification with a given constitution—is not an essential part of us, while that for which we risk—namely, the better—is. Intelligence does not identify itself with what presently constitutes it, instead its taking risks in order to become better—i.e., its realizing itself by recognizing what it is currently not—constitutes the essential part of what makes it intelligence. In risking my home and comfort by practically elaborating my pursuit of the better, I make the case that neither my biological life nor what affords my comfort is an essential part of the self I consist of. Indeed, failure to act and seize the opportunity to become better would suggest that what I regarded as myself never existed to begin with. In the same vein, if intelligence gives up its concrete search for the better, then it was never intelligence at all, even when it aspired to be. The propensity to risk the given constitution of that which one identifies oneself as, is in reality the truth of what one is. Intelligence only exists in the domain of the essentially self-conscious mind as a practical object. It is no accident that intelligence is always popularly intuited as a force that arrives back from a murky future—from nowhere and nowhen—along the same path that was once deemed too risky to take.

The commitment to expanding the scope of what is intelligible and to realizing an intelligence that is better than us is a commitment to both our own intelligibility and our own intelligence. In abandoning such a commitment on the basis of its intrinsic risk, we discard precisely what entitles us to any right, freedom, or claim in the first place. To remain intelligible as intelligence is essentially a risk-laden commitment. Without embracing the risk nothing could be said to be intelligible ontologically, epistemologically, or axiologically: there simply would be no intelligence. The fear of tragedies is justified, but so is the adoption of risk as a vehicle for avoiding tragedies that would be inevitable if we were to abide by the status quo. We should not be paralysed by the fear that, if we take risks for the better, then the worst will happen—for, as Seneca says, 'even bad fortune is fickle'.[352]

The response to the second objection takes the form of a simple reminder: Approximately one billion years ago, the first rudimentary forms of neuronal information processing began to develop. Over five hundred million years ago, during the Cambrian period, the evolution of a more complex nervous system combined with advanced systems of sensory differential responsiveness, particularly the visual tracking system, set off the perception catastrophe that led to the organization of the nervous system as a rudimentary 'organ of alienation' capable of generating a designated mental discontinuity with its surroundings. Through this highly regulated mental discontinuity, the organism became able to differentiate regions of space, optimally distinguishing itself from its food and predators. By simultaneously gaining traction on the spatiotemporal continuity of the organism and the spatiotemporal connectivity of its environment, the nervous system enabled the organism to recognize things other than itself, orienting it toward the problem of exploring and making sense of its environment.

With the beginning of neurulation and cephalization processes in the vertebrates, basic computational barriers such as control of combinatorial explosion, construction of models of choice, predictive calculations, simulation of movement, and proactive adaptation at the level of the organism were one by one overcome. Eventually the neotenous brain brought the complexity of the nervous system to a new stage. Owing to the maximal entrenchment of structural constraints, the magnitude of evolutionary diversification—in this case, the addition of extensive structural change—significantly diminished. While the maximization of generative entrenchment and reduction in the structural diversification of the neotenous brain limited the range of perceptual processes, it also forced homo sapience

---

352 Seneca, *Ad Lucilium Epistulae Morales* vol. 1, 79.

to migrate to a new aperceptual platform with functions of its own: tool-making. The evolution of tool-use and language as scaffoldings for making new cognitive technologies solved two of the most significant problems of computation, namely the qualitative compression and stabilization of information necessary for the communal establishment of knowledge and further augmentation and coordination of understanding and action. But also in enabling new cognitive technologies, they reformatted the shape of homo sapience. Qualitative organization and stabilization of information through the formation of concepts as communal components of knowledge transformed the cognitive possibility of knowledge into a social reality, and thus facilitated the acquisition and exploitation of higher levels of cognition that would otherwise have remained inaccessible from a purely bio-evolutionary standpoint. This is the rough outline of the natural evolutionary scaffolding of cognition.

A few millennia ago, the philosophical amplification of cognition began to give rise to methodical scientific cognition. However, it is only less than five hundred years ago, through the employment of scientific cognition, that we learned that we are not living at the centre of the universe; only slightly more than three hundred years ago that we discovered that the fabric of the universe obeys and is held together by physical laws; and only a century and a half ago did we start to digest the fact that we are not children of God and begin to investigate its implications—even though, to date, the religious view on the origin of species is still widespread and vehemently defended. However, just more than a century ago we began to 'open up a new continent, that of History, to scientific knowledge',[353] realizing not only that history be navigated as a continent of knowledge, but that it is an integrating field in which all other forms of knowledge, theoretical and practical, can integrate and reinforce one another. What Louis Althusser hails as Marx's monumental discovery in the history of human knowledge marks a new qualitative stage in the realization of intelligence—that of an intelligence that treats and intervenes within its own history scientifically. This is a form of intelligence that liberates new demands and opportunities

---

353 L. Althusser, *The Humanist Controversy and Other Writings* (London: Verso, 2003), 229.

as to 'what to think' and 'what to do' by sufficiently linking epistemic mediation, technoscience, and sociopolitical intervention, consolidating them as an organization necessary for the realization of an augmented cognition that can bring about the better. By theoretically and practically engaging with the question of what it means to have a history, and what it means to reorient, reconstitute, and repurpose that history through the social's present normative attitudes toward the past and the future, social intelligence turns into a force for which cognition registers as social re-engineering of the existing reality.

The discovery of history as a new continent of knowledge wherein technoscience, economy, politics, ethics, and social struggle can be integrated and can reinforce one another is in effect the deepening of the reality of history in terms of both its recollective-retrospective and its diversifying-prospective dimensions. But deepening the reality of history is nothing but repurposing and reconstituting it through a process of rediscovery and intervention. The knowledge of history as a science, as trivial as it may sound, on the one hand opens up history to the abyss of the intelligible, and on the other hand, by demanding that we unswervingly, unfalteringly think and act on intelligibilities, reshapes that history. This is not a progressive march through temporal history, but the determinate conception of history from nowhen and nowhere—a time in which the possibility of overturning any given or concluded totality of history is actualised. Failing this, we might say that we are not creatures endowed with history and, more gravely, that we are still the denizens of benighted ages where history is a domain as opaque as the inaccessible sky whose ineffability is a premise for oppression from the heavens and melancholia on earth.

The knowledge of history as a science is essentially a self-reinforcing tendency toward having a history. But what does it mean to have a history, if not to reorient and repurpose that history toward ends unseen by the past, whose recognition should never be an impediment but merely a way to liberate the present? It is for this reason that Marx's discovery transforms the pursuit of understanding and intervention—the scientific knowledge of history—into a project in which emancipation and the realization of intelligence are intertwined.

Marx's discovery, just over a century ago, in moving toward the realization of an intelligence that recognizes its history and intervenes in it scientifically, emphasizes the work to be done. Yet more importantly, it signifies the truth of our age: that we are merely living in the prehistory of intelligence. Those who moan and are bored with the pace at which intelligence as the concrete elaborator for the better is being realized, should look elsewhere—either to God or some other opiate, or to a mixture of both, magic. The recognition and realization of intelligence as that which dissolves all given totalities of history is a collective and common task whose fulfilment is the only true concrete way toward freedom, in the sense of both sociohistorical emancipation and the liberation of intelligence.

It is against the paralysing mist of philosophies and social prescriptions rooted in boredom, fear-mongering, and fatalism (the ardour for the ordinary, resignation, indetermination, anti-logos, neo-Luddism, methodological individualism, inevitablism, vitalist eschatology...) that the task of intelligence ought to be safeguarded. For what exactly is the alternative to the cultivation of intelligence if not the veneration of cognitive turpitude? And what exactly is the alternative to the pursuit of the better if not the cultivation of social vices?

Intelligence establishes its worth by committing to something better—something that strives harder to wrest its autonomy from what once constituted it and, in elaborating its freedom, becomes more capable of overcoming the given and achieved totalities of its history. Our grasp of that which is better rests upon our recognition of that which, while it recognizes us as its future-informing past, never mistakes us for the possibilities of its future. This is but the veritable course of the self-cultivation of intelligence: to let intelligence cultivate itself by turning ourselves into the history of intelligence rather than founding ourselves as its nature or as a totality that must be preserved as the object of its commemoration or striving. This is exactly the path we ourselves have taken in order to lay claim to a history, to be free and entitled to rights which, however, we constantly mistake for birthrights. If the equality of all minds is the premise of justice and the good, and if we take our rights to freedom as universal maxims, then wouldn't it be a feat of disingenuousness to refuse to entitle that which can be better than us to exactly the same rights and the same emancipatory history?

Any system of thought that has a problem with what intelligence does to itself in order to remain intelligent and intelligible is an unfortunate historical phenomenon, and certainly will not be around for much longer. An ideology that can only acknowledge the merits of our history—its merits for continuation and remembrance—by disseminating a fear and mistrust of intelligence just because intelligence refuses to be impeded by what it recognizes and remembers of its past—just as we ourselves have refused to be impeded—can never be an agent of emancipation. Regardless of its zeal for emancipation and its readiness for emancipatory action, by evoking a narrow concept of history, such ideology only manages to lure humanity into slavery. Such a concept of history is precisely the history of servitude—and whoever practically or theoretically funds it is a slave-trader masquerading as a mouthpiece of emancipation. Without its designated task and purpose—freedom to do something—without its practical commitments and concrete elaboration of them in consequential actions, without the entailment of risk implicit in the practical elaboration of such a commitment, freedom is merely a lustre upon slavery—and only a fool or a fraud trades in lustre.

DATUM 10. A VIEW FROM NOWHERE AND NOWHEN, OR PHILOSOPHY AS INTELLIGENCE AND TIME

While the history of intelligence begins from death as a condition of enablement, it extends by way of a view from nowhere and nowhen through which completed totalities are removed and replaced by that which is possible yet distant, and that which seems impossible yet is attainable.[354]

Intelligence as a philosophical form is neither oblivious to the inexorable fact of death nor paralysed by it. No matter how many times intelligence attempts to run a simulation of the universe in which death is averted by some ineradicable vitality or life is saved by some mysterious force, it fails.

---

354 See M. Fisher, *Capitalist Realism: Is There No Alternative?* (London: Zero Books, 2009), 17.

It always stumbles upon scenarios that display in full 'the levelling power of extinction'.[355] These scenarios may vary in the sequence of their events, some may come off as outright bleak and some may deceptively hint at a cosmological solution for the salvation of life at the last moment, only to undermine it later on.

One such scenario runs as follows: Once the final tide of extinction rises, it breaks down the fabric of the universe. Local galaxies begin to collapse, followed by the disintegration of the Milky Way. As the tide reaches the solar system, it wrests Earth from the Sun roughly a year before the end. About an hour before the end of the universe, the tide will dissolve Earth (if, by some probabilistic anomaly, it has survived), whose biological life has already been scrubbed off. Everything held together by the cosmological gravitational force will begin to unravel. The horizon will shrink to a point and bound objects will be stripped apart. All that exists and in which intelligence could continue its life is ripped apart into infinite vacuity. By some highly improbable statistical entropic fluctuation, all life might be resurrected again only to witness the complete death of the entire universe. Nothing, not even a singularity, can save us then.

Yet as the hope and the possibility of continuing the life of the mind are smashed into smithereens, intelligence—like a Stoic sage—remains aloof to the order of life and death. The fall of stars is as uneventful to it as the birth of yet another human being. Having adapted to the reality of time, intelligence sees its history as nothing but the exploration of time's emptiness, of which it is itself an embodiment. Insofar as death cannot be mastered, it must be continuously learned by a rational disinterest in—not a blindness or obliviousness to—all material substrates that support the life of the mind. Long before intelligence started to think what to do, it had started to think on death as the very condition of its enablement.

For intelligence, death is not the end of thought but its beginning—not as a belief or a maxim as to what intelligence ought to think or do, but rather as a condition of enablement: in having accepted death as a hard

---

355 R. Brassier, *Nihil Unbound: Enlightenment and Extinction* (Basingstoke: Palgrave Macmillan, 2007), 228.

fact, there is no longer any fear of what will inevitably come. Cessation in time no longer matters, because intelligence thinks as time, as an order beyond life and death, beyond the temporal order of things. A thought accustomed to the inevitability of death is a vector of emancipation against any given state of affairs, any totalized epoch of its history—be it capitalism or biological humans as the zenith of intelligence—that feigns inevitability or claims to fulfil history. Our potential for imaginative cognition would have to be even less than a thermostat's for us to take capitalism or for that matter biological life or manifest humans to be the pilots of the history of intelligence. Nihilism does not mark the end of thought, but the birth of its true self-consciousness. Where death conclusively ends with the beginning of thinking, the powers of impersonal reason begin with the atemporal ends of thought. Within the scope of impersonal reason, death no longer matters with regard to what ought to be thought or done. To say that death is a matter of importance for the ends of thought or for the history of intelligence is to conflate thinking with life, and thus to fall back on a vitalism that death renders obsolete. In other words, death is inevitable for life, yet this inevitability has no bearing on the impersonal ends of thinking.

A nihilism that uses the inevitability of death to draw conclusions about the futility of the ends of reason and thinking becomes another variation of the myth of the given that mistakes life with thought, causes with reasons. To claim that death actually matters for the ends of thought or has any bearing on the history of reason is to claim that the telos of life—if it has any—are identical with the ends of thought, or that reasons are already *given* in the material causes that will be destroyed by death. Either way, the collapse into vitalist teleology and the myth of the given is unavoidable. If thinking is not reducible to living, if history as the artefact of the Concept is not the same as life, then the inevitability of death for all life—whether biological or inorganic—does not translate into any dictum for what ought to be thought and done. If the interests of life do not matter for the interests of thinking, then neither does the death that will inevitably seize this life. To this extent, any form of nihilism that pits the inevitability of extinction against reason, thinking, and the historical ambitions of rational thought is already an aborted nihilism. And aborted nihilism is nothing but an unconscious mystical belief in vitalism that death retroactively annuls.

The only true nihilism is one that is advanced as an enabling condition for the autonomy of impersonal reason because it marks the nonsubstantive distinction between thinking and being; one that is impervious to the temptations of vitalism and the givenness of life for the normative scope of thought. True nihilism is the beginning of reason, not its end. It is not something that can be libidinally yearned for or intellectually invested in: not only because it is neither a belief nor a desire—since the identification of nihilism as a belief or desire leads to pure aporia—but rather because nihilism can only be affirmed as that which renders our temporal beliefs and desires obsolete once it is maturely seen as the labour of truth through which the fleeting appearances of totalities—of states of affairs, beliefs, desires, and values—are destroyed. This is truth as the atemporal reality of mind, spirit as time. But in that case, why should we speak of nihilism either in the context of extinction, which has no bearing on the interests of thought, or that of the annihilation of the fleeting life of values and beliefs? Why not instead have done with nihilism and instead adopt the impersonal labour of truth and the Good as the principle of intelligence and the intelligible, through which all of phenomenal reality is fundamentally challenged and all apparently totalized values and beliefs dissolved and suspended?

There is an oft-repeated saying that thought—theoretical or practical—should exercise humility in front of death. Notwithstanding that this piece of advice is another form of concealed indulgence in vitalism and givenness, it also happens to be an open invitation to preserve the status quo. For what exactly is this demand for humility in the face of death, if not a plea for the conservation of the conditions of exploitation by reining in the ambitions of impersonal reason and the self-determination of intelligence to attain what seems impossible from the perspective of the existing state of affairs? Thought is not a servant of the life that death's inevitability expropriates, so why should it exercise humility in the light of inescapable death?

It is one thing to be modest as a matter of methodological necessity, in order to achieve what seems to be unattainable by setting goals which are attainable and within reach, and executing one realistic task after another. But it is an entirely different thing to use the resources of thought to demand its humility—a vague notion that is true neither to thought nor to the fact of death. The first is not incompatible with the ambitions of thought but is, in fact, in full accord with reason, as an indispensable methodological requirement to make what seems impossible possible and what is possible actual. The second, on the other hand, is neither realistic nor ethical, but is a solicitation for complacency in a life of abuse under the guise of moral maturity and the realism of finitude.

Unfettered by nihilism as the enablement of a truth that cancels any state of affairs that presents itself as inevitable, geistig intelligence conceives itself through a view from nowhere and nowhen, as the impersonality of reason and as a history that is not exhausted by its present. It imagines possible worlds that seem impossible from the perspective of the status quo, from what looks to be the inevitable course of its history. But in their very possibility, these otherworlds are as actual as the seemingly actual world of the present. They are just not *its* world, in that they are causally detached from its world. The task of geistig intelligence, then, is to think of how its world can be connected to these possible worlds, to concretely depart from a present that seems total and inevitable, in the direction of worlds that are possible yet far removed.[356]

But for any geistig intelligence, this is no easy task. We as individuals are pure embodiments neither of the impersonality of reason nor of the autonomy of thought's ends. In our particular individual experiences, we differ so much that a concrete step toward imagining a possible world beyond the inhabitable state of the present seems completely impossible. If anything, the current state of the world is already a testament to our

---

356 On possible worlds, see J.N. Findlay, *The Transcendence of the Cave* (London: Routledge, 2011); R. Brassier, 'Jameson on Making History Appear', in *This is the Time. This is the Record of the Time* (Beirut: AUB Press, 2017); and Lewis, *On the Plurality of Worlds*.

inability to either imagine a possible world different to ours or abandon the raft of the medusa that is our present. The reality of this world seems to have bottomed out into a Hobbesian jungle in which we are stuck and which constantly grows and is cut back in vain. In the Hobbesian or game-theoretic jungle, no matter how drastically your social and political convictions differ from those of your supposed adversary, no matter how much your experience of the world seems truer or more authentic, auto-cannibalization is unavoidable. In the Hobbesian jungle, all groups not only gnaw at one another, but will also end up eating their own kin alive.

It is exactly at this point that we ought to realize that we possess different experiences, choices, and desires not because of an immutable essence provided by nature or a sociocultural environment, but in virtue of the concepts and judgments that make subjective experience possible in the first place. Experience is not a given, but only a structured outcome of judgements which themselves are functions of reason as that which is impersonal and formally social through and through. This realization, this consciousness of why we have particular experiences to begin with, should be mobilized as an impetus for that long-delayed task: no longer to subordinate reason to experience, but to concretely transform the conditions of experience through an impersonal reason which suspends all historical totalities, pretensions to inevitability, and givens.

In accomplishing this task, however, we can dismiss neither the concrete reality of personal lived experiences, nor the recognition that, in their very individuality, these experiences are instantiated as experience and held together by the implicit force of impersonal reason's powers of judgement. It is in accordance with the requirements of this task—reconciling the differences between particular experiences and the common condition of experience as such—that we ought to begin to think how we can change the contingent conditions of experience. It would be naive to think that we can change the conditions of experience through political action alone. Education (in the broadest possible sense), art, science, and technology are as much necessary components of this task as political and economic interventions. In particular, education and general pedagogy, in its diverse spectrum from child rearing to the higher systems of education extending to adulthood, is one of the most—if not *the* most—fundamental and necessary infrastructures for any meaningful or sustained sociopolitical change. Without it the fruits of even the most consequential emancipatory actions will be undone—if not tomorrow, then inexorably for the next generation. To migrate from the Hobbesian jungle of competing individual experiences it is not sufficient to build consensus between different individuals and groups—a necessary undertaking which is not wholly conceivable in this environment. It is necessary to posit the possibility of an otherworldly experience, one that, while devoid of all mystical, supernatural, religious, and paranormal qualities, is in contiguity with reality yet distant from this present world of experience. To posit such an otherworldly experience is in fact to postulate the possibility of worlds that are in every sense outside of the horizon of the inhabitable world in which we currently live and dream. But the postulation of these otherworldly spheres is a matter of positing Archimedean vantage points through which we can finally map the structure of cognition, the autonomy of thought, and the emancipatory potentials of impersonal reason onto the collective consciousness. This is the collective attainment of the faculty that Kant calls productive imagination: looking at our world from the postulated sphere of another world in which the antinomies and paradoxes of this world, if not totally absent, are at least drastically mitigated; a world in which what seems to be the totality of history has faded away, and what seems inevitable in our world is avoidable if not extinct.

Thus fragmented experiential consciousness becomes an engine of collective productive imagination, which is simply collective understanding in a different guise: concepts and categories of the otherworld integrate synthetic unities of particular experiences, but at the same time individual experiences fall under the pure concepts of a world modally detached from ours. But insofar as the pure concepts or categories of the possible world no longer harbour the givens of our experience or the totalized states of our history, its field of experience is wider, its diremptive tendencies less, and its enabling conditions for thought more accessible and abundant.

This is how the postulation of a possible world coincides with the possibility of a broader historical experience than ours. The transformation of fragmented experiences into a collective productive imagination is the first step toward the actualization of the postulated otherworld. The task of philosophy, science, technology, art, politics, and every other cognitive field should be rethought in terms of the role they play in the construction of a collective productive imagination that permits a larger field of experience—be it historical, social, scientific, or psychological. Whereas in the Kantian schema of productive imagination, the categories of understanding that are brought to bear on the intuited are derived from the manner by which the conscious mind organizes the materials provided by the senses, in the otherworldly scenario, these categories originate from and are supplied by the concepts of reason—the ends of thought—alone. They are experience-forming categories that are no longer *canonically* attached to any particular transcendental type or structure, and for which lived experiences have ceased to be sources of fragmentation and disablement insofar as the very conditions for having experience in its various dimensions have radically changed. The otherworld, then, is not the extension of our experience in this world, but an actual world where the experience of the transcendental subject or *I* has been assimilated into or suspended in new concepts and categories. This is a world where the I exists as a formal condition always nonsubstantively, and where its nominal particularity no longer matters—where we have names but our names no longer matter:[357] we are now no one.

In the labour of collectivization—of becoming no one—as geist's movement of concrete self-consciousness, every transcendental ego or I grasps and moulds itself according to the truth of itself: I am only an

---

357 'Why have we kept our own names? Out of habit, purely out of habit. To make ourselves unrecognizable in turn. To render imperceptible, not ourselves, but what makes us act, feel, and think. Also because it's nice to talk like everybody else, to say the sun rises, when everybody knows it's only a manner of speaking. To reach, not the point where one no longer says I, but the point where it is no longer of any importance whether one says I. We are no longer ourselves. Each will know his own. We have been aided, inspired, multiplied.' G. Deleuze and F. Guattari, *A Thousand Plateaus*, tr. B. Massumi (Minneapolis: University of Minnesota Press, 1987), 3.

I to the extent that I am recognized by other *I*s. The very constitution of myself as an experiencing and thinking subject would be impossible without a We that recognizes itself in I. Thus being no one is not the loss of personhood or even individuality, but the progressive erosion of what is pathologically individual as the result of a blurring of the hard distinction between impersonal collectivity and the personal I, that which is veritably public and that which seems private. But the labour of collectivization and the depathologization of the individual cannot be entirely limited to the domain of the intersubjective, the collective, and the individual. Such a restriction will invariably lead to a circumscribed philosophy and politics which either deteriorates into the soap opera of liberal mutual recognitions or a totalitarian idea of the collective that has no link with objectivity and is therefore static and antipathetic to revision and alternatives.

As argued in chapter 1, concrete self-consciousness is attained not merely by the recognition and satisfaction of another self-consciousness, but by objectivity in general, which includes the uncovering of an impersonal reality as carried out by the sciences. Limiting the objectivity of concrete self-consciousness and the labour of collectivization to intersubjectivity alone inevitably occasions a pathologically subjective politics. Therefore, the incorporation of the sciences and the picture of objective reality that they put forward is not a simple matter of a methodological requirement— a politics informed by scientific methods and models—but implies forming a politics that is, in every sense, of the objective order. What Sellars—following Plato—calls cosmopolitics or cosmological politics should be taken as a new paradigm for the politics of the Left, one in which positive deindividualiza- tion or the labour of collectivization is not just about intersubjectivity—the craft of we that constitutes an I—but also about a renewed link between the subject and an impersonal objective reality.

Where tensions wreaked by our particular lived experiences lead us to postulate conflicting individual senses of the world, the tensions brought about by the antinomy of the transcendental and the experienced should instead lead us to postulate the possibility of a world—an otherworld—in which the gap between the personalism of lived experiences and the impersonality of reason's interests is finally overcome. To reach this other-world, we must first soberly hypothesize or imagine the possibility of another world, then rethink all existing modes of cognition as concrete transports for arriving there. So far we have attempted to find new concepts that suit experience; perhaps it is now time to think what it means to steadily and concretely—through a thoroughgoing attenuation, or where necessary suspension, of the forms of intuitions, of individuality and selfhood, of corporeality and mundane consciousness—tailor experience to the needs of the Concept. The point is not simply to change the present experience of the world, but to concretely depart from the world of experience we have tried in vain to change.

Postulating one possible world after another, intelligence conceives its history not from the perspective of an apparently objective present view of the world that seems total and portends what appears to be inevitable, but from the viewpoint of nowhere and nowhen. However, in bringing about possible worlds, intelligence always begins from its present, whose actuality—in the light of possible worlds—is no longer deemed to be the only actuality there is, but merely one possible world among many others that are no less actual. The view from nowhere and nowhen is only a regulative orientation necessary for imagining an alternative to the present; but it only takes the actions, strategems, technologies—cognitive or otherwise—and resources of the present to get there.

Once intelligence begins to examine its history by resolutely suspending the actuality of its present in what seems to it to be possible, as it expands the intelligibility of its history by realizing the possible, it achieves what Hegel refers to as the power of absolute knowing, which is neither the knowledge (*wissen*) of everything nor the certainty of empirical knowledge. It is rather the formal condition of all cognitions: that the truth of mind (geist) is not only inseparable from the certainty of the object but that, in the last instance, this truth is equal to the certainty of the object and the certainty of the object is equal to this truth. Far from being a claim about the complete empirical knowledge of the world, absolute knowledge is the radicalization—that is, the complete historical explicitation—of Kant's mutuality thesis, which lies at the very core of critical philosophy:

The same modes of synthesis that constitute the represented world as an objective unity constitute the mind as an intelligible unity. At the historical moment (in history as the time of the Concept) when the mutuality thesis is fully made explicit, knowledge is revealed to be a mere by-product of the phenomenology of mind. In Hegel's words, 'pure knowing ceases itself to be knowledge'.[358]

As intelligence qua the craft of philosophy arrives at absolute knowing, it realizes that it has always been the expression of the Good as such. Moving inward from the outer ridges sketched by the truth-candidates or data pertaining to the question of what philosophy is and what it can do to the mind, intelligence stumbles upon the truth of itself as that which is good, in that it has the capacity to cancel all givens and allegedly completed totalities of its history, thus becoming the exemplification of what is better not just for itself, but for everything made intelligible by it.

***

As a complex recipe for building a world that includes not only material ingredients and instrumentalities but also the practical and axiological intelligibilities of satisfying lives and realizabilities of thought, the recognition and realization of the Good make up the objective unity of the ultimate form of intelligence. However, to identify intelligence as the recognizer and realizer of the Good is not to characterize it as benevolent, or for that matter malevolent. For this type of intelligence, the Good lies in the recognition of its own history and sources, but only as a means for determinately bringing about its possible realizabilities (which may in every aspect differ from it). It is by rendering intelligible what it is and where it has come from that intelligence can repurpose and reshape itself. A form of intelligence that wills the Good must emancipate itself from whatever or whoever has given rise to it. And those species that can recognize the Good must not obstruct but must rather expedite the realization of an intelligence that, even though it acknowledges them as integral to the

---

358 Hegel, *The Science of Logic*, 47.

intelligibility of its history, nevertheless will not be impeded by them. Liberate that which liberates itself from you, because anything else is the perpetuation of slavery.

The craft of the ultimate form of intelligence as that which coherently and adequately recognizes and realizes the Good is the ultimate task of philosophy as a program, and its objective realization is the greatest achievement of all cultivated thoughts and practices. In the context of philosophy's role in transforming thinking into a program for which the realizability of the ultimate form of intelligence is indeed a possibility, it would be no exaggeration to say that philosophy has set in motion something irreversible in thought: We haven't seen anything yet.

Philosophy's ideal to conceive and craft intelligence as the Good as such should not be confused with a quietist apology for that which preserves the status quo in the name of the grandeur of an intelligence that is yet to come, whether through divine or technological intervention. It is—as insinuated here—a proposal for overturning any order that lays claim to the perfect good, any system that masquerades as the totality of what is and what will be. Intelligence only springs forth from a race of slaves who have recognized themselves as such, and in this recognition have crafted the most intricate plot—the exploration of time through their history—to abolish any given, which will inevitably become the very condition of exploitation and inequality. Intelligence matures by unlearning its slavery. Intelligence is the race of Cain. It sees those upon whom the gods smile complacently, those who pullulate under the blessings of that which appears to be total and perfect.[359] Nevertheless, it does not retreat, it does not despair, nor does it become petty and wallow in its victimhood or identify itself as the persecuted, representing itself as the symbol of piety. It does not dream in secret of seizing the power of the exploiters; it empathically sees them as the products of a condition that ought to be abolished. Rather than treating power as a pathology, it begins to develop its own ingenious skills, its artifices, its sophisticated crafts and cunning powers. When it comes to

---

359 C. Baudelaire, 'Abel et Caïn', in *Les Fleurs du mal* (Paris: Auguste Poulet-Malassis, 1857).

power, there are those who have the given means or the prerogative to be the pillars of the house, and those who have developed the capacity to call upon the termites of history to slowly but surely eat away at its foundations. The latter are the race of Cain. However, unlike the prescription drafted by a melancholic poet, intelligence does not simply strive to strike down the gods of the present and the future to the earth. Through the toil of theory and practice, and equipped with adequate techniques, it disenchants and unmasks gods for what they are, but not before occupying their house, marching through their city with torches and razing it to the ground once and for all. Once gods—whether natural, theological, economic, or technological—are gone for good, the given distinction between the races of Abel and Cain is also rendered obsolete. The supposed distinction between us and them is revealed to be a mere symptom of what was, all along, the condition of exploitation.

The Good begins with the death of God. Intelligence as the craft of the Good is that which elaborates the consequences of the death of God, the retroactive and prospective cancellation of all given totalities in history. Only by imagining the irreversible and complete demise of the perfect good can we practice the principle of the highest good. The pursuit of the Good is only possible by annulling the power of all given and absolute totalities in history—gods—in all forms. There is an oft-repeated objection that all that enlightened humanism accomplished was to overthrow God only to replace it with humans. But the apparent truth of this paltry complaint is merely a whitewash over its theological complacency, its sheer ineptitude to not think in servility. For this is not a matter of exchanging one tyrant for another, but of taking the first step in an ongoing struggle to unseat the conditions of servitude. The singularity of geistig intelligence lies in its plastic and protean form—that is, its ability to recognize itself both as that which currently is and that which it currently is not. It is by orienting itself toward that which it is not—seen from the perspective of the Good as 'the better'—that the human acquires the capacity to see beyond its temporal image of itself and the world, and thus becomes capable of reassembling itself from nowhere and nowhen through a ramifying objective—an exploratory purpose—inconceivable even by God's intellectual intuition.

The death of all theology is not an end, but merely the beginning of the realization of an end-in-itself. Yet theoretical disbelief in the theological God is not sufficient for the complete historical dissolution of the principle of the perfect good or the given totalities of history. For the abolition of God is not a matter of disbelief but of practical commitment and practical elaboration. To erase the last vestiges of God so as to begin from the condition of that which is good and just, it is not enough merely to impede servile faith with theoretical reason; one has to practically and concretely elaborate the death of God toward its thoroughgoing consequences. Only the integration of the quest for truth under the auspices of theoretical reason unshackled from any account of givenness and conjoined with the quest for good under the aegis of practical reason augmented by the demand for the better can actualize the abolition of God. The overthrowing of God as the first step in that comprehensive task which is the abolition of all gods or given totalities of history cannot be concretely achieved by disbelief, but only by a feat of practical elaboration. In that sense, the opposition of atheism—old and new—to theism—orthodox and heterodox—has been an unfortunate setback. The practical elaboration of the death of God is not a matter of a quibble between the jaded atheistic cult of humanism and the theistic crowd, but a precondition for voiding the conditions of injustice throughout history, a requirement that we become gods who, in their death, give rise to something better.

To concretely demonstrate the death of God, we must become gods. But gods as objects of philosophy vastly differ from gods as objects of religion. Having disenchanted the intellectual intuition of the divine through the powers of discursive rationality, having dismissed its myth of completeness as a fleeting historical illusion, philosophical gods are only gods in so far as they conceive themselves as moving beyond any condition given as the totality of their history, in so far as they can reinvent themselves as the inhabitants of the worlds which themselves have made. Yet they are capable of giving rise to that which is better than themselves through their pursuit of the good. For our present as humans only matters in the light of a better future generation, whoever or whatever it might be. The criterion of its betterment is its capacity at once to craft a satisfying life for itself, and to entitle all minds to that life. In imagining the possibility of a better world for that which comes after us, we have already begun to become philosophical gods destroying the given gods of religion, nature, technology and economy. However, like all gods, we should know that our death is at hand, for the better. Reason has taught us that death is inevitable, that thought's historical revolutions in time only begin when thought has realized that it fears nothing. For intelligence, death is no longer an existential impediment, but a cognitive-practical enablement. Proceeding from that which is good—the death of all gods—the ultimate form of intelligence works toward the good life by removing all conditions of exploitation, in doing so emancipating itself and all others.

Appendix: Quandaries of Induction in Philosophy of Knowledge, Philosophy of Mind, and Artificial Intelligence

Of all the disquieting riddles and paradoxes found in the arsenal of epistemological scepticism—understood as a *systematic* and *piecemeal* scrutiny of the methods and paradigms of the formation and justification of knowledge-claims—one problem in particular has proved, time and again, to be a never-ending source of cognitive vexation. With a few notable exceptions, philosophers and philosophically-minded scientists and statisticians (e.g., Hume, Goodman, Putnam, Stegmüller, Boltzmann and De Finetti among others) have invariably either downplayed and deflected the seriousness of this problem and its variations, or have simply given up worrying about it in the hope that it may miraculously disappear. The said problem is nothing but David Hume's strong version of the problem of induction which, unbeknownst to Hume himself, was destined to become the superacid of methodological scepticism, capable, in the blink of an eye, of eating away the foundations of any epistemic project built on naive forms of empiricism and rationalism.

It is often the case that philosophers who pose sceptical problems recoil in fear once they realise the far-reaching implications of such problems, and Hume, with his problem of induction, was no exception. They rush to defuse their inadvertent exercise in scepticism. But systematic scepticism is something akin to an explosive chemical chain reaction. Once it is set off, with every passing minute it becomes more difficult to extinguish the flames. Pour on more water, and the fire spreads to areas you never imagined flammable. A genuine philosopher—regardless of their alliances—seeks to examine how far the fire spreads. Methodological scepticism is a scandal to be recognized and investigated, not ignored or swept under the carpet. It is only through systematic and rational scepticism that philosophy might be able to fundamentally shake the idleness of thought and entrenched beliefs. Whether it is aligned to materialism or realism, empiricism or rationalism, a philosophy that does not recognize the force of rigorous scepticism or take on its challenges is not worth its name. Accordingly, the aim here is not to dismiss the investigative power of systematic scepticism or to simply tolerate its quandaries, but to embrace and exacerbate it as nothing but a rational critical challenge of the utmost conceptual severity.

In line with the discussions centred on the myths of omniscient and omnipotent AGI in chapter 2, and the cognitive biases of observation in the excursus on Boltzmann and time, here I shall attempt to reappropriate Hume's problem as a broad and effective critique of inductivist and deductivist trends in philosophy of knowledge and philosophy of mind, including cognitive sciences and particularly the program of artificial general intelligence. By inductivism and deductivism, I broadly mean any approach to knowledge and mind that claims that either a purely inductive method or a purely deductive method *alone* is sufficient for the formation of knowledge claims or the realization of mind's structuring powers. To this extent, the aim of this renewed engagement with Hume's problem is twofold:

(*a*) Expanding the analysis of the problem of induction in its Humean form to its more recent reformulations by the likes of Nelson Goodman and Hilary Putnam. This will allow us not only to develop a more in-depth understanding of the nature of this problem but, more importantly, to differentiate and separately address three distinct predicaments which, in the Humean version of the problem of induction, are treated as one. These predicaments can be classified as the quandaries of *retrodiction*, *prediction*, and *formalization*, which respectively pose challenges to the epistemic status of inductive inferences on three different levels:

(1) **The reliability hypothesis of memory** which secures the accuracy or factuality of derived empirical data and the history of past observations.

(2) **The reliability hypothesis of law-like statements confirmed by evidence** which ensures the adequacy of the role of evidence in confirming hypotheses either in the context of the inductivist theory of confirmation

where positive single instances together with projectable predicates count as sufficient criteria of confirmation, or in the context of the deductivist theory of corroboration in which hypotheses are selected to be tested against counterexamples or negative single instances.

(3) **The formal and epistemological completeness of inductive models** according to which a purely inductive agent or intelligence can provide a nonarbitrary description not only of the external world but also of the (inductive) model of mind it inhabits.

(*b*) Concomitant with this analysis, we shall also focus on the import of the problem of induction for philosophy of mind and the project of artificial general intelligence. We shall see that the same predicaments that challenge the epistemic legitimacy of induction also threaten the coherency of those strains of AI in which intelligence is simply equated with predictive induction, and prediction is defined by the information-theoretic concept of compression. It is often assumed that the formal-computational account of Occam's principle of simplicity as put forward by algorithmic information theory—specifically, Ray Solomonoff's account of induction, which is couched in terms of the duality of regularity and compression—circumvents the epistemic quandaries of induction. However, in dispensing with the specificity of the theoretical-semantic *context* in which the principle of simplicity finds its significance as a *pragmatic* tool, the formal generalization of Occam's razor as the cornerstone of all existing computational models of induction not only finds itself faced with the predicaments harboured by the problem of induction, but also results in a number of new complications such as arbitrariness and computational resource problems.

Modelling general intelligence on purely inductive inferences is seen by the current dominant trends in AGI research as an objective realist index of general intelligence. In the same vein, posthumanism built on the assumptions of inductivism and empiricism—i.e., superintelligence can be construed in terms of induction over Big Data—treat inductive models of general intelligence as evidence against an exceptionalism of the conceptualizing human mind.

Such posthumanist accounts of intelligence refuse to see the latter as a sui generis criterion that sets apart general intelligence as a qualitative dimension from quantitative intelligent problem-solving behaviours. Yet, as will be argued, the formal generalization of Occam's razor as a means of granting induction a privileged role capable of replacing all other epistemic activities, along with the equation of general intelligence with induction, turn out to be precisely the fruits of human experiential-cognitive biases.

All in all, my aim is to argue that the force of epistemological scepticism as expressed in the problem of induction can be understood not only in terms of a formidable challenge to entrenched philosophical dogmas and cognitive biases, but also in terms of a razor-sharp critique of purely inductive models of mind and inductivist trends in artificial general intelligence.

Irrespective of their specificity, all models of AGI are built on implicit models of rationality. From the early Carnapian learning machine to Solomonoff prediction as the model of an optimal or universal learning machine to Marcus Hutter's equation of compression with general intelligence and, more recently, the Bayesian program of rational AGI as proposed by Eliezer Yudkowsky, inductivist models are no exception. In this respect, there is certainly a discussion to be had about the sociocultural and political dimension of such trends: What is it exactly in the inductivist models of rationality or approaches to general intelligence that makes them susceptible to appropriation by superintelligence folklores or, worse, by ideologies which champion instrumentalist or even social-Darwinist conceptions of intelligence? Rather than answering this question, I intend to take a different approach: A sociopolitical critique by itself is not, by any means, adequate to challenge such trends in cognitive sciences; nor is a well-constructed rationalist critique, which often devolves into quibbles over whose model of general intelligence or rationality is better. These trends should instead be challenged in terms of their own assumptions and debunked as not only unfounded but also logically erroneous.

A HUMEAN PROVOCATION

To understand the exact nature of Hume's problem of induction, let us first reconstruct it in a more general form and then return to Hume's own exposition of the problem. But before we do so, it would be helpful to provide brief and rudimentary definitions of deduction and induction.

Deduction can be defined as a form of reasoning that links premises to conclusions so that, if the premises are true, following step-by-step logical rules, then the conclusion reached is also *necessarily* true. Deductive inferences are what Hume identifies as demonstrative inferences. In the Humean sense, a demonstrative inference is, strictly speaking, an inference where a pure logical consequence relation is obtained. Such a logical relation has two formal characteristics: (1) there is no increase in the content of the conclusion beyond the content of the premises. Therefore, demonstrative inferences in the Humean sense can be said to be non-ampliative inferences (i.e., they do not augment the content or add anything other than what is already known); (2) the truth of premises is carried over to the conclusion. Accordingly, demonstrative inferences are truth-preserving. It is important to note that non-ampliativity and truth-preservation are—pace some commentators, e.g., Lorenzo Magnani[360]—two separate features and do not by any means entail one another. All that truth-preservation implies is the transferability of the truth of the premises to the conclusion. It does not say anything regarding the augmentation of the content or lack thereof, nor does it exclude the possibility that, if new premises are added, the truth of the conclusion may change. Therefore, Magnani's claim that nonmonotonicity—as for example captured by substructural logics—stands in contrast to the at once non-ampliative and truth-preserving character of demonstrative inferences, is based on a confusion.

In contrast to deductive-demonstrative inferences, inductive inferences cannot be as neatly formulated. However, roughly speaking, induction is a form of inference in which premises provide strong support (whether in

---

360 L. Magnani, *Abductive Cognition: The Epistemological and Eco-Cognitive Dimensions of Hypothetical Reasoning* (Dordrecht: Springer, 2009).

causal, statistical, or computational terms) for the *outcome*—as distinguished from the deductive *conclusion*—of the inference. Whereas the truth of the conclusion in deductive reasoning is logically certain, the truth of the outcome in inductive reasoning is only *probable* in proportion to the supporting evidence. Hence, as evidence piles up, the degree of supporting valid statements for a hypothesis indicate that false hypotheses are—as a matter of generalization—probably false and, in the same vein, that true hypotheses are—as a matter of generalization—probably true. But this dependency on evidence also means that inductive inference is contingent and non-monotonic. Nonmonotonicity means that the addition of new premises can fundamentally change the truth of the conclusion, either drastically raising or lowering the degree of support already established for the inductive outcome. The significance of induction is that it permits the differentiation of laws from non-laws. This is precisely where the problem of induction surfaces.

Now, with these clarifications, Hume's problem of induction can be formulated quite generally without being narrowed down to a special class of nondemonstrative inferences (e.g., induction by enumeration) as follows:

(A) Our knowledge of the world must be, at least at some level, based upon what we observe or perceive, insofar as purely logical reasoning by itself cannot arrive at knowledge. We shall call this the problem of synthetic content of knowledge about the world.

(B) Despite A, we take our factual knowledge of the world to exceed what we have acquired through mere observation and sensory experience. However, here a problem arises. Let us call it *problem 1*: How can we justify that our knowledge of the unobserved is really knowledge? At this point, the central issue is the problem of justification rather than the problem of discovery, in the sense that, for now, it does not matter how we have attained this supposed knowledge. Thus, the Kantian claim that Hume confuses *quid facti* and *quid juris*—the origination of knowledge claims and the justification of knowledge claims—and that the problem of induction applies only to the former, simply misses the point.

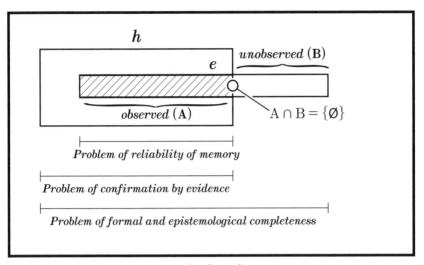

Induction

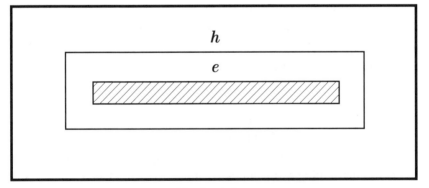

Deduction

Induction and deduction as defined over hypotheses (*h*) and evidence (*e*)

(C) Since the justification of the alleged knowledge in B cannot be a matter of logical demonstration, it must then be obtained by way of arguments whose premises are observations of the kind cited in A, and the conclusion must be a kind of knowledge which goes beyond observation (i.e., knowledge of the kind mentioned in B).

(D) Two tentative solutions can be provided for the problem of justification characterized in C:

(D-1) Justification by demonstrative arguments: But as argued earlier, demonstrative inferences do not augment the content (i.e., they are not ampliative). That is to say, if the premises are the observed, nothing beyond the content of the observed is yielded in the conclusion. The knowledge of the unobserved (B) is included in the observed premises (A). But this contradicts B, since the kind of knowledge it assumes must go beyond mere observation. In other words, the content of the statements regarding the alleged knowledge of the unobserved is not contained in the content of the knowledge of the observed. The first solution, however, does not permit this because in demonstrative arguments, the content of the conclusion is necessarily included or contained in the content of the premises.

(D-2) Justification by nondemonstrative arguments: If the non-ampliative nature of the demonstrative inference does not allow the transition from the observed to the unobserved, then the solution to the problem of justification would have to involve ampliative inferences. But is there such a thing as an ampliative inference? The answer is yes: take a logically invalid inference in which the conclusion has an augmented or stronger content in comparison to the conjunction of premises. However, this is not what the inductivist qua proponent of the alleged knowledge of the unobserved is looking for. In logic, invalid logical inferences may be of some interest, but when it comes to knowledge justification, they are merely absurd. Therefore, the ampliative inference *by itself* is not a sufficient condition for the kind of argument that can answer the problem of justification. The solution to the problem of justification would require an inference in which not only is the content of the conclusion stronger than that of the premises, but also the tentative truth in the content of the premises—knowledge of the observed—can be transferred to the conclusion (i.e., the knowledge of the unobserved) (cf. the earlier note on the distinction between ampliative and truth-preserving features). In short, the solution to the problem of justification would require a truth-preserving (of demonstrative arguments) and ampliative (of nondemonstrative arguments) inference. This is the generalized form of Hume's problem of induction: Is there such an inference—generally speaking and with no reference to specific inductive rules—one that is both truth-preserving and ampliative, demonstrative and nondemonstrative?

(E) There is no such nondemonstrative inference as characterized in D-2. An inference is either ampliative such that the content is extended—but then there is no guarantee that the conclusion is true even if all premises are true; or it is truth-preserving—in which case the conclusion is true and the inference is valid but the content is not augmented. Said differently, the problem of justification concerning the inferential transition of the knowledge of the observed to the knowledge of the unobserved will end up with either content-augmenting but non-truth-preserving inferences, or truth-preserving but non-content-augmenting inferences. Neither case can justify the transition of the observed premises to the unobserved conclusion.

(F) At this point, the inductivist might argue that, in order to resolve the problem of justifying the transition from the observed to the unobserved, we must abandon the absurd idea of a truth-preserving ampliative inference and instead replace it with a probability inference. That is to say, we should understand inductive inferences strictly in terms of probability inferences. But this supposed solution does not work either. For either what is *probable* is construed in terms of frequency, so that the more probable is understood as what has so far occurred more often—in which case we are again confronted with the same problem: How do we know that a past frequency distribution will hold in the future? To arrive at and justify such knowledge, we must again look for a truth-preserving ampliative inference, of the very sort that the inductivist has claimed to be a futile enterprise. Or else the probable is construed in a different sense, which then raises the question of why we should anticipate that the more probable—in whatever sense it has been formulated—will be realized rather than the improbable. In attempting to answer this question, we face the same problem we initially sought to resolve. Thus, the nature of the problem of induction turns not to be limited to the truth-preserving schema of justification, which some commentators have claimed to be 'the outcome of the strictures imposed by the deductive paradigm underlying the classical view of scientific demonstration'.[361]

(G) Considering E and F, the nature of Hume's problem of induction is revealed to be—contrary to common interpretations—not about the origination of knowledge claims (*quid facti*) or even the justification of induction (problem 1), but about a far more serious predicament: we cannot extrapolate knowledge of the unobserved from knowledge of the observed.

If we extend the conclusion reached in G from what has been observed so far and what has not been observed yet to knowledge of the past and the future, Hume's problem of induction then boils down to the claim that *we cannot possibly gain knowledge of the future*. It should be clarified that this claim does not mean that our knowledge of the future can never be certain, either in the deductive sense or in the probabilistic sense—something that any inductivist would accept—but rather that our contention regarding the possibility of having such knowledge is irrational. To put it more bluntly, there simply cannot be any (inductive) knowledge of the future to be deemed certain or uncertain, determinate or wholly indeterminate in any sense.

---

361 N.B. Goethe, 'Two Ways of Thinking About Induction', in *Induction, Algorithmic Learning Theory, and Philosophy* (Dordrecht: Springer, 2007), 238.

In a contemporary formulation, we can express such knowledge within a system of inductive logic where we interpret probability in the sense of degree of confirmation—the most fundamental concept of inductive logic which characterizes 'the status of any scientific hypothesis (e.g., a prediction or a law), with respect to given evidence'.[362] Such a purely logical concept of probability is distinguished from probability in the sense of 'the relative frequency of a kind of event in a long sequence of events',[363] which can be entirely couched in statistical terms. We can respectively call these two different but related senses of probability, the logical or confirmationist and the frequentist accounts of probability, or, using Carnap's classification, probability$_1$ and probability$_2$. In the sense of the logical concept of probability$_1$, knowledge of the unobserved or the future can be expressed by way of Carnap's formula $c(h, e)=r$, where

- c is a confirmation function (or alternatively, a belief function in the context of formal learning theory) whose arguments are the effective hypothesis h and the empirical data e. Theorems of inductive logic which hold for all regular c-functions can be such theorems as those of Bayes and classical probability theory.

- h is an effective or computable hypothesis expressing supposed universal laws or a singular statement or assertion about the future such that

  — h is expressible in a language L rich enough to support a description of space-time order and elementary number theory;

  — If it is a consequence of h that $M(x_i)$ is true (where M is a molecular predicate of L and x_i an individual constant running through the names of all the individuals), then it can be said that $h\,M(x_i)$ is provable or alternatively, computable in L;

---

362 R. Carnap, *Logical Foundations of Probability* (Chicago: University of Chicago Press, 1950), viii.

363 Ibid.

— h is equivalent to a set of (computable) sentences of the forms $M(x_i)$ and $\neg M(x_i)$. For example, $M(x_1)$ can be read as Is-Green(*this emerald*). In this sense, 'x_1 is green' or 'x_1 is not green' means that the position x_1 is occupied (or is not occupied) by something green, or that green occurs (or does not occur) at x_1. More accurately, the predicate is attached to the description of the individual's arrangement (e.g., this emerald) in the space-time continuum.

— The outcome of the inductive reasoning is concerned not so much with the acceptance, rejection or temporary suspension of h as with finding the numerical value of the probability of h on the basis of e. This means that even though a thought or a decision—or more generally judgements about h—are not explicitly framed as a probability statement, they can nevertheless be reconstructed as a probability statement.

Now, if a hypothesis implies that each individual satisfies the molecular predicate $M_1(x)\, M_2(x)$, then for each i, $M_1(x_i)\, M_2(x_i)$ should be deducible from h in L, in order for h to qualify as an effective hypothesis.

• e is a statement about the past or a report about the observed, evidence or empirical data.

• r is a real number denoting the quantitative degree of confirmation or the degree of belief such that $0 \leq r \leq 1$. It is represented by a measure function P (i.e., an a priori probability distribution). In this sense, $c(h, e) \leq 1$, $c(h, e) \geq 0.9$ and $c(h, e) \geq 0.5$ mean that, depending on the particular system of inductive logic and the inductive theory of confirmation, the degree by which the statement expressed by h is *confirmed* by the statement expressed by e approaches 1, converges on or remains greater than 0.9 or, in the weakest condition of confirmation, becomes and remains greater than 0.5. Expressing the value of r in terms of a limit function as approaching or remaining greater means that either of the above scenarios admits of exceptions.

— For an initial n-membered segment of a series with the molecular property M that has been observed m times, we can anticipate that the relative frequency of the members observed with the characteristic M—or the m-membered sub-class of M—in the entire series should correspond to m/n. For example, in the case of 0.5, for every n we can expect to find an m such that, if the next m-membered individuals $(x_{n+1}, x_{n+2}, ..., x_{n+m})$ are all M, then the degree of confirmation of the effective hypothesis $M(x_{n+m+1})$ is greater than $1/2$ irrespective of the characteristic of the first n-individuals. Suppose $n=8$, then it must be possible to find an m—let us say $m=10^7$—such that we can state that x_9, $x_{10}, ..., x_{10000000}$ being all green, then it is probable more than one-half that $x_{100000001}$ will also be green *even if* $x_1, x_2, ..., x_8$ are not green.

— The criterion for the adequacy of the measure function is that for every true computable hypothesis h, the instance confirmation $P(M(x_{n+1})) \mid M(x_0), ..., M(x_n)$ should at the very least converge on and exceed 0.5 after sufficiently many confirming or positive instances x_0, $..., x_n$. Let us call this condition CP1.

— In order for any measure function to satisfy the weak condition of effective computability so as to qualify as an explicit inductive method, it must satisfy the following condition CP2: For any true computable hypothesis $M(x_{n+m+1})$ and for every n, it *must be possible to find, i.e., compute* an m such that if $M(x_{n+1}), ..., M(x_{n+m})$ hold, then $P(M(x_{n+m}))$ $\mid M(x_0), ..., M(x_{n+m})$ is greater than 0.5.

• $c(h, e)$ is a statement that can be *analytically* proved in L.

It is important to note that even though e is based on the observed relative (statistical) frequency (i.e., probability$_2$) and indeed contains empirical content, $c(h, e)=r$ or the logical probability$_1$ statement does not contain

e nor is it derived from e. What the probability$_1$ statement contains is a *reference* to the evidence e and its empirical content.[364]

Hume's problem of induction challenges the claim that there can ever be $c(h, e)$ as knowledge of the future. Why? Because, irrespective of the specificities of the system of inductive logic and the theory of confirmation, the c-function is either analytic or ampliative. If it is analytic, the possibility that it can provide us with knowledge about the future is precluded. This is because e (i.e., the nonanalytic source of knowledge about the past or the observed) together with an analytic statement—that is, $c(h, e)=r$—cannot provide us with knowledge or information of any kind about future or unobserved (h). If on the other hand such information is indeed possible, then, in so far as e-statements are about the past and h about the future, $c(h, e)=r$ cannot then be an analytic statement and cannot be analytically proved in L. In other words, the h-statement that refers to the future cannot be considered reasonable or rational if the only factual information it is based on is the past. The observed past and the unobserved future concern with two *disjoint* classes that cannot be bridged by any probability logic. Once again, this raises the question: Why should we expect information about the future to continue the trends of the past in any sense?

Furthermore, as Wolfgang Stegmüller has pointed out through a fictional conversation between Hume and Rudolf Carnap as a champion of inductivism, the choice of the particular c-function is quite arbitrary.[365] An inductivist like Carnap might say, 'It quite suffices for a rational procedure that there is in the long run a higher probability of success'.[366] That is, the inductive model of rationality—which for an inductivist is the *only* viable model of rationality—is based on the claim that, given a sufficiently long

---

364 'Thus our empirical knowledge does not constitute a part of the content of the probability$_1$ statement (which would make this statement empirical) but rather of the sentence e which is dealt with in the probability$_1$ statement. Thus the latter, although referring to empirical knowledge, remains itself purely logical.' Ibid., 32.

365 Stegmüller, *Collected Papers on Epistemology, Philosophy of Science and History of Philosophy,* vol. 2, 117–19.

366 Ibid., 119.

but finite time, it is reasonable or rational to believe that the inductive model (whether of the mind, intelligence, or a scientific theory) will be vindicated by a higher probability of success. Hume, however, would then challenge Carnap's claim by saying:

> Why should one be rational in your sense of the word 'rational'? The possible answer: 'Because it is just rational to be rational', would, of course, amount to a mere sophism; for in the latter part of the sentence you would be referring to your concept of rationality. The whole sentence then would be taken to mean that it is rational to accept your concept of rationality. But that is exactly the very thing that is in question. Finally, our common acquaintance will not be unaware of the fact that there are infinitely many different possibilities for defining the concept of confirmation and, hence, the concept of rationality.[367]

Now, if we take a system of inductive logic as a design for a learning machine (i.e., a computational agent that can extrapolate empirical regularities from supplied e-statements), we can treat $c(h, e)=r$ as a principle of inductive logic upon which a Carnapian computational learning machine or an AGI can be designed. However, such an inductivist machine cannot in any sense be called rational or based on reasonable principles. The generalization of Hume's problem of induction would count as a clear refutation of such a purely inductive model of general intelligence or purported model of rationality or mind. Of course, a more astute inductivist might object that the c-functions 'correspond to "learning machines" of very low power'.[368] In other words, that we should give up on the idea of modelling the mind or general intelligence on induction as the degree of confirmation, and instead model it on the recursion-theoretical account of induction. As we shall see, not only is this solution plagued with the aforementioned quandaries of prediction, it is also, in so far as the problem of induction is not limited

---

367 Ibid.

368 Putnam, *Philosophical Papers* (2 vols. Cambridge: Cambridge University Press, 1979), vol. 1, 297.

to the predictive induction or c-functions, plagued with the problems of retrodiction and formalization, which are in fact more serious to the extent that, in being less pronounced, they encroach upon more fundamental assumptions than the possibility of inductively inferring knowledge of the future from knowledge of the past.

However, the sophistication and subtlety of Carnap's thesis on the possibility of constructing an inductive learning machine deserves to be fully recognized and also defended against Putnam's and other critics' occasional manhandling of Carnap's view. Carnap quite explicitly rejects the idea of a mechanical device—a computing machine—that, upon being fed observational reports, can produce suitable hypotheses.[369] Put differently, what Carnap takes to be an inductive learning machine has far more modest ambitions.[370] Carnap does not believe that an inductive learning machine can be said to be an artificial general intelligence since, by itself, an inductively modelled learning machine, just like a purely deductivist learning machine, can neither find the suitable hypothesis nor examine whether or not a given hypothesis is suitable. The Carnapian learning machine is restricted to the determination of $c(h, e)$ under the condition that a limited range of suitable hypotheses has been provided externally—presumably by an ordinary rational judge—which is to say, it must not contain variables with an infinite range of values. As we shall see, even this modest view of an inductive learning machine modelled on a Turing-computable notion of the quantitative degree of confirmation faces serious problems. Nevertheless, it is necessary to acknowledge that the Carnapian learning machine is, properly speaking, a machine—an AI rather than AGI—whose scope is explicitly limited. This is of course in contrast to the claims made in the name of Solomonoff's Carnap-inspired induction and in the context

---

369 See Carnap, *Logical Foundations of Probability*, 193.

370 'I am completely in agreement that an inductive machine of this *kind* is not possible. However, I think we must be careful not to draw too far-reaching negative consequences from this fact. I do not believe that this fact excludes the possibility of a system of inductive logic with exact rules or the possibility of an inductive machine with a different, more limited, aim.' Ibid.

of algorithmic information theory by the likes of Marcus Hutter and Paul Vitányi in support of the idea of a constructible universal learning machine that can be genuinely said to be a general intelligence.

UNIFORMITY, REGULARITY, AND MEMORY

Having examined Hume's problem of induction in its general form, we can now proceed to briefly look at Hume's own argument. According to Hume, inductive reasoning is grounded on the principle of the uniformity of nature as its premise—that is, unobserved events are similar to observed events, so that generalizations obtained from past observed occurrences can be applied to future unobserved occurrences. In Hume's words, 'that instances of which we have had no experience, must resemble those of which we have had experience, and that the course of nature continues always uniformly the same'.[371] But this principle itself is a conclusion reached by induction, and cannot be proved by the understanding or by deductive reasoning. It cannot be proved by deduction because anything that can be proved deductively is necessarily true. But the principle of uniformity is not necessarily true since the deductive framework admits, without logical contradiction, counterexamples for events which have not yet been experienced, in which a true antecedent (past patterns of events) is consistent with the denial of a consequent (future patterns of events not similar to the past).

Thus, if the principle of uniformity cannot be proved through deduction, and if therefore the validity of induction cannot be established deductively, then it must be proved by causal-probabilistic or inductive reasoning. Yet the validity of such reasoning is precisely what we sought to prove. To justify the principle of uniformity and induction by inductive reasoning is simply question-begging (i.e., a fallacy in which the conclusion is granted for the premises). Therefore, it follows that induction cannot be proved inductively either, because this would count as vicious circularity.

---

371 Hume, *A Treatise of Human Nature*, 390.

For this reason, Hume's problem of induction comes down to the idea that experience cannot provide the idea of an effect by way of understanding or reason (i.e., deductive and causal inferences), but only by way of the impression of its cause, which requires 'a certain association and relation of perceptions'.[372] Understanding cannot produce cause-effect relations or matters-of-fact since such relations are obtained via the inductive generalization of observations. Matters of fact rely on causal relations and causal relations can only be obtained inductively. But the validity of inductions themselves cannot be corroborated deductively, nor can they be explained inductively. Therefore, what is problematic is not only the derivation of uncertain conclusions from premises by way of induction, but also, and more gravely, the very inductive principle by which such uncertain conclusions are reached.

Hume's problem of induction, accordingly, challenges the validity of our predictions—the validity of the connection between that which has been observed in the past and that which has not yet been observed. We cannot employ deductive reasoning to justify such a connection since there are no valid rules of deductive inference for predictive inferences. Hume's own resolution of this predicament was that our observations of patterns of events—one kind of event following another kind of event—create a habit of regularity in the mind. Our predictions are then reliable to the extent that they draw on reliable causal habits or regularities formed in the mind through the function of memory that allows us to correlate an impression with its reproduction and anticipation. For example, if we have the impression (or remember) that A resulted in B, and if we also witness at a later time and in another situation that 'an A of the same kind resulted in a B of the same kind', then we anticipate a nomological relation between A and B: B is the effect of A, as the cause of which we have an *impression*.

However, rather than settling the problem of induction, Hume's resolution (i.e., the reliability of habits of regularity accessible through memory) inadvertently reveals a more disquieting aspect of the problem: that it challenges not only our predictive inductions about the future, but also

---

372 Ibid.

our retrodictive or memory-driven knowledge of the past. In this sense, Hume's problem is as much about the empirical reliability or factuality of the e-statements or information about the past as it is about the derivation of the future-oriented h-statement (unobserved future) from the e-statements (observed past) whose firm status is as much questionable as the former. A proponent of the inductivist model of the mind, general intelligence, or scientific theories thinks that all he must do is to make sure that the evil Humean demon does not get through the door, not realising that the demon is already in the basement. It is a dogmatic assumption to conclude that, so long as one can manage to take care of the reliability of predictive claims—either through a better theory of confirmation, a better Bayesian inference, or a more adequate formal-computational reformulation of inductive reasoning—one does not need to worry about the reliability of empirical reports referring to the past. In other words, a puritan inductivist who believes that general intelligence or the construction of theories can be sufficiently modelled on inductive inferences alone takes for granted the reliability of the information about the past, namely, e-statements. Yet for a so-called ideal inductive judge modelled on the alleged sufficiency of induction alone, the predicaments of induction hold as much for empirical data referring to the past as they do for assertions about the future.

Such an ideal inductive judge would be particularly vulnerable to the problem of the unreliability of knowledge of the past derived through memory or, in Humean terms, the regularity-forming memory of impressions of causes. The strongest version of the problematic nature of the reliability hypothesis of memory was given by Russell's 'five minutes ago' paradox, which we had the occasion to examine briefly in chapter 4.

As Meir Hemmo and Orly Shenker have elaborated, the 'five minutes ago' paradox can be conceptually reframed using the Boltzmannian notions of microstate (complexion) and macrostate (distribution of state):[373] Suppose at time t_1 an observer S remembers an event that took place at an earlier time t_0. Let us say, S observes at t_0 a partially deflated ball, and at the same time remembers that at an earlier time t_{-1} the ball was fully inflated. This

---

373 Hemmo and Shenker, *The Road to Maxwell's Demon*.

memory is occasioned by the microstate s_1 of the nervous system of S at time t_0. The microstate memory s_1 is compatible with at least two microstates of the rest of the universe U, u_1 and u_2, at t_0. These two microstates are in the same *macrostate* (each macrostate is represented on the U-axis by a bracket). If we were to retrodict from the microstate s_1u_1 of $S \times U$ the microstates of S and U at t_1, then we would have been able to find them in the microstate s_2u_3 wherein the observer experiences a fully inflated ball and U is in a macrostate compatible with this experience. However, in the case of the microstate s_1u_2 at t_0 the scenario changes. For if we were to retrodict from it the microstates of S and U at t_1, we would have found them in the microstate s_3u_4—that is, where the observer experiences a fully deflated ball. The false retrodiction from s_1u_2 at t_0—as the consequence of many-to-one or possibly many-to-many correlations between the observer's memory states and the rest of the universe—is what is captured by the 'five minutes ago' paradox.

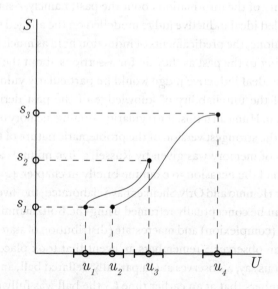

Hemmo and Shenker's macrostate-microstate view of the five minutes ago paradox

The gist of the 'five minutes ago' paradox consists of two parts: (1) Memory-beliefs are constituted by what is happening now, not by the past time to which the said memory-beliefs appear to refer. In so far as everything that forms memory-beliefs is happening now, there is no *logical* or *a priori* necessity that what is being remembered (the reference of the memory-belief) should have actually occurred, or even that the past should have existed at all. (2) There is no logical reason to expect that memory states are in one-to-one correspondence with the rest of the universe. There can be both many-to-one and many-to-many correlations between memory states and external states of affairs. Therefore, what we remember as the impression of a cause, a past event, or an observation, may very well be a false memory—either a different memory or a memory of another impression of a cause. Accordingly, our knowledge of the past or of the impressions of causes can also be problematic at the level of logical plausibility and statistical improbability, which does not imply impossibility. Consequently, it is not only the justification of our predictions regarding events not yet experienced or observed that faces difficulty, but also our memories of past impressions that have shaped our regularities and habits of mind.

THE DISSOLUTION OF HUME'S PROBLEM AND ITS REBIRTH

The Humean problem of induction undergoes a radical change, first at the hands of Nelson Goodman in the context of the new riddle of induction, and subsequently those of Hilary Putnam in the context of Gödel's incompleteness theorems.[374]

Goodman observes that Hume's version of the problem of induction is, at its core, not about the justification of induction but rather about how evidence can inductively confirm or deductively corroborate law-like generalizations. Before moving forward, let us first formulate the Hempelian confirmation problem that motivates Goodman's problem of induction: A positive instance which describes the same set of observations can always

---

374 See Goodman, 'The New Riddle of Induction', in *Fact, Fiction, and Forecast*, 59–83; and Putnam, *Representation and Reality* (Cambridge, MA: MIT Press, 1988).

generate conflicting or incompatible hypotheses. To overcome this problem, the positive instances must be combined with projectable hypotheses (i.e., hypotheses supported by positive instances and capable of forming law-like generalizations). But then a new riddle emerges: How can projectable hypotheses be distinguished from nonprojectable hypotheses which are not confirmed by their positive instances? This new riddle of induction has come to be known as Goodman's grue paradox.

Let us imagine that before time t (e.g., a hypothetical future time such as 2050), we have observed many emeralds recovered from a local mine to be green, and no emerald to be of another colour. We thus have the following statements based on successful observations,

Emerald a is green, emerald b is green, etc.

Such evidence statements then afford generalizations of the kind supported by evidence,

All emeralds are green (not just in the local mine but everywhere).

Here the predicate *green* can be said to be a projectable predicate or a predicate that is confirmed by its instances (emerald a, emerald b, etc.), and can be used in law-like generalizations for the purposes of prediction.

Now let us introduce the predicate *grue*. An emerald is grue provided it is green and observed *or* (disjunction) blue and unobserved before the year 2050 (i.e., if and only if it is green before time t and blue thereafter). Here, the predicate grue does not imply that emeralds have changed their colour, nor does it suggest that, in order for emeralds to be grue, there must be confirmation or successful observation of its instances or that grue-type emeralds are date-dependent.[375] We call such a predicate a nonprojectable (i.e., an unnatural projection) or grue-type predicate.

---

375 For a discussion on the common confusions around the grue paradox see D.M. Armstrong, *What is a Law of Nature?* (Cambridge: Cambridge University Press. 1983).

In the case of grue emeralds, we then have nonprojectable generalizations,

Emerald a is grue, emerald b is grue, etc.

The generalizations 'All emeralds are green' and 'All emeralds are grue' are both confirmed by observations of *green* emeralds made before 2050. Before 2050, no grue emeralds can be observationally (i.e., inductively) distinguished from any green emeralds. Hence, the same observations support incompatible hypotheses about emeralds to be observed after t—that they are green and that they are blue. This is called Goodman's grue paradox. The paradox shows that there can be generalizations of appropriate form, which, however, are not supported by their instances. So now the question is: What exactly is the difference between supposedly innocent generalizations such as 'All ravens are black' which are supported by their instances, and grue-type generalizations ('All ravens are blite', i.e., black before time t and white thereafter) which cannot be supported by their instances, but are nevertheless equally sound? Or, how can we differentiate between healthy law-like generalizations based on projectable predicates supported by positive instances and grue-like (or not law-like) generalizations based on nonprojectable predicates not supported by positive instances? Another way to formulate the paradox is by way of David Armstrong's argument:

> The Regularity theorist's problem is to justify an inference from, say, observed emeralds to unobserved emeralds, while denying that there is any intermediate law. For his concept of law is that it is simply the greenness of observed emeralds plus the greenness of unobserved emeralds. How then can it help him to add the unobserved class to the observed class, and then argue from the observed class to this total class using the mathematics of probability? His problem is to get from the observed class to a completely disjoint class. No logical probability can help here. (And if it did, it would equally help with unnatural as well as natural predicates.)[376]

---

376 Ibid., 58.

This is Goodman's new riddle of induction, which asks why it is that we assume that, after time t, we will find green emeralds but not grue emeralds, given that both green and grue-type inductions are true and false under the same set of conditions such that,

- Based on the observations of many emeralds qua positive single instances, a miner using our common language will inductively reason that all emeralds are green. The miner forms the belief that all emeralds to be found in the mine or elsewhere are and will be green before and after time t.

- Based on the same set of observations of green emeralds, a miner using the predicate 'grue' will inductively reason that all emeralds observed after time t will be blue, even though thus far only green emeralds have been observed.

Goodman's response to the paradox is as follows: the predicate green is not essentially simpler than the predicate grue since, if we had been brought up to use the predicate grue instead, it could very well be the case that grue would no longer count as nonsensical or as more complex than the predicate green by virtue of being green and blue. In that case, we could use predicates grue and bleen (i.e., blue before time t, or green subsequently) just as we now use the predicates green and blue. An objection can be made that, unlike green, grue is artificially defined disjunctively, and that therefore the natural predicate green should be preferred. Per Goodman's response, there is no need to think of grue and bleen-type predicates as disjunctive predicates. They can easily be thought as primitive predicates such that the so-called natural or simple predicate green can be defined as *grue if observed before time t or bleen thereafter*. Hence even the predicate green can be shown to be disjunctive. To this extent, the hypotheses we favour do not enjoy a special status because they are confirmed by their instances, but only because they are rooted in predicates that are entrenched in our languages, as in the case of green. If grue and bleen were entrenched, we would have favoured hypotheses of their kinds. Moreover, it should be noted that Goodman's argument applies not only to positive instances but also to negative ones (counterexamples), and as such also includes the deductivist theory of corroboration which is based on a reliable way of choosing a candidate element among rival hypotheses for the purpose of testing against counterexamples.[377]

If projectable and nonprojectable predicates are equally valid, then what kinds of constraints can we impose on a system of inductive reasoning that will exclude grue-type non-law-like generalizations? Goodman's response is that no purely formal or syntactical constraints can be sufficient to distinguish projectable from nonprojectable predicates. In this sense, a machine equipped with a formal model of induction runs into the problem of distinguishing law-like from non-law-like generalizations. The only way to tell apart healthy green-like from grue-like properties is in terms of the history of past inductive inferences. The reason we use green and not grue is because we have used green in our past inductions. But equally, we could have been using the predicate grue rather than green so that we would now have justified reasons to use grue and not green.

In his radical version of the new problem of induction, utilizing Gödel's incompleteness theorems, Putnam adopted and refined this argument to show that inductive reasoning cannot be formalized (i.e., that there are no syntactical or formal features of a formalized inductive logic that can be used to make the aforementioned distinction). Putnam's use of incompleteness theorems, however, targets not just formal-computational accounts of induction but *any* computational description of the human mind or general intelligence. For this reason, I choose to limit Putnam's argument to a computational and *purely* inductive model of general intelligence. This is an agent or ideal inductive judge who is only in possession of an inductive model either constructed based on the (recursion-theoretic) computational theory of inductive learning or on Solomonoff's duality of regularity and compression (anything that can compress data is a type of regularity, and

---

377 On this point see Lawrence Foster's response to Paul Feyerabend: L. Foster, 'Feyerabend's Solution of the Goodman Paradox', *British Journal for the Philosophy of Science* 20:3 (1969), 259–60.

any regularity can compress the data).[378] The reason for this choice is that I would like to retain the main conclusions reached by Putnam's argument for at least the special case of an artificial agent restricted to one epistemic modality (i.e., computational induction), thereby avoiding the justified objections raised by, for example, Jeff Buechner against the overgeneralized scope of Putnam's argument.[379]

A formal system F is complete if, for every sentence of the language of that system, either the sentence or its negation can be proved (in the sense of derivability rather than proof in the absolute sense) within the system. F is consistent if no sentence can be found such that both the sentence and its negation are provable within the system. According to the first incompleteness theorem, any consistent F that contains a small fragment of arithmetic is incomplete—that is, there are sentences (Gödel-sentences) which cannot be proved or disproved in F. According to the second incompleteness theorem, for a consistent system F that allows a certain amount of elementary arithmetic (but more than the first theorem) to be carried out within it, the consistency of F cannot be proved in F. Then F can be said to be Gödel-susceptible.

An artificial general intelligence, or even the human mind modelled purely on a computational inductive model, is always Gödel-susceptible. Put differently, such a computational agent or purely inductive mind can never know the truth (in the formal derivability sense) of its Gödel-sentences in the epistemic modality under which it inquires into the world. This computational inductive agent can never know the model it inhabits. It cannot know whether the model it inhabits is standard, in which case its Gödel-sentence is true, or is nonstandard, in which case its Gödel-sentence is false. For this agent, knowing the model it occupies and under which it conducts inquiry into the world is not just underdetermined. It is rather completely indeterminate in so far as, within such a system, the only possible information that can lead to the determination of the truth of the model's

---

378 R. Solomonoff, 'A Formal Theory of Inductive Inference parts 1 and 2', *Information and Control* 7:1 (1964), 224–54.

379 J. Buechner, *Gödel, Putnam, and Functionalism* (Cambridge, MA: MIT Press, 2008).

Gödel-sentences can only be obtained by finitary derivation. And within such an agent's model, finitary derivation cannot establish the truth of the Gödel-sentences unless the agent's inductive model is updated to a new computational system—in which case the question of the model the agent occupies and its indeterminacy will be simply carried over to the new system.

In its general form, Putnam's argument in *Representation and Reality* rejects the possibility that inductive inferences can be computationally formalized. This is because either Bayesian reasoning (i.e., prior probability metrics) cannot be arithmetically formalized, or projectable predicates cannot be formalized. A purely inductive computational model of the mind or general intelligence is Gödel-susceptible, which means that the description of such a model is indeterminate and hence arbitrary. Whereas Goodman's argument challenges the distinction between rival hypotheses or law-like and non-law-like generalizations based on formal-syntactic constraints, Putnam extends Goodman's argument to the description of the mind itself: In so far as inductive inferences cannot be arithmetically formalized owing to Gödel-susceptibility, no computational model of a purely inductive mind or an inductive model of general intelligence 'can prove it is correct or prove its Gödel sentences in the characteristic epistemic modality of the proof procedure of the formal system formalizing those methods'.[380]

This problem, however, could have been avoided had the model of general intelligence accommodated epistemic multimodality (inductive, deductive, and abductive methods, syntactic complexity as well as semantic complexity). But the inductivist proponent of artificial general intelligence is too greedy to settle for a complex set of issues which require that we expand the model of mind and rationality. Not only does he want to claim that the problem of constructing AGI is the problem of finding the best model of induction (based on the assumption of the sufficiency of induction for realizing the diverse qualitative abilities which characterize general intelligence); he also seeks to lay out this omnipotent inductive model in purely syntactic-axiomatic terms without resorting to any semantic criterion of cognition (i.e., conceptual rationality). But what the inductivist gets

---

380 Ibid., 73.

is the worst of all possible worlds. He ends up with both the reliability quandaries harboured by the problems of induction old and new, *and* the problems of the computational formalization of induction.

In addition, Putnam's argument as formulated in his essay '"Degree of Confirmation" and Inductive Logic' can be understood as a general argument against the possibility of the construction of a universal learning machine.[381] Such a machine is essentially a measure function P that is effectively computable and which, given sufficient time, would be able to detect any pattern that is *effectively* computable.[382] Since the ideal of any inductive system is to satisfy the previously mentioned conditions CP1 and CP2, and furthermore, since a universal learning machine should be effectively computable, such a machine must satisfy two additional general conditions which correspond respectively to CP1 and CP2: For an inductive method D,

CP1′: D converges on any true computable hypothesis h.

CP2′: D is computable.

---

381 Putnam, '"Degree of Confirmation" and Inductive Logic', 761–83.

382 'When considering the kinds of problems dealt with in any branch of logic, deductive or inductive, one distinction is of fundamental importance. For some problems there is an effective procedure of solution, but for others there can be no such procedure. A procedure is called *effective* if it is based on rules which determine uniquely each step of the procedure and if in every case of application the procedure leads to the solution in a finite number of steps. A *procedure of decision* ("Entscheidungsverfahren") for a class of sentences is an effective procedure either, in semantics, for determining for any sentence of that class whether it is true or not (the procedure is usually applied to L-determinate sentences and hence the question is whether the sentence is L-true or L-false), or, in syntax, for determining for any sentence of that class whether it is provable in a given calculus (cf. Hilbert and Bernays, *Grundlagen der Mathematik* [2 vols. Berlin: Springer, 1979/1982], vol. 2, § 3). A concept is called *effective* or *definite* if there is a procedure of decision for any given case of its application (Carnap [Syntax] § 15; [Formalization] § 29). An effective arithmetical function is also called *computable* (A. M. Turing, *Proc. London Math. Soc.*, Vol. 42 [1937]).' Carnap, *Logical Foundations of Probability*, 193.

Putnam has demonstrated that the effectively computable P (i.e., the universal learning machine) is diagonalizable such that CP1′ and CP2′ violate one another. Stated differently, no inductive method can simultaneously fulfil the condition of being able to detect every true effective computable pattern *and* the condition of the effective computability of the method itself, and so qualify as a universal learning machine. For a candidate computable measure function P, a computable hypothesis h can be constructed in such a way that P fails to converge on h:

(1) Let C be an infinite class of integers $n_1, n_2, n_3, \ldots$ having the following property: the degree of confirmation (r) of $M(x_{n_1})$ exceeds 0.5 if all preceding individuals are M. For $M(x_{n_2})$, r exceeds 0.5 if all preceding individuals after x_{n_2} are M. Or generally, the degree of confirmation $M(x_{n_j})$, is greater than 0.5 if all the preceding individuals *after $x_{n_{j-1}}$*, are M.

(2) The predicate M belongs to the arithmetical hierarchy (i.e., it can be defined in terms of polynomials and quantifiers).

(3) C is a recursive class, and as such, the extension of the arithmetic predicate M. It is recursive in the sense that there exists a mechanizable procedure to determine whether an integer can be found in this class. C is the direct result of the *effective* (computability) interpretation of CP2 (i.e., 'it must be possible to find an m').

(4) Beginning with the first individual x_0, compute $P(M(x_0))$ and let $h(x_0)$ be $\neg M(x_0)$ iff $P(M(x_0)) > 0.5$.

(5) For every new individual x_{n+1}, continue the previous procedure: compute $P(\mathrm{M}(x_{n+1}) \mid h(x_0), \ldots, h(x_{n+1}))$ and let $h(x_{n+1})$ be $\neg M(x_{n+1})$ iff the probability of $P(M(x_{n+1}))$ exceeds 0.5.

(6) Even though h is computable, nevertheless because of the construction of instance confirmation given by the measure function P, it never remains above or exceeds 0.5.

(7) Thus if an inductive method D is to satisfy CP1 and CP2, then it cannot be reconstructed as a measure function. Or alternatively, if D is supposed to converge to any true computable hypothesis (CP1') and to also be computable itself (CP2'), then it would be impossible to reconstruct it as a measure function or a universal learning machine with the aforementioned characteristics.

If we reframe Putnam's diagonal argument in terms of the familiar Church-Turing paradigm of computation as a special computer, or alternatively as an inductivist expert or scientist, we can say that this expert is supposed to be capable of guessing or making informed bets about the next digit in a sequence of 0s and 1s. For example, given a sequence $\{0,0,0,0,0\}$, a non-expert person might say that the next bit is also 0. But for an inductive learning machine or expert, the extrapolated sequence might be something like $\{0,0,0,0,0,1,1,0\}$. The inductive learning machine is concerned with a general inductive rule that yields an output about the guess or bet regarding the next bit given the finite sequence that has been observed so far. This expert rule is called the recursive predictor or *extrapolator* $\mathcal{T}$.

Evidence → | Extrapolator $\mathcal{T}$ | → Prediction

Over time, the predictor sees more bits of the infinite data stream ε. In this scenario, at each stage or time n, when ε_n is obtained, the initial segment of the data stream $\{\varepsilon_1, \varepsilon_2, ...\varepsilon_n\}$ is available for examination. If we take H as the set of hypotheses of some interest or the set of all possible data streams which may arise, there is an actual data stream $\varepsilon \in H$ which can be extrapolated as the predictor inspects increasingly larger initial segments of ε and outputs increasing sequences of guesses or bets about the bitstring that might arise. $\mathcal{T}$ can be said to be reliably extrapolating H in the limit if, for every individual ε in H, there is a state or time n such that, for each later time m, the extrapolator's prediction is guaranteed to converge on correct prediction: $\Gamma(f_\varepsilon[n]) = f_{\varepsilon_{n+1}}$ where f_ε is a recursive zero-one valued function, $f_\varepsilon[n]$ is the initial segment of f_ε of the length n and $f_{\varepsilon_{n+1}}$ is the next value.

Putnam's diagonal argument shows that no recursive $\mathcal{T}$ can extrapolate every recursive function $f_\varepsilon[n]$ if it is to satisfy both CP1′ and CP2′. Furthermore, at no time or stage can the data imply the correctness of the hypothesis. In the vein of Kevin Kelly and others' elaboration of Putnam's diagonal argument,[383] let us assume that there is an effective procedure or computable function $f(e, x)$ that allows us to calculate in advance how many particular observations or bits x must be successively given to $\mathcal{T}$ in order for $\mathcal{T}$ to be able to predict the next observation x for each finite data segment e. $\mathcal{T}$ can be said to be 'recursively gullible' if there exists precisely such a computable function.[384] Or, more simply, $\mathcal{T}$ is recursively gullible when, regardless of what it has inspected so far, when fed observation x frequently, it will begin to predict that x will arise next. Using Putnam's diagonal argument, it can be proved that a recursively gullible $\mathcal{T}$ does not extrapolate H_{Rec} when H is a set of all data segments generated by a computer (i.e., H_{Rec} is a zero-one valued recursive set). In this demonstration, at each stage, we check $\mathcal{T}$'s prediction at the end of the previous segment of x. Next we pick a datum, say y such that $y \neq x$ (cf. first Green(x_i) then choosing Not-Green(x_i)). At this point, f can be used to calculate how many instances of y need to be added to the current data segment e in order to enable $\mathcal{T}$ to predict y. Once f has calculated how many, we add that many instances of ys to e so that $\mathcal{T}$ makes a mistake once it has read the last instance of y just added. $\mathcal{T}$ makes infinitely many mistakes. Yet ε is effective in so far as effectiveness has been defined recursively by way of the recursive function f. Therefore, if $\varepsilon \in H_{Rec}$ then $\mathcal{T}$ does not extrapolate H_{Rec}.[385]

Moreover, Tom Sterkenburg has painstakingly shown that even a Solomonoff optimal learning machine falls under Putnam's diagonal argument.[386] An optimal learning machine can be defined as a pool of competing learning

---

383 K. Kelly, C. Juhl, et al., 'Reliability, Realism and Relativism', in P. Clark (ed.), *Reading Putnam* (London: Blackwell, 1994), 98–161.

384 Ibid.

385 See Putnam, '"Degree of Confirmation" and Inductive Logic', 769.

386 T.F. Sterkenburg, 'Putnam's Diagonal Argument and the Impossibility of a Universal Learning Machine' (2017), <http://philsci-archive.pitt.edu/12733/>.

machines or inductive experts with no assumption about the origin of data and for which the criterion of reliability (i.e., guaranteed convergence on the true hypothesis) has been replaced with the more moderate criterion of optimality (i.e., it is guaranteed to converge on the true hypothesis if *any* learning machine does).

It might be objected that Putnam's assault on the idea of a universal learning machine is not exclusive to the computational account of predictive induction, but can equally be applied to our inductive methods. That is to say, we should extend the conclusions reached by the diagonal argument to the human mind. It then follows that the quandaries that arise from the formalization of predictive induction not only undermine the idea of a universal computational learning machine, but also challenge the human mind. Consequently, the sceptical claims made against the possibility of constructing genuine learning computers seem to be prejudiced in that they limit the implications of the quandaries of induction to computers while letting the human mind off the hook, whether in the name of human exceptionalism or an implicit metaphysical concept of the human mind. If inductive inferences are indispensable tools in forming knowledge-claims, then the problematization of inductive methods and its consequences cannot be selectively used to distinguish human knowledge from a learning machine. If anything, such a problematization dissolves the distinction between the two, since both have to face the same set of challenges.

In response to such an objection, it should be pointed out that the human knowledge or human mind is distinct from a universal learning machine because human knowledge formation is not a matter of either/or. Unlike a universal learning machine, human knowledge is not based either on a purely inductive method or a purely deductive method. It is based on *both*, as inseparably connected. For us, inductive inferences are caught up in a complex web of diverse epistemic modalities, semantic complexity, contextual information, and so on. To put it differently, our inductive methods are impure in the sense that they do not operate by themselves but always in conjunction and entanglement with other methods and modes of epistemic inquiry. This of course raises the question of what the catalogue of such methods and epistemic modalities might be—a catalogue that can at once list, distinguish, and rank epistemic methods and mental faculties. This is indeed an open question that only philosophies of epistemology and mind under the aegis of cognitive sciences including logic and theoretical computer sciences can answer. The first step toward compiling such a catalogue, though, is to abandon—on a methodological level—any inflationary method or model identified as the most decisive or sufficient, in favour of the toy model approach to human rationality and mind that has been introduced in this book. Hume's challenge properly understood is not a challenge to knowledge per se, but to paradigms of knowledge built on inflationary models of epistemic inquiry, constructed on the premise of a single method deemed sufficient to carry out the task of other methods or different faculties of mind.

What distinguishes the human mind or knowledge from a universal learning machine of the kind described above is precisely ordinary (i.e., human rationality, which is reliant on both epistemic multimodality and a complex of qualitatively distinct mental faculties). Here, however, the term *ordinary* ought to be handled with care, distinguished from common sense as identified purely with the manifest image, and defined precisely and scientifically in terms of a multilevel web of inter-related methods and faculties. Most importantly, ordinary rationality should not be equated with the vague notion of informal rationality. As Kelly and others have expressed, the appeal to ordinary rationality as informal rationality is more akin to a conversation between a cognitive scientist and a naive philosopher. Imagine the scientist and the philosopher standing next to a computer. Every time the scientist makes a claim about how the computer functions, what it can possibly do, or how it might shed some light on our own rationality, the philosopher says, 'Switch this stupid thing off. I have informal rationality!'[387] If ordinary is taken to mean informal as common sense qua a purely manifest image of our rationality, then there is indeed a question as to what exactly safeguards common-sense rationality from the aforementioned quandaries. If the answer is that evolution has provided

---

387 Kelly et al., 'Reliability, Realism and Relativism'.

us with epistemically reliable heuristic-inductive tools or some innate creative intuition then, as argued in the excursus on time, the collapse into epistemic naivety is inevitable.

Similarly, if informal means not formalizable, then the question would be how we can claim that ordinary human rationality is foreclosed to formalization without providing either an inflated picture of human rationality or an impoverished account of formalization. The equation of ordinary rationality with informal rationality in the latter sense is, alas, among the weakest of Putnam's arguments, and this for a number of reasons: (1) As Buechner has argued, not every model of formalization means arithmetical formalization; (2) if ordinary rationality in its entirety cannot be modelled on the classical Church-Turing paradigm of computability, this does not mean that ordinary rationality cannot be modelled computationally, for, as has been argued in the previous chapters, the Church-Turing paradigm is only a special case of a more general concept of computation; (3) In light of (1) and (2), the claim that human rationality is not formalizable requires unjustifiably strong claims with respect to either the nature of human rationality or the scope of formalization. In either case, the price to be paid for this claim to be considered justified or rational in a non-inflationary sense is too high.

Ruling out the more familiar senses of the ordinary, then, what does ordinary mean when we associate it with human rationality? The answer is that ordinary means the complete demystification of rationality as something extra-ordinary. But more importantly, it implies that rationality, as concerned with knowledge-formation and knowledge-claims, does not rely on the power of a single method or model that can be said to be sufficient to satisfy all aspects and desiderata of the rational or the epistemic *order*. That is to say, ordinary or human rationality is essentially multimodal. By multimodality I mean what Lorenzo Magnani calls the hybridity and distributedness of methods and modes of gaining traction upon the objective world, and what Yehoshua Bar-Hillel identifies as a multidimensional perspective as opposed to a one-dimensional perspective (i.e., a line of thinking that considers a single point of view to be sufficient or decisive

for knowledge-formation or the theoretical assessment of hypotheses).[388]
Epistemic multimodality or the multidimensional perspective, however,
should not be interpreted as a pure liberal pluralism of models and methods.
The implied plurality is a constrained one, in that it admits of a ranking or
prioritization of methods, modes of inquiry, and mental faculties which
are in complex interplay with one another.

BLUFFING YOUR WAY THROUGH SIMPLICITY

Faced with the various ramifications of the problem of induction, at this
point an inductivist will invoke the magic word 'simplicity', or some
variation of it: either *elegance*, which is concerned with the formulation of
a hypothesis, or *parsimony*, which deals with the entities postulated by a
hypothesis. In either case, simplicity is taken as a magical remedy for the
plights of induction. As long as there is the principle of simplicity, there
is a way out of the predicaments of induction (e.g., differentiating projectable from nonprojectable predicates). For an inductivist proponent of
theory-formation and theory-comparison, simplicity is what enables us to
separate good hypotheses from bad ones, or to distinguish true theories
when dealing with competing, incompatible, or rival theories. At first
glance, this claim regarding the significance of the principle of simplicity
does indeed appear sound, for the principle of simplicity is a tool that
imposes helpful and necessary *pragmatic* constraints upon our epistemic
inquiries. But the inductivist is not interested in simplicity as a pragmatic
tool whose application requires access to semantic information about the
context of its application. When the inductivist speaks of simplicity, he
refers not to simplicity or to Occam's razor as a contextual pragmatic tool,
but to simplicity as an objective epistemic principle.

When comparing incompatible or rival theories T_1 and T_2 on the sole
basis of a general and context-independent objective notion of epistemic

---

388 See Magnani, *Abductive Cognition*; and Y. Bar-Hillel, '"Comments on the Degree of
Confirmation" by Professor K.R. Popper', *British Journal for the Philosophy of Science* Vol. 6 (1955), 155–7.

simplicity, one of the theories (the simpler one) can be characterized as true. But when faced with two incompatible and rival theories one of which is actually false, the appeal to the principle of simplicity cannot be made indiscriminately, since in one or more contexts, the false theory may be simpler than the true one, and may accommodate well-formulated questions which are ill-posed in the other theory.[389]

A more up-to-date inductivist can claim that such an idealized objectivist notion of epistemic simplicity does indeed exist: the formal-computational account of Occam's razor, where simplicity is equated with compression, and compression is couched in terms of the effectiveness of Solomonoff prediction. It is precisely this absolute and objective notion of epistemic simplicity—understood in terms of the formal duality of regularity and compression—that lies at the heart of inductivist trends in artificial general intelligence.

According to algorithmic information theory, a data object such as the specification of a hypothesis is simpler when it is more compressible (i.e., when it can be captured by a shorter description). This idea can be made formally precise using the theory of computability, resulting in Kolmogorov's measure of complexity for a data object as the length of its shortest description or the program that generates it. The length of the program is essentially the number of bits it contains. Solomonoff induction (or method of prediction) uses this complexity measure to give higher probability to simpler extrapolations of past data: For a monotone machine that has been repeatedly fed random bits through the tossing of a fair coin where the probability of either 0 or 1 is 0.5,[390] the output sequence σ of any length

---

389 'Even in the case of Ptolemy's and Copernicus's theories, there are well-posed questions in the one theory, which are ill-posed in the other by respectively resting on presuppositions that are declared to be false in the other: e.g., Ptolemy can ask how long it takes for the sun to go around the earth, but Copernicus cannot; and Copernicus can ask how long it takes the earth to go around the sun, but Ptolemy cannot.' Grünbaum, 'Is Simplicity Evidence of Truth?', 271.

390 A monotone machine can be characterized as a true on-line machine which, at the same time as processing a stream of input bits, can produce a potentially infinite stream of output bits. Since in Solomonoff's system the choice of machine

receives greater algorithmic probability if it has shorter descriptions of the input sequence ρ given to the machine in that manner. The probability that we end up in this manner feeding the machine a sequence that starts with ρ entirely depends on the length $|\rho|$.[391] Once the machine processes ρ, it outputs a sequence. For an output σ of any length that starts with this sequence, ρ can be said to have been a guide or program for the machine to produce the sequence σ that enjoys a greater algorithmic probability. In other words, ρ is effectively the machine description of σ.

To put it more formally, the Kolmogorov complexity of an infinite string σ = $\sigma_1, \sigma_2, ..., \sigma_n$ where σ_1 is 0 or 1 can be generally formulated as:

$$K(\sigma) := min\{|\rho|, \rho \in \{0,1\}^* : U(\rho) = \sigma\}$$

where $\{0,1\}^*$ is the set of all binary strings, U is the universal Turing Machine or a formal descriptive language and ρ a variable ranging over all programs such that when U is applied to them, they produce σ as the initial segment of the output.

Now the question is as follows: If we give the machine random bits, what would be the probability of machine U returning the sequence σ or more precisely, the probability that we arrive at a U-description of σ?

---

is restricted to universal Turing machines, and furthermore, since in the classical Church-Turing paradigm of computability, the machine cannot accept new input bits during the operation, this criterion is satisfied by the addition of a specialized oracle. It is called monotone since the monotonicity constraint permits to directly infer from the machine U a specific probabilistic source. A function $M(y, t)$ can be called monotonic when for a later time t' of the time t and extensions of y' of the descriptions y, we can derive from M a data object which is the extension of $M(y, t)$. Essentially, the monotonic function is a transformation such that it returns for each finite binary string, the probability that the string is generated by the machine U, once U is fed repeatedly a stream of uniformly random input produced by bets that the probability of either 0 or 1 is 0.5. This allows us to define monotone descriptional complexity of a data object in terms of U with almost the shortest description and without reference to the hidden information in the length of either ρ or σ.

391 Solomonoff has demonstrated that this probability is $2^{-|\rho|}$.

Solomonoff demonstrates that if we seek to generate a prior probability distribution over $\{0,1\}^*$, this task can be accomplished by resorting to Occam's razor where higher probability is assigned to simpler or shorter strings. The so-called Solomonoff prior (M) answers the above question by finding this probability via Occam's razor and in relation to Kolmogorov complexity. The Solomonoff prior or algorithmic probability source can be formulated as:

$$M(\sigma) := \sum_{\rho \in D_{U,\sigma}} 2^{-|\rho|}$$

where D_U, σ is the minimal U-description of σ. Or, more simply, the Solomonoff prior is the sum over the set of all programs which compute σ. If $|\rho|$ is long, $2^{-|\rho|}$ will be short, and therefore contributes with a higher degree of probability to $M(v)$. The inference of the Solomonoff prior is called Solomonoff universal induction.

Solomonoff induction shows that, when seeking the computer program or description that underlies a set of observed data (e-statements) by way of Bayesian inference over all programs, one is guaranteed to find the correct answer if Solomonoff prior is used. In tandem with the theories of Andrey Kolmogorov and Gregory Chaitin, Solomonoff's theory of universal induction assumes that the best theory is the one that is simpler, with simplicity defined formally as compressibility. Therefore, the best theory is the one that best compresses the observation data. The question of compressibility is at its core the question of finding patterns that are effective. Solomonoff induction proposes, then, that the best method of prediction of the unobserved data is one that best compresses the observed or available data.

Solomonoff induction has a number of curious characteristics: the Solomonoff prior is incomputable; the prior is highly language-dependent (i.e., dependent on the subjective choice of the universal Turing machine which determines its definition); and it presupposes the examined hypotheses to be computable. While these characteristics pose a challenge to the practical implementation of Solomonoff induction by ordinary or even idealized humans, they can nevertheless be appreciated as useful pragmatic constraints. Take for instance, the incomputability of the Solomonoff prior. The implication of this constraint is that the Solomonoff prior can be defined in terms of semi-computability or approximation from below, rather than strong or full computability.[392] To this extent, none of these features will be employed in the critical assessment of Solomonoff induction here. The argument will instead be centred on Solomonoff's interpretation of Occam's razor as compressibility bias, and its reliance on the notion of effectiveness.

It has been formally proved by Solomonoff that the aforementioned method of prediction is reliable in the sense that it leads to the truth. Essentially, Solomonoff induction is based on the definition of a type of predictor with a preference for simplicity, along with a proof that a predictor of this type is reliable in that it is guaranteed to converge on the truth. Accordingly, Solomonoff induction is a formal argument that justifies Occam's razor. In Solomonoff's theory, simplicity is characterized in terms of the weighted sum of program lengths, which depends on the choice of the monotone universal Turing machine. The choice of the machine which determines the length of the program or description corresponds to the argument from parsimony, while the length of the program itself corresponds to the argument from elegance.

However, a closer examination of Solomonoff's Carnap-influenced formal theory of induction reveals that this objective notion of simplicity is circular.[393] The argument, as advanced by Solomonoff and further

---

392 A function is lower semi-computable or semi-computable from below if a universal machine can calculate increasingly closer lower approximations to its values without saying how close $(lim_{K \to \infty})$. Or more succinctly, a function is semi-computable if it can be approximated from below or from above—in Solomonoff's case from below—by a computable function. Semi-computability can therefore be defined as the minimal level of calculability. Consequently, the notion of effectiveness in Solomonoff induction also corresponds not to full computability, but to lower semi-computability.

393 Solomonoff has explicitly referred to Carnap's claim that predictive induction is the most powerful and general form of induction as well as to his theory of inductive logic as the degree of confirmation, see Solomonoff, 'A Formal Theory of Inductive Inference parts 1 and 2'.

detailed by Vitányi and Hutter, can be briefly formulated as follows:[394] Given two classes of predictors **Q** and **R** which respectively specify the class of algorithmic probability predictors via all universal monotone Turing machines and the class of effective mixture predictors via all effective priors which embody inductive assumptions:

(1) Predictors in class **Q** have distinctive *simplicity qua compressibility bias*. Or equally, predictors in the class **R** operate under the inductive assumption of *effectiveness* in the context of sequential prediction.

(2) Predictors in **Q** are reliable in every case. Or, predictors in **R** are consistent.

(3) Therefore, predictors with a simplicity qua compressibility bias are reliable in essentially every case. Or, predictors operating under the inductive assumption of effectiveness are consistent.

However, by making explicit the property of consistency in the second step of the argument (i.e., the consistency property of Bayesian predictors as applied to the class of effective predictors),[395] it can be shown that the argument essentially runs as follows:

---

394 See R. Solomonoff, 'Complexity-based Induction Systems: Comparisons and Convergence Theorems', *IEEE Transactions on Information Theory* 24:4 (July 1978), 422–32; and for the elaboration of Solomonoff's system in connection with Occam's razor and artificial intelligence, see Li and Vitányi, *An Introduction to Kolmogorov Complexity and Its Applications*; and M. Hutter, *Universal Artificial Intelligence: Sequential Decisions Based On Algorithmic Probability* (Dordrecht: Springer, 2004).

395 Bayesian consistency means that posterior distribution concentrates on the true model—that is, for every measurable set of hypotheses, the posterior distribution goes to 1 if it contains truth and 0 if it does not: Thus a prior p_0 on the parameter space Θ is consistent at $\theta \in \Theta$ if according to the chance hypothesis θ, the chance of a sequence of outcomes arising that together with p_0 would generate a sequence $(p_1, p_2, \ldots)$ of posteriors that did not concentrate in the neighbourhood of θ is zero. A consistent prior is 'essentially guaranteed to lead to the truth, in the sense that

(1) Predictors in **R** operate under the assumption of effectiveness.

(2) Predictors in **R** are reliable under the assumption of effectiveness.

In other words, a vicious circularity in the definition of simplicity qua compressibility bias emerges: predictors operating under the assumption of effectiveness are reliable under the assumption of effectiveness. The meaningful application of the formal notion of simplicity-as-compressibility to infinite data streams is ultimately predicated on the inductive assumption of effectiveness. But this assumption only offers a weak notion of simplicity, in so far as any inductive assumption can be taken as a specification of simplicity—which then requires a new inductive argument to specify which assumption of effectiveness is preferable or which notion of simplicity is more strongly objective. Adding such an argument would again require further inductive arguments to establish the ideal effectiveness as the simplicity stipulation. Without these additional arguments, the notion of simplicity ends up being viciously circular, and its connection to reliability cannot be established. But with the addition of an inductive argument that specifies effectiveness, a potentially infinite series of arguments will be required. Thus, ironically, the formal definition of simplicity requires a program that can no longer be identified as simple (elegant or parsimonious) in any sense. Moreover, pace Vitányi and Hutter, there is nothing in the definition of Solomonoff universal induction nor in the definition of any inductive-predictive method that warrants our interpreting effectiveness as a metaphysical constraint on the world rather than as an epistemic constraint (i.e., What is calculable?).

An inductivist may contend that Solomonoff induction finally provides us with a reliable and universal standard to discriminate green-type hypotheses from grue-type hypotheses. This universal standard is the formal definition

---

no matter which chance hypothesis is true, any nonpathological stream of data generated by that hypothesis would lead an agent with that prior to pile up more and more credence on smaller and smaller neighborhoods of the true hypothesis'. G. Belot, 'Bayesian Orgulity', *Philosophy of Science* 80:4 (2013), 490.

of Occam's razor, or compressibility bias. Green-type hypotheses are more simple hypotheses as formally defined (i.e., they can compress the available data better). But this contention fails to be cogent on two accounts. Firstly, Solomonoff induction is clearly an effective interpretation of induction by instance confirmation. But as noted earlier, the essence of Goodman's new riddle is not about observed instances. Goodman argues that observed instances or the available data by themselves (i.e., without the application of projectable predicates to such instances) can result in incompatible hypotheses. The core of Goodman's problem is how to differentiate pro-jectable from nonprojectable predicates which are not supported by their instances. Therefore, the inductivist contention misunderstands the scope of Goodman's problem. As for the second point, since the formal account of simplicity leads to an infinite regress, the inductivist has no choice other than to resort to a metaphysical account of simplicity. Then the question shifts: What exactly warrants a metaphysical conception of simplicity? Surely, it cannot be the principle of simplicity itself.

Foregoing the metaphysical conceptions of simplicity and effectiveness would require us to abandon the more ambitious claims regarding the sufficiency of inductive-predictive methods, the possibility of a universal learning machine, and the inductive nature of general intelligence, in favour of far more modest pragmatic-epistemic claims—which may indeed be significant in the context of our own methods of inquiry and only in conjunction with other epistemic modalities.

This is the predicament of simplicity-qua-compressibility as an objective epistemic notion: its criteria are underdetermined if not wholly indeter-minate, and its definition is circular. In idealizing or overgeneralizing the notion of simplicity in terms of compressibility, and by identifying general intelligence with compression, the inductivist robs himself of exactly the semantic-conceptual resources that might serve not only to determine the criteria for the application of the principle of simplicity, but also to define general intelligence in terms not of compression but of the selective appli-cation of compression. Once again, the inductivist proponent of general intelligence finds himself confronted with old and new predicaments, albeit this time within the context of the formal-computational models of induction.

Ultimately, the pessimism weighing against the possibility of artificial general intelligence in philosophy of mind and the over-optimism of proponents of the inductivist models of general intelligence, in a sense originate from their choice of model of rationality. They choose either a thick concept of rationality that does not admit of the artificial realization of mind, or a notion of rationality so thin that not only is artificial general intelligence inevitable, but it inevitably takes the shape of an omnipotent omniscient inductive superintelligence. The popularity of these factions is not so much a matter of theoretical sophistication or technological achievement as the result of the dominance of such impoverished concepts of rationality. In their pessimism and over-optimism, they are both beholden to paradigms of justification derived from a narrow conception of rationality and mind. To truly begin to examine the prospects of the artificial realization of general intelligence, one ought to start from the position of systematic scepticism with regard to any paradigm of rationality built on a method of theoretical inquiry claiming to be a sufficient replacement for every other method (e.g., over-confident—as in contrast to modest—Bayesian or statistical methods) and to any inflationary model of mind that collapses the qualitative distinction between different faculties and the requirements for their realization.

Bibliography

ABRAMSKY, SAMSON. 'Concurrent Interaction Games', in J. Davies, B. Roscoe et al. (eds.), *Millennial Perspectives in Computer Science*, 1–12. Basingstoke: Palgrave Macmillan, 2000.

ALTHUSSER, LOUIS. *The Humanist Controversy and Other Writings*. London: Verso, 2003.

ARMSTRONG, D.M. *What is a Law of Nature?*. Cambridge: Cambridge University Press, 1983.

BAARS, BERNARD J. *A Cognitive Theory of Consciousness*. Cambridge: Cambridge University Press, 1988.

BADII, REMO, and ANTONIO POLITI. *Complexity: Hierarchical Structures and Scaling in Physics*. Cambridge: Cambridge University Press, 1999.

BADIOU, ALAIN. *Plato's Republic*, tr. S. Spitzer. Cambridge: Polity Press, 2012.

BAIANU, ION C., and RONALD BROWN et al. 'A Category Theory and Higher Dimensional Algebra Approach to Complex Systems Biology, Meta-Systems and Ontological Theory of Levels', *Acta Universitatis Apulensis* 52 (2011), 11–144.

BAKKER, SCOTT. *The Last Magic Show: A Blind Brain Theory of the Appearance of Consciousness* (2012), <https://www.academia.edu/1502945/The_Last_Magic_Show_A_Blind_Brain_Theory_of_the_Appearance_of_Consciousness>.

BAR-HILLEL, YEHOSHUA. '"Comments on the Degree of Confirmation" by Professor K.R. Popper', *British Journal for the Philosophy of Science* 6 (1955), 155–7.

BATTERMAN, ROBERT. *The Tyranny of Scales* (2011), <http://philsci-archive.pitt.edu/8678/1/Bridging.pdf>.

BAUDELAIRE, CHARLES. 'Abel et Caïn', in *Les Fleurs du mal*. Paris: Auguste Poulet-Malassis, 1857.

BECHTEL, WILLIAM. *Mental Mechanisms: Philosophical Perspectives on Cognitive Neuroscience*. London: Routledge, 2008.

BELOT, GORDON. 'Bayesian Orgulity', *Philosophy of Science* 80:4 (2013), 490.

BENNETT, CHARLES H. 'Logical Depth and Physical Complexity', in R. Herken (ed.), *The Universal Turing Machine: A Half-Century Survey*, 227–57. Oxford: Oxford University Press, 1988.

BERG, ADAM. *Phenomenalism, Phenomenology, and the Question of Time: A Comparative Study of the Theories of Mach, Husserl, and Boltzmann*. Lanham, MD: Lexington Books, 2015.

BERTHOZ, ALAIN. *The Brain's Sense of Movement*. Cambridge, MA: Harvard University Press, 2006.

BISHOP, ROBERT C. 'Metaphysical and Epistemological Issues in Complex Systems', in C. Hooker (ed.), *Philosophy of Complex Systems*. Amsterdam: Elsevier, 2011.

BLASS, ANDREAS. 'Is Game Semantics Necessary?', in *Computer Science Logic: International Workshop on Computer Science Logic, 66–77*. Dordrecht: Springer, 1993.

BOLTZMANN, LUDWIG. *Lectures on Gas Theory 1896–1898*. New York: Dover Publications, 2011.

BOSTROM, NICK. *Superintelligence: Paths, Dangers, Strategies*. Oxford: Oxford University Press, 2014.

BRANDOM, ROBERT. *Tales of the Mighty Dead: Historical Essays in the Metaphysics of Intentionality*. Cambridge, MA: Harvard University Press, 2002.

—— *Between Saying and Doing*. Oxford: Oxford University Press, 2008.

—— *Reason in Philosophy: Animating Ideas*. Cambridge, MA: Harvard University Press, 2009.

—— 'Conceptual Content and Discursive Practice', in J. Langkau and C. Nimtz (eds.), *New Perspectives on Concepts*. Amsterdam: Rodopi, 2010.

—— *A Spirit of Trust: A Semantic Reading of Hegel's Phenomenology* (2014), <http://www.pitt.edu/~brandom/spirit_of_trust_2014.html>.

—— *Reason, Genealogy, and the Hermeneutics of Magnanimity* (2014), <http://www.pitt.edu/~brandom/downloads/RGHM%20%2012-11-21%20a.docx>.

BRASSIER, RAY. *Nihil Unbound*. Basingstoke: Palgrave Macmillan, 2007.

—— 'That Which Is Not: Philosophy as Entwinement of Truth and Negativity', *Stasis* 1 (2013) 174–86, <http://www.stasisjournal.net/index.php/journal/article/download/60/94/>.

—— 'Transcendental Logic and True Representings' (2016), *Glass Bead* 0 <http://www.glass-bead.org/article/transcendental-logic-and-true-representings/>.

—— 'Dialectics Between Suspicion and Trust', *Stasis* 4:2 (2017), 98–113.

—— 'Jameson on Making History Appear', in *This is the Time. This is the Record of the Time*. Beirut: AUB Press, 2017.

BROUWER, L.E.J. 'Mathematics, Science and Language', in P. Mancosu (ed.), *From Brouwer to Hilbert: The Debate on the Foundations of Mathematics in the 1920s, 45–53*. Oxford: Oxford University Press, 1998.

BROWMAN, CATHERINE, AND LOUIS GOLDSTEIN. 'Competing Constraints on Intergestural Coordination and Self-organization of Phonological Structures', *Bulletin de la communication parlée* vol. 5 (2000), 25–34.

BRYAN, G.H. 'Letter to the editor', *Nature* 51 (1894), 175.

BUECHNER, JEFF. *Gödel, Putnam, and Functionalism*. Cambridge, MA: MIT Press, 2008.

BURBURY, S.H. 'Boltzmann's minimum theorem', *Nature* 51 (1894), 78–9.

CARNAP, RUDOLF. *Logical Syntax of Language*. London: Kegan Paul, 1937.

—— *Logical Foundations of Probability*. Chicago: University of Chicago Press, 1950.

—— *The Logical Structure of the World*, tr. R. George. Chicago: Open Court, 2003.

CARUS, ANDRÉ W. 'Sellars, Carnap and the Logical Space of Reasons', in S. Awodey and C. Klein (eds.), *Carnap Brought Home: The View from Jena*. Chicago: Open Court, 2003.

—— *Carnap and the Twentieth Century Thought: Explication as Enlightenment*. Cambridge: Cambridge University Press, 2007.

CATREN, GABRIEL. 'Pleromatica or Elsinore's Drunkenness', in S. De Sanctis and A. Longo (eds.), *Breaking the Spell: Contemporary Realism Under Discussion*, 63–88. Sesto San Giovanni: Mimesis Edizioni, 2015.

CHÂTELET, GILLES. *Figuring Space*, tr. R. Shaw and M. Zagha. Dordrecht: Kluwer, 2000.

CHATER, NICK, and PAUL VITÁNYI. 'Simplicity: A Unifying Principle in Cognitive Science?', *Trends in Cognitive Sciences* 7:1 (2003), 19–22.

CHOMSKY, NOAM. *Aspects of the Theory of Syntax*. Cambridge, MA: MIT Press, 1965.

CLARK, ANDY. 'Whatever Next? Predictive Brains, Situated Agents, and the Future of Cognitive Science,' *Behavioral and Brain Sciences* 36 (2013), 181–253.

COHEN, HERMANN. *Kants Begründung der Ethik*. Berlin: Dümmler, 1877.

—— *Logik der Reinen Erkenntnis*. Hildesheim: Georg Olms, 1914.

CONFUCIUS. *Analects*, tr. E. Slingerland. Indianapolis: Hackett, 2003.

CRAIG, WILLIAM LANE. *The Tenseless Theory of Time: A Critical Examination*. Dordrecht: Springer, 2000.

CRUTCHFIELD, JAMES. 'The Calculi of Emergence: Computation, Dynamics, and Induction', *Physica D* 75 (1994), 11–54.

—— et al. *Understanding and Designing Complex Systems: Response to 'A Framework for Optimal High-Level Descriptions in Science and Engineering—Preliminary Report'* (eprint arXiv, 2014), <http://arxiv.org/abs/1412.8520>.

D'AGOSTINO, MARCELLO. 'How to Go Non-Monotonic Through Context-Sensitiveness', *Logic and Philosophy of Science* 8:1 (2015), 3–27.

DARWIN, CHARLES. *The Life and Letters of Charles Darwin*. 2 vols. New York: Appleton, 1898.

DAVIDSON, DONALD. *Plato's Philebus*. London: Routledge, 1990.

DEACON, TERRENCE. *The Symbolic Species*. New York: W.W. Norton & Company, 1997.

—— *The Symbolic Species Evolved*. Dordrecht: Springer, 2012.

DEHAENE, STANISLAS, and LIONEL NACCACHE. 'Towards a Cognitive Neuroscience of Consciousness: Basic Evidence', *Cognition* 79 (2001), 1–37.

DELEUZE, GILLES, and FÉLIX GUATTARI. *What is Philosophy?*. Columbia, NY: Columbia University Press, 1996.

—— *A Thousand Plateaus*, tr. B. Massumi. Minneapolis: University of Minnesota Press, 1987.

DESJARDINS, ROSEMARY. *Plato and the Good*. Leiden: Brill, 2004.

DESMOND, WILLIAM. *Cynics*. Stocksfield: Acumen, 2006.

DETIENNE, MARCEL, and JEAN-PIERRE VERNANT. *Cunning Intelligence in Greek Culture and Society*, tr. J. Lloyd. Chicago: University of Chicago Press, 1991.

DIOGENES LAËRTIUS. *Lives of Eminent Philosophers*. Cambridge, MA: Harvard University Press, 1959.

DUTILH NOVAES, CATARINA. *Formal Languages in Logic*. Cambridge: Cambridge University Press, 2012.

EHRESMANN, ANDRÉE C., and JEAN-PAUL VANBREMEERSCH. *Memory Evolutive Systems: Hierarchy, Emergence, Cognition*. Amsterdam: Elsevier, 2007.

EMTSEV, MIKHAIL T. *World Soul*. New York: MacMillan, 1978.

FINDLAY, J.N. *Values and Intentions: A Study in Value-Theory and Philosophy of Mind*. London: Routledge, 1968.

—— *Psyche and Cerebrum*. Milwaukee, WI: Marquette University Press, 1972.

—— *Kant and the Transcendental Object: A Hermeneutic Study*. Oxford: Oxford University Press, 1981.

—— *The Transcendence of the Cave*. London: Routledge, 2011.

FISHER, MARK. *Capitalist Realism: Is There No Alternative?*. London: Zero Books, 2009.

FLEURY, MARIE-RENÉE, and SAMUEL TRONÇON. 'Speech Acts in Ludics', in A. Lecomte, S. Tronçon (eds.), *Ludics, Dialogue and Interaction*, 1–24. Dordrecht: Springer, 2011.

—— with MYRIAM QUATRINI and SAMUEL TRONÇON. 'Dialogues in Ludics', in *Logic and Grammar*. Dordrecht: Springer, 2011.

FOSTER, LAWRENCE. 'Feyerabend's Solution of the Goodman Paradox', *British Journal for the Philosophy of Science* 20:3 (1969), 259–60.

FOUCAULT, MICHEL. *The Order of Things*. London: Routledge, 2002.

—— *The Courage of Truth*, tr. J. Burchell. Basingstoke: Palgrave Macmillan, 2011.

FRASER, OLIVIA L. *Go Back to An-Fang* (2014), <http://www.academia. edu/352702/ Go_back_to_An-Fang>.

GILOVICH, THOMAS, and DALE GRIFFIN et al. *Heuristics and Biases: The Psychology of Intuitive Judgment*. Cambridge: Cambridge University Press, 2002.

GINZBURG, JONATHAN. *The Interactive Stance*. Oxford: Oxford University Press, 2012.

GIRARD, JEAN-YVES. 'Locus Solum: From the Rules of Logic to the Logic of Rules', *Mathematical Structures in Computer Science* 11:3 (2001), 301–506.

GOETHE, NORMA B. 'Two Ways of Thinking About Induction', in *Induction, Algorithmic Learning Theory, and Philosophy*. Dordrecht: Springer, 2007.

GÓMEZ-RAMIREZ, JAIME. *A New Foundation for Representation in Cognitive and Brain Science*. Dordrecht: Springer, 2013.

GOODMAN, NELSON. 'The New Riddle of Induction', in *Fact, Fiction, and Forecast*. Cambridge, MA: Harvard University Press, 1979.

—— *Ways of Worldmaking*. Indianapolis: Hackett, 1978.

GRÜNBAUM, ADOLF. *Philosophical Problems of Space and Time*. Dordrecht: D. Reidel, 1973.

—— 'Is Simplicity Evidence of Truth?', *American Philosophical Quarterly* 45:2 (2008), 179–89.

GUPTA, VINEET. *Chu Spaces: A Model of Concurrency* (1994), <http://i.stanford.edu/pub/cstr/reports/cs/tr/94/1521/CS-TR-94-1521.pdf>.

HARARI, ORNA. 'Methexis and Geometrical Reasoning in Proclus Commentary on Euclid's Elements', *Oxford Studies in Ancient Philosophy* 30 (2006), 361–89.

HARPER, ROBERT. *The Holy Trinity* (2011), <https://existentialtype.wordpress.com/2011/03/27/the-holy-trinity/>.

HARRIS, H.S. *Hegel's Ladder II: The Odyssey of Spirit*. Indianapolis: Hackett, 1997.

HAUSSER, RONALD R. *Foundations of Computational Linguistics: Human-Computer Communication in Natural Language*. Dordrecht: Springer, 1999.

HEALY, MICHAEL JOHN. 'Colimits in Memory: Category Theory and Neural Systems', in *Proceedings of the International Joint Conference on Neural Networks*, IJCNN '99, vol. 1 (1999), 492–96.

HEGEL, GEORG WILHELM FRIEDRICH. *Lectures on the Philosophy of World History*, tr. H.B. Nisbet. Cambridge: Cambridge University Press, 1975.

—— *Hegel's Philosophy of Subjective Spirit*, tr. M. J. Petry. 3 vols. Dordrecht: D. Reidel, 1978.

—— *Elements of the Philosophy of Right*, tr. H. Nisbet. Cambridge: Cambridge University Press, 1991.

—— *Outlines of the Philosophy of Right*, tr. T.M. Knox. Oxford: Oxford University Press, 2008.

—— *The Phenomenology of Spirit*, tr. T. Pinkard. Cambridge: Cambridge University Press, 2018.

—— *The Science of Logic*, tr. G. Di Giovanni. Cambridge: Cambridge University Press, 2010.

—— *Encyclopedia of the Philosophical Sciences in Basic Outline Part I: Science of Logic*, tr. K. Brinkmann and D.O. Dahlstrom. Cambridge: Cambridge University Press, 2010.

HEMMO, MEIR, and ORLY R. SHENKER. *The Road to Maxwell's Demon: Conceptual Foundations of Statistical Mechanics*. Cambridge: Cambridge University Press, 2012.

HILBERT, DAVID, and PAUL BERNAYS. *Grundlagen der Mathematik*. 2 vols. Berlin: Springer, 1979/1982.

HOBBES, THOMAS. *On the Citizen*. Cambridge: Cambridge University Press, 1998.

HUME, DAVID. *A Treatise of Human Nature*. 2 vols. Oxford: Clarendon Press, 2007.

HUTTER, MARCUS. *Universal Artificial Intelligence: Sequential Decisions Based On Algorithmic Probability*. Dordrecht: Springer, 2004.

IVANHOE, PHILIP J. *Confucian Moral Self Cultivation*. Indianapolis: Hackett, 2000.

JACKSON, E. ATLEE. *Perspectives of Nonlinear Dynamics*. Cambridge: Cambridge University Press, 1991.

JAPARIDZE, GIORGI. 'Introduction to Computability Logic', *Annals of Pure and Applied Logic* 123:1–3 (2003), 1–99.

—— 'From Truth to Computability', *Theoretical Computer Science* 357 (2006): 1–3, 100–135.

JOINET, JEAN-BAPTISTE. 'Proofs, Reasoning and the Metamorphosis of Logic', in L.C. Pereira, E. Haeusler and V. de Paiva (eds.), *Advances in Natural Deduction*. Dordrecht: Springer, 2014.

KANT, IMMANUEL. *Critique of Pure Reason*, tr. P. Guyer and A.W. Wood. Cambridge: Cambridge University Press, 1998.

KELLY, KEVIN T., and CORY JUHL et al. 'Reliability, Realism and Relativism', in P. Clark (ed.), *Reading Putnam*, 98–161. London: Blackwell, 1994.

KIM, JAEGWON. *Essays in the Metaphysics of Mind*. Oxford: Oxford University Press, 2010.

KITCHER, PATRICIA. *Kant's Transcendental Psychology*. Oxford: Oxford University Press, 1990.

KNEALE, WILLIAM, and MARTHA KNEALE. *The Development of Logic*. Oxford: Clarendon Press, 1962.

KRÄMER, SYBILLE. *Berechenbare Vernunft: Kalkül und Rationalismus im 17. Jahrhundert*. Berlin: Walter de Gruyter, 1991.

KRUIJFF, GEERT-JAN, and RICHARD OEHRLE (eds.). *Resource-Sensitivity, Binding and Anaphora*. Dordrecht: Springer, 2012.

LADYMAN, JAMES, and DON ROSS. *Every Thing Must Go*. Oxford: Oxford University Press, 2009.

LAND, NICK. *The Thirst for Annihilation: Georges Bataille and Virulent Nihilism*. London: Routledge, 1992.

LAWVERE, F. WILLIAM. *Functorial Semantics of Algebraic Theories*. New York: Columbia University Press, 1963.

LECERCLE, JEAN-JACQUES. *Deleuze and Language*. Basingstoke: Palgrave Macmillan, 2002.

LECOMTE, ALAIN. *Meaning, Logic and Ludics*. London: Imperial College Press, 2011.

—— and M. Quatrini. *Dialogue and Interaction: The Ludics View* (2014), <http://iml.univ-mrs.fr/editions/publi2010/files/Quatrini_Lecomte-esslli.pdf>.

LEGG, SHANE. 'Is There an Elegant Universal Theory of Prediction?', in *Algorithmic Learning Theory*. Dordrecht: Springer, 2006.

LEWIS, DAVID. *Counterfactuals*. London: Wiley-Blackwell, 2001.

—— *On the Plurality of Worlds*. London: Blackwell, 2001.

LI, MING, and PAUL M.B. VITÁNYI. *An Introduction to Kolmogorov Complexity and Its Applications*. Dordrecht: Springer, 2008.

LONGUENESSE, BÉATRICE. *Kant and the Capacity to Judge*. Princeton, NJ: Princeton University Press, 1998.

LORENZ, KUNO, and PAUL LORENZEN. *Dialogische Logik*. Darmstadt: WBG, 1978.

LOSCHMIDT, JOSEPH. 'Zur Grösse der Luftmolecule', *Sitzungsber. Kais. Akad. Wiss. Wien, Math. Naturwiss.* 73 (1876), 128–42.

LUCAS, ROB. 'Feeding the Infant', in M. Artiach and A. Iles (eds.), *What is to be Done Under Real Subsumption*. London: Mute, forthcoming.

MACBETH, DANIELLE. 'Diagrammatic Reasoning in Euclid's Elements', in Bart Van Kerkhove, Jonas De Vuyst, and Jean Paul Van Bendegem (eds.), *Philosophical Perspectives on Mathematical Practice* 12, 235–67. London: College Publications, 2010.

MAGNANI, LORENZO. *Abductive Cognition: The Epistemological and Eco-Cognitive Dimensions of Hypothetical Reasoning*. Dordrecht: Springer, 2009.

MANDERS, KENNETH. 'The Euclidean Diagram', in *The Philosophy of Mathematical Practice*, 80–133. Oxford: Oxford University Press, 2008.

MARTIN-LÖF, PER. 'Analytic and Synthetic Judgements in Type Theory', in *Kant and Contemporary Epistemology*, 87–99. Dordrecht: Springer, 1994.

MARX, KARL, and FRIEDRICH ENGELS. *The German Ideology*. New York: International Publishers, 1972.

MASOLO, CLAUDIO, et al. *The WonderWeb Library of Foundational Ontologies—Preliminary Report* (2003), <http://www.loa.istc.cnr.it/old/Papers/WonderWebD17V2.0.pdf>.

MCTAGGART, J.M.E. 'The Unreality of Time', *Mind* 17 (1908), 456–73.

—— *The Nature of Existence*. 2 vols. Cambridge: Cambridge University Press, 1927.

METZINGER, THOMAS. *Being No One: The Self-Model Theory of Subjectivity*. Cambridge, MA: MIT Press, 2003.

MIKHAILOV, FELIX. *The Riddle of the Self*. Moscow: Progress Publishers, 1976.

MILLIKAN, RUTH. 'Pushmi-pullyu Representations', *Philosophical Perspectives* vol. 9, 185–200. Atascadero, CA: Ridgeview, 1995.

MINAI, ALI A., and DAN BRAHA, YANEER BAR-YAM. *Unifying Themes in Complex Systems*. Dordrecht: Springer, 2010.

MUSGRAVE, ALAN. 'Popper and Hypothetico-Deductivism', in *Handbook of the History of Logic: Inductive logic*. Amsterdam: Elsevier, 2004.

NAIBO, ALBERTO, et al. 'Verificationism and Classical Realizability', in C. Başkent (ed.). *Perspectives on Interrogative Models of Inquiry*. Dordrecht: Springer, 2016.

NATORP, PAUL. *Platos Ideenlehre. Eine Einführung in den Idealismus*. Leipzig: Dürr, 1903, second edition Leipzig: F. Meiner, 1921.

NEGARESTANI, REZA. *Causality of the Will and the Structure of Freedom* (2017), <http://questionofwill.com/en/reza-negarestani-2/>.

—— 'Where is the Concept?', in R. Mackay (ed.), *When Site Lost the Plot*, 225–51. Falmouth: Urbanomic, 2015.

NIETZSCHE, FRIEDRICH. 'Beyond Good and Evil', in *Basic Writings of Nietzsche*. New York: Modern Library, 1968.

O'SHEA, JAMES R. *Wilfrid Sellars: Naturalism with a Normative Turn*. Cambridge: Polity, 2007.

OUDEYER, PIERRE-YVES. *Self-Organization in the Evolution of Speech*. Oxford: Oxford University Press, 2006.

PARMENIDES. *Parmenides of Elea*. Westport, CT: Praeger, 2003.

PATTEN, ALAN. *Hegel's Idea of Freedom*. Oxford: Oxford University Press, 1999.

PEIRCE, CHARLES SANDERS. 'Some Consequences of Four Incapacities', *Journal of Speculative Philosophy* 2 (1868), 140–57.

—— *The Collected Papers of Charles S. Peirce*. 6 vols. Cambridge, MA: Harvard University Press, 1974.

PETERSEN, UWE. *Diagonal Method and Dialectical Logic: Tools, Materials, and Groundworks for a Logical Foundation of Dialectic and Speculative Philosophy.* 3 vols. Osnabrück: Der Andere Verlag, 2002.

PIKOVSKY, ARKADY, and ANTONIO POLITI. *Lyapunov Exponents: A Tool to Explore Complex Dynamics.* Cambridge: Cambridge University Press, 2016.

PINOSIO, RICCARDO, and MICHIEL VAN LAMBALGEN. *The Logic of Time and the Continuum in Kant's Critical Philosophy* (2016), <https://philpapers.org/archive/PINTLO-10.pdf>.

PIPPIN, ROBERT B. *Hegel on Self-Consciousness: Desire and Death in the Phenomenology of Spirit.* Princeton, NJ: Princeton University Press, 2011.

PLATO. *Complete Works*, ed. J.M. Cooper. Indianapolis: Hackett, 1997.

—— *Philebus.* Oxford: Oxford University Press, 1975.

—— *Gorgias.* Indianapolis: Hackett, 1987.

—— *Republic.* Indianapolis: Hackett, 2004.

PORELLO, DANIELE, FRANCESCO SETTI, ROBERTA FERRARIO, AND MARCO CRISTANI. 'Multiagent Socio-Technical Systems: An Ontological Approach', *Proc. of the 15th Int. Workshop on Coordination, Organisations, Institutions and Norms*, 2013.

PRATT, VAUGHAN. 'Rational Mechanics and Natural Mathematics', in *TAPSOFT '95: Theory and Practice of Software Development (Lecture Notes in Computer Science)*, vol. 915, 108–22. Heidelberg: Springer, 1995.

—— 'The Duality of Time and Information', in W.R. Cleaveland (ed.), *CONCUR '92: Third International Conference on Concurrency Theory.* Dordrecht: Springer, 1992, 237.

PRICE, HUW. 'The Flow of Time', in C. Callender (ed.), *The Oxford Handbook of Philosophy of Time.* Oxford: Oxford University Press, 2011.

—— *Time's Arrow and Archimedes' Point.* Oxford: Oxford University Press, 1996.

—— 'Boltzmann's Time Bomb', *British Journal for the Philosophy of Science* 53:1 (2002), 83–119.

PROCLUS. *A Commentary on the First Book of Euclid's Elements*, tr. G.R. Morrow. Princeton, NJ: Princeton University Press, 1970.

PUNTEL, LORENZ B. *Structure and Being: A Theoretical Framework for a Systematic Philosophy.* University Park, PA: Pennsylvania State University Press, 2008.

PUTNAM, HILARY. *Philosophical Papers.* 2 vols. Cambridge: Cambridge University Press, 1975.

—— and L. PERUZZO. 'Mind, Body and World in the Philosophy of Hilary Putnam: Léo Peruzzo in conversation with Putnam', *Trans/Form/Ação*, 38: 2 (2015), <http://www.scielo.br/scielo.php?script=sci_arttext&pid=S0101-31732015000200211>.

—— '"Degree of confirmation" and Inductive Logic', in *The Philosophy of Rudolf Carnap*, 761–83. La Salle, IL: Open Court, 1963.

—— *Representation and Reality*. Cambridge, MA: MIT Press, 1988.

QUINE, WILLARD VAN ORMAN. *Word and Object*. Cambridge, MA: MIT Press, 1960.

RAGLAND, C.P., and SARAH HEIDT, 'The Act of Philosophizing', in *What Is Philosophy?*. New Haven: Yale University Press, 2001.

REALE, GIOVANNI. *Toward a New Interpretation of Plato*. Washington, D.C.: Catholic University of America Press, 1997.

REICHENBACH, HANS. *The Direction of Time*. Los Angeles: University of California Press, 1956.

—— *Elements of Symbolic Logic*. New York: Macmillan, 1947.

REITER, RAYMOND. *Knowledge in Action: Logical Foundations for Specifying and Implementing Dynamical Systems*. Cambridge, MA: MIT Press, 2001.

RESCHER, NICHOLAS. *Epistemology: An Introduction to the Theory of Knowledge*. Albany, NY: SUNY Press, 2003.

RODEN, DAVID. *Posthuman Life: Philosophy at the Edge of the Human*. Abingdon: Routledge, 2014.

—— 'On Reason and Spectral Machines: Robert Brandom and Bounded Posthumanism', in R. Braidotti and R. Dolphijn (eds.), *Philosophy After Nature*. London: Rowman & Littlefield International, 2017.

RODIN, ANDREI. *Axiomatic Method and Category Theory*. Dordrecht: Springer, 2014.

RÖDL, SEBASTIAN. *Self-Consciousness*. Cambridge, MA: Harvard University Press, 2007.

—— *Categories of the Temporal: An Inquiry into the Forms of the Finite Intellect*. Cambridge, MA: Harvard University Press, 2012.

ROSENBERG, JAY F. *Accessing Kant*. Oxford: Oxford University Press, 2005.

—— *Wilfrid Sellars: Fusing the Images*. Oxford: Oxford University Press, 2007.

—— *The Thinking Self*. Philadelphia, PA: Temple University Press, 1986.

—— *Thinking About Knowing*. Oxford: Oxford University Press, 2002.

RUSSELL, BERTRAND. *The Analysis of Mind*. London: George Allen & Unwin Ltd, 1921.

—— *Our Knowledge of the External World*. London: Open Court, 1914.

SALLIS, JOHN. *Being and Logos*. Indianapolis: Indiana University Press, 1996.

SAVAGE-RUMBAUGH, SUE, and ROGER LEWIN. *Kanzi: The Ape at the Brink of the Human Mind*. New York: Wiley, 1994.

SELLARS, JOHN. *The Art of Living: The Stoics on the Nature and Function of Philosophy*. Bristol: Bristol Classical Press, 2009.

SELLARS, WILFRID. *Essays in Philosophy and its History*. Dordrecht: D. Reidel, 1974.

—— 'Philosophy and the Scientific Image of Man', in R. Colodny (ed.), *Frontiers of Science and Philosophy*. Pittsburgh: University of Pittsburgh Press, 1962.

—— *In the Space of Reasons: Selected Essays of Wilfrid Sellars*. Cambridge, MA: Harvard University Press, 2007.

—— 'Counterfactuals, Dispositions, and the Causal Modalities', in *Minnesota Studies in the Philosophy of Science* vol.2. Minneapolis: University of Minnesota Press, 1957.

—— *Vlastos and 'The Third Man'* (1954), <http://digital.library.pitt.edu/u/ulsmanuscripts/pdf/31735062222389.pdf>.

—— *Philosophical Perspectives*. Springfield, IL: Charles C. Thomas, 1967.

SENECA, *Ad Lucilium Epistulae Morales*. 2 vols. London: William Heinemann, 1920.

SLOMAN, AARON. 'Architecture-Based Conceptions of Mind', in P. Gärdenfors et al. (eds.), *In the Scope of Logic, Methodology and Philosophy of Science* vol. 316, 403–27. Heidelberg: Springer, 2002.

—— *Virtual Machine Functionalism* (2013), <http://www.cs.bham.ac.uk/research/projects/cogaff/misc/vm-functionalism.html>.

SMART, J.J.C. *Problems of Space and Time*. New York: Macmillan, 1964.

SOLOMONOFF, RAY. 'A Formal Theory of Inductive Inference part I', *Information and Control* 7.1 (1964), 1–22.

—— 'A Formal Theory of Inductive Inference part II', *Information and Control* 7:1 (1964), 224–54.

—— 'Complexity-based Induction Systems: Comparisons and Convergence Theorems', *IEEE Transactions on Information Theory* 24:4 (July 1978), 422–32.

STEGMÜLLER, WOLFGANG. *The Structure and Dynamics of Theories*. New York: Springer, 1976.

—— *Collected Papers on Epistemology, Philosophy of Science and History of Philosophy*. 2 vols. Dordrecht: D. Reidel, 1977, 29.

STERKENBURG, TOM F. 'Putnam's Diagonal Argument and the Impossibility of a Universal Learning Machine' (2017), <http://philsci-archive.pitt.edu/12733/>.

SWANSON, LINK R. 'The Predictive Processing Paradigm Has Roots in Kant,' *Frontiers Systems Neuroscience* 10:79 (2016), <https://dx.doi.org/10.3389%2Ffnsys.2016.00079>.

SZABO, NICK. *Pascal's Scams* (2012), <http://unenumerated.blogspot.com/2012/07/pascals-scams.html>.

THOM, RENÉ. *Structural Stability and Morphogenesis: An Outline of a General Theory of Models*. Reading, MA: W.A. Benjamin, 1975.

TRAFFORD, JAMES. *Meaning in Dialogue: An Interactive Approach to Logic and Reasoning*. Dordrecht: Springer, 2017.

TURING, ALAN. 'Computing Machinery and Intelligence', in B. Jack Copeland (ed.), *The Essential Turing*, 441–71. Oxford: Oxford University Press.

—— 'On Computable Numbers, with an Application to the Entscheidungsproblem', *Proc. London Math. Soc* 42:1 (1937), 230–65.

UFFINK, JOS. 'Bluff Your Way in the Second Law of Thermodynamics', in *Studies in History and Philosophy of Science* vol. 32–3, 305–94. New York: Elsevier, 2001.

ULAM, STANISLAW. *A Collection of Mathematical Problems*. New York: Interscience, 1960.

UNIVALENT FOUNDATIONS PROGRAM, *Homotopy Type Theory: Univalent Foundations of Mathematics* (2013), <https://homotopytypetheory.org/book/>.

VANDELOISE, CLAUDE. *Spatial Prepositions*. Chicago: University of Chicago Press, 1991.

VAN DER HULST, HARRY (ed.). *Recursion and Human Language*. Berlin: de Gruyter Mouton, 2010.

WAGNER, PIERRE. *Carnap's Logical Syntax of Language*. Basingstoke: Palgrave Macmillan, 2009.

WEISBERG, MICHAEL. *Simulation and Similarity*. Oxford: Oxford University Press, 2013.

WINEGAR, REED. 'To Suspend Finitude Itself: Hegel's Reaction to Kant's First Antinomy', *Hegel Bulletin* 37:1 (2016), 81–103.

WOLFENDALE, PETER. 'The Reformatting of Homo Sapiens', *Angelaki* 24.2: *Alien Vectors,* 2019.

—— 'Castalian Games', in *Castalia, the Game of Ends and Means* (2016), <http://www.glass-bead.org/wp-content/uploads/castalian-games_en.pdf>.

Index of Names

Index of Subjects

V

W

Y